MENNONITES IN CANADA, 1939–1970

A PEOPLE TRANSFORMED

T. D. REGEHR

Mennonites in Canada, 1939–1970: A People Transformed

Volume 3 of
Mennonites in Canada

UNIVERSITY OF TORONTO PRESS
Toronto Buffalo London

Printed in Canada
ISBN 0-8020-0465-2

Printed on acid-free paper

The first two volumes of *Mennonites in Canada* are available from
University of Toronto Press and the Mennonite Historical Society:

Volume 1: Frank H. Epp, *Mennonites in Canada, 1786-1920: The History of
a Separate People* (Toronto: Mennonite Historical Society of Canada, 1974).
ISBN 1-55056-013-1

Volume 2: Frank H. Epp, *Mennonites in Canada, 1920-1940: A People's
Struggle for Survival* (Toronto: Macmillan of Canada, 1982).
ISBN 0-7715-9708-8

Canadian Cataloguing in Publication Data

Regehr, T. D.
    Mennonites in Canada, 1939–1970

    Includes bibliographical references and index.
    ISBN 0-8020-0465-2

    I. Mennonites – Canada – History – 20th century.
    I. Title

FC106.M45R44 1996 289.7'71 C95-932790-8
F1035.M45R44 1996

University of Toronto Press acknowledges the financial assistance to its
publishing program of the Canada Council and the Ontario Arts Council.

Contents

List of Tables

Preface

The dream of writing a new history of Mennonites in Canada originated in the mid-1960s. Canadians were preparing to celebrate the centennial of Confederation, while Mennonites in the United States had begun work on a four-volume history project called the Mennonite Experience in America. There was growing interest in things historical, and a small but dedicated group of Canadian Mennonites decided that the story of their people should also be written and shared with their fellow citizens.

The research and writing of a new scholarly history of Mennonites in Canada were sponsored by a joint committee of the Mennonite Historical Society of Ontario and the Mennonite Historical Society of Manitoba. That body appointed Frank H. Epp, then pastor of the Ottawa Mennonite Church, to begin work in 1967. The committee was subsequently expanded to include members of Mennonite historical societies in Saskatchewan, Alberta, and British Columbia, and was renamed the Mennonite Historical Society of Canada.

The first volume, which covered the period from 1786 to 1920, was published in 1974, when many Mennonites in Manitoba celebrated the centennial of the arrival of their ancestors in Canada. The second volume appeared in 1982, and Frank Epp planned to complete the third volume in time for the bicentennial of the coming of the first Mennonites to Ontario. Ill health made it impossible for him to complete the project.

The Mennonite Historical Society of Canada invited me to complete the third volume, and I began work on it in 1988. The society has, throughout this entire time, given the project its unwavering support. It solicited funds to cover some of the research costs, paid the salaries of research assistants, appointed and paid the expenses of a reading committee, and underwrote some of the publication costs. Over the years many members of the society have given assistance and advice, but I want to make particular mention of two of the society's presidents, J. Winfield Fretz and T.E. Friesen, who provided strong leadership for the project.

The Mennonite Central Committee, Canada (MCC [Canada]); the Ontario Mennonite conferences, which are now merged in the Mennonite Conference of Eastern Canada; the Conference of Mennonites in Canada (CMC); the Canadian Conference of the Mennonite Brethren Church in North America; the Evangelical Mennonite Conference (EMC); and the Evangelical Mennonite Mission Conference (EMMC) provided much-appreciated financial help. They also made their archives available and provided information and advice.

Historians cannot do their work without archives and libraries. In the research and writing of this book I have been served exceptionally well by archivists at the three major and several smaller Mennonite archives in Canada. The staff at the National Archives of Canada, various provincial archives, the Archives of the Mennonite Church in Goshen, Indiana, the U.S. National Archives, the Bundesarchiv in Koblenz, Germany, and various libraries all helped to make the research easier and more pleasant.

Several agencies provided financial support. The Social Sciences and Humanities Research Council of Canada gave me two research grants, which made possible research in Germany and at the National Archives in Canada and in the United States. A grant from Multiculturalism Canada paid the salary of my replacement for one year of leave from my regular duties at the University of Saskatchewan. A sabbatical leave in 1988–9 was also devoted to this project. The generous support and office space made available to me that year at Conrad Grebel College in Waterloo allowed me to become better acquainted with the Mennonite communities of southern Ontario.

Particular thanks must go to Marlene Epp, who served as a research associate of the project for a number of years before going on to doctoral studies at the University of Toronto. She increased my sensitivity to the place of women in Mennonite history. More recently Paul Regehr served as a research assistant, bringing his interest in Far Eastern and religious studies to research assignments on Mennonite missionary work and also helping in the editing, proofreading, and indexing of the manuscript.

The Mennonite Historical Society of Canada appointed a Reading Committee, which read, commented on, and gave advice about the manuscript as work proceeded. Members of that committee proffered much useful advice and saved me from numerous errors. The group was chaired by Sam Steiner and John Friesen. Its members included Peter Bargen, Leo Driedger, Abe Dueck, Marlene Epp, David Fransen, Reginald Good, Harry Loewen,

Royden Loewen, Lucille Marr, Lorraine Roth, Rodney Sawatzky, and Paul Toews. My colleague at the University of Saskatchewan Michael Hayden also read the entire manuscript and gave me much wise counsel. All this advice has made the text much better than I could have made it alone. I must, of course, bear responsibility for any remaining errors of fact or interpretation.

This project would not have been undertaken but for the vision, the energy, and the commitment of Frank H. Epp. He was a friend, mentor, and example. I dedicate this volume to his memory.

A Personal Prologue

All historians struggle with the problem of objectivity. The factual information they include in their work, and the stories they tell, comprise only an infinitesimally small part of all that happened. Even the archives and libraries housing millions of books and documents provide only a distillation of what others believed was worthy of recording and preserving on paper. Personal recollections, newspaper accounts, pictures, maps, films, and, alas, 'machine readable archives' provide much more information than any historian of our modern times can ever use. And yet they too comprise only a fraction of all that people experienced. There is, inevitably, much selection, evaluation, arranging, and explaining to be done, and all those functions are subject to individual bias.

In the nineteenth century the German historian Leopold von Ranke challenged his professional colleagues to write history only as it had actually happened ('wie es eigentlich gewesen'). Yet his student Heinrich Treitschke wrote exceedingly nationalistic and, in the view of others, biased histories of the German people.

The problem of objectivity is particularly difficult for those writing about the experiences of their own people. Historians engaged in such work are also participants in the events they write about. Readers may better understand such history if they are informed and warned about the historian's own experiences.

This history of Mennonites in Canada from 1939 to 1970 is a part of my history. It is a story of change, adaptation, and accommodation. I am a part of that story, but it is one that no two people experienced in exactly the same way. Many hours of archival research and reading have informed, broadened, and changed my knowledge and understanding of the Mennonite experience in Canada during and after the Second World War. In some important respects the interpretations offered are not what I thought they would be when I began. The story as told in these pages is nevertheless the story as I, with my particular experiences and insights, have come to understand it. No other historian reading the same material would have written a history exactly like the one I have written.

Almost all Mennonite histories to date have been written either by complete outsiders or by insiders, usually preachers, teachers, or leaders in Mennonite communities. I am neither an outsider nor fully an insider. My parents were devout members of the Mennonite Brethren Church. I grew up in the Mennonite community at Coaldale, Alberta, participated in many services at the Coaldale Mennonite Brethren Church, and attended the Alberta Mennonite High School for five years. Those experiences shaped and still inform much of what I cherish and consider important, but they were also problematic. When I graduated from high school I desperately wanted and needed to get away and leave it all behind. While attending university, I deliberately chose to study subjects far removed from my own heritage. As an undergraduate, I first chose economics as my major, in part because I had been warned that it was 'the theology of Mammon.' When I discovered that many economic theories and models assume hypothetical conditions I turned to history to study what had actually happened. Business history, and specifically the careers of Canada's most notorious entrepreneurial buccaneers, became my specialty. That, however, did not mean that the values and ideals inculcated in childhood disappeared. Several experiences and new insights led to a new understanding and appreciation of a heritage that I had rejected.

SETTING THE MOULD

One of my earliest childhood memories concerns the events of the first week of September 1939. I was almost two years old. Mother was kneading bread dough in the lean-to addition that served as the kitchen of our small home on a 23-acre irrigation farm. Father came home with terrible news. Mother stopped her work, and both of my parents knelt down on the rough wood floor to pray. Their anguished entreaties continued for a long time. I understood nothing of the crisis, except that something very bad had happened.

The events of that day, however, are the starting point of this history. War had broken out, and my parents knew something about war. The First World War and the Russian Revolution had destroyed their childhood homes and resulted in their immigration to Canada. They could not foresee the impact of this new conflict but responded to news of another war with prayer. They believed that prayer and a strong faith in God should permeate all aspects of life.

I got an early impression of that faith in an unusual way. The construction of church and community buildings was done by the members. On larger projects the congregation was divided into smaller groups to perform assigned tasks. My father was one of the coordinators, and on days when his group worked he sometimes took me along. At the building site I spent time playing in the sand piled up for cement work or with bits and pieces of construction material that became imaginary cars, trucks, or whatever. I got my glass of milk when the men had their coffee or lemonade breaks. A number of the fellows took time to talk with me, share some of my enthusiasms, or bring me new pieces of material suitable for my play. They also showed great concern when I stepped on a board with a protruding nail. They were, I concluded, very good, hard-working people, who applied their religious convictions in practical activity.

Several of the church leaders and preachers also provided good role models. The church had a number of lay preachers. One of my favourites was Jacob (Jash) Dueck. One of his sermons remains particularly vivid in my memory. The weather had been dry, and everyone had been irrigating all week. Jash Dueck had not had time to prepare a proper sermon. So he spoke about what he had seen, thought, and experienced while irrigating. That was the sort of thing even a youngster could understand. In those days the farmers still irrigated by flooding their fields. As it happened, Jash Dueck had been widowed and had remarried, and shortly thereafter his second wife had also died. Now, as he was irrigating, he flooded the nest of a field mouse who had helpless babies. The mother tried frantically, but in vain, to save herself and her brood. Her desperation brought into unusual focus the word of scripture, which tells us that God sees even the little sparrow fall. Did He also see the field mouse? Where was He when disaster overwhelmed her? Where is He when people feel as helpless and desperate as that field mouse? Where is He when good people suffer terrible loss or perish under circumstances they cannot control or even influence? No amount of praying could save that field mouse. Nor, I thought, had it saved the preacher's two wives, or the thousands of Russian Mennonites about whom we heard again and again in the late 1940s who had perished or endured horrible suffering in Soviet exile or in the murderous atrocities of the Second World War.

Jash Dueck gave us no clear answer to such questions that Sunday morning. In fact, as I remember it, he ended with an observation that was not altogether encouraging to his farmer friends. He thought there would still be mice in his field next year, and life would be as good, or as bad, for those mice as it had been before disaster overwhelmed the mouse that had drowned. What was really good and true before the disaster remained good and true.

That sermon forced the listeners to ponder the larger mysteries of life. I thought that it was a much more profound and realistic affirmation of faith than the stories that we heard much more often about people who had escaped miraculously after praying desperately to God. We knew that in Russia and during the Second World War many had escaped, but also that many more had perished. Jash Dueck's sermon seemed more firmly rooted in what actually happened than did the stories of miraculous rescue.

There was another, older preacher whom I very much appreciated. He was Abram Willms, a retired farmer who wrote poetry and was a great lover of nature. As Willms walked along the small irrigation ditches in the Coaldale suburb of Nortondale where he lived, he enjoyed, examined, and shared with passers-by such as I the wonders of animal and plant life. Willms, I discovered, was the kind of man who could find God, the creator and sustainer of life and nature, even in the bubbles that formed in the dirty water in our irrigation ditches. He and others like him applied their religious faith in everyday life. Their practical Christianity formed the matrix in which my religious understanding and values were cast and received their form.

THE MOULD IS BROKEN

There were, unfortunately, some things said and taught in the Mennonite Brethren Church at Coaldale that did not seem to meet the critical test of practical Christianity. I was not a well-behaved child. Maybe I was hyperactive; maybe my parents were too busy to give me the attention that I craved; perhaps I was envious of my better-behaved younger siblings when they received parental love and attention; or maybe I was simply a bad boy. Whatever the reason, I often did things that resulted in seemingly countless spankings. That, however, brought only temporary behavioural changes. The real solution to my problems, according to Mennonite Brethren theology, was a conversion experience. That normally happened in adolescence. Until then the stick had to do service.

In adolescence my understanding of what it meant to be saved or converted became problematic. It is quite possible that I misunderstood some of the religious training I received. As a professor who has taught thousands of students over a twenty-eight–year teaching career, I realize that what an instructor tries to communicate in lectures is not necessarily what students answer in an examination. It is quite possible that I misunderstood what our teachers, preachers, and community leaders tried to communicate. Perhaps I was unduly influenced by my behavioural problems, but it seemed to me that some of the things that I heard in church were contrary to the teachings of the scriptures and my own experiences.

In Sunday school we were taught that there was a fundamental dichotomy in human beings. People were spiritual, and they were fleshly or carnal. Life was a constant struggle between these two forces. One Sunday school teacher described it colourfully when she told us that there is, in each of us, a battle similar to a fight between a black and a white dog. It required constant effort to make sure that the bad black dog was kept under control.

This fundamental human dichotomy was linked closely to a theology that made a clear distinction between Christian living and 'the world.' 'Worldliness,' or the gratification of 'fleshly' lusts and desires, was constantly denounced. Our church had an impressively long list of worldly activities that must be avoided by Christians. Smoking, consumption of alcoholic beverages, radio, movies, local tractor shows, television, various forms of personal adornment and beautification by females, card playing (except 'Rook'), and above all, any form of pre- or extramarital sexual gratification were forbidden. Rules alone, however, were not enough. True liberation from the bondage and temptations of the flesh was achievable only through a religious conversion, which was presented as a radical and magical transformation. The old nature, the black dog of the Sunday school lesson, would pass away, or at least lose much of its power. All things would become new. Even the worst and most perverse person became 'whiter than snow.'

In my case those notions of conversion converged with troublesome adolescent sexual experiences. Since I grew up on a farm I had some practical knowledge about sexual matters. In addition, my parents had a book of scripture readings that they used for daily family devotions. Scripture passages deemed unsuitable for children, including stories of numerous interesting Old Testament sexual misdeeds, were not included. But for me the book became an interesting guide. One simply had to look up in a real Bible what had been left out. And much of it was certainly interesting, but not entirely consistent with the limited instruction we were given regarding sex.

When I reached the age of puberty my father asked me to read the pamphlet written by Abram Nachtigal, the contents of which are discussed below, in this history. It was not consistent with the Bible stories or with farmyard observances. And then I fell in love with a girl who, I thought, personified all the virtues that I lacked. While I was under that influence, evangelistic services were held in town. I had reached the right age, and if I got saved my troublesome behaviour at home would end and happy, romantic dreams might become reality. So I responded to the altar call, but the experience was an unmitigated disaster. None of the promised things happened. There was neither a transformation, nor a startling spiritual breakthrough. Nothing the counsellors said, or advised me to say or do, generated the promised magic. I felt only profound disappointment and a growing sense of outrage. Then, after the mandatory confession of sins and penitential prayer, I was told that now I must believe and tell people that I was 'saved.' All would be well if I gave a stirring testimony the next evening. That advice struck me as utterly dishonest. I thought that I was being told to testify to something that had not happened. The evangelist, I concluded, was a charlatan.

In 1951 the local Alberta Mennonite High School added grades seven and eight to the curriculum. My parents, desperate about my situation, were determined that I should take the rest of my education in that Christian school. My experiences there were decidedly contradictory. I enjoyed school and learning and felt both empathy with, and great yearning for, many of the social, cultural, and religious values taught there. There were, however, also numerous evangelistic and revival services.

My response to the high school's evangelistic meetings was perhaps unusual. My parents had given me a Bible with a concordance, and I began to compare what the evangelists said with references to the same topic in the concordance. The Bible is a remarkably rich and diverse book, and it was not difficult to find scripture verses that differed from those cited by the evangelists. The threat of hell-fire was one of their favourite subjects, but I discovered that the Old Testament concept of hell was not the kind of place described by the speakers and that only some of the New Testament references described a terrible, fiery pool. So, after a particularly hot sermon, I confronted the evangelist with what I had found. He responded by saying that clearly the Holy Spirit was working in my heart but that I seemed determined to harden my heart and to pervert the scripture. The only choice available to me, he insisted, was to believe or reject God's word, presumably as he interpreted it, and to ignore verses that did not fit. I came away convinced that the man was not honest and that he used only those Bible verses that suited his purpose. I concluded that if there really were such a place as hell he was more likely than I to end up there.

I also found the emphasis of the evangelistic speakers on a single, dramatic, life-changing conversion experience troublesome. Most of the biblical references to conversion are in the Old Testament and deal with group, mass, or national, not individual, conversions. Several references, in both the Old and the New Testament, speak not only of the need for children to accept the faith of their elders, but also of converting the hearts of the fathers to the children. Could it be that the evangelist needed to be converted to my ideas and understanding of the scriptures, rather than the other way around?

There was another puzzling matter. The scriptures did not document the conversions of Jesus' disciples, or of many other God-fearing people. They almost always omitted what was regarded as the most important part of the obituaries read at funerals in our church – whether the individual had been converted. Saul's experience on the road to Damascus, which was constantly held as the model, was clearly an exception.

The many rules of conduct were also problematic, not only because they forbade things that I wanted to do, but because they seemed remarkably similar to the many rules and laws of the scribes and Pharisees in Jesus' time. The harsh manner in which our church leaders enforced some of those rules also seemed similar to the tactics of Jesus' opponents. Our leaders did not physically stone church members guilty of sexual misconduct, but they certainly did not treat them the way Jesus treated the woman caught in adultery. Indeed, what our preachers said about sexual matters, and specifically what Abram Nachtigal had written in his pamphlet, seemed to be simply wrong. So on a number of things it seemed to me that what the preachers and evangelists said and did was not right.

It was clear that my classmates did not react to the methods used by the evangelists in the same way I did. For most there seemed to be no conflict between what was preached and what the scriptures or Anabaptist/Mennonite theology had to say. What to others appeared as a seamless whole appeared to me dissonant and contradictory. At times that situation resulted in terrible despair and anguish because I was an outsider, but these feelings alternated with other times when I firmly resolved to work out for myself what was, and what was not, believable, honest, good, and true.

Immediately after graduation from high school I went to Calgary in search of a job and at the end of the summer registered at the University of Alberta. It was my hope and expectation that I would be able to forget, ignore, or at least put behind me the religious struggles of the past. The university, city, books, and ideas all seemed new, interesting, and liberating. I was suspicious of all churches, particularly those of the Mennonite Brethren.

RECOVERY OF A LOST HERITAGE

There was a return. An important new insight came in a philosophy of religion course. One of my assignments that year was to write an essay on religious theories and ideas of the resurrection. It took me more intimately into various religious theories of death and the relationship between the body and the soul or spirit. The key point was whether the Christian faith promised only a spiritual or both a bodily and a spiritual resurrection. Sunday school teachers, preachers, and the evangelists had emphasized the fundamental conflict between the spiritual and carnal elements of life. That approach suggested a future existence in a pure, disembodied, spiritual state. A book comparing the deaths of Jesus and Socrates convinced me that the Judeao-Christian tradition differed from Greek philosophy. Christianity stressed the unity and wholeness of humans, rather than the differences and conflict between body and mind.

This holistic philosophy, harmonizing physical and spiritual aspects of human existence, made far more sense to me than the Greek philosophy of mind (or soul) over matter. At the time I thought such a holistic philosophy was contrary to the Mennonite theology with which I had grown up. Then, to my surprise, I discovered that it was consistent with historical Anabaptist and Mennonite theology. That was the beginning of my reconciliation with a religious tradition that I thought I had abandoned.

The second major insight came after I began work at the Public Archives in Ottawa in 1960. There was a small group of Mennonites in the city, and one couple, Peter and Helen Wiens, made a determined effort to contact any new arrivals bearing a Mennonite name and to invite them to delicious Sunday dinners. Occasionally they rented a local school auditorium for a worship service. What a different Mennonite group that was! Almost all the men had at least one university degree, most worked in the civil service, and their approach to religion was open, tolerant, holistic, and easy-going. These were good people, and my wife and I, after our marriage in 1961, became particularly good friends with the first pastors of the group, Bill and Mary Dick. That church was one whose values and ideas I found compatible with the teachings of the scriptures.

There was one more important new insight. At home there had been much talk about worldliness and the importance of remaining separate from the world. The long lists of rules designed to maintain that separation never made much sense to me, and my studies at the university quickly demonstrated that so-called 'worldly' affairs were not very different from the everyday experiences of believers. Good and evil existed in both worlds.

In 1962 the Mennonite World Conference met for the first time in Canada. The gathering was held in Kitchener, Ontario, and my wife and I decided to go. The theme was 'The Lordship of Christ.' It was memorable for many because of the presence of Harold S. Bender, president of the Mennonite World Conference, who was in failing health (he died later that year). I had not heard of the man before and knew little about his work. But he was obviously a significant Mennonite scholar, and after the World Conference I began to read some of the things he had written.

In his celebrated presidential address to the American Society of Church History in New York in 1943 Bender had identified three great principles which, he argued, constituted the 'Anabaptist Vision.' The first, and for me the most important, was emphasis on holistic Christian discipleship. All of life must be brought into a fundamental harmony under the lordship of Christ. As I understood it, that meant that spiritual and carnal, sacred and secular aspects of life were not necessarily in conflict with one another. They must all be brought into a holistic, Christian harmony in a life of radical discipleship.

The other principles of Anabaptism are discussed below. There was, however, one specific aspect of Bender's 'Vision' that remained problematic for me. Bender, like many of the preachers in Coaldale, talked and wrote a great deal about nonconformity to the world. At the Mennonite World Conference, however, I was pleased to hear one of the European Mennonite leaders emphasize the lordship of Christ over all of life. He made no distinction between secular and sacred matters – all was subject to the Lord. That made more sense to me than sectarian Mennonite theology.

CONCLUSION

In reflecting on my experiences, I now particularly cherish those that fashioned a holistic, integrated, and harmonious understanding of life. Jash Dueck struggling with his grief in a workaday setting, Abram Willms rediscovering the creator in the muddy water of an irrigation ditch, new philosophical insights, the scholarship of Harold Bender, and the insights of the European theologians who spoke at the Mennonite World Conference are a part of my spiritual heritage. For a time those older and more traditional Mennonite values and ideals were obscured. I lost sight of the holistic elements of the Anabaptist heritage, but the struggle to reconcile and harmonize values and beliefs in new circumstances was not only a part of my personal experience; it has been part of the collective Canadian Mennonite experience since 1939.

Frank H. Epp, 1929–1986, to whose memory this volume is dedicated

The Hoffnungsfeld (Field of Hope) Mennonite Church, Glenbush, Saskatchewan

First Mennonite Church, Kitchener, Ontario, which also housed the Ontario Mennonite Bible School

A Mennonite barn raising at Elmira, Ontario, 1989

An Old Mennonite sewing circle, 1994

Exodus, by Agatha Schmidt

First Mennonite Church, Greendale, BC, during the flood of 1948

Mennonite Brethren baptism in the Sumas River, BC

R. Musselman Ltd., Excavating and Grading

Mennonite Disaster Service at work in LaRivière, Manitoba, 1966

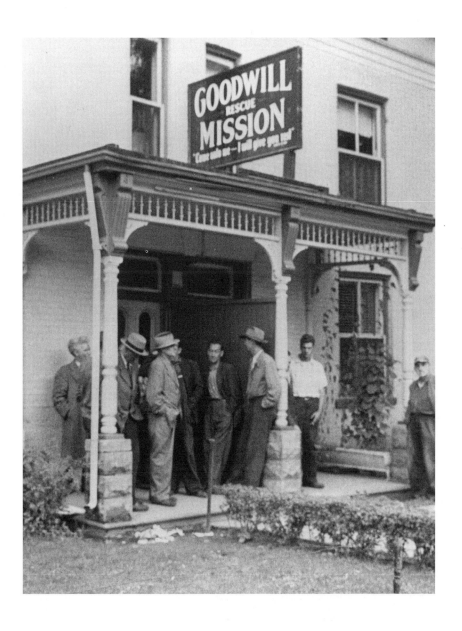

Amish Mennonite Goodwill Rescue Mission, London, Ontario

Mennonite Pioneer Mission, Pauingassie, Manitoba

Saskatchewan Bergthaler Mennonites preparing to leave for British Honduras

Johann H. Enns receiving the Order of Canada

A Mennonite quilting bee

Mrs H.I. Dueck of Kleefeld, Manitoba, with completed Centennial quilt

The Mennonite delegation that met with Prime Minister Diefenbaker, 1960

The Mennonite delegation that met with Prime Minister Trudeau, 1970

The Coaldale Mennonite choir and orchestra, at Southminster United Church, Coaldale, Alberta, for their performance of Handel's *Messiah*, 1956

The Japanese religious and cultural centre at Strawberry Hill, BC, which was purchased and used as a church by the Mennonite Brethren

A.D. Penner's Dodge-DeSoto car dealership

Queen Elizabeth, visiting the Mennonite community of Steinbach, Manitoba, on 14 June 1970, receives flowers from Lisa Epp; Mayor Barkman looks on.

Elven Shantz with Old Order Amish leaders

The Brunk Tent Campaign, 1957

Mennonite World Conference in Kitchener, Ontario, 1962

Introduction:
A People Transformed

Canadian Mennonites in 1939 were overwhelmingly rural and agricultural people living in relatively isolated communities. The 1941 Canadian census reported that 86.9 per cent of Canada's 111,380 Mennonites lived on farms or in small rural towns and villages.[1]

J. Winfield Fretz, an American Mennonite sociologist who visited Canadian Mennonite communities in the early years of the war, believed that their churches and communities survived best in 'agricultural areas where the pull of the church in a community tends to draw its members into community and by degrees drive out by processes of competition, invasion and succession, the non-Mennonite populations.' He warned: 'Where Mennonites have gone to the cities, the solidarity of the communities has been shattered ... Mennonites moving to the cities have in large numbers lost their identity as Mennonites.'[2]

E.K. Francis, another American sociologist who undertook a major study of the Mennonites of southern Manitoba in the 1940s, concluded: 'If the Mennonites today are relatively well-adjusted to Canadian social and economic life, and constitute hardly any problem, this is largely due to the fact that they were allowed to settle in solid communities, and that these communities have been preserved.'[3] Francis thought that it was good that Canadian Mennonites had readily distinguishable occupational, residential, linguistic, religious, and attitudinal characteristics and that, as a result, 'neither the Mennonites nor their neighbours in Manitoba will ever have the slightest difficulty in determining precisely who is one of them and who is not.'[4]

This situation changed dramatically in the three decades following the outbreak of the Second World War. Canadian Mennonites abandoned their farms and rural communities in such large numbers that by 1971 the Canadian census found slightly less than 30 per cent of Canadian

Mennonites living on farms. More than 47 per cent lived in cities, while 23 per cent were rural, non-farm people.[5]

This massive migration involved much more than a mere change of residence. Mennonite and non-Mennonite commentators alike realized, and lamented the fact, that an entire way of life was changing.[6] Moreover, many of the alterations also affected those who stayed but modernized their farms.

Two distinguished Canadian historians, Robert Craig Brown and Ramsay Cook, have argued that Canada was transformed from an essentially rural and agricultural nation into a modern, industrialized, and urban country in the twenty-five years from 1896 to 1921. The hallmarks of the transformation were urbanization, industrialization, new investment patterns, application of new technologies, massive immigration, and, more generally, unprecedented economic expansion, diversification, optimism, and prosperity.[7]

Canadian Mennonites resisted that shift and experienced great difficulty in the period described by Brown and Cook. Indeed, for more than 7,000 of them in Manitoba and Saskatchewan, the changes became so threatening that they abandoned their homes and farms to seek new and more accommodating conditions in Mexico and Paraguay. Those who stayed had to adjust to the new conditions and circumstances in Canada, but that decision did not lead to their assimilation. Instead, E.K. Francis found evidence that the isolated, rural, and agricultural character of their communities was reinforced in the 1920s and 1930s and that Manitoba's Mennonites 'did not to any considerable extent mingle with Canadians of different backgrounds, mainly because their colonies and towns had, if anything, become more homogeneous ethnically than they had been twenty years earlier.'[8]

During the years covered in this study, beginning with the outbreak of war in September 1939, Canadian Mennonites experienced a sea change that paralleled that of their fellow citizens a generation earlier. It took them out of their former isolation and into the mainstream of Canadian life. Not all responded in the same way, but all were dramatically affected.

Sociologists have shown how small minority groups interact with dominant host societies by making a useful distinction between 'assimilation' and 'accommodation.' Assimilation is the process whereby individuals are absorbed, incorporated, and harmonized to become an indistinguishable part of the dominant culture, society, or nation. It implies loss of a unique identity and integration into that of the dominant culture. That process describes the experience of a minority of Canadian Mennonites in the three decades following the outbreak of the Second World War.

There is another pattern of adjustment – that of an entire minority group making major adjustments and changes while still retaining its own identity, values, and traditions.[9] This process is now generally labelled 'accommodation.' It accurately describes the internal dynamics of change in the majority of Canadian Mennonite communities, congregations, and families after 1939. Fundamental alterations occured, but leaders of Mennonite factions and groups retained sufficient influence and control to ensure that 'when culture change was forced upon them, they changed as a group, thus sparing individual members the misery and mental agonies of the marginal man.'[10]

This accommodation was made easier by several changes in Canadian society. First, assimilationist pressures in the educational system became less threatening. The established churches, which had advocated fairly aggressive assimilationist educational policies, lost much of their influence. At the same time the larger Mennonite groups developed new educational initiatives to perpetuate distinctive religious values.

Foreign and Canadian diplomatic policies also became less threatening after 1945. Previously, Canadian Mennonites had difficulty with unquestioned Canadian support for British imperialist political and military adventures and misadventures. After 1945 Soviet communism became the main target of Canadian military and diplomatic initiatives. Many Canadian Mennonites, especially those who had experienced the Russian Revolution and subsequent communist governments, found it much easier to support Canadian foreign and military policies when these involved resistance to communist aggression or participation in United Nations–sponsored peacekeeping operations.

In domestic affairs Canadian and Mennonite values also converged after 1945. Scholars tell us that peace, law, order, and good government have been fundamental social goals and ideals for Canadians.[11] When stripped of their British imperialist and military biases, those values were also very important to Mennonites.[12]

Canadian society, in short, was perceived as becoming more friendly and tolerant of distinctive Mennonite values. Mennonites still experienced much hostility when refusing to take part in the war, but when reviewing the alternative-service experience afterwards their leaders and government officials said so many complimentary things about one another that it resembled a love-in.

Minorities react differently when confronted by a basically friendly rather than a hostile dominant culture. Before 1939 many Mennonites regarded the surrounding society as hostile or, at best, reluctantly tolerant. After 1949 they saw it as basically friendly. In situations where minorities live in well-disposed societies they almost always begin to emphasize those aspects of their own heritage that are in harmony with or that complement those of the host while playing down other aspects that are not in step. Religions have virtually limitless possibilities, and leaders must choose which to highlight. After the war Canadian Mennonites increasingly paid attention to, and sometimes rediscovered, those aspects of their culture that were consonant with the rest of Canadian society. As a result, their post-1939 transformation brought them more fully and enthusiastically into the mainstream, through a process of accommodation, not assimilation.

Not all Mennonite groups responded in the same way. Significant numbers were simply assimilated, and others maintained a determined separatist stance. Most, however, accommodated themselves, modifying, but not losing or abandoning, what they considered essential elements of their own heritage. Canadian Mennonites thus became a people transformed, but not assimilated, in the thirty years following the start of the Second World War. This volume tells the story of that transformation.

PART ONE
THE SETTING

1

Canadian Mennonites in 1939

Wars have been likened to a crucible or a blast furnace within which peoples and nations are subjected to intense heat and from which none emerges unaltered.[1] Historians have suggested that Canada, perhaps more than the nations devastated by war, became a different country in the 1940s. They say that most of the pieces were still the same, but they had been changed and rearranged so that 'the effect of the picture is quite different.'[2]

Canadian Mennonites were one of the pieces that was altered and rearranged by the war. Their place in Canadian society and in the Canadian economy, their understanding of and relationship to the government or the state, and their attitude toward what many still called 'the world' all changed in quite fundamental ways during and after the war. This chapter seeks to describe Canadian Mennonite life at the time they entered the crucible of war.

A PEOPLE OF 'THE WAY'

In the Epilogue to *Mennonites in Canada, 1920–1940*, Frank Epp described the situation in which Canadian Mennonites found themselves at the end of the 1930s: 'Mennonites had survived and were surviving. The visible continuity of the Mennonite communities, congregations, and conferences was obvious. The loyalty of the young people was impressive, in terms of both the quantity and the quality of their responses. Within and across the five main provinces in which they were now scattered, the Mennonites were tied together by informal networks and formal organizations, which contributed both to identity and to solidarity. The culture was being preserved. The faith was being taught.'[3]

Canadian Mennonites in 1939 were a diverse people but they shared many common beliefs and practices. They were practical, mostly rural, people, who, in their own relatively isolated churches and communities, tried to apply directly and quite literally the things taught by Jesus. For that reason some writers have described them as 'A People of the Way.'[4] 'We believe,' one of their leaders wrote later, 'in an embodiment of the good news in the way we live – in the way we present ourselves as persons, families and church community.'[5]

Mennonites' understanding of what it meant to live as Jesus had taught had been shaped by their troubled historical experiences. Persecution had scattered their sixteenth-century Anabaptist ancestors. Many had fled from the Netherlands, Switzerland, and southern Germany and found refuge on remote settlement frontiers in Poland, Prussia, Russia, and North and South America, where they secured religious privileges and concessions in return for pioneering economic services. While many of the earliest Anabaptists were urban artisans and professionals, centuries of life on a succession of agricultural settlement frontiers made their Mennonite descendants a rural and agricultural people. Farming had become not only a preferred way of life but to many an almost sacred vocation. It afforded more than a liveli-hood. A rural and agricultural way of life, in the opinion of one Mennonite scholar, provided 'an ideal environment in which to carry out their church and family ideals.'[6]

In many respects the faith of Anabaptists and Mennonites was similar to that of members of other Christian denominations. They shared a belief in God as the supreme being who created and sustains all; in Jesus, the fully human and fully divine saviour; and in the Holy Spirit, who guides human beings to faith and convicts them of sin. They also believed in the sinfulness of human nature and in the need for repentance, divine forgiveness, and sal-vation, followed by a life of holiness. The scriptures were, in their under-standing, divinely inspired and the absolute authority for life and faith.[7]

The Anabaptists of the sixteenth century had become convinced that the unreformed church placed undue emphasis on 'good works.' While acknowl-edging the importance of good works, the Anabaptists thought that Roman Catholicism did not emphasize sufficiently an unconditional commitment to applying all the teachings of Jesus in a holistic way of life. It permitted, and often demanded, that Christians participate in warfare and do other things that were, they believed, not consistent with Jesus' ethic of love and forgiveness.[8]

The reformed churches, in the view of the Anabaptists, corrected some of the errors of the unreformed church but also failed to apply the teachings of Jesus to all of life. For that reason, sixteenth-century Anabaptists were re-garded as radicals. They called for a return to the scriptures and to all the teachings of Jesus and of the Apostolic church. Their most important differences from other Christians focused on five main principles.

The first distinctive Anabaptist principle was biblicism.[9] Anabaptists believed that the entire Bible, including both the Old and the New Testaments, was the word of God and the only reliable guide for life. This stance, according to one of the best-known Mennonite theologians of the 1930s and 1940s, 'was not unique with them for the Lutherans and the Reformed, as well as Catholics, also believed in divine inspiration. The Anabaptists, however, made their attitude toward the Bible operate in daily life to a degree which seemed fanatical to other sixteenth century Christians.'[10]

Their high view of the scriptures led directly to their second principle – that of a Christ-centred discipleship. All of life, in its many and varied contexts, must be brought into harmony with the teachings of the scriptures and therefore under the Lordship of Christ. Christianity was a way of life, and the way of salvation. Discipleship, or the more powerful German concept of *Nachfolge*, was central to Anabaptist theology.[11] Religion and faith meant 'following Jesus' teachings and example day by day, no matter where the path may lead.'[12] They applied this principle in a more radical way then either Catholics or Lutherans.

The third characteristic was an ethic of love and non-resistance, based primarily on Jesus' teachings in the Sermon on the Mount, which was closely and directly linked to their emphasis on discipleship. Mennonites did not expect those who had not voluntarily committed themselves to Jesus' way to follow and do all that he had taught. They recognized that secular or worldly societies could not be governed by such principles. Regeneration, renewal, or rebirth involving a voluntary commitment to the Jesus Way was a prerequisite – the gate – whereby the believer entered into the new spiritual life based on love and non-resistance. Anabaptists believed that in their own relations with fellow believers and non-believers alike, they must not depart from 'the Way,' even when it seemed foolish or difficult. Jesus had taught that love, including love of one's enemies, would be the chief mark of his followers. Anabaptists and Mennonites understood that to mean that they could not participate in armed self-defence, violent revolution, or the killing of other human beings, even in war. Love and non-resistance thus became a fundamental principle of Anabaptism.[13] Some critics have, in fact, suggested that the Mennonites' peace or non-resistance teachings provide the only acceptable justification for continuing their separate denominational identity.[14] Non-resistance and/or peacemaking became the distinguishing and most controversial doctrine. At its core, however, the principle had less to do with the evils of warfare than with the simple insistence that Jesus' teachings be applied in all situations.

The most frequently told and illustrated story coming out of sixteenth-century Anabaptist history was that of Dirk Willems, who ran across a frozen waterway while fleeing would-be captors. One of the pursuers followed but fell through the ice. Willems 'returned and aided him in getting out, and thus saved his life,' only to be seized and, 'after severe imprisonment and great trials proceeding from the deceitful papists, put to death at a lingering fire.'[15] Few stories more completely captured the Mennonite understanding of the essence and the difficulty of living in accordance with Jesus' ethic of love and non-resistance.

It was clear to Anabaptists that the unregenerate in their natural human condition, whether acting individually or collectively through the state, could not be expected to adhere to such a standard of conduct. This led to a fourth teaching. Anabaptists did not regard any secular state or government as the Kingdom of God on earth, even when headed by Christian princes. Secular governments, they believed, were ordained of God. Their essential function was to maintain order and make possible a decent human society: 'to punish the evil, to protect the good, to administer a righteous justice, to care for the widows, the orphans, and the poor, and to provide a police force that is not against God and His Word.'[16] This mandate sometimes required force and punitive actions which were not neccessarily consistant with Jesus' teaching. The state had to deal with evildoers differently from the way it treated true believers. Anabaptists thus held a dualistic view of secular governments. Governments were ordained of God but operated on principles 'which parallel the principles of Christ's kingdom, and are not in accord with it.'[17]

The fifth principle pertained to ecclesiology – specifically to teachings that the church must be an accountable community of believers who had voluntarily committed themselves to follow Jesus' way in all aspects of life and who had signified that commitment through adult baptism.[18] Anabaptists and Mennonites rejected the notion of a state church, insisting that the true church comprise only believers who had made a mature, adult decision. They believed that the church, rather than a nation led by a Christian prince, was 'the society in which Christ exercises His glorious reign.'[19] The church, however, could fulfil that mandate only if it remained pure, holy, 'all glorious, with no stain or wrinkle.'[20] Anabaptist ecclesiology thus placed greater emphasis on holy living, peoplehood, local church autonomy, and relatively democratic and egalitarian forms of leadership than did other Protestants.[21]

This understanding of the church also created much tension. It sometimes seemed to be in conflict with emphases on individual free choice and the responsibility of each believer to follow his or her understanding of the scriptures. Salvation, church membership, and much else in Mennonite life depended on individual choice and responsibility. Attitudes described by some scholars as 'the Protestant ethic' were pervasive in Mennonite thinking. But there was also a strong sense that in matters involving the church members had collective responsibilities to ensure that the church be kept pure. The determination to keep and safeguard the church as the Kingdom of God on earth sometimes led to conflict and fragmentation.

A SCATTERED AND FRAGMENTED PEOPLE

Core Christian and Anabaptist beliefs and practices were greatly affected by the historical experiences and diverse theological influences to which Mennonites were exposed on a succession of eastern European and North American settlement frontiers. Since most Mennonites lived in a diaspora and had no central church structures, it was not surprising that the gospel came to be applied differently in different situations.

Persecution in the early years, religious intolerance, and economic opportunities on eastern European and North American trade and agricultural frontiers led to numerous Mennonite migrations. The Hanseatic trading centres of northeastern Europe, and the virgin but flood-prone lands of the Vistula and Nogat valleys, brought Dutch Mennonites to north German, Prussian, and Polish territories. Later, after Russia conquered Polish and Ukrainian territories held by the Turks, that country opened new agricultural frontiers that attracted Mennonites from Prussia and, in smaller numbers, from Switzerland and southern Germany. William Penn's great colonization experiment in North America brought not only Quakers but also many Mennonites from Switzerland and southern Germany. After the American revolutionary war some of them came to what was then British North America.

Major religious revivals or awakenings rooted in European Pietist, German Baptist, English Methodist, and North American Evangelical rather than in Anabaptist teachings swept the Mennonite communities in both Russia and North America in the mid-nineteenth century.[22] Those revivals or awakenings resulted in new tensions and in establishment of two large Mennonite conferences – the Mennonite Brethren in Russia and the General Conference in the United States – and several smaller conferences. Some appreciated the new spiritual emphases while others feared that cherished, sixteenth-century Anabaptist insights were lost or modified beyond recognition. As a result, Mennonites in the early twentieth century were a scattered and diverse people, which none the less retained some common beliefs and practices.

The most important new religious influences affecting Mennonites in the nineteenth and twentieth centuries came through a movement broadly defined as evangelicalism. 'Evangel' means simply glad tidings or the good news of the gospel, and evangelicals are those who have heard and accepted that good news. That presumably includes all Christians, but 'evangelicalism' became a term used to define a particular section of the Protestant churches. While definitions in Europe, particularly Germany, and in the English-speaking world differed somewhat, the term generally referred to Protestants who believed in the corruption of human nature through the fall, regeneration and personal salvation through the blood of the Saviour, the inspiration and authority of the Bible, and a life of personal piety and witness to non-believers.[23]

Some Mennonite groups, particularly those most affected by nineteenth- and twentieth-century revival movements, identified strongly with evangelical thought and institutions, while others tried to distinguish themselves from evangelicalism. The strongest appeal of evangelicalism for Canadian Mennonites was its biblicism. One of its weakest links was the strong and uncritical support that many evangelicals gave to military and imperialist policies. Evangelicalism thus affirmed unconditionally one of the most cherished and time-honoured Mennonite articles of faith (biblicism) while contradicting another (the ethic of love and non-resistance). Evangelicals and Mennonites differed also over the importance of an emotional conversion and life-long Christian discipleship. Evangelicals emphasized the significance of a salvation experience in which the individual accepted Christ as his or her personal saviour. Many, but not all Mennonites placed greater emphasis on what they called 'the Way of the Cross,' by which they meant a holistic application of Jesus' teachings to all aspects of life.

Nineteenth- and early-twentieth-century evangelicalism was a diverse movement of religious renewal of which three substreams – pietism, fundamentalism, and dispensationalism – had particular relevance to Mennonites. Pietism originated in the Reformed and Lutheran churches, mainly in Europe, and emphasized conversion, application of this experience in daily life through good works, and nonconformity through avoidance of such things as dancing, card playing, the theatre, worldly literature, and use of alcoholic beverages and tobacco. Pietists also focused on the second coming of Christ.[24]

Fundamentalism, as discussed here, was a particular branch of North American evangelicalism devoted mainly to resisting all forms of liberalism and modernism. Fundamentalists believed in the literal inspiration and inerrancy of the scriptures, fighting some of their greatest battles against proponents of Darwin's theory of evolution. They also stressed personal experience of salvation. Their methods were militant, and they gave exceptionally strong support to American military and nationalist policies.[25]

Dispensationalism had its roots in the Plymouth Brethren and held that God has dealt and will deal differently with humans in various eras. Its adherents specifically divided human history into seven eras, or dispensations, arguing, among other things, that the teachings of Jesus in the Sermon on the Mount did not apply directly to the church of the present era but referred to a future, perfect age. They were passionately interested in the nature of future dispensations and devoted much time and study to scriptural teachings of the end-times.[26]

Evangelicalism in these various manifestations had a major impact on Russian and North American Mennonites. In the early twentieth century there was intense controversy in (Old) Mennonite churches in the United States over some forms of religious fundamentalism.[27] That resulted in a search for, and rediscovery of, sixteenth-century Anabaptist beliefs and practices. The work of Harold S. Bender and his associates at Goshen College in Indiana was particularly influential.[28] Recovery of what Bender called 'the Anabaptist Vision' provided an escape from bitter religious controversies between fundamentalists and modernists. The more important long-term product, not yet fully understood in 1939, was a new point of reference for Mennonites living in diaspora.

Bender's ideas were most clearly and concisely defined in an essay that he presented as his presidential address to the American Society of Church History in 1943.[29] He identified three great principles of sixteenth-century Anabaptism. The first was holistic Christian discipleship. All of life must be brought into basic harmony under the Lordship of Christ. The second was voluntary church membership, based on true conversion and voluntary commitment to living in accordance with Jesus' teachings. The third focused on Jesus' ethic of love and non-resistance and on abandonment of all warfare, violence, and taking of human life.

Bender's work, based mainly on Swiss and south German Anabaptist sources, had an enormous impact on Mennonite scholarship, but other researchers soon pointed out that sixteenth-century Anabaptism also had roots in other regions of Europe.[30] Anabaptism, they argued, had multiple origins, and there were significant differences of opinion on many matters even in the earliest days. Bender's work nevertheless was the catalyst that led to rediscovery of a religious heritage that had been influenced and sometimes radically altered by the religious revivals of the nineteenth and early twentieth centuries.[31]

Bender had his greatest influence on the (Old) Mennonite Church in North America, but several Canadian scholars and teachers from other Mennonite conferences publicized his ideas.[32] Bender defined, or redefined, some of the most important doctrines held by scattered and fragmented Mennonite people around the world.

MENNONITE GROUPS IN CANADA

Most of the Mennonites living in Canada in 1939 traced their history to one of four migrations, but there had also been intermittent migrations between the major waves and smaller movements of people back and forth between Canada and the United States. The four major migrations of Mennonites (plus the fifth, after 1945) to Canada are shown in Table 1.1 and described in Appendix A.

The first migration of (Old) Mennonites from the United States to Ontario also included several hundred Tunkers who later adopted the name 'Brethren in Christ.' They too had Anabaptist roots and maintained close relations with Canadian Mennonite organizations.[33]

Each group came with its own history, religious practices, and congregational or conference organizations and leaders. Each contained serious divisions. In 1939 there were no less than twenty distinct conferences or organized Canadian Mennonite and related branches. They are listed in Table 1.2 by the migration from which the majority of their members were descended or to which they belonged, and are described in greater detail in Appendix B.[34]

Schisms have been a persistent problem for Mennonites, but the fragmentation evident in Canada in 1939 can also be attributed to the time of immigration and to religious movements of renewal on widely separated Russian and American settlement frontiers in the nineteenth and early twentieth centuries.

When Mennonites first established new, largely isolated, frontier communities, some of the religious leaders dreamed of utopias – of miniature Kingdoms of God on earth. But it soon became evident that even in their own churches and communities serious problems and blemishes remained, and new ones appeared as people dealt with changing circumstances. Shortcomings led to demands for reform, which created new divisions.

The reforms that swept the Russian and American Mennonite churches in the nineteenth century were not a result of studying original Anabaptist texts or of explicit attempts to return to the doctrines of the founding leaders.[35] The Great Awakenings that deeply affected Mennonites in Canada and the United States were part of the German and Pietist influences, though English Wesleyan and Methodist evangelists also preached in North American Mennonite communities. In Russia and eastern Europe, German Pietists,

Table 1.1
Major Mennonite migrations to Canada

Dates	Name in Canada	Group(s)	Place of origin	Destination	Numbers
1786–1825	'Swiss'	(Old) Mennonites, Brethren in Christ	United States	Ontario	2,000
1824–50	'Swiss'	Amish Mennonites	Europe	Ontario	1,000
1874–80	'Kanadier,' 'Dutch'	Mennonites	Russia	Manitoba	7,343
1923–30	'Russlaender'	Mennonites	Russia	Canada	20,201
1947–51	–	Mennonites	Russia and eastern Europe	Canada	7,698

Sources: Based on Frank Epp, *Mennonites in Canada, 1786–1920* (Toronto: Macmillan, 1974), Mennonites in *Canada, 1920–1940* (Toronto: Macmillan, 1982), and *Mennonite Exodus: The Rescue and Resettlement of The Russian Mennonites since the Communist Revolution* (Altona, Man.: Canadian Mennonite Relief and Immigration Council, 1962); Orland Gingerich, *The Amish of Canada* (Waterloo, Ont.: Conrad Press, 1972); and the *Mennonite Encyclopedia* (Scottdale, Penn.: Herald Press, 1959).

Baptists, and Lutheran Evangelicals exerted great influence in Mennonite communities. In their broader contexts, English Methodist, German Pietist, Baptist, and other evangelical revivals represented a protest against the growing problems of urbanization and industrialization. They proclaimed ideals that also had great appeal in the Mennonite communities, even though Mennonites in Russia and Canada remained almost entirely a rural and agricultural people throughout the nineteenth and early twentieth centuries.[36]

The divisions almost always pitted those who demanded changes because they believed that the old, established Mennonite churches had lost the zeal of the original church against those who feared that major changes would undermine their cherished faith and ways of life. These disagreements were often intensified by serious personality conflicts and by the ambitions of frustrated leaders. Geography and place of residence also played an important role.

Three distinct nineteenth-century waves of reform and fragmentation in the Russian and American Mennonite churches, each helping to explain Canadian Mennonite fragmentation, can be identified. In 1812 John Herr in the United States[37] and Klaas Reimer in Russia[38] led groups that broke away from the established Mennonite churches to form the Reformed Mennonite Church and the Kleine Gemeinde, respectively. Then, in 1847 and 1860, John Oberholtzer and John Holdeman, respectively, provided the leadership that resulted in formation in the United States of what would become

Table 1.2
Branches of Mennonites in Canada in 1939

Conference/branch	'Souls'[a]	Members[b]	Number of congregations
Majority of members from the first migration, 1786–1820			
(Old) Mennonites – Ontario	6,000	2,775	25
(Old) Mennonites – Alberta and Saskatchewan	1,000	584	7
Reformed Mennonites – Ontario		200	
Old Order Mennonites – Ontario (includes Markham-Waterloo and David Martin groups)		1,047	
Mennonite Brethren in Christ – Ontario (now Missionary Church)	4,000	2,241	46
Mennonite Brethren in Christ – Alberta (now Missionary Church)	1,000	500	20
Majority of members from the second migration, 1824–50			
Amish Mennonites – Ontario	4,000	2,000	18
Amish Mennonites – Alberta and Saskatchewan	200	100	4
Old Order Amish – Ontario (includes Beachy Amish)		350	
Majority of members from the third migration, 1874–80			
Sommerfelder – West Reserve Manitoba	6,000	2,500	1
Sommerfelder – Saskatchewan	3,000	1,500	5
Old Colony – Manitoba	1,060	390	1
Old Colony – Saskatchewan	2,500	1,200	2
Chortitzer Mennonite Conference East Reserve	2,769	1,207	1
Kleine Gemeinde – Prairies	2,449	1,102	2
Bergthaler – Saskatchewan		1,956	
Rudnerweider – Prairies	2,829	1,162	1
Holdeman (Church of God in Christ)	1,572	781	4
Members from various migrations			
Conference of Mennonites in Canada (includes Bergthaler of Manitoba and Rosenorter of Saskatchewan)	21,921	11,376	77
Mennonite Brethren – Prairies	14,000	6,250	75
Mennonite Brethren – Ontario	850	500	8

Table 1.2 (concluded)

Conference/branch	'Souls'[a]	Members[b]	Number of congregations
Evangelical Mennonite Brethren	1,810	1,000	7
Krimmer Mennonite Brethren	400	250	5
Related groups			
Brethren in Christ		700	
Hutterian Brethren	4,506		

Sources: See the discussion of sources in note 34.
[a] The term 'souls' includes all members and adherents.
[b] 'Members' refers to those who had received adult baptism and voluntarily joined a congregation.

the Eastern District of the General Conference of the Mennonite Church of North America[39] and of the Church of God in Christ, Mennonite.[40] Also in 1860, reform-minded Mennonites in Russia left the Mennonite church there to organize the Mennonite Brethren Church.[41] In Canada, Daniel High led a holiness revival that resulted in his expulsion from the Old Mennonite Church in 1848 and the founding of the New Mennonite Church, which became the Evangelical Missionary Church.[42]

A third wave of reform and fragmentation occurred in the 1880s and 1890s when several groups dissatisfied with changes in their churches diverged from the more culturally assimilated Mennonites to form Old Order Mennonite[43] and Old Order Amish groups[44] in the United States and Ontario. In western Canada, the Mennonites who had come from Russia in the 1870s experienced their own turmoil, leading to the founding of Mennonite Brethren, Church of God in Christ, Mennonite (Holdeman), Sommerfelder, Chortitzer, and Evangelical Mennonite Brethren churches.[45]

Some common themes or concerns emerged in the various reform movements and became part of the Canadian Mennonite identity. There were, first of all, frequent charges that churches had become lax in their discipline and tolerated unacceptable activities. Individuals were admitted to membership or allowed to retain it even though their life-style seemed offensive. Many reform-minded dissidents called for more rigorous practices of excommunication. They wanted rigorous codes of conduct, prohibiting 'worldly' activities such as dancing, smoking, alcohol consumption, card

playing, membership in fraternal organizations, participation in political activities, higher education, acceptance of modern technology, wearing of clothing according to the latest styles, reading novels, and attendance at country
fairs, horse races, movies, and theatrical performances. The objective was to
cleanse and purify the church, but the result was often a narrowly legalistic
and judgmental approach to religion.

Some dissidents also denounced discontinuance of such traditional practices as footwashing, the kiss of peace, observance of holy days, catechism,
forms of baptism, styles of worship, and models of church governance. For
the Old Order Amish in Ontario, for example, one issue that led to schism
was a decision to build separate meeting-houses. Old Order Amish, also
called 'House Amish,' continued to meet for worship in the homes of members. Some found establishment of Sunday schools and preaching in the
English language unacceptable.

Demand for return to historic practices and modes of conduct was matched,
and sometimes overpowered, by other dissident or reformist demands that
the church accept new methods and approaches. The 'Great Awakening' in
North American congregations was, according to one Mennonite theologian, 'borne on the wings of the Sunday School, an institution which gained
general acceptance in the Mennonite Church in the years from 1865-95.'[46]
But Sunday schools were controversial. Reform-minded U.S. Mennonites
accepted them, but the more conservative groups pointed out that neither
the original apostolic church nor sixteenth-century Anabaptists had them.
They were convinced that religious instruction was primarily a family responsibility and worried about use of the English language in the Sunday
schools. They were not convinced that Mennonites needed Sunday schools,
and some of the fastest-growing Mennonite and Old Order groups were
those that rejected such schools.[47] Rapid growth in the Mennonite and Old
Order groups that rejected Sunday schools, however, depended almost entirely on retention of the youth raised in large Old Order and other traditional families.

Those groups that accepted Sunday schools attributed much of their subsequent growth to them. An influential American Mennonite scholar has
argued that they had a decisive impact on groups that accepted them. The
Sunday school 'saved the church from great disaster by the new life, new
spirit, new activity, and new visitation which it put into the church. Many of
the congregations that rejected the Sunday School either have died out or
have gradually declined.'[48]

Itinerant and winter Bible conferences and Bible schools were also a by-
product of the Sunday school movement. These were primarily designed as

training and educational institutions for active or prospective church workers. Ministers' and deacons' conferences provided opportunities for leaders to meet, talk, and compare insights. Often a particular portion of scripture was studied, and its relevance to contemporary conditions discussed. The Bible schools also trained prospective Sunday school teachers, youth leaders, and music or choir directors. In addition, some groups set up secondary and post-secondary educational institutions where young people hoping to serve their communities as professionals, initially mainly as teachers, could receive more of their basic training in an acceptable context.

Sunday schools were not a significant factor in nineteenth-century renewal movements in Russian Mennonite communities, but other prayer and Bible study activities, and new educational institutions for youth, were as important there as in North America. These developments were complemented, and strongly reinforced in both Russian and American Mennonite communities, by a new style of evangelism. Itinerant preachers and evangelists, often from other denominations, organized special evangelistic services that stressed the necessity of a personal conversion experience. Conversion was usually defined as an emotionally charged and introspectionist event. It involved a deep sense of personal sinfulness and repentance, followed by deliverance and intense joy.

Evangelistic concerns, reinforced by more mundane, assimilationist pressures, hastened a change in the language of worship in the older Canadian Mennonite churches. As long as separation from the world, and the building of the Kingdom of God in their rural enclaves, were the main concerns of Mennonite leaders, the German language not only was cherished as a unique and familiar way in which people expressed their faith but also kept out new ideas and influences. Effective evangelistic witness to outsiders, however, was possible only in their language. As a result, by 1939, the (Old) Mennonite, Amish Mennonite, and most other 'Swiss' Mennonite churches in Canada, except for the Old Orders, were using English as the main language in worship. Churches founded by immigrants of the 1870s and 1920s still worshipped in German, but some were beginning to feel pressure to include English services.

The bitter disputes in North American Protestantism between 'fundamentalists'[49] and 'modernists'[50] created much tension but did not further fragment Canadian Mennonites. Possible exceptions were the Evangelical Mennonite Brethren church in Steinbach and the Evangelical Mennonite Mission Conference, both products of new evangelical influences.

The Mennonites who had come from Russia to Canada in the 1870s were less affected by Fundamentalist controversies. For them, schooling and participation in municipal politics proved more divisive in the early twentieth century.[51]

The immigrants of the 1920s had brought with them strong Pietist influences,[52] intensified by their traumatic experiences during the Russian Revolution, civil war, migration, and economic struggles in Canada during the 1930s. Physical survival had been their uppermost concern and brought Russian Mennonite groups closer together than they had been since the Mennonite Brethren had separated from the old Mennonite church in Russia in 1860. Fundamentalist-Modernist controversies were too distinctively North American to cause serious new divisions among the most recent immigrants.

The distinctive and separate historical experiences of various Mennonite immigrants, together with new influences, accounted for most of the fragmentation among Canadian Mennonites up to 1939.[53]

Mennonite historians and sociologists have sometimes described those groups that readily accepted religious and technological change and were tolerant of diversity as 'liberal' or 'progressive.' Those who resisted change, rejected new religious ideas and methods, and attached greater importance to traditional ways are described as 'conservatives.'[54] There are, however, several problems with such designations. Many of the new ideas and practices brought in by Methodists, Pietists, and other evangelicals were reactions against industrialization and urbanization, not acceptance of the social changes of the time. Evangelists talked much about a return to an 'Old Fashioned' gospel message. The saintly mother and her simple faith rooted in Bible reading, or the heart-broken, honest father with calloused and work-weary hands folded in prayer for an erring son who had gone astray in the city, reappeared constantly in Gospel songs and evangelistic sermons.

Juxtaposed against those traditional virtues were sharp denunciations not only of the evils of the cities and of non-agricultural industrial endeavours but also of modernists, liberals, and humanists who preached a social gospel that sought to reform social conditions rather than seek sectarian escape and renewed emphasis on personal salvation of individuals caught in the toils of urban and industrial life. Many of the evangelists were highly intolerant of anyone whose religious ideas differed from their own.[55]

All this raises serious problems when a 'liberal' label is attached to those Canadian Mennonites who responded positively to the new evangelicalism. New religious ideas and practices facilitated and hastened integration and sometimes assimilation of Canadian Mennonites into one particular stream of North American religious life. But that religious stream was largely rural, agricultural, traditional, and conservative. It stood in opposition to many

forms of modernity. Evangelicalism and Fundamentalism for some Mennonites were 'a transitional theology between an inherited nineteenth century
[Mennonite] theology, less doctrinal and precisely formulated, and the emergence of a theological biblicism rooted in a rediscovered Anabaptist herme-
neutical tradition.'[56]

The most significant result of the new evangelical influences in Canadian
Mennonite communities was not an embrace of liberal or progressive principles by those who accepted the new ideas. Rather, by 1939, new and different religious ideas and practices had already created considerable ideological
and theological confusion in those very groups. That confusion would in-
tensify in the following decades.

LEADERS

Mennonites could not look to a Pope or to centralized church authorities
for guidance when dealing with confusing and divisive issues. Their patterns
of leadership were more democratic, but also more diffuse. These historic,
long-accepted, but unique patterns were described thus in a Mennonite Brethren report on leadership:

The leaders, teachers, and servants of the church were chosen by the church out of
their own midst after much prayer, trusting that Christ by His Spirit would give to
His flock, in the words of Jeremiah, 'pastors according to mine heart, which shall
feed you with knowledge and understanding.' (Jer. 3:15) From among the teachers
they appointed an Elder to carry the leadership responsibility for the flock, the other
teachers and ministers being their helpers. New workers, teachers and ministers, chosen from within the church, trained and matured under the influence and leadership
of the Elders of the church, grew into the work of the local church and Conference
thoroughly indoctrinated with all Scriptural principles of belief and practice.[57]

The leaders chosen in this way usually served without financial remuneration, and their call demanded lifelong commitment. This method of selection tended to elevate the most influential, the wealthiest, and the most
talented members of the community to leadership. Some groups chose their
leaders by lot, but in such cases there was usually careful screening of the
names placed in the lot.[58]

Congregations and churches often included more than one meeting place.
The Bergthaler Church of Manitoba, for example, had as many as twenty
meeting places and more than 3,000 members, all subject to the leadership of
one elder (*Aeltester*) and a council (*Lehrsdienst*), which included all the or-

dained preachers, teachers, and deacons in the various meeting places. The elder had exclusive responsibility to conduct baptisms, serve communion, and officiate at weddings and funerals, ordinations, and other important church functions. He usually, but not always, chaired meetings of the council and exerted great ecclesiastical as well as economic, social, and political power in both church and community.

(Old) Mennonite and Amish Mennonite churches introduced the title of 'bishop' to designate their leading congregational leaders. Those coming from Russia or the Soviet Union in the 1870s and 1920s were more likely to use the title *Aeltester* (elder), but there was not complete consistency in the use of either term.[59] The functions and powers of bishops and elders varied over time and place and among groups.[60] The ordained officials were responsible for ongoing spiritual matters only, but in closed Mennonite communities their power and influence often extended to other aspects of congregational, family, and community life. They could refuse the rites of the church to recalcitrant individuals, and expulsion carried serious social and economic as well as religious consequences. Members in some Mennonite communities were not allowed to do business with excommunicated individuals, and in some Russian, Mexican, and South American Mennonite colonies non-members could not own land in the colony.

The power and authority of the religious leaders were further increased by the fact that they were almost always chosen and ordained for life. There was no generally accepted way in which they could be removed for misconduct, incompetence, or abuse of power. Rivalries, conflict, and quarrels, ending in schism, were a frequent result.[61]

The label 'church council' was not used in Canadian Mennonite churches in 1939. The administrative body usually consisted of all the ordained officers and, sometimes, evangelists and elected lay members. Most Russian Mennonite groups referred to this administrative body as the '*Lehrdienst*'; Swiss Mennonites called it 'the bench'; and still others called it the '*Vorberat.*' The main responsibilities were similar and related mainly to the ongoing ministry of the church.

All important matters, including selection of new leaders, were subject to democratic control of the membership. Membership meetings were therefore an important part of church life, but in many Canadian Mennonite churches in 1939 only men were allowed to participate, and gatherings were commonly called 'brotherhood' meetings. A few congregations allowed women to participate fully.

Canadian Mennonite leaders depended on local congregations. The administrative structure was unusually flat or non-hierarchical, but in 1939 it was in a process of modification by three seemingly contradictory trends.

The first had to do with localization. Churches with many meeting places but only one bishop or elder were subjected to considerable pressure to grant more authority and power to their larger local congregations. Numerous church functions were performed only by the bishop or elder. Churches with many meeting places made inordinately heavy demands on these officials, who rarely received adequate financial remuneration. So they had to look after their own farm or business in addition to their church work. It was also inconvenient when all important congregational celebrations had to be planned to suit the crowded agenda of the bishop or elder.

Larger local bodies with leadership talent quite naturally sought independence and ordination of their own bishop or elder. This process of devolution had been going on for years in Canadian Mennonite churches.[62] Sometimes the unpopularity, death, or increasing age and frailty of the bishop, or geographical scattering, hastened the process, while a young, vigorous, administratively talented and charismatic bishop or elder delayed it. But the desire for local autonomy had resulted in localization in some groups by 1939. The larger, geographically scattered churches were among the first to grant local autonomy, but even the Kleine Gemeinde, which had only four meeting places relatively near one another, recommended in 1942 that the congregations at Steinbach, Gruenfeld/Kleefeld, Prairie Rose, and Blumenort each accept responsibility for their own affairs.[63] Thus the old system, in which large churches with numerous meeting places were held together through the work and influence of a common bishop or elder, was giving way to greater local autonomy.

Localization, however, increased the need for new structures and institutions to coordinate joint activities of common interest to various autonomous congregations. Bishops and elders had provided personal links. Now conferences came to provide coordination on matters of mutual interest.

Conferences and bishop- or elder-led churches with multiple meeting places were not mutually exclusive organizational structures. The Rosenorter Mennonite Church of Saskatchewan and the Bergthaler Mennonite Church of Manitoba, each led by strong and influential elders and possessing numerous meeting places, joined in 1903 to form what would become the Conference of Mennonites in Canada (CMC). Canada's Mennonite Brethren (MBs), in contrast, never really endorsed elder-led governance, though they had had such a structure in Russia and some of their leaders ordained in Russia functioned as elders in Canada. In North America the Mennonite Brethren looked instead to their conferences for leadership in matters requiring joint action.

By 1939 some of the larger Mennonite groups, particularly in western

Canada, were slowly replacing the bishop- or elder-led multiple-meeting-place churches with autonomous local congregations voluntarily joined into larger conferences. Other large groups, such as the Bergthaler in Manitoba, who had an exceptionally strong and capable leader in Elder David Schulz, and almost all the smaller groups retained the elder system throughout the 1930s, even though some were or became members of conferences as well. Since some joint projects required cooperation and support on a national or international basis, while others were of an essentially regional or provincial nature, the largest Mennonite groups also found it prudent to create regional or provincial, national, and international conferences.[64]

Canadian Mennonites had also created several inter-Mennonite organizations. Some were purely local, mutual aid or cooperative ventures, in which members from different conferences or churches worked together. These local, joint undertakings were complemented by major national and international inter-Mennonite organizations. The dire problems of Mennonites during and after the Russian Revolution and civil war led to the organization in both Canada and the United States of inter-Mennonite committees to coordinate emergency relief aid. The Mennonite Central Committee (MCC) was organized in the United States in July 1920, followed in October by founding of what was initially called the Canadian Central Committee.[65] Both bodies provided urgently needed relief assistance, as did the parallel Nonresistant Relief Organization in Ontario.

The First World War, the Russian Revolution, civil war, and economic disasters in Russia made emigration an increasingly attractive option, but only Canada seemed willing to accept more Mennonite immigrants. In order to facilitate such a migration, and, after an offer of substantial transportation credits came from the Canadian Pacific Railway (CPR), the Canadian Central Committee was reorganized as the Canadian Mennonite Board of Colonization on 17 May 1922. This board conducted negotiations with the Canadian government and, with the help of the CPR, arranged for the immigration of more than 20,000 Russian Mennonites who came to Canada in the 1920s. The board was assisted by the Conference of Mennonites in Canada, the Mennonite Brethren, the Mennonite Church, the Church of God in Christ, Mennonite, and the Evangelical Mennonite Brethren.[66] Other groups also provided assistance, even though they were not officially represented on the board.

The MCC, which had coordinated the relief aid extended to the Mennonites in the Soviet Union in the 1920s, subsequently expanded its activities, and by 1939 it was the largest and most important North American inter-Mennonite relief organization.[67]

These and other inter-Mennonite organizations were usually created to deal with a specific problem. Some completed their work and ceased operations, but the MCC and the Canadian Mennonite Board of Colonization remained in 1939.

A curious phenomenon associated with the growing importance of Mennonite conferences and inter-Mennonite organizations was the rise of a relatively small cadre of exceptionally influential leaders. The bishops, elders, and other elected leaders usually represented their churches at conferences and were named as representatives of their denomination or group on the boards of inter-Mennonite organizations. The fact that these leaders received railway passes meant that it was cheaper for churches to send them as delegates to conferences and meetings in distant places. As a result, a few leaders came to occupy key executive and committee positions in their conferences and in inter-Mennonite organizations. They got to know one another well, forming what in another Canadian context might well have been called a 'Family Compact.'

The case of the Conference of Mennonites in Canada (CMC), the nation's largest Mennonite conference, is indicative. Its most senior leadership positions came to be dominated during the first fifty years of its history by five men – Benjamin Ewert, H.H. Ewert, Jacob Gerbrandt, J.J. Thiessen, and David Toews. H.H. Ewert served as a member of the conference executive from 1906 until 1913, four of those years as chairman. His brother Benjamin sat, with only a few short interruptions, on the executive from 1903 until 1942. Jacob Gerbrandt was a member of the executive committee, again with only a few breaks, from 1908 until 1951. David Toews served from 1904 until 1940, usually as chairman, and after his retirement J.J. Thiessen was first vice-chairman and then, from 1943 until 1959, chairman.

These five men also represented the CMC on the boards of important inter-Mennonite organizations, such as the Board of Colonization, which was chaired by either David Toews or J.J. Thiessen for decades, and the U.S.-based MCC, on whose executive Ewert, Gerbrandt, Thiessen, and Toews also served.

In the large, multi-meeting-place Bergthaler Mennonite Church of Manitoba, which was a founding member of the CMC but refused to join the North American General Conference, Elder David Schulz, who also served on numerous national, regional, and provincial committees, gained similar prominence and influence.

Thus a small group of men, who were of course associated with and assisted by others, dominated the CMC's affairs and numerous inter-Mennonite ventures for decades. There were very few major CMC or inter-Mennonite committees on which these men did not sit, often as chairmen. Their influence would become even greater during the Second World War because they also dominated the inter-Mennonite organizations that negotiated wartime alternative service and other arrangements with the Canadian government and arrangements for postwar immigration of Mennonite refugees from Europe. These men travelled extensively, visited and spoke in hundreds of churches, including many in small, rural communities, and were thus able to build an exceptionally strong support base.

The situation in the CMC was not unique. The other Mennonite groups and conferences also produced a small number of exceptionally influential leaders. In the (Old) Mennonite Church in Ontario the well-known quartet of Oscar Burkholder, S.F. Coffman, C.F. Derstine and J.B. Martin provided strong leadership,[68] as did Bishop E.J. Swalm of the Brethren in Christ.[69] Affairs of Canadian Mennonite Brethren were largely controlled in 1939 by men such as John A. Harder, B.B. Janz, C.F. Klassen, J.B. Toews, and A.H. Unruh,[70] while histories of the Rudnerweider/Evangelical Mennonite Mission Conference highlight Wilhelm H. Falk, Gerhard J. Froese, Isaac Hoeppner, and Peter S. Zacharias, the four founding ministers.[71]

These leaders all had only limited formal theological or other training. Most were community leaders, chosen by members of their home communities, but already in 1939 there were some exceptions. The nature and extent of the work demanded of their leaders had prompted some congregations to offer remuneration if those leaders would devote all, or at least most, of their time and energy to church-related work. In the case of the (Old) Mennonite leaders, limited remuneration was closely linked to special collections taken at evangelistic meetings conducted by those leaders or to tuition fees paid by students attending the Ontario Bible School at which some of them taught.

However, those sources of income were unreliable and insufficient, so a few local congregations began to provide some regular support. The first leader or pastor called from outside the local community to serve as a paid pastor in a Canadian Mennonite church on a long-term basis was probably Clayton F. Derstine. Derstine was an evangelist and pastor of the Roanoke Mennonite Church at Eureka, Illinois, when he was called to serve as pastor of the First Mennonite Church in Kitchener, which had suffered a painful division. A few other urban Mennonite congregations had also hired pastors before 1939, in part because they wanted individuals with at least some relevant theological training. But Mennonite churches with paid pastors were still a decided minority in 1939.

EVERYDAY LIFE

The separatist, rural, and agricultural communities in which Canadian Mennonites lived in 1939 were sometimes very different from the utopias they had hoped to establish. Some were prosperous and well ordered, particularly those in Ontario and in southern Manitoba, where the settlers were well established. But large families and difficult economic conditions during the Depression had left many of the younger families without adequate resources to acquire farms of their own. An American sociologist who visited the Mennonite communities of Canada in 1943 expressed grave concern about 'an excess population that had no place to establish itself.' The problem was particularly serious on the prairies. The plight of landless Mennonites from the former Mennonite reserves north of Saskatoon was described thus:

Rev. J.J. Thiessen in Saskatchewan told me of some sixty families from the Old Colony people who had settled on the periphery of the city of Saskatoon and were living in tragically wretched conditions. Not only are they all extremely poor economically but their spiritual and moral level is absolutely pathetic . . . I was also told by one of the librarians at the University of Toronto who had made a study of some of the religious groups in western Canada that she had never seen anything more wretched than some of the impoverished Mennonite communities in Saskatchewan.[72]

Many Mennonite farm families on the prairies, particularly among those who had migrated from the Soviet Union in the 1920s, had acquired land and equipment at high prices in the late 1920s. In the 1930s they were so burdened with debt that they had to seek legal protection under special legislation designed to prevent banks, mortgage companies, and other creditors from taking over farms if all reasonable efforts were being made to make the required payments.

Even in the older communities in Ontario a growing number of young couples could not set up farms of their own. Instead they had to seek employment in farm-related service activities in the villages and towns. Others began to look to the cities. Winnipeg, Saskatoon, Kitchener, and the larger rural service towns in Mennonite districts all had sizeable Mennonite 'halfway' settlements in which the poor lived on subdivided one- or two-acre plots where they planted gardens and kept a cow, a pig, and a few chickens while earning whatever they could at odd jobs in the town or city. Urbanization, however, encompassed only a small minority of Canadian Mennonites in 1939.

Mennonites in older communities, with their strong sense of community and commitment to mutual aid, probably faced fewer serious economic problems than most Canadian farmers in 1939. But the same conditions that had already resulted in a massive migration of Canadians from the countryside were also clearly evident in the Mennonite communities. Those pressures would be greatly intensified during the war and in the succeeding decades and would sweep most Canadian Mennonites into the cities. In the process both family and community life would be dramatically altered.

The family, the family farm, and occasionally the small agricultural service business were the core of Mennonite social organization. Religious, social, cultural, and economic concerns all had a common focus in the family and in the role of each of its members. Life in the traditional, separated rural and agricultural context, it was hoped, would be integrated and wholesome, not fragmented as it often was in industrial and urban settings. On the farm everyone worked together, everyone had a place, and everyone made a contribution.[73]

Gender roles were clearly defined and carefully maintained. The male head of the family had final responsibility and authority for all aspects of family life. On occasion that facilitated arbitrary and even abusive behaviour, but overriding concerns for the success and welfare of the family farm or small-town business limited exploitative behaviour. The traditional farm family in 1939 was patriarchal, but the important place of women in the farm economy gave them greater influence than was the case in many non-farm urban families.[74]

Farm wives were taught to be submissive and to obey their husbands, but they performed absolutely vital and essential tasks on the farm. They managed the household, child care, large-scale gardening, food preservation, farm chores, and even field work, when extra help was needed. They were indispensable in subsistence activities and in reproduction of children to provide the hands that maintained the system. In 1939 they still had to do most of this work without the new household conveniences that were making life easier for middle-class city women. In 1941, for example, only 20.2 per cent of farm homes had electric lighting, 12.2 per cent inside running water, 29.3 per cent a telephone, 22.2 per cent refrigeration, and only 8.1 per cent flush toilets.[75] The figures for Mennonite homes are not given separately but were probably even lower, particularly among the 1920s immigrants, because expenditures on land, farm machinery, and stock tended to take precedence. Cooperation between spouses was essential in labour-intensive farm operations, and Mennonites were a 'conspicuous exception' to the general decline in 'day to day co-operation of spouses' in farming households.[76]

Mennonite women in 1939 were little affected by the modernization taking place in home economics and in childrearing. While other Canadian women were bombarded with the prescriptions of experts on 'correct methods for mothering,' exemplified in the raising of the famous Dionne quintuplets born in 1934, Mennonite mothers probably shared the opinion of a working-class immigrant of the late 1920s who rejected 'silly psychological books' in favour of 'instinct, tradition, and observation.'[77]

Table 1.3
Percentage of adherents under the age of 15
in the major religious denominations, 1941

Mennonites	38.7
Roman Catholics	32.9
Baptists	26.1
United Church	24.5
Anglicans	22.6
Presbyterians	20.3

Source: Census of Canada, 1941.

In any case, the new, 'scientific' methods really only worked for women with small families who had the time needed to meet each child's 'proper' care and education. Labour-intensive Mennonite farming made children an economic asset, and large families were still the norm. So, in 1941, Canadian Mennonites still had a larger percentage of adherents under the age of 15 than other major Canadian religious denominations, as Table 1.3 demonstrates.[78]

Larger families were common among the less wealthy, less educated, rural and newer immigrant communities. In Ontario, the proportion of adherents under the age of 15 was approximately 31 per cent, while on the prairies, where most of the more recent immigrants were located, it averaged 40 per cent. As well, urban Mennonites were having smaller families,[79] confirming that urbanization was a factor in the decline of family size for Mennonites as well as for other Canadians.

The rural-urban split does not fully account for Mennonite family size. Whether Mennonites were shying away from modern birth control methods, which were becoming more widely available during the 1920s and 1930s, is difficult to document. The fact that A.R. Kaufman, a leading disseminator of birth control information in the country, employed a number of Mennonites at his Kitchener rubber factory,[80] suggests that at least those working in that factory and their closest friends and relatives may have been aware of the new birth control methods.

The appointment of a special Birth Control Committee by the (Old) Mennonite Conference of Ontario in 1944 suggests that family planning was becoming an issue, at least for that conference. The committee, made up entirely of men, argued against use of birth control on the basis of scriptural calls to 'be fruitful, and multiply, and replenish the earth.' A normal marriage, they said, should be blessed with children.[81] Another writer insisted that the main purpose of marriage was propagation of the human race through 'a well-ordered succession of child-bearing in the fear of the Lord.'[82] Large families were regarded as a sign of God's blessing and of obedience to his injunctions.

That a woman's primary role was to be a wife and mother was not seriously questioned. One woman, writing in the *Gospel Herald*, blamed current economic problems partly on the fact that too many girls were looking forward to a 'business career.' To counter this trend, she suggested that girls be taught from infancy that 'the highest rank in life for women is that of homemaker and motherhood.'[83] Certain vocations, however, such as nursing, teaching, and missionary work, were acceptable for Mennonite women, particularly if they were single, or for those few years of adulthood prior to marriage. Because these were nurturing professions, they prepared a woman for her ultimate vocation. One writer to the *Christian Monitor*, describing the ideal wife, noted that though his own wife had a high school education, had taught school, and had a talent for music and painting and a love for literature, these were 'but accessories' to her primary role as 'homekeeper.'[84] A woman's primary influence in the community and in the world was through the raising of her children; as one woman put it, 'Being queen of a nation pales in comparison to the opportunity we have, that of shaping and moulding young lives to go out into life to work for God and His Church.'[85]

For Mennonite women in 1939 issues concerning nonconformity or separation from the world had unique implications. Cosmetics, jewellery, fashionable clothing, and other means of enhancing appearance were widely regarded as worldly and therefore forbidden. For female members of the (Old) Mennonite Church, the Old Orders, or other conservative groups in Ontario, a devotional head covering became the most visible outward symbol of their nonconformity. Head coverings were also prescribed for western Canadian Holdeman and Kleine Gemeinde women. Old Colony and Sommerfelder women had to wear kerchiefs in church.

Distinctive clothing for men was never stressed to the same extent. In 1939 ordained men in the (Old) and Amish Mennonite conferences in Ontario were expected to wear the plain coat, and most did so until the late 1950s; in the 1960s it became optional. Other male members were urged to wear plain or simple clothing but did not face as much pressure as did the women, for whom the devotional head covering became a symbol of humility, submission, and obedience. One woman even compared it to the crown of thorns worn by Christ. In other conferences, where the wearing of a head covering in public did not receive the same emphasis, simple, unostentatious, and modest apparel was expected, and adornments that might denote pride, vanity, or arrogance were firmly rejected.

Women were not expected to participate in the business meetings of their congregations. Several conferences included the name 'Brethren' in their official name, and business meetings were often referred to as 'Brotherhood' meetings, but some of the MB churches in Russia had permitted women to participate in their business meetings and continued that practice in Canada. Women, of course, attended the regularly scheduled worship services and were active participants in congregational choirs and Sunday school programs. In addition, they had developed their own women's organizations, which became parallel church undertakings. 'The desire of ... Mennonite women to perform "willing service" in their home and beyond'[86] led to organization of sewing circles, *Frauenvereine*, ladies' aids, or ladies' auxiliaries, which allowed talented women to learn new skills, to participate actively, and to lead in some aspects of church life. The work of these groups would grow after the outbreak of war. The women provided relief to war sufferers and later to postwar refugees.

CONCLUSION

Canadian Mennonites in 1939 were still a simple, rural and agricultural people who sought to separate themselves as much as possible from outside influences and to build their own communities, churches, and families in the way that Jesus and the scriptures taught. They had survived the difficulties of the 1920s and 1930s, but powerful new influences already at work would end that separation and transform them. They were at a turning point, though many regarded it more as a fork in the road. One path led to accommodation and integration with the outside world, loss of faith, and ultimately eternal punishment. The other, much more difficult, path required renewed commitment to a separatist strategy. But even those most strongly committed to the old way of life would be drawn into closer and more frequent contacts with the outside world. For the majority of Canadian Mennonites the advice of baseball great Yogi Berra seemed appropriate: 'When you come to a fork in the road, take it.'

PART TWO
THE CRUCIBLE OF WAR

2
Wartime Alternative
and Military Service

The Canadian census of 1941 reported that there were 16,913 Mennonite males between the ages of 15 and 35 living in Canada.[1] During the war approximately 4,500 Mennonite men enlisted for active military service,[2] while 7,543 were drafted for alternative service.[3] Thus more than 70 per cent of Canadian Mennonite men of military age rendered either alternative or active military service during the Second World War. An unknown but significant number obtained wartime work in Canadian towns and cities; still others provided voluntary service at home and abroad. Most expected to return to their cherished rural communities when peace came, but only a minority were able to do so.

Leaving home during the war was a common, often traumatic, and, for many of Canada's Mennonites, permanent experience. The manner in which they did so varied greatly. Noah Bearinger departed his southern Ontario home on 4 January 1943. Together with other conscientious objectors he boarded a train at Galt at 9 p.m. 'It was,' he recalled, 'a cold winter evening and many parents had gathered to see their boys leave. They sang farewell songs as we were loaded and started moving into the dark.'[4] This group of 'conchies' was on its way to the Montreal River camp near Sault Ste Marie. They travelled by train as far as the Sault and from there on cattle trucks with tarpaulins over the top and bales to sit on. En route, as the cold, darkness, apprehension, and feelings of homesickness deepened, the young men tried to keep up their spirits by singing gospel songs. The lyrics of a favourite, which expressed the feelings of many conscientious objectors, were:

It may not be on the mountain height,
Or over the stormy sea.
It may not be at the battle front,

My Lord will have need of me.
But if by a still small voice he calls,
To paths that I do not know,
I'll answer, dear Lord, with my hand in thine,
I'll go where you want me to go.
I'll go where you want me to go, dear Lord,
Over mountain, or sea or plain,
I'll say what you want me to say, dear Lord,
I'll be what you want me to be.[5]

Henry Pankratz of Langham, Saskatchewan, embarked under completely different circumstances in 1941. He enlisted in the Royal Canadian Air Force in defiance of the traditional religious beliefs of his family, but with the approval of friends and community leaders. Unfortunately, his plane was shot down over Germany on 6 December 1944. An emergency parachute jump saved his life, but he became a prisoner of war. In spite of some difficult experiences, he regarded his air force experience as 'the highlight of my life' and explained his decision to enlist thus: 'I and my brothers always felt that Canada gave our parents a new life and an opportunity to live in peace and harmony and raise a family in the best country in the world, and therefore worth fighting for. As a result we often found ourselves at variance with Mennonite tradition and/or religious beliefs.'[6]

Fred Snyder from Ontario also signed up with the Canadian air force in 1941, went overseas, and served as a radar mechanic. For him the reality of war was restricted in the early years to impersonal blips on a radar screen. But after VE Day he saw the bombed-out German cities and said: 'We moved into Germany and I can recall ... Dueren, a town the size of Kitchener at that time, a beautiful place, but as we approached, it seemed ... it was just a pile of rubble one storey deep ... The stench of the dead, five months later, was sickening. We were bombing very precisely and just slaughtering that whole population. Canadians, British and Americans were doing this! That's when I first sensed that it was sickening on both sides, that we were not better than the Germans.'[7] When he set out in 1941 Snyder believed that it was his patriotic duty to serve. But he said later that when a person enlists, 'You park your brains at the door and you change overnight ... In the military you don't think, you just follow instructions.'[8] After the war, he became a peace activist.

Gerhard Ens, David Schroeder, and William Unrau from southern Manitoba spent part of the war working as conscientious objectors in Manitoba mental hospitals.[9] Ens and Schroeder found the work meaningful and satisfying, and Ens later observed: 'I learned to know another group of people. I learned to know about the whole area of mental retardation which has given me a great many insights for later years.'[10] The two colleagues went on to distinguished teaching careers. Unrau, however, was killed while burning garbage at the St Boniface Hospital. Something in one of the garbage containers apparently exploded, injuring him. When calling for help he inhaled poisonous gases produced by the explosion, and he died a few days later.[11]

Rudolf Goetz of Yarrow, British Columbia, joined the restricted medical corp and was sent overseas in 1944. He was killed in action in March 1945. Acquaintances from Yarrow say that Goetz died when a live grenade landed in a crowded spot. Goetz dropped on it, and his body absorbed the explosion, which otherwise would have killed many others.[12] Goetz lies buried in a Canadian military cemetery near Nijmegen, Holland.[13]

Jacob G. Enns of Altona, Manitoba, is also buried in a European military cemetery. Jacob and four of his brothers, sons of dragline operator William Enns and his wife, Kathleen, all enlisted. Jacob, at 26 years of age, was killed in action at Gruppenbuhren, Germany, on 26 April 1945, only days before the end of the war. He was serving with the 1st Battalion of the Calgary Highlanders and was one of six Highlanders killed in action, all on that date, in that place. The distinguished historian who has written the history of the Highlanders describes what happened: 'It was all a great tragedy, really. The war was almost over and the objective given to the battalion was not especially important. Basically, the men were advancing over an open field under cover of smoke when the wind suddenly shifted – fortunes of war. The men were caught in the open and cut down in a crossfire of German machine guns. Of course, no one knew the war was about to end or that the advance would have so little meaning in the long run.'[14]

These eight men, with their varied experience of war, were part of a massive movement of more than 12,000 young Mennonites who served their country.

MENNONITE LEADERS DISAGREE

The divergent responses of Canadian Mennonite men was, in part at least, a result of divided opinions among their denominational leaders. In the United States the largest Mennonite Conference, popularly known as the (Old) Mennonites, had adopted a resolution on peace, war, and military service at a general conference held at Turner, Oregon, in August 1937. A later meeting of representatives from other Mennonite conferences in Chicago endorsed these principles, with a few minor modifications.[15] The American Mennonites declared flatly that they would not participate in military or cadet training and would not cooperate with organizations such as the YMCA or the Red Cross, whose medical and relief work was closely linked to war. Nor would they help finance war operations through purchase of war bonds. Instead they would devote themselves 'to aid in the relief of those who are in need, distress or suffering, regardless of the danger in which we may be placed in bringing such relief, or of the cost which may be involved in the same.' They also expressed the hope 'that if service be required of us it may not be under the military arm of the government, and may be such that we can perform it without violating our conscience.'

The meetings of U.S. Mennonites prompted their Canadian co-religionists to hold a special gathering to decide what they would do in the event of war. More than 500 delegates and observers, including a sizeable U.S. delegation, met at Winkler, Manitoba, on 15 May 1939.[16] The Americans pleaded with the Canadians to stand in unity with them by endorsing the Chicago declaration. The Canadians readily reaffirmed their historic refusal to participate in active military service, but they were not agreed on appropriate forms of alternative service.

These differences were not surprising. Mennonites had arrived in this country over a period of 150 years under varying circumstances. They had no common leadership or organizational structure, and groups had responded differently to the problems of military and alternative service in Canada, or in their country of origin, during previous wars.

Those whose ancestors had come to British North America in the first two major migration waves identified in the previous chapter had been granted special exemptions from active military service, but not from alternative, non-combatant service or payment of special taxes in lieu of military service.[17] These provisions had been maintained in Canadian legislation, though the specific type of service that might be required of them in wartime had never been clearly defined. At the May 1939 meeting in Winkler, descendants of these people, most of whom still had close links with the Americans, urged acceptance of the Chicago statement.

Mennonites ('Kanadier') who had come from Russia to southern Manitoba in the 1870s had obtained written ministerial assurances, followed by an order in council, which provided 'That an entire exemption from any military service, as is provided by law and Order in Council, will be granted to the denomination of Christians called Mennonites.'[18] It was not clear whether this document exempted these Mennonites from all service in the event of war, but those to whom the 1873 order in council applied believed that they could not, even in wartime, be conscripted for state service of any kind. That interpretation had, at least in practice, been accepted by the Canadian government in the conscription crisis of the First World War.[19] Descendants of this group argued that they need not offer service of any kind. Even the limited scope of service proposed by the American Mennonites seemed to them a dangerous compromise. War, if it came, was none of their business. At Winkler, they were prepared to concede that a letter might be written asking Ottawa to confirm their complete exemption from all active or alternative service.

Immigrants who had come to Canada from the Soviet Union in the 1920s ('Russlaender') had been informed, at the time of their arrival, that the exemptions of 1873 would not apply to them. The deputy minister of justice had written in 1924 that 'more than half a century has elapsed and conditions have changed so much that I do not think it could reasonably be held that the Government is now inviting immigrations upon the terms then stipulated.'[20] It was agreed, however, that the more general legislation under which members of the historic peace churches were exempt from combatant service but could be called for alternative service would apply to the Mennonite immigrants of the 1920s.

These Mennonites had accepted alternative Russian state service after 1870 at the demand of the tsarist government. Initially their service had been performed in Mennonite-financed and -administered forestry projects, but in the First World War members had also funded and operated a wide range of Red Cross medical, ambulance, and first aid services at the front, on special hospital trains, and in military hospitals. These services seemed constructive, and most of those involved were convinced that they had rendered an effective witness to the historic tenets of their faith.[21] What they had done was more positive and constructive than either doing nothing or participating only in services that had no links with the military. They were prepared to serve Canada as they had served Russia.

The Winkler meeting thus revealed three distinct approaches. Those covered by the 1873 order in council claimed exemption from all state service, even in time of war. The descendants of the earliest Mennonite migrations were willing to render some form of alternative service if it were entirely non-military, while those who had arrived in the 1920s were willing to render a much broader range of services, including medical and ambulance work at the front.

The failure of Canadian Mennonites to agree in May 1939 on acceptable forms of alternative service in the event of war had no immediate consequences. The country was not yet at war, and the government was as uncertain about alternative services as the Mennonite leaders. In the 1920s and 1930s Mennonite leaders had tried to get Ottawa to indicate what might be expected but were told bluntly: 'In the event of war, there would be plenty of time then for persons who are exempt under the law to claim that exemption.'[22]

Prime Minister William Lyon Mackenzie King, who had grown up in Berlin (Kitchener) and appreciated Mennonite contributions in building that community, thought that members of the historic peace churches should be exempt from combatant military service. His government, nevertheless, had no policy regarding conscientious objectors except that services required of them would be established 'upon such conditions and under such regulations as the Governor in Council may, from time to time, prescribe.'[23]

The outbreak of war in September 1939 did not lead to immediate clarification of manpower policies. The prime minister, remembering how divisive conscription had been in the First World War, was determined to avoid a similar crisis.[24] He announced that Canada, being far from the conflict, would adopt a 'limited liability' war policy, which would not include compulsory military or alternative service. That made it unnecessary to define what might be required of members of the historic peace churches and temporarily eased the pressure to devise a common policy.

CANADA DEMANDS WARTIME SERVICE

The Nazi Blitzkrieg (lightning war) unleashed on Poland early in September 1939 quickly ran its course. Within weeks western Poland was occupied, and Germany fortified its new eastern borders. Thereafter, for seven months, there was a lull in the fighting. In Europe the Blitzkrieg gave way to the Sitzkrieg (sitting war), while leaders in Britain, France, and Canada spoke of a 'phoney war.' Nazi attacks in the west were expected, and during the winter both sides prepared for more fighting in the spring.

The Sitzkrieg on Germany's western front ended abruptly on 10 May 1940, when combined air, land, and parachute attacks against Holland, Belgium, Luxembourg, and France once more unleashed the fury of the Blitzkrieg. Within a week triumphant German forces crossed the French border, advancing relentlessly on Paris. Italy entered the war as an ally of Germany on 10 June, and six days later the government of France fell. The difficult and costly withdrawal of the remaining British and French forces from Dunkirk lessened allied military losses but also demonstrated that the allies had suffered a catastrophic defeat.

With France reeling, and the Soviet Union and the United States remaining neutral, only Britain and its colonies and dominions stood in Hitler's path to world domination. Massive air attacks on Britain seemed a certainty, but the country was ill prepared. The French collapse seemed but a prelude to a similar British disaster. Under such grave conditions any notion of a limited Canadian involvement in the war seemed entirely inappropriate, and officials in Ottawa were instructed to prepare legislation authorizing a massive conscription of men and resources for the war effort. That legislation, entitled the National Resources Mobilization Act (NRMA), authorized Ottawa to conscript or expropriate all necessary national resources. In an effort to appease French Canadians who were strongly opposed to conscription for overseas service, the NRMA provided for conscription of men only for home defence.

For conscientious objectors any distinction between compulsory military service overseas or at home was irrelevant. Passage of the NRMA in June 1940 meant that they faced compulsory military or alternative service. They were assured, however, that the government would respect exemptions from bearing arms 'which are enjoyed by members of certain religious groups in Canada, as for example the Mennonites.'[25] These assurances were warmly received in Mennonite communities, many of which had come under increased criticism and occasionally fallen victim to vigilante attacks in the dark days of May and June 1940. Sensational newspaper accounts of German collaborators who had allegedly expedited German success in Europe fed a growing war hysteria as one European country after another fell to the Nazi juggernaut.[26]

There were particular concerns about western Canadian Mennonites who had come to Canada only in the 1920s and maintained strong German cultural, linguistic, and social traits. Hitler's aggressively anti-communist stance also appealed to these people, who had suffered much at the hands of the communists in their former homeland.[27] The older Ontario Mennonite communities, where people knew each other and where questions regarding Mennonite loyalty had been worked out during the First World War, were largely immune to the vigilantes of 1940. Elsewhere, in May and June 1940, there were serious incidents. A Mennonite church in Leamington, Ontario, was ransacked,[28] and two Mennonite churches at Vauxhall, Alberta, fell victim to arson.[29] Several Mennonite teachers with alleged German sympathies were dismissed,[30] and Saturday German-language schools in a few Mennonite communities were closed by members of local branches of the Royal Canadian Legion.[31] Police surveillance in German-speaking Mennonite communities was increased,[32] and pressure was exerted on the young men to enlist.

The response of Canadian Mennonites was almost always conciliatory. Where Saturday German schools created tension they were temporarily closed. In communities where Mennonites had established their own German libraries they reviewed their holdings and burned some of their books. Members of Parliament from constituencies with a large Mennonite population were contacted, reassured, and kept informed about demonstrations of Mennonite loyalty to Canada. Mennonites cooperated closely with law-enforcement agencies.[33] Their major concern after June 1940, however, was the new policy of conscription. That could lead to a major confrontation between conscientious objectors and government officials.

MENNONITES AGREE TO ALTERNATIVE SERVICE

Mennonite leaders, except of those covered by the 1873 order in council, thought it prudent to negotiate with Ottawa the kind of service that they would find acceptable, but they were seriously hampered by their own disagreements and by the government's preoccupation with urgent military and political problems.

Mennonite and peace church leaders whose members were not protected by the 1873 order in council arranged an interview with the prime minister for Monday, 10 June 1940, just as government officials were drafting the final clauses of the NRMA. But 10 June turned out to be one of the worst days of the war for Canada, and particularly for the prime minister. Nazi military forces had encircled and were bombarding Paris. The bedraggled survivors of the Dunkirk evacuation were limping back to Britain. And then, just before the prime minister's morning briefing, word was received that Italy had entered the war as Germany's ally. King's policy of a 'limited liability war' was in shambles. Canadians everywhere except in Quebec were clamouring for conscription, and there were ominous demands that King be replaced as prime minister if he did not introduce a more aggressive war policy.

The prime minister had a series of cabinet and political conclaves that day, in which Canadian responses to the probable fall of France, and the entry of Italy into the war, were discussed. Those meetings left him utterly exhausted.[34] He had a late lunch, cut short by news of a further disaster. Norman Rogers, the exceptionally able Canadian minister of national defence, had just been killed in an airplane crash near Newcastle, Ontario. The prime minister was asked to break the sad news to Mrs Rogers. Before he could go to see her, or inform the House of Commons of Rogers's death and Italy's entry into the war, he met with the Mennonites. King's diary makes clear his state of mind: 'There seemed to be a curious sort of deadness in my mind; nothing seemed, at the moment, to quite break through it. I confess I am terribly worried about the government. Rogers was the best man I had in the administration, bar none, for this period of war. No loss could possibly be greater to the ministry.'[35] King's meeting with the Mennonite leaders was brief. They assured him that, while unwilling to kill, they would ameliorate human suffering. They were, in turn, reassured that conscientious objectors would not be required to bear arms and that any service required of them would be established only under the Rules and Regulations drawn up after Parliament passed the NRMA. There was still time to negotiate acceptable forms of alternative service.[36]

The Mennonite delegates were apparently unaware of the tremendous strain under which the prime minister was labouring. One of them reported simply that King had again promised that the Mennonites would not be required to render wartime services that violated their religious principles.[37] Neither that leader nor King, when reflecting on the day, considered those things that were of greatest concern to the other.

When the NRMA was passed no one knew how it would affect conscientious objectors (COs). Its first requirement was that all men between the ages of 16 and 60 be registered.[38] That registration took place in August 1940 and created much confusion for COs. A few western Mennonites insisted that under the terms of the 1873 order in council they were entirely exempt from all wartime service and refused to register. Mennonite leaders did their best to persuade such individuals to register, but a few cases ended up in the courts.[39]

In Ontario the Mennonite, Brethren in Christ, and Quaker leaders established the Conference of Historic Peace Churches (CHPC) and asked their members and adherents to register twice – first with their local NRMA board and then with the CHPC.[40] The CHPC thus obtained a complete list of all the men from their churches who had complied with the national registration. In western Canada, Mennonite leaders suggested that their members and adherents write the word 'Mennonite' across the face of their registration forms, but not all the Mennonites were informed of this suggestion. In addition, several registrars refused to accept forms marked in this way. The result was that some western Mennonite registrants marked their cards, but most did not.[41]

Registration was, of course, only the first step. It provided the information needed by the government to use the manpower and other resources of the country. The procedures to be followed by NRMA boards when calling up men for service were spelled out in 'National War Services Regulations, 1940 (Recruits).'[42] There were, of course, hundreds of thousands of Canadians doing critically important non-military work. The war effort would have been seriously hampered if key business executives, government administrators, factory workers, miners, farmers, and others had been conscripted for active military service. Mobilization boards were therefore instructed to review the work done by prospective conscripts and to grant postponements of military training to those engaged in work vital to the war effort. Those not granted a postponement were ordered to undergo a medical examination and, if found fit, to report for military training.

The 'Regulations' included two sections outlining procedures to be followed by the registrars when dealing with conscientious objectors. Section 17 dealt with 'Members of the Community of Doukhobors and the sect or denomination of Christians called Mennonites who had immigrated to Canada pursuant to the arrangements evidenced by the Order in Council of August 13, 1873.' These people, if they had 'continued without interruption to be members of the said Community or the said sect or denomination ... and ... resided without interruption in Canada, shall be entitled ... to the indefinite postponement of their military training.'[43] The government had apparently not yet decided in August 1940 whether these people would be called to any form of alternative service or whether their claim for complete exemption would be recognized.

Other Mennonites and members of historic peace churches were governed by section 18 of the 'Regulations,' which also allowed an individual to obtain indefinite postponement of military training, provided that 'such person is compellable to do non-combatant duty either with the Naval, Military or Air Forces or with any civil authorities or both.'[44]

There were immediate and persistent difficulties in interpreting these two sections of the 1940 regulations. It was difficult in churches that practised adult baptism to define who was, and who was not, a Mennonite. Many of the young men called before National War Services Boards were not yet baptized. Others had been baptized only recently and were vulnerable to a charge that they had joined the Mennonite church only to escape military service.

It was even harder to determine who was, and who was not, included in the 1873 order in council. While there had been four major waves of Mennonite migration, there had also been intermittent movements of smaller groups. Many of the people in the large Mennonite church at Rosthern, for example, had come from Prussia in the 1890s and early 1900s, while others in the same church had ancestors who had arrived from Russia in the 1870s. Still others had migrated at various times from the United States or Ontario, or from Russia in the 1920s. Members of these various groups had intermarried, further complicating claims under section 17.[45]

Serious problems also arose because, in western Canada, those seeking postponements under section 18 had to appear in person and demonstrate, to the satisfaction of the registrar, that they really were conscientious objectors. Recalling their experiences with such procedures in the First World War, Mennonite leaders were not hopeful about the ability of their young men to make a convincing case. There had been too little teaching of peace principles in the churches, and most of the young men had only an elementary school education. They were not likely to respond effectively to intense questioning by skilled lawyers. It would be much easier if peace church ministers could simply certify which young people were members or adherents of their congregations.[46] Several registrars, however, felt that many young Mennonites were willing to enlist but were prevented from doing so by their leaders. A formal hearing would make it easier for such individuals to break with their elders and for mobilization boards to identify those making insincere claims.[47]

Immediately after their appointment, the thirteen registrars were called to Ottawa, where all the provisions and requirements of the conscription procedure were reviewed and explained. Each registrar studied and then explained specific sections of the 'Regulations' to his colleagues. Judge Adamson, the Manitoba registrar, studied and reported on the provisions pertaining to conscientious objectors.[48] Adamson was a devout Protestant churchman with a strong personal antipathy to pacifists and COs. He set the tone for the early proceedings. In Manitoba he subjected conscientious objectors to rigorous interrogations, lecturing them on what he believed their patriotic duties were, ridiculing their responses, and objecting if religious leaders tried to intervene to ensure consistency in the answers given by the young men.[49] Registrars in the other western provinces initially followed a similar strategy but gradually became less aggressive.

The first serious difficulties arose when a large group of Alberta COs had their claims rejected. B.B. Janz, leader of the largest Mennonite Brethren church in the province, made strong representations on behalf of these men to the Alberta board and to sympathetic politicians. Eventually sufficient political pressure was exerted that the board agreed to rehear the rejected applications. Most of the claims were then granted, and after that the Alberta registrar adopted a more generous approach, though there were more disputed cases in that province.[50]

The situation in British Columbia was similar. After serious initial difficulties, the BC boards granted postponements in a reasonably consistent and generous manner. The task of Alberta and BC boards was made easier by the effort expended by B.B. Janz in Alberta and John A. Harder in British Columbia to ferret out dubious and fraudulent claims before they reached the board. Harder was appalled when candidates, shortly after having their claims as COs recognized, volunteered for active military service. He warned the young men in his province not to claim CO status if they were not absolutely sure of their religious convictions on the matter.[51] Some of the young men later claimed that the grilling they got from Janz or Harder was worse than that at the formal hearing.

In Saskatchewan and Manitoba the determination of Registrars Embury and Adamson to interrogate and then judge the sincerity of individual conscientious objectors created problems throughout the war. Hutterite and Doukhobor claimants generally encountered less difficulty in dealing with these registrars, in part because they had a well-defined, often memorized, position. Greater diversity in the responses of Mennonite claimants gave the judges more opportunities to point out inconsistencies.

The situation in Ontario was much easier for COs who had registered with both the government and the CHPC. They were not required to appear personally if it could be shown that they had registered with the CHPC. They thus escaped difficult interrogations. But conscientious objectors anywhere who failed to persuade members of their mobilization board of the sincerity of their beliefs were ordered to undergo military training and were subject to military discipline if they refused. Several dozen were imprisoned, some repeatedly. There was no formal appeal mechanism,[52] and troublesome cases continued to involve much vexatious work throughout the war.

An immediate and pressing concern of peace church leaders arose following passage of the regulations because men granted postponements under section 18 could be compelled to render non-combatant service under military or civilian supervision. The regulations did not define such service, and initially those qualifying under section 18 received postponements pending establishment of suitable programs. Mennonite leaders were worried, however, that the government might set up a non-combatant service under military supervision, which they would find unacceptable. Most thought it prudent to begin negotiations regarding acceptable forms of alternative service.

Leaders of CHPC in Ontario met on 8 October 1940 to draw up proposals.[53] The plan they agreed to was called the 'Christian Fellowship Service.' A program run by CHPC would be active in relief, construction and reconstruction, highway and public works, reclamation and forestry, farm service, public health and welfare, and medical, hospital, industrial, and mechanical services. This plan was modelled on the Civilian Public Service plan that U.S. Mennonites had submitted to the president, the details of which were still being negotiated. The key feature of the Ontario plan was that individual projects, once approved, would be administered by the CHPC rather than by the military or by civilian agencies with links to the military.

Mennonite leaders from western Canada met six days later in Winnipeg, but they came to no agreement.[54] Those protected by the 1873 order in council had already created their own committee of Elders (*Aeltestenkomitee*). They were not willing to make any offer of alternative service. Those not covered by the order in council wanted to offer a program involving not only the work outlined in the Ontario proposal but also medical and ambulance work at the front, preferably under their own or Red Cross supervision. They argued that the medical and ambulance service rendered by Mennonites in Russia during the First World War provided them with an opportunity 'to practice brotherly and Christian love and to face danger side by side with other fellow citizens, and what was of the main importance in this respect: it need not violate the conscience of a non-resistant Mennonite.'[55] They were also worried that failure to devise an imaginative and effective service program which alleviated the suffering caused by war would prompt many more of their young people to enlist for active military service.

The Ontario plan was suggested as a compromise between the divergent positions advocated by the two groups of western Mennonites, but neither western group endorsed it at their Winnipeg meeting. They agreed only to meet again a week later in Saskatoon. There a formal break between the two western groups occurred, with representatives of those Mennonites within the purview of the 1873 order in council withdrawing. Those that remained then drew up an alternative service program that included both the non-military work proposed in Ontario and ambulance or medical service.

The separate gatherings in Ontario and western Canada were preparatory for crucial meetings with federal politicians and officials on 12 and 13 November 1940, at which details of alternative service were to be formulated. The CHPC and the group of western Mennonite leaders willing to accept some form of alternative service each sent four delegates to Ottawa, who at first met privately. They agreed that all would endorse the Ontario plan with a strengthened reference to medical help 'in the event of epidemics or other emergency resulting from the war'[56] but not to offer to do medical or ambulance work at the front.

The eight Mennonite and peace church leaders first met with two deputy ministers of national war services, T.C. Davis and L.R. Lafleche, on 12 and 13 November 1940. It became immediately apparent that the proposal was not acceptable. Davis and Lafleche suggested non-combatant service under military control. This was firmly rejected by the Mennonite leaders, leaving both sides frustrated.[57]

One Mennonite delegate was particularly upset by this turn of events, but several others shared his concern. Benjamin B. Janz, the influential MB leader from Alberta, was strongly committed to some form of ambulance and medical service at the front. He preferred that it be under the supervision of the Red Cross but was willing to accept military control. He tried to persuade the other delegates to broaden their proposal and to seek further meetings with political leaders and bureaucrats. But the others left Ottawa after the inconclusive meetings of 12 and 13 November 1940.

Janz delayed his departure and, on his own, drew up a new, nine-point memorandum proposing an ambulance and/or medical program.[58] With this memo in hand, he arranged a private meeting with departmental officials and with several sympathetic senators and members of Parliament. Janz emphasized that 'our Mennonite Red Cross workers should do their duties allways [sic] unarmed and never be transferred to the Active Service Force or other non-combatant service neither in Canada nor overseas.' Informally he also intimated that he and the Mennonites whom he represented would not object if their young men served in military uniform and under military control.[59]

This was precisely what Davis and Lafleche had in mind, but the other Mennonite leaders were appalled when informed of what Janz had proposed. Another meeting of all eight delegates was hastily arranged. There was bitter talk of removing Janz because he had breached the solidarity of the group, but further fragmentation of the Mennonite position would undermine the credibility of the delegation. So it was agreed that Janz would accompany the others when the group met again with National War Services officials in Ottawa on 22 November 1940. The delegation again offered Ontario's Christian Fellowship Service plan, but with an indication that a minority of their people might also be willing to undertake medical and ambulance work.[60]

The interview with the bureaucrats on 22 November 1940 did not go well. The bureaucrats tried to exploit Mennonite divisions but were frustrated when the delegation remained united. The discussion became heated and culminated in a harsh exchange between Lafleche and Jacob H. Janzen, one of the leaders from Ontario, whose personal views were close to those of Janz but who was determined to preserve unity. Lafleche asked the delegates: 'What will you do if we shoot you?' That was too much for Janzen, who had survived several desperate situations in the Soviet Union. Obviously agitated, he replied: 'Listen General, I want to tell you something. You can't scare us like that. I've looked down too many rifle barrels in my time to be scared in that way. This thing is in our blood for 400 years and you can't take it away from us like you'd crack a piece of kindling over your knee. I was before a firing squad twice. We believe in this.'[61]

A stalemate seemed inevitable, but the delegation later met with Jimmy Gardiner, the minister of national war services. Gardiner had grown up in

Ontario, where he had gotten to know and respect the Brethren in Christ. As premier of Saskatchewan in the 1930s he had enjoyed good relations and strong support in Mennonite communities. He listened intently as the delegates explained their position. His response was reassuring: 'There's one hundred and one things that you fellows can do without fighting; we'll see that you get them.'[62] With those words ringing in their ears, the other members of the delegation left Ottawa. Janz again stayed behind, determined to have some form of medical and ambulance service included. He had further meetings with the bureaucrats and politicians, but on 1 December 1940 he too left Ottawa without any firm indication of what the government would do. On the CPR train going west Janz wrote and sent another appeal to Davis: 'pardon me to express my sore feeling that the willingness of many of the Mennonite Churches for the great work for the wounded and sick soldiers, even on the battlefield, even in the army – an unheard thing in North-American Mennonite history – could not gain any more recognition of the authorities then [sic] some other entirely different work. We must feel it a setback at home.'[63]

These negotiations in Ottawa in November 1940 seriously undermined the position of those Mennonites in western Canada covered under the provisions of the 1873 order in council. Their *Aeltestenkomitee* still hoped to obtain complete exemption but had no voice in the formulation of the policies negotiated between government officials and the Mennonite delegates willing to accept some form of alternative service.

ALTERNATIVE SERVICE

The government acted on 24 December 1940, with the passage of an order in council amending the National War Service Regulations, 1940 (Recruits).[64] Three types of training in lieu of military training were provided for postponed conscientious objectors. They could be sent to a military camp for non-combatant military training, they could be ordered to take first-aid training of a non-combatant nature at a facility other than a military camp, or they could be assigned to civilian labour service at facilities other than a military camp.

The new order in council applied to all COs, effectively destroying the unconditional exemption for those exempted by the 1873 document. The *Aeltestenkomitee* immediately sent a delegation to Ottawa but was told that complete exemption was no longer an option. The delegates then reluctantly agreed to accept alternative service, provided that it were of a civilian nature under civilian control.

The government and the military authorities were preoccupied with the war itself and with the training and equipping of thousands of newly conscripted men. They had given little thought or attention to the establishment of facilities for special non-combatant training in military camps and were taken aback when senior military officers expressed strong opposition to any non-combatant service under military supervision by conscientious objectors. This opposition at least temporarily made impossible any alternative service under military control, including the medical and ambulance work so strongly advocated by B.B. Janz and listed as the first option in the order in council of 24 December 1940. The military sentiment was simple and corresponded with the views of those Mennonite leaders who also opposed this option: 'There is no conditional service in the army ... All personnel therein must be subject to transfer from one arm to another in the interest of the service ... No branches or units of a modern army can be considered entirely non-combatant. Modern warfare makes all branches the object of direct attack, and, therefore, all units must be responsible for their own defence. They are trained to bear arms with the idea that these weapons will some day have to be used by the men so trained.'[65]

The second alternative also proved impractical. There were no non-military camps where conscientious objectors could receive first-aid training of a non-combatant nature, and none was set up during the war. COs were left only the option of civilian labour at a facility other than a military camp, but even for such service no administrative arrangements were made until mid-1941.

The result was unfortunate. There was no useful training or work that conscientious objectors could do until the government established appropriate civilian labour camps, but National War Service Boards were increasingly reluctant to grant postponements for individuals who, according to the regulations, should be conscripted for some sort of service. As a result, many of the conscientious objectors who appeared before boards in the first six months of 1941 were given a difficult time. Those whose status as a CO was approved were sent home, subject to recall and assignment of alternative service work once an appropriate program were founded. In the meantime word spread that married men were less likely than single men to be drafted for alternative service. There were, as a result, numerous weddings in some Mennonite communities.

Conscientious objectors who were also farmers could obtain postponement of military service if their board deemed that they were needed on the farm. But anyone whose postponement as a farmer was denied could not then claim postponement as a CO. A number of Mennonites, however, obtained postponements as farmers rather than as conscientious objectors. Many who obtained CO status were also allowed to remain on their farms if they were the only male operator. Similarly, the first son on a family farm was usually assigned or allowed to continue to work there. If there was a second son of military age who was not needed at home but was working on a neighbouring farm where the operator had enlisted or urgently needed help, he too could be granted a postponement and assigned to appropriate farm work. All such assignments were subject to periodic review and became scarcer as the military manpower situation deteriorated.

No approved alternative service program was set up for conscientious objectors until the government announced, in May 1941, work in national parks and on highway construction. This program used and expanded Depression-era work camps. Unemployed men 'riding the rails' in search of work had been the most conspicuous and potentially dangerous victims of the Depression in the 1930s. Work camps had been set up to keep the men busy and to maintain control over them, but unsatisfactory conditions led to a much-publicized On-to-Ottawa trek and subsequent closure of the facilities. In 1941 they were reopened, and others established, to house conscientious objectors. After 1942 there were also camps for Japanese evacuees from British Columbia, interned enemy aliens, and prisoners of war.

The camp administrators were convinced that their most important task was to maintain control and give as little publicity as possible to the program. The result, according to the chief alternative service officer, was that the general public was not aware of the work done by conscientious objectors.[66] As a result, Judge Embury, the Saskatchewan registrar, complained that work in these camps 'produces no noticeable public benefit, annoys the old soldier, is of no value as a War Effort, and is unsuited to the many educated Mennonites, who have expressed to our Board their desire to serve the country in any dangerous war service except that involving the actual taking of life.'[67] Work as nursing orderlies, stretcher-bearers, ambulance drivers, and truck drivers, and in coastal forestry fire protection services, might all be more useful, but in 1942 a sympathetic MP explained: 'under the circumstances which existed last year I am free to confess I do not know to what other type of work they could have been turned. But I feel they should be put to something more useful in the future.'[68] These were sentiments shared by many of the conscientious objectors, but it seemed to some that they were being called to be faithful in small things before being called to greater things.

The first three CO camps were a highway construction camp at Montreal River north of Sault Ste Marie, Ontario, a National Parks camp in Riding Mountain National Park in Manitoba, and a road construction camp at Lac La Ronge in Saskatchewan. The first groups sent to these camps were young men who were between 21 and 24 years of age on 1 July 1941. Initially they were obliged to serve only the same length of time as the men called up for military training. Most were therefore able to return home after three or four months, subject to recall as needed.[69] That situation changed in November 1941, when the men were informed that 'each and every one of them is subject ... to alternative service work for the duration of the war.'[70]

The type of work conscientious objectors were asked to do changed in the spring of 1942. Anticipated manpower shortages at home and overseas prompted the government to broaden and enlarge the work assigned to COs. In British Columbia the Japanese attack on Pearl Harbor in December 1941 raised fears that Japanese-Canadian saboteurs or airborne incendiary bombs from Japan would set vital forest resources on fire. The BC Forestry Service did not have sufficient staff to deal with the new threat, and conscientious objectors were assigned to 'assist in the protection of British Columbia forests from fires started by enemy action or sabotage.' Conscientious objectors fought a total of 234 fires in 1942 and 1943, but there is no evidence that any had been started by enemy action. They also did much reforestation work and, during winter, cleared snag and deadfall and built truck trails to facilitate fire fighting.[71] And they did that work so well that, in 1943, when the men were withdrawn and assigned other work, the *Victoria Times* reported: 'Withdrawal of conscientious objectors from B.C.'s forestry camps on Selective Service orders returning them to their farms, will cost the provincial forestry branch the most effective fire fighting service it has ever had.'[72]

The men were initially withdrawn from the BC forestry camps to help with seasonal farm work on the prairies. But after April 1943 critical wartime labour shortages in agriculture and industry prompted the government to assign COs to those sectors.[73] Mennonite leaders, when invited to identify industries that they would find acceptable, provided the following list: agriculture, canning factories, cheese-making, creameries and dairies, experimental farms, feed mills, food processing, hospital service, meat packing, medical and dental services, teaching.[74] The list was subsequently expanded to include teaching at United Church mission schools in the north, where former teachers and missionaries had enlisted for active military service. Shipyards, airfields, and other civilian facilities with obvious military functions were not on the approved list, but some Mennonites accepted work at such facilities.

Mennonite COs were not necessarily told the purpose or objectives of some of the projects on which they worked. Some of the BC fire fighters were assigned work in and around the Esquimalt Naval base on Vancouver Island. Efforts to guard against and, if necessary, counteract the efforts of enemy incendiaries intent on setting forest fires were easily diverted into other

Table 2.1
Disposition of postponed conscientious objectors, 1945

Agriculture	6,655
Miscellaneous essential industries	1,412
Sawmills, logging, and timbering	542
Packing and food-processing plants	469
Construction	269
Hospitals	86
Coal mining	63
Grain handling at Head of the Lakes	15
Alternative service camps	170
Serving jail sentences	14
In hands of or being prepared for Enforcement Division	34
In hands of RCMP or agencies to locate whereabouts	201
Under review	921
Total	10,851

Source: NAC RG 35/7, Vol. 21, 'Historical Account of the Wartime Activities of the Alternative Service Branch, Department of Labour, 11 April 1946,' p. 19.

surveillance or defensive work cloaked in official military secrecy. Some COs were involved in painting or cleaning, repairing and assisting in construction of naval facilities whose ultimate role in the war they did not know. Some worked briefly on a bizarre scheme to build hollow 'bergships' out of a mixture of ice and wood chips, which were allegedly more resistant to submarine attacks than conventional battleships.[75]

The alternative service workers in approved jobs were paid regular wages by their employers, but they were allowed to keep only a small monthly allowance. The rest of what they earned had to be donated to the Red Cross. Between 1 May 1943 and 31 December 1945, $2,222,802.70 was paid to the Red Cross under this arrangement.[76]

The changes in 1943 provided for a much more diverse alternative service, and some of the camps became little more than temporary facilities holding men until they could be assigned elsewhere. Others remained if the work done was of national importance or if they were difficult and obstreperous. The Jehovah's Witness COs were deliberately uncooperative. As a result, at the end of the war, only 170 men, almost all Jehovah's Witnesses, remained in the CO camps.[77]

Conscientious objectors were among the last conscripts to be demobilized. The government wanted to give returning soldiers preference over COs in the search for postwar jobs. The work done by conscientious objectors at various times changed, but on 31 December 1945, 10,851 postponed COs, approximately 7,500 of them Mennonites, were employed as shown in Table 2.1.

The increased scope of alternative service after 1943 resulted in virtually full conscription of medically fit Mennonite young men between the ages of 18 and 35 who were not needed in agriculture at home or already employed in essential industries and services.

The desire to use COs more effectively also led to a change of military policy regarding restricted non-combatant service and hence provided new service opportunities. An order in council on 16 September 1943 made it possible for conscientious objectors to enlist in the Royal Canadian Army Medical Corps or in the Canadian Dental Corps 'with all the obligations and duties of a soldier on active service with any unit or formation of the Army except that he was not under any circumstances required to bear arms.'[78]

COs were divided in their response. The Conference of Historic Peace Churches in Ontario rejected any kind of service, either non-combatant or combatant, in the army or under military direction.[79] One of the first enlistees, however, expressed another view. He believed that the restricted medical corps 'opened up the whole possibility of sharing the misery that the world was experiencing at the time and not be sheltered by doing something else out in the bush or safely behind the lines in Canada.'[80]

The military authorities accepted, but did not vigorously promote, non-combatant medical service. That lukewarm endorsement, and divided opinions among the COs, resulted in enlistment of only 227 men in the restricted medical and dental corps.[81] Those who did enlist were faced with some confusion and hostility on the part of military instructors and fellow trainees, described by one of the participants: 'It was all arms training. Marching. So what are you going to do with these guys. And there must have been about close to 30 of us in by that time. From all denominations, not just Mennonite. So in the end we ended up carrying stretchers. Two guys to a stretcher. Our poor platoon was very ashamed of us at the beginning because here were all these guys with their guns and then right in the tag end was our ... platoon of about 30 guys, two guys to a stretcher, marching along. We caused many stares and curiosity.'[82] These fellows nevertheless earned a good reputation and were warmly commended by their commanding officer: 'There hasn't been one mark against any of these guys. No one has shirked his duty. No one has been up for detention ... It's the only platoon that's ever gone through this camp with a perfect record.'[83]

Rudolf Goetz, referred to above, served in the restricted medical corps. He died, and several other corps members sustained less serious wounds at the front.[84] Those involved regarded their service as consistent with the peace witness of their churches.

Alternative service drew 7,543[85] young Mennonite men into new and unfamiliar environments. It broadened their social, intellectual, and spiritual horizons. Some were surprised and perplexed when they discovered a great diversity of beliefs and practices, even among those sharing non-resistant principles. One of the camp preachers noted that working with men from other denominations provided 'a wonderful opportunity to free themselves of denominational bigotry.'[86]

The world, even as experienced in a CO camp, was obviously more complex and diverse than many of the young men had thought. The home congregations tried to provide some spiritual guidance and support for them, but since men from different backgrounds served together in the camps, visiting pastors or preachers sometimes personified differences in the Mennonite world. Noah Bearinger, for example, recalled how members of the (Old) Mennonite Church were admonished when one of their ministers saw them playing ball on a sunny Sunday afternoon.[87] Sports, even on Sunday, seemed a harmless diversion to others.

There was another issue that broadened the religious experience of many conscientious objectors. Some Mennonite Brethren and Brethren in Christ had embraced fairly evangelistic religious practices, which emphasized personal 'crisis' conversion. That was alien to the traditions of the socially and culturally more traditional and conservative groups. Yet it was often younger evangelists who accepted the challenge of visiting the camps to hold religious services.[88] Some men reacted negatively to the emotional, evangelistic appeals; others responded positively but later had difficulty fitting into their home congregations; while others responded positively and later exerted great influence back home.[89]

Some COs with evangelistic inclinations from several camps used their free time to conduct street services 'to save the sinning populace' of nearby towns.[90] This created serious tensions. The new evangelical style was uncomfortable for many, and aggressive wartime proselytization by members of a pacifist sect seemed impolitic. Both those who supported aggressive evangelical methods, and those who opposed them, were forced to re-evaluate how they related to their fellow Canadians and how they could make their religious insights relevant to those around them. No clear consensus emerged among the COs but an awareness of divergent approaches forced many to extend their intellectual horizons not only to consider the dynamics within their own isolated communities, but also to look at broader problems. Alternative service was thus a broadening and maturing experience, which brought COs into 'contact with people outside of what for many men were circumscribed intellectual and social boundaries.'[91]

In retrospect the experience seemed to many quite positive. In the official government report on the wartime activities of the Alternative Service Branch, Mennonite COs received high praise: 'The Mennonites co-operated in every way from the beginning of Alternate Service. There was very close co-operation between the Mennonite Bishops and the Alternative Service Officials. Perhaps it can be said that this group has contributed more than any other group to alternative service.'[92]

Mennonite leaders responded with letters and official resolutions thanking the government for the provisions that it had made for them. Even those covered by the 1873 order in council who believed that they should be exempt from any state service during the war were moved to write a letter of thanks: 'The Mennonite people who were invited to this country in 1870 by the Government are well pleased to live in a democratic country that still maintains the liberties of all classes of people, especially liberty in religion. We are glad to live under the British government as there is no country that protects religion like the Governments of Great Britain and the British Dominions.'[93]

Alternative service allowed Mennonites 'to see themselves as participants in a society much broader than their own. Christian responsibility now required not only ministering to one's own people, but to society in general.'[94]

'LOST SONS AND DAUGHTERS'?

Before the outbreak of the war, Peter J. Klassen, a Mennonite author, wrote a novel entitled *Verlorene Soehne* (Lost Sons).[95] He sought to elucidate the Mennonite doctrine of non-resistance and particularly to point out the errors and problems that had arisen when Mennonite young men had departed from those principles during the difficult years of the Russian Revolution and civil war. That novel ended in a reconciliation, complete with a forgiving girlfriend and a prospective happy marriage. But Klassen was clearly worried that a new war would once again raise the same difficult issues.

He was right. Approximately 4,500 young men and women of ethnic Mennonite background were drafted or enlisted voluntarily for active military service in the Canadian armed forces during the Second World War.[96] Their reasons varied, but very few Mennonite young men enlisted in the early months of the war or during the heightened war hysteria in May and June 1940. They responded in significant numbers only when compelled by the provisions of the National Resoures Mobilization Act.

The military career patterns of these men strongly suggest that they did not find the armed forces a congenial atmosphere. Few achieved officer rank, and after the war almost all left the service as quickly as possible. Many, particularly those from more isolated rural communities, suffered considerable personal anguish as they tried to cope not only with the demands and dangers of military life but also with rejection and condemnation at home.

Mennonite leaders found it difficult to deal with these young people, some of them desperately sincere members who could not accept official dogma. All the Mennonite conferences and many congregations had official policies that terminated the membership of those who enlisted for active military service. But implementation of such a policy was the responsibility of individual congregations, and difficulties and inconsistencies quickly arose. A Mennonite journalist who had extensive contact with young Mennonite men in military training at Camp Borden near Toronto complained: 'One well-known Mennonite church has removed the teaching of non-resistance from its confession of faith and allows its members to serve in any military capacity. Another automatically expels members who participate in active military service, but not those enlisted in the medical corps. A third expels anyone who dons the uniform, irrespective of the service involved. Is it any wonder that our young people are confused?'[97]

Leaders and congregations, with a few notable exceptions, did little to provide spiritual support and nurture for these young people but demanded that they apologize and admit their guilt before being readmitted. Most returning soldiers would not or could not honestly comply with this requirement. As a result, most were permanently lost to their home congregations. They had to look to other sectors of Canadian society and to other churches in which to establish themselves after the war. Altona United Church, for example, gained a number of energetic and enthusiastic new members when Mennonite soldiers who could not return to their home congregations joined that church. Veterans' educational and civil re-establishment allowances eased their adjustment to civilian life, but for their home congregations many of these young people remained 'lost sons.'

Some of these men, including Henry Pankratz, mentioned above, returned with pride in their military achievements and regarded Mennonite leaders and conscientious objectors with disdain. A few flaunted that disdain, as an incident in Steinbach, Manitoba, shows:

I have an even more vivid memory of a young Mennonite soldier, that same summer [1940] standing arrogantly in our churchyard one Sunday morning in full military dress complete with a long, wicked-looking dress sword (probably worn against regulations), basking in the envy of the older youths and defiantly returning the disapproving stares of older people. He was a young man whom I had not seen in church for many years, and I guessed even then that he had only come to show off and to mortify his elders. And he had not miscalculated. Had a Martian suddenly dropped into our midst he could not have created a more startling or alien effect. The war had come to Steinbach.[98]

But others, such as Fred Snyder, also referred to above, deepened Mennonites' and peace churches' understanding of difficult and ambiguous wartime choices. Still others felt that defence of a cherished religious principle was not balanced in most Mennonite churches by a spirit of love, forgiveness, and reconciliation. 'Oh yes, they prayed for me. They certainly prayed,' one Mennonite soldier wrote later, 'but their prayers took no practical form.'[99]

Active military service during the war involved mainly the men, but fifty-five women of Mennonite ethnic background also enlisted. They earned proportionately more promotions to officer rank than did their male counterparts. Those promotions, however, came mainly in nursing and medical services, which were closer to Mennonite occupational and ideological traditions. But there are almost no published or recorded stories of Mennonite women who enlisted and later returned to membership and participation in Mennonite churches. In most published histories of Mennonite communities and congregations these women are either not mentioned at all, or their enlistment is mentioned and then they disappear from the narrative. The local history of Altona, Manitoba, is typical: 'Two Altona women joined the Canadian Women's Army Corps. Anne Dick was the daughter of Peter P. and Mary Dick, Jacquelin Johnston, the daughter of Fraser and Merle Johnston, the CPR station agent and his wife.'[100] That is all we are told about these two women. Some excellent studies on the wartime role and work of women in the Canadian armed forces have been prepared,[101] but the contribution made by Mennonite women has not yet been examined in any systematic manner.

CONCLUSION

More than 12,000 persons of Mennonite ethnic background left their homes for active military or alternative service during the Second World War. Most of the 4,500 who enlisted for active military service did not return permanently to their home communities or to membership in a Mennonite church. Many of these may have been alienated from their home churches long before the war, but others were rejected and condemned when they enlisted and did not return for that reason. Some returned, but often only after considerable spiritual turmoil.

The 7,543 who claimed CO status also responded to changes wrought by the war. Most expected to return after the war, but serious problems in rural and agricultural endeavours, and attractive opportunities in the outside world, persuaded many to look for new places to live and new ways to earn a livelihood. Many of the young men who left parental farms found on their return that the family had managed for years without them and that they were no longer needed. Few had sufficient funds to acquire farms of their own. Increased mechanization and rising capital costs made agriculture impractical.

Fortunately, the returning young people had learned new skills, and the demand for skilled and reliable workmen in a host of urban and industrial undertakings remained high. Young Mennonites returning from alternative or active military service discovered attractive new opportunities, which were enhanced by the greater social ease they felt as a result of exposure to the outside world. They had survived and many had excelled in strange new work and social conditions. Modern urban industrial society was no longer an alien or hostile environment.

3

Voluntary Service

The disasters of the Great Depression had for a time turned Canadians in on themselves. They blamed governments, business leaders, bankers, capitalists, speculators, and one another for their troubles.[1] Mennonites, while somewhat removed from the most controversial conflicts of the 1930s, had been engaged in their own desperate struggles for survival, both in Canada and in the Soviet Union.[2] In 1939 most Canadian Mennonites wanted to live in peace and quiet in their cherished rural enclaves. They wanted to be 'in the world, but not of it.'[3]

The war forced Canadians, including Mennonites, to broaden their perceptions of the world. They had to look beyond their own immediate problems and aspirations and work together in a common endeavour that required great sacrifice. More than 400,000 Canadians, including approximately 4,500 Mennonites, served in the armed forces. An additional 7,500 Mennonites were conscripted into alternative wartime service. War, however, also involved millions of Canadians who participated in a vast array of activities that directly or indirectly supported the war effort, kept the economy and the government functional in the absence of hundreds of thousands of men, and provided support, relief, and rehabilitation for the victims of war. Voluntary service, particularly by women, was an essential feature of wartime and postwar society. Like military or alternative service, it too broadened perceptions. Even Mennonites who did not leave their rural communities became more familiar with distant places and with massive foreign problems which made their domestic discontents seem more manageable by comparison.

Mennonites who participated in voluntary service projects came to see the outside world less as a hostile and threatening place to be avoided and more as a suffering, damaged, and violated place in desperate need of Christian love and compassion.[4] As a result, voluntary service, 'In the Name of Christ,' became a central feature of Mennonite life. After leaving home, often involuntarily, Mennonites discovered that they could make useful and appreciated contributions to the world through voluntary service.

WILLING SERVICE AT HOME BY CANADIAN MENNONITE WOMEN

A basic assumption of the Canadian Military Service Acts is that in time of war all citizens, not only those conscripted for active military or alternative service, are at war. 'Rosie the riveter' and 'the Bren gun girl' in Canada symbolized the wartime contributions of women who became factory and industrial workers.[5] Few Mennonite women assembled Bren guns or worked as riveters in military-industrial factories, but many faced the daunting prospect of maintaining family life and keeping the family farm or business going without the help of their men. Traditional gender roles had to be modified as women accepted and did managerial, mechanical, administrative, and heavy manual work pertaining to the operations of the family farm or rural family business formerly the responsibility of the men. This was an experience they shared with the wives of Canadian enlisted men.

Mennonite family farms had always required the day-to-day cooperation of wives in ways that were undergoing general decline in other communities and occupations.[6] That cooperation and the sense that they were engaged in a partnership, albeit often one in which the wife was only a junior partner, significantly changed during the war. Wartime exigencies modified gender roles because rural women everywhere had to do more and different work. About Canadian women in general, one historian wrote: 'They have worked harder at farm work than ever before. They have driven tractors, made hay, picked fruit, raised wonderful gardens and increased the poultry and egg production of all Canada. Yet they have found time to make tons of jam for overseas, clothing for refugees and thousands of articles for the Red Cross.'[7]

Some wives and mothers of conscientious objectors (COs) faced acute economic hardship, particularly after alternative service was extended for the duration of the war while the monthly allowances of the men remained at or below subsistence levels. The dire financial difficulties of their families persuaded some COs to enlist in the armed forces, thus obtaining a much higher allowance.[8] Others refused to return to the camps after a weekend or longer pass, insisting that they were needed at home. One Rosthern-district woman warned the authorities that 'unless my son is permitted to return [home] for the period suggested [three months], it will have the effect of wrecking the health of myself and my children.'[9] A Waterloo woman wrote irate letters to officials in Ottawa until the embarrassed son asked the local church leader for help.[10] Some COs, in making requests for leave from the camps during particularly busy seasons on the farm, wrote of mothers, sisters, and wives experiencing great difficulty in running the operation on their own. Such situations, however, were not unique to the families of conscientious objectors, and men were allowed to return home only if their work there was deemed to be essential to the war effort.

Normally Mennonites looked to the church to step in and assist those in their congregations who were in need. During the war, however, the plight and legal problems of COs whose claims had been rejected by mobilization boards kept the leaders busy and overshadowed the problems of families at home. One conscientious objector wrote to his minister: 'I don't know what happened to the promises that were made to us before we left as far as support for our wives goes or that they would be looked after.'[11] The minister proposed establishment of a special committee to look after the needs of dependants of the men in the camps, but there were only sufficient resources to deal with a few cases of acute hardship. An increase in the monthly allowance for COs, authorized by the government in July 1944,[12] did more than any organized church or conference activity to relieve the economic distress of wives, mothers, and children of COs.

An important new form of financial assistance for many of the women came in the form of Family Allowance benefits, universalized in 1944. The cheques were issued in the name of the mother and gave many women greater financial independence.[13] Mennonites, however, were sharply divided on the advisability of accepting the allowance.[14] For some women those small cheques were a real God-send. But some Mennonites feared that those receiving the cheques would become liable to military or some other unacceptable service.

The wives, mothers, and daughters who maintained essential farm and family operations developed new skills, new confidence, and a sense of achievement and self-reliance. Many did not simply return to their previous roles when the war ended. During the Depression many farms, particularly some of those of Mennonite immigrants of the 1920s, for reasons discussed below, had become so heavily indebted that the operators lost them or had to apply for protection under mortgage moratorium schemes. During the war prices for many farm products rose, and some women showed much better results than had their husbands before the war. Such women were understandably reluctant to return to the role of helpmeet.

Historians also tell us that increasingly acute labour shortages allowed or forced many women to seek employment in government or industry. Many became wage earners with a salary of their own.[15] Paid employment outside the home or off the farm, however, was less of an option for most Mennonite women than it was for urban Canadian women.

Mennonite women volunteered for a great deal of wartime work and service. Women's organizations, also known as sewing circles or women's missionary societies, were a part of almost all Mennonite congregations; women could get together to visit while doing useful and necessary needlework. They sewed and knit clothing for needy persons at home or aboard and did fine needlework and other handicrafts which were sold at church or community sales and bazaars to raise money for relief or mission work.[16]

During the war the scope of work done by women's organizations expanded greatly. Women across Canada were encouraged to knit and sew for their distant menfolk and for citizens and soldiers of allied countries overseas.[17] Mennonite women, naturally, were most concerned about the plight of their men in alternative service. They sewed and knitted thousands of items of clothing – with woollen socks, mittens, and scarves being particularly popular – and packed countless packages of baked and canned goods, which were sent to the men.[18] Christmas packages were particularly popular. The women in the Erb Street Mennonite Church in Waterloo, and perhaps elsewhere as well, transcribed Sunday morning sermons, which were then sent to the men in the camps.

Voluntary service allowed some women to develop business and administrative skills when undertaking large-scale sewing, knitting, canning, and other food preparation or Red Cross–related medical and relief programs. The organizational work of Ida Frey Martin Bauman in Ontario provides an example. Bauman had been born into an Old Order Mennonite family but converted to the (Old) Mennonite church, where she was very active in the sewing circle. She enjoyed shopping and scoured the countryside looking for bargains in textiles and other materials needed by sewing circles. She sometimes bought thousands of dollars worth of material at special sales and then resold it at cost to other sewing circles.[19] She also helped persuade Mennonite relief organizations to buy a special cutting machine and to open a cutting room which supplied the women in sewing circles with pre-cut garments. She was one of many women who, with the help of their husbands or fathers, 'loaded their sewing machines into their cars and gathered in each other's homes or in the churches – at least once a month. Between times they did more sewing at home.'[20]

Some of the women extended their aid beyond their own denomination. Those in Yarrow, British Columbia, for example, prepared special Christmas packages for every young man from that community who was in active military or in alternative service.[21] Those at Coaldale, Alberta, prepared special gift packages. Most were sent to the men in the alternative service camps, but others were distributed to some of the men in the nearby prisoner of war camp at Lethbridge and to Japanese Canadians who had been relocated from their homes in British Columbia.

The needs of the Canadian Red Cross became a particularly important concern for almost all Mennonite women's organizations. Many old cotton sheets were washed and cut or torn and folded into bandages. During the war the Red Cross always had more than enough work, and it came to rely heavily on the Mennonite women's organizations.[22] Participants cherished the afternoons or evenings of fellowship when they worked and visited together.

This work inevitably made the women more aware of events beyond their own communities. Letters from alternative service workers and others who had received packages, or from the Red Cross[23] explaining its work overseas, were read with interest and familiarized the women with distant problems and events. When the Mennonite Central Committee (MCC) opened overseas relief programs, the reports of its workers who distributed the supplies made or packed by the women were read with particular interest, since several Canadian women had volunteered for work overseas, to help orphaned, homeless, and relocated children and the elderly in England and, later, other war sufferers on the continent. After the war, MCC's massive material aid programs providing food, clothing, housing, shelter, and some medical and educational help for European refugees and war victims[24] received very strong support from Canadian women's societies and sewing circles.

Prior to 1939, women's societies had undertaken local projects, but much of their effort was devoted to denominational mission programs overseas.[25] That emphasis obviously changed during the war. Areas of relief work previously ignored were now addressed, and in a sense sacralized. Alternative service and relief workers were not missionaries, but their efforts to heal the wounds and lessen the suffering caused by war were regarded as integral to the building of God's Kingdom. Missionary interests did not disappear, but priorities shifted, social perspectives were broadened, and women became more active participants in the affairs of peoples and societies victimized by war.

OVERSEAS RELIEF AND REHABILITATION

Older members in Ontario and southern Manitoba remembered how, in the 1920s, they had been able to extend desperately needed and much appreciated help to Mennonites in the Soviet Union. They responded enthusiastically and generously to the urgent needs and opportunities for service during and after the Second World War. Those who had received help in the 1920s and had subsequently immigrated to Canada understood better than most the havoc, pain, and suffering that follow military conflict and political upheavals. They too were eager to help, particularly through Mennonite agencies, which ensured that the aid would be given to alleviate real need. And young people who felt uncomfortable with a form of non-resistance that allowed them to escape the sacrifices of active military service enthusiastically embraced opportunities to demonstrate the values and principles of their faith.

Almost all the Mennonite relief organizations drew support from more than one conference or group. Most sought to help war sufferers, to aid Mennonite victims of war and political or military upheavals in eastern Europe seeking to reach Canada, and to speak with a united voice to government.

In the 1940s there emerged a plethora of Mennonite relief organizations, which was confusing even to those directly involved.[26] The largest and most important was the MCC. It had been organized in 1920 to assist suffering Mennonites in the Soviet Union and established its head office in the small rural Pennsylvania town of Akron.[27] During the Second World War it coordinated the shipping and distribution overseas of relief supplies gathered by North American Mennonite relief organizations. MCC also looked after most of the negotiations in Europe related to postwar emigration of Mennonite refugees.

In Canada the organization of relief work reflected divisions that had become obvious in the debates over alternative service. The Amish, (Old) Mennonite, and members of other Ontario peace churches whose ancestors had come to British North America in the first two migration waves coordinated their relief work through the Non-Resistant Relief Organization (NRRO), which they had established during the First World War. Those Canadian Mennonites covered by the terms of the 1873 order in council organized the Canadian Mennonite Relief Committee (CMRC) in 1940, while the immigrants of the 1920s set up in 1940 the Mennonite Central Relief Committee (MCRC).[28] Overseas the goods gathered by these three committees were distributed by MCC.

Another cluster of inter-Mennonite committees divided along the same lines. The Conference of Historic Peace Churches (CHPC) in Ontario; the *Aeltestenkomitee*, representing those exempted by the 1873 order in council; and the Mennonite Board of Colonization, which represented the immigrants of the 1920s, conducted most of the negotiations with Ottawa pertaining to alternative service and postwar immigration.[29] Overseas negotiations with government, military, and United Nations organizations concerning emigration were again in the hands of MCC.

When the Second World War broke out American MCC leaders moved quickly to undertake relief work. Their first project was in Poland. This quick response was at least partly due to concern about the thousands of Mennonites living in Poland, East and West Prussia, and the Free City of Danzig (now Gdańsk), all of which were occupied by Germany in the first month of the war. Approval in principle to begin a Polish relief program was given by the Germans in October 1939, and in November an MCC commissioner was sent to investigate and report on needs in occupied Poland. His instructions set the pattern for MCC relief: 'Our work, as you know, is entirely non-partisan – relief to be extended without preference as to race, nationality, or otherwise, with particular attention to relief needs among war suffering women and children. In case, of course, that there should be relief needs among the Mennonite folks of Europe, these should also receive prior consideration.'[30]

This project created immediate problems for Canadian Mennonites. Canada was a belligerent in the war. The United States remained neutral until December 1941, and the first relief project undertaken by the U.S.-based MCC was in territory occupied by the enemy. Canadian currency and customs controls, particularly for money and supplies destined for enemy-occupied territory, made it difficult for Canadian Mennonites to work through the U.S. offices of MCC. A second MCC project, to assist refugees from the Spanish civil war who had fled to France, was equally problematic for Canadians after the fall of France in June 1940.

None of the three Canadian Mennonite relief organizations had its own overseas connections. All were willing to allow MCC to look after overseas arrangements, but that became increasingly difficult. Canadian gathering, packaging, inspection, customs clearance, and shipping facilities were needed. As long as the United States remained neutral in the war it was easier to satisfy wartime trade restrictions if Canadian relief supplies were shipped to approved destinations from Canadian ports in Canadian or allied ships.

Two initiatives facilitated shipment of Canadian Mennonite relief supplies. The first was the opening of a Canadian regional office of MCC at Kitchener, Ontario, and a sub-office in Winnipeg. The Kitchener office reviewed applications from Canadians willing to serve overseas as MCC relief workers, making the appropriate recommendations to MCC officials in Akron; served as the Canadian gathering, processing, and shipping centre for clothing to be sent overseas; handled the gathering and shipping of food butchered, canned, processed, or preserved in numerous smaller Canadian centres; and was responsible for MCC public relations and fund-raising in Canada.

The second major initiative involved establishment in 1940 of a wartime relief program in England. This was an effort that Canadians could support and in which they could participate. The first MCC work in England involved caring for 120 displaced Polish boys between the ages of 16 and 18.

Then, in the dark days of the London Blitz, thousands of children, the sick, and the elderly were evacuated from large industrial centres to temporary facilities in the countryside. These evacuees, particularly those from poor social and economic backgrounds, urgently needed care. British authorities accepted an MCC offer to open and operate several homes for some of these orphan boys and other evacuees.

The initial appointments of people serving in the British Isles included several Canadians. The first was John Coffman, son of Ontario Mennonite patriarch S.F. Coffman, who arrived in England in October 1940. It was Coffman who suggested that MCC relief goods sent to England be stamped 'In the Name of Christ.'[31] Others who joined Coffman in England included three Canadian nurses, Elfrieda Klassen (later Dyck), Edna Hunsperger (later Bowman), and Mabel Cressman. All were active in the care of youngsters or elderly people evacuated from potential targets of German bombing raids. Edna Hunsperger returned to North America in 1946 and, after further training at Goshen College, joined the Victorian Order of Nurses in Kitchener, where she married Henry Bowman.[32] Mabel Cressman also returned to North America in 1946 but subsequently became a missionary in Argentina.[33] Elfrieda Klassen married MCC co-worker Peter J. Dyck, and together they had a long and distinguished record of service with MCC.[34]

John Coffman operated a mobile canteen in Birmingham for a time, but the main MCC wartime relief efforts in England involved care for impoverished children and the elderly.[35] A total of twenty-four MCC workers served there during and immediately after the war, the first arriving in May 1940 and the last leaving in July 1947.[36]

U.S. entry into the war made any MCC relief work on the continent increasingly difficult, and in 1942 the last of those projects was closed when two MCC workers there, neither of them Canadian, were interned at Baden-Baden. Canadians became involved in relief work on the continent only after the liberation.[37]

During the war Canadian Mennonites also generously supported the Canadian Red Cross, particularly in projects directed at women's mission groups and school children.[38] Earnings by alternative service workers, beyond the subsistence allowances established by the Department of Labour, were also paid to the Red Cross.[39]

POSTWAR RELIEF AND REHABILITATION

The unconditional surrender of Germany in May 1945 left enormous relief and rehabilitation problems. Much of Europe lay in ruins, and an estimated forty million individuals, many of them women and children, had been uprooted and were outside their home country.[40] The international agency with primary responsibility for relief and rehabilitation was the United Nations Relief and Rehabilitation Administration (UNRRA). It had been created under an agreement signed by forty-four governments on 9 December 1944 and given responsibility to 'plan, co-ordinate, administer or arrange for the administration of measures for the relief of victims of war in any area under the control of any of the United Nations through the provision of food, fuel, clothing, shelter and other basic necessities, medical and other essential services.'[41]

UNRRA's first task was to assist citizens of any of the United Nations who had been displaced by the war and those who had become refugees because they had supported the allied cause. The objective was to repatriate as many of the displaced persons and refugees as quickly as possible. UNRRA staff worked in close cooperation with the victorious allied military forces, providing interim aid until the displaced people could return home. As a result, little was done by the UNRRA teams in the terrible winter of 1945–6 to assist or provide emergency aid to citizens of former enemy nations.[42]

UNRRA never had sufficient resources to discharge even its primary obligations, and it was anticipated from the beginning that various non-governmental organizations would also play an important role. But the military situation in Europe remained unstable for months, as the allies divided Germany, Austria, Berlin, and Vienna into occupation zones. In many cases the occupying military forces were not from the country into whose zone those territories fell. The Americans, for example, held substantial German territory in May 1945 which became part of the Soviet zone, and adjustments created uncertainty and occasionally conflict. The last thing the allies needed was an uncoordinated inundation of relief workers with priorities, objectives, and policies formulated without reference to military or strategic considerations.

It took time and careful planning before an orderly system for non-governmental relief and rehabilitation was established in occupied enemy territories. In the American zone a Council of Relief Agencies Licensed for Operations in Germany (CRALOG) was organized in January 1946. Parallel councils were established in the French and British zones later the same year. In the first two years of CRALOG's operations MCC was one of the largest contributors of private relief supplies to Germany and was represented on the CRALOG council by a young, keenly observant, American volunteer named Robert Kreider.[43]

Responsibility for the citizens of enemy countries was to be assumed by new local civilian governments. Relief agencies wishing to establish a refugee camp or distribution centre were expected to work in cooperation with these civilian authorities. In addition, special local relief distribution committees could be set up to receive aid from overseas relief agencies. Members of a particular parish or congregation, or employees of a factory, could form such a committee, explain their needs, and then receive and distribute relief supplies provided either directly by one of the North American charities or, more often, through intermediary relief committees in Germany. The result was a fairly elaborate system of local and more broadly based Mennonite relief committees.

Most of the European aid provided by MCC was in the defeated countries of Germany and Austria, but numerous short-term relief and material-aid distribution efforts also emerged in Denmark, Holland, France, Belgium, Switzerland, Hungary, Poland, and Italy.[44] Canadian volunteers, screened by the MCC office in Kitchener before going on to Akron for orientation and training, participated in many of these projects.

Mennonite interests and attitudes in postwar activities often focused on two main objectives. The first was the simple humanitarian and Christian impulse to feed the hungry, cloth the naked, house those without shelter, provide medical care for the sick and wounded, and generally to help those suffering and in need, without regard to race, colour, or creed.[45] This policy was tempered, however, by a second objective, which was to help their own people – 'those of the Mennonite household of faith.' Stories of the terrible suffering of Mennonite refugees from the Soviet Union in the dreadful collectivization programs of the 1930s, and of the terror that they had endured in their escape to the West, deeply moved MCC officials, who took a special interest in these refugees. Numerous accounts of encounters between MCC workers and the Mennonite refugees have been preserved.[46] The MCC workers in Europe, and certainly Mennonite supporters in North America who had friends and relatives among the refugees, made very generous donations to MCC but then also expected that MCC programs would meet the needs of these severely tested people. Robert Kreider described the attitude of MCC workers in 1946:

As an MCC we are happy to cooperate fully with other agencies in this joint relief distribution effort of CRALOG. As demonstrated by our work in England, France, Italy, Belgium, etc. – our relief concerns go far beyond the needs of our own group … At the same time, we are interested in investigating the needs of Mennonite folk in Germany and developing indigenous Mennonite relief distribution committees among the Mennonites. Without disrupting our joint CRALOG effort, we are concerned that we obtain supplies for distribution thru these indigenous Mennonite committees.[47]

Many years later C.J. Dyck, another MCC worker, wrote: 'There have been times when Anabaptist-Mennonites defined community to include their own in-group people only, but MCC has rejected this narrow definition from the time of its first work in Russia in 1920 to the present. Help is indeed given to the "household of faith," but to others too, as possible.'[48]

MCC relief officials found themselves pushed in one direction by UNRRA, the military authorities, local governments, and their own announced determination to distribute relief supplies only on the basis of need, and in the opposite direction by European Mennonite leaders and refugees and their constituents at home. In two of his letters, Robert Kreider wrote of these diverse pressures and the way in which MCC officials responded:

The first concern of this committee [a local Mennonite relief committee in the French Zone] is to minister to Mennonite need, but their service extends to others in need who live in the vicinity of Mennonite congregations ... Undoubtedly many Menno-nites in Germany have written to folk in the United States and Canada, telling of their need. In any case of need which comes to the attention of donors at home, the name may be sent to the MCC representatives in the field ... and the names will be for-warded immediately to the responsible Mennonite relief committee representative. One can be assured that immediate attention to the need will be given.[49]

The MCC effort to distribute scarce resources via CRALOG to the most needy was incredibly impartial. MCC and AFSC [American Friends Service Committee] were seen as the agencies most resistant to politicizing relief. The Catholics unapologetically sent aid as *Papstspende* and the Lutherans were ready to have its relief used to polish the image of the Protestant church. MCC pressed for inter-agency child feeding projects that would transcend parties and churches.[50]

As MCC workers in Europe struggled to maintain an impartial and balanced relief program, there was little doubt about the interest, sentiment, and concern of the Mennonites in North America, particularly of those who had close relatives and friends among the refugees.[51] Overseas, however, those distributing supplies had to balance the desire of the folks back home to help their own people and field policies that provided aid on the basis of need, giving preference to United Nations nationals. Robert Kreider described one early proposal to balance these objectives:

The big news of the week – and this is definitely off the record – is that General Clay has requested Washington approval for a scheme of contributing food packages to Germans by donors in the U.S. Perhaps this all has long since come to your attention. A U.S. donor may send 15 pound food packages to friends, relatives, acquaintances, anyone in the American Zone of Germany. The number of packages is not limited. Individual food packages are permitted *if* the donor prepares an identical package for distribution through CRALOG and German Central Committee channels to the neediest families. Obviously, the persons who receive the most packages from abroad are the ones with the best international connections. The duplicate package will serve to balance that tendency toward unfair distribution. Public Health and Welfare is appreciative of any scheme which brings more food into this Zone. This scheme may be a direct answer to our Mennonite concern that we have opportunity to help those of the 'household of faith.'[52]

Administration of such a scheme would have been difficult, and it was not implemented. Instead, American relief agencies, among which MCC was prominent, created a new, cooperative organization. CARE provided 'a nonprofit, safe, personalized, packaged relief service with delivery to specific recipients guaranteed.'[53] Initially CARE distributed mainly surplus army rations and individual gifts, but it soon developed its own food and textile packages which individual donors in North America could prepare or pay for and designate for delivery to specific refugees. In this way the donors in North America could send packages to specific individuals or a designated Mennonite committee or congregation, while official MCC relief programs in war-ravaged countries distributed food, clothing, and medical supplies on the basis of need.

MCC also established a registry for the refugees, facilitating the search for missing relatives and family members. Where possible they expedited the movement of Mennonite refugees out of eastern European countries, particularly from Poland, to Germany. And, as is shown in the next chapter, MCC became intimately involved in emigration of thousands of these refugees from Europe to Canada and to several South American countries.

The tragic experiences of the Prussian, Polish, and Danzig Mennonites were also of great concern to North American Mennonites. These people had participated with or given strong support to the German military and wartime occupation forces and were evacuated, forced to flee, or expelled from their homes during the last months of the war. There was no immediate prospect that they would be allowed to return, but an effective Mennonite relief program in Poland might begin the process of reconciliation. In addition, there was a natural curiosity regarding the fate of the material and, perhaps more important, the cultural, artistic, and religious possessions that these Mennonites had left behind.

Since farming communities in Europe had been devastated by the war, many farmers urgently needed good-quality livestock, mainly for breeding purposes. A Church of the Brethren farmer from Lancaster County, Pennsylvania, suggested that he and his people could provide both cattle and attendants if UNRRA provided the ships to take the stock to Europe. Thousands of animals were sent, mainly to Poland, Yugoslavia, Greece, Albania, and Czechoslovakia, under the program.[54] Several Canadian young men served as attendants and were called 'seagoing cowboys.' On the long trips, the seagoing cowboys, in the words of one historian, 'had their horizons widened and became more acutely aware of the extent of evil in the world as well as of the great need for relief in war-stricken Europe.'[55] Several whose interest in their own Anabaptist background was stimulated by that experience subsequently went to college and then did research and wrote about European Anabaptist and Mennonite history.

A second MCC-sponsored relief program in Poland, also begun in 1946, involved training Polish peasant farmers in the use of tractors. UNRRA agreed to supply the tractors, while MCC provided 25 tractor mechanics to instruct the Poles. Wilson Hunsberger, a native of Waterloo, Ontario, became director of this project. It was not an easy assignment. First there were difficulties and delays in the delivery of the tractors. Then Hunsberger reported ruefully that 'one can hardly underestimate the ability of the Poles as ... mechanics.'[56] Many of the tractors were reportedly put into 'disuse' almost as quickly as they arrived, mainly because of the students' inexperience and ignorance concerning lubrication and cooling. The project was nevertheless seen as a means to reopen dialogue between Mennonites and the Polish people. The MCC workers were also encouraged to identify, and sometimes rescue, Mennonite church books and other religious artifacts.

North American Mennonites responded generously to the desperate victims of war. At the busiest times MCC provided a daily meal to approximately 100,000 people in Germany. It supplied clothing, arranged for housing, secured medical supplies, and offered school and language instruction for tens of thousands of refugees and war victims.

The extensive publicity regarding the suffering of Mennonite refugees from the Soviet Union made Mennonite congregations particularly sympathetic to all victims of war. Mennonites who during the war had sometimes been severely criticized for not making an adequate contribution to the war effort generously supported the relief work.

CONTINUING VOLUNTARY SERVICE

There was always a close link among alternative service, voluntary service, and mission work. Nowhere was that more obvious than in a unique program that introduced Canadian Mennonites to the suffering and poverty of Native people in northern Manitoba. After the war some of those who had worked in those northern missions persuaded their conferences to begin their own Native mission programs. The results, discussed below, were mixed, but alternative and voluntary service had revealed to Mennonites many areas of great and continuing need, both at home and abroad. Some of those needs remained long after the war was over, and many Mennonites became convinced that they should continue to serve in peacetime as they had during the war. Were some of the services that they had been compelled to provide during the war the kinds of things that responsible Christians could and should do for their country in both war and peace?

One response was continuation, strengthening, and expansion of Voluntary Service (VS) programs. During the war growing hostility from non-Mennonite neighbours, and the ridicule sometimes heaped on the work of conscientious objectors by hostile politicians or local newspapers, hit a raw nerve. It stung when, for example, the Prince Albert *Daily Herald* reported sarcastically in 1943 that 'references to the Conchies helping win the war by cutting bridle paths in the park always gets [*sic*] a laugh.'[57] More helpful voluntary service in peacetime would quieten such criticisms.[58] So new programs 'organized use of different lengths of contributed time for various types of relief and peace needs at home and abroad. Priority is given to the younger workers; so this is to a great extent youth service. Periods of service vary from the "short" winter or summer terms of about ten weeks to the "longer" term of a year or more. Projects are chosen in places of need to provide a variety of opportunities in skills and interests. Strong emphasis is given to group witness and fellowship.'[59]

Workers in peacetime, like those in wartime alternative service, received basic out-of-pocket expenses and a modest personal allowance. Many worked on projects in which services were rendered free of charge, but some tasks offered a salary. Where the work was unpleasant, difficult, or in remote areas, remuneration far exceeded the allowances given VSers. The difference between salary and expenses/allowance went no longer to the Red Cross but into the MCC treasury to fund MCC projects where workers were paid inadequately or not at all. Most voluntary service was administered by MCC, but conferences also operated some of their own denominational programs – usually those closely associated with missionary endeavours.

Some of the earliest MCC-administered postwar VS assignments involved construction in Europe. The first exclusively Canadian unit, however, opened in 1948, when thirty-three young Mennonites accepted summer work in mental hospitals in North Battleford, Saskatchewan; Brandon, Manitoba; and London, Ontario. This was the first time in peace that Canadian hospitals allowed special groups to serve as medical and nursing support staff and to do maintenance and other work. The quality of the work by COs done during the war smoothed the way for the peacetime volunteers.

In 1954 new teaching and nursing Mennonite programs were initiated in Newfoundland. They involved VS teaching, health care, and social work in impoverished communities, where the volunteers worked for up to three years at activities similar to those of VSers in northern Native communities. Like the Native programs, those in Newfoundland were begun because the United Church was having difficulty finding qualified teachers for its schools. The memory of Mennonite alternative service teachers during the war in northern Manitoba encouraged Max Dawe, superintendent of the United Church mission in Newfoundland, to contact Harvey Taves, Canadian director of MCC, with a request for Mennonite teachers and nurses. Taves and Dawe put together a VS program under which Mennonite teachers, nurses, and social workers would work in Newfoundland communities under conditions similar to those of alternative service. The worker would receive transportation, accommodation, other expenses, and a $10-per-month allowance. The school, however, would pay normal salaries, with the difference going to MCC, to be used in VS programs that were not self-sustaining. Taves estimated that this would yield $70 per month per VSer. Though the amount of the monthly allowance later changed, the basic principles remained.[60]

VSers were not expected to serve for more than two or three years. Most attended the local United Church. The program was designed to provide an opportunity for dedicated young people to serve their country and to witness to their faith in a practical way in an area of need. Approximately thirty teachers and health workers, including several medical doctors, were placed in Newfoundland communities each year throughout the 1960s. Normally workers were placed in groups of four or five.

The efforts of the VSers were complemented by MCC support for a broadcast on Radio Station CJON in St John's. The tapes were prepared in close collaboration with the Twillingate Presbytery of the United Church. MCC agreed that the program must be worthy of the United Church in both musical quality and messages. They included a good deal of music, mainly choral groups singing 'old line hymns.' The objective, according to MCC officials, was 'to strengthen the hands of the ministers within the Presbytery with whom we have already been working in the past.'[61]

Most VS programs, including those in Newfoundland, did not aim at establishment of new Mennonite churches or at bringing students or patients to a religious conversion experience. The workers were to model Christian-

ity in their lives and in their work. One of the Newfoundland students recalled the work of VS teachers: 'I shall always be grateful for the Mennonite
work in Newfoundland. I believe that the first Mennonites came to Baie
Verte, Nfld. when I started Grade 10 in 1955. Bill [Miller] taught me in grades
10 and 11 and I'm absolutely convinced that if he hadn't come at that critical
time in my development that I might not even have come to university, let
alone get a Ph.D ... Bill worked extremely hard and because of that he forced
us to work, not by threats but by his example.'[62]

In inspections and other reports MCC officials assessed the program. A
1970 report, for example, said:

MCC teachers have been assigned to 16 different communities in Newfoundland
and Labrador. Our 30 volunteers without exception find the work and life in this
rather underdeveloped province both challenging and meaningful. Most of our VSers
have been placed in very backward and isolated spots but a few have been placed in
rather good schools, a departure from the former practice. The rationale is that not
only the pupils but also teachers, school boards and supervisors benefit from new
methods, fresh approaches and from the dedication and enthusiasm that comes with
the Christian volunteers. Stock in 'Mennonite' teachers is very high – even to a point
where these teachers are overrated, making it problematic for our people to live up to
this image.[63]

Officials of the Department of Northern Affairs and National Resources
inquired whether ten or fifteen Mennonite VSers could be placed in the Arc-
tic. MCC officials indicated willingness to discuss the matter, but the proposal had to be dropped when the Treasury Board refused to fund the program.[64]

A few VSers were also assigned to geriatric-care facilities and in homes for
deprived children in Quebec. These were not integrated with mission programs that Mennonite conferences had in that province, though VSers there
and elsewhere were encouraged to attend and become involved, where possible, in a nearby Mennonite church.

Canadian VS workers also continued to participate in international relief,
reconstruction, nursing, medical, teaching, agricultural, and community assistance programs, including several designed to assist the struggling Mennonite communities in Mexico and Paraguay. The concept of voluntary service has, according to an assessment written in the late 1980s, 'gained wide
acceptance in the churches as a way for persons, especially youth, to commit
their lives voluntarily and sacrificially for a period of Christian service in
situations of human need.'[65]

Canadian Mennonites learned a great deal about the world and the meaning of Christian discipleship and servanthood through voluntary service. What they learned has enlightened, enriched, and changed Mennonite churches around the world. Instead of trying to separate themselves from the world, young Mennonites have gone out to serve and heal the wounds of a war-torn and strife-filled world.

MENNONITE DISASTER SERVICE

During the war MCC developed an administrative and financial organization that permitted quick and effective responses to disasters at home and abroad. That organizational structure was modified after the war. A small permanent staff became an autonomous organization called Mennonite Disaster Service (MDS) in 1950.[66] When a disaster occurred anywhere in the world, this small core staff, aided and assisted when necessary by MCC personnel, could immediately mobilize volunteers willing to help and raise funds by publicizing the need in Mennonite communities. The objective was to give lay persons an opportunity 'to aid the victims of natural disasters such as floods, tornadoes, storms, earthquakes, and fire by cleanup and reconstruction work, largely in damaged homes.'[67] Special emphasis was placed on assistance to those least able to help themselves, such as children, single parents, the handicapped, and elderly persons. The organization was decentralized, with local units and directors able to respond quickly to local disasters. But other skeletal regional organizations staffed by lay persons could swing into action quickly in case of disasters requiring a response that exceeded the capacity of the local unit.

Creation of a flexible, quick-response organization took time, but one was clearly in place by 1970. A devastating flood in Rapid City, South Dakota, in 1972, illustrates how MDS worked. Syd Reimer, living in Rosenort, Manitoba, and chairman of the Manitoba Mennonite Disaster Service, received a phone call soon after the flood. The South Dakota MDS unit was overwhelmed and needed volunteers to help in clean-up, repair, and reconstruction. Syd, a divisional manager with Investors Syndicate Limited, obtained immediate short-term leave to help coordinate the work. About 1,500 volunteers from across North America, including 309 from Canada, responded. Students just out of school for the summer, entire families, and other volunteers went to Rapid City for varying periods – some for only a long weekend, others for several weeks.[68]

It was a policy of MDS to work closely with government civil aid agencies and with other disaster service organizations. Its workers were sometimes the first on the scene. They served without pay and often stayed longer than most emergency workers to help in longer-term rebuilding.

The work had immediate beneficial results for those receiving help and provided unique opportunities for practical Christian witness. That kind of service, rooted in part in rural and agricultural mutual aid and cooperative traditions, but also addressing modern urban problems, enjoyed continuous and strong support in Mennonite communities. Basic human empathy, reinforced by Christian love and concern, resulted in substantial support if people became aware of suffering and need. Administrative, personnel, and overhead costs were held to a minimum, allowing MDS to escape the scandals that discredited some non-Mennonite relief organizations and disaster services. MDS and other MCC-sponsored relief and disaster services also tried very hard to maintain a neutral political stance in local and international conflicts. The objective was simply to provide aid where and when people most urgently needed it.

RELIEF SALES

The funds to support Mennonite relief, voluntary, and disaster services came mainly from charitable donations. Such gifts were, however, significantly enhanced by special MCC-sponsored relief sales. These sales originated in Morgantown, Pennsylvania, in 1957, but spread to Canada a decade later. They were, and still are, unique ethnic, social, cultural, and philanthropic events that are held 'wherever North American Mennonites are clustered together, whether rural or urban.'[69] They have become popular 'because people can serve in a worldwide ministry at home in a way reminiscent of earlier community efforts such as barn raisings, butcherings, and threshings.'[70]

These sales have become ethnic fund-raising festivals. Ethnic Mennonite foods are served. Quilts, needlework, crafts, handiwork, artistic work, and farm produce are offered for sale. Special ethnic musical, literary, social, even physical fitness and athletic events have become a part of these sales. The primary objective, however, is to raise money for relief programs, and the central feature of the sales is the auctioning of the numerous items donated. Special funds are raised within the supporting Mennonite congregations beforehand to cover all overhead costs. Thus all receipts for items sold at the sales go directly and entirely to programs designed to help needy people. The first relief sale in New Hamburg, Ontario, in 1967 raised $28,000, with 10,000 people visiting, but in 1991 MCC Ontario received $324,000 from the New Hamburg sale alone.

The relief sales embody 'several things dear to the Mennonite soul: a deep desire for togetherness and comradery [*sic*], celebration of family, church, tradition, and service, and the impulse to help others.'[71] Like many Mennonite material aid and relief programs, the support they receive crosses age, gender, and Mennonite denominational boundaries. Men, women, young people, children, and the elderly contribute their diverse skills in quilting, sewing, knitting, needlework, hog butchering, pancake making, arts, crafts, gardening, and home baking, establishing new networks and friendships among Mennonites, Amish, and Brethren in Christ. Local committees arrange these sales, sometimes designating which MCC-approved or -administered program is to be supported with the funds raised.

CONCLUSION

Wartime and postwar alternative service, material aid, and voluntary service changed the Canadian Mennonites. Their eyes and hearts had been opened to worldwide need and suffering, and that altered some of their basic responses to the outside world. Separatist and sectarian principles – nonconformity and non-resistance – gave way to more interventionist, charitable, and supportive strategies.

Scripture verses that had been cited frequently to support Mennonite teachings regarding nonconformity included 1 John 1:15, in which Christians are admonished: 'Love not the world, neither the things that are in the world. If any man love the world, the love of the Father is not in him.'[72] Alternative and voluntary service focused attention more clearly on other verses, such as Matthew 25:40: 'Inasmuch as ye have done it [fed the hungry, given drink to the thirsty, clothed the naked, welcomed strangers] to the least of these my brethren, ye have done it unto me.' If, according to John 3:16, 'God so loved the world that he gave his only begotten son,' was it not incumbent on Christians also to love the world and to express that love in healing and redemptive ways? The editors of a new Mennonite periodical that began publication in 1970 clearly expressed the new attitudes: 'We believe we have been placed in this world to rejoice in all of its beauty and goodness and to heal and transform it through our love. Love seeks to enfold what it loves, it doesn't turn from the world to protect its own purity but reaches out to embrace it.'[73]

When Canadian Mennonites were conscripted or volunteered for wartime and postwar service they found that, through love, even the worst hellholes on earth could be, and sometimes were, transformed into sacred places.

4

Refugee Immigrants

Canadian Mennonites experienced significant disruptions during the war, but theirs were far less painful and difficult than those of Mennonites in the Soviet Union, Poland, the Free City of Danzig (now Gdańsk), and Prussia. Almost all the Mennonites living in eastern Europe, including the European part of the Soviet Union, in September 1939 were forcibly relocated, evicted, or expelled from their homes during the war. Many of those from the European part of the Soviet Union were exiled to far eastern and northern labour and concentration camps, while most of those expelled from Danzig and Prussia eventually emigrated to South America or re-established themselves in West Germany. There were, however, 7,698 Mennonites from eastern Europe who became refugees[1] in western Europe and emigrated to Canada in the five years from 1947 through 1951.[2]

In Canada the European refugee immigrants hoped to settle in rural farming communities. Most, in fact, had to commit themselves to two years as agricultural workers, as domestic servants, or, in a few cases, as labourers in designated industries with serious labour shortages, but few were able to acquire their own farms. Instead, they joined, and sometimes led, the Mennonite migration into the cities.

MENNONITE REFUGEES FROM THE SOVIET UNION

One of the Mennonite refugees who came to Canada in the 1940s was Agatha Schmidt, who recaptured in original oil paintings some of the most moving and difficult aspects of the lives of her people. She also wrote an account of the story behind her art[3] – a tale similar to that of many other Mennonite refugee-immigrants from eastern Europe.

Schmidt was one of about 100,000 Mennonites, and of approximately one million ethnic Germans, living in the Soviet Union when war between Germany and the Soviet Union broke out in June 1941.[4] The village in which she lived had already lost many of its men under Joseph Stalin's enforced policies of agricultural collectivization in the 1930s. German military successes after June 1941 led to Soviet attempts to evacuate eastward German and Mennonite settlers living in territories likely to be captured by the Germans. The men were evacuated first, but the German advance was so fast that many of the villages on the west side of the Dnieper River fell before evacuation was completed. Villages and settlements on the eastern side of the Dnieper lost almost all their men and about half of their women and children to the evacuation. Agatha's village was overrun by the Germans before the women and children could be moved east.

By the end of October 1941 most Soviet Mennonite communities were occupied by the Germans.[5] They remained under German occupation for two years. German administrators regarded ethnic Germans living in the Soviet Union, many of whom had suffered greatly under Stalin, as natural allies of the Reich, giving them major civilian responsibilities and encouraging eligible young men to enlist in German military units.

Defeat of the German forces at Stalingrad in the winter of 1942–3 resulted in a general retreat westward. Approximately 350,000 Soviet Germans, including an estimated 35,000 Mennonites,[6] were removed from their homes and taken westward under German military escort in September and October 1943. The plan was to resettle these people further west in a portion of central Poland that the Germans hoped would become part of postwar Germany.[7] Schmidt described the organization of the trek in September of 1943: 'We were 4 persons in our wagon, my mother and we three girls, aged 16, 18 and 20. Ahead of us in the trek was my Aunt Tina with her daughter and further back my old grandfather lay in a wagon driven by his daughter, Aunt Elizabeth, and her young son and daughter.'[8]

The long trek in the muck and cold of a rainy Ukrainian autumn and winter became a nightmare as exhausted draught animals and refugees fell by the wayside. Agatha Schmidt's old grandfather died after two months of this misery and was hurriedly buried in a shallow pit beside the churned-up mud of the road. Successive rear-guard, defensive lines were thrown up at strategic points by the retreating Germans to slow the Soviet advance, which was stopped at key river crossings for weeks or even months. But gradually the Germans were pushed further and further west. Schmidt's group spent the coldest winter months of 1943–4 in temporary accommodations near the Ukrainian–Polish border. Then, in March 1944, they were resettled in the Wartegau district of central Poland. There they remained for almost a year before the collapse of the eastern front along the Vistula River precipitated flight to escape the approaching Red Army.

The departure from central Poland was poorly coordinated. Some of the refugees made their way west with hurriedly requisitioned and poorly fed or equipped horses and wagons. Others were taken west by train. Thousands perished, and many thousands more were overtaken by the Soviets. The treatment accorded the refugees by Red Army units varied considerably, in part because the exigencies of continuous and often difficult military action against retreating German defenders had to take priority over refugee policies and concerns. Many refugees died or were sent back to the Soviet Union if arrangements could be made without weakening the military effort.[9] Some received relatively generous care and treatment, at least up to the time of their forced repatriation and exile to Siberia. Others were harassed and physically and sexually abused but then allowed to continue westward or to find shelter with local people.

Schmidt and members of her family, travelling sometimes by horse and wagon, but at other times on foot, in trucks, and finally by train, crossed the Oder River and experienced the final collapse of the Reich in the American zone but wrote sorrowfully that 'very many of our people were not able to escape the Russians.'[10] After Germany's unconditional surrender they found shelter and essential material aid in one or other of the large refugee camps established by the occupying military authorities or by United Nations or private relief agencies. With the help of the Mennonite Central Committee, the remnants of the Schmidt family made contact with relatives in Canada and emigrated there in 1948. Schmidt's experiences, while unique in some respects, were typical of what happened to many of those who came to Canada in the immediate postwar period.[11]

The suffering and hardship of the Mennonite refugees from the Soviet Union who were evacuated westward by the retreating Germans were part of much larger wartime strategies in which innocent people became pawns used to advance rival Soviet and Nazi territorial ambitions. (A statistical summary of the fate of Soviet Germans and Mennonites is given in Table 4.1.) Two

Table 4.1
Fate of Soviet Germans and Soviet Mennonites, 1941–5

	Soviet Germans	Mennonites
Living in the Soviet Union in 1941	1–1.1 million	100,000
Deported by the Soviets	650,000	55,000
Evacuated by Germans or fled westward	350,000	35,000
Overtaken by the Red Army	200,000	?
Forcibly repatriated by the Allies	80,000	?
Remaining in the west, Sept. 1945	70,000	12,000

Sources: See discussion of sources in note 6, page 458.

specific documents set the framework for much of that suffering. The first was the agreement negotiated between the Soviet and German foreign ministers in September 1939. Under the secret articles of the so-called Molotov-Ribbentrop accord, the two nations divided eastern Europe into spheres of influence, each agreeing not to interfere with aggressive initiatives undertaken by the other in its own sphere. Germany thus gained a free hand in the western two-thirds of Poland, while the Soviet Union was given similar privileges in the eastern third of Poland and in the Baltic republics of Estonia, Lithuania, and Latvia. The two powers also agreed to population exchanges whereby Slavic peoples in German zones of influence would be removed to Soviet zones and ethnic Germans in Soviet-controlled areas would be moved to German territory.[12]

Both Hitler and Stalin believed that there would be strong pressure from the Western allies to draw new postwar boundaries in eastern Europe in accordance with the ethnic composition and the freely expressed political and national preferences of the local people. That expectation was reinforced when Winston Churchill and Franklin Delano Roosevelt, at a meeting in August 1941, announced their war aims, which were incorporated into the Atlantic Charter on 1 January 1942. In it the Western allies renounced territorial aggrandizement and committed themselves 'to oppose territorial changes that do not accord with the freely expressed wishes of the people concerned.'[13]

The principles of the Atlantic Charter were noble, but the consequences in eastern Europe disastrous. Both Hitler and Stalin wanted to retain all or most of the Polish and some of the other eastern territories that they had occupied in 1939 and 1940. It was the desire to strengthen German claims to western and central Poland that prompted the retreating Germans to order the forcible expulsion of millions of Poles from the Wartegau region of central Poland early in 1944 and then to resettle evacuated Germans from the Soviet Union and other occupied Slavic countries in that region. If, at war's end, the territory was actually occupied and settled by Germans, it should, according to the Atlantic Charter, become part of postwar Germany. Most of the refugees who were resettled in Poland were consequently sworn in as German citizens.[14] The Polish expulsions, and the resettlement of their lands by Germans evacuated from territories further east, naturally caused intense suffering, resentment, and retaliatory measures when the Red Army gained control.

Some estimates hold that at least five million, and perhaps as many as seven million, Soviet citizens were outside the boundaries of their own country at the end of the war. The majority had either been conscripted for hard labour in Germany or been taken prisoners of war by the enemy and were eager to return home. But at conferences in Teheran and Yalta, Stalin had persuaded

Churchill and Roosevelt that all 'liberated Soviet citizens' be repatriated, whether they wished to return or not. Stalin, whose regime had been fiercely criticized by dissident émigrés following the 1917 revolution, feared the influence that embittered and hostile former Russian/Soviet citizens might have in the West. He also sought a measure of revenge on those whose loyalty during the war had come into question or who had actively helped the enemy. He readily admitted at Yalta that traitors and collaborators would be punished. Others, he insisted, had nothing to fear.

Churchill and Roosevelt were eager to maintain friendly relations with their Soviet ally. In addition, the Western allies had no effective way of dealing with hundreds of thousands of refugees who were unwilling to return to their home country. So they agreed to Stalin's demands for repatriation of all 'liberated Soviet citizens.'[15]

Most of the involuntary repatriations took place in the first five or six months after the German surrender. Some American and British military officials were never enthusiastic about them, while others lost whatever enthusiasm they had when they saw the brutality and adverse publicity associated with the repatriations.

The policy of forced repatriation was unofficially modified in November 1945 by the American military authorities. Those changes became official, but were not publicized, in January 1946. Thereafter Soviet repatriation officers had to provide irrefutable proof that an individual had voluntarily rendered aid and comfort to the enemy before that person could be involuntarily repatriated.[16] These new instructions did not entirely end the threat of involuntary repatriation for Mennonite refugees from the Soviet Union. Soviet repatriation officers were still granted access to alleged former Soviet citizens. The refugees, moreover, were not informed of the changed policy, and American officers were told not to try and persuade anyone to reject Soviet offers of repatriation. But after January 1946 it was no longer the official policy to repatriate involuntarily refugees from the Soviet Union unless there was clear evidence of voluntary, disloyal wartime behaviour.

The threat of involuntary repatriations became particularly difficult for a number of Mennonite refugees from the Soviet Union trapped in the American sector of Berlin. Soviet officials wanted these people repatriated. The American military officers were reluctant to comply but had no way of getting the people out of Berlin. In the end an informal arrangement, made possible because of harmonious personal working relations between General Lucius Clay, the senior American military commander in Berlin, and his Soviet counterpart, Marshal Sokolovsky,[17] allowed the refugees to leave for the West on a special sealed train. The refugees and MCC officials directly involved had not been informed of the changed policy and had no knowledge of the arrangement between Clay and Sokolovsky. They interpreted the rescue as a divine and miraculous event. Their view of the Soviet Red Army and its commanders was entirely negative, and most would have regarded Sokolovsky's collaboration, had they known about it, as perhaps even more miraculous than they did the unknown circumstances of the Berlin rescue. What the refugees knew was that they had prayed desperately. God had heard their prayers, and they had been rescued.

Ignorance of Sokolovksy's intervention, however, made it possible to tell and retell the story in ways that fitted into Cold War political rhetoric and sharpened and focused anti-communist and anti-Soviet sentiments in Mennonite communities around the world. It became the best-known, albeit incomplete, Mennonite story of the Second World War. It captured more completely than any other story or document the spirit, the sentiments, and the religious convictions of the Mennonite refugees who escaped to western Europe, and eventually emigrated to North or South America.

PRUSSIAN AND DANZIG MENNONITES

The refugees from the Soviet Union made up the overwhelming majority of the Mennonite immigrants who came to Canada in the late 1940s. They were, however, joined in western Europe by others driven from their ancestral homes in Danzig, East and West Prussia, and Poland. A few of these were also able to emigrate to Canada after 1950.

In September 1939 there had been approximately 665 Mennonites in East Prussia, 2,500 in West Prussia, 6,000 in the Free City of Danzig, and 2,000 in central Poland.[18] Virtually all these people fled, were evacuated by the retreating Germans, or were expelled from their homes by the new, Soviet-backed Polish government during the last months of the war or shortly thereafter.

The Mennonites living in East and West Prussia were, of course, citizens of the Third Reich, while those in Danzig and in Polish territories occupied by the Germans were incorporated into the Reich during the first weeks of the war and were thereafter treated by the Germans and allies alike as citizens of the Reich.[19] They suffered relatively little property damage or economic hardship during the first five years of the war, but many of their young men were drafted or joined the German military voluntarily and suffered relatively high casualty rates. The Prussian Mennonites had made participation in the military a matter of individual conscience after the Franco-Prussian War of 1870, and only a small minority objected to military service in the Second World War. The Prussian Mennonite community of Heubuden, for example, had approximately 250 young men in the German military, of whom 100 were killed before the end of 1944.[20]

It was only during the last six or seven months of the war that the property and lives of the Danzig and Prussian Mennonites were devastated. The victorious Red Army reached the eastern borders of the Reich in October 1944. Once they crossed into Germany the Soviet troops committed terrible atrocities against the local populace, comparable to those committed earlier by the Germans in the occupied eastern territories. The Soviets were in part motivated by revenge, but the atrocities also furthered the diplomatic and state purposes of the Soviet Union. Stalin had no intention of surrendering the portions of eastern Poland and the Baltic states that he had annexed and incorporated into the Soviet Union after the signing of the Molotov-Ribbentrop Accord. Instead, he proposed that postwar Poland be compensated for the lost eastern territory by moving the country's western boundary to the banks of the Oder and of the western branch of the Neisse rivers. That land, however, was populated mostly by Germans. It would be difficult to apply the principles of the Atlantic Charter to the proposed new borders unless the Germans east of the Oder-Neisse line were killed or driven from their ancestral homes and the territory resettled by Polish and other Slavic peoples. Thus state policy was combined with motives of revenge to create a hell on earth for the German populations of Danzig, East and West Prussia, Pomerania, Silesia, and northern Poland.

Soviet atrocities varied in time and place and according to the general military situation and the control individual officers exercised over their troops. The Red Army first broke through German defensive lines and entered East Prussian territory on 19 October 1944. This first thrust into German territory was rebuffed, and the Soviets were forced to withdraw within two weeks, but lurid accounts of events during those two weeks were widely publicized by the Germans.[21]

The subsequent advance of the Red Army, and fear of further atrocities, set in motion a mass flight of terror-stricken Germans from the eastern provinces of the Reich, from Danzig, and from Poland. Soviet German evacuees, temporarily resettled in the Wartegau, mingled with new Prussian and Danzig refugees in a desperate struggle to escape to the West. The military defeat of the Reich seemed inevitable, but any fate in western Europe seemed preferable to capture by the advancing Red terror.

The flight took two main forms. Those fleeing in November and December 1944, particularly if they came from the more southerly regions of Poland and the eastern provinces of the Reich, mobilized whatever horses, wagons, and other means of land transport they could and fled westward by land. Often the refugees were only a short distance ahead of the advancing Red troops, and their convoys were harassed by low-flying Soviet bombers, which killed many and terrorized more. The land routes during the last two months of 1944 were difficult. Thousands died on the way, or were overtaken by the advancing Soviet troops and killed or, if they were Soviet citizens, repatriated.

Millions of Germans from the northeastern German territories and from Danzig were unable to escape overland. The Soviet advance through central Poland, Silesia, and Pomerania was faster than further north, where the major Baltic ports and large portions of Prussia resisted longer. Soviet troops first reached the Baltic seacoast at Stolp in January 1945, cutting off all overland escape routes for millions of Germans from Danzig and the northeastern corner of the old Reich.[22] The Germans fled to the hopelessly congested ports on the Baltic and in the Gulf of Danzig, desperately hoping for rescue by sea.

The German navy and merchant marine and owners of private ships and boats moved every available vessel to the open winter ports in the Gulf of Danzig. A total of 790 ships were placed in this service, but the rescue was fraught with multiple dangers. Along both the northwestern and southeastern sides of the Gulf of Danzig, and also further north between Koenigsberg and Memel, there are huge lagoons or bays. These bodies of water lie between the mainland and narrow peninsulas of land about 15 to 25 miles from the mainland. The Vistula Lagoon (Frisches Haff) extends from the mouth of the Vistula northward to Koenigsberg, while further north the Courland Lagoon (Kurishes Haff) stretches northward to Memel.

The rescue operations by sea took place between January and May 1945, when these lagoons were partially or completely frozen. Due to winter ice and military conditions, the rescue ships could operate only in open water beyond the peninsulas. The major ports available there were those of Pilau and Hela. There the ships lay at anchor, awaiting refugees who had to make their way across the lagoon from the mainland and then across the narrow peninsula. In the winter months the lagoons were covered with ice, and the refugees tried to cross them on sleighs or wagons. Later in the spring they used small boats, which also carried refugees from the peninsula to the ships lying at anchor in the deeper, ice-free waters of the Gulf.

The ice on the bays of the Vistula Lagoon was not always thick enough to carry the refugees, and many with heavier wagons, or when travelling together in large numbers, broke through the ice and drowned or died of exposure. As well, there were Soviet bombing raids. The nightmare did not end when refugees reached the peninsula or the harbours at Pilau and Hela. Here too there was constant strafing and bombing by Soviet aircraft. Historians readily admit that there were military objectives in bombing the Baltic ports, but they also suggest that 'it is difficult to see sufficient military necessity that could have justified constant bombardment of a port where tens of thousands of refugees were being evacuated.'[23]

Both the retreating Germans and the advancing Soviets had laid numerous mines in the Gulf of Danzig, and Soviet submarines operated in the Gulf and further out in the Baltic. Several of the largest ships, and many smaller ones, were sunk. On 30 January 1945 the *Wilhelm Gustloff*, with about 7,000 refugees and wounded soldiers on board, was hit by a submarine torpedo. Even though it was travelling in convoy, only 838 of the passengers were rescued. Then, on 16 April 1945, the *Goya*, again with approximately 7,000 passengers, was sunk by a submarine; there were only 183 survivors. Many of the ships shuttled back and forth, some as many as twelve times, and between 1.5 and 3 million refugees were saved,[24] while 20–30,000 perished in the attempt. These statistics suggest that the sea rescue was, in fact, much safer than the overland treks, but huge ships, crammed to capacity with defenceless refugees, wounded soldiers, and evacuees, going down with enormous loss of life have made the sea rescue more poignant.

Approximately 1,800 Prussian and Danzig Mennonites were involved in this rescue.[25] Most were taken to large refugee camps in Denmark, Schleswig-Holstein, or northern Germany. The unexpectedly fast military collapse, the precipitate flight into the unknown, and then a prolonged sojourn in miserable refugee camps, surrounded by barbed wire, proved traumatic for these people. The Polish government would not allow them to return to their former homes; the Danish government resented their presence; and the weak civilian German authorities had great difficulty integrating their own people, let alone refugees, into the shattered economy. United Nations agencies providing relief and planning for emigration were expected to help first refugees who were citizens of one of the United Nations. So the unhappy Germans from territories that had become part of postwar Poland sat and waited, many for three to five years, before they could emigrate or find work and homes within the shrunken borders of West Germany. As well, Mennonite refugees from Prussia, Danzig, and Poland were scattered in various camps, and all efforts by MCC workers to bring them together failed.

PREPARATIONS FOR EMIGRATION

There may have been as many as 40 million refugees in Europe immediately after the war, but of that number between 850,000 and 1 million were unwilling or unable to return home.[26] Not included in that number were roughly six million Germans who had fled or been evacuated or expelled from the eastern provinces that had become part of postwar Poland and were languishing in Danish and north German refugee camps. Among those unwilling to return home were approximately 12,000 Mennonites from the Soviet Union and 1,800 to 2,000 Prussian and Danzig Mennonites.

The first concern of the military authorities, of United Nations agencies, and of voluntary relief organizations was to provide emergency relief for the destitute refugees. The prospects of integration into the war-ravaged countries of Western Europe, however, were very poor for many. Emigration was regarded as the best way to assist many of the refugees.

The United Nations established several agencies to assist in emigration of European refugees, the most important being the International Refugee Organization (IRO).[27] The IRO and its predecessors provided facilities for the medical and political screening of refugees by officials of prospective host countries and paid for transportation to the point of disembarkation in the host country. The IRO's mandate was, however, restricted to citizens of one of the United Nations. The emigration of other refugees was still possible, but only if those interested could arrange screening, cover transportation costs, and find a country that would accept the refugees. Prospective host countries, however, were under considerable pressure to give preference to refugees within the mandate of the IRO.

The IRO's restricted purview created awkward problems for the Mennonite refugees from the Soviet Union. As citizens of the Soviet Union they were eligible for assistance from the IRO and the United Nations Relief and Rehabilitation Agency (UNRRA), but many were convinced that an admission that they were Soviet citizens would also make them vulnerable to involuntary repatriation. If, however, they were classified as German citizens, or as Volksdeutsche (ethnic Germans) who had collaborated with the enemy, they were not eligible for United Nations, and specifically IRO, assistance. Most hoped to receive United Nations relief and emigration assistance without risking repatriation.

C.F. Klassen, the senior officer of the Mennonite Central Committee (MCC) in Europe, thought that there was a way to circumvent the difficulty. Mennonites in the Soviet Union in the 1920s had successfully claimed Dutch ancestry.[28] That claim had allegedly expedited the migration of the 1920s. Immediately after the Second World War approximately 420 refugees from the Soviet Union had fled to the Netherlands, claiming they were of Dutch ancestry.[29] When the Soviets heard of this they quickly put a stop to it, threatening to hold Dutch soldiers who had been taken prisoner by the Germans and later liberated by the Soviets. That threat effectively closed the Dutch borders to Mennonite refugees from the Soviet Union, but not the possible utility of claiming Dutch ancestry.

When the Dutch border closed, some Mennonite refugees were given emergency assistance in UNRRA camps. Others found help in a large, MCC-administered camp at Gronau, near the Dutch-German border.[30] Another large Mennonite refugee camp, Lager Backnang, was established near Stuttgart and also accommodated refugees who had tried, unsuccessfully, to escape to Holland.[31] These camps provided immediate help, but no long-term solutions. Most of the refugees were eager to migrate to Canada, where many had close relatives. Many were also willing to consider Brazil, Paraguay, or some other South American country if they could not go to Canada.[32]

The claim of Dutch ancestry was successfully advanced on behalf of the refugees who had escaped from Berlin in February 1947. The Inter-Governmental Commission for Refugees (IGCR), a predecessor of the IRO, had paid the $160,000 that it cost to charter the Dutch ship *Volendam*, which transported those refugees to South America early in 1947.[33] That encouraged C.F. Klassen, other senior MCC officials, and many of the refugees themselves to build their claims for migration assistance around their Dutch ancestry. These claims, nevertheless, resulted in prolonged and bitter disputes and controversies, particularly between MCC officials, who were strongly supported by U.S. State Department officials, and officials of the IRO and its predecessors, who were subjected to considerable pressure from Jewish, Ukrainian, and other ethnic groups, which had suffered at the hands of Volksdeutsche during the German occupation of the eastern territories.[34] MCC insisted that Mennonite refugees from the Soviet Union were of Dutch ancestry, 'unmistakeably other than German.'[35] It was impossible to deny that many had collaborated with the Nazis, but MCC officials insisted that the refugees had done so only under duress. They allegedly had also registered themselves or accepted German citizenship 'exclusively and only in order that they might protect themselves from the Bolshevik agents.'[36]

At first the Mennonite claims were accepted, at least tacitly, but then information from captured German documents, held at the huge Berlin Document Centre, came to light. That information contradicted some of the claims made by Klassen and other MCC officials that the refugees had acted under duress. As a result, some IRO officials became convinced that MCC had deliberately withheld important information. MCC officials hotly denied that charge.[37] The emotional climate can be deduced from Klassen's insistence that he was compelled to wage 'an honest fight against ignorance, prejudice, stupidity, and not seldom, even wickedness of IRO officers.'[38] It was, to put it mildly, a nasty fight, the details of which are beyond the scope of this book and are being published elsewhere.[39]

MCC officials had established their own registry of Mennonite refugees from the Soviet Union. That registry did not include information about military service; the time, place, and circumstances under which German citizenship had been acquired; or other information pertaining to possible collaboration with the Nazis. MCC officials did not know, at least not officially, and probably did not want to know, such things. Duress and voluntary collaboration in conditions of war were themselves flexible concepts, but much of the information allegedly withheld was not available in official MCC records. That, however, did not alter the facts that there was damaging information in captured German records that documented Mennonite wartime collaboration with the German occupation forces and that some Mennonites had accepted German citizenship long before their resettlement in the Wartegau and at times when there was no compulsion for them to do so. MCC's claims that collaboration or acceptance of German citizenship had occurred only under duress were thus refuted.[40]

The hard facts of the case were that IRO researchers and officials were closer to the truth, as revealed in the surviving captured German documents, than the disclaimers in the MCC documents. The MCC officials did not deliberately withhold information available in their files, and they expressed more accurately the emotional and spiritual state of the refugees. These were people who had suffered intensely under Soviet rule and for a time saw the Germans as God's instrument to free them from tyranny. The desperate fear of Soviet capture or repatriation became their overriding concern during the last stages of the war and the period immediately following. Neither the refugees nor MCC officials had been informed of changes in involuntary repatriation policies, and the cold and impersonal classifications of the IRO did not seem to fit or take into account their sad plight and their unique experiences. MCC's efforts to establish Dutch identity for them were, nevertheless, regarded sceptically or as outright deception by some IRO officials.

The fight over eligibility created much tension, but, thanks largely to effective intervention by U.S. State Department officials who were impressed and grateful for the massive relief and rehabilitation activities of MCC, almost all the refugees from the Soviet Union who wished to do so were able to migrate to North or South America with support and assistance from the IRO or one of its predecessors. Thus the migration of the 1940s, unlike that of the 1920s, did not leave Canadian Mennonites with another large transportation debt.

IMMIGRATION TO CANADA

The preferred destination of the Mennonite refugees was Canada, where many had close relatives and friends. Ottawa, however, was not prepared to admit large numbers of immigrants immediately after the war. The disastrous unemployment problems of the 1930s, and memories of serious labour disturbances after the First World War, were very much on the minds of Canadian politicians and bureaucrats as they formulated new immigration policies. Their first priority was demobilization and industrial reconstruction, which would absorb returning Canadian soldiers and the many workers in wartime industries that had to be converted to meet peacetime requirements. Immigrants should be admitted only if they could be integrated into the economy. 'Absorptive capacity' became the overriding concern of immigration policy makers, and officials at the Department of Labour were involved in formulation of immigration policies.[41]

A further concern was the desperate shortage of suitable shipping immediately after the war. Priority had to be given to Canadian soldiers returning home from Britain and Europe. Thousands of these men had been stationed for most of the war in the British Isles, where they had married British war brides and fathered children, all requiring transportation to Canada.

The first non-Canadians allowed to come or stay as postwar immigrants were Polish veterans unable or unwilling to return to communist-controlled Poland. They, returning soldiers, and workers in military production plants were absorbed with unexpected ease into a surprisingly buoyant economy. After fifteen years of depression and war, Ottawa was eager to rebuild the economy to meet postponed civilian demands, and consumers responded enthusiastically. The difficult labour situation of 1919 and 1920 was not repeated in 1946. Instead, key sectors of the economy continued to face serious labour shortages.[42] Military expenditures also remained unexpectedly high with the increase of tensions between the Western allies and the Soviet Union.

The plight of the refugees in Europe, the relative strength of the Canadian economy, and continuing labour shortages, particularly of farm workers, forestry and mining labourers, and domestic servants, made possible liberalization of Canada's cautious immigration policies.[43] Also, business leaders believed that a larger domestic labour pool would blunt strident demands by organized labour for large salary increases. Both the Canadian National Railways (CNR) and Canadian Pacific Railway (CPR) were still eager to resettle immigrants on their own marginal frontier lands or simply to generate more traffic for transportation systems that had expanded dramatically during the war but faced a serious loss of traffic with demobilization. Various ethnocultural groups concerned about the plight of kinfolk in European refugee camps also demanded that Canada admit more immigrants.

Canadian Mennonites were among the most effective and persistent pressure groups. They worked through the MCC in Europe and the Canadian Mennonite Board of Colonization in Canada, where an effective partnership with the CPR, begun in the 1920s, was renewed. When Mennonite leaders contacted the CPR for assistance in bringing refugees from Europe immediately after the war, the response was exceptionally cordial and cooperative. 'You can be assured,' the chairman of the Board of Colonization was told, 'of the fullest possible support and help of the Canadian Pacific Railway.'[44] In the next months Mr Cresswell of the CPR, together with a sympathetic MP and C.F. Klassen, visited the officers of the Inter-Governmental Committee on Refugees (IGCR) a number of times to set up procedures for medical and political screening. The IGCR's officials noted that 'there are certain technical difficulties, but Mr. Klassen did not appear too much daunted.'[45] The problems concerned eligibility of Mennonite refugees from the Soviet Union for United Nations assistance.

Canadian Mennonite leaders, on the advice and with the support of CPR officials, launched intensive lobbying to ease immigration regulations. Prime Minister King and key cabinet ministers were visited repeatedly, but in 1946 the response remained cautious.[46] 'It has been decided,' the sympathetic Jimmy Gardiner informed one Mennonite leader, 'that it would be very difficult to attempt to settle very many here while we are re-establishing our own troops. It is thought that it will take most of this year [1946] to accomplish that.'[47]

The first major breakthrough came in June 1946, when an order in council permitted immigration from Europe of refugees who had close relatives in Canada willing to sponsor their immigration. The order in council said nothing about UNRRA or IGCR eligibility (the IRO was not yet established) but stipulated that the prospective immigrants had to have sponsors who would assume responsibility for travel from the point of disembarkation and for the care and support of the immigrants after their arrival in Canada. In the case of Mennonite immigrants who had close relatives in Canada, such sponsorship was arranged through the Canadian Mennonite Board of Colonization.[48]

The CPR offered immediate help for Mennonite refugees who lacked UNRRA or IGCR (later IRO) assistance. It had granted substantial transportation credits to the Mennonite immigrants of the 1920s. That debt, which together with interest charges, totalled $1,767,398.68,[49] had been renegotiated and adjusted in the 1930s. The Mennonites had already paid $180,000 in interest charges, but the CPR agreed not to assess further interest charges. If the entire amount still owing were repaid, the $180,000 would be placed in a Special Suspense Account 'for use as collateral for the value of transportation furnished by the company for new movements under the auspices of the Board.'[50] The last of that transportation debt was repaid in November 1946. Thereafter the Canadian Mennonite Board of Colonization had an assured $180,000 line of credit with the CPR, which could be used to pay for transportation of any refugees not eligible for UNRRA or IRO assistance. CPR officials and some federal politicians were willing to set up alternative medical and political clearing offices in Europe for prospective Mennonites who could not be screened in the UNRRA camps or at IRO facilities because they were outside the IRO's mandate.

Several groups with links to refugees outside the mandate of the IRO also established the Canadian Christian Council for Resettlement of Refugees Outside the IRO Mandate (CCCRR), but the Mennonites participated only half-heartedly. They hoped and expected that their refugees from the Soviet Union would come to Canada with IRO assistance and would use the CCCRR only if their claims for IRO assistance were rejected.[51] In the end, almost all the Soviet Mennonite refugees had their travel costs up to the point of disembarkation in Canada paid by the IRO. Those costs exceeded $1 million.[52] The $180,000 credit with the CPR remained on the books until 1951, when $125,390.68 was used to pay for the transportation of 703 Danzig and Prussian Mennonites not eligible for IRO assistance.[53]

Once it became clear to Ottawa that the overwhelming majority of Mennonite and non-Mennonite immigrants alike who had been admitted in the late 1940s were being successfully absorbed, and serious labour shortages remained in key Canadian industries, it was decided to admit additional and perhaps more controversial immigrants. German nationals, including those expelled from Prussia and Danzig, were admissible after 1950. That opened the door for the Danzig and Prussian refugees still stuck in Danish and north German refugee camps.

The Canadian Mennonite Board of Colonization worked with the CCCRR, under whose auspices 777 Danzig and Prussian Mennonites were brought to Canada, including some of the 703 whom the board assisted through its credit with the CPR. The preoccupation of the board and of the MCC with the eligibility disputes with the IRO over the Soviet refugees probably delayed the admission of Prussian and Danzig refugees, while saving the board and/or MCC over a million dollars in transportation costs. Those delays, and conditions in the Danish camps, led many Prussian and Danzig Mennonites to settle in Uruguay, even though most wanted to come to Canada. Other expellees were integrated into (West) German life, thanks in part to innovative MCC rehabilitation work.

The Mennonite refugees who came to Canada in the late 1940s and early 1950s were part of a much larger wave of immigrants from war-ravaged Europe (see Tables 4.2 and 4.3).

Table 4.2
Canadian and Mennonite immigration, 1947–51

Year	Total Canadian immigration	Mennonite immigration
1947	71,719	542
1948	125,414	3,828
1949	95,217	1,632
1950	73,912	580
1951	194,391	1,116
Total	560,553	7,698

Sources: Canadian immigration figures: M.C. Urquhart and K.A.H. Buckley, *Historical Statistics of Canada* (Toronto: Macmillan, 1965), Series A254; Mennonite immigration figures: MHC Canadian Mennonite Board of Colonization, 1348/1109.

Table 4.3
Composition of Canadian Mennonite immigration, 1947–51

Close Relatives Scheme	6,101
Sugar-beet workers	308
Farm Labour Scheme	73
Domestic servants	35
Forestry workers	41
Railway workers	2
Mine workers	6
Danzig, Prussian, and German nationals after 1950	1,132
Total	7,698

Source: MHC Canadian Mennonite Board of Colonization, 1348/1109.

THE IMMIGRANTS IN CANADA

Canadian Mennonites welcomed the immigrants with great sympathy, love, and warmth but sometimes also with misunderstanding and prejudice. Mennonite periodicals had extensively covered the suffering endured by the refugees during the war and their plight afterward. C.F. Klassen in a nationwide speaking tour in 1946 reported on the experiences and problems of the refugees, drawing very large crowds. His frequent written reports, which appeared under the ironic heading 'Brueder in Not' (Brothers in Need – ironic because most of the refugees were women and children), were read with great interest, particularly by the immigrants of the 1920s who had many relatives, friends, and acquaintances among the refugees. Peter J. Dyck, intimately involved in the rescue and migration to Paraguay of the refugees trapped in Berlin, made skilful use of pictures, including many taken with his own movie camera, when he toured North America.

Sponsors or the Canadian Mennonite Board of Colonization had to pay for travel from disembarkation to the new place of residence in Canada. Between 1947 and 1951 that task involved total expenditures of $1,316,448.34, only some $400,000 less than the debt incurred in the 1920s. Loans by the board for which the immigrants themselves were responsible, however, amounted to only $176,822.34. The rest was covered by payments made by sponsors and by special donations.[54]

Newly arrived immigrants needed jobs. That was not generally a serious problem for those sponsored by relatives or who came under one of the Department of Labour's special labour schemes, so long as they were physically able to work and not encumbered by child care needs and concerns. Those sponsored by relatives were given accommodation and work, at least until they could be placed in positions as farm workers or domestic servants. Such jobs did not require more than a rudimentary knowledge of English, and many of the immigrants had already begun to study the language in the refugee camps and on board ship. Some seasonal farm labour was suitable for both male and female adults, while domestic service was done mainly by younger, usually unmarried, women. Many of the immigrants, fearing possible deportation, were fiercely determined not to become a burden to the government or in any other way to jeopardize their status as landed immigrants. They worked remarkably hard, often under adverse conditions, but the first jobs held by most of the immigrants involved agricultural labour or domestic service. This was not attractive or particularly remunerative, and most of the immigrants moved on as quickly as possible to other work, which was, however, almost always available only in urban areas.

Many of the immigrants, and certainly some of the Mennonite colonization board officials, hoped and expected that the immigrants would somehow become farmers, perhaps on new northern frontiers. Both major Canadian railways also hoped that new agricultural settlements would generate traffic for them. That, however, did not happen. The immigrants lacked the capital to acquire even marginal land and the machinery to begin farming. As well, their commitment to traditional, rural and agricultural life-styles had been weakened greatly under Soviet collectivization, terror, and the forced evacuation. Their life-styles and work habits had more in common with factory and industrial workers than small, independent farm operators. Most therefore found cities more attractive, particularly if they could work in an urban, Mennonite-owned factory or business, where they could still use the

German language, at least until they learned English. Some of the Mennonite urban businesses, in fact, fostered their own chain migration,[55] and the immigrants accelerated Mennonite urbanization while also increasing the landless and proletarian element in many of the rural congregations.

EXPERIENCES OF REFUGEE IMMIGRANT WOMEN

Many of the immigrants were women, often with small children, but without a husband or father. Employment and the challenge of earning a livelihood were much more difficult for such 'families.' Seasonal farm labour was an option, and older children could do some of the arduous work in sugar beet and other row-crop or fruit-farming operations. Some of these single-parent families, however, obtained accommodation in the small houses of the landless that had been built on the edges of many Mennonite communities before the war. The improved economic conditions nationally made it possible for many of the former occupants to find jobs in the city, and immigrant families could plant a garden, raise chickens, and keep a cow and perhaps a pig on the old, half-way rural-urban town lots. In some communities new two-acre lots were laid out and occupied by single-parent immigrant families. Even a mother who could not take a job could produce many of the things that she and her family needed on such a town lot. Church deacons' funds were sometimes used to supplement what could not be scratched out of such marginal operations. Once the children were old enough, immigrant mothers accepted menial labour wherever they could find it.

The single-parent families, however, did not fit prevailing assumptions about family life. In Canada generally, and certainly in many Mennonite communities in the late 1940s, women were not expected to seek paid employment outside the home. Nationally, labour shortages and the exigencies of war had made employment outside the home acceptable and necessary during the war, but afterwards there was an expectation that women would return to hearth and home.[56] Female domesticity once again became the acknowledged ideal. That ideal was strongly held in Mennonite communities, but it was not readily available to impoverished, recently arrived, single-parent families.

Marrying, staying home, having babies, raising children, and providing domestic support and security for the breadwinner were the vital ingredients of the dream of domesticity.[57] Failure to live up to these expectations, and some unfamiliar social and cultural practices, marginalized many Mennonite immigrant women and their families. That marginalization became particularly painful for some who had shown exceptional strength and remarkable qualities of leadership and spiritual toughness in trying conditions. In the darkest winter days of 1943, for example, refugee women temporarily housed near the Polish border worked exceptionally hard to prepare and organize a special Christmas Eve and Christmas Day service. On Christmas Day a special women's choir, consisting almost entirely of women who had lost fathers, husbands, and sons in the Stalinist terror of the 1930s or during the war, sang the old and familiar German songs and read appropriate scripture passages. This event moved one of the few older men in the group to write: 'These women and girls, frightened, harassed and emaciated after years of Soviet slavery and desperate refugee living are the real heros of the trek.'[58]

Canadian Mennonites were not ready to give women, and certainly not impoverished immigrant women, comparable positions of responsibility and leadership in their churches and communities. Several factors created suspicion and difficulties. Canadian Mennonite leaders knew that many of the immigrants had grown up on Soviet collective farms without the benefit of regular church services. Some of them, moreover, took pride in at least some of their pre-war achievements. But in North America any evidence of success in the atheistic Soviet system was regarded with suspicion. A more important concern, however, was that these people had not received satisfactory religious instruction in their youth, and many had participated in questionable or worldly activities not permitted in Canadian Mennonite churches.

Even more disconcerting were the marital status and some of the tragic sexual experiences of many, perhaps most, of the immigrants. Many refugee women and girls had been raped, and some of the children who accompanied them to Canada were the result of those experiences. Desire for survival, for better provisions for their dependants, or for protection from gross abuse had prompted some women to seek or at least to acquiesce in sexual liaisons with military and other officials who could provide protection and provisions.

The heroine of a semi-autobiographical Mennonite novel was not alone when she consented to a sexual liaison with a military officer to protect herself from repeated rapes. She defended this form of prostitution in a simple and direct manner: 'Seven, eight, ten brutes used me every day. Now it's only one. And we have shelter. And food. And protection. Don't talk to me about honour, mother.'[59] There are accounts by children who were protected and given food because their mothers suffered and submitted to violence: 'I have never seen her scream for fear, and she went through dreadful times, or panic. She trusted God and quietly, submissively, resigned herself to the situation that presented itself ... She knew she had to resign herself and do whatever was required of her. If she resisted, she would lose the last two children.'[60]

Canadian male Mennonite leaders did not know how to deal with these women and their experiences. In many Mennonite congregations there was a kind of conspiracy of silence regarding the darkest aspects of the refugee experience. But there was also reluctance to entrust such women with major roles in the churches, even though many had shown remarkable practical and leadership talents as refugees and in the care of their families in Canada. Few of the refugee women have said or written much about their worst war-time experiences.

In a few isolated instances, where it became known that refugee women had actually preached when no men were able or willing to do so, or that they had participated in activities not sanctioned by the local Canadian congregation they had joined after their immigration, they were obliged to make a public apology. The story that Harry Loewen has told about his mother was, unfortunately, not an isolated incident. In desperate times and conditions she had done things that male Mennonite leaders did not understand but found offensive: 'One day my mother had to appear before the congregation and repent for the "worldly" life she had lived during the war years. Mother submitted humbly and apologized for having "failed the Lord" repeatedly over the years. She was, of course, forgiven and restored to full fellowship in the congregation. Other women had to do the same.'[61]

Exclusion from leadership and influence and criticism for dubious war-time activities were not, for most of the refugee women, their most difficult problems. Subservience and obedience – to church leaders or to Soviet collective farm administrators or to refugee camp directors – were part of their lives. What made all of this much more difficult was the fact that they were alone, many without word regarding their spouses. Some had learned that a husband who had disappeared had subsequently remarried or established conjugal relations with another woman. These women desperately needed the practical and emotional security and pleasures of marriage, but church leaders – all male and married – sought to formulate and defend marital policies that did not meet those needs.

Since almost all the refugees were affiliated with either the Conference of Mennonites in Canada (CMC) or the Mennonite Brethren (MBs), leaders in those two conferences were particularly hard-pressed to deal with problems of remarriage of women who either did not know the fate of their spouses or whose spouses had remarried. Leaders in both conferences initially took a legalistic position. In the 1940s they condemned outright any common-law relationships and refused to sanction any remarriages as long as it was uncertain whether the first partner was dead. This, however, created such serious problems, particularly when North American Mennonite leaders tried to impose the policy on the congregations in South America, that a special commission consisting of sixteen Mennonite leaders, all men, from the two continents was asked to formulate guidelines. The result was a new policy that sanctioned remarriage if, after a seven-year waiting period, no word had been received that the other partner was still alive. The same length of time was also suggested in cases where the absent partner had remarried in Europe or in the Soviet Union.[62] Those guidelines, however, were not officially accepted by the North American conferences. As a result, refugees who remarried when there was no proof that their first partner was dead faced the threat of excommunication.

Refugee women with illegitimate children also faced legal problems in Canada. Initially these offspring were not admissible as close relatives. The Canadian Mennonite Board of Colonization had to make special representations on behalf of these women and children, including guarantees for the continuing support of such women and children.[63] It did so in a number of cases without the knowledge or consent of church leaders in the communities in which such refugees tried to establish themselves after their immigration. Mennonite leaders, preachers, and pastors were not trained or equipped to deal with the emotional trauma of these violated women.[64]

There has been no systematic study of the impact that the immigrant women, with their painful stories, had on Canadian Mennonites. Many, of course, wanted only to forget the worst of what had happened, but in some of the larger communities they were able to create a subculture that provided mutual support and comfort.

CONCLUSION

It is not easy to assess the general impact of the post–Second World War immigrants on Canadian Mennonite communities and congregations. Unlike the migrants of the 1920s, those who came after 1945 did not have an immediate or strong effect on church or conference leadership.[65] A disproportionate number of the Mennonite leaders in the Soviet Union had come to Canada in the 1920s. Many of those who remained fell victim to Stalinist terror or to war. The immigrants of the 1940s, mostly women and children, did not challenge established leaders, and few had the type of training or resources possessed by younger Canadian Mennonites who rose to leadership in the 1950s.

The immigrants did, however, have some influence on an increasingly contentious issue in western Canada. The three largest Swiss Mennonite Conferences in Canada had already made the transition from the German language to English in their worship services, but in western Canada that difficult process had begun only before the outbreak of the Second World War. English was used in some western Sunday schools, at some youth endeavour meetings, and even occasionally in Sunday morning worship before the immigrants arrived. The immigrants slowed the transition.

The immigrants also reinforced some conservative theological and social ideas and practices. A religious renewal in the Soviet Union during the German occupation, and special religious services and numerous baptisms in European refugee camps,[66] were firmly rooted in traditional Mennonite values and beliefs. Religious survivors of events that have carried off thousands of their fellow believers often develop strong convictions that they were rescued for some divine purpose, as was evident in the attitudes and actions of some post-1945 Mennonite immigrants. It has been said that people are most religious in situations in which powerlessness, uncertainty, and material insecurity are most apparent.[67] Religion, at least in such circumstances, is often focused on the supernatural. Only divine intervention that defies human logic seems to offer an escape, and the refugees talked a great deal about how, in desperate situations, they had prayed and then been saved through God's intervention. The story of the Berlin rescue became the defining myth of what many of these refugees believed and how they interpreted their experiences. Their conviction reinforced some conservative and traditional elements of Mennonite popular and practical theology.

The immigrants had, however, also seen and experienced much in the outside world, and they did not regard many things in the same way as Canadian Mennonite leaders, who had never or only rarely ventured beyond their rural enclaves. So-called worldly issues and activities about which Mennonite leaders in Canada became agitated seemed trivial to them.

The refugees needed above all to earn their own livelihood. Almost none could establish their own farms. Instead, the majority found work that involved a move to the towns and cities. There some achieved prosperity and security, and most also became continuously and intimately involved in the larger Canadian society. As a result, their acculturation was remarkably rapid, but into an urban environment. Some became leaders and many were participants in the urbanization of Canadian Mennonites.

The immigrants also reinforced the already-hostile feelings of many Mennonites toward the Soviet Union, communism, and socialism. Stories of suffering under Stalinist collectivization, uprooting of the people, destruction of the Mennonite commonwealth, and Soviet wartime atrocities all fostered fiercely anti-communist attitudes. The immigrants arrived in Canada with a view of the world that would become more and more popular in North America in the days of the Cold War. That eased their entry, and that of their fellow church members, into the modern, urbanized, industrialized, and capitalistic Canadian society and economy.

5

Wartime Changes in Agriculture

The Mennonite young men who left home during the war for military, alternative, or voluntary service were expected to return to their rural communities and agricultural pursuits. There was also an expectation that land and work would be found in rural Mennonite communities for postwar refugee immigrants.

Some Mennonite leaders, however, realized that all was not well in the existing communities. There was not enough land to accommodate many of the younger families. Small satellite communities of the landless had sprung up on the fringes of the larger towns in Mennonite districts. New colonization schemes were urgently needed if these people were to become farmers, but those most in need of land could not afford it. A collective solution was needed.

In an effort to deal with the problem, the MCC commissioned a young Mennonite sociologist, J. Winfield Fretz, to study communities and the prospects for new colonization.[1] Fretz wrote a fairly optimistic report. Others were more keenly aware of fundamental problems, not only among the landless, but also for many who had acquired their own farms but were barely surviving. As a result, little came of Fretz's proposals.

Some farmers who had acquired their own land were also in serious trouble, as was demonstrated at a meeting of farmers from 13 districts in Alberta on 14 and 15 July 1939.[2] Aron A. Toews of Namaka had prepared a careful but fundamentally pessimistic paper on the economic problems of the farmers. Alberta farmers and their families had worked very hard but were barely surviving. Many had already lost their farms. Large debts and high interest rates, low commodity prices, and widespread frustration and despair threatened to force more and more Mennonites into the ranks of the proletariat – a term that Toews chose deliberately because of its emotional impact on Menno-

Table 5.1
Hours of labour required to produce 100 bushels of wheat, 1800–1958

Year	Hours
1800	370
1840	230
1880	150
1900	100
1940	43
1958	26

Source: *The Albertan*, 15 October 1959.

nite settlers who had experienced the revolution and civil war in Russia.[3] These were experienced farmers, but even their survival seemed in peril.

The 1930s were, of course, a disaster for all prairie farmers, but even higher commodity prices during and after the war did not improve the prospects of thousands of Canadian Mennonites who hoped to acquire their own farms. Labour shortages and new technology made most prospective farmers redundant. The full impact of what some historians have called 'the great disjuncture' was not yet obvious to the Mennonite farmers of Alberta in 1939. Almost twenty years later, on 15 October 1959, *The Albertan* newspaper carried an article that reported on the problem facing those who wished to farm.[4] American agricultural economists had calculated the number of hours of labour required to produce 100 bushels of wheat at various times (see Table 5.1), and had shown that, by 1958, one farmer with modern machinery could produce what it had taken fifteen to grow in 1800.

North America needed far fewer farmers, and that at a time when Canadian Mennonites were already faced with a growing landless class. Some of the more traditional Canadian Mennonites understood the threat and resisted the new technology as best they could, but, for most, developments in agriculture set in motion massive migration into cities and towns, with new occupational opportunities and different life-styles.

Great migrations are generally a result of both 'push' factors, which persuade people to leave their homes and communities, and of 'pull' factors, which draw or attract them to new opportunities and new worlds. Profound and massive changes in Canadian agriculture during the Second World War[5] pushed hundreds of thousands of Canadians, including thousands of Mennonites, off their farms and out of their traditional rural communities. This chapter deals with those changes. Later chapters deal with the 'pull' factors. Since agriculture in different regions was affected differently by the war, it is necessary to examine developments in the three regions of Canada where large numbers of Mennonites lived.

THE PRAIRIES

Prairie agriculture in the 1940s experienced major and often completely un-expected changes. These disruptions placed disproportionate burdens on indebted Mennonite farmers who had migrated from Russia in the 1920s. Those who had been on their farms longer, or had diversified their opera-tions, generally found it easier to maintain traditional practices or to make the necessary adjustments.

Farmers on the prairies, unlike their counterparts in Ontario, produced primarily for international markets, which were much more variable than domestic markets. So they were among the first to experience serious war-time disruptions. There had been widespread expectation that the outbreak of war would result in greater demand and higher prices for wheat, as had been the case in the First World War.[6] 'Wheat,' Dominion Agriculture Min-ister Jimmy Gardiner told prairie farmers as late as August 1940, 'is the one material resource that is of greater importance than any other, in order that this war might be prosecuted to a successful conclusion.'[7] He urged farmers to grow as much wheat as they could, and many followed his advice. A scant six months later Canada had a huge, 700-million-bushel surplus, and the collapse of international wheat prices seemed imminent. Gardiner had to admit that wheat had become 'Canada's most troublesome war casualty' and to tell farmers that 'the government would be best pleased if you did not grow any wheat this year.'[8]

Two major factors accounted for this unexpected turn of events. The first was the defeat and fall of France and the occupation of western Europe by Hitler's armies in 1940. The resulting allied blockade closed continental Eu-ropean markets to Canadian wheat and other agricultural exports, leav-ing Great Britain as Canada's only major overseas agricultural market. The second factor related to those British markets. The British were no longer as eager to buy Canadian wheat as they had been during the First World War. Extensive nutritional research had convinced food administrators that in any future war people would need more than 'essential' cereal foods that were rich in calories and proteins. They must also have meat, dairy, poultry, and other animal products containing vitamins and minerals that were classified as 'protective' foods.[9]

Once it was decided that both cereal and animal products were needed, British food administrators had to decide what domestic farmers should grow, and what should be imported. Since shipping was expected to be a serious wartime problem, and because animals need between three and ten pounds of feed to produce one pound of meat, cheese, or eggs, the limited shipping space would obviously be best used if animal products, rather than cereal and feed grains, were imported. British farmers were therefore told to plough up their grasslands, slaughter their livestock, and turn to production of grains and potatoes.[10] That significantly reduced British demand for wheat.

There was a bright side for Canadian farmers. The change in British food policies meant that Britain imported less wheat and more bacon, eggs, cheese, and similar animal products. Demand was further and greatly increased when Hitler's conquest of Europe cut Britain's bacon trade with Denmark and its imports of cheese and dairy products from the Netherlands. If Canadian prairie farmers could convert their wheat production to pork, dairy, and poultry products, they could serve enormous British demand.

Changing from wheat to animal products required new technology and considerable capital. Ottawa stood ready to offer advice and limited financial assistance, but not all prairie grain farmers were willing or able to take advantage of the new opportunities. Those prairie Mennonite farmers who had come from the Soviet Union in the 1920s were particularly hard hit by the Canadian wheat crisis of 1941. They had come west, borrowed money, and acquired land, livestock, and farm equipment at the relatively high prices prevailing in the late 1920s. In the 1930s large debts, high interest rates, the collapse of international grain prices, and drought left many in desperate straits.[11]

The grain crisis dashed any hope of the kind of increase in grain prices that these indebted farmers desperately needed. Dominion controls set grain prices at 'the rock bottom income the prairie farmers must have.'[12] That was not enough for those carrying large debts, and dominion assistance for economic diversification was not made available to farmers already seriously in debt.[13]

The Mennonite immigrants of the 1920s were also burdened with a huge debt to the Canadian Pacific Railway, which they had incurred to gain passage to Canada.[14] Much of that debt had not yet been repaid, further limiting the ability of these farmers to switch production.

Prairie dryland farmers who made that shift early in the war earned attractive returns. Prairie hog production increased from 1,959,000 animals in 1939 to a wartime high of 4,409,000 in 1944.[15] There were comparable increases in poultry and dairy operations. Mennonite farmers not seriously encumbered by debt were in a good position to take advantage of these new opportunities. Most had long operated mixed farms, where the family provided for as many of its own needs as possible and then sold surpluses. Small poultry and dairy operations were common in Mennonite communities, often served by local cooperative cheese factories and egg-grading stations. Sharply increased British demand[16] allowed them to expand their cheese and egg production.

Mennonite cheese producers in Alberta took particular advantage of improved markets, as did several in Manitoba. During the war years an average of twenty cheese factories operated in Alberta. At least half of these, including several of the largest, were owned and operated by Mennonite cooperative organizations.[17] The largest was set up at Coaldale in 1928; it also secured a large and lucrative government contract to supply milk and cheese to the nearby prisoner-of-war camps at Lethbridge and Medicine Hat.[18]

Several types of Mennonite cheese won major provincial and national prizes and awards. Many of the factories became centres for other cooperative services and community ventures. The grounds of the Coaldale cheese factory, for example, at one time also housed an egg-grading station, a cold storage plant, a lumber yard, a credit-union, a fuel-oil depot, offices for mutual hail, fire, medical, and hospital insurance, and a German-language lending library. The factory was not only an economic but also a social and cultural centre.

Egg-grading and candling stations handled the third agricultural commodity greatly needed in wartime Britain. Early in the war whole eggs dipped in oil, which served as a preservative, were shipped mainly from eastern Canada to Britain. Scarcity of shipping facilities and inevitable breakage during the rough, north Atlantic crossing led to innovations that made it possible for prairie shippers to benefit from British egg contracts. Refrigeration allowed for new ways to ship prairie eggs. They could be broken, melanged, or scrambled, poured into huge, eight-foot by four-foot by four-foot containers lined with heavy waxed paper, and frozen solid. Such blocks, shipped frozen, permitted a reduction of 75 per cent of the space needed for egg exports. On arrival in Britain the frozen blocks were stored in huge mess-hall freezers, and cooks 'shaved' off, thawed, and then cooked, fried, or otherwise prepared and served 'shaved eggs.'[19] In the later years of the war dehydration and shipping of powdered eggs and milk saved even more shipping space, but neither shaved nor dehydrated Canadian eggs were regarded as a dietary delight. The new technology and the temporary wartime markets that it opened nevertheless made it possible for Mennonite farmers to expand production and for other small businessmen to establish or expand ancillary businesses such as hatcheries and poultry feed mills.

Wheat, in reduced quantities between 1941 and 1944, and bacon, cheese, and eggs, all in increased quantities, were the most important agricultural products that prairie farmers raised for domestic and export markets during the war. But the same farmers were also called on to begin or expand production of many other commodities. In the irrigation districts of southern Alberta and in the Red River Valley of Manitoba a struggling sugar-beet industry had operated for several decades. Cane sugar from the Caribbean supplied most Canadian requirements, but wartime shipping and supply problems and the vital nature of sugar supplies provided enormous impetus to the sugar-beet industry on the prairies.

Another initiative involved the growing of oilseeds, particularly sunflowers. Before the war, Canada's oilseed product needs were met through imports and from approximately 10,000 acres of soya beans grown in southern Ontario. With wartime restrictions on imports, the need for domestically produced edible vegetable oils, lubricants, and oil-based components in explosives and other military requirements increased substantially. The Mennonites of southern Manitoba had grown sunflowers to meet their own domestic need for many years. Dominion administrators encouraged substantial expansion of the acreage in 1942 and the building several years later of a Mennonite-controlled cooperative oilseed-crushing plant. In 1944 contracts for 25,000 acres of sunflower seeds were signed, and by 1949 the industry had grown to 60,000 acres in southern Manitoba.[20]

A second major oilseed crop that expanded significantly during the war was flax. Government encouragement and high prices led to a substantial increase in acreage after 1942, but the market remained volatile throughout the 1940s. Alberta's Department of Agriculture promoted production vigorously but conceded in 1944 that weeds, difficulty of handling, and low market prices remained serious problems. As a result, flax was not grown extensively.

Numerous other minor agricultural products also found a ready market during the war. Irrigated districts in southern Alberta, and southern Manitoba farms, produced a variety of vegetables and other row crops. Major canning facilities were established, and late in the war the government promoted and encouraged technology whereby vegetables could be dehydrated and hence shipped overseas more efficiently. Farmers willing to try new crops were given expert advice, information, and some financial assistance. Cultivation of these crops was none the less highly labour intensive and thus provided particular opportunities for farmers with large families. Equally important, growers' contracts, reviewed and approved by the dominion Wartime Prices and Trade Board, guaranteed a market at fixed prices.

Agricultural diversification also encouraged local processing of many of the new products. The oilseed-crushing plant at Altona was only one of many new farm-related industries. Processing of honey and beeswax, a factory manufacturing cheese boxes at Steinbach, a dehydration plant converting potatoes into potato chips at Winkler, a dozen cheese factories in Alberta and at least one in Reinland, Manitoba, several canneries and an egg-grading station, and even a small factory making puffed wheat at Steinbach were examples of such diversification in prairie Mennonite communities.[21]

The prairie agricultural economy nevertheless remained volatile. British wartime purchases of Canadian agricultural products, military supplies, and services were all made possible through export credit arrangements between the two governments. But as the war progressed and Britain's debts mounted, the strength of the pound sterling fell. This resulted in increased pressure on the quantities and prices of all British imports, making those markets less attractive. At the same time, other branches of prairie agriculture became more attractive.

The Japanese attack on Pearl Harbor, and a massive American military and civilian build up in the Pacific northwest, created major new opportunities and markets for prairie farmers. An estimated 30,000 Americans were sent north to build a highway 2,333 km (1,458 mi) from Dawson Creek, British Columbia, to Fairbanks, Alaska; an oil pipeline 1,000 km (625 mi) from Norman Wells to a refinery in Whitehorse, Yukon; and numerous military installations throughout the Pacific northwest. All those men had to be fed, and the military and civilian suppliers and contractors created huge new markets for Canadian agricultural produce.[22] American tastes, however, differed from those of the British. They wanted steaks, hamburgers, chicken, and turkey.

Astute prairie grain farmers soon began to switch from pork, cheese, and eggs to beef, broilers, and turkeys that could be sold at much more attractive prices to the Americans. Alberta's turkey farmers, for example, reaped an unexpected bonanza when American military purchasing agents scoured the countryside for traditional American Thanksgiving and Christmas turkeys in 1942. Surplus supplies that had accumulated over several years in cold storage plants in Calgary and Edmonton were cleaned out, and additional supplies had to be brought in from eastern Canada.[23]

The new American markets in the Pacific northwest, of course, lasted only as long as large numbers of Americans were stationed there. Frenzied activity made Edmonton's Namao airport briefly the busiest in the world. Colossal food shortages in Europe immediately after the war resulted in sharply increased demand for cereal grains, but too many prairie farmers shifted back to grain in the 1950s, once again creating huge surpluses.

Market instability, together with insistent wartime calls for active military or alternative service, drove thousands of prairie farmers off the land. Farmers who entered the war years with large debts and who depended on a single commodity were more vulnerable than those on long-established and diversified farms served by strong, community-based economic support and mutual aid institutions. As a result, Mennonites whose ancestors had come to western Canada in the 1870s suffered fewer economic disruptions than those who had arrived in the 1920s. An American sociologist, E.K. Francis, reported that the latter group 'did not show any signs of serious or permanent disorganization.'[24] This seemed to suggest that a postwar return and strengthening of traditional Mennonite rural and agricultural ideals and practices was possible for that group.[25] The war had, however, unleashed other economic forces that would overtake the older communities as surely as wartime market problems affected the more recent arrivals.

Alternative service claimed many workers on the traditional, mixed, comparatively self-sufficient, but labour-intensive Mennonite farms. Such shortages could be somewhat overcome through purchase of new and much more efficient machinery. Wartime priorities, however limited resources that factories could devote to making new farm machinery, but farmers acquired machinery – or at least knowledge about it – that could do the work formerly done manually. After the war, factories that had made military hardware were encouraged to apply the latest technologies and made machines that could do work more efficiently and at lower costs than hired manual labourers. Mechanization, however, led to larger and more specialized operations, in which expensive new machinery could be used most efficiently. Prairie Mennonite farms accordingly became much more capital intensive, requiring only limited labour.

Rural electrification was carried out on the prairies after 1945. When farms were first hooked up, farmers, or their spirited offspring, might go out into the middle of a distant field and ceremoniously bury one of the old kerosene barn lanterns. Mechanization drastically reduced farm labour, and many youngsters themselves became redundant and had to look elsewhere for work.

Farming had been a family- and community-based, labour-intensive way of life. Families and communities, engaged in common and mutually supportive endeavours, were an expression of Mennonite faith and of social, cultural, and spiritual values. During the 1940s, however, farming became more market-oriented, mechanized, capital intensive, individualistic, and business-like, in spite of the admonitions of Mennonite leaders: 'It should be our mission to keep our people away from the city and affairs of the world, and to help them as best we can so that all can establish their homes on their own land, where they can live in accordance with the customs and practices of our fathers.'[26]

Those most strongly committed to traditional agricultural values initiated new migrations to northern Canadian or southern Latin American settlement frontiers. Others rejected new technologies in an effort to preserve a cherished but threatened life-style. But prairie farmers, irrespective of their religious commitments, had become inextricably bound up in the markets, the technology, and the economic affairs of the outside world.[27] Thousands of Mennonites who had grown up on prairie farms left during the war and did not return afterwards.

BRITISH COLUMBIA

The experiences of Mennonite farmers in British Columbia in the mid-1940s had many parallels with those of their prairie co-religionists. Total cash income from the sale of BC farm products grew steadily, increasing from $30,238,000 in 1939 to $72,469,000 in 1945 and to $104,399,000 in 1951.[28] Increases were on a similar scale in most sectors of the agricultural economy. The proportion of cash income derived from hogs, cattle, and vegetables grew slightly, while fruits, dairy products, grains, potatoes, and poultry dropped somewhat.[29]

Mennonites engaged in dairy or poultry farming enjoyed steady growth. Others, particularly those in berry and tree-fruit farming, faced more instability. For them, the war brought unprecedented economic growth and development, followed by collapse. The experiences of all farmers in the lower Fraser Valley, however, were also dramatically influenced by the evacuation of more than 20,000 Japanese farmers and fishermen after the Japanese attack on Pearl Harbor in December 1941.[30]

Only 5,119 of Canada's 111,554 Mennonites lived in British Columbia in 1941. Most farmed in a cluster of communities in the lower Fraser Valley, the largest being at Yarrow. Almost all those living in the Fraser Valley or on Vancouver Island were immigrants of the 1920s who had settled first on the prairies but had moved west in the late 1920s or in the 1930s. In 1939, most were eking out a living on small, mixed farms that produced the food that they needed and small quantities of berries, vegetables, and dairy and poultry products for sale on local markets.[31] Most had to supplement their income through paid employment as berry and hop pickers or, for the younger women, as domestic servants in the homes of wealthier Vancouverites.[32]

The situation had improved slightly in the late 1930s with introduction of a new variety of raspberry that produced well on the wet and heavy soil around Yarrow[33] and with the slow expansion of Mennonite strawberry farming on rough but cheap, logged-over land south of Abbotsford, where the berries were planted from stump to stump.[34] Pre-war returns, nevertheless, remained marginal. Agricultural officials noted in 1938 that a bountiful harvest, combined with continuing financial problems in the prairie provinces where much of the fruit was sold, resulted in serious problems of overproduction.[35]

The market for raspberries was equally discouraging. 'The raspberry,' according to departmental officials, 'is not as popular as the strawberry, and as they can be grown at many Prairie points and ripened almost as early as in British Columbia, there is little likelihood of profit by acreage increase.'[36] Moreover, the taste and appearance of Newburgh raspberries, which were best suited for the soil conditions at Yarrow, made them less desirable for fresh-berry markets. They were best used in the manufacture of jam.

The problems of the markets were threefold – serious overproduction; dumping of American surpluses, which periodically destabilized the market; and seasonal and economic limits of prairie markets for fresh berries. All these factors resulted in sharp price fluctuations.[37]

Overproduction was blamed mainly on Japanese berry farmers, who dominated the BC markets. They had started small, with almost no capital. Hard work and frugal living had resulted in success. In 1934 a BC inspector estimated that Japanese farmers cultivated 63 per cent of all farm lands in the Fraser Valley and produced 85 per cent of the berries.[38] A later estimate held that in 1942 the Japanese produced 83 per cent of the strawberries and 47 per cent of the raspberries grown in the province.[39]

The Japanese tried to stabilize prices through the Pacific Co-operative Union. A large handling, packing, and marketing facility was built at Mission, and smaller ones at Abbotsford, Chilliwack, Hammond, Hatzio, Matsqui, and Whonnock.[40] When Mennonite farmers at Yarrow began to cultivate Newburgh raspberries, Ed Shimek, the congenial general manager of the Pacific Co-operative Union, encouraged them and helped them to form the Yarrow Growers' Co-operative, which then worked in harmony with the Japanese-owned venture.[41] In 1938 the two co-ops negotiated a contract to sell berries packed in barrels in sodium dioxide to British jobbers. After the war started, managers of the co-ops worked hard to have their berries covered by export credit arrangements between Canada and Great Britain.[42] They succeeded, but prices authorized by the Wartime Prices and Trade Board were so disappointing that the growers complained that receipts did not even cover production costs.[43] The board responded with a two-cent-per-pound subsidy for berries used in manufacture of jam or packed for export in sodium dioxide. This, they believed, would allow the industry as a whole to survive.[44]

Agriculture on the lower Fraser was radically altered in 1942 when Ottawa decided, for reasons of national security, to evacuate all the Japanese.[45] The expulsion created a vacuum and, with it, remarkable opportunities for others.

When the evacuation orders were first announced early in 1942 the Japanese were told that they would be in effect only for the duration of the war. That led many of them to make arrangements whereby their property would be looked after while they were away. Their farms were mostly small hold-ings producing berries, row crop vegetables, poultry, and dairy products, though they also operated several large greenhouses. Such farms required constant work and attention, and the Japanese tried to negotiate rentals or make other arrangements so that competent and knowledgeable farmers would look after their farms. Some such arrangements, and even a few sales, were negotiated privately, but in most involving berry farms the Pacific Co-operative tried to negotiate rentals.

A scheme worked out by Mr Shimek of the Pacific Co-op was designed for experienced but impoverished farmers willing to operate berry farms. The co-op paid the Japanese owner his or her rent immediately, requiring of the renter only an agreement to deliver the crop, when harvested, to the co-op. The co-op would then calculate appropriate payment, deduct the rent al-ready paid to the Japanese owner, and pay the renter the remaining balance. The plan proved particularly attractive to drought- and Depression-ravaged Mennonites from the Prairies, though a federal official exaggerated their in-volvement: 'The majority … appear to be Mennonites. Some apparently ar-rived in the district from the Prairies only a year or two ago.'[46] Lists of those leasing or renting Japanese farms are available; 37 of 215 leases were held by persons with ethnic 'Mennonite' names.[47] Participation by Mennonites was greater than that for any other identifiable group and disproportionate to the number of Mennonites in the province. The difficulties of Mennonite prairie grain farmers, the proximity of small but growing Mennonite communities in the Fraser Valley, the minimal capital requirements of the leasing scheme, a farming heritage, and willingness to commit themselves and their families to hard manual labour account for their response. But the influx also prompted sharp protests from local residents. An editorial in the *Abbotsford, Sumas and Matsqui News* even suggested that 'between Japanese and Mennonite settlers, the Jap was the lesser evil in building up the community.'[48]

The leasing plan was not a success. The BC and Canadian governments decided, while the leases were still being negotiated, that the Japanese should not be allowed to return after the war. Instead, government officials proposed that the Japanese receive compensation and their farms be held for returning veterans. That decision, particularly the method of valuation and the terms under which 817 former Japanese berry farms in the Fraser Valley were sold to the Veterans' Land Administration (VLA)[49] in June 1942, has been the sub-ject of bitter controversy[50] and of a federal apology decades later.

The VLA was highly critical of the relatively open-ended Japanese leases for the duration of the war. It wanted maximum flexibility in administering lands so that they could be made available when veterans needed them. After taking over the farms, the VLA made a particularly destructive decision. It refused to recognize leases of more than one year. That effectively removed any incentive by the lessee to do new planting or even to keep weeds under control. The holder of a one-year lease simply tried to get whatever he or she could out of the farm that year. Even a local VLA administrator complained: 'A one season's lease on a berry farm is positively violent and destructive to these farms.'[51] The results became obvious immediately: 'All one has to do is drive the byways and highways where berry patches a year ago were properly cared for and this year they are nothing more or less, in the great majority of cases, than weed patches. Between weeds and disease, there won't be much left. Another very serious item, of course, is replanting. Berry plants are only good for three real good crops and there was a negligible replanting this season, so at the outside, 2 to 3 years and berries will be through.'[52]

Veterans' Affairs officials tried to deflect some of the criticism, blaming lack of experience on the part of the recently arrived farmers who had signed the Japanese leases, singling out Mennonites recently arrived from the prairies for particular criticism.[53] The one-year leases offered by the VLA, however, had much less appeal to the Mennonites than the earlier, longer leases, and their participation was considerably reduced for the 1943 crop year.[54] They preferred to acquire their own farms. Those without funds could get wild land at very low cost, while those with some capital were able to buy established farms from owners who enlisted for active military service, took remunerative urban employment, or simply could not find reliable workers.[55] A few Mennonite farmers holding leases for the length of the war negotiated purchase agreements with veterans to whom the VLA granted the farms.

Destruction of the former Japanese berry farms through racial intolerance and bureaucratic bungling resulted in serious shortages of berries. That forced the Wartime Prices and Trade Board in 1943 to establish higher price ceilings, designed to give farmers a net return approximately equal to that obtained in the relatively prosperous period between 1926 and 1929. The new prices were 'approximately 90% above the average for the four years [1938–41].'[56] This arangement opened attractive opportunities for Mennonite farmers willing to engage in labour-intensive farming. The tiny Yarrow Growers' Co-operative became the most visible symbol of Mennonite success. In 1941 it handled less than 1 per cent of the local berry crop, but in 1943 it had more than half.[57]

The year 1943 was a turning point for BC Mennonite berry farmers. Evacuation of the Japanese farmers had created an economic vacuum. The leasing arrangements of 1942 had not been successful, but with higher prices in 1943 the returns on adequately tended leased farms, and on previously marginal, privately owned farms, improved dramatically. The Yarrow co-op more than doubled its assets, built new storage facilities, bought new sodium dioxide equipment, and put up a jam factory, all in 1943.[58]

Mennonite berry farmers also participated in the government's 1943 Victory Bond drive. The quota for Chilliwack and district was $712,450, of which $15,000 had been allocated to Yarrow, but that overwhelmingly Mennonite community bought $28,600 worth.[59] The years of desperate poverty and deprivation were over. Church correspondents reported: 'The crops were good again this year, and with the exceptionally high prices many have not only been able to repay all their debts, but also to expand substantially their farms and businesses. Wages were also very good. People could acquire things that previously had been impossible.'[60]

Increasing prosperity also changed local attitudes. The *Abbotsford, Sumas and Matsqui News*, which at one time had denounced the Mennonites for their pacifism and poverty, published friendly feature articles lauding their economic success. The feature story on one family indicates the changed attitude: 'Until Tuesday the family had shared the long chicken house with the chickens, but through thrift and careful cultivation, have now been able to build their own home. With seven cattle and ten acres of land, Falk says "we can make our own living." An old-timer in the district sold the land to the Mennonites.'[61]

It was not surprising that the annual Thanksgiving celebrations in BC Mennonite churches included recitals of the many economic and spiritual blessings that God had bestowed on his busy, hard-working, and frugal people. But professional thieves thought it worth their while to break into the offices of the Yarrow Growers' Co-operative, blow open the safe, and steal at least $700 in cash![62]

Mennonites had somewhat less spectacular successes in dairy and poultry farming but evacuation of the Japanese also created opportunities there. The Japanese had been almost as prominent in the highly labour-intensive dairying and poultry operations as in berry farming. Their dairy and poultry farms, their large and flourishing greenhouses, and community cultural and religious buildings were not sold to the VLA. Mennonite and other prospective farmers purchased these properties, including several cultural centres, which were converted to Mennonite churches, from the Custodian of Enemy Property. Those who wanted only to sell some products from their farms also found the economic vacuum created by removal of the Japanese beneficial, as shortages and prices increased.

The dairy and poultry farmers did not face the same violent market fluctuations as did the berry farmers. During the Depression producers in the

Fraser Valley had established pools and a quota system, and prices remained fairly stable. Demand increased sharply during the war, particularly after removal of the Japanese and arrival of many Americans in Alaska and the Pacific northwest. New opportunities emerged, and one Mennonite correspondent in 1943 wrote that Mennonite chicken houses and dairy barns were growing in the Fraser Valley like mushrooms: 'We are making a living, and often more than just a living, with the chicken, berry and dairy businesses.'[63] Prices for eggs, chickens, milk, butter, and cheese, like those for berries, were controlled by the Wartime Prices and Trade Board, but people with access to reliable and inexpensive labour prospered.

Almost all BC Mennonites were or hoped to become farmers, and the operations that they chose allowed all family members to be employed. One of the province's senior Mennonite leaders assessed the experience of his people in 1946:

We were witnesses to the utter poverty of the greater part of the settlers – a poverty which drove them to seek aid for the very necessities of life. We marvel when today we view the well established, independent Mennonite farmer of British Columbia ... Today each Mennonite settlement in British Columbia is a landmark of unprecedented development. Neither the strongest optimist nor the dreamer could have fancied such stupendous progress. This improvement is not due so much to the easier flow of money during war years, but rather to the untiring efforts of settlers, to their integrity, practical sense, and complete trust in God.[64]

Evacuated Japanese farmers and their families could have suggested other reasons for such progress. And the confident Mennonites of 1946 did not foresee a painful and bewildering lesson in financial management, market fluctuations, and community and church disintegration.

Berry farmers had faced oversupplied markets in the 1930s. Surpluses were eliminated in 1942, but only because of the evacuation of the Japanese farmers and the neglect or destruction of many of their farms. Wartime domestic and export markets created increased demand, much of which was met by Mennonite farmers. Berry production again expanded dramatically. The Yarrow Growers' Co-operative, for example, had shipped only 146 tons of raspberries to Britain in 1940 but had more than 6,000 tons available for export in 1948.[65]

Only continuing large export contracts could absorb the rapidly increasing supply of berries. But Ottawa was reluctant to grant further export credits, and British purchasers were becoming alarmed as the pound sterling lost value against the dollar. As a result, Canadian and British officials agreed late in 1947 that further Canadian export credits for non-essential food contracts should be curtailed. Canadian farmers, including BC berry producers, thus lost almost all the British markets opened during the war.

The Yarrow co-op was particularly hard hit. Its Newburgh raspberries were best suited for export in sodium dioxide or for immediate manufacture into jam, and it had purchased expensive equipment to serve the British market. North American jobbers, however, were becoming more interested in fresh or quick-frozen berries. The Yarrow co-op purchased some quick-freeze equipment, but markets everywhere on the Pacific coast were badly oversupplied. And Yarrow's Newburgh raspberries were not well suited for changing demand.

The federal government tried to ease the loss of the British market for sodium dioxide–packed berries in 1948 by 'guaranteeing the cost of the barrels and packing baskets which are used in British Columbia for the packing of SO_2 berries, which is a particular variety of berry used for making jam.'[66] The co-op in fact used the guarantees to pack exceptionally large quantities of berries in sodium dioxide, even though there was no domestic or export market in sight. The Yarrow growers still hoped that Ottawa would extend the British export credits or that other markets might be found, but none emerged and the co-op was left with more than 5,000 barrels of unsold sodium dioxide–packed berries and hundreds of tons of frozen berries at the end of the 1948 crop year. The barrels filled the warehouse and spilled over into the open yards, where they remained for the winter, while the co-op scrambled to rent all available cold-storage space in the valley and in adjacent northern Washington state. Prices were drastically reduced until, in 1949, the Saskatoon grocery wholesaling firm of Shelly Western bought some of the berries, paying only for processing, packing, and shipping.[67] The rest were eventually sold to the government of Ireland under temporary federal export credits.[68]

Immediately after the collapse of the market, all the producer organizations, including the Yarrow co-operative, were instructed by government officials to take effective steps to limit production. So hundreds of acres of flourishing berry fields were ploughed up. Many Mennonite farmers were confused, and some became very angry when given such instructions. They had never really understood international commodity marketing. Some simply insisted that 'Whether we will sell the crop or not, we can only farm the good and proper way. Our berry fields are in beautiful shape and we mean to keep them that way.'[69] A flood in the spring of 1948 created much misery and loss, which was more difficult to repair because farmers could not sell their berries. But the flood also destroyed hundreds of berry fields. As well, a fungus spread to which the Newburgh raspberries were particularly vulnerable. Supply and demand for berries gradually moved back into balance. The federal government offered to assist the farmers, but only if they switched to other crops.[70]

One of the principal victims of the 1948 disasters was the Yarrow Growers' Co-operative. The co-op had been the most important instrument of economic growth during and immediately after the war and had enjoyed strong community support.[71] But most of the producers tended to blame the co-op's managers for the problems, and it was forced to wind down.[72] The disaster also created other tensions in the community and in the local Mennonite congregations. As is discussed in a later chapter, two new Mennonite private high schools were forced to close, and Yarrow lost its position as the largest and most influential Mennonite community in British Columbia.

The evacuation of the Japanese farmers, the phenomenal expansion of Mennonite berry farming to fill seemingly unlimited British wartime contracts, and then the loss of the British markets and the collapse of their most important economic, educational, and cultural institutions took the farmers on a wild economic roller-coaster ride. That was an experience that they shared with prairie grain and hog farmers but that differed markedly from the more placid and stable markets enjoyed by dairy and poultry farmers, who produced mainly for domestic markets under careful supply-management schemes.

The 1948 berry fiasco shattered cherished Mennonite agricultural ideals. The proper rewards for honest toil had been lost because of international market fluctuations. Farming had changed, and many of those affected just wanted to forget and get on to something else. Often that something else was neither rural nor agricultural.

ONTARIO

The wartime experience of most Mennonite farmers in Ontario resembled that of BC dairy and poultry farmers. Ontario farmers sold most of their produce on domestic or, in some cases, American specialty markets, which were quite stable. The physical volume of production remained remarkably stable throughout the war and showed steady progress afterwards (see Table 5.2).[73]

Agricultural historians tell us that 'in Ontario there were fewer changes of any magnitude in the relative importance of various products than in any of the other provinces'[74] in the 1940s. Southern Ontario had become a thriving urban and industrial region. Domestic markets absorbed the bulk of agricultural products grown in the region. Those markets were greatly strengthened by war related industrial and manufacturing activities. As a result, Ontario farmers including Mennonite farmers in and near Kitchener-Waterloo,[75] be-

Table 5.2
Index numbers of physical volume of agricultural
production in Ontario, 1941–50 (1961 = 100)

1941	65.6
1942	77.1
1943	58.4
1944	71.8
1945	64.4
1946	70.4
1947	66.6
1948	70.3
1949	73.5
1950	73.0

Source: Ontario, Ministry of Agriculture and Food, *Agricultural Statistics for Ontario, 1941–1978* (Toronto: Queen's Printer, 1979).

came even less dependent on exports, producing almost entirely for provincial markets.[76]

Ontario set up effective supply-management and marketing arrangements for most agricultural commodities. In 1937, after Ottawa's failed attempt to control agricultural marketing, the province passed the Ontario Farm Products Control Act, which created supply-management and marketing schemes. These programs included quotas, producer contracts, protective tariffs that kept out cheap American imports, and export subsidies for surplus commodities to control production and prices. The resulting system used 'monopolistic marketing procedures to operate on the producers' side of the market, presumably to counteract the monopolistic practices of the large food-processing and retailing organizations on the other side.'[77] It was, of course, much easier to run such programs when most of the produce was sold on local and domestic markets subject to provincial or wartime federal jurisdiction.

Establishment of these boards created social and ethical problems for some Mennonite farmers. They appreciated the economic stability and price predictability but worried about undue state interference and their increased economic integration into secular programs.

The first developments of this kind had occurred on the prairies in the 1920s, when the cooperative wheat pools were created. The (Old) Mennonites in the Alberta-Saskatchewan Conference had taken a firm stand against the pools, but the developments in Ontario in the 1930s and 1940s were more problematic. The prairie wheat pools were organized by the farmers, and membership was voluntary. Some Mennonites participated, but the (Old)

Mennonites and other culturally conservative Mennonite groups refused to join, arguing that this constituted an unequal yoking of believers with unbelievers.[78]

The boards and agencies set up by Ontario in the 1930s to deal with severely depressed agricultural prices were accepted by even the most conservative and separatist Mennonite groups without serious objection. The orderly marketing of agricultural products was regarded as a proper exercise of government authority. Such programs protected honest and hard-working small producers against exploitation and disaster at the hands of speculators and commodity price manipulators. Adherence to and respect for such schemes were a matter of 'rendering unto Caesar the things that are Caesar's.' Order, stability, and continuity, not quick windfall profits made possible by short-term wartime scarcities, were the values cherished by the Mennonite farmers of Ontario. For them, perhaps more than for almost any other Canadians, farming represented an idealized and separatist way of life: 'Love of the soil has become an acquired value through a long heritage of dependence upon the soil for survival. To them [referring specifically to the Old Order Mennonites and the Old Order Amish living in Waterloo and surrounding counties] the soil is like an old friend that responds to nurture, faithfulness, and care. Hard work is rewarded with harvest year in and year out. Farming and religious principles such as separation from the world, frugal and simple living, the ethics of love and nonviolence all go well together.'[79]

In the 1940s stability and reasonable prosperity, under the watchful eye of provincial marketing and federal regulatory agencies, protected that cherished way of life. There were, however, several Mennonite farmers whose farming and farm-related operations expanded in the 1940s to the point where they became large-scale agro-businesses. Several Mennonites, for example, became very active in the Waterloo County Holstein-Frisian Association, which wanted to increase the export of pure-bred Holsteins to the United States. A.B. Brubacher was appointed field man in 1928, and Lorne Brubacher served from 1938 to 1962. 'It was during that period,' Brubacher wrote, ' ... that the foundation of popularity for the Canadian Holstein was established in the United States,'[80] and the average price per head rose from $95 to $350.

Another Mennonite from southern Ontario, Roy G. Snyder, was a pioneer in cattle breeding through artificial insemination. This technology was tested successfully at the Central Experimental Farm at Ottawa in 1936. The first commercial application in Ontario came in the Waterloo region in 1941.[81] Other agro-businesses in the Waterloo region in the 1950s included the large turkey farm of Milo and Ross Shantz and the dairy processing business of Etril Snyder. These operations all showed steady and substantial growth after the war and led the way for modification of the traditional family farm.

Available markets and the prices received for their produce by fresh fruit and vegetable growers in the Holland Marsh northwest of Toronto, in the Niagara Peninsula, and in the Leamington area were not rigorously controlled by provincial agencies and therefore less stable. Many of the Mennonite immigrants of the 1920s had settled in the latter two areas. In the Niagara peninsula large farms had been purchased and then subdivided into five-, ten-, or fifteen-acre plots. In some of these acquisitions and in other financial matters, the Mennonite immigrants of the 1920s were helped by a former Saskatchewan Mennonite farmer named Peter Wall, who purchased, subdivided, and then resold large farms to destitute Mennonites on so-called Mennonite terms. There was no down payment, and repayment schedules were related to income received by the renter. In the early years, and on into the 1940s, many farmers also took jobs in local factories to earn additional income.

The Mennonite farmers at Virgil also organized their own producer co-op, alleging that the existing one did not give adequate service. The Mennonite-owned Niagara Township Fruit Co-operative quickly outgrew the other producer co-ops in the area, but wartime transportation problems made it difficult to get all the fresh fruit and vegetables to markets in Hamilton, Toronto, and other urban centres. There was also considerable demand by the armed forces and by local jobbers for canned fruit of all kinds. As a result, Peter Wall financed construction of a new cannery about three miles from Niagara-on-the-Lake. It was organized in 1940 as a cooperative, managed and operated by Wall, and grew quickly. In 1943 this cannery employed about 200 women and 50 men for five months every year and processed about $500,000 worth of produce. And there were plans to enter new lines of work, notably preparation of baby foods, which would make year-round operations possible. A subsidiary facility to process tomatoes was also built at Dunnville. Buoyant wartime markets ensured good returns for Niagara Mennonite farmers.[82]

Other Mennonite communities in Ontario, notably those in the Leamington area, enjoyed comparable growth, though local canneries and fruit- and vegetable-processing plants were built by non-Mennonites. The big Heinz cannery at Leamington provided a ready market for locally grown tomatoes and other vegetables, while a large vegetable-canning, quick-freezing and dehydration facility was put up at Tecumseh. That venture, which pioneered in the marketing of its unusual new corporate symbol, 'the Green Giant,' was promoted by John Wall. This John Wall, whose correspondence exudes quaint, homespun folk wisdom and short, pithy sayings expressing rural values that sound distinctly Mennonite, was a Roman Catholic born in Wales.[83]

The big fruit and vegetable canneries built during the war years faced turbulence afterwards, and several Mennonite-promoted plants eventually closed. Wartime food contracts disappeared, and, more important, domestic consumers came to prefer fresh or quick-frozen fruit and vegetables to canned produce. As a result, there was more instability unless growers could negotiate reliable contracts with the new and expanding urban grocery chains.

Overall, Ontario agricultural prices during the war rose gradually but steadily. Agriculture nevertheless underwent a transformation. Labour became a serious problem everywhere, as men who had worked on farms were drawn into active military or alternative service and wartime industries offered wages that farmers could not match. Farm wives and daughters helped to alleviate labour shortages, in many cases taking over management and operation of the farm when husbands and sons enlisted or were called to alternative service. Many farmers, nevertheless, turned increasingly to machines to do at least some of the work previously done manually. In the process Ontario agriculture became much more business-like and integrated into provincial, national, and international economic systems.

Thus, in Ontario, the farm labour force, which had been thought woefully inadequate in 1946, fell from 334,000 that year to only 217,000 ten years later. Even a 500 per cent increase in average farm wages could not stem migration of rural workers to the cities.[84] On most Ontario farms, including those of most so-called progressive Mennonites, milking machines, milk coolers, pumps, feed grinders, tractors, combines, hay balers, forage harvesters, corn pitchers, chemical weed sprayers, manure loaders and spreaders, beet thinners and toppers, potato planters and diggers, and a variety of automated livestock and poultry feeders did the work of the departing labourers. All these machines, of course, cost a great deal. In 1939 Ontario farmers used machinery and implements valued at only $144,235,000. By 1945 that figure had risen, despite severe wartime manufacturing restrictions and military priorities, to $213,717,000, and it climbed to $445,278,000 in 1951.[85]

The Old Order Amish and Old Order Mennonite farmers in Ontario generally moved more slowly than their neighbours in mechanization and capitalization. Farming to them was a way of life, and the new technology often disrupted cherished aspects of rural and agricultural life. The culturally most conservative Old Order Amish and Mennonite farmers very deliberately, and with considerable success, countered the general trend: 'These farmers have a comparatively low capital investment because of their generally smaller acreages and their use of older and more limited kind and amount of machinery. Since the labour used is almost all supplied by the family or by the exchange of labour with relatives and neighbours, labour costs are low. Even where farmers must hire help, they do so by hiring young teen-age boys from other church members' families who work for modest wages.'[86]

CONCLUSION

In 1959 a Mennonite history professor published an article entitled 'The Agricultural Revolution of Our Day.' Citing *Time* magazine, he stated:

In the last twenty years farming had changed more radically than in the previous two centuries ... Farming will be less and less a way of life and more and more a business, and as a business it will depend more and more on capital and less and less on labour. Whether we like it or not, agriculture is changing from an art and a craft to a science and a business. In summary we can say that this means that farmers will be pushed either by inward compulsion or outward necessity to farm wholeheartedly, either intensively with the use of fertilizers, irrigation, and practices of specialization, or extensively. Those who fail in this will, of course, migrate to the city or remain as itinerant farm or city workers.[87]

The old ideal of the family farm did not die easily, nor was it abandoned by all Canadian Mennonites, but three developments of the early and mid-1940s undermined this idyllic way of life. First, overseas export markets for some Canadian agricultural products were volatile and unpredictable. On the prairies many Canadian Mennonite farmers who produced grain, hogs, beef, and poultry products, in British Columbia those who grew raspberries and strawberries, and the Ontario vegetable and tree-fruit growers in the Niagara peninsula and at Leamington faced serious problems through no particular fault of their own when international market conditions suddenly changed. Farmers who produced primarily for domestic markets, or operated mixed and diversified farms where low prices for one commodity might be offset by higher prices for another, were sheltered from the worst of these disruptions and tended to stay longer on their farms than those devastated by international trade upheavals. But after the war it became obvious that there were other, more predictable and secure ways of making a living. Business and the professions seemed to reward the old virtues of hard work, honesty, integrity, and comparative independence in ways that seemed more reasonable, fair, predictable, and therefore more appealing.

A second major change involved mechanization and the resulting higher capital costs of farming. In the 1940s many of those who wanted to farm lacked the necessary capital, and some the technical expertise, to engage in mechanized agriculture. There were, even before the war began, hundreds and perhaps thousands of Mennonites who lacked the capital needed to establish themselves on their own farms. The sharply increased capital requirements during and after the war made farming impossible for these people.

A third factor was the labour involved. On the old family farm all members worked together and then also shared the fruits of their labours. Mennonites had succeeded as farmers in part because, in comparison with many other Canadian farmers, their family members worked exceptionally hard while living simply and frugally. The everyday reality of life on marginal, labour-intensive, under-capitalized, and poorly equipped farms was, however, far removed from the idyllic rural scenes pictured in the literature.

On mixed farms there was, first of all, the tyranny of the twice-daily chores, dictated by the needs of farm livestock and poultry. Those tasks seemed to many children and teen-agers a vicious form of slavery, which kept them from hockey, baseball, and many other after-school activities. Even when the family went on vacation, one member usually had to stay home or a neighbour or relative had to be found to do the chores. Perhaps those farm duties fostered a sense of responsibility, a feeling of participation in the joint family farming ventures, and a more disciplined approach to life generally. But they also roused resentment and great relief for many who managed to escape.

The heavy manual labour during the summer could be even worse. Much of it was physically demanding but intellectually depressing.[88] Long days under a hot sun hoeing vegetables or sugar beets, picking berries or vegetables, pitching hay or working on threshing crews prompted more than one young Mennonite to resolve 'to seek work that would be useful, would be somewhat enjoyable, would provide opportunities for personal growth and development.'[89] Labour-intensive farming for unpredictable commodity markets achieved too few of those goals. Other, more attractive opportunities beckoned for those who left the farms, and also for those who chose to stay but adjusted their practices to the new conditions.

PART THREE
YEARS OF PROSPERITY

6

The Continuing Agricultural Base

In the decades following the Second World War Canadian Mennonites became a prosperous people. Not many achieved great wealth, but the struggle for survival that they had waged in Canada, in the Soviet Union, and in post-war Europe was over. They emerged from the crucible of war stronger and more flexible. Their increased strength was based on greater confidence in their ability to participate productively in Canadian society. Flexibility was achieved because of their changing perceptions of Canadian society and government.

The early years of wartime alternative service had been difficult, in part because the conscientious objectors (COs) were treated as if they were an embarrassment, tolerated by the government but relegated to perform menial tasks on the periphery of Canadian society in a time of national emergency. As the range of services performed by the COs increased, and as many Mennonites were able to render much-appreciated voluntary services, it became clear that they could help, and were helping, the war effort without violating their religious principles. Even the more frustrating aspects of alternative service seemed more worthwhile after Mennonites heard official accolades. They too had served their country and in the process learned a great deal about it and about economic as well as religious opportunities beyond their own communities.

These experiences altered Mennonite perceptions of both the outside world and of the Canadian government. The world came to be seen less as an evil place to be avoided and more as a place of great suffering in need of the love and healing that Jesus had exemplified in his ministry on earth. A tribute by Theodor Heuss, president of the Federal Republic of Germany, affirmed not only the political and economic, but also the religious dimensions of the changing Mennonite perspective of the world. Heuss sent the Mennonite Central Committee (MCC) and other agencies that had provided relief to his people immediately after the war a gift of fifty works of art, together with an acknowledgement: 'These acts of brotherly love saved the lives of many Germans and helped the exhausted and the despairing to gather fresh courage.'[1]

Canadian Mennonites naturally appreciated that the Canadian government had respected their religious principles, but their wartime experience went further than alternative service. The government had maintained stability and enforced basic economic fairness through effective wartime controls. Great sacrifices had been demanded, but honest endeavour was also rewarded. Prime Minister King was the only democratically elected leader who was in power at the beginning of the war, remained in power throughout, and won another election immediately afterwards. Ottawa had done what Mennonite theology prescribed as the proper role of the secular state.[2] In the mid-1940s the government planned and regulated demobilization in ways that avoided the economic instability of 1918–19. Its postwar policies provided stability, order, and unprecedented prosperity. Mennonites participated in that prosperity, but it radically altered where and how many of them lived and how they earned their livelihood.

Agriculture, their preferred vocation, was transformed in the decades following 1945. It did not benefit to the same extent as other industries from the economic boom. Total net farm income, for example, stood at $478,958,000 in 1941, rose to $1,053,097,000 in 1946 and $1,931,377,000 in 1951, but gradually declined thereafter. In 1971 it was only $1,615,289,000.[3] These figures did not match sharply increased values of farm capital: in 1939, $4,298,763,000; in 1971, $23,886,381,000.[4] Net farm income was therefore 11 per cent of farm capital in 1941 but had fallen to only 7 per cent in 1971. Clearly it did not keep pace with capital costs, and the return on capital invested in agriculture, even if labour costs are ignored, was not as great as it was on other investments.

Farmers responded by sharply reducing their labour costs and purchasing machines that increased the efficiency of their operations, but only if they significantly expanded operations. The number of men in agricultural occupations fell from 1,064,847 in 1941 to 405,250 in 1971,[5] while total farm population, which was 3,152,491 in 1941, dropped to 1,489,565.[6]

Canadian Mennonites were part of these statistics, but for them the changes were even more rapid. In the 1941 census almost 87 per cent of them were still listed as rural residents. Thirty years later only 53 per cent were, and only a little more than half of those actually lived on farms. The agricultural base of Canadian Mennonite communities was shrinking.

Statistics and graphs often seem cold, impersonal, and devoid of human interest. Yet each of the tens and hundreds of thousands of Canadians who

Figure 6.1
Mennonite urban-rural statistics

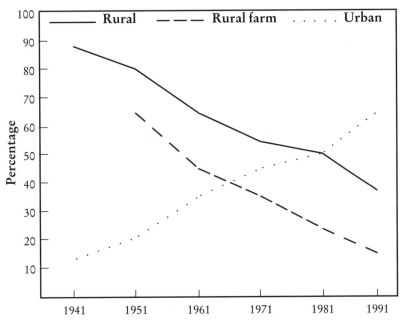

left the countryside had his or her way of life changed. Adjustments had to be made, both by those who stayed and by those who left the rural areas. This chapter focuses on the adjustments made by Mennonites who stayed on their farms or in farm-related businesses.

Figure 6.1 shows the decline of the Mennonite rural population and the increased urban population, as reported in the Canadian census. Also shown is the rural farm population, part of the total rural population. See Appendix F for Mennonite urban-rural statistics for all of Canada and for each province.

MOVING ONCE MORE

Some Canadian Mennonite farmers opted for emigration rather than change their farming operations. They moved either to remote new agricultural frontiers in northern Canada or to isolated new settlements in Central and South America. The immediate issues in almost all these migrations were availability of affordable land and concerns about education.

Land was cheaper in remote and marginal frontier communities. The sale of a farm in an older community brought in enough money to enable grow-ing families to acquire more remote land for growing sons. Mennonites un-derstood that the constant subdividing of family farms to accommodate all the male members of large families was not practical.

Education also was a matter of concern. Its primary purpose was to pre-pare and train children for life. Mennonites believed that all aspects of life should be brought under the Lordship of Christ in a harmonious and inte-grated way. The public schools, however, made a clear distinction between secular and religious training, formally offering little or none of the latter. That was bad enough, but many schools taught children how they could and should become good and productive citizens of this world. Some Menno-nites wanted their offspring trained to become productive and faithful mem-bers of the church and of the sectarian communities of their people.

A further concern pertained specifically to agriculture. Traditional Men-nonite parents hoped and expected that their children would become farm-ers. Yet much of what was taught in schools was of little or no value in an agricultural setting. The curriculum was designed to prepare children for a productive life in modern, usually urban society. Such an education was, at best, useless for children who would become farmers, and it might well make it easier for the children to break away from their home communities.

School attendance at an approved public school had become mandatory during the First World War, but Mennonites living in compact communities were usually able to influence the locally elected school boards. In addition, settlers living more than three miles from an organized school district were not usually subjected to legal action if their children did not attend an ap-proved public school. In new Mennonite frontier settlements where there were no public schools it was possible to arrange for education as parents and community leaders deemed best.[7]

In the years after 1945 Mennonites usually emigrated individually or in small groups. There were no mass migrations, and some were poorly planned. A few ended in failure, and more in serious losses. A group of farmers from the Bergthaler Mennonite Church of Saskatchewan, for example, opened negotiations with the government of British Honduras. They wanted to es-tablish an agricultural community along the Mosquito Coast and in 1948 obtained permission to do so. But disagreements and difficulties in the sale of their assets in Canada delayed their departure. Meanwhile, in British Honduras, stiff opposition from the Roman Catholic hierarchy led in 1949 to rescinding of permission to immigrate.

A small group of the most determined prospective emigrants in Saskat-chewan was either unaware or chose to ignore information about the change in policy. In 1951 these people sold their farms, loaded four large and specially equipped trucks with their remaining possessions, and set out for British Honduras.[8] They were stopped by authorities on the outskirts of Mexico City and informed that their admission to British Honduras had been annulled. Canadian diplomatic officials who met with them described them as 'extremely naive.'[9] When told that they could not go to British Honduras, they asked the Canadian officials to send a telegram to Costa Rica, seeking permission that they be admitted there as immigrants. Nothing came of that request, and the group, which had gone to Mexico on tourist visas, was deported back to Canada. The diplomats could do little more than shake their heads.

It is most unusual, to say the least, that a group of 70 people should undertake a trek of more than 4,000 miles after having sold their farms, without at least having bothered to make sure that the Honduran authorities would still be willing to accept them, especially after a lapse of three years. It is also surprising that they should wish to settle permanently in one of the most inhospitable regions of Central America, with practically no knowledge of tropical agriculture nor of Gulf Coast hygienic conditions ... They had not even enquired as to whether there were highways to Honduras or to Costa Rica.[10]

The Canadian ambassador admitted, however, that this migration was similar to that of the ancient Israelite exodus from Egypt, noting that 'the whole venture has been quite biblical and it is indeed unfortunate that these good, but naive, people should have met with so many rebuffs.'[11]

The Bergthal Mennonites from Saskatchewan were more successful in the early 1960s, when another pioneer group left, this time to found a colony at Santa Cruz, Bolivia. They were joined, in 1969, by approximately 200 Old Colony Mennonites who sold their Canadian properties in the Peace River country, loaded their remaining possessions and implements on trucks, and drove south.[12] One scholar estimates that about 2,500 Sommerfelder, Chortitzer, Kleine Gemeinde, and Old Colony Mennonite farmers[13] emigrated from Canada to Mexico and Paraguay after 1945. Others went to Bolivia, to British Honduras (Belize), and later to other Latin American countries.[14]

Central and South American agricultural settlement frontiers attracted only a handful of Canadian Mennonites. Others sought new homes on northern frontiers. Beginning in the late 1930s, some Old Colony Mennonites from Saskatchewan moved north to La Crete and Buffalo Head Prairie, both close to Fort Vermilion, near the northern border of Alberta. By 1947, 377 Mennonites lived there.[15] They located their homestead claims beyond the boundaries of any organized school district. That, they hoped, would make it possible to establish German-language schools in which only traditional Mennonite school subjects would be taught.

The Alberta government was concerned about the absence of any approved public schools in these communities. It proposed elected trustees on boards that would levy local taxes for support of their schools. The Mennonites at La Crete and Buffalo Head Prairie resisted all such attempts until the early 1950s.

Then, in 1953, two ministers of the Alberta/Saskatchewan (Old) Mennonite Conference visited the communities. The (Old) Mennonites had accepted public schools in their northern Alberta communities and visited La Crete and Buffalo Head Prairie with the encouragement of the provincial Department of Education. They explained to the Old Colony people that the local trustees would retain effective control even if the schools became public and that the government would appoint only teachers who understood and respected Old Colony values. The (Old) Mennonites suggested that acceptance of a public school would not destroy local control, but it would provide money from local taxes and government grants to improve the schools. The Old Colony leaders reluctantly agreed.

No Old Colony or Sommerfelder teachers with the requisite qualifications were available, and almost all the instructors initially appointed were members of the Conference of Mennonites in Canada (CMC), who regarded the Old Colony people as a prospective mission field. Two of the leading ministers in Rosemary, Alberta, J.D. Nickel and D.P. Neufeld, were particularly enthusiastic about this new missionary endeavour, and by 1960 at least five CMC teachers were working in these northern schools. There was also talk of starting a CMC mission church in the community. The Old Colony parents had not, of course, agreed to send their children to school in order that they be converted to the gospel as understood by CMC teachers.

Since local Old Colony Mennonites dominated the school board, and thus had effective control over hiring of teachers, they recommended removal of the Mennonite teachers. It seemed better to have non-Mennonite teachers than the meddlesome, mission-minded, CMC teachers.

Mennonite Brethren (MBs) from Coaldale, Alberta, followed up the rejection of CMC teachers by sending one of their Bible school teachers who needed summer work to the northern communities to do mission work there. He reported that though these people read the same 'pure and unadulterated Word of God' as the Mennonite Brethren, their 'narrow and legalistic' insistence on specific forms and life-styles prevented the Word from bearing fruit.[16]

Introduction of the public school system in La Crete and Buffalo Head Prairie, construction of improved roads and other transportation facilities, and arrival of more settlers, including Mennonites who did not share Old

Colony values, destroyed the isolation of these communities and prompted those most committed to the old ways to move once more. A few left for British Honduras between 1958 and 1962, and then, in 1969, families with about 200 people sold their Canadian properties, loaded their trucks, and left for Bolivia, driven to this extreme action, in part at least, by the missionary activities of other Canadian Mennonites. Bishop Wiebe of the Old Colony church at La Crete expressed the attitude of many of his people: 'We cannot stop you from coming and establishing a church here, but we wish you would leave us alone.'[17] The plight of Mennonite groups intent on preserving their traditional theology and life-style in the face of aggressive teaching and missionary efforts by other Mennonites who had embraced North American evangelicalism has been described thus:

The groups which did not accept the evangelical theology, namely in Manitoba, the Chortitzer, Sommerfelder and Old Colony, and in Saskatchewan the Old Colony, Bergthaler and Sommerfelder, attempted to stem the influence of evangelical theology as much as possible. However, the more they resisted this theology, the more they became the object of subsequent evangelistic campaigns by those who had accepted the evangelical theology ... A common weakness of all the conserving Kanadier groups was that they frequently were unable to express their beliefs theologically, and thus the theology they were trying to express was misunderstood.[18]

The resulting turmoil created restlessness and frustration for Old Colony people who remained in northern Alberta, particularly among the younger people. In communities that offered few social activities, youth turned to the streets: 'Drag racing of pick-up trucks down the main street of town, as well as tailgate parties, became popular pastimes. The combination of drinking and driving needed to be curbed, but most parents tended to turn a blind eye to these activities.'[19] Departure of those most strongly committed to a separatist, agrarian way of life, and arrival of other Mennonite settlers with different ideas, left the Old Colony people at La Crete and Buffalo Head Prairie confused and angry. It seemed that there was no longer a viable place in western Canada for them.

Mexico, Paraguay, and other Latin American countries, for reasons beyond the scope of this book, did not provide a satisfactory solution either. As a result, there was considerable movement back and forth between long-established Canadian Mennonite communities, the new northern frontier settlements, and Latin American colonization ventures. In the course of these migrations those involved suffered considerable cultural, social, religious, and economic loss. That impoverishment made them even more vulnerable to the blandishments of those who advocated greater accommodation to Canadian conditions and to new styles of religious renewal.

Efforts by Old Order Amish and Old Order Mennonite groups in Ontario to maintain their traditional way of life seemed equally drastic but more successful. These groups steadfastly rejected modern farm machinery and agricultural technology, especially electricity and modern automotive and communications innovations. Their way of life had for hundreds of years been based on a horse-powered economy, and for them the horse and buggy, rather than physical isolation, became the means to preserve their cherished communities and congregations. Eventually, on their farms, they accepted some modern labour-saving devices but insisted that these be pulled by horses: 'The horse slows things down, imposes limits, and symbolizes some of the deepest meanings of Amish life. Riding in a horse-drawn carriage is a visible symbol of ethnic identity, unmistakeable to the insider and outsider alike. As a good ethnic badge, the horse both integrates and separates. It leaves no doubt about the boundary lines of Amish society. As the blinders over the horse's eyes shield out roadside distractions, so the horse has blinded Amish society from worldly distractions and kept it bound to tradition.'[20]

The horse, preservation of their own dialect, distinctive clothing, and the buggies in which they travel have become Old Order Amish and Old Order Mennonite 'armaments of defense,' which 'draw the boundary lines between church and the world.'[21] The cars driven by Waterloo-Markham Mennonites, which must be black and for a time had to have all the chrome and other shiny decorations painted black, serve a similar, though perhaps somewhat less effective, function.

A second safeguard for the Old Orders has been their strong commitment to community and congregational interests. In a time when individual interests and rights were increasingly emphasized by others, the Old Orders stubbornly insisted that community and congregational interests take precedence over the interests and rights of the individual. And they set up their own effective system of social rewards and punishments to encourage or compel conformity. 'The Amish,' one scholar has argued, 'are social engineers who have masterminded an effective program of cultural survival without the benefits of higher education or the advice of professional consultants.'[22]

The Old Order Amish and Old Order Mennonites in Canada were small groups in 1950, but the number of Old Order Amish was significantly augmented by an unusual migration from the United States which began in 1953.[23]

Before that year there may have been as many as 350 Old Order Amish living near Milverton in Perth County, Ontario.[24] After 1953, eight new Old Order Amish settlements were established in Ontario – at Aylmer, Chesley, Norwich, Lakeside, Tavistock, Gorie, Wallacetown, and Mt Elgin.[25] The Wallacetown settlement was abandoned in 1964, but in 1966 the number of Old Order Amish living in Ontario had grown to 141 families, made up of about 1,000 individuals in seven settlements.[26] There were also attempts to establish Old Order Amish settlements in other provinces, but none of these succeeded.[27]

A number of reasons have been given to explain why Old Order Amish migrated from the United States to Canada after 1953.[28] First, land and the cost of establishing new farms had become too expensive in the United States. Prices were lower in Ontario, and available land was allegedly better. That made it easier for young couples to acquire farms of their own. Most of the immigrants came with some capital resources, realized through the sale of U.S. properties.

Second, Canada, unlike the United States, did not have conscription after the Second World War. The Old Order Amish in the United States were not drafted for active military service, but they were called up for civilian public service, which many found unsatisfactory. Such service took their men off the farms and exposed them to new ideas and religious practices. It was feared that 'short hours, much leisure time, and an unwholesome environment away from parents and fellow believers, all tended to make [the civilian public service camps] a potentially dangerous situation.'[29]

Third, Old Order Amish knew that Ontario, like most U.S. states, had compulsory school attendance. But until 1960, rural schools in Ontario were run by local school boards with minimal direction from Toronto. Hence, in areas of heavy Amish and Mennonite settlements, small local school boards were controlled by Amish or Mennonite representatives. In their new Canadian communities the Old Order Amish were able to organize their own boards in the 1950s.

Old Order Amish historians also referred to a fourth consideration. Canada in 1953 allegedly did not have an individualized and compulsory social security program, or agricultural and farm assistance programs, like the U.S. ones, which the Old Order Amish found unacceptable. Canada, they thought, 'trailed the U.S. by perhaps ten years, and though these things might have discouraged other settlers, the Amish were pleased.'[30] In fact, Canada's social security, agricultural, and farm assistance programs were by 1953 more extensive than those in the United States, but they had evolved and were administered differently. The financial benefits of tariffs and of government supply-management, marketing, and price-support schemes in Canada were usually incorporated into the price that the farmer received for his or her product and did not require applications by individual farmers or direct government payments to them.[31]

The Old Order Amish who moved to Canada after 1953 demonstrated that it was still possible to sustain their cherished way of life, at least for those with sufficient funds to acquire land without going seriously into debt. Their rejection of labour-saving technology meant that their farms required smaller capital outlays and remained more labour intensive – and thus supported many more people – than highly mechanized operations. Rejection of modern technology nevertheless resulted in occasional problems. The most obvious example occurred in the 1970s when the Ontario Milk Marketing Board established new hygienic standards which required that fluid milk be cooled on the farm in bulk tanks. The Old Order Amish objected not to improved hygienic standards but to the proposed bulk cooling tanks, which were electrically powered – a technology they rejected. In the end some congregations allowed members to install bulk milk-cooling tanks if they were powered by electricity generated by on-farm, diesel-powered generators. Others rejected this compromise, and their farmer-members had to switch from dairy to other agricultural products.[32] The Old Order Amish and similar groups in Ontario thus showed that geographical isolation was not essential to maintaining the old ways. It could be accomplished through rejection of modern technology, effective community control, and migration.

RETURNING MEXICAN MENNONITES

During the years after 1945 another major group of Mennonite immigrants returned to Canada. These were people, or their children and grandchildren, who had left Manitoba and Saskatchewan in the 1920s as a result of school disputes.[33] They had obtained from the Mexican government a guarantee of religious freedom, or Privilegium. Approximately 7,000 had emigrated to Mexico and founded two large colonies in the provinces of Chihuahua and Durango, and numerous smaller ones. By 1945 the Mennonite population in Mexico had reached 12,000.[34]

The early pioneer years were difficult. Drought, dubious land transactions, and church schisms prompted many people to return to Canada, either permanently or to visit relatives and earn some much-needed cash. Canada was much more prosperous than Mexico, and some estimates suggest that up to 20 per cent of the emigrants of the 1920s returned before 1940.[35] That return migration was interrupted during the 1940s but resumed early in the 1950s when population pressures caused by high birth rates and restrictions on new land purchases, combined with severe drought and church tensions, struck the settlements.[36]

Many of the returning Mennonites in the early 1950s arrived at the Canadian border impoverished, sick, and without proper passports or other legal documents.[37] The earliest difficulties occurred at BC border points, where large numbers began to arrive after 1951. A.A. Wiens, secretary of the Mennonite Provincial Relief Committee of British Columbia, described what sometimes happened:

Palm Sunday. The Border officials from Blaine-Douglas phoned me to come there to help them with a special case ... During the night a Mennonite family from Mexico had arrived. Ticket to Vancouver. No other destination given. They came by bus. No food. No money. Nobody could speak English. Dirty. Husband a Canadian Citizen. Wife a British Subject through marriage; a baby Canadian citizenship; the other children not registered – Mexican citizens. Their belongings – a heap of old dirty trash, spread out in the customs to be sprayed against foot and mouth disease. I assumed responsibility for them. But before we were through with all the regulations required it was 4 p.m. Many curious spectators were around. But fortunately no newsmen with cameras. This family is in Yarrow now.

It came worse on Good Friday. The traffic at Blaine-Douglas is usually very heavy. Late Thursday evening along came an old Mexican Studebaker with 3 adults and 6 children. No one spoke English. The gasoline tank empty. The borrowed Mexican car a pile of junk. The mother of the children in a terrible state of health. She had given premature birth somewhere in Arizona. The youngest baby only 9 months old. She was badly haemorrhaged and here nobody to understand them. So around half past 11 p.m. my phone rang.[38]

Canadian immigration officers checking the status of these returners discovered that most of those born in Canada had not become Mexican citizens, thus retaining their Canadian citizenship.[39] By the Canadian Citizenship Act, 1947, first-generation children born abroad, with parents who were Canadian citizens, could apply for citizenship. But they must do so between their twenty-first and twenty-second birthdays,[40] or they lost their citizenship rights. Very few Mennonites born in Mexico had made an application before 1952. They were not, therefore, Canadian citizens, but Mexican Mennonites, once they became aware of this requirement, took care to make sure that young people made the necessary application when they reached twenty-one.

Those Mennonites in Mexico who had not made the required application at the right time, but whose parents kept Canadian citizenship, retained some unusual rights based on British legislation. The Nationality Act of 1948 provided that first-generation children of British subjects born abroad remained British subjects if they had not become citizens of their country of residence. Thus Mennonites born in Mexico who were over the age of 22 but were neither Mexican nor Canadian citizens had become 'citizens of the United Kingdom and Colonies' at the time the Canadian Citizenship Act, 1947, which deprived those who had not applied of their Canadian citizenship, took effect.[41]

Unpleasant border incidents prompted some Mexican Mennonites, Canadian Mennonite leaders, and immigration officials to seek a solution. The tone of the negotiations may be deduced from a letter that Johann Fehr, a Mexican Mennonite, addressed to 'Beloved Gentlemen in Ottawa' in 1954:

My grave task is to get on my way and say, as did the prodigal son, 'Father, I have sinned in Heaven and before Thee; I am unworthy of being called Thy son, make me into one of Thy day-labourers.'

Beloved gentlemen, would you still be able to make it possible for us to come to Canada again which was once so dear to us? We would come as farm workers, weak as we are, as defenceless German Mennonites. We number 18,337 souls. Pray, gentlemen, accept mercifully this request from your weak servant. We left Manitoba, Canada, to settle in Mexico. Again I ask you, grant my request, weak as its foundation may be.[42]

Fehr received no official encouragement from immigration officials, who nevertheless realized that the original migrants were still Canadian citizens and that most of the first-generation, Mexican-born Mennonites had Canadian or British citizenship rights. They asked Mennonite leaders in Canada to look into the matter and make recommendations. These leaders became very concerned and were willing to help. 'It is,' one wrote, 'a very serious thing for Canadian government officials to become disturbed about the public relations problem that these Mennonites present.'[43] Canadian immigration and American State Department officials also worried about the inadequate and unsanitary conditions in which the migrants made their way across the United States. All too frequently old trucks or vans, crammed to capacity with large but destitute families, broke down en route, leaving local social agencies with the task of providing help.

The Canadian Mennonite organizations could do little about confusing citizenship status, but they worked with government officials to facilitate issuance of proper visas and work permits, and they accepted responsibility for care of those needing help. Efforts by Canadian Mennonites to assist were made more difficult by the opposition of the Mexican Mennonite church leaders, who threatened to excommunicate any returners who accepted such

aid. And within the Canadian Mennonite oraganizations there were serious
tensions and disagreements between people descended from the immigrants
of the 1870s who had close family connections with the Mexican Mennonites and those who had come to Canada in the 1920s and tended to be much
more critical of the returnees, their destitute condition, their seemingly irresponsible travel patterns, and their determination to retain the old ways.[44]

When some of the Mennonites from Mexico began to take up migrant agricultural work in Ontario, members of the Old Order Mennonites and Amish
were sympathetic and pleased 'to become acquainted with other Christians
who are so nearly like-minded.'[45] But some soon made derogatory comments
about the personal habits and hygiene of the Old Colony Mennonites.

The earliest Mexican immigrants became migrant farm labourers in the
Abbotsford, Burns Lake, and Yarrow areas of British Columbia, in the sugar-
beet fields of southern Manitoba, and on fruit, vegetable, and other row-crop
farms of southern Ontario. Attempts to obtain work in the sugar-beet industry
of southern Alberta were thwarted by the federal government, which was bringing Native people from northern Saskatchewan to work there. Local hostility
and competition from other immigrants, mainly from India and Asia, made
British Columbia less attractive to the Mexican Mennonites after 1956.

In 1955 some returnees started an unsuccessful agricultural settlement at
Matheson, Ontario. A new farming community on marginal land in the Rainy
River area of Ontario survived, but only after concerned Mennonites in
Ontario provided emergency funding through the Mennonite Assistance
Agency, created for that purpose.[46]

In the 1960s the Mexican Mennonites who were engaged in seasonal farm
work in southern Ontario set up a rapidly growing but impoverished and unstable community at Aylmer, Ontario, where migratory farm work was available but where it also seemed possible for at least the more prosperous families
to follow the example of the Old Order Amish immigrants in acquiring their
own farms. MCC, Old Order Amish, and Old Order Mennonite support, and
missionary initiatives by several Mennonite conferences with strong links to
the Mexican Mennonites, expedited partial integration of returnees living in
and around Aylmer. The Rudnerweider Mennonite Church (renamed the Evangelical Mennonite Mission Conference in 1959), an offshoot of the
Sommerfelder Church in Manitoba, launched aggressive missionary work
among the returning Mexican Mennonites and started a Bible school and a
church at Aylmer to serve these people. Other Mexican Mennonites joined
disgruntled farmers from the prairies in opening up new agricultural frontiers
in the Peace River and more northerly Alberta and BC districts.

One of the most serious problems confronting those Mennonites who returned from Mexico was the schooling of their children. The communities into which most of them moved had schools which these immigrants found unacceptable. Some Mennonite families engaged in seasonal agricultural labour in Canada tried to avoid schools by remaining in Mexico during winter and coming to Canada only in time for spring farm work. By the time authorities learned of their arrival, summer vacation had usually begun.

School attendance was made more attractive when the mothers of children in school became eligible for the family allowance. Most of the Mexican Mennonites were poor but had large families, so the prospect of receiving social benefits became an incentive to send the children to school. In contrast, harsh or punitive measures by the authorities tended to reinforce historic notions of persecution and led to non-violent but stubborn non-compliance. Kindness and modest monetary inducements proved much more effective.

The returnees reinforced rural and agricultural communities in several different ways. Some acquired land and established farming communities of their own. Others, at least temporarily, provided cheap labour for the better-established farmers. Most originally came with only temporary work permits or tourist visas, but after several years of life as migrant farm workers more and more decided to settle in Canada. Their situation in 1975 was described in this way:

The majority of Mexican Mennonites in Manitoba and Ontario appear to work as farm labourers in the summer and as unlicensed tradesmen, semi-skilled, and unskilled factory workers in the winter. Only a minority have farms or businesses of their own, but this is the goal that most labourers are striving towards as well.

The men seem to be especially efficient in carpentry, welding, and mechanics, but because of their low level of formal education are unable to be certified for this work. Women are most frequently employed in unskilled and semi-skilled factory and farm labouring positions, although some have excellent sewing skills and a few have trained as nurses aides. In addition to working full time in the fields during the harvest season, the women take care of large families and do all of the cooking, cleaning and washing. When the long hours of work in the fields are combined with the physical strains of bearing and raising so many children, it is not surprising that the women frequently look much older than their age and much older than men of the same age.[47]

HELPING ONE ANOTHER

Canadian Mennonites generally, particularly those who valued collective community interests, strongly supported mutual aid and cooperative efforts. Such programs assisted community members who had suffered some misfortune, as well as younger members unable to set up their own farms or businesses. At Aylmer, Ontario, for example, the Old Order Amish pooled their resources in the 1950s to purchase a seventy-acre farm, complete with buildings, from one of their older members. They wanted to save the farm for an Amish family that might need it, rather than allowing it to be sold 'to an English buyer.' An Old Order Amish family from Iowa subsequently bought the farm with payments arranged to take into account the productive capacity of the property and the purchaser's ability to pay.[48]

When Mennonite settlers first came to Canada they created mutual aid organizations, and these were still common in the 1940s and 1950s. Most of these church- or community-based bodies were of two types – separatist/historical congregational organizations and more broadly based, cooperative organizations.

Separatist Mennonite mutual aid allowed churches and sectarian communities to structure their own internal economic relationships in order to achieve common objectives. Care of orphans, the elderly, and those suffering serious economic hardship, illness, or other disasters was institutionalized in separatist, usually church-sponsored or -supported, mutual aid programs.[49] Such organizations were expected to operate according to scriptural principles, not according to prevailing economic policies of materialistic individualism. J.W. Fretz referred to their underlying assumptions as 'brotherhood economics': 'The New Testament principle described in the Book of Acts as the brethren helping each other, each according to his ability and each according to his need, has not been the principle on which business has operated ... A program of mutual aid whereby we are made continually conscious of our obligations one to another and where we are engaged in actively helping each other in the Name of Christ will eliminate much of selfish materialism. Christian love applied to economic relations will change these practices.'[50]

Fretz took many of his ideas from the writings of a Russian revolutionary, Prince Peter Kropotkin.[51] Kropotkin, while accepting Darwin's theory of evolution, launched a vigorous attack against 'the widely accepted Darwin theory of survival of the fittest.'[52] He argued 'that competition is always injurious to the species and that the best way to insure safety, security, and progress is to practice mutual aid.'[53] Kropotkin advocated cooperation and vigorously attacked the allegedly individualistic and competitive practices of Western civilization and particularly of Christian teachings. He later became an anarchist.

Fretz, writing in the 1940s, did not accept Kropotkin's anarchist ideas, but he did argue that mutual aid was 'a social relationship built on mutual faith and common trust ... It is an opportunity for the natural expression of human sympathy and common love toward one another.'[54] His pamphlets exerted considerable influence, and in 1964 he was instrumental in establishing in Kitchener a Mennonite Savings and Credit Union that reflected his ideas.[55]

For Fretz, church or congregation and community were largely the same. That, however, was not necessarily the case in many Mennonite communities, and many mutual aid societies included non-Mennonites. A cooperative cheese factory, basic medical facilities, municipal road-building projects, and cooperative ventures, such as the oilseed-crushing plant at Altona, usually had a broadly based membership. These programs were created to deal with practical local problems. The Rhineland Agricultural Society, for example, was formed to protect farmers facing bank foreclosures and bankruptcy during the Depression. When it was organized in 1931, 626 of 1,240 farmers in the municipality had reportedly already lost title to their farms and another 455 were so heavily in debt that mortgage payments alone took a third of their crop. The co-op was a vehicle to make the financial resources of the wealthier members of the community available to those threatened with foreclosures on terms that took into account community interests.[56] Later, Mennonite cooperative credit unions provided community- oriented financial services.

Community-based co-ops that dealt with outside organizations and institutions usually operated in accordance with accepted business practices and principles. They were not charitable institutions and did not define their operating principles solely on the basis of scripture. Some restated old scriptural principles but added secular and socialist 'class' analysis. Others candidly admitted that they were being run in accordance with what utopians such as Kropotkin and Fretz had denounced as 'prevailing economic policies of materialistic individualism.'[57]

The conflict between rival concepts was particularly clear in southern Manitoba. David Schulz, long-time elder of the Bergthaler Mennonite Church of Manitoba, defended separatist and closed programs. His church had established a *Waisenamt* (orphans' fund), *Feuerversicherung* (fire insurance), and a burial society, all run on the principle that 'the strong had a responsibility to share, serve without pay on community structures, and support the weak so that their dignity and worth as persons could be protected.'[58]

Schulz often found himself in conflict with J.J. Siemens, southern Manitoba's best-known advocate of more broadly based, secular co-ops. Siemens, the driving force behind the Rhineland Agricultural Society, dreamed of community-based co-ops not restricted to individuals in good standing with a Mennonite congregation. His ideology was secular and socialist. His views 'stemmed primarily from an analysis of the flaws of capitalism, but they also owed much to the Mennonite tradition of mutual aid and community building.

For him, the co-operative movement was a way of reviving an old practice for a new situation.'[59] Cooperatives, Siemens believed, should build and strengthen rural communities,[60] whereas the older, separatist programs supported by David Schulz and other Old Order and traditional Mennonite groups were designed to strengthen the congregation.[61]

Cooperative and mutual aid programs sometimes exhibited divergent aspirations. J.J. Siemens and the Rhineland Agricultural Society offered a socialist alternative to free enterprise, but other Mennonite co-ops, most notably the Steinbach Credit Union, were to 'boost and further private enterprise.'[62] Co-ops could create the economic infrastructure for other businesses, much as crown corporations have provided basic postal, transportation, energy, and telecommunications facilities at prices set to meet community needs rather than to generate maximum profits for capitalist promoters. Credit unions have, for that reason, been described as 'an instrument in the hands of the common man to free himself from the shackles of big business,'[63] even though their promoters supported different ideologies.

Initiatives to solve specific problems or to create new opportunities for Mennonites engaged in farming covered a wide range of activities. The largest was almost certainly Co-op Vegetable Oils. The growing and processing of sunflower seeds and other vegetable oils dramatically changed agriculture in and around Altona. In 1956 Manitoba's Department of Industry and Commerce measured the impact of this co-op on Altona. It found that the 46 employees and their 136 dependants comprised 30 per cent of the town's population increase during the previous decade and that these people indirectly accounted for 13.2 per cent of the town's total retail trade, while taxes paid by the plant amounted to 13 per cent of the town's revenue.[64]

The Saskatchewan Youth Farm at Rosthern and the Ailsa Craig Boys Farm in Ontario were probably the most unusual co-ops. In the 1940s Saskatchewan Mennonites, specifically the Saskatchewan Mennonite Youth Organization (SMYO) of the Conference of Mennonites in Canada, got permission to use the beautiful grounds and public facilities of the federal experimental farm at Rosthern to hold youth retreats,[65] which were characterized by evangelistic services, singing, and fellowship.

During the war it became clear that Ottawa would consolidate its experimental farm operations and that the Rosthern farm might be sold. The government, however, was reluctant to offer the farm to the highest commercial bidder during the war, when land prices were low. It hoped that the farm might be used for some public service or charitable purpose. The SMYO had already been active in daily vacation Bible schools, including some in northern Native communities, and there was also interest in establishing charitable health-care facilities. So the SMYO offered to purchase the farm and use the proceeds of farming operations for charitable purposes.

Jimmy Gardiner, the federal minister of agriculture, was well disposed towards the Mennonites, as was Prime Minister William Lyon Mackenzie King, who represented the nearby constituency of Prince Albert, which included many Mennonite voters. Negotiations in 1942 resulted in a government decision to sell the experimental farm and all associated buildings to the SMYO at a fraction of their market value. The SMYO in turn agreed to use farming proceeds to build and operate, as finances permitted, homes for orphans, the elderly, the mentally retarded, and troubled youngsters. The operations of the homes, particularly the ones for orphans and troubled youngsters, were to be integrated with those of the farm. Proceeds from those facilities, in addition to fees paid by residents and limited government grants, would pay operating costs. Inmates were encouraged to participate in the farm work as they were able. The SMYO also wanted to use the facilities for daily vacation Bible school and retreat and camping activities.

Eventually some activities and programs on the Youth Farm were curtailed. The main facility was a nursing home for the aged, and it was significantly expanded several times. During the Vietnam War, American conscientious objectors did some of their civilian public service work at the farm. Mennonites and many other members of the community benefited from this unique venture, which embodied 'brotherhood economics' in a practical way.

The boys' farm at Ailsa Craig, Ontario, began as a project of the local Amish Mennonite community. It was similar to other home mission projects of the (Old) and Amish Mennonites in the United States, where farms had been converted to charitable institutions. The venture proved successful, but the cost of modifying existing farm buildings and constructing new ones exceeded the resources of the local Amish. The Conference of Historic Peace Churches (CHPC) was invited to accept the major responsibility for the farm, which was 'to meet the spiritual and social needs of adolescent youth.'[66] Since the CHPC was not incorporated, title was transferred to MCC, while the CHPC began running the farm. New, enlarged facilities, including a recreation hall, renovated farm-house and barn, and new housing for staff and boys, were dedicated in 1955.

Mutual aid societies helped preserve traditional values and allowed controlled adjustment to new economic conditions. The continuing strength and distinctiveness of Mennonite communities with strong cooperative institutions, and the disintegration of such an identity in communities where such institutions have failed, are testimony to their value.[67]

Cooperatives often introduced Mennonites to the financial aspects and complexities of farming and operating small, rural, service businesses. Most of the people who used the services offered were not particularly concerned about ideology or theology. They were more likely to evaluate such institutions pragmatically; those that solved problems received their support. Those that did not, or occasionally resorted to offensive separatist, capitalist, or socialist rhetoric, were avoided. There was, however, a gradual shift away from separatist institutions to more broadly based consumer and producer co-ops. That change, particularly in cooperative organizations in which Mennonites did not have control or even significant influence, marked growing accommodation to changed conditions.

FARMERS AS BUSINESSMEN

Canadian farmers were bombarded after the war with literature and public addresses that insisted that those who wanted to succeed as farmers had to become more business-like. They must take advantage of new technologies, which in turn required much larger capital investments. That made careful planning and cost-benefit analyses essential. Machinery, and its efficient use, often made the difference between success and failure.[68]

Prevailing opinion was that agricultural success and the survival of rural communities depended on the willingness of farmers to accept and implement new ways of doing things without losing the most precious aspects of farming as a way of life. The strategies and policies adopted by the Co-operative Commonwealth Federation (CCF) government of Saskatchewan offered one approach. A Royal Commission on Agriculture and Rural Life in 1952 was charged with studying rural and agricultural problems and prescribing policies to preserve and protect, but also to modernize and revitalize, agriculture and rural life. The commission produced 22 book-length studies dealing with everything from rural transportation and electrification costs and problems with rural credit and finance to education, health care, and social development.[69]

The recommendations were fairly simple. Rural and farm people did not enjoy the amenities available in the city. Rural electrification was too slow and expensive, fuel and heating costs were too high, few farm houses had running water, and many still lacked reliable telephone service. The solution proposed (and subsequently adopted) called for new policies to be followed by the utility companies, most of which were publicly owned. It was readily admitted that extending and maintaining services to scattered rural farmsteads were more expensive than providing the same services in the cities. But if people were to remain on the farm it was necessary that they have the same basic services and amenities as their urban counterparts. Since the utilities enjoyed local monopolies, they could set provincial rates that equalized costs of the service to various users. In effect, it was recommended that urban users subsidize less cost-efficient rural rates. The commission, in the tradition of the CCF, also recommended financial incentives for cooperative initiatives to modernize rural life. Tax exemptions for co-ops were proposed and later implemented. Other provinces, while not tying their policies as closely to a carefully formulated strategy, adopted similar approaches.

Some rural and agricultural experts had doubts about Saskatchewan's 'socialist' and 'co-operative' strategies, which sought to preserve what was best in traditional rural life while also accepting change. Farmers, they said, faced 'vast technological upheaval that ... overwhelmed traditional family and village life.'[70] Attempts to prop up old rural ways built around mixed family farms were futile. Successful farms had to be appropriately capitalized, mechanized, and specialized.[71]

The debate involved more than political ideology. It focused on the very nature of farming and rural life. Should farming be regarded essentially as a wholesome way of life, or as a business?[72] Several CCF initiatives were designed to strengthen rural communities but in fact undermined them. New and improved highways, consolidation of schools, closure of small, rural hospitals, and construction of larger, union hospitals all made living and shopping, studying or recovering from illness in the larger towns and cities easier and more attractive than what was available in smaller rural centres. The policies helped some of the larger, rural, service towns but severely damaged hundreds of smaller villages and hamlets.

Highway, educational, and health-care programs all further broke down physical barriers that had isolated rural Mennonite communities. In Ontario, and in settlements close to large cities or flourishing smaller trade centres, that isolation had been broken even before 1940, but after 1945 new roads, automobiles, radios, newspapers, television, telephones, and other means of modern transportation and communication easily penetrated the remaining barriers. Extensive contact with the outside world became a fact of life for rural Canadians.[73] For those who cherished the isolation of their sectarian rural enclaves these developments were disconcerting.

The two technological advances that most affected Canadian farming were tractors, or more generally tractive power, and electricity.[74] Tractors required less and different care, lasted longer, and worked harder than horses. With hydraulic and power take-off, they could also provide rotary power for implements that performed tasks that horse-drawn, ground-driven machines could not do.[75] Gasoline- or diesel-powered machines, moreover, could be operated by one person. In grain harvesting a self-propelled combine operated by one person could now do the work previously done by large threshing crews, which had made the harvest a collective experience. Haying technology now allowed one or two operators to do the labour that had been done by an entire crew when horse-drawn hayracks took the hay to the barn door, whence it was hoisted by horse-powered slings for storage in the commodious lofts of hip-roofed barns.[76]

What gasoline- or diesel-powered tractive power did for field work, electricity accomplished in the barn and farm-house. Milking machines, automated watering and feeding systems, electrically powered and monitored heating systems, household cleaning, cooking, baking, refrigeration, and a host of other tasks could now be done by machines. Such devices changed family and community life. Fewer farm labourers were needed. Activities that had once seen neighbours working together could now be carried out by each farmer on his or her own – provided that he or she had the machines.

Family life was even more dramatically affected. With the new machines field work became the responsibility of the men, while women looked after the children and the household. Children could no longer provide as much help, but the cost of raising them increased. Royden Loewen has written about these changes in Hanover, Manitoba: 'In pre–World War II days ... [the local] economy had been indelibly linked to self-sufficient, mixed farm households. By 1960 Hanover had a new appearance. Its countryside was dotted with modern farms that specialized in either poultry, egg, dairy or hog production and which now often sported low-lying, white-coloured barns of plywood construction located across the farmyard from the modern bungalow.'[77]

Gender roles became more specialized. Men were breadwinners and producers, while women became housekeepers, consumers, reproducers, and child nurturers.[78] That plan fitted postwar secular expectations.[79] Well-defined differences between 'Town Ladies' and 'Farm Women' faded when modern technological advances were extended to farm homes.[80]

The changing patterns of farm operations also resulted in much more continuous and intimate involvement with outside agencies. Farmers had to learn about prices, interest rates, commodity markets, new machinery, advances in weed and insect control, higher quality standards and regulatory changes, new accounting and financial methods, changes in tax laws, new government reporting requirements, and many more things designed to make farming more businesslike. Secular concerns, values, and institutions threatened to dominate affairs and influence farmers' decisions.

The credit arrangements made by Mennonite and non-Mennonite farmers alike to finance purchase of land and machinery illustrates some of these changes. In 1959 Ottawa established the Farm Credit Corporation (FCC), which provided funds to farmers at a preferred rate of interest. The FCC imposed strict operating, accounting, and reporting conditions on borrowers. All expenses over $100, whether personal or business, had to be approved by the corporation.[81] Failure to comply had serious consequences. The Old Orders and other like-minded groups rejected FCC terms and excommunicated members who accepted them. Many other young Mennonite farmers, however, saw such arrangements as the only way in which they could secure the capital needed to have their own farms. Credit unions and other community-based financial institutions provided some alternatives, but they too were constrained by the realities of the marketplace.

Increased mechanization almost always led also to greater specialization. Machines were expensive but, once acquired, could do far more specialized work than was available on more or less self-sufficient mixed farms. There were economies of scale that farmers could achieve only if they expanded one branch of their operations and withdrew from others.[82] The results were often dramatic. The traditional association among family, farm, and community was broken. Mechanization, capitalization, intensification, and rationalization forced most Canadian Mennonite farmers to pay more attention to the dictates of the market than to family, church, or community concerns.

CONCLUSION

In 1971 Canada had half as many Mennonite farmers as it had had thirty years earlier. For a people who for generations had looked to farming as an almost sacred vocation, that was an exceptionally important change. The majority of those Canadian Mennonites still engaged in agriculture had become more business-like. That meant, among other things, that priorities established by their congregations and communities had to be reconciled and, if that was not possible, altered to meet the dictates of economic efficiency, the tyranny of commodity markets, the capital requirements of increased mechanization, and a significantly reduced need for labour previously provided by family and community members.

Most Canadian farmers in 1971 were more prosperous than their counterparts thirty years earlier, but they had invested far more capital. They also employed fewer hired hands and relied less on the labour of family members than had their parents and grandparents. Farming, in short, had changed for most of Canada's Mennonites.

There were exceptions. The Old Order Amish, and to a lesser extent the Old Order Mennonites and the Markham-Waterloo (black-bumper) Men-

nonites, maintained traditional practices, which reinforced their sectarian religious community and family patterns. Rejection of technological advances
became the most visible aspect of their increasingly distinctive, unusual, and
for many observers romantic Canadian life-styles. The immigration of several
hundred Old Order Amish from the United States reinforced and validated
this radical dissent, but it gained few converts from the outside world.

Those groups that sought geographical isolation in order to maintain an
old way of life met with less success. Outside influences, often coming
through other Mennonite groups, undermined the separatist aspirations of
Chortitzer, Sommerfelder, Saskatchewan Bergthaler, and Old Colony agri-
culturalists who sought refuge in the north. And many of those who moved
south, either in the 1920s or in the 1950s, found that Latin America provided
less-than-ideal conditions for their utopias.

Agriculture changed, but it survived. And many Canadian Mennonite farmers survived, but even in rural and farm homes new, different, and essentially
urban hopes, aspirations, practices, and attitudes were evident. The rural and
agricultural sector did not disappear, but for most farmers it became more
modern and essentially more urban.

7

New Economic Opportunities

Reuben Musselman of rural Waterloo county in Ontario was typical of many Mennonites who were unable to establish their own farms but who discovered other possibilities after the Second World War. Reuben was a member of the second group of Mennonite conscientious objectors sent to the Montreal River camp, about eighty miles northwest of Sault Ste Marie.

The men were placed in a former lumber camp and put to work building a portion of the highway along the north shore of Lake Superior, which was expected to become part of a proposed trans-Canada highway. Few preparations had been made for their arrival, and the men were given little more than hand tools and asked to do rough manual work. Matters improved considerably when they got an old bulldozer, which did much of the heaviest and roughest work. The old machine, however, required constant care and attention, particularly during winter. Musselman was one of the mechanically competent fellows who kept that bulldozer operating. A fellow camp worker remembers that on one cold and frosty morning Musselman gathered a pile of oily rags, placed them under the machine's oilpan, and lit them. The resulting, unseasonable change of temperature roused the old machine from short-lived hibernation.[1]

When he returned home Musselman found little opportunity to acquire an economically viable farming operation of his own. He first took jobs with local companies but then started his own company, which used skills he had learned at Montreal River. He acquired a bulldozer and specialized in the digging of farm ponds. These ponds or dugouts helped conserve water during spring run-offs or heavy rains and provided a more secure supply of water for livestock and for general domestic farm use. The company never became large, but it employed as many as forty men, and Musselman was periodically invited to give guest lectures on the subject at the Ontario Agricultural College in Guelph. He thus became a small businessman, applying new skills learned during the war to constructive peacetime use.

In the alternative service camps Musselman had also seen much waste and needless destruction, as lumber, newsprint, and wood products companies tried to maximize wartime production with no thought of conservation. After the war, Musselman promoted conservation when he acquired some sandy land near St Agatha, Ontario, and there planted thousands of trees, again using knowledge and skills learned in the camps. Those and other adjacent lands are now beautifully forested areas extensively used by the public for skiing and hiking.

The details of Reuben Musselman's story are unique, but the broader pattern of his career is not. He was part of a remarkable flowering of Canadian Mennonite entrepreneurship and economic diversification in the late 1940s. Almost all the Mennonites who took advantage of these new opportunities had grown up on farms. They knew and understood the farming community and were able to adapt and apply technological advances to solve specific problems and perform important tasks on the farm.

Prospective Mennonite businessmen had natural contacts and some unique market and labour advantages in the rural communities. Mennonite farm people were still somewhat suspicious of outsiders. Some non-Mennonite businessmen had been sharply critical of the Mennonite peace position during the war. So rural Mennonites were more likely to trust one of their own when making a decision about some new technology. A deal negotiated in southern Manitoba in the Low German language, or with someone who knew and found ways and means to accommodate the idioms and nuances of (Old) Mennonite and Amish culture in Ontario, while selling new machines seemed much more reliable than one negotiated in a less familiar form.

Haggling over prices is a fine but culturally sensitive art. In the late 1940s and the 1950s the homogenizing effect of radio and television advertising had not yet engulfed rural Mennonite communities. People there knew how to deal with their own, and many had also learned, either in Russia or in Canada, how to haggle with pedlars and rural salespeople. Some Mennonites and Hutterites had themselves sold farm produce door to door in the cities or specialized items to neighbourhood farmers. In the more prosperous times after 1945 rural Mennonite businessmen found ways of selling in their home communities, in part because they understood the mentality of their customers.

Nascent Mennonite entrepreneurs, particularly in the late 1940s and early 1950s, could also rely on an at least partially protected labour supply. Capital requirements for acquiring and equipping farmsteads were prohibitive for many Mennonite young people. Work for a Mennonite businessman, often one who shared denominational values, seemed an attractive alternative – a way either to earn sufficient funds to buy and equip a farm or to pursue further education and a profession. Inexperienced and insecure Mennonites found it easier to fit into rural services and later urban businesses operated by Mennonites.[2]

Mennonite businessmen in the mid-1940s could expand or enter businesses that were relatively closely related to traditional ways. That, however, was often only the first step in a progression that quickly let them expand into other, usually at least vaguely related business activities, such as urban construction or furniture companies that tried to replicate in an urban context some of the rural, agrarian methods.

THE INCREASED ROLE OF GOVERNMENT

The Canadian government played a major part in the planning and management of the economy after the Second World War. It was a widely accepted perception that the government's management of the economy during the Depression had not been a success.[3] Late in the 1930s, however, Ottawa had accepted and began to implement some of the counter-cyclical economic theories of the British economist John Maynard Keynes. In times of slow economic growth and high unemployment, Keynes argued, governments should stimulate the economy by spending more. Military service and vast increases in government spending during the war had, at least temporarily, solved the problems of depression and unemployment. The federal government had also controlled prices and wages to combat inflation and windfall profits. There were, however, fears that the economy might revert to the conditions of the 1930s, or experience the economic disruptions that had followed the First World War, if controls were abruptly lifted after the war.

Ottawa began to plan reconstruction policy as early as 1942. There were imaginative proposals made for conversion of the massive Department of Munitions and Supply into a new Department of Reconstruction and Supply. The huge factories producing military hardware should not simply be shut down after the war. They were to be converted, with government assistance and under government regulation, into automobile assembly plants and factories for a wide range of durable consumer goods.[4] Ambitious new housing and highway construction programs, and innovative educational and health-care initiatives, would allow returning veterans and workers in war industries to earn a livelihood. Restructuring of the economy was to take place under a watchful eye and with careful direction, encouragement, and regulation by the federal government.[5]

A central feature of transition policy was comprehensive social security. The primary motivation for what has since become known as the social safety net was, aside from the obvious political considerations, economic, rather than humanitarian. The things manufactured by the reconstructed industries and the services offered by professionals and civil servants all had to be sold. A major problem of the 1930s had been inadequate purchasing power. The new social security system was designed to address that problem.[6]

A commission appointed in 1942 produced a *Report on Social Security for Canada*[7] and other economic planning studies. Implementation of such programs helped re-elect the Liberals in 1945.[8] Some of the key components were put in place during the mid-1940s. Implementation varied among provinces, which had administrative jurisdiction, even though most of the money and basic guidelines came from Ottawa. Four initiatives were particularly important: national pensions, comprehensive unemployment insurance, government-supported hospital and medical insurance, and family allowances. Together they gave millions of Canadians purchasing power to buy the cars, durable consumer goods, and services provided by the reconstructed economy.

Canadian Mennonites, while sometimes reluctant to accept social welfare benefits, gained greatly from policies that stabilized farm income, created new opportunities in automotive, home-building, and retail businesses, and provided employment for many more educational, health-care, and government workers. The policies met the needs of upwardly mobile members of the middle class. The interests of large corporations and wealthy capitalists were not neglected, but the Mennonites benefited mainly from the middle-class opportunities created by the policies.

Canadian governments after the Second World War managed the economy in a manner that most Mennonites found acceptable and from which they derived significant gains. Few believed that the government was building the Kingdom of God on earth, but it was doing what Mennonites believed good governments in their proper sphere of authority should do. That included creation of an economic and social environment that was peaceful, stable, orderly, and prosperous. Between 1945 and 1970 Canadian Mennonites accepted, participated in, and gave support to the new economic order, even though that drew them more intimately into activities that earlier generations had sought to avoid. Their increased economic involvement was nevertheless quite varied.

SERVING THE NEEDS OF FARMERS

Canadian Mennonite young people everywhere, whether they accepted or rejected key aspects of agricultural modernization after the Second World War, found that only a few families could place all younger family members on farms of their own. Even the Old Orders, labour intensive though their farms might be, could not do so. The Old Orders, however, set up a host of rural and agricultural service businesses. Their commitment to horses and buggies provided some obvious business and commercial opportunities. Harnesses and buggies had to be manufactured locally, and machinery designed for electrical or tractive power had to be modified, creating work for local blacksmiths and machine-shop operators. Distinctive household arrangements encouraged those skilled in woodwork to run small furniture-manufacturing and -repair shops, often built on Old Order farms to provide work for younger, landless family members or for middle-aged and older men who had turned the farm over to adult sons. This arangement complemented the work of the women, who were skilled quilt makers and also created other masterpieces of needlework.

The commodities produced in Old Order Amish and Old Order Mennonite shops and homes were intended mainly for their own people, but outsiders also became customers. Racetrack operators, for example, began to look to Old Order buggy shops for special supplies for harnesses and sulkies. In addition, supply and repair shops, blacksmith and farm-equipment manufacturing and repair work, metal shops, and meat-processing and -butchering plants were common ventures of the Old Orders and of other Mennonite groups strongly committed to a rural way of life. Farm-related processing, manufacturing, repair, and service industries helped to sustain, and sometimes to modify, the traditional life-style.[9]

Farm-related business was also an alternative for other Mennonites. Even in the earliest days farming communities had included small, independent, rural and agricultural service businesses. A private store and a blacksmith shop were standard features of village life, and more diverse services were offered in the larger towns as need and opportunity arose.

These operations were sometimes run by individuals who also had their own farms, or by family members, often younger sons. At Rosthern, Saskatchewan, Gerhard Ens opened a retail store and post office in a borrowed railway box car in the 1890s, while an amateur blacksmith used the rails on the local siding, a sledge hammer, and a primitive forge to beat out dull ploughshares.[10] Grist and feed mills, seed-grain merchants, brick works, lumber yards, coal and fuel merchants, machine repair shops, furniture makers,

leather, shoe and harness merchants and repairers, and other small enterprises were common and greatly appreciated.[11]

J. Winfield Fretz's 1943 report described some of the local businesses at
Steinbach, Manitoba. A local lumber yard had spawned woodworking shops,
which made compartments for hives used by local beekeepers, boxes in which
to pack cheese produced at a local factory, a sash-and-door shop, and a small
business building cabinets and cupboards. The local bee industry had also led
to establishment of a small tin and metal shop manufacturing honey extractors,
smokers, and other beekeeping equipment and a small beeswax factory, all of
which sold products in many parts of Manitoba. Steinbach also had farm-machinery repair, modification, and manufacturing shops. In another Manitoba
town a farmer bought a machine that manufactured puffed wheat, thus 'dis-
posing of a crop that is grown on one's own farm at a much greater income than
could be realized if sold on the open market.'[12]

The number of small businesses in Steinbach and in many other Mennonite
communities doubled in the 1940s.[13] Most of them, like pre-war family farms,
were highly labour intensive. The earliest and most common were the local
blacksmith shop and a grocery store, which often doubled as the post office. At
Coaldale, Alberta, for example, John Neufeld started blacksmithing with an
anvil and a coal forge in a backyard cow shed. Sharpening ploughshares, shoe-
ing horses, repairing old machinery, and modifying or even manufacturing new
parts and sometimes entirely new machines to meet specific local requirements
kept Neufeld and other blacksmiths busy.

The old blacksmith shops, however, began to lose business once tractors
replaced horses, welding technology replaced older blacksmithing techniques,
and franchised farm machinery dealers replaced itinerant, commissioned machinery salesmen. But blacksmiths and other rural service people often became
franchised machinery dealers and expanded operations. Thus blacksmith John
Neufeld's sons became expert welders and franchise dealers and greatly expanded their father's business. On the fiftieth anniversary of the founding of
the original blacksmith shop, the sons noted that 'these first 50 years have seen
many changes and Neufeld Industries has continued to respond to the changing needs in the community and contribute to the growth of its economic base.'[14]

Small rural businesses generally demanded hard work rather than large capital resources. A simple, industrious, and frugal life-style that did not unduly
offend the social and religious norms of the community, and the quality of the
service offered, determined success or failure. Relations between farmers and
rural service businessmen were not entirely harmonious, especially if credit
was extended. Both parties were none the less members of the same community, and often of the same church.

After the war Canadian factories were converted, frequently with government help, from manufacture of military equipment to production of modern farm machinery, trucks, cars, and durable consumer goods. The availability and the manner in which new farm machinery was sold and serviced greatly affected rural blacksmith shops. Before the war farm machinery was generally sold by commission agents – typically travelling salesmen who earned a commission on whatever they sold. The machines were relatively simple. If they required servicing or repairs the farmer or the local blacksmith or mechanic, not the agent, made them. 'The tractor in 1945,' according to one expert, 'consisted principally of an engine, a simple transmission, some sort of a fixed or swinging drawbar, a set of wheels and a steering wheel, and that was about all.'[15] Manufacturers set up depots in the large urban centres where they stocked replacement parts and also employed a few troubleshooters who could be called in case of serious trouble with an expensive or experimental machine. But the agent rarely accepted any responsibility for service or repair.

In Mennonite communities that attitude by commission salesmen created much ill-will and facilitated a quick and easy transfer of business to local blacksmiths and mechanics as soon as they became sellers of machinery. Mennonite and many other farmers wanted those who sold them the equipment to provide parts and repairs, particularly for new machines with which they were not familiar.

The desired changes came quickly after 1945. The commission agent, 'who had very little in the way of stock or repair parts or service facilities,' and who was rarely interested in taking a used machine in trade when selling a new one, gave way to a franchised dealer, who provided a broader range of services and facilities. Often that dealer was the old blacksmith. After the war he was expected to carry a reasonable line of repair parts and to offer competent mechanical and maintenance service. He was expected also to accept old trade-in machines and to refurbish and then resell them, and, as the cost of new machines increased and manufacturers developed new credit arrangements, the franchised agent was expected to accept major responsibility and much of the risk in the administration of factory-sponsored credit schemes.[16]

The shift from commission agents to independent, franchised farm-machinery dealers had taken place in the United States after the First World War but occurred in Canada only after the Second. Independent, franchised dealers provided much more continuity and stability in the sale and servicing of farm machinery, thanks to their continuous and increasingly institutionalized contacts with the technology, credit, and commercial markets of the outside world.

In the towns and villages where they lived and where they had extended family, congregational, and community contacts, mechanically adept and ambitious young Mennonites quickly set up as franchised dealers of farm machinery. They became an invaluable source of information about new farm technology, and they provided safe but useful business contacts with the outside world. Together with the franchised automobile dealers discussed below, they became conduits of innovative and sometimes revolutionary technological information.

More ambitious dealers could apply their technological and inventive abilities. After the Second World War the larger pieces of modern farm machinery were mass produced in assembly-line factories in eastern Canada or the United States. The machines were designed to serve large markets with diverse requirements. But assembly-line production allowed for few deviations from standard patterns and designs. As a result, many new machines had to be modified and adapted to meet local requirements. That forced many of the local franchised agents, with the help of farmer customers, blacksmiths, and local mechanics, to refit standard machines.

The agricultural implement and machinery industry specialized increasingly after 1945. A few full-line companies came to dominate manufacture of major machines such as tractors and combines.[17] These firms, however, did not supply, manufacture, or modify machines that could harvest specialty crops or cope with unusual conditions. Eventually the industry came to be divided into four groups – full-line, long-line, short-line, and short-short-line companies – depending on the type and range of machines or parts manufactured. In the 1940s rural Mennonite entrepreneurs established short-short-line and short-line farm-machinery companies, producing only a single line of specialized equipment for local markets or doing specific modifications.

Modifications were also necessary if farmers did not convert all their machinery at the same time. Introduction and growing use of gasoline tractors made horses obsolete, but many of the implements used for tillage, seeding, and harvesting had been designed so that farmers would sit on them. When they sat on the tractor all the levers and handles controlling the old horse-drawn implements were beyond their reach unless appropriate modifications were made. Local mechanics, welders, and craftsmen thus found much remunerative work.

The pace of adaptation varied considerably. In Ontario many Mennonite farmers used both horses and tractors and only gradually replaced machines as they wore out. On western Canadian farms change proceeded more rapidly after 1945, due in part to shortages of labour. Tractors, power take-offs, and hydraulics could be applied to older machines only if they were modified.

There were other needs as well. In southern Manitoba specialized harvesting equipment was required to harvest sunflower seeds, and manufacture of attachments or modifications for combines designed for grain harvesting became a profitable venture for George Janzen of Reinfeld. Janzen's Big J. Industries conducted experiments that allowed him not only to serve local farmers but also to develop a considerable export market.[18]

The Monarch Machine Company of Winnipeg, later Monarch Industries, was founded by John J. Klassen in 1935 to manufacture feed mills but eventually manufactured pumps for flood-prone regions of rural Manitoba. During the war, Monarch obtained lucrative contracts to build bilge and marine pumps for the Canadian navy. After the war the firm expanded into specialized manufacturing ventures.[19]

Franchised dealerships in rural Canada were not restricted to major farm machinery. C.A. DeFehr, selling cutlery and hardware in the farming districts of southern Manitoba, obtained an exclusive franchise to sell the imported Standard Import Cream Separator, which proved superior to those already available and launched DeFehr's exceptionally successful career.[20] His move was typical of what happened to small rural businessmen across Canada. In his case, however, an exclusive import contract rather direct franchising got him started.

Villagers operating general stores also had to adapt to new conditions. The early stores depended for supplies on jobbers and wholesalers in Toronto, Winnipeg, or Vancouver. Most stock was purchased from travelling agents, and the stores simply marked up whatever price they were charged. In most villages, and even in some larger towns, they faced little direct competition.

The great bane of early operators, and of most other rural Mennonite businessmen in the 1940s, was sale on credit. Farmers do not have regular income, and most need credit during the months before they receive payment for harvested crops. Banks and other rural credit institutions seemed unwilling to provide credit, but general store owners, farm machinery dealers, and all other rural business operators sustained heavy losses when selling on credit. Many rural businessmen accordingly supported establishment of local Mennonite credit unions and credit facilities extended by machinery manufacturers.

Loblaws, an eastern Canadian grocery chain, was the first to adopt a cash-only basis – an example quickly followed by others. Some of the Canadian Mennonite general stores that went cash only were those owned and operated by the Schellenbergs[21] in Osler and other small Saskatchewan Valley towns. They did so after a visit to the Loblaws stores in the east. Most owners found it difficult to wean customers from old practices, but those who did almost invariably increased their returns. The Schellenbergs in Hague and Saskatoon, for example, expanded into the large O.K. Economy chain.[22] The Schellenbergs also pioneered in other ways. They found the service offered by salesmen and jobbers unsatisfactory and began to buy in bulk directly from the larger wholesalers or manufacturers. They set up their own grocery wholesale business, which proved more profitable than the retail stores and remained in their hands even after they sold O.K. Economy stores to Loblaws.

Other Mennonite grocery stores near large wholesaling centres found that reliable trucking assured them of fresh goods. Zehr's grocery store chain in Waterloo county, for example, built up its business through sound connections with Toronto and Montreal, while in Manitoba the Reimer trucking company was similarly reliable. Availability of fresh goods linked small stores with the larger wholesale and transportation companies.

The successful grocery and general stores followed the example of the larger chains, again led in Canada by Loblaws, by allowing customers to serve themselves rather than storing goods on shelves behind a counter. Home delivery of groceries for shut-ins and others also spurred growth of Zehr's stores in Kitchener-Waterloo[23] and was tried with apparently less dramatic results by other Mennonite-owned stores. Even village store owners delivered some groceries.

A final innovation was introduction of profit sharing. Initially such plans involved mainly the managers of individual stores or branches of a particular business, but it soon became apparent that there were advantages to bringing in other employees as well. Most such plans, however, left control firmly in the hands of the founder and his family, who were not eager to divulge all aspects of their business or to share decision making with employees. As a result, profit sharing needed frequent clarification and modification, but giving hired managers and employees a direct stake in a venture was accepted as good business practice and introduced many more people to the fundamentals of business administration.

The Schellenbergs and the Zehrs, both of whom eventually sold out to Loblaws, had counterparts in all the Mennonite communities. Service, hard work, and competitive prices were stressed again and again in the recollections and histories of these businesses, but these stores were also in the forefront of closer economic integration with the business world. They broadened the economic horizons of owners, operators, and consumers.

Operators of groceries and general stores, like the franchised dealers and short-short-line farm-machinery manufacturers, still had their roots in the villages or larger rural centres. They still controlled their own work environment, where hard work, integrity, honesty, and intelligence were more important than large capital investments. Henry Nikkel of Coaldale adopted a typical approach when he chose as a slogan: 'The Store on the Corner that Deals on the Square.'[24] William DeFehr, on the fiftieth anniversary of his family's business, said: 'Honest, hard toil does pay off in the long run. Laying ground-work in business takes time, no instant success. Integrity and fair play have combined to establish a business fairly well insulated against the ups and downs of the economy.'[25]

When John Klassen of Monarch Industries died it was noted that early in his career he had spent a large part of most days working with his employees in the shop. When times were difficult he allegedly paid himself only two dollars per week while his best workers got four dollars. His success was attributed to 'that kind of frugality, combined with integrity and hard work, that enabled him to transform his small operation into a major manufacturing firm by the late 1940s.'[26] Employees were treated more as members of a community, rather than as mere hirelings. C.T. Loewen, founder of the Loewen Millworks in Steinbach, provided time and a place where employees could worship, at company expense, some fifteen to twenty minutes one morning each week.[27]

Attempts to run rural services in ways that retained aspects of rural life on family farms facilitated the transition from farm life to paid employment, but employers also retained and sometimes increased less attractive aspects of rural life. Most rural service businesses were labour intensive, and while Mennonite employers might be concerned about the motivation and spiritual welfare of their employees, they rarely had any sympathy with labour unions or collective bargaining of any kind. They were the bosses, rewarding employees according to what they believed was fair and equitable, much as the head of a farm family expected every member to contribute to the success of the farm and then to be rewarded as the head of the household saw fit. Employees were expected to think first and foremost of the business and, beyond that, to trust the goodwill and generosity of their employer. Adversarial relations, owners believed, would destroy the sense of common endeavour.

There were probably practical limits to the exploitation to which Mennonite employers in small businesses could subject their workers, but concepts of employees' rights, and particularly any right to disrupt work, were vehemently rejected. Wages in the smaller towns were generally lower than those paid for comparable work in the city, but some Mennonite employers building up their businesses paid very meagre wages.

Mennonite employers expected that in times of difficulty they and their staff alike would make sacrifices, but most were not nearly as keen about sharing benefits when times were good. And in the matter of hiring and firing workers, with or without good cause, employers insisted on virtually unfettered authority. As a result, in a religious denomination that preached egalitarian doctrines of the 'priesthood of all believers,' workplace relations were certainly not equal. Thus, while employers introduced new technologies and created jobs, they also contributed to changes in power relations that were typical of modern industrialized societies.

The small rural businessmen and franchised dealers, like the farmers whom they served, depended on hard work, honesty, integrity, and fair play, rather than on large capital resources or exploitation of a large labour force. They were not capitalists in a Marxist 'class' sense and almost never thought of themselves in terms of 'class.' If they had any abiding ideology, it was a strong commitment to conducting their affairs as they saw fit, to hard work, and to reliance on the quality and integrity of everyone involved in their businesses. While behaving in ways that Marx argued were typical of the petite bourgeoisie, they thought of themselves as productive members of their communities rather than as members of any economic class. They were small, independent, rural, service-oriented operators.

THE AUTOMOTIVE INDUSTRY

Numerous new business opportunities arose or expanded dramatically in the years following the Second World War, but the automotive industry proved exceptionally attractive and profitable for Mennonites. Small rural businessmen in Mennonite communities had become involved in the sale and servicing of automobiles long before 1939. Initially they did so as a service to their own people, in much the same way that they sold and serviced farm machinery. During the war automobile sales languished as manufacturers turned to military production, while rationing of fuel, tires, and parts severely limited civilian driving. After the war, factories were converted to produce cars, trucks, and other consumer goods.

Mennonite businessmen found easy entry into the selling and servicing of cars and trucks. In the 1960s they also began to modify or adapt cars, trucks, and vans in ways comparable to the short-short-line agricultural-implement business.

Automobiles, like farm machinery, had been sold mainly by commission agents. After 1945, cars and trucks were sold principally by franchised dealerships, in which the values that particularly appealed to small, independent operators still prevailed. But, as one American writer complained, 'the car changed our dress, manners, social customs, vacation habits, the shape of our cities, consumer purchasing patterns, common tastes, and positions in intercourse.'[28] Armin Wiebe, in a novel written in southern Manitoba Mennonite idiom, reveals cultural practices that became possible only after young people gained use of their parents' cars:

The Dairy Dell is the place where everybody goes in the summer time after anything is over and there is always somebody there that knows you and will come to talk you on, for sure if you have a woman along. I mean it's always that way on Sunday nights if you are lucky enough or brave enough when you are driving through all the darps or up and down the main street to hold still by some girls that are walking the road along and you find enough nerve to talk them on in a nice way and sometimes you get full of luck and they will get in the car and you can go driving the sunflower fields through on the middle roads but you always go to the Dairy Dell before the night is over. And at the Dairy Dell all those that didn't pick up some girls crowd the cars around where the girls are in.[29]

A Canadian historian has suggested that after 1945 Canadians regarded CAR (capitals are his) as if it were a new god: 'CAR threatened to turn us all into nomads, and his wheels, like Juggernaut, levelled every physical and psychical obstacle they met. They invaded every urban open space and threatened to destroy every blade of urban grass. They knocked down houses. They called imperiously for straight, wide roads to be carved out of our diminishing fertile fields. They tore up our precious peach orchards and ordained that factories for making new parts of CAR should be erected in their place.'[30]

Next to television, the automobile probably did more to break down the isolation of rural communities than any other modern invention. Canadian Mennonites wanted separation from the influences of the outside world, but most embraced the automobile with remarkable enthusiasm, though there were some sceptics.

During and immediately after the war there were severe shortages of cars and trucks, but production increased steadily, and after 1950 millions of new cars rolled off factory assembly lines each year, and some Canadian Mennonites particularly enjoyed selling, trading, and servicing cars. Competitive, franchised dealerships sprang up like mushrooms in most Mennonite communities, and in the big cities some of the largest dealerships carried ethnic Mennonite names.

This suggests that a distinctive milieu had developed in rural Mennonite towns and villages, and among their aspiring businessmen, which proved responsive to the challenges and opportunities of franchised car dealerships. The local dealerships were pre-eminently institutions of vigorous, small, independent operators. They offered sales, service, trade-in allowances, and factory-sponsored credit, but salesmen, who received most of their remuneration on the basis of the number of sales finalized, were the heart of the dealerships. In an age of prosperity, car dealerships became a veritable petty bourgeois heaven. Ability, effort, and integrity brought rewards. As well, franchised car dealers enjoyed far more security than most farmers, thanks to contractual agreements with both manufacturers and consumers, but retained their independence and their influence within the system.[31]

Automobile dealerships and garages had an enormous impact on almost all the larger Mennonite towns and villages. In Altona, for example, A.B. Klassen began to sell Meteors and Mercurys in the late 1940s but changed to Studebakers a few years later. J.J. Bueckert opened Bueckert Motors in 1952, and A.J. Thiessen relocated his Chrysler dealership from Rosenfeld to Altona a few years later. Numerous garages and service stations, among them E.J. Braun's Service, George P. Wiebe's Imperial Service, P.H. Dyck's Esso Drive-In, Henry Friesen's Royalite Service, and the Tri-lite Garage were opened to meet growing need.[32] All this in a town that had a 1946 population of only 1,065.

Steinbach, Manitoba, earned a reputation for offering the best car deals in the province. J.R. Friesen had become the first Ford dealer in western Canada in 1914. His enthusiasm resulted in threats that he would be excommunicated from the Kleine Gemeinde, but reconciliation came within a year, after several ministers bought cars themselves.[33] Friesen apparently offered them particularly attractive deals.

After 1945, the major car manufacturers introduced volume selling: the aim was to reach a 'target point' in sales, which for most firms was 500 vehicles per year. At that point, the dealer received a substantial bonus. In anticipation Steinbach car dealers offered higher trade-in allowances and sold both new and used cars at lower prices.[34]

The success of some Steinbach dealers lay also in unconventional sales techniques. Dodge dealer A.D. Penner, for example, invited prospective customers home for dinner. 'After a hefty meal we were usually able to close the deal without arguing about price cuts,' he said. On other occasions Mrs Penner agreed to milk a customer's cows while A.D. was demonstrating a car to the animal's owners.[35] Other promotional ventures included the 'Automobile Extravaganza' of October 1960, in which people came all the way from Alberta to buy a car and in return had their hotel, restaurant, and transportation bills paid. The pitches paid off. In 1955 two Steinbach men won awards for being among Canada's top salesmen, and Elvin Fast, then working for Friesen, averaged 250 sales a year in 1952, 1953, and 1954.[36]

Mennonite businessmen also did well in the late 1940s in another part of the automotive industry – repair, operation, and modification of trucks and buses. The earliest Mennonite ventures into trucking were related to rural service requirements. A.J. Thiessen, for example, collected dairy and poultry products in the rural communities and then sold them door to door in the larger towns and in Winnipeg. For that he needed a reliable truck that could also haul other things as space and time permitted. Later he established a general store and hatchery in Rosenfeld but found transportation unsatisfactory. So he purchased additional vehicles, hauled his own supplies and, when opportunity offered, supplies needed by others from Winnipeg to Rosenfeld and other southern Manitoba villages. This initiative generated return freight for the trucks, which took eggs, milk, butter, and cheese into the capital. Thiessen also established a Chrysler dealership to get the best possible price for new trucks and, of course, to sell cars and trucks to others.

Immediately after the war, Thiessen saw possibilities in repair and operation of passenger buses. In the 1950s, his interests shifted to manufacture and operation of specially modified trucks used as sanitation service vehicles.[37]

Don Reimer, another southern Manitoban, became involved in trucking as an adjunct to the family's general store, this time in Steinbach. The store was operated by Don's father, who often purchased supplies, including food, in bulk. He needed to move perishables quickly and efficiently. Less than satisfactory service by the railways and other transportation companies prompted the Reimers to do their own hauling. Much of the produce came from the United States, entering Canada at Windsor, whence it had to be hauled to other Canadian points. Don Reimer, then only 18 years old, decided to start his own trucking company and provide regular service between Windsor and Winnipeg. He was helped greatly by a national rail strike in 1950, which, in his own words, 'made a lot of people rethink their transportation requirements. It was with that impetus that we began our transportation business from Winnipeg, Manitoba, to Windsor, Ontario.'[38]

Huge public expenditures resulting in improvements on major highways, including the Trans-Canada, a small portion of which at Montreal River had been built by conscientious objectors, further expedited growth of the trucking industry. But even after Reimer's company had become one of the largest transportation outfits in Canada, he credited most of his success to honesty, diligence, and integrity. The company's slogan – 'On Time or It's Free' – reflected a marketing strategy rooted in the small-town grocery-store owner's frustrations. It assumed that every employee would do everything possible to meet the promise of reliability. Reimer, like many other small Mennonite businessmen of the late 1940s and the 1950s, tried to perpetuate traditional family and community relationships in his dealings with employees: 'We may have the means to buy the best equipment there is but that is far less important than that we have good people. A good driver in a poorly manufactured truck is a better combination than a poor driver in the most expensive rig.'[39] He added: 'We hire as skilfully as we know and select people as appropriately as we can. After that there's a great responsibility on us to try to minister to them, nurture them, build them up and do everything we can to make them more successful people ... We have two full-time chaplains ... We believe the total health of the employee is important, physically as well as spiritually and emotionally. We do as much as we can to make sure an employee is a successful employee in every sense of the word.'[40]

Key factors in the success of truck and bus operations were careful handling, reliability, and punctuality. It was never easy to provide that kind of service. Good and reliable employees, keen to provide first-class service and meet tight schedules, particularly for time-sensitive shipments, certainly helped. Immediately after the war, however, there was a serious shortage of reliable vehicles. Manufacturers had concentrated on production of urgently needed military vehicles during the war, and after 1945 manufacture of automobiles was given priority. There were, however, thousands of military vehicles, or parts for them, that, with suitable alterations, could serve civilian trucking and passenger transportation.[41] As a result, at least during the 1940s, trucking required skills similar to those of short-short-line farm-machinery manufacturers. Mechanics, welders, and shop workers were as important as drivers and handlers.

In the early days of trucking and busing, as in the franchised automobile dealerships, large sums of investment capital were not required. Skilled labour, reliable and punctual service, hard work, and a dedicated staff, all in an era of general prosperity, allowed Mennonite entrepreneurs to establish themselves in business. In the 1940s such businesses were small, but they became a basis for phenomenal expansion later.

URBAN HOUSE CONSTRUCTION

In the decades after the Second World War many Canadians dreamed of a car and a bungalow in the suburbs. Mennonite businessmen sold many a dream car, and perhaps also some mechanical nightmares. They also built thousands of bungalows in the suburbs to house their own families and those of fellow Canadians. Government housing policies, moreover, were exceptionally well suited to the business interests, aspirations, and methods of Mennonite builders.

Housing had become a great problem in Canada. Few new units had been built during the Depression, so Canada entered the war with a serious shortage, which was further aggravated by curtailment of civilian building during the war.[42]

The shape and structure of postwar housing construction were determined by two federal initiatives – a National Housing Act and the Central Mortgage and Housing Corporation. These programs originated in pre-war efforts to promote building of houses. In 1935 Ottawa had created a special mortgage fund that made credit available for improvement of existing housing or construction of new homes on easier terms than those offered by financial institutions, which, it was thought, responded much too cautiously to the problems of the Depression. Interest rates were lowered, amortization periods lengthened, and higher loan-to-value ratios authorized. The key feature, however, was a government guarantee 'which eliminated all risk of capital and interest loss on funds advanced by institutions.'[43] This legislation was enlarged and modified in 1938, making possible construction of approximately $100 million worth of residential housing before wartime priorities made the program inoperative.

The return of thousands of demobilized soldiers, growing and strong civilian demand for housing, and the unpopularity of rigid wartime rent controls created a crisis immediately after the war. In response to public demand, and in an effort to prevent massive unemployment, Parliament in 1944 passed An Act to Promote the Construction of New Houses, the Repair and Modernization of Existing Houses, the Improvement of Housing and Living Conditions, and the Expansion of Employment in the Postwar Period.[44] Again, as in 1935 and 1938, the objective was to provide guaranteed loans or mortgages for individuals who wished to build or repair housing for themselves. The money went to the prospective homeowner, not to large private developers or construction firms. That gave the individual the power to determine, subject to federal guidelines and local building codes, how his or her new or used house should be built or repaired, and by whom. The National Housing Act, 1944, provided for loans for up to 95 per cent of the first $2,000 needed for repair or construction, 85 per cent of the next $2,000, and 70 per cent on approved sums in excess of $4,000. Interest rates were set at 4 1/2 per cent, and loans were amortized over twenty years.[45]

In English Canada the privately owned, single, detached, urban family dwelling became the mainstay. Very little funding was provided for low-cost rental accommodation, except in Quebec, where different social policies and priorities prevailed.[46] The objective of federal housing policies was, in the words of one critic, to transform Canada from 'a nation of tenants to a nation of homeowners, with the exception of Quebec.' This, he notes, 'was a fundamental revolution in our living patterns and a tremendous stimulus to the development of our national economy.'[47] The National Housing Act, 1944, became the most important instrument in implementation of that objective.[48]

Administration of the policy was entrusted to the Central Mortgage and Housing Corporation (CMHC) in 1945, and until the mid-1960s politicians and CMHC administrators alike 'devoted much of their formal speechmaking and laudatory pronouncements to the encouragement of the house-building industry in its efforts to provide hundreds of thousands of homes for sale during the years 1946–1959. Every effort was made to provide adequate supplies of mortgage money, to manipulate interest rates, and to set forth appropriate terms to encourage individual home ownership.'[49]

A privately owned, detached dwelling made the city relatively amenable to Mennonites. Like a privately owned quarter-section homestead, it allowed some independence to those hoping to maintain a degree of separation from the rest of society. It was its owner's castle, which could be defended against unwelcome, worldly intrusions. Mennonites living in their own houses, communicating mainly with Mennonite friends and relatives, working in Mennonite-owned businesses, and worshipping in urban Mennonite churches where German was still used could, if they chose, remain as separated from 'the world' as their rural cousins.

Postwar housing policies nevertheless opened up business opportunities. The way in which CMHC made guaranteed funding available seemed tailor-made for individuals who lacked capital but were willing to work hard to acquire housing. Prospective homeowners providing their own labour could usually get a mortgage to cover all land and material costs for a modest dwelling. If they had a job, they could build the house during the hours not spent on the job. Individuals who began simply by putting up a house for their own family sometimes helped friends and relatives or others willing to use their services. Materials salvaged from abandoned or obsolete military camps and facilities, or other derelict buildings, sometimes had to suffice. Financing was made possible by the CMHC.

Once rudimentary accommodation for their own families had been provided, emerging Mennonite builders could sell the house just completed and use the capital thus raised to acquire another derelict house or a new place to repair or build again. In many cases the family had to make do for years in houses in various stages of construction. Such builders rarely invested large amounts of their own money. Several of those early builders also acknowledge that they were greatly helped by the almost complete absence of any effectively enforced building codes or standards. Canada was desperately in need of housing. Ottawa provided basic funding for prospective homeowners and builders. Inspection and enforcement of housing codes and standards, beyond the general standards of the CMHC, were responsibilities of municipal or provincial governments, which did not establish effective standards until the late 1950s. A statement by Alberta's minister of economic affairs in 1945 is indicative: 'There is only one solution to the national housing crisis, and that is a national housing programme free from bureaucracy, red tape, regulation and State interference at every turn.'[50]

In other countries inadequate technical expertise, lack of funds, or development and zoning policies formulated by or for the benefit of large developers kept new and undercapitalized entrants out of house construction. In the late 1940s Canadian government action removed or significantly lowered all such barriers.

Successful builders soon moved beyond the limited operations described above. Once they had sufficient capital and experience, they could hire additional workmen, particularly skilled tradesmen, and achieve economies of scale by constructing several houses at the same time. The more ambitious employed thousands of Mennonite immigrants who came to Canada from Europe in the late 1940s and in the 1950s. Many of these newcomers did not know enough English, or were not sufficiently familiar with Canadian practices, to enter other employment and thus became a pool of reliable and inexpensive labour. In addition, many of the men returning from alternative service, as well as others no longer needed on family farms, had valuable practical skills.

A host of small construction companies involving Mennonite builders, mostly unincorporated, were established in the late 1940s and early 1950s in all the major cities west of Toronto. A few subsequently became very large and wealthy, but initially the typical venture was a small family or extended-family operation which sought to replicate in an urban setting many of the values and characteristics of rural and agricultural communities. Working for some of these builders was more like being involved in a joint family-community project than a typical employer-employee relationship.

The industry also fostered creation or expansion of small businesses that operated as subcontractors or suppliers. Lumber yards were, of course, nothing new; nor was manufacture of furniture or special housing supplies such as windows and doors.[51] Plumbers and electricians were needed on all housing projects, and subcontracting became popular. The sale and servicing of household appliances offered other opportunities, particularly in the 1950s, for those without much money who wanted to establish their own businesses.

PROFESSIONS AND PUBLIC SERVICE

There was also a significant increase in the number of Canadian Mennonites who entered the professions or government service after the war. A 1989 study indicates that 28 per cent of all Mennonites in North America, and more than 40 per cent of those living in urban centres, were active in one of the professions.[52] That has caused sociologist Leo Driedger to refer to the rapid professionalization of Canadian Mennonites after 1945 as an urban professional revolution.[53]

Before 1939 only two professions – teaching and health care – had been regarded as appropriate for those unable or unwilling to become farmers. Good teachers, either in their own separate schools or in public schools attended by Mennonites, were needed in all communities, and the first two Canadian Mennonite private high schools were established primarily to train young people who would become teachers. The status of a teacher, however, varied considerably. In some Mennonite communities such a career was thought appropriate only for the weak and the sickly, and when a small, scrawny baby boy was born it was not uncommon to surmise that he might not be good for anything but teaching.[54] In other communities teachers were accorded considerable respect, but rarely generous salaries. Teaching nevertheless was a necessary and appreciated profession, which those so inclined had been encouraged to enter. Since most teachers in Mennonite communities had received at least some training in the outside world, they became intermediaries from that realm. Improved educational opportunities, and huge increases in government expenditures on schools, made teaching increasingly attractive following 1945.

Health care in the traditional Mennonite communities had always been a curious mix of professional and folk medicine. The eagerness with which some communities organized mutual aid hospital and medical plans was indicative of the importance attached to good medical care, but most communities also had their own bonesetter or chiropractor and many relied on midwives and home cures for the care of women in childbirth. Spirits of nitre and *Alpenkreuter*, both alleged wonder drugs good for any ailment, still jostled for space with more modern medicines in many Mennonite medicine cupboards, but there was growing realization that serious illnesses required more professional care.[55]

First World War experiences by Mennonites who had served on Russian ambulance or Red Cross trains and in veterans' hospitals greatly increased interest in medicine, and a medical or nursing career was accepted and valued in most pre-1939 communities. Alternative and voluntary service in Canadian hospitals and insane asylums further broadened interest in the health-care professions.

After 1945 better education and more advanced professional training, together with rapidly growing demand for professional services, fostered at least in part by the emerging social welfare system, encouraged many more young Mennonites to enter the favoured professions as well as many new ones. Those entering the teaching, caring, or supporting professions generally encountered less resistance from their elders and had less difficulty in reconciling their religious principles with the demands of their professional work than was the case for those entering what might be broadly called the more adversarial professions. Lawyers, for example, had greater difficulty than social workers.[56] The adversarial nature of the legal system seemed to threaten collective community or congregational values.

Professionals operated in the larger Canadian society, usually lived in cities or larger towns, and were generally much more open to new and different ideas and influences than their rural and agricultural cousins. In many of their values, however, farmers and professionals were in substantial agreement. Most professionals, like most farmers, lived in an environment in which hard work, integrity, order, stability, and fairness were highly valued.[57]

CONCLUSION

Thousands of Canada's Mennonites were not able to find satisfactory employment and careers in their rural, agricultural enclaves. Many found more attractive possibilities after the war and achieved greater prosperity than ever. They certainly helped to build the Canadian economy, but the fundamental factors that made the nation prosperous were beyond their control. They, like other Canadians, benefited from buoyant world markets for resources and services and from reconstruction. Together with their fellow citizens, and with the encouragement and guidance of their governments, they figuratively beat swords into ploughshares.[58]

In practice, however, the old military and agricultural images were no longer appropriate. After 1945 Canadians transformed their munitions, airplanes, naval vessels, tanks, and guns into houses, automobiles, durable consumer goods, improved health care, and educational and social services. Mennonites participated enthusiastically and gained significantly from that transformation. That same process, however, took the majority out of their rural and agricultural communities and placed them in the larger towns and cities of the country.

8
Lure of the Cities

In 1956 American sociologist J. Winfield Fretz warned: 'Where Mennonites have gone to the cities, the solidarity of the communities has been shattered ... Mennonites moving to the cities have in large numbers lost their identity as Mennonites.'[1] In the 1960s, however, Fretz became founding president of Conrad Grabel College, a Mennonite liberal arts college affiliated with the University of Waterloo. He had discovered that Canadian Mennonites moving to the cities had not lost their identity and that the urban Mennonite experience in Canada differed significantly from that in the United States.[2] Some aspects of traditional life were lost, but others were not only retained but strengthened.[3] The migration to the city was nevertheless difficult and fraught with controversy.

PERCEIVED DANGER

In November 1942 Jacob G. Thiessen, the Mennonite Brethren (MB) city missionary in Vancouver, submitted a report to the MB churches of British Columbia:

I joyfully note that the number of working girls has decreased. But I regret the influx of young men, and many families, attracted by available jobs in shipyards, sawmills, etc. It is not beneficial for our people. City atmosphere is hazardous for our young men and family fathers who, attracted by greater earnings, settle down in the city and gamble with the future of their children ... In closing, allow me to express the concern of my heart: May the hour soon come when none of our people can be found in Vancouver, or any other large city, except for a few missionary companions. I become anxious at the thought of a Mennonite 'proletariate' in the city. May the Lord guide us back into a quiet country life and help us to serve Him in Christian simplicity.[4]

Thiessen and others feared not only loss of a Mennonite identity but that those moving to the city would succumb to the pressure to accept and do many things that were regarded as 'worldly' and sinful in traditional Mennonite communities and churches. It seemed to be getting more and more difficult to keep 'worldly' things out of rural churches, but things were allegedly much worse in the cities. Some of the supposed urban dangers seem, at least in retrospect, petty, if not downright silly. In 1954, for example, John Hess, the popular young associate pastor at First Mennonite in Kitchener, received a sternly worded letter:

The true prophets of the Lord in Bible times were *never* popular, and I dare say if a preacher (or layman too) takes an out and out stand for God today against sin and worldliness, the sport craze, fads & fashions, personal ornamentation, corsages, flowers in church assemblies, jewellery and artificial ornamentation, he won't be very popular either ... I wonder how pleased God is with us when we have so much trash in his sanctuary. We are departing fast from the simple worship of our blessed God ... I shall continue to pray that you will help to bring about a change for the better instead of allowing more worldliness.[5]

There was cause for concern. Some of those who had gone to the city had renounced their religious heritage. The Schellenbergs in Saskatoon, for example, became patriotic zealots during the war, decidedly hostile toward employees who attended German Mennonite church services.[6] Like some others, they anglicized their name, to Shelly. They had renounced their religious and ethnic heritage. Rudy Wiebe, in his novel *The Blue Mountains of China*, tells the story of a fictional Mennonite land speculator and car salesman named Dennis Willms who changed his surname to Williams.[7] The Lehn family became Lane, a few Schmidts became Smiths, and a Janz was legally transformed into a Jones, giving unique meaning to the desire of some Mennonites to keep up with the Joneses.

A few Mennonite students had gone to urban universities, usually to prepare for a career in teaching or health care. Some had allegedly lost their faith. Such losses confirmed fears that cities were dangerous places in which traditional, plain, simple, frugal, and temperate life-styles, separate from the rest of the world, seemed inappropriate. Many of the concerns, however, were based on ill-informed suspicions and were often expressed in simplistic and unsophisticated language.

Theologians, sociologists, and other social scientists who have studied urbanization have provided more scholarly analyses of what happened when people moved to the cities.[8] Urbanization, they have suggested, was part of fundamental societal changes closely linked to the often-misused word 'modernization.'[9] 'Modernization' refers to the massive changes made possible by new technology, which transformed 'the social arrangements and collective consciousness of an entire society over time ... [It] consists of new social patterns which are produced by technologically induced growth.'[10] Technology, as noted in the previous chapter, also transformed rural life, but it was in the cities that its effects were most obvious.

Sociologists have identified three facets of modernity. The first is differentiation, or specialization. People, organizations, and institutions concentrate on work that they, with their specialized knowledge and understanding of a particular technology, can do best and depend on others for goods and services that they themselves cannot produce or provide economically and efficiently. Henry Ford's assembly-line automobile factories, where each worker had a specialized task, became an example of efficient, modern economic and social organization. Traditional societies, it is argued, cohere around commonalities, while modern societies are characterized by differences.[11]

In rural and traditional Mennonite communities people followed basically the same life-style and shared common values, interests, and concerns, but the glue that had held them together seemed to be missing in modern, urban societies. In the cities, a new, different, and potentially dangerous substance held societies together. It was called 'rationalization' and involved secular attempts to control, plan, 'strategize,' predict, and calculate the probable consequences of particular policies, priorities, and activities. Rationalization was based on the assumption that human beings, with their intelligence and with the appropriate technology, could create and maintain civilized communities and a modern, prosperous, and good society. It seemed to reduce sharply the place and role of those forms of Christian discipleship that might be regarded as inefficient or 'irrational,' and it left little room for reliance on miraculous or divine guidance and intervention. Rationalization implied that human beings, with the help of new technologies, could control what previous generations had left in the hands of God, fate, or charity. It seemed contrary to traditional Mennonite attitudes of *Gelassenheit* and discipleship – of trusting abandonment and yielding to the will of God and of unconditional obedience to his Word, regardless of consequences. Where is the place of faith in a modern world where people try 'by whatever ways and through all possible means ... to take charge of things and control their environments, tossing aside any residual traces of fatalism'?[12]

Mennonites, particularly in times of persecution and suffering, had accepted a Christian form of fatalism comparable to the acceptance of military discipline memorialized by Alfred, Lord Tennyson, in his verses on the charge of the Light Brigade at Balaclava during the Crimean War: 'Theirs not to reason why, / Theirs but to do and die; / Into the valley of Death / Rode the six hundred.' In the end God will set all things right. In the meantime the Christian's responsibility rests in faithful discipleship, which semed out of step with modern urban society. 'The transition from traditional to modern ways,' scholars tell us, 'is ultimately a shift from fate to choice, from destiny to decision.'[13] When the Berlin refugees and MCC officials talked of the miraculous rescue in 1947 they tried to restore a faith that they feared was being lost. In the cities, however, people were more likely to demand what a prominent member of the Mennonite church in Hamburg, Germany, asked after Peter Dyck had told the story of the Berlin rescue. She demanded, rather loudly: 'Now tell us what really happened.'

A third characteristic of modernity is individualization. People specialize and make their best contribution to society if they exercise their talents and abilities in a rational manner. They must be willing to go where their knowledge, experience, and abilities are needed. The predictability of modern social, economic, and political life is likely to be upset if people, as individuals, do not behave in a rational, self-interested way. Modernization, it has been argued, 'unhooks individuals from the confining grip of custom and kin, and champions free-spirited individualism. In non-modern societies individual behaviour – regulated by religion, tribe, and village – must yield to collective goals ... Specialization, mobility, and technology in the modern world unravel the structural ties that knot the individual into long term relationships with permanent groups.'[14]

Individualization seemed to threaten Mennonite commitments to collective concepts of family and of congregational and community life. It changed what many thought were desirable and God-pleasing personal characteristics: 'Self-denial, humility, obedience, meekness, lowliness, and forbearance were the esteemed virtues of the Mennonite personality ... Modern culture championed individual achievement, personal fulfilment, self-esteem, and individual rights above virtually all other values ... Moderns wanted to take charge of things, control outcomes, assert rights, and prevent injustice – not wilt in the face of threat.'[15]

Canadian Mennonites were not, of course, aware of all these and other differences between traditional rural and modern urban societies when they moved, usually individually but in rapidly growing numbers, to the cities. But some perceptive and concerned leaders realized that the move would lead to redefinitions of Mennonite articles of faith and to modifications of their way of life.[16]

Eight major Canadian metropolitan centres had, by 1971, attracted more than 50,000 Mennonites. There were ten times as many urban Mennonites in 1971 as there had been in 1941, while the Mennonite population in Winnipeg had increased almost fourteenfold (see Table 8.1).[17]

Table 8.1
Mennonite population in Canadian metropolitan
centres with more than 100,000 people, 1941–91

	1941	1951	1961	1971	1981	1991
Winnipeg	1,285	3,460	13,595	17,850	19,190	21,900
Kitchener/						
Waterloo	1,472	1,646	4,480	5,235	9,760	10,645
Vancouver	559	1,624	5,260	8,880	9,515	12,505
St Catharines	200	510	2,515	5,955	5,985	6,525
Saskatoon	871	1,663	4,765	5,697	5,380	10,665
Calgary	91	233	1,220	2,650	3,635	3,735
Toronto	326	267	1,375	2,540	2,950	2,585
Edmonton	29	85	455	1,590	1,920	2,145
Montreal	54	65	140	580	750	1,015
Regina	87	90	240	520	685	1,125
London	13	45	115	645	485	630
Hamilton	41	66	250	425	420	745
Victoria	10	14	45	145	320	405
Ottawa/Hull	12	28	60	230	285	565
Windsor	62	49	85	210	–	165
Sudbury	13	7	55	160	–	210
Thunder Bay	22	13	34	70	–	95
Halifax	–	1	7	40	–	180
Quebec	–	–	–	20	–	70
St John's	–	–	9	10	–	10
Saint John	–	16	1	5	–	–
Oshawa	–	–	–	–	–	80
Chicoutimi	–	–	–	5	–	–
Trois-Rivières	–	–	–	–	–	–
Sherbrooke	–	–	–	–	–	15
Total	5,147	9,888	34,706	53,462	61,195	

Source: Based on Leo Driedger, 'Post-War Canadian Mennonite: From Rural to Urban
Dominance,' Journal of Mennonite Studies, 6 (1988), 70–88. Where there were fewer than 200
Mennonites in a metropolitan centre in 1981, they were grouped together with 'Other
Protestants.'

URBAN BEGINNINGS

The urban experience of Canadian Mennonites before 1940 was decidedly
mixed. When, apparently in 1811, Benjamin Eby built the original log building that served as both a school and a place of worship in Waterloo county,
the church served a rural community.[18] But soon thereafter Ebytown, renamed Berlin and later Kitchener, became a flourishing trade and market

centre. The city in effect came to the agricultural Mennonite community in Waterloo county. Elsewhere larger service towns also brought urban influences into rural settlements.

The earliest encounters of Canadian Mennonites with the cities were often restricted to basic economic activities. In the nineteenth century, however, some Ontario Mennonites chose to go to the cities to do mission work among the poor, and by 1900 they had five mission programs in Kitchener-Waterloo, Toronto, and St Catharines.[19] These early missions by the Swiss Mennonites usually responded to specific needs and did not necessarily result in establishment of a permanent church or mission program. More Mennonite city missions were set up early in the twentieth century, and a few of those evolved into local churches. Membership growth, however, was slow, and after fifty years the (Old) Mennonite mission in Toronto, which had been founded in 1907 and later became the Danforth Mennonite Church, had only twenty-five members.[20]

In the 1930s the (Old) Mennonite Church, the Amish Mennonite Conference, the Conference of Mennonites in Canada (CMC), and the Mennonite Brethren (MBs) all launched mission programs in one or more cities. They served the needs of the homeless, the poor, and those afflicted with alcoholism and other health problems endemic to urban slums in Toronto, London, Winnipeg, Calgary, and Vancouver. During the war years these missions faced serious difficulties, and the Mennonite Board of Missions and Charities (MBMC) reported in 1946: 'The war years have been fraught with difficulties for our city workers. Economic prosperity and the unpopularity of our position on war have perhaps been factors that have militated against a normal development of our city churches during the recent past.'[21]

A unique project was begun in Kitchener-Waterloo in the late 1930s. A Polish Jew named Joseph Cramer had been converted to Christianity and wanted to provide what became known as a 'House of Friendship,' where homeless men could obtain food, shelter, and counselling. Food hampers were also to be distributed to needy people in the city. Cramer was able to secure the enthusiastic support of C.F. Derstine, the dynamic and influential pastor of First Mennonite Church in Kitchener. The venture met obvious needs, was expanded several times, and became a distinctive feature of that city and of Mennonite efforts to help those who seemed unable to cope with the complexities and temptations of modern life.[22]

Some Mennonite Brethren who had come to Canada from the Soviet Union in the 1920s became aware of great poverty and need among some Russian immigrants living in Vancouver and of others at Blaine Lake, Saskatchewan. Their knowledge of the Russian language and culture, it was thought, made these immigrants a logical mission field,[23] and endeavors were established in both places. Missions to urban poor, culturally marginalized, non-Mennonite people confirmed some pessimistic ideas about the evils of city living, but they did not provide Canadian Mennonites with encouraging or realistic information about urban life.

Missions to the urban destitute also did not provide a satisfactory base for establishment of Mennonite churches that would meet the spiritual needs of Mennonite people who moved to the city.[24] Some churches did begin as 'home missions,' designed to serve urban migrants. The purposes and methods of such efforts, however, were quite different from those of the skid-row missions.

One group of urban Mennonites became a focus of concern for the immigrants of the 1920s who arrived in Canada impoverished and with a heavy transportation debt. Farm income, especially in the 1930s, was low, and jobs were few for people who had not yet mastered the English language and had few other marketable skills. But there was a demand for domestic servants – usually in the cities – and many young Mennonite women reluctantly accepted such employment. Parents and church leaders worried about the welfare of these young women; most had room and board at their place of employment, but they needed a place where, on their days off, they could meet others in a similar situation and receive counselling and participate in religious services. To meet this need, rooms or houses were rented or purchased and matrons or city workers appointed in Toronto, Winnipeg, Saskatoon, Calgary, and Vancouver. The homes also provided limited accommodation and served as employment agencies for women looking for work or between assignments.[25] In Vancouver a similar home for young men on short-term leave from alternative wartime service or working in the Vancouver area also operated for several years in the 1940s.[26]

The young domestic servants became the vanguard of a mass movement after the war. During the war, with improved economic conditions in their home communities, fewer young Mennonite women entered domestic service, but numbers rose when the postwar immigrants arrived. Once the young immigrant women acquired a working knowledge of English, secretarial, health-care, and educational jobs proved more attractive than domestic service.[27]

The situations of these young women varied greatly. In Vancouver Jacob G. Thiessen reported instances of physical and sexual abuse and problems with wages and other contractual difficulties. In Saskatoon and Winnipeg the city missionaries or Mennonite Girls' home matrons established good relations with prospective employers, mediated difficulties, and blacklisted abusive employers and particular types of work.[28]

A number of the young Mennonite women in Saskatoon served at various times in the residence of Walter Murray, president of the University of Saskatchewan. The late Professor Jean Murray, Murray's daughter, recalled that one of the women helped to finance the university expenses of her brothers. The young men apparently spent the first weeks of university in temporary shelters they had dug out of the banks of the nearby South Saskatchewan River, before finding slightly more suitable accommodation in the badly overcrowded city. But on occasion they dined in style, though not always on the most nutritious fare. If there were leftovers after some formal reception at the president's house, their sister made sure that her brothers got them. Later, when one brother became a respected biology professor at the university, he got to sample the appetizers and hors-d'oeuvres the first time they were served.[29]

Work in the homes of the wealthy and influential, or in other places of paid employment, gave these women a greater degree of urban and worldly sophistication than the men who remained on the farms or sought alternative winter employment in northern bush camps cutting cord wood or in prairie coal mines. One of the women later recalled: 'Suddenly I was wearing a black and white uniform and emptying ashtrays and serving cocktails at a dinner party. I'd never even heard of hors d'oeuvres before, let alone made them. And a cucumber sandwich! What kind of thing was that to eat? At home we had always spoken German and now I had to answer the phone, place orders at the butcher shop, and deal with the milkman, the baker and the Eaton's delivery boy. I learned English pretty quickly.'[30] Another recollected: 'When my husband married me some people who knew how many years I had worked in Winnipeg asked him "And what do you want with a city girl?" '[31]

The information about urban living that these trail-blazers carried back home was radically different from that conveyed by workers in the urban slum missions. The former came to feel not only economically but also socially and intellectually inferior to their refined 'English' employers. The latter were bearers of a message of spiritual salvation and social and economic improvement. Often the same city mission worker was expected to minister to both young domestics and the older males on skid row. He should not, however, allow his two types of clients to meet or fraternize too freely. Parents and conference leaders certainly did not want any of the women to form close friendships or to marry even a converted but former alcoholic, homeless, and alien man. So it was both prudent and convenient to arrange Bible study, prayer meetings, and worship services for the young women on Thursday afternoons and/or evenings – that being their day off – and to hold evangelization services on Sunday evenings.

There was yet another way in which urban Mennonite churches got started. Mennonites who obtained work or came to study in the city began to meet informally in homes for worship, Bible study, and fellowship; casual gatherings led to organization of churches. At first many of these emerging urban churches received limited financial assistance and were served by visiting ministers from rural churches or from one of the conferences.[32]

Mennonites moving to the cities did not find skid-row missions appealing. They wanted Mennonite churches 'similar to the churches we are familiar with in our denomination,'[33] but the ones they established, and the policies adopted, were different enough that they created tension with rural ministers and conference leaders.

The city missions were generally conference projects. Mission workers usually received at least some financial support, but they were then also accountable to the rural ministers who dominated the conferences. Those leaders were often suspicious about the things that were said and done in the cities. The experience of the Mennonite Brethren in Vancouver illustrates the nature of the problem. Franz Janzen, the MB mission worker in Vancouver in the 1930s, was appalled when several of the Mennonite men worshipping at his mission called for creation of a permanent church in the city. He was convinced that such a development would destroy the missionary focus of his work and encourage even more Mennonites to come to the city. The derelicts saved as a result of his work would not fit into a traditional MB church. So Janzen excommunicated the troublemakers.

Janzen's pre-emptory and unauthorized excommunications resulted in appointment of a committee consisting of a leader from each of the rural MB churches in the Fraser Valley. They quickly determined that Janzen's actions had been too hasty. Janzen asked for forgiveness, but a vote to reappoint him for another year was lost 39 to 40.[34] Thereafter church leaders in the valley made determined efforts to control and direct developments in Vancouver. They arranged the appointment of Jacob G. Thiessen from Dalmaney, Saskatchewan, as city missionary.

Thiessen gave a sermon or led Bible study on Thursdays at the home for Mennonite women working in the city. On Sunday mornings he preached to Russians living in one of the poorest districts, and on Sunday evenings there were evangelistic services at the mission for destitute men who were encouraged 'to separate themselves from ungodliness and worldly lusts and to lead a disciplined, righteous and godly life.'[35]

The rural church leaders approved of Thiessen's efforts, but urban family heads were not satisfied. The work at the mission had limited appeal for them, their families, or the young women in the Girls' Home. Thiessen's efforts to involve these people in his missionary work were not popular. In 1940, for example, he initiated a program in which the Mennonite young women were to distribute Christian literature to combat 'the ever increasing threat of unbelief fostered by evolutionary teaching, which causes some to lose faith.'[36] The young women were not interested. What they and other Mennonite Brethren working in the city wanted was their own church. But Thiessen and conference leaders still feared the city and felt that they must retain control over developments there. That seemed possible because most new or prospective urban churches needed financial and other support from the conferences and the rural churches. That support was generously given, but with it also came warnings, advice, and instructions from conference leaders who did not understand life in the city but were fundamentally suspicious about it.

One of the issues that created conflict and misunderstanding involved greater tolerance in the city churches for ideas and activities that were not acceptable in the rural churches. A bitter dispute between the leaders of the Schoenwieser (First) Mennonite Church in Winnipeg and provincial, Canadian, and North American conference leaders greatly exacerbated rural-urban tensions in Manitoba. The Schoenwieser church had rural origins but had become an urban church with rural affiliates.[37] Its first elder, Johann P. Klassen, was popular in his own church[38] but was regarded by some rural ministers as too liberal theologically and too willing to accept new ideas and practices. Dancing, social drinking, card playing, movie attendance, theatrical productions, and many other similar activities were allegedly tolerated in his church, and young men who had enlisted for military service were welcomed without a demand that they apologize for the error of their ways.

In the 1940s and 1950s the Schoenwieser Mennonite church was unique, but it seemed to represent the more open and tolerant urban characteristics that rural Mennonite leaders found offensive. In addition, there were charges that the church exhibited imperialistic tendencies and sought to dominate the affairs of the provincial conference. In Steinbach, members irritated by the socially restrictive rules of the church introduced a motion that, had it passed, would have allowed them to hold dual memberships in the Steinbach church and another church – presumably the more tolerant Schoenwieser Church.[39]

The Johann Klassens moved to British Columbia for health reasons in 1939. Johann H. Enns, Klassen's assistant from 1932, was chosen as leader and elder of the Schoenwieser Mennonite Church. Enns had taught Bible school in

Altona and Winnipeg and was active in Mennonite education, mutual aid, health care, the girls' home, mental health, and other charitable activities in Winnipeg. As an immigrant who had come to Canada in the 1920s, Enns sought out and helped other recent arrivals or people facing problems in the city. He was a kind, caring, loving, and self-sacrificing pastor. But some feared that he was too tolerant[40] and had 'a somewhat sentimental understanding of the Christian faith.' He allegedly had 'romantic illusions about evil ... because he believed that in the end no evil was more powerful than God.'[41]

In May of 1945 Enns was invited to prepare a *Referat*, or study paper, for the annual Manitoba ministers' and deacons' conference. He had just read and been greatly impressed by Ludwig Keller's biography of Hans Denk, an early Anabaptist leader.[42] So he prepared a presentation on Denk's life and work. Denk had been greatly troubled by the apparent contradiction between the many biblical references that described God as a God of love and the teaching of Christian churches that the great majority of humans created by that loving God would be condemned to the most horrible and never-ending torment in hell.[43]

Questions regarding the reality and certainty of eternal punishment in hell for all unbelievers were exceptionally controversial. The Methodist, Presbyterian, and Baptist churches in Canada had held bitter and controversial heresy trials in the 1890s, when their people began to move into the cities and some of the professors in the urban theological colleges raised questions regarding the interpretation of some of the biblical references to hell and eternal damnation.[44] Similar questions had been raised, albeit surreptitiously, by some urban American Mennonites in the 1920s, and in 1945 Enns raised them in Canada. That was too much for several of the rural Manitoba ministers, who registered a strong protest with the executive of the conference. They alleged that Enns subscribed to the doctrine of universalism (Die Lehre von der Wiederbringung aller Dinge).[45] They also questioned whether he still accepted the literal, divine, and infallible inspiration of the scriptures and whether he still accepted and believed in Christ's virgin birth and in all the biblical miracles. They demanded a special meeting of elders and ministers at the approaching annual sessions of the Conference of Mennonites in Canada (CMC), to be held in Eigenheim, Saskatchewan, in July 1945.

J.J. Thiessen, chairing the conference, tried to postpone the matter, but the dissidents insisted and a special meeting was called on very short notice. Enns took a conciliatory stance, but the other ministers prepared a lengthy resolution that was sharply critical of universalism and of preachers who supported such ideas. Only the elderly David Toews, who was hard of hearing and missed much of what was said, seemed to support Enns. Since Enns had been notified of the special meeting only minutes before it was held, Toews asked him to prepare a longer statement. This Enns did in a three-page letter that was sent to all those involved.[46]

The resolution passed by the ministers and deacons at Eigenheim roused the ire of Enns's fellow ministers, friends, and supporters in Winnipeg. Benjamin Ewert and Isaac I. Friesen, both of whom worked at the Bethel Mennonite Mission, which had been established in Winnipeg to serve those moving to the city in search of work, feared that the affair might disrupt various CMC programs and tried to mediate. Enns was conciliatory, but neither his supporters nor his critics wanted a compromise. Several of the former sent intemperate letters to the conference executive, and a special meeting of the ministers of a number of Schoenwieser-affiliated and a few other CMC churches prepared a resolution supporting Enns.[47]

The situation got entirely out of control in September, when Johann G. Rempel, the respected teacher at the Rosthern Bible School and a member of the CMC's executive, responded publicly to the criticisms made by of the Schoenwieser preachers and their supporters. In an article published in three major Mennonite papers Rempel equated what he understood to be the teachings of Johann H. Enns with the words of the serpent to Eve in the Garden of Eden, as recorded in Genesis 3:1: 'Hath God Said?' Enns's ideas, Rempel wrote, marked the beginnings of modernism and rationalism and must be condemned unequivocally.[48]

Rempel's article, which he said had been reviewed and approved by all members of the conference executive, provoked numerous published and personal responses. Some were written in the heat of the moment, and Rempel later complained that critics had called him a liar, a slanderer, a hypocrite, the devil, swine into which the devil had entered, Beelzebub, and a Pharisee.[49] Rempel was not, however, a man to be intimidated and promptly wrote and published a second, even more inflammatory newspaper article.

The Schoenwieser church council responded with a resolution to withdraw from the Canadian conference. That resolution, however, was not immediately accepted, pending further discussion. Enns apparently also drafted a reply to Rempel's first article but was persuaded not to send it to the papers. His attitude throughout was much more conciliatory than that of other Schoenwieser ministers and members, who, it was alleged by their opponents, constituted a small clique that wanted to dominate and dictate to the entire conference.[50]

On 8 December 1945 Rempel followed up his two articles with an appeal to all the elders and ministers of the CMC, suggesting that further polemics were futile and that a meeting of elders and ministers should be called to seek reconciliation. He insisted, however, that all participants must commit themselves in advance to two conditions. First, their only objective must be to seek harmony, and second, all must agree that there could be no compromise whatever regarding the teaching of universalism.[51] The Schoenwieser naturally declined the invitation, suggesting instead that the conference agree that human knowledge of the end times and eternity is incomplete, that they should be regarded as a great mystery of God, and that the primary concern of Christians should be the discharge of their responsibilities during their short span of life on earth. Conference leaders found that unacceptable, and meetings early in 1946 failed to resolve the impasse.[52]

At the 1946 annual sessions of the CMC, held in Beamsville, Ontario, four resolutions pertaining to the dispute were passed. The most controversial explicitly repudiated universalism and declared that 'we expect that only such churches will join or belong to our Conference that as a whole, and in particular their leaders, stand on the foundation expressed in the foregoing three points.' When that resolution passed by a vote of 369 to 23, it precipitated a formal break between the Schoenwieser church and CMC.[53]

The break created numerous problems in Winnipeg, particularly for the Bethel Mennonite Mission,[54] the Mennonite Girls' Home, the Concordia Hospital (built at the initiative of former students of the Halbstadt Kommerzschule in Russia, many of whom were members of the Schoenwieser church), and a Schoenwieser-sponsored initiative to build a Mennonite Invalid Home. Benjamin Ewert, the CMC mission worker in Winnipeg, was particularly concerned about a serious fragmentation of CMC work in the city.

The problems were further aggravated by the fact that the Schoenwieser were members of both the CMC and of the General Conference of Mennonites in North America, but not of the Conference of Mennonites in Manitoba.[55] The Bergthaler Mennonite Church of Manitoba, which exercised great influence in both the CMC and the Conference of Mennonites in Manitoba and included many critics of the Schoenwieser, had never joined the General Conference of Mennonites in North America. But it was the North American conference that held title to the Girls' Home and several other institutional properties in Winnipeg, and leaders in that conference knew that there was considerable sympathy for the Schoenwieser in some of their U.S. churches.

The General Conference had some experience with conflicts of this kind and had already established a Church Unity Committee. That body was asked to seek reconciliation in the Manitoba dispute. It arranged meetings involving CMC executive members, the Schoenwieser ministers, and other concerned ministers. These culminated in a decisive meeting held in the Bethel Mission Church on 26 March 1949.[56] At that gathering Johann Enns read a careful and conciliatory statement,[57] which most of the Manitoba ministers and elders rejected. The committee then prepared its own resolution, which asked Enns to 'teach the Bible as it was written and without trying to explain everything,' and to 'faithfully, through teaching and warnings against all unholy living, strive to encourage our people to live according to Biblical principles.'[58] Enns accepted immediately, but the Manitoba ministers insisted that he must also personally and explicitly endorse all the conference resolutions, including the one that had condemned universalism. After long and difficult discussions Enns capitulated, but even that was not enough for some of the ministers. They demanded a formal apology and an explicit admission of error. That was too much for members of the committee. They rejected categorically any demand that Enns apologize for sincerely held convictions. Most of the Manitoba ministers acquiesced, but one resigned all his positions with the conference in protest. Several BC ministers, when they heard about the re-entering of the Schoenwieser church into the conference, also threatened to take their churches out of the conference.

The Church Unity Committee, and the two ministers from the Bethel Mennonite Church in Winnipeg, were convinced that the specific issue of universalism provided a convenient target for a broader and more fundamental conflict – between an open and tolerant urban church and more traditional and legalistic rural churches. At one point Jacob H. Janzen, a visiting minister from Ontario, reported that he had met with some of the Schoenwieser ministers only to discover that they did not share Enns's view on universalism but adamantly insisted on his right to hold such views and on the duty of the congregation to support him as their elder because he had been an exceptionally good and faithful minister to them.[59]

Resolution of the dispute about Enns's views on universalism allowed the numerically superior rural congregations to claim a victory. But it did not result in significant theological or practical changes in the large and influential Schoenwieser church, which continued to serve urban, professional, educated, and progressive members, as well as many recently arrived immigrants whose grim wartime experiences defied the simplistic theological formulations accepted in the rural churches.

The conflict began as a theological disagreement, but as time went on various leaders, in their letters, described it as a dispute 'between the Mennonite churches in the Province of Manitoba and of the City of Winnipeg.'[60] Other rural leaders referred to various new practices and ideas that they did not like as 'Winnipegish.' Few disputes in Canadian Mennonite history revealed the three key facets of modernity and urbanization identified by social scientists – differentiation, rationalization, and individualization – more clearly than the support that the Schoenwieser church gave to its minister and his religious ideas.

The Schoenwieser Mennonite Church in Winnipeg was not typical of Mennonite churches in Canada, and universalism was not a major issue in other city churches. What was typical, however, was that the urban churches generally were more open and tolerant of new and different ideas and less insistent on adherence to inherited ideas and practices. Differences in occupation, economic status, way of life, worship, and involvement in secular activities and institutions were more readily accepted.

URBAN MENNONITE CHURCHES

A survey of metropolitan Mennonite churches in Canada undertaken by sociologist Leo Driedger has shown that fifty-seven urban churches were created in the three decades following the outbreak of the Second World War, and sixty more in the next two decades (see Table 8.2).

Histories of Mennonite urban churches differed significantly, but some gen-

Table 8.2
Mennonite churches and church membership in Canadian metropolitan centres, 1981

Cities	Pre-1920	Churches established in:							Total	No. of members in 1981	1981 census
		20s	30s	40s	50s	60s	70s	80s			
Winnipeg	1	2	1	2	8	11	7	11	43	9,352	19,105
Vancouver	–	–	2	2	3	5	6	6	24	4,780	9,515
Kitchener/Waterloo	3	3	–	–	1	1	–	3	11	2,725	9,760
Saskatoon	–	–	2	–	4	3	1	4	14	2,565	5,380
St Catharines	1	–	–	2	1	1	2	–	7	2,180	5,985
Calgary	–	–	–	1	2	–	3	3	9	1,193	3,635
Toronto	2	–	2	1	–	–	–	5	10	826	2,950
Edmonton	–	–	–	–	2	1	1	2	6	654	1,920
Montreal	–	–	–	–	–	1	1	–	2	200	750
Regina	–	–	–	1	–	1	–	1	3	366	685
London	–	–	–	–	–	–	–	–	–	–	485
Hamilton	–	–	–	–	1	1	1	–	3	170	420
Victoria	–	–	–	–	–	–	1	–	1	48	320
Ottawa	–	–	–	–	–	1	–	1	2	139	285
Quebec	–	–	–	–	–	–	–	1	1	25	
Total	7	5	8	9	22	26	23	37	136	25,223	61,195

Source: Driedger, 'Post-War Canadian Mennonites: From Urban to Rural Dominance,' *Journal of Mennonite Studies*, 6 (1988), 70-88.

eral observations are possible. A few that had begun as slum mission projects remained firmly committed to that mandate. Such churches grew only slowly, if at all, but they provided much-needed help. Most urban missions moved to new church buildings in the suburbs after enough ethnic Mennonites became members and recast the mission church to meet their needs.[61]

Churches that grew out of home mission initiatives, usually either as a service to young women working in the Girls' Homes or attempts by itinerant home mission workers to call together scattered members of their denomination living in the city, also faced problems when more permanent residents moved into the city and began to agitate for traditional churches with worship services on Sunday mornings rather than on convenient evenings, as was usually the case in the Girls' Homes. The interests, educational levels, and occupational choices of those associated with the early home missions did not always coincide with those of new arrivals seeking employment or advancement in the city.

The histories of new urban Mennonite churches have some striking similarities, particularly in the close friendships that developed in a new urban setting. Early meetings tended to be informal. University students, single young people, and young families were disproportionately represented. Picnics, family outings, skating parties, literary evenings, amateur theatrical productions, visiting, and fellowship fostered bonds of friendship; opportunities and insights were shared with people of similar ethnic background. It could be exciting to move from an often-restricted and separatist rural environment into the wide-open world of the city.

Since these groups were not at first organized as churches, individuals remained members of their home rural churches, where there were sometimes rumblings about forbidden things done in the city. In modern urban communities, the old boundaries between sacred and secular became blurred. For centuries Mennonites had sought to 'withdraw from the worldly system and create a Christian social order within the fellowship of the church brotherhood,'[62] but many of the traditional rural boundaries seemed either irrelevant or impractical in the city. As a result, Canadian Mennonites devoted much time and energy to the question of how they could remain true to the tradition while also becoming constructively involved in the world. Rural leaders were more inclined to insist on strict boundaries between sacred and secular concerns, but they lacked means to enforce them on their city-dwelling members.

An example of this kind of development occurred in Edmonton, where a group consisting mainly of university students from the exceptionally legalistic and restricted rural environment of the Coaldale Mennonite Brethren

Church[63] formed a core group that was organized in 1962 as the Lendrum Mennonite Brethren Church. Peter Bargen, a leader of the group, later recalled: 'We sincerely believed the Mennonite Brethren Confession of Faith even though we strongly rejected the legalistic mold within which it so often found expression ... It was felt that in the past people had been excessively forced into a mold. The church must stress individual responsibility, thus allowing a freer expression of one's spiritual outlook. The church must encourage and insist on religious and intellectual honesty.'[64]

The whole notion of boundaries between sacred and secular affairs was questioned by leaders such as Bargen, who radically redefined holistic Anabaptist teachings. 'A sacred-secular distinction,' he wrote, 'is not supported in Scripture. God is a dimension which enters into every sphere of the Christian life, therefore there is nothing secular for the Christian.'[65] Where many complained that modern life resulted in greater secularization, others emphasized the need to make sacred the things formerly thought of as secular or 'worldly.'

Small groups where people knew one another and appreciated differing backgrounds gave emerging urban churches a strong sense of unity and common purpose, which might, unfortunately, be of only short duration. People had moved to the city with many different ideas and preferences. Some chafed under social and cultural restrictions in their home communities but had not abandoned their sectarian theology. It was very difficult, however, to move old social boundaries and then establish new ones. Greater openness or tolerance often became controversial. In the 1940s and 1950s, for example, most urban Mennonite churches still expelled, or at least demanded an admission of wrong-doing and evidence of contrition, from those experiencing marriage breakdowns and divorce, even though they no longer insisted on traditional courtship and marital patterns enforced in many of the rural churches.

The determination of some to maintain what they regarded as essential and proper church discipline, and the weakening of the means to enforce such discipline, created much uneasiness and conflict in the late 1950s and early 1960s. Radio and television were acceptable; movie attendance was still dubious but tolerated; social drinking remained unacceptable to many; membership in professional associations was acceptable; but trade-union membership remained a problem, particularly for the (Old) Mennonites and in churches with many urban employers. Use of cosmetics, jewellery, other items of personal adornment, and fashionable, faddish, or outlandish clothing were accepted in moderation but still regarded as symbols of 'worldliness' by some, and visiting rural preachers or evangelists were inclined to link spiritual renewal with return to more rigorous avoidance of dubious and 'worldly living.

In other instances, the simple fact that more and more people joined a particular group could create problems. Numerical growth placed increasing strains on intimate and informal small-group experiences. Sometimes newcomers felt that the original group had formed a relatively closed 'clique.' In other cases members of the original group felt slighted when new arrivals took over positions of leadership. The early intimacy and friendliness was thus lost. People were disappointed, and differences of background, beliefs, practices, education, or current occupation created fissures. The fault lines, in most cases, had been there all along, but they became obvious when the group increased in size or organized itself into a church and applied for membership in a conference.[66]

Disagreements often focused, directly or indirectly, on two structural problems. When a group organized itself as a church it was customary to draw up a constitution, which defined and institutionalized objectives and governance. But writing and adoption of a constitution and by-laws often proved more divisive than expected. There was, first of all, the problem of defining membership, and inevitably of excluding those who did not meet the specified conditions. Mennonite Brethren (MB) conferences insisted on a conversion experience confirmed through baptism by immersion as a condition of membership, but early MB urban missions and church groups attracted individuals from other Mennonite and occasionally non-Mennonite backgrounds. A formal constitution barred such people from membership.

Constitution writing was also made more difficult by doctrinal issues, often introduced by people influenced by non-Mennonite evangelists or by training in dispensationalist or fundamentalist Bible schools. In addition, clauses stressing standards and methods of personal conduct and church discipline that were rooted in separatist, rural-based Mennonite ideals caused controversy. Those trying to write constitutions lived in a rapidly changing world, but such documents threatened to 'freeze' the situation as it then existed.

Leadership, about which more is said below, also underwent major changes and also became problematic. The system of a multiple lay ministry, common in the rural churches, rarely worked well in the city, where church leadership functions, like so many other things, became specialized and professionalized. Members with more education and greater intellectual, social, and cultural sophistication, dealing with new and different issues and problems, needed and demanded pastoral care and preaching based on appropriate professional training. Paid pastorates seemed appropriate, but early arrangements were exceptionally unstable. The pastor was a paid employee, dismissable at the pleasure of the membership or, more often, at the whim of a few wealthy and influential members of the church board.

In the old rural communities the preachers, elders, and bishops were the natural leaders of the community, served without remuneration, and could mobilize economic and social, as well as religious, sanctions against dissidents. In urban congregations the pastor was expected to provide prophetic and sometimes unpopular leadership to uphold the faith and standards of behaviour. But he was also a hireling, dependent on leaders sometimes guilty of the very things that other members demanded and expected him to denounce. Under such circumstances bland and inoffensive, but erudite and respectable, preaching all too often replaced the earlier rough, uneducated, but hard-hitting preaching rooted in everyday experiences of the worshippers in rural churches. So, when there was any kind of trouble in the church, it was often pastors who got blamed and were dismissed. They were expected to be spiritual leaders, but few urban congregations gave them the means to exercise and enforce that leadership.

Pastors also faced another problem. They were expected to be exemplary in their personal and family life. In urban churches, where members disagreed sharply on acceptable behaviour, the pastor risked censure if he or members of his family did things that half the congregation condoned but perhaps only a vocal minority condemned. And if he faced personal or family problems, or was assailed by doubts and spiritual uncertainty, there was no one in whom he could confide without exposing faults and weaknesses that pastors should not have.

The results were unfortunate. Far too many churches tried to solve their problems and generate spiritual renewal by making the pastor a scapegoat and loading on him burdens of sin, misunderstanding, disagreement, and wrong-doing that should have been borne by the entire congregation.[67]

URBAN INSTITUTIONS

Only a few Mennonite economic self-help and mutual-aid institutions were established in Canadian cities before 1970. The most notable was the Concordia Hospital in Winnipeg, founded as a maternity home in 1928. A house was rented and suitably modified to provide for five beds. Two midwives/nurses made up the original staff. Interested persons were encouraged to become members of the sponsoring society, which offered a contract system under which members would receive hospital care at reduced rates.[68] The language of communication in the early years was German, and most members were Mennonites.

Demand for hospital services increased sufficiently that in 1934 the society acquired larger facilities. The new hospital provided public service, thereby qualifying for tax concessions and limited municipal support, but the contract system for members remained in force, providing desperately needed funds for the hospital during the worst years of the Depression.

In 1939 the hospital entered a twenty-year period of consistent growth. Then, in 1958, compulsory government hospital insurance forced the hospital to terminate its own contract system and to operate under the government scheme. That raised numerous questions about the purpose and policies of the hospital and whether it could still provide a unique service to the Mennonite constituency if the basic terms and conditions of operation were set by the government.[69] Like numerous other city hospitals operated by nursing and health-care orders of the Roman Catholic church, Concordia had to provide services to the general public, but a new chaplaincy program provided a denominational identity by offering a spiritual as well as a physical health service.

Concordia's supporters were also involved in establishing, in 1945, a home for the elderly – the Bethania Nursing Home, later renamed the Bethania Mennonite Personal Care Home Inc.[70] A second Mennonite home for the elderly, built next door to First Mennonite Church, was established in 1968, and after 1970 numerous Mennonite retirement homes and geriatric centres were set up in many Canadian cities. Urban family and residential life made it difficult for family members or neighbours to provide the care needed by elderly people. Grandfather and grandmother did not fit into the standard, CMHC-approved suburban bungalow.

Canadian Mennonites launched a number of health-care facilities in the years after 1945, ranging from mental-care homes to homes for disturbed children, the elderly, and the handicapped, but until 1970 these were almost always located in towns such as Abbotsford, Altona, Clearbrook, Coaldale, Didsbury, Leamington, Milverton, Preston, Rosthern, Steinbach, Tavistock, Vineland, Warman, Winkler, and Yarrow.

Much the same thing happened with mutual aid or cooperative institutions, usually founded in larger towns where Mennonites comprised a sizeable percentage of the population. Winnipeg did have a Mennonite burial and cemetery society, and credit unions were set up in Winnipeg and Kitchener-Waterloo – in the latter case only in 1964. Prairie Mennonites living in the city could also remain members of the rurally based Waisenamt of their denomination, but there were no direct transplants of most such institutions to urban environments.

Mennonites also established strong urban educational institutions in the 1940s. These are discussed in greater detail in a later chapter, but they helped members adjust to urban life. Similarly, artistic, musical, theatrical, publication, and literary organizations sprang up in the cities after 1945. And numerous urban service, self-help, and charitable activities and programs were initiated by the Mennonite Central Committee. These too are described in later chapters.

SUBURBAN CAPTIVITY?

When Canadian Mennonites came to work in the cities they rarely bought houses and settled in the core areas where the early missions and some of the Girls' Homes were located. Social conditions and services in poorer areas were unsatisfactory, while the prices of homes in more affluent districts were beyond the means of most. Instead, most Mennonite newcomers settled in new suburban areas. Canadian housing policies were, as explained above, particularly well suited for would-be homeowners. Those policies, however, have also been credited or blamed for the massive, land-consuming and automobile-dependent suburban sprawl that became characteristic of postwar North American urban development.

Mennonite patterns of home acquisition differed somewhat from one city to the next, but most members acquired homes in good, solid, middle-class suburbs.[71] After decades of Depression- or wartime-induced poverty and housing shortages, a home of their own, complete with wonderful modern conveniences, seemed a dream almost too good to come true. Those uprooted by the war who had suffered homelessness and statelessness particularly cherished their new homes and their citizenship in a prosperous country. Mennonite folklore also told of a mythical, utopian place called Schlarraffenland. It was not exactly heaven, with golden streets, heavenly choirs, and myriad saints offering glory and praise to the Lamb of God, which had conquered evil and death. No, it was a decidedly earthly place, inhabited by apes who had so arranged things that all necessary work got done without any exertion on their part. There were all kinds of creature comforts, and all the inhabitants lived as only royalty had been able to live in real life. After the disasters of the 1930s and 1940s a secure job with a steady income, a new house with modern conveniences, in a community that provided sound educational, social, religious, and recreational facilities, resembled the fabled Schlaraffenland, at least when viewed from afar.

Those who moved to this fabled land soon discovered that it was not quite as they had imagined it, and some may have recalled ruefully that their new houses, like the fabled Schlaraffenland, was the home not of real people but of apes. Social scientists have even spoken of a suburban captivity. Personal freedom, traditional family patterns, and community living, they tell us, were all adversely affected by block after block of look-alike neighbourhoods and 'boxes,' each with the mandatory, CMHC-approved 'three bedrooms, an L-shaped living/dining room, and, in most areas of the country, a full basement.'[72]

Women, in particular, found aspects of suburban life difficult. An Ontario suburbanite housewife wrote: 'I began to feel as if I were slowly going out of my mind. Each day was completely filled with child and baby care and keeping the house tidy and preparing meals.'[73] And things did not necessarily improve when the babies and children grew up. A Mennonite suburbanite in Winnipeg described her frustrations: 'Modern appliances have taken over long and arduous household tasks, but instead of being freed from domestic duties, women now spend hours polishing already shining floors, baking calorie-rich dainties for dieting friends, and sewing yet another garment to add to the bulging closets. Mennonite women, in particular, have clung almost desperately to domesticity as if there were intrinsic value in zwieback and home-sewn dresses.'[74]

During the war women had frequently been called on to step out of traditional gender roles.[75] Once the war was over, the exigencies of suburban life forced them back into domestic life. Suburban living separated male-dominated places of 'productive' work downtown or in the factory from residential suburbs, where women did their reproductive and support work. 'Tracts of new housing,' feminists tell us, 'embodied a separation of the sexes that held women particularly responsible for home and family and men for economic support and community leadership.'[76]

This spatial segregation was a departure from traditional Mennonite life. On the farms all family members had worked together for the common good. Farming had been a partnership, even when the wife was only a junior partner. Genders were more clearly segregated in suburbs and downtown employment. The postwar baby boom, which tied more women down longer with child care, reinforced the segregation of male and female spheres of work.

Postwar housing policies were nevertheless popular, and Mennonite contractors and house-builders helped to make them acceptable to their people. The popular press, commercial advertising, the practical advice on child rearing given by Dr Benjamin Spock, and many a sermon preached at Mennonite weddings all reinforced the notion that women belonged in the home while the men held the jobs and earned the money to sustain a supposedly idyllic suburban life-style.

The suburb was made possible only by the automobile and by improved public transportation. Urban workers had traditionally been forced to live within walking or commuting distance of their work. After the war, if they owned a car or had adequate urban bus service, they could buy a house in the suburbs, far removed from their place of employment. But most suburban families could afford only one car. Sometimes the working male needed it for his work and thus controlled its use. In such cases the wife was trapped in the suburb, free only to visit such places as she, often encumbered by one or several infants or toddlers, could reach on foot or by public transport. Appointments or shopping forays requiring transportation over longer distances had to wait and be fitted into the husband's busy schedule.

Men living in the suburbs who did not need a car for their work were more likely to rely on buses to get to and from work. That left the cars for the women and obviously gave them greater freedom of movement, but that movement was still largely restricted to local errands. The division of female and male workplaces remained intact.

Some women flourished in the nurturing and caring roles that were typical of suburban housewives and mothers. Others felt trapped and resentful because they were not able to exercise other talents. Still others replicated the role of junior partner, answering telephone calls, doing some of the accounting and other paper work for husbands engaged in businesses of their own, and, alas, typing and proof-reading the essays and theses of husbands earning university degrees. If honorary degrees are ever awarded for such service there would be many suburban Mennonite wives entitled to a PHT (Putting Hubby Through).

The suburbs often fostered a narrowing of intellectual, cultural, and spiritual horizons which limited the witness and influence of urban Mennonites. One suburban housewife noted: 'Suburbia tended to narrow our vision of the outside world. We thought we had the ideal life ... We knew little about the world of poverty, culture, crime and ethnic variety. We were like a brand new primer, "Dick and Jane."' [77]

The suburbs, with their single-family bungalows or split-levels, also undermined traditional extended-family living arrangements. CMHC houses were designed for a father, mother, and two or three children. It was difficult to make room in such houses for grandparents or other family members, particularly if they needed special care. Even for members of the 'nuclear' family, life became more fragmented. Each person could pursue his or her own interests and activities, while conversations with next-door neighbours might concern the state of the crabgrass in the lawn, the loan of a garden tool, or daytime excursions by mothers and children to the local playground, library, or skating rink. The vital joys and concerns of everyday life that had been shared by all members of traditional rural communities were shared selectively, if at all, with other family members and neighbours in the city.

There were certainly times, such as the great Winnipeg flood of 1950, when neighbours worked together and developed common bonds of friendship and trust, but they were exceptional. Suburban living in single, detached family dwellings, made possible by better roads and automobiles, created a way of life that, whatever its merits or faults, differed significantly from the rural family and community life of earlier generations.

MENNONITE VALUES AND URBAN INSTITUTIONS

When Mennonites first moved to the cities in large numbers there was great concern that they would lose their identity as Mennonites. A look at a map of any Canadian city to which they moved in large numbers quickly demonstrates that that identity has not been lost but has in fact been strengthened.[78] In 1971 Winnipeg had the largest concentration of Mennonites in Canada, and quite possibly in the world. There were then twenty-six Mennonite churches, two Bible and liberal arts colleges, two high schools, a hospital, a personal-care home, a printing press, a radio studio, several newspaper editorial offices, MCC headquarters, and a large number of private businesses with a Mennonite identity. And that was not a passing phenomenon: in 1990 the number of Mennonite churches in Winnipeg had almost doubled, and stood at forty-seven.[79]

There was comparable growth in other Canadian cities. Mennonites did not lose their identity in the cities. That identity was, however, significantly modified. Isolationism was no longer a prominent feature of Mennonite life; it was no longer possible to identify a Mennonite by his or her nonconformist clothing, occupation, or life-style, even though urban adherents continued giving strong support to and using their institutions to perpetuate many traditional values.

In a recent article, based on a major statistical study of Mennonite identity and modernization, Leo Driedger asserts that urbanization and professionalization were highly correlated and that in 1989 four times as many Mennonites worked in the professions as toiled on the land.[80] Urban professionals were found to be generally more tolerant and open than rural people regarding issues of personal morality such as premarital sexual intercourse, gambling, smoking, moderate drinking, divorce, attendance at movies, social dancing, masturbation, political participation, and the swearing of oaths.[81] More surprising, they also tended to be less individualistic and more concerned about community interests and problems than their rural co-religionists. They gave stronger support to historic Anabaptist and Mennonite peace principles and to the work of Mennonite organizations, such as the

Mennonite Central Committee and the Mennonite Disaster Service. They were also more open to equal roles for women in the church and more sympathetic to the demands for equality by persons of other races. And finally, urban professionals were more supportive of programs of outreach and evangelism than those living in rural communities. Driedger argues that 'exposure to the larger society tends to expand the world view, making Mennonites less preoccupied with ingroup preservation and giving them greater sympathy for the plight of others ... Contact with a diversity of faiths, races, and ideologies also makes them more tolerant.'[82] He points out that professionals work more with people and their needs, which also contributes to their greater openness.[83]

All this suggests that while urban Mennonites, particularly professionals, have abandoned sectarian doctrines, they are more strongly committed to other distinctive Anabaptist and Mennonite doctrines. It can therefore be argued that urbanization strengthened, rather than weakened key elements of Mennonite faith and life.

CONCLUSION

Mennonites moved in rapidly increasing numbers from rural farms, villages, and towns into the cities after the Second World War. Life in urban and suburban communities proved neither as idyllic as some hoped nor as destructive of distinctive values as others feared. What is clear is that when Mennonites moved to the cities they gave up some aspects of their former way of life but transplanted other, essential aspects of their faith into their new environment.

Urbanization was made easier because it occurred in a time of prosperity, but material success also raised new and awkward questions about Jesus' hard sayings about wealth. Those hard sayings were gradually softened by talk of responsible 'Christian stewardship.' The question was not whether or not it was good to be prosperous but how one used available material resources. One important way in which Canadian Mennonites sought to use their unprecedented prosperity involved training, nurture, and education of their children.

PART FOUR
PREPARING THE NEXT GENERATION

9

Nurture and Training of Youth

The years of economic prosperity after 1945 made it possible for Canadian Mennonites to devote substantial thought, energy, and resources to the nurture, training, and education of their children and young people. The rapidly changing circumstances of many Mennonites, particularly new city dwellers, led to changed attitudes, new church and conference programs, and much stronger support for a variety of educational institutions. Child-rearing practices, methods used to bring young people to a mature religious commitment, and attitudes toward human sexuality all changed significantly, while the number of Mennonite young people attending secondary and post-secondary educational institutions increased dramatically. As a result, the generation that came to maturity, and perhaps prematurely to power, in the 1950s and 1960s had very different preparation for their work, and a different outlook on the world and their place in it, than their parents and grandparents.

All religious people are concerned about the best ways in which to transmit to their children and grandchildren the most precious and meaningful aspects of their heritage. Voluntarist religious groups face particular challenges because a conscious adult decision is needed for full fellowship. That message seemed particularly relevant when our grandson was born and my wife and I received a card that said: 'A grandchild is a message to a time to which we cannot go.' That card expressed the joy in seeing the beginning of another generation, and it hinted at concerns every parent and grandparent has at such a time. What will the message be that we send to another time through our grandchildren? Will it include those things that we regard as most precious and meaningful in our lives? What are the appropriate nurture, training, and education that will ensure that the values and ideals that we cherish will live on in succeeding generations?

These questions become particularly urgent in a time of rapid change. In the postwar years Canadian Mennonites were very much concerned about the training given their children, but they were not always in agreement about the relative importance of various aspects of their faith and religious practice. Some groups clung tenaciously to the old rural and sectarian way of life. Others accepted and placed increased emphasis on selective aspects of pietist and evangelical Christianity, which moved them closer to a particular substream of North American religious life. Still others were strongly influenced by renewed emphasis on and appreciation of their Anabaptist heritage, as rediscovered by Harold S. Bender and his associates. And finally there were some who moved, albeit cautiously, toward assimilation into mainstream North American Christianity.

How people adapted and accommodated themselves to the changing needs, conditions, and opportunities, and how maturing young people were integrated into the adult community of believers, varied a great deal, but there were also crucial shared developments and influences that provide useful insights into the processes of change in the individual and collective lives of Canadian Mennonites. Such developments were rarely linear or one-directional; evolution tended to be erratic, inconsistent, and dialectic in nature. There were, however, key times and events in the lives of individual adherents and members, especially in infancy, childhood, and adolescence, which were marked by special celebrations and ceremonies, as individuals passed from one stage of life to another. Those were times when both the continuities and changes in family, congregation, and community life were important.

BIRTH

Children born in Mennonite homes and communities in the period 1939–70 began their religious lives differently from most other Canadian children in one important respect. They were not baptized as infants and hence were not officially members of the religious community in which they grew up.[1] The Anabaptist and Mennonite refusal to baptize infants was not rooted in a negative attitude toward the newborn. Children were in fact highly cherished and regarded as special gifts of God entrusted to the care of parents, extended family, and congregation.

Mennonites accepted the doctrine that even infants shared in the sin and fall of Adam and Eve, but they rejected the doctrine that infants and children were accountable for that original sin, since they neither understood nor participated in it. Mennonites therefore did not believe that infants needed the special grace bestowed through infant baptism.[2] Their rejection of infant baptism, however, left a gap in the formal celebrations marking arrival of a new member of their community of faith. That gap was gradually filled in many of the larger conferences by special infant dedication ceremonies. Practices varied widely. More traditional congregations rejected the concept outright. Others, beginning in the 1950s or the 1960s, made it optional. The ceremony itself was also conducted in different ways. Some ministers hugged the child and blessed it with the laying on of hands: some blessed the child through the laying on of hands while it was held by its parents: still others invoked God's blessing with uplifted hands. In general, the emphasis was on the obligations and duties of the parents and of members of the congregation in the rearing of the child.[3] Child dedication did not obviate the need for the child to make his or her own decisions and commitments later in life, nor did it replace adult baptism as marking formal entry into the fellowship of the community of believers. Child dedication nevertheless became a semi-official ceremony marking acceptance of the infant as a participant in the religious community.

CHILD REARING

Since they experienced urbanization at least one generation later than most of their fellow citizens, Canadian Mennonites during and immediately after the Second World War tended to follow late-nineteenth- and early-twentieth-century Canadian, American, and European child-rearing practices. They were not particularly innovative in applying Anabaptist principles when raising their children, other than to insist on adult baptism.

Mennonites believed that the primary responsibility of parents and of the church in the training of young children below 'the age of discretion' – usually puberty and adolescence – was to love, educate, nurture, direct, and prepare the child for the time when it reached the age of discretion, when it could make the appropriate choice of its own free will. Jesus' invitation to let the little children come to him was often cited. The child was to grow up in an atmosphere that fostered understanding and appreciation of the Christian heritage, thus predisposing it to make the right decision when it achieved the age of discretion and accountability:[4] 'Given an emotional climate of love, trust, and acceptance in the home, the developing individual will come to accept the values of the social system, not because he is required to do so under pain of punishment if he does not, but because he has warm and kindly feelings toward those people (parents, teachers, etc.) who model and teach the system's prevailing values.'[5]

There was, however, another side to the Mennonite understanding of what it meant to be a child. Infants may be innocent, but there is, from the beginning, a propensity to sin, selfishness, and rebellion. It was therefore also the responsibility of parents, and of the congregation, to protect children from sin and wrong-doing and to punish them when they misbehaved. Obedience, respect, and compliance with family, congregational, and ultimately God's spiritual rules and instructions must be not only taught but also enforced if the child's natural propensity to sin was to be curbed. Parents, congregational, and community leaders who were influenced by or accepted a spiritual-carnal or mind-body duality became particularly concerned about the need to curb or thwart manifestations of carnal and fleshly desires.

Sometimes this approach resulted in child-rearing practices that degenerated into psychologically, spiritually, and physically abusive confrontations between parents and children, most notably if a child were high-spirited, rebellious, or simply strongly independent.[6] Fear of the Lord and submission to His will and to the will of His church were basic principles of Mennonite child rearing. Menno Simons, for example, wrote: 'A child unrestrained becomes headstrong as an untamed horse. Give him no liberty in his youth, and wink not at his follies. Bow down his neck while he is young lest he wax stubborn and be disobedient to thee. Correct thy son and keep him from idleness lest thou be made ashamed on his account.'[7]

In the underground gossip and folk wisdom of many communities there are, unfortunately, numerous stories of serious abuse in the implementation of this method of child rearing. An extreme case in a large Canadian Mennonite community involved a father who took seriously the admonition of that Old Testament profligate, King Solomon, not to spare the rod lest that spoil the child. The father believed strongly that the rod ought to be applied until the young son capitulated – in other words, until his stubborn wilfulness and rebellion were broken. But pain and anger drove the child instead to an infuriated kicking, scratching, and spitting attack on the father. The ensuing discipline was so severe that the child was beaten into unconsciousness, but the father was not able to achieve the desired objective. The resulting resentment and hostility on the part of the son haunted the father until his death, but all attempts at reconciliation failed, even though the two men lived in the same community until the father died decades later.[8]

Parental punishment and correction could be justified by reference to the all-knowing, righteous, and judgmental characteristics attributed to God. Even the worst corporal punishment could never compare with the horrors of eternal damnation in the fires of hell. One victim of this school, which was, unfortunately, also common to other evangelical traditions, came to think of God as 'an omnipresent judge with x-ray eyes who missed no speck of wickedness in my evil little heart'[9] and of his stern father as that jealous

God's agent on earth. This God could demand a reckoning at any moment. 'You might die in your sleep or the sound of the trumpet might come between mouthfuls of porridge at breakfast.'[10] The resulting anxiety and fear were terrible for some children. One described his experiences thus: 'My nights were filled with nightmares and the sound of my teeth gnashing. I wet my bed until I was ten or eleven. I walked in my sleep. As a boy of 10, I had countless nights I could not sleep at night for fear of hell.'[11]

These were extreme, but not isolated, experiences. Sometimes other members of the congregation were also drawn into the disciplining of children. Some churches, for example, appointed monitors who were charged with responsibility to ensure that the children behaved in church. Those who misbehaved could be taken out and spanked by the monitor. Such practices were, for a time, carried to extremes in the Yarrow Mennonite Brethren Church, where one of the monitors, well known for his violent temper, sometimes dragged boys out of the church and beat them severely. Only rarely did a father intervene to rescue his son. There was tacit approval of such actions.[12]

Such disciplinary tactics were also extended in Yarrow to adolescents, and even to older men who violated accepted community standards of conduct. A vigilante group of masked Mennonite Brethren men operated for a time in the town, administering severe beatings to individuals who brought liquor into the community and husbands who beat their wives or consorted with prostitutes.[13] These practices were rooted in the Russian Mennonite experiences of some of the members. Yarrow was an extreme case, but relatives, community leaders, and teachers elsewhere did spank or otherwise punish children and adolescents who misbehaved.

Some of these practices, quite aside from their dubious legality, were eventually recognized as abuse, particularly where children below the age of accountability were involved, and in the 1950s several Mennonite authors published books that placed increasing emphasis on the nurture of children.[14] The focus on love, nurture, and support also received strong support from more secular sources. In his enormously influential baby- and child-care books Dr Benjamin Spock[15] advocated a loving, accepting, and permissive approach to child-rearing: 'When I was writing the first edition, between 1943 and 1946, the attitude of a majority of people toward infant feeding, toilet training and general child management was still fairly strict and inflexible. However, the need for greater understanding of children and for flexibility has been made clear by educators, psychologists, and pediatricians, and I was trying to encourage this.'[16] Spock urged parents to 'love and enjoy your child for what he is, for what he looks like, for what he does, and forget about the qualities that he doesn't have … The child who has never quite been accepted by his parents, who has always felt he is not quite right, will grow up lacking confidence.'[17]

On the important question of discipline Spock insisted that children needed love, understanding, affirmation, and a sense of pride and self-confidence and that harsh punishment was apt to be self-defeating.[18] He also attacked the issue of parental responsibility if the child did not make appropriate choices later in life. Passages, particularly from the wisdom literature of the Old Testament, which stressed the honour that comes to parents when their child does what is right, were frequently cited by Mennonite authors and preachers. The implication was that if the child rebelled it brought shame and raised serious questions about the spirituality of the parents. This implication, in fact, forced a number of Mennonite leaders, most notably some of the lay preachers, to withdraw from the ministry if their children rebelled or they could not keep order in their own households.[19] Sermons at weddings and family celebrations dealt forcefully with the awesome responsibilities of husbands and fathers as spiritual leaders in ways that reinforced authoritarian and patriarchal child rearing.

Spock would have none of this. 'The Bible,' he wrote,

speaks ominously of the sins of the father being visited on the children, and many of us parents were warned in similar words in our own upbringing. Rarely does slow development have anything to do with inadequate child care or inherited defects or the sins of the parents (real or imaginary).[20] ...

The main source of good discipline is growing up in a loving family – being loved and learning to love in return ... I may as well let the cat out of the bag right away as far as my opinion goes and say that strictness or permissiveness is not the real issue. Good-hearted parents who aren't afraid to be firm when it is necessary can get good results with either moderate strictness or moderate permissiveness. On the other hand, a strictness that comes from harsh feelings or a permissiveness that is timid or vacillating can each lead to poor results. The real issue is what spirit the parent puts into managing the child and what attitude is engendered in the child as a result.[21]

Child-rearing practices emphasizing love and nurture in early childhood training appealed to many modern Canadian Mennonites. Parents took seriously their responsibilities, but children ultimately had to be given the freedom to make their own decisions and commitments. Parents and congregations were not necessarily at fault if some made unfortunate choices.[22] Most accepted the advice offered by some Mennonite and secular writers alike in the 1950s.

The ultimate objective of Mennonite child rearing was 'the inculcation of the basic beliefs, values, attitudes and social mores that will guide the individual into socially accepted and responsible adult roles.'[23] Traditionally the major role in this regard had rested with the immediate and extended family, but after the war congregations became more active in that process, shouldering some of the tasks previously vested almost entirely in the family. Sunday schools, daily vacation Bible schools, summer camps, special junior services or stories for children in the worship services, colourful illustrated talks by visiting missionaries, evangelistic services, and later short films brought the congregation into the child-rearing process.

ADOLESCENCE: AN AMBIGUOUS TIME

Adolescence was the most critical and also the most ambiguous time in the raising of Mennonite young people. All early child rearing was designed to prepare the child for the time when it would make its own adult decision, commitments, and vows and thus become a full member of the congregation and community. That time came during adolescence. Adolescence, however, was a time of great uncertainty, since there was no agreement regarding the age at which innocent children became accountable adults or what should be done when they reached that age. Calvin Redekop, a Mennonite sociologist, has described the situation in which Mennonite adolescents found themselves: 'The child, as long as it was innocent, was a natural child of God, but when that child entered adolescence and began to express his or her own will and autonomy, he or she moved from a "saved" condition to one of being "pagan." This ambiguity during the adolescent years created great concern for Mennonite parents and tended to develop pressures upon children to experience a religious conversion, and quite early to minimize the period of the "uncertain" group.'[24]

In traditional and isolated communities where parental, congregational, and community controls remained strong and effective, the time at which an individual was expected to make fundamental religious and spiritual decisions and commitments was between the ages of 17 and 21.[25] Young people received special religious instruction, often with the aid of a series of questions and answers called the catechism, which prospective members were expected to memorize.[26] A satisfactory response, and willingness to make a commitment to the teachings of the scriptures and the discipline of the church, were the prerequisites for baptism and church membership.

In congregations that exercised less social and religious control, the ages at which Sunday school teachers, preachers, evangelists, and parents began to put pressure on adolescents to make commitments tended to be lower than in traditional rural communities, and a variety of supportive and sometimes coercive measures were taken to ensure that adolescents made the right decision or at least had the necessary knowledge and understanding to make such a decision.

Anabaptist theology indicated that only those who had accepted baptism and the responsibilities of membership were subject to church rules and to discipline for transgressions. The time before baptism and full membership was therefore a period of somewhat greater freedom, in which the status of the individual was unclear. During that phase, 'sowing a few wild oats' was tolerated and, in some traditional communities, tacitly encouraged. The theology of personal choice and personal commitment implied a deliberate turning away from sin and evil. That did not fit the experiences of those who had been relatively well behaved throughout childhood and youth. The Apostle Paul's dramatic experience on the road to Damascus had been possible only because of his earlier sinful ways, and groups that were confident that the social controls in place in their communities would bring erring young people back into line at the appropriate time were willing to tolerate adolescent behaviour not acceptable once the person became a member of the congregation. Youthful tampering with the outside world became 'a form of social immunization. It provides some teen-age excitement, but also a minimal dosage of worldliness that strengthens resistance in adulthood.'[27]

SPECIAL CHURCH PROGRAMS FOR ADOLESCENTS

The integration of adolescents into congregations with less rigid and effective social, economic, and occupational controls was different. Some of those who advocated tactics of love, nurture, support, and guidance in childhood also favoured those same approaches and methods vis-à-vis adolescents. A Mennonite psychologist and long-time instructor at Eastern Mennonite College, whose writings enjoyed a wide circulation in Swiss Mennonite communities in both Canada and the United States, clearly defined this approach: 'Adolescents resist authority and superiority. But the adult who accepts them as persons and not as problems, who shares their experiences, who likes them for what they are and not for what he would like to see them be, who believes that they can accept responsibility – to that person they will give respect. They will seek his counsel and accept his guidance.'[28]

Support and nurture included a range of youth activities and programs organized by individual congregations or by the conferences. During the Depression and throughout most of the 1940s and on into the 1950s, special Christian endeavour societies, *Jugendvereine*, and literaries provided opportunities for fellowship and for developing leadership skills. Special evening church services devoted to the reading of literary and devotional materials, the playing of musical instruments, singing, picnics, field trips, special youth projects, personal testimonies of spiritual trials and triumphs, and participation in local evangelistic services might be arranged. Meetings sponsored by the Christian endeavour societies were generally open to all members and adherents of the congregation, and many of the societies or literaries were run by individuals well past the age of adolescence. The Saskatchewan Mennonite Youth Organization, for example, found it necessary to make special efforts to ensure that only members under the age of thirty served on the executive.

The literaries, Christian endeavour societies, and *Jugendvereine* became a means whereby individuals could test and apply their talents and gradually become integrated into the active work of the congregation. Congregational and community choirs, orchestras, and musical ensembles provided another means of socialization. Choir practices allowed young people of both sexes to meet and socialize, and larger regional or provincial songfests, or *Saengerfeste*, became a social highlight even for those with only limited musical abilities and interests.

ADOLESCENTS AND CHURCH CAMPS

A new way in which leaders of the more accommodating Mennonite churches sought to socialize and integrate young people was through church or Bible camps. Camping evolved somewhat differently in various Mennonite conferences. The earliest North American Mennonite camp was part of a mission program of the General Conference to the Hopi Indians in 1903,[29] and efforts to serve children who had no other church contact remained an important aspect of Mennonite camping programs, but they were also designed to serve children and adolescents in the church.

As long as Mennonite children and young people spent their summers working on parental farms, leaders felt no great need to establish wholesome outdoor experiences for their own children and young people. Weekend retreats seemed appropriate for adolescents, but only if they did not interfere with farm work. Once more and more people moved to the cities, and mechanization on the farms left time in summer for other things, support for summer camps increased. Wholesome outdoor experiences could include both physical activities and religious services. There were also suggestions that camping programs supplemented regular church services from which young people did not always get all the help and guidance they needed to make the appropriate religious commitments in a radically changed modern context. In the immediate postwar era Mennonite camps tended to value specific conversion or Christian-commitment experiences.

Mennonites learned or borrowed from the larger society ideas about Christian recreation. Historically they had regarded many forms of recreation with suspicion. A great variety of 'worldly amusements,' including organized sports and popular forms of entertainment, were denounced in numerous congregational and conference resolutions. But a mix of religious and physical activities in a wholesome setting made camping more attractive, and it was consistent with a holistic theology. A 1955 editorial in the *Canadian Mennonite* defined the basic purpose of such camping programs: 'Camps vary in program, but their broad objectives are the same. Camps offering a balanced program share the universal aim of designing their activities to contribute to the preparation of the camper, to take his place in society. Through this balanced program effected in an outdoor environment under skilled leadership, camps seek to develop attitudes, habits, skills, and concerns which will aid in the proper growth and development of campers.'[30]

The editor said that the best results occurred when directors used the recreational approach: 'Hiking, cookouts, sleepouts, nature study, are ways of recreation that are very good to teach about God through nature in the out-of-doors.'[31] One director reported that 'something that excites the child on natural grounds, provided a great opportunity for learning, growth and promotion of educational and moral values.'[32]

In some camps children and young people were subjected to considerable emotional pressure to make the desired religious decisions and commitments, sometimes long before they had reached the maturity to do so.[33] Mennonite Brethren camp directors, for example, kept track of the number of children and young people 'saved,' and camp workers were encouraged to achieve the highest numbers possible.[34] That, unfortunately, led on occasion to pressure that was experienced not as an expression of Christian love and concern but as emotional and spiritual abuse. At a biannual convention of the Mennonite Camping Association in 1967 counsellors complained about the pressure to which they were subjected to produce measurable results. One of them noted, 'We don't hurry childbirth. Even so we should be patient with a camper coming to faith.' Another said, 'We are not called upon to save all campers, but only to be faithful witnesses.' It was noted that, 'From various quarters came stories which indicate spiritual violation of young lives upon which Jesus placed immense value. Spiritual rape someone called it.'[35]

No accurate statistical account can be drawn up, but personal recollections, memoirs, and testimonies by baptismal candidates indicate that, in spite of numerous instances of dubious pressure tactics, the camps became an effective and increasingly popular means to bring many children and youth into the fellowship of the church. And over time camp directors developed greater sensitivity to abusive practices. Excessive, premature, or inappropriate pressure to force a child to make a commitment that he or she did not fully understand, or was not yet ready to make, did violence to fundamental Mennonite and Anabaptist theology, which stressed personal choices and commitments, freely made, without outside pressure or compulsion.

The Amish Mennonites and the Brethren in Christ had both been somewhat suspicious but began to use some of the facilities of (Old) Mennonite or United Mennonite camps in the 1950s. The results were sufficiently encouraging that, in 1962, the Ontario Amish Mennonite mission board purchased a farm site near Shakespeare, Ontario, to develop a camp for children and youth,[36] while the Brethren in Christ purchased Camp Kahquah on the shores of Lake Ahmic near Magnetawan, also in 1962.[37]

Camping gave concerned Mennonite leaders the freedom to experiment with new ideas in programming. While diverse in origin and method, the camps had sufficient common interests that the Mennonite Camping Association mentioned above was organized in the 1960s to share ideas, experiences, and techniques and to deal with leadership training, tactics, and abuse by overly zealous counsellors. The executive secretary noted in 1977: 'The camping program is uniquely suited to model the church's goals with regard to the simple life-style, conflict resolution, the building of the community, the teaching of the stewardship of creation, and an awareness of a responsibility regarding natural resources.'[38]

ADOLESCENTS AND EVANGELISTIC CAMPAIGNS

Evangelistic or revival meetings, sponsored either by individual congregations or by community ministerial organizations, were another means whereby adolescents were drawn into the life of the congregations. Such campaigns were not new to most Canadian Mennonites in the 1940s. Some conferences and congregations were in fact a product of nineteenth-century religious revivals. Some had been greatly influenced by such revivals, while others had only accepted the new religious influences reluctantly. And a significant minority of both the more traditional or conservative Canadian Mennonites, and of those who were more open and tolerant and found the dogmatism and anti-intellectual propensities of many evangelicals offensive, rejected evangelistic methods and doctrines, which they regarded as contrary to the faith of their forebears.

Evangelistic services became more popular as other means of social control in Mennonite communities weakened. Many of the older Mennonite leaders, even in accommodating congregations, found the theatrical and emotionally coercive tactics of North American evangelists offensive. Jacob H. Janzen of Ontario, for example, after sitting through a diatribe against the theory of evolution in the course of which the evangelist brought live monkeys onto the stage, simply said, 'Christianity is no monkey business.'[39] John A. Harder from British Columbia insisted that 'conversion is not a matter primarily of one's feelings, but rather it is a free choice of the human will, as the scriptures repeatedly point out.'[40] Churches that still conducted worship services in German also worried that English-language revival meetings would increase the pressure to change the language of services, and some brought in German-speaking evangelists.[41]

Ambitious younger Mennonite preachers, however, began to emulate the tactics of American evangelists, often after attending non-Mennonite Bible schools where they learned how to whip up the emotions of their listeners.[42] One of these evangelists quickly recognized the powerful effect that the new methods had on younger listeners and published a paper in which he cited statistics which indicated that in North American evangelical churches a few members had been converted before the age of four, and 85 per cent between the ages of four and fifteen.[43] And so even very young adolescents became targets for the evangelists. At Yarrow and elsewhere, in spite of Harder's warnings, the new trends were defined thus: 'Conversion of children became the main focus of many parents and of the Sunday school. Once the conversion process was formalized by reducing it to several simple steps, the Sunday school could teach it to the young children. Although the church rejected infant and child baptism, conversion of children was stressed even to the point of including on occasion preschool children. Early conversion, according to one observer, became one of Yarrow's answers to the danger of assimilation.'[44]

Several popular evangelists with Mennonite antecedents also gained entry into, and enormous influence in, Mennonite communities in Canada. The large Janz family living near Herbert, Saskatchewan, included several brothers who attended the Mennonite Brethren Bible School at Herbert in the late 1920s or early 1930s. From Herbert they went on to the Prairie Bible Institute in Three Hills, Alberta, and from there to evangelistic careers. The fine singing of the Janz brothers gospel quartet, combined with aggressive evangelistic preaching, reached Mennonite audiences at a time when many church leaders were still suspicious about non-Mennonite evangelists. The brothers took care neither to endorse or to refute historic Mennonite peace principles. Sometimes they preached in German but said little about distinctive Mennonite social and cultural practices, leaving the impression that these were peripheral matters. The main concern, according to the Janz team, was to invite people to a conversion experience. In many western Mennonite communities the Janzes introduced hitherto-alien North American evangelistic techniques. They came from Mennonite stock and understood the Mennonite people. That gave them openings in communities that were still denied other evangelists.

The most impressive breakthrough of North American evangelistic tactics in Canadian Mennonite communities, however, came through the Brunk Brothers of Harrisonburg, Virginia. They had become involved in successful evangelistic campaigns in the United States in the early 1950s, and in the mid-1950s there were increasingly insistent demands that they be invited to conduct services in Canada. Many Mennonite leaders had grave doubts and concerns about their theatrical methods and about the way in which they had reduced 'conversion' to what seemed to some critics to be little more than a few ritualistic procedures. But strong support from the Swiss Mennonites in Ontario eventually led to an invitation to conduct a series of revival meetings in Ontario. One Ontario Mennonite church leader who found George Brunk's methods distasteful wrote, rather sadly, after one of their campaigns to a fellow minister:

You think people should be encouraged to heed not only the lively antics and hammering – the thunder and lightening –, but also the still small voice of God. I too think we must test what is done and do what is right. But when I think how the sensitivities of our people have been dulled through radio-jazz, the viewing of murder stories on TV, and our material prosperity, I must ask myself if the time has come when watchmen on Zion's ramparts must sound the alarm ... We must use all available means to rouse and awaken people. We live in very serious times in which the sabre-rattling from Satan's underworld is becoming louder and louder.[45]

The impact of the Brunk Revivals was somewhat different among the Swiss Mennonites of Ontario from what it was among the Russian Mennonites, particularly in southern Manitoba. George Brunk understood, accepted, and gave strong support to Swiss Mennonite teachings pertaining to nonconformity and worldliness, especially with regard to dress. In that sense his messages in Ontario were essentially separatist, but he used modern methods of mass evangelism.

In western Canada his message was received and interpreted differently. Brunk, like most Swiss Mennonites, had no commitment to the German language, and he neither understood nor appreciated the distinctive social and cultural heritage of the Russian Mennonites. He thought that most Mennonite congregations in western Canada were trapped in linguistic, social, cultural, and religious traditions that had lost their relevance. Severe criticism of the established Mennonite churches was an essential part of his message. People were not getting what they needed. Mass revivalistic methods were designed to meet the spiritual needs of modern North Americans.[46]

In southern Manitoba many saw and interpreted the Brunks' message as a liberating influence. Specifically, the evangelists clearly preached and emphasized the importance of conversion and new spiritual life that was not tied to the German language, to old and seemingly obsolete cultural traditions, or to the rules and prohibitions that had been drawn up to enforce what was becoming an increasingly artificial separation of the church from the outside world. In a series of reports on the Brunk Revivals in Manitoba in 1957 Frank H. Epp, editor of the *Canadian Mennonite*, emphasized the liberating elements:

Tradition can be either master or servant of the Christian faith. In the lives of many Mennonites in southern Manitoba tradition was definitely assuming the master role. This expressed itself in various ways. Church membership, some thought, sufficed for salvation. That the mission of the church was cultural rather than spiritual, was the opinion of others. The practices of the past were authority enough for the individual, said some. In all of the campaigns these falsehoods were exposed. The exposure struck deep into the heart of a formalistic and traditionalistic Mennonite community life, but thus became part of the ongoing revival.[47]

Young people were uncomfortable with the rigid rules and prohibitions in their old rural communities. The evangelists seemed to offer a safe and spiritual way to escape while not only remaining true to the essentials of their faith but recapturing aspects of it that had been weakened, lost, or obscured. The 1957 Brunk campaigns in southern Manitoba garnered 907 recorded conversions and 1,650 recorded dedications or recommitments. The sponsors were confident that the results would be in evidence for a long time to come, 'as the seed which has been sown will grow and mature into the firm, ripe fruit of Christian character.'[48]

Not everyone experienced the campaigns in a positive way. Assessments published in 1957 emphasized that 'the altar call was clear and definite and not overworked.'[49] Later recollections by many of those affected indicate that, for some, that was simply not true. One person, who was 'saved' later recalled: 'Aching inside I joined the shamed few who struggled to the front. But it was a tainted acceptance – the condition was that I abandon my real self, my self-respect. I crawled to the Father and joined the spiritually raped, emotionally castrated, pathetic people huddling at the altar in shame.'[50] Another who resisted later wrote:

I knew I was risking eternal damnation by not submitting, but somehow the public shame of making that long guilty march to the front of the hangar-shaped "tabernacle" long enough to house a squadron of Spitfires, and baring my soul to the whole community was more frightening than eternal damnation. I quaked and cowered even more when I saw my cousins and schoolmates – sometimes even my buddies – doing it. At such moments I would not have been surprised if the fiery pit had opened at my feet and the cackling fiends had pulled me down forever. I knew it was what I deserved. And still I sat, irrevocably condemned, too terrified to make my move ... By refusing to conform, by not submitting to the blunt tactics of family, school, and tabernacle, I was early branded a rebel at large.[51]

These were not isolated cases. The evangelistic campaigns of the late 1940s and 1950s undoubtedly became the occasion on which many Mennonite adolescents made life-long commitments to the Christian faith and to their church. But the evangelists also did terrible damage. They were in positions of power and authority, claiming to speak on behalf of God himself. And they used powerful methods. For some adolescents the message responded to their own growing awareness of sin and failure and of youthful rebelliousness. But in other cases the message was inconsistent with the training that the young people had received as children, and contrary to the state in which they found themselves as adolescents. Children raised in a loving and supportive atmosphere, who had responded positively to that training, did not suddenly become lost, utterly depraved, and wicked pagans. For such people spiritual growth and maturation were more likely to be incremental rather than revolutionary. They could not honestly replicate the intense sense of guilt and evil of the apostle Paul on the road to Damascus, or of hardened criminals whose stories were a stock in trade of the evangelists. Nor could the results of a positive response be as dramatic or as radical as the evangelists promised. Spiritual, like physical cleansing was not a radical, once-in-a-lifetime experience for most people. It was an ongoing necessity of Christian life.

The Brunk revivals were often described as fires.[52] It was an apt metaphor. In western Canada they burned and destroyed much that was formalistic and traditionalistic in Mennonite community life. They removed much accumulated debris, thus making new growth possible. They also seared and severely damaged many people. In his study of enthusiastic religion in western New York in the nineteenth century Whitney R. Cross documented how destructive the fires of the spirit could be.[53] Those conflagrations left many people as spiritually burned out or intellectually hardened hulks in need of healing and rehabilitation. Revivals drew some into the Kingdom of God while alienating others.

The Janz and Brunk revivals, however, opened the gates of Mennonite communities for other evangelists. Mennonite congregations and Bible schools produced a number of home-grown evangelists eager to emulate the Janz and Brunk crusades, and Mennonites also began to listen to evangelists from outside the Mennonite community. The most important and influential of these were undoubtedly Theodore Epp's 'Back to the Bible' broadcasts, Charles E. Fuller's 'Old Fashioned Gospel Hour,' Billy Graham's 'Hour of Decision,' and Graham's widely publicized evangelistic crusades. Over time these American evangelists, particularly Graham, also helped to focus some fundamental problems facing Mennonites as they tried to accommodate themselves to North American evangelicalism. That, however, is discussed in more detail in a later chapter.

PUBERTY AND SEXUALITY

The gospel as proclaimed by North American evangelists often emphasized spiritual concerns, which were seen as being in conflict with carnal, or worldly things. Frequent denunciations of the pleasures of the flesh resulted in difficult, convoluted, and confusing attitudes toward puberty and sex.

As long as people lived close to nature in rural and agricultural communities there seemed no need for leaders to say much about sexual matters, other than to emphasize that sexual intercourse should take place only within the bonds of marriage.

Several factors led to sharply increasing Mennonite anxiety on this subject during and immediately after the Second World War. The most obvious was that the old social controls became much less effective once people moved out of traditional rural communities, or found new means of transportation, particularly automobiles, which allowed young people to escape the watchful eye of community elders.[54]

Those Mennonites who had come to Canada from Russia or the Soviet Union became particularly alarmed. In the old country they had looked down on the peasantry, in part because of their allegedly disgusting and animalistic sexual behaviour. That revulsion was greatly intensified during the revolution and civil war, when rape, torture, gross abuse of women and girls, and spread of venereal diseases, as well as murder, robbery, and other forms of violence, characterized the reign of terror of Nestor Makhno and his anarchist followers.[55] The repetition, and perhaps even increased magnitude, of sexual crimes against German refugees and civilians by Red Army soldiers in their westward march during the last months of the Second World War left Canadian Mennonites with a terrible impression of what might happen if human sexual behaviour were not firmly controlled. These appalling experiences reinforced social ideas that accepted a fundamental dualism between the human spirit, or mind, and the body, or the lusts of the flesh.[56] Carnal desires must be suppressed if one were to achieve spiritual purity. Sexual activity was for purposes of procreation only.[57]

Anti-sex attitudes are deeply engrained in Christian theology and have found strong expression in times of rapid social or economic change during and following the industrial revolution.[58] In sexual matters, perhaps more than in many other things, Mennonites have always been 'a great deal more reactive than proactive, reacting to the mores and practices of the society in which they lived.'[59] Since they experienced urbanization and industrialization a generation later than most North Americans, they tended in the 1940s and 1950s to accept ideas about human sexuality that had been widely held a generation earlier but were being modified or abandoned by other Canadians.[60]

The first open and public discussion about 'the sexual problem' was initiated by Jacob H. Janzen of Waterloo in December 1941. Janzen noted that when Mennonite young people were obliged to leave their home communities where standards of appropriate behaviour were well understood they needed appropriate instruction on a subject hitherto largely avoided.[61]

Janzen had been a teacher in one of the largest private Mennonite girls' schools in Russia. He had observed and been forced to deal with adolescent girls trying to cope with their developing sex drives. Those observations had led him to some unusual conclusions. He believed that the sex drive in young women was stronger than in young men but that menstruation provided women with urgently needed relief while no comparable natural relief was available to young men.[62] He attributed various mental and spiritual problems faced by women, particularly during adolescence and among spinsters, to a strong but unfulfilled sex drive.[63]

Janzen's main argument, however, was that sex in its proper place was a noble gift of God. He acknowledged that, in addition to the basic biological function of propagating the race, it also provided pleasure and fostered gentler, more loving, and more civilized actions and sentiments. He advocated sexual activities consistent with natural human needs and inclinations but also believed that birth control, masturbation, coitus interruptus, and other unnatural disruptions of the cycles of nature could cause serious mental and spiritual anguish and distress. The main point of his pamphlet, however, was to urge parents to talk openly with their children about sexual matters. He also defended the Mennonite circle games (*Schluesselbund*) played by the young people in some communities at weddings and on other social occasions. He believed that such games and other mixed-gender activities allowed young people to meet and get to know each other in a wholesome atmosphere.

Janzen's pamphlet is perhaps most notable for what it did not say. He did not endorse prevailing vitalist concepts, which were a basic part of much of the religious literature about human sexuality in the early decades of the twentieth century. That literature insisted that vital forces, or life substances, united and enervated all parts of the human organism. All sexual activity – masturbation, nocturnal emissions, and sexual intercourse itself – resulted in the outpouring of this vital energy and could lead to catastrophic consequences.[64] The religious writers reported that care-givers in insane asylums knew that many of the patients under constant surveillance masturbated, and they attributed the insanity to the loss of too many vital forces. Some asylum administrators, dietitians, and medical doctors believed that the eating of red meat particularly stimulated sex drives and that inmates should be given only bland foods.[65] The search for such foods resulted in the invention or introduction by the Kellogg brothers, who ran a big asylum catering mainly to more affluent but troubled Americans at Battle Creek, Michigan, of two foods that have become staples in North American diets – peanut butter and corn flakes.[66]

Janzen did not specifically reject vitalist ideas, but he did not endorse them either. A shortened version of his paper was published in *Der Bote* and elicited generally favourable reviews.[67] He was urged to expand the 22-page paper but declined, arguing that he lacked the necessary medical training. He had written on the basis of his experiences and observations as a teacher in a Mennonite girls' school and felt that he had no comparable competence to discuss the sexual problems of adolescent boys.

Another Mennonite preacher was not so reticent. C.F. Derstine, the well-known evangelist and pastor of the First Mennonite Church in Kitchener, Ontario, wrote three short sex manuals in the 1940s.[68] These were not based on original research, nor were they the product of thoughtful reflection based on personal observation and experiences. Instead, Derstine relied mainly on material written by other North American evangelists, preachers, and self-proclaimed sex specialists such as Dr Sylvannus Stahl, Oscar Lowry, and John R. Rice. Derstine accepted the vitalist concepts held by those writers, trying only to dress them up in appropriate, nonconformist Mennonite clothes. The tone of his books, and of the authors whose ideas he promoted, was unscientific and blatantly anti-sexual. The central idea was stated very succinctly by Oscar Lowry, whose book was used in several Canadian Mennonite Bible schools and colleges: 'Because of the extravagant waste of their sex energy we have in this generation altogether too many of the mamby-pamby, wishy-washy, aimless, shiftless, purposeless, stunted, dwarfed, unambitious specimens of humanity, who have no higher ambition than to hang around pool rooms, saloons, gambling dens, racetracks and the brothels.'[69]

Girls as well as boys were warned about the evils of masturbation, which these writers described as 'an abominable sin against God and nature [which] has no parallel except sodomy.'[70] Anything short of procreation made even the 'sacred intimacies of life nothing more or less that licensed prostitution.'[71] Birth control and abortion were, of course, vehemently denounced. These were the kinds of ideas that Derstine, the most popular evangelist of the (Old) Mennonite church, promoted in his writings. But he linked them closely to Mennonite nonconformist teachings.

In 1947 a Mennonite Brethren preacher and teacher used some of the least scientific aspects of this type of sex education to prepare his own pamphlet, which was to be distributed among Mennonite Brethren young people.[72] Abram Nachtigal of Yarrow, British Columbia, however, became obsessed with masturbation. His fascination with the prophecy, eschatology, and the alleged biblical significance of the number seven, led him to list seven different ways in which masturbation was sinful.

Some of the evangelists writing about sexual matters also developed a peculiar fixation about women's hair, which gained wide currency in some Canadian Mennonite churches. John R. Rice, citing scripture, attributed all manner of social ills to the fact that women cut or 'bobbed' their hair.[73] According to him, long hair for a woman meant submission to her husband or father. Short hair meant rebellion against the God-given authority of fathers and husbands. Women with such attitudes made bossy, and therefore unsatisfactory, wives. Some might even aspire to become preachers, in direct contradiction of the scriptures, as interpreted by Rice, which clearly taught that women should not be allowed to speak in church.

Canadian Mennonite anxieties and misinformation regarding sexual matters collided in the 1940s with rapidly changing attitudes and concerns by other Canadians. As early as the 1920s some social scientists advocated better and more accurate information on human sexuality. Most Canadians were not ready for such advice in the 1920s, but public attitudes changed significantly during the war years. Military authorities were appalled at the sexual ignorance of some recruits and offered tough, realistic, often crude instruction dealing particularly with sexually transmitted diseases and the very unpleasant ways in which military doctors dealt with such problems.

School boards were also encouraged to provide better sex education. Mennonite leaders, however, protested vigorously against all forms of sex education in the schools. They feared that it would teach students only how to avoid the consequences of sexual sin, rather than provide stern warnings against such sins. They also feared that sex education might increase the curiosity of those taught. In 1949, for example, the Mennonite Brethren Conference of Alberta, meeting at Linden, passed a resolution protesting against any form of sex education in high schools. B.B. Janz was instructed to bring this protest before the government, which he did in a long, revealing, but also remarkable letter in which he described sex education as a communist plot designed to undermine the moral and physical fibre of the West.[74]

There were, fortunately, also some Mennonite writers who offered more sensible advice about human sexuality and the role of women in society. An early American Mennonite contributor was H. Clair Amstutz, a medical doctor, who wrote in the 1950s. In the 1960s several conferences and symposia were held, in which Mennonite medical doctors, theologians, and ethicists sought to dispel the old myths and superstitions. The old mind-body dualism was questioned, and new understanding and interpretations designed to reunite sexuality and spirituality were developed. There was a new emphasis on wholeness and 'shalom.'[75] 'Sexuality,' according to a recent Mennonite encyclopedia article, 'has within it those elements, both physical and spiritual, that can be used to fulfil God's will for individual lives.'[76] This understanding led many leaders and educators to abandon harshly judgmental principles and rigid prohibitions when dealing with sexual problems, opting instead for premarital counselling, seminars, retreats, and marriage encounters, designed to improve sexual relationships within marriage and to strengthen feelings of self-worth and responsibility by both partners.[77]

But the changes were not easy. In 1970 the English-language *Canadian Mennonite* carried a feature article entitled 'Sex Is Great.' The message was simple and explicit. 'Sex is a beautiful fact of life, and when actualized in marriage adds magnificent dimensions to man/wife relationships. But outside of marriage? Sex can be explosively destructive.'[78] The article elicited numerous letters from readers. Some were highly supportive, but others were furious. Several immediately cancelled their subscriptions. A Winnipeg reader wrote, 'We have children growing up and if you can't print anything better than sex articles ... we want none of it.'[79] Another reader described the article as 'plain filth and dirt.' After reading it, she felt 'as though one has been wading in a gutter.'[80]

These responses prompted a Mennonite pastor, marriage counsellor, educator, and broadcaster to explain that he had encountered numerous instances where sexual problems led to marriage and family breakups and that such people needed help. That message was obviously very different from the one proclaimed by C.F. Derstine several decades earlier.[81]

FROM ADOLESCENCE TO MEMBERSHIP

Three widely recognized steps marked the end of the uncertain adolescent period in the lives of Canadian Mennonites. First, there should be an informed, voluntary, adult acceptance or affirmation of salvation and a conscious decision or commitment to order one's life in accordance with the principles and teachings of Jesus. This was followed by adult baptism – public affirmation of the personal decision – and initiation into membership. Baptism was followed, often in only a short time, by marriage, and thus entry into the approved, if often idealized, pattern of adult Mennonite life.

In traditional communities these three critical steps – affirmation of faith, baptism, and marriage – tended to take place in a fairly short period and were closely linked. The post-1940 changes tended to weaken the links and extend the period over which these three steps were taken. The significance and meaning attached to each step, particularly baptism, also changed.

The first step postulated a personal decision to turn from an 'unsaved' adolescence to a committed life of Christian discipleship. The term 'conversion' was used to signify 'the changing of purpose, direction, and spirit of life from one of self-seeking and enmity toward God to one of love toward God and man.'[82] Some Mennonites saw conversion as a one-time, revolutionary, and intensely emotional experience; others believed that such a decision should be the logical outcome of a longer, evolutionary process in which education and nurture were critical. But there was general agreement that there must be a personal decision, however arrived at, and that only God's grace and forgiveness of sins made it possible for the individual to begin a new life.

Some form of conversion was regarded as essential before baptism. Baptism was not regarded as an indispensable prerequisite of salvation, but it was widely accepted as one of the most important and meaningful experiences of special grace in the life of a Christian. It was thus a sacrament in some sense of that term and, like most sacraments, also a formal rite of passage, in this case from adolescence to adulthood and from an uncertain and dependent status to one of full membership in the congregation.

Two elements are integral to Mennonite adult baptism. First, it signifies a conscious and deliberate decision and commitment by the person being baptized to accept and follow the scriptures and, especially, all the teachings of Jesus. In addition, the candidate accepts and makes a commitment to obey and respect the rules, practices, and teachings of the local congregation and of the larger conference of which that congregation might be a member. The relative emphasis placed on the two commitments varied, though there was a general assumption that the two would not be in conflict with one another.

Changing circumstances, however, made specific prohibitions increasingly impractical and virtually impossible to enforce, particularly in urban congregations with mobile memberships, and many congregations abandoned such legalisms.

There were other elements or interpretations of the meaning of baptism where there was disagreement between Mennonite congregations and conferences. Those who viewed the growth of their members to maturity as a gradual or evolutionary process, and life as a spiritual journey in which individuals commit sins and experience failures and need divine forgiveness or cleansing both before and after making a mature personal commitment to the faith, normally pour or sprinkle water on the head of the individual being baptized, thereby signifying that individual's spiritual cleansing or washing. There were, however, some congregations and conferences that baptized by pouring or sprinkling but also supported 'crisis' conversions.[83]

Those who attached greater importance to one or perhaps several cataclysmic emotional conversion experiences, and who defined such an event as a spiritual death and resurrection, baptized by immersion. According to their theology, the individual had been 'dead in sin' but resurrected or reborn to new spiritual life. Baptism by immersion in the waters of a river, lake, or baptismal tank in the church signified the believer's spiritual death, burial, and resurrection.[84]

These differing interpretations of the meaning and consequences of baptism generated considerable controversy when individuals baptized in one way applied for membership in a congregation practising another form. Sometimes intermarriage was the reason for such transfers. In other cases individuals who had been baptized and become members of one conference, perhaps still in the Soviet Union or in a postwar European refugee camp, found themselves in a community where their conference had no congregation or where they found another Mennonite church more attractive. Those churches practising baptism by pouring or sprinkling were generally willing to accept into membership individuals who had been baptized by immersion, but for many years the reverse was not true. The problem probably had less to do with the form of baptism than with the importance that immersionist groups attached to dramatic conversion.

The immersionist churches, however, began to soften their position in the 1960s, manifesting greater openness on both the form and meaning of baptism. In part this was a response to the fact that some members found the death-and-resurrection theology implicit in baptism by immersion inconsistent with their own, more evolutionary experiences. A Mennonite Brethren college president, for example, urged that churches emphasize in their teaching and preaching the meaning of baptism as a sign of one's coming to faith and then give sufficient latitude with regard to the specific form so that the experience would reflect the spiritual experience of the candidate. He argued that sprinkling or pouring may be more appropriate for someone who is born and reared within the community of faith, and immersion for the adult convert coming from the non-Christian world, as did converts in the New Testament.[85]

Baptism and full membership in the local and world-wide community of believers were traditionally seen as prerequisites to marriage and the commencement of family life in a manner supported and approved by the congregation and the community. Marriage was the second important ceremony of special divine grace in the lives of most Mennonites: 'Fundamentally the Anabaptist-Mennonite view of marriage reflects and represents the concern for the voluntary "community of the saints." In this perspective marriage is seen as its germ cell. It is cared for and cultivated as a religious *Gesinnungsehe*, a community of the spirit. Marriage and the family are submitted to rules of conduct arising from the New Testament and are also dedicated to the principles of the Sermon on the Mount.'[86]

Community, congregational, and family life and activities were integral and interrelated aspects of Christian living. Mutual support and reciprocal expectations and assistance were assumed and widely practised in traditional Mennonite communities. But there were defined boundaries that, if crossed, deprived the individual of such support. In the 1940s and 1950s none of the Mennonite conferences sanctioned divorce or the remarriage of divorced people. In such matters official positions tended to be legalistic, judgmental, and rigid, rather than supportive, sympathetic, loving, forgiving, and redemptive, unless the individuals involved first confessed their 'sins' and humbly sought forgiveness.

The terrible ambiguities and problems of war refugees whose matrimonial partner had either disappeared in the vast Soviet labour camps, or of families torn apart by the exigencies of war, created serious problems for congregations where large numbers of these people became members. In many cases the survivor, usually female, who had escaped to Canada did not know whether her partner was dead or alive. In other cases new liaisons had been formed. These difficult situations created seemingly insoluble problems for leaders who were intent on maintaining traditional principles but were also sensitive to the pain and suffering that rigid insistence on those principles might cause. Relatively young people who had lost a spouse whose fate was unknown were condemned to a life alone, with only limited means of support, even though there was little or no prospect of a reunion.

The rigidity exhibited by those dealing with such cases had less to do with the specifics of those cases than with concerns that deviations from the accepted norms would communicate the wrong message to young people. But adherence to accepted marital standards did not shield congregations from the realities of modern life. In the 1940s, divorce was almost invariably followed by excommunication of the offending partner and advice to the other partner to persevere and to bear whatever burdens had to be borne. In the following decades, divorce became an inescapable reality.

The resulting turmoil was often painful. There were many who feared that any relaxation of marital standards would destabilize family and congregational life. Several documented cases in church minutes in the 1950s pertain to couples who were guilty of premarital sex and were then forced to confess their sins, in detail, before the assembled brotherhood. Sometimes the individuals involved were then banned for periods of between a month and a year from any church work and sometimes from social contacts with other members. Ordained ministers who transgressed in this regard were banned for life from further preaching or teaching in some Canadian Mennonite churches.

The punishment meted out was often much harsher for women than for men, apparently because the leaders feared that such transgressions threatened family, congregational, and community stability in a more fundamental way. In one documented case of incest the father was forced to confess his sins before the assembled 'brotherhood,' and then his membership was suspended for three months. The young daughter, who was then a teenager but whose abuse began while she was a child, was barred from any participation in the choir, Sunday school, or other church work for a year. In another instance, a young preacher allegedly visited a prostitute but, according to his own testimony, lost the desire at the last moment. His punishment was far less onerous than that of the female victim of incest. In confidential conversations, a number of older ministers also reported cases in which sexual offences by leading ministers were dealt with quietly and without public notice, lest the scandal tarnish the reputation of the church in the community. This method stood in sharp contrast to the harsh treatment accorded less influential offenders, particulary women – in some cases by the very same leaders who had themselves 'fallen' but whose affairs had not been made public.[87]

Harsh condemnation of individuals who were weak, confused, and vulnerable prompted concerned church members, often those closest to the people involved, to recall Jesus' response when a woman taken in adultery was brought to him. Under Jewish law the woman should be stoned, but Jesus simply asked that any person without sin cast the first stone. None did, but an adjustment towards that kind of thinking was difficult for many Canadian Mennonite leaders, who thought primarily of family, congregational, and community controls, which seemed to be weakening. Nevertheless, almost all Mennonite churches in urban centres, and later those in rural communities, eventually had to re-evaluate their position.

There were, however, some groups that retained firm standards, even if they lost many members. Those groups practising a rigid 'ban' or 'avoidance' of excommunicated members also applied it to sexual relations between married couples if only one partner was excommunicated. Accounts of methods used to ensure marital avoidance in such cases suggest that it was difficult to enforce and usually led to withdrawal from membership or excommunication of the partner who had not been initially banned. Religious sanctions alone were not as effective as they had once been when people had lived in relatively closed communities, where leaders exerted not only religious but also economic, social, political, and cultural authority.

CONCLUSION

Canadian Mennonites found that many of the methods whereby they passed on their heritage of faith to the next generation had to be modified as the traditional social controls of small, relatively isolated, rural, and closed communities weakened. Education, nurture, and training replaced some of the harsher, paternalistic methods of child training. The normal difficulties, confusion, and uncertainties of adolescence became more intense for many Mennonite young people because some preachers, evangelists, leaders, and teachers, fearing the weakening of traditional methods of social control, opted for conversion-oriented religious doctrines and practices that either did not fit the childhood training and experiences of their young people or accentuated and reinforced dubious aspects of patriarchal and evangelical/ecclesiastical tyranny and abuse. There were substantial but largely undocumented losses of children born into Mennonite families who did not join the churches of their parents. But there were many more children who were trained, nurtured, educated, and disciplined in ways that led them to question and challenge but then to accept the faith of their parents and forebears.

Statistics are, at best, a crude and imprecise measure of success in propagating the faith. The arrival of thousands of immigrants from war-torn Europe further complicate any assessment of the effectiveness of Canadian Mennonite attempts to transmit the faith to their offspring. But in 1941, 111,554 Canadians told census takers that they were Mennonites; in 1971, 168,150 did so. Membership figures show a comparable increase. Those statistics suggest that Canadian Mennonites propagated the Gospel among their own young people with results that would delight most voluntarist religious groups.

10

Church and Community Schools

Mennonites in Canada have always attached much importance to the education that their children received in private, secular, or church schools.[1] They believed that schools had a responsibility to prepare children for a productive life as adults and also to preserve and perpetuate the religious and cultural values of their communities and congregations. Canadian Mennonites have not, however, always agreed on the occupation or productive work that their children should do as adults, particularly as members moved to cities. As a result, ideas about schooling also diverged.

In 1939 Canadian Mennonite schools, except for two private high schools, were local or community-based institutions. They offered instruction at the elementary and intermediate levels, or specialized and practical religious training at the post-intermediate level. After 1939 there emerged more broadly based secondary and post-secondary institutions of learning. Local congregational or community schools changed; some flourished after the war and exercised increased influence in Mennonite communities, while others prospered for a time but then fell into decline. This chapter deals with community- or congregation-based elementary, Sunday, German, and Bible schools. The next chapter tells the story of Mennonite high schools and colleges.

ELEMENTARY SCHOOLS

The pattern of Mennonite elementary schooling in Ontario evolved slowly, while in western Canada it was set during and after the first World War.[2] Though education is primarily a provincial responsibility, elementary schooling was similar everywhere in Canada except in Quebec and Newfoundland.

The earliest elementary schools were organized by local community leaders, who hired teachers and determined curriculum. In many rural districts of Ontario local control had remained strong, even after small rural schools became public schools eligible for financial assistance from local and provincial governments. Local trustees still hired teachers, who had to follow the provincial curriculum, which allowed considerable flexibility. There was some patriotic and nationalist sentiment during the first World War, but Ontario Mennonites living in relatively compact rural communities could organize and operate their schools pretty much as they saw fit.[3]

The situation was more difficult on the prairies, mainly because of mixed settlement by homesteaders. It was impractical for each group to establish its own school in such communities, and many English-speaking settlers and government officials thought that all groups should learn English and how to function in a Canadian environment. So-called national schools, many thought, could help achieve these assimilationist objectives. As a result provincial and territorial governments in western Canada established a tax-supported public or 'national' school system in the 1890s. The legislation did not prohibit private schools, but their supporters were not exempt from public school taxes.

Increased nationalistic fervour during the Great War sharply increased public demands that elementary schools, particularly in immigrant communities, more effectively foster national integration.[4] New legislation made it compulsory for all children of designated school age to attend an approved school that followed the official curriculum and hired only qualified teachers. Patriotic exercises such as flag raising, the singing of the national anthem, recitation of the Lord's prayer, and in some schools promotion of cadet and other para-military activities were components of public education.

Mennonite leaders recognized that the public schools were designed to educate and integrate children from many racial, ethnic, and religious backgrounds into the mainstream of Canadian life. In their own private schools they stressed nonconformity to the world and within their own communities an integrated and holistic life-style in which all learning was permeated by religious knowledge, wisdom, faith, and insights. They did not think 'national' public schools met their needs.

Provincial authorities eventually accepted a compromise, allowing a half-hour of special religious instruction before or after the regular school day but still insisting that all young people attend public school. That, obviously, was not satisfactory to those demanding a fully integrated religious and secular curriculum, but it seemed the only practical course, given such religious diversity in the schools.[5]

Mennonites responded to these changes in several ways. Those most

strongly committed to the old ideals moved to agricultural frontiers in northern Canada or in Latin America. Others accepted the new arangements but
found ways to mitigate them. Curricula provided some flexibility and choices
in material and the way it was covered and regarding school activities. In
small, compact Mennonite communities served by a one- or two-room school,
notably those of the Old Order in Ontario and in the Manitoba and
Saskatchewan Mennonite reserves, residents could serve on the local school
board or elect people sympathetic to their wishes and thus have a voice in
selecting teachers, choosing curriculum, and planning school activities. Qualified Mennonite teachers who had studied at Mennonite high schools at
Gretna, Manitoba, or Rosthern, Saskatchewan, or other qualified teachers
sympathetic to Mennonite principles, could be, and were, hired by many
boards in Mennonite communities. Such teachers could avoid patriotic exercises and school activities such as school dances which parents found offensive. And there could be religious instruction during the half-hour before or
after the regular school day. In many schools in southern Manitoba the pattern was one-half hour of religious education before and half an hour of
German after the school day, which ran from 8:30 a.m. to 4:00 p.m. This was
not the system that Mennonites wanted, but most reluctantly accepted it
while arranging supplementary religious instruction for their offspring.

A new threat – school consolidation – emerged in the 1930s and created a
crisis for Ontario Old Order Mennonite and Amish groups in the 1960s.
The consolidations of the 1930s, which occurred mainly in western Canada,
were made necessary by the Depression and depopulation of rural districts.
Those of the 1960s in Ontario were motivated by concern about the quality
of education offered in one- and two-room schools. Modern education, it
was argued, required proper but expensive library, laboratory, and gymna-
sium facilities. Those were viable only if the many small rural schools were
closed and consolidated facilities were built in the larger centres. On the
prairies, consolidation was carried out gradually, and Mennonite opposition
was a little slower but differed little from that in other small communities
that regreted loss of their little school.

In Ontario consolidation became official policy in the 1960s. But people in
some rural communities, including many Mennonite ones, clung tenaciously
to their schools. They felt strongly that courses offered in large, consolidated
schools were not designed for farm children. The *Milverton Sun*, for example,
complained: 'The educational system as we know it offers very little for the
farmer. Many students, and all Amish Mennonite students in this rich farmland
area of ours, are wasting their time in our schools ... when they graduate they
have learned absolutely nothing about their chosen field – farming.'[6]

The Ontario government nevertheless in 1964 established township area schools, operated by local boards. This change resulted in the closing of rural one- and two-room schools and greatly weakened the influence of local people over their children's education.

Almost all the Old Order people refused to send their children to consolidated schools. They decided instead to set up private elementary schools. Similar developments in the United States had already resulted in major challenges in the courts. Canada had no guarantees similar to those enshrined in the U.S. constitution. There was consequently much greater pressure to garner public support, to negotiate, and to compromise rather than to litigate. The Old Orders received support in the press, among the general public, and from other Mennonite and community organizations.

Elven Shantz, a Waterloo Mennonite businessman, and Douglas Snyder, director of the Mennonite Central Committee (Ontario), handled most of the negotiations. Much of the discussion centred on competing views of which educational system would best serve the local community and how the objectives of the Old Order people could be harmonized with the desires of other members of the community. There was concern that without Old Order enrolments and tax support there would not be sufficient funding for construction of consolidated schools, with appropriate laboratory, library, and physical education facilities.

A negotiated compromise placed the Old Order people under a system of double school taxation. They still had to pay regular school taxes, but if, at their own expense, they wanted their own system, the old school-houses were made available to them if those facilities were in suitable locations. Where appropriate buildings were not available, private schools were built and paid for by the Old Orders. There was also at least one rural school near St Jacob's where the school board negotiated with the county board of education at the time of consolidation to keep the school in the public system but to retain local autonomy. Since the school was of a substantial size and solidly Mennonite, the board acquiesced.[7]

In their private schools Old Order Amish and Old Order Mennonites appointed teachers and approved the curriculum. The schools were subject to government inspection and review and could be closed by the minister of education if instruction were deemed unsatisfactory.

The Old Order people received invaluable help from James Bauman, a well-qualified and able public school teacher and administrator who 'offered his services as a supervisor of the proposed schools, and as a mediator between them and the Ministry of Education. During the summer of 1966, he conducted a two week course for preparing would-be teachers for the classroom. Seven trainees attended, six of them taught school for the coming year while James taught in the seventh.'[8]

After the first year, Bauman regularly ran two-week summer programs for new teachers and selected and made sure that appropriate textbooks and supplies were available and that proper timetables and student registers were prepared for each school. He also administered standardized tests which made it possible to compare the performance of pupils in the private schools with that of students in the public system. This was possible because the basic curriculum of the private schools met the province's rather vaguely defined requirements: 'The Ministry of Education has set no special rules or guidelines for us. The school law states, as nearly as I can quote it, that a child must attend school from age six or seven until he reaches the age of sixteen, unless in the opinion of the Minister, he receives satisfactory education otherwise. By this, I would surmise that the Minister has been sitting back for these eighteen years, to see what the results are. Obviously, the results are proving satisfactory, or the Minister would have closed down our schools long before this.'[9]

There was some grumbling when Ontario increased the minimum age at which children could leave school from 14 to 16. The provision had been that children must attend school until 16 unless it could be demonstrated that they were needed for work on their parents' farm. Old Order parents had generally availed themselves of this provision to end their children's education at age 14. Even the limited mechanization of Old Order farms, however, had reduced the need for such labour, and in an appropriately planned curriculum there was much that 14- and 15-year-olds could learn about modern farming. So the requirement that these children remain in school until their sixteenth birthday was accepted after discussions about the instruction to be offered in the additional two years.

The private Mennonite schools met the interests of those who believed that elementary school was sufficient for students who would become farmers, mechanics, or housewives in rural farming communities. The children learned the basic things that they needed to know but remained ignorant of much that would be of use to them only if they left their farms and communities.

Scattered Mennonite settlement patterns and provincial legal impediments, particularly in western Canada, made it impossible to establish private elementary schools in many communities there. Parents and church leaders had to find alternative means to provide religious instruction once offered in Mennonite private schools. Sunday schools, German Saturday schools, and Bible schools were set up to provide what had been lost.

SUNDAY SCHOOLS

In the larger Mennonite settlements in Ontario, Sunday schools were begun, usually before 1900, in those churches where the new evangelistic influences were welcomed. Where members retained effective control over local schools, the transition tended to be slower, but services, even in large, central (Old) Mennonite and Amish Mennonite congregations, were held only on alternate Sundays, so that Sunday school could fill the space every other week. In some Amish Mennonite congregations, the excuse that German could be taught to the children was also used to justify Sunday schools, which ironically became vehicles for more rapid change to English. Sunday schools nevertheless filled perceived gaps in the school and/or congregational instruction offered to children.

Sunday schools originated in the late eighteenth century, where they were created to teach poor factory children in England something about morals and religion and to keep them off the streets. Early-nineteenth-century British and American Sunday schools were organized by private individuals, mainly to evangelize the poor and unchurched. Leaders in the established churches provided catechetical instruction for their own young people, and many opposed the Sunday schools because they did not observe denominational boundaries.

After 1840 Sunday schools came to be seen more as an appropriate vehicle for the religious instruction of children. The first Mennonite Sunday school in North America was apparently established in Waterloo county, Ontario, in 1840. Growth in Ontario was uneven, with some congregations and conferences giving enthusiastic support, while others resisted. In western Canada Sunday schools grew rapidly in most Mennonite communities that had lost their private elementary schools.

Sunday schools were not common in Mennonite churches in pre-revolutionary Russia, in part because Mennonites controlled their own elementary and secondary schools. Mennonites who immigrated to Canada in the 1870s tried to replicate that model, but loss of control over their own elementary schools and arrival of immigrants from the United States led to opening of Sunday schools in some of the 'Kanadier' churches (Kanadier were the immigrants of the 1870s). Other Kanadier congregations resisted Sunday schools until consolidation. The immigrants of the 1920s ('Russlaender') quickly and enthusiastically accepted Sunday schools. As a result, almost all but the most traditional Mennonite churches in Canada had them by the late 1930s.[10]

Sunday schools provided basic religious training, but they also became effective instruments of change, innovation, and renewal.[11] Religious instruction in the old parochial Mennonite elementary schools had included the learning of selected Bible stories and, in more advanced classes, memorization of a series of questions and answers that constituted the Mennonite catechism. Such instruction, by most accounts, was not exciting or intellectually stimulating.[12] The new Sunday school curriculum materials prepared by evangelical churches and conferences were much more colourful and interesting.[13] They also introduced new ideas, approaches, and influences.[14] Stories pertaining to experiences familiar to the children were added to those from the Bible. New and more lively music and other artwork, and some new methods of child evangelism, were introduced.

The three major North American Mennonite conferences each devoted much time and thought to preparation of their own material, while the smaller ones depended on material from the larger conferences, from other denominations, or from interdenominational Sunday school associations. In preparation of pupil and teacher guides Mennonites in Canada encountered two serious problems. The first pertained to language. In the 1940s, only the larger and long-established Mennonite churches in Ontario conducted their worship and educational programs in English. German was preferred elsewhere. Sunday school literature coming from American Mennonite or non-Mennonite sources, however, was almost all written in English. Only the Canadian Mennonite Brethren made a determined effort in the late 1930s and the 1940s to develop complete Sunday school lesson materials in German. But their material was less colourful or interesting than some of the English materials, and the rather elaborate work booklets required a competence in German that many children did not possess. There were also obvious problems if neighbourhood children of non-Mennonite background, or Mennonite children whose parents spoke English at home, came to Sunday school. As a result, the language transition in churches usually began in the Sunday schools.[15]

The language problem was further complicated by theological difficulties. Materials from non-Mennonite publishing houses did not nessesarily reflect Mennonite values and doctrines, particularly those relating to war and peace.[16] Some Canadian Mennonites also felt somewhat uneasy about some of the materials published by the North American Mennonite conferences. In the 1920s fundamentalism had created bitter controversies in Mennonite churches and conferences in the United States and, to a lesser extent, in the Swiss Mennonite churches in Ontario. U.S. Sunday school materials disseminated these influences in Canada in ways that those who had come from Russia sometimes found disconcerting.

Sunday schools introduced new ideas and opened valuable opportunities for service by younger, often highly idealistic and motivated, church members, including many young women who became teachers there at a time when most other church activities were male dominated. [17] Younger teachers found there a means of expression for their creative, artistic, leadership, and pedagogical talents. Alternative worship experiences were tolerated and even encouraged in Sunday schools at a time when they were not yet allowed in male-led adult worship services. The singing of gospel choruses with a lively beat, accompanied at times by children clapping their hands or acting out parts of the chorus, created a cheerful and exciting atmosphere. Dramatic productions, particularly enactment of the Christmas story for the annual Christmas Eve program or Sunday school promotion services, provided further creative outlets at a time when theatres and movies were still forbidden. These activities placed Sunday schools 'at the cutting edge of new developments in the churches,'[18] but some leaders feared that they trivialized the Gospel.

Memorization remained important. Children, even those only four or five years old, were encouraged to memorize a short scripture verse each week, while older ones were offered rewards for memorizing longer passages. In some Sunday schools the older children were also encouraged to memorize the catechism, but in others that was done in special church membership classes, while still others dispensed entirely with the catechism.

There was rarely any doubt regarding the basic objectives of Sunday schools. Their first and most important task was to familiarize children with the Bible and the events recorded there. Those tales were often told in a didactic fashion, as were other stories from everyday life, but students did become familiar with the accounts in the Bible. In some Sunday schools students were also placed under considerable pressure once it was thought that they were mature enough for a conversion experience. There were, however, also warnings about possible abuses if excessive emotional pressure were brought to bear on young children.[19]

Another topic that received much attention was missionary activity.[20] The objective was to increase the children's love of other needy people, but much of the material also described in colourful and graphic detail the ignorance, superstitions, and bizarre behaviour of 'the heathen.' These were people who were expected to change their entire way of life and accept the 'superior' Western and Christian outlook of the missionaries; only then could they achieve success and happiness. Rarely was there any mention of insights or spiritual understanding that these people may have had before the coming of the missionaries. They were portrayed as people living in spiritual and intellectual darkness and economic squalor, simply awaiting the coming of the missionaries who would dispense light and understanding and thus help them to a happy and fulfilled life. The most gripping missionary stories involved contests of wills between the missionary and some local chieftain or witch doctor, with the missionary and his or her God always coming out victorious.

Children were curious about strange people and far-away places. They dreamed of excitement and adventure and rejoiced in the victories of the missionaries. It all seemed so much more interesting, exciting, and worthwhile to rove the plains and jungles of some African mission field in an open land rover than to spend the week hoeing weeds in the family vegetable garden or thinning sugar beets under a hot sun.

Sunday schools opened new horizons, introduced new ideas and teaching methods, and provided a cherished avenue of service for many young people, particularly young women. They offered the religious instruction that children in many Mennonite communities had previously received in elementary school. Some Mennonite groups, notably the Old Order Amish and the Old Order Mennonites, steadfastly rejected the Sunday school, but their children usually went to private rather than public elementary schools.

At first Sunday schools represented outside influences about which at least some leaders were apprehensive. Over the years, however, a few conferences modified the curriculum to include more frequent references to distinctive Mennonite doctrines, ideas, and values.

GERMAN SATURDAY SCHOOLS

Preservation of the German language, as the preferred language of religious instruction and worship, or as a spiritual, cultural, and ethnic treasure, or simply as the necessary means to communicate with older members of immigrant communities, was still a matter of great concern to some Mennonite leaders in the 1930s. That concern became somewhat muted during the war years but was renewed in several of the larger Mennonite communities afterward.

The amount of German, if any, that could be taught in the public schools was demonstrably inadequate, and the Sunday school, even if conducted in the German language, was not the place to teach German grammar and vocabulary. Yet survival of German as the language of worship and communication required training in these essential but mundane aspects of the language. The preferred place for such instruction in immigrant Mennonite communities was in special Saturday, or in some cases Friday evening, schools. This meant, of course, that Mennonite children attended school every day of the week, but it was generally accepted that Sunday school must not exact a rigour inconsistent with the theology of a day of rest. Saturday schools were never restricted or inhibited in that regard. Vocabulary, grammar, reading aloud, penmanship, and the recitation of memorized scripture and folk verses and songs were the typical ingredients. A German-language primer, *Die Fibel*, and later increasingly advanced readers (*Lesebuecher*), which included mainly cultural and literary material, were used in the schools.[21]

A number of these schools came under attack from patriotic zealots during the early years of the second World War. In some communities, where Mennonites used the public schools or other public buildings and facilities for their Saturday schools, continued use was denied them, and they had to close the schools or move them into their own churches.[22] Opposition was, however, not widespread. B.B. Janz, for example, offered to close the German Saturday schools at Coaldale, Alberta, as a gesture of goodwill but was never asked to do so.[23]

German-language Saturday schools included extensive teaching of Bible stories and elementary training in Christian ethics. The year-end programs included German secular as well as religious recitations, short dramatic presentations, and much folk and religious music.[24] But those who hoped that the schools would ensure that German remained the language of worship and everyday communication must have regarded these schools as failures. The schools functioned reasonably well in the largest immigrant Mennonite communities, but not in more isolated settlements. And even in the largest communities there were always many Mennonite children or parents who could think of other, more interesting or necessary things to do on Saturdays. Interest and support waned as English became the language of everyday communication, of instruction in the Sunday schools, and eventually of worship in the churches. As a result, few German Saturday schools remained in 1970, and those that did attracted children from ethnic German, rather than exclusively German-speaking Mennonite, backgrounds.

For school children of the 1940s, English became the primary language of communication, but the Saturday schools familiarized a generation of Canadian Mennonites with aspects of their German heritage. Students did not necessarily appreciate them, but those who attended came away with a useful knowledge and understanding of a second language that they could use elsewhere. University classes in German, and even the language exams for Ph.D candidates, were much easier for students with a Saturday school training than for those without such exposure to the language.

BIBLE SCHOOLS

Mennonite children received their elementary schooling either in public or in private schools. In many congregations that training was supplemented by Sunday and German Saturday schools. There was, however, a feeling by some parents that children did not get sufficient biblical instruction. Effective work and participation in the churches required further and more intensive study of the Bible and practical training for prospective preachers, Sunday school teachers, choir conductors, and other church workers. Bible conferences of varying duration, and short-term courses during winter, when farm people had more time free, became popular. There was, moreover, a gap between completion of elementary schooling and marriage. During summers such young people normally worked on parental or other farms, but there was time in winter for further study.

Bible schools typically offered 'a Bible-centred, intensely practical, lay-oriented program of post-secondary theological training.'[25] It is estimated that Protestant groups set up more than 140 in Canada after 1885, at least 90 of them in the West. Forty-four of the latter were started by Mennonites. The Mennonite Brethren (MBs) established more Bible schools than any other denomination.[26]

The first Canadian Mennonite Bible school was started in Ontario. S.F. Coffman, then an itinerant evangelist, preached frequently in the province in the 1890s. Beginning in 1899, he was instrumental in arranging Bible conferences which would 'instruct Christians to appreciate the Bible, to know the will of God, understand the Christian life, and then give faithful testimony both in life and service.'[27] In 1907 the (Old) Mennonites added to the annual Bible conference a Bible study class, which was to last for several weeks. That class grew and flourished, eventually becoming the Ontario Mennonite Bible School.

In the west the first Mennonite Bible school was started at Herbert, Saskatchewan, in 1913. Unlike the Ontario Bible study class, the Bible school at Herbert sought to teach preachers, missionaries, Sunday school teachers, and other church workers. It was closed in 1918 but reopened in 1921 and operated continuously until 1958.[28] After the First World War many new Mennonite Bible schools were opened in Ontario and on the prairies.[29] Table 10.1 identifies the schools that opened between 1900 and 1976.[30]

The responsibilities of the Bible schools were threefold. First and most important, they imparted basic biblical knowledge and understanding, to enrich and guide individuals who would become parents, farmers, housewives, and supportive church members. Second, they prepared or trained future preachers, church leaders, choristers, choir conductors, Sunday school teachers, missionaries, and other church workers. Finally, they helped preserve a distinct Mennonite identity and witness during a time of rapid change.

Table 10.1
Canadian Mennonite Bible schools, 1900–70

Date opened	Place	Name	Affiliation	Date closed
1907	Kitchener, Ont.	Ontario Mennonite Bible School/Institute[31]	MC	1969
1913	Edmonton, Alta.	Edmonton Bible Institute[32]	MBC	>1940
1913	Herbert, Sask.	Herbert Bible School[33]	MB	1957
1913	Markham, Ont.	Winter Bible School[34]	MC	>1940
1921	Didsbury, Alta.	Mountain View Bible School[35]	MBC	>1940
1925	Winkler, Man.	Peniel Bible School[36]	MB	–
1927	Hepburn, Sask.	Bethany Bible School[37]	MB	–
1928	Dalmeny, Sask.	Tabor Bible School[38]	Int.	1954
1929	Gretna/Altona, Man.	Elim Bible School[39]	CMC	1988
1929	Coaldale, Alta.	Morning Star Bible School[40]	MB	1965
1930	Winnipeg, Man.	Winnipeg German Bible School[41]	MB	1942
1930	Yarrow, BC	Elim Bible School[42]	MB	1955
1931	Steinbach, Man.	Steinbach Bible School[43]	Int.	–
1932	Springvale/Gormley Ft Erie, Ont.	Ontario Bible School/ Niagara Christian College[44]	BIC	–
1932	Glenbush, Sask.	Glenbush Bible School[45]	MB	>1940
1932	Rosthern, Sask.	Rosthern Bible School[46]	CMC	1961
1932	Tavistock, Ont.	Winter Bible School[47]	AM	195?
1932	Rosemary, Alta.	Rosemary Bible School[48]	CMC	1942
1932	Winnipeg, Man.	Mennonitische Religionsschule[49]	CMC	1947
1933	La Glace, Alta.	La Glace Bible School[50]	MB	1946
1933	Gem, Alta.	Bethesda Bible School[51]	MB	1946
1933	Baden, Ont.	Winter Bible School[52]	AM	195?
1934	Aberdeen, Sask.	Aberdeen Bible School[53]	CMC	>1940
1934	Wembley, Alta.	Wembley Bible School[54]	CMC	>1940
1934	Alberta (itinerant)	Winter Bible School[55]	MC	1954
1935	Springridge, Alta.	Springridge Bible School[56]	CMC	>1940
1935	Crowfoot, Alta.	Crowfoot Bible School[57]	MB	1937
1936	Wellesley, Ont.	Winter Bible School[58]	AM	196?
1936	Leamington, Ont.	Leamington Bible School[59]	CMC	194?
1936	Abbotsford/ Clearbrook, BC	South Abbotsford Bible School/ Mennonite Brethren Bible Institute of BC[60]	MB	1970
1936	Swift Current, Sask.	Swift Current Bible Institute[61]	CMC	–
1936	Didsbury, Alta.	Menno Bible Institute[62]	CMC	1967
1936	Vineland, Ont.	Vineland Bible School[63]	CMC	1946
1937	Vauxhall, Alta.	Vauxhall Bible School[64]	MB	1943
1937	Speedwell, Sask.	Bible School[65]	MB	>1940
1937	St Elizabeth, Man.	St Elizabeth Bible School[66]	CMC	>1940
1938	Virgil/Kitchener,Ont.	Virgil Bible School/Mennonite Brethren Bible Institute of Ontario[67]	MB	1955
1938	Sardis, BC	Greendale Bible Institute[68]	MB	1943
1938	Eigenheim, Sask.	Bible School[69]	CMC	194?
1939	Silberfeld, Sask.	Congregational Bible School[70]	CMC	1945

Table 10.1 (concluded)

Date opened	Place	Name	Affliation	Date closed
1939	Vineland, Ont.	Vineland Bible School[71]	MB	1941
1939	Coghlan/ Clearbrook, BC	Bethel Bible School[72]	CMC	1970
1939	Countess, Alta.	Countess Bible School[73]	CMC	>1940
1939	Drake, Sask.	Drake Bible School[74]	CMC	>1940
1939	Sardis, BC	Mennonite Bible School[75]	CMC	1952
1939	Yarrow, BC	Mennonite Bible School[76]	CMC	>1940
1940	Kitchener, Ont.	Emmanuel Bible College[77]	Miss.	–
1942	Black Creek, BC	Black Creek Bible School[78]	MB	1945
1942	Toronto, Ont.	Russian Bible Institute[79]	MB	1946
1942	Hochfeld, Sask.	Bible School[80]	MB	194?
1943	Eagle Creek/ Arlee, Sask.	Russian Bible School[81]	MB	194?
1947	East Chilliwack, BC	East Chilliwack Bible School[82]	MB	1959
1950	St Catharines, Ont.	United Mennonite Bible School[83]	CMC	1956
1970	Clearbrook, BC	Columbia Bible Institute[84]	Int.	–
1976	Aylmer, Ont.	Aylmer Bible School[85]	EMMC	–
1976	Ville St Laurent,Que.	Institute Biblique Laval[86]	MB	–

There were considerable differences in the relative emphasis given to these responsibilities in the various schools.

Mennonites had always esteemed the authority of the scriptures as the ultimate guide in life and death. When the Winkler Bible School stated that its general purpose was 'to lead men and women into the Holy Scriptures and to assist them in making God's Word effective in their lives,'[87] it stated the purpose of all the schools. And when it was stated at the 25th anniversary celebrations of the Coaldale Mennonite Brethren Bible School that it was their task to fill the gap created because children did not receive religious instruction in the public schools, they expressed another widely held concern.[88] Walter Klaassen described the attitude not only of members of the Eigenheim Mennonite church when he wrote: 'The Bible was for them both road map and navigation system ... The Bible gave a place for whatever occupied their minds. In a discussion of the desperate economic situation in which they found themselves in 1938, Elder Gerhard G. Epp never went beyond the biblical frame of reference in trying to make sense of it.'[89]

But Urie Bender's critical comments about the way in which a teacher at the Ontario Mennonite Bible School sometimes used the scriptures also reflected a fairly common attitude:

Oscar Burkholder lived and served in an era when a *thus saith the Lord* was often the last word instead of a beginning point from which to search openly for the guidance of the Holy Spirit. It was an era when a firm *the Scriptures say* was used as confirmation of applications already made instead of affirmation of principle to be applied in a different place and at a different time. An era when, for some, the question, 'What does the Bible say?' led less often to a diligent searching of the Scriptures than it did to a quoting of proof texts. An era when 'It's in the Book' could be used to punctuate pronouncements to end a discussion, or forestall an argument. In any case, such words sounded convincingly final.[90]

The ideal nevertheless was clearly understood, as the following quotation from the history of the Ontario Mennonite Bible School demonstrates: 'The Word of God is our light and life, applicable in all our experiences. It is God's way for all mankind, for salvation, and for Godly living in salvation. So many people are turned aside from the Word by human interpretation. Never forsake the Word to follow men. Learn to understand what the Word of God says. Let its own light illuminate your hearts and minds.'[91]

The Bible schools also trained future ministers and church workers. The MBs estimated in 1963 that 90 per cent of their missionaries serving abroad, 86 per cent of missionaries at home, 59 per cent of ministers, and 67 per cent of Sunday school workers had some Bible school training.[92] Those statistics were matched by the Mennonite Conference of Ontario, where, at one time, 85 per cent of the ministers were graduates of the Ontario Mennonite Bible School. Eight former students became moderators of the conference.[93] What Urie Bender said of the Ontario Mennonite Bible School was true of the other larger schools also: 'Successive waves of graduates and former students settling into Ontario church life brought with them increased and specific Bible knowledge, enlarged vision, a unique camaraderie developed on campus, as well as a commitment to service which found much of its application in the local setting.'[94] The schools were the major training ground for an entire generation of Mennonite church leaders, preachers, and lay workers who developed and maintained for many years close and intimate contacts with one another.

The Bible schools also sought to preserve a distinct Mennonite witness and heritage during an era of swift change. On their success the evidence is mixed and controversial. Reviews of curricula and course outlines indicate relatively little emphasis on Anabaptist or Mennonite history or on distinctive Mennonite theological principles. In the three years from 1965 to 1967 the Ontario Mennonite Bible School, for example, offered only one elective course on American Mennonites, in 1965, and one on Mennonites in Europe, in 1967. There was no course offered that focused on Anabaptist theology or on Canadian Mennonite history.[95] The situation was similar at the Steinbach Bible School, where in 1942 only one course in Mennonite history was offered, for students in their final year.[96]

Mennonite and Anabaptist subjects were not entirely ignored, but the emphasis was elsewhere. Among the Swiss Mennonites in Ontario and in western Canadian communities to which significant numbers of U.S. Mennonites had migrated before the First World War, American evangelical and fundamentalist doctrines received a great deal of attention, while German pietism was emphasized in the Bible schools established by the Russlaender. Evangelism, missions, atonement, personal conversion, personal piety, and eschatology received far more attention in the Bible schools than did careful teaching about a holistic approach to all of life, Christian discipleship, Anabaptist understanding of the nature of the church, the ethic of love, non-resistance, or Anabaptist teachings about the state.[97]

The curriculum and the theological orientation of teachers varied considerably. In the 1940s and 1950s leaders of the Mennonite Brethren and the Conference of Mennonites in Canada (CMC) each tried to develop a common curriculum for the Bible schools in their conferences, but there were no minimum academic qualifications for teachers or students. Textbook materials were borrowed from various sources, some not in complete agreement with historic Mennonite and Anabaptist doctrines. Library collections were haphazard and inadequate. Scheduling was often influenced by local agricultural conditions, such as a late harvest or an early spring. Personal piety and appropriate deportment were held in greater esteem than intellectual brilliance or academic achievement. And, since the Bible schools often depended for their survival on a few dedicated teachers and supporters, these teachers had considerable freedom to teach what and how they thought best.[98]

As a result, none of the conferences developed a comprehensive or coherent single curriculum for their Bible schools. Offerings nevertheless became more similar over the years, because many of the younger teachers had received additional training at one of the new Mennonite Bible colleges. In addition, Bible school students who hoped to go to those colleges wanted academic credit for their classes. As a result, courses came to resemble the introductory courses offered at the Bible colleges, which in turn were modelled on introductory classes at American Mennonite liberal arts colleges.[99]

The history courses offered in the Bible schools tended to focus on Bible history, church history, and the history of missions, rather than distinctly Mennonite history.[100] There were relatively few courses in systematic theology, and the textbooks most frequently used were written by non-Mennonites.[101] The usual approach was to study individual books of the Bible. Courses on

Psalms, Acts of the Apostles, the epistles, and the Gospel of John were frequent, but these did not lend themselves readily to the teaching of distinctive Mennonite or Anabaptist theology.

Many of the schools also offered courses named variously 'False Cults' or 'Departures from the Faith.' These courses tended to convey the message that there was one true faith, which was usually equated with those articles of faith on which almost all evangelicals agreed, and then to contrast that with the errors of other Christian denominations and non-Christian religions. Distinctive Mennonite teachings that differed from those of other evangelicals tended to confuse the dichotomies established in these courses and were not given prominence.

The Bible schools emphasized missions and evangelistic work. Students learned much about distant places, other peoples, and world events, and many felt challenged to take up missionary work. But the unique and distinctive beliefs of various Christian denominations made little or no sense to 'the heathen' to whom the Gospel was to be preached. Mennonite missionaries on furlough frequently visited the Bible schools. They had worked in close partnership with missionaries from other evangelical denominations in the mission field and stressed what they regarded as the essence or the core of the Christian message, rather than Anabaptist-Mennonite distinctives.[102]

Evangelization at home, whether through the Sunday schools, the daily vacation Bible schools, or the camps that gradually replaced or complemented vacation schools, also highlighted what teachers regarded as core values and beliefs. As long as worship services in Mennonite churches were conducted in German, non-Mennonites converted through these evangelization efforts had little choice but to attend non-Mennonite evangelical churches. It was therefore impractical to value distinctive Mennonite doctrines. Missionary and evangelistic efforts, as a result, tended to play down any distinctive doctrines that were rooted, and had been applied, in unique historical experiences.

There was another serious problem. Teachers themselves had no clear understanding of Anabaptist and Mennonite ideas, beliefs, and values. For many, being a Mennonite had more to do with rigid codes of conduct, personal behaviour, and distinctive cultural or ethnic practices. Swiss Mennonites emphasized nonconformist dress and personal adornment, especially for women. In western Canada there was a determination, at least in some churches, to preserve German as the language of religious worship. There was also much talk about worldliness in all the Bible schools, but equating Mennonitism and Anabaptism with the German language, a separatist agricultural life-style, and long lists of social, cultural, and personal prohibitions gave students a mistaken understanding of their distinctive theological insights and teachings.

The linking of Mennonitism and Mennonite history with defence of sectarian values was strengthened in 1939 when the Youth Movement of the Rhineland Agricultural Society in southern Manitoba commissioned a series of 'lectures for the instruction of Mennonite history.' These lectures were published in four booklets under the title *Woher? Wohin? Mennoniten!*[103] The author was Paul Schaefer, a teacher and later principal of the Mennonite Collegiate Institute at Gretna. Schaefer was a strict disciplinarian who supported preservation of the German language and an agricultural way of life with exceptional vigour and determination.

Before 1970 most Mennonite Bible schools in Canada paid little or no attention to Harold S. Bender's reinterpretations of Anabaptist history and theology. Some teachers at the Ontario Mennonite Bible School, however, had studied at Goshen College and were therefore familiar with his work. Several instructors at the new Mennonite Bible colleges in Winnipeg also became familiar with the new scholarship. They in turn influenced some of their students who became Bible school teachers. For most in western Canada, however, Paul Schaefer and Walter Quiring, author of numerous books praising the pioneering exploits of German Mennonites on South American farming frontiers, defined what it meant to be a Mennonite.

The indifferent or critical attitudes toward Mennonite distinctives were reinforced by the things taught to students who attended non-Mennonite Bible institutes. Over the years up to 25 per cent of the students at the Prairie Bible Institute, Calgary Prophetic Bible Institute, Berean Bible Institute, Briercrest, Winnipeg Bible College, and other fundamentalist and/or evangelical Bible schools came from Mennonite homes, and some returned as pastors to Mennonite churches or to teach in Mennonite Bible schools. The result has been described thus:

An honest report of the influence of the Bible institutes must say that the influence has been mixed, sometimes helpful and sometimes harmful. Not having any interest in or responsibility for the historic heritage and particular doctrines and practices of the Mennonites, they have never promoted the Mennonite cause as such, have occasionally been the source of divisive and polemic influence, and have imported some foreign and even dangerous doctrines and emphases. On the other hand, they have often had a good influence in the promotion of spiritual awakening and increased evangelistic and missionary activity.[104]

The Bible schools were very strongly influenced by German pietist and American evangelical and fundamentalist theology. If they dealt at all with distinctive Anabaptist-Mennonite history and doctrines they tended to emphasize aspects that most Canadian Mennonites were abandoning – the German language, nonconformist dress, separatist rules for personal behaviour, and a rural/agricultural life. They only rarely focused on distinctive Mennonite doctrines that differed from those held by other evangelicals[105] but that had far greater relevance for young people entering secular, urban, and, particularly, professional communities.

Canada's bigger Mennonite Bible schools had their largest enrolments, and probably also their greatest influence, in the immediate postwar years. By the mid-1950s, however, enrolments began to decline, and by 1970 all but a few of the schools had folded. Some of the very small schools in remote communities had closed before 1940, and during the war the number of male students fell so sharply because of military or alternative service that some teachers began to think that their institutions would become girls' schools.[106] In the cities the young women in the Girls' Homes became the core group in evening Bible classes, while in rural areas young, unmarried women made up the overwhelming majority of students in day Bible schools. After the war, however, there was a great influx of male students, especially to the larger schools. Increased prosperity and better transportation permitted students to travel from greater distances to attend the larger, better-staffed, and better-equipped institutions. But those same factors led to the demise of more of the smaller, more remote schools. Consolidation affected Bible schools as much as it did public elementary and high schools.

Support for the early Bible schools usually had come from local congregations or a consortium of local churches. Consolidation increased the burden for the larger congregations, which now also accommodated students from smaller churches in their conferences. That led to restructuring, under which conferences rather than individual or groups of congregations supported the schools. Mennonite Brethren, for example, merged a number of theirs until, eventually, they had only one in each of Ontario, Manitoba, and Saskatchewan and a joint school (with the CMC) in British Columbia.[107] The Saskatchewan-Alberta (Old) Mennonite Conference retained its itinerant Bible school, but for most Swiss Mennonites the Ontario Mennonite Bible School became their denominational Bible school.

Consolidation took place mainly in the 1950s, but it was driven not just by a desire for greater efficiency and better instruction. Student enrolments also began to fall, in several cases dramatically, at mid-decade. Those that survived either added high school classes or transformed themselves into Bible institutes that offered courses designed for high school graduates and were recognized for academic credit by the Mennonite Bible colleges in Winnipeg or by Mennonite liberal arts colleges in the United States.[108] A number of the schools ran parallel and overlapping programs – a Bible school program designed for students without a high school diploma who had no immediate intention to pursue further studies, and a Bible institute curriculum for high school graduates who intended to go on to college or university. Consolidation and the raising of academic standards saved at least half a dozen of the former Bible schools, but they had become Bible institutes.

Several factors account for the decline of the Bible schools. First, and probably most crucial, more young people went to high school and university. The Bible schools served young people who had completed their elementary schooling but were too young to get married or establish their own farms. Students attending high school, of course, stayed in school longer, though there was still usually a gap of several years between school leaving and marriage. But the maturity and level of instruction for 18- and 19-year-old high school graduates were not the same as that of younger students who had completed only grade seven or eight, and it was difficult for teachers to integrate their Bible school and Bible institute programs.

In communities where new Mennonite private high schools were established, tensions sometimes developed between supporters of the Bible school and those of the high school. The latter accepted more changes and wanted an education that would prepare their children for urban, secular, and professional work, while the former tended to be more strongly committed to traditional rural values.

The attitudes of some high school students also changed. If they went to Mennonite high schools they received religious instruction there, and some regarded that as an alternative to Bible school training. More significant, students needed many more years of schooling. High school, followed by university or professional education, filled the years that earlier generations had devoted to Bible study.

The two new Mennonite Bible colleges in Winnipeg also undermined support for, and attendance at, the Bible schools. They offered more advanced training, and some courses were recognized for university credit. The colleges initially offered training needed by students who intended to become pastors or take up other full-time work in the church, whereas the Bible schools were designed to train lay people. However, in the 1970s, when the Bible colleges strengthened their relationship with the two universities in Winnipeg, and shifted more clearly to lay education and the training of young people for a wide range of vocations, the Bible schools were undermined even further.

Students planning a secular, academic, or professional career could also take courses at the Bible colleges that better fitted their needs and interests than did the general Bible instruction given in the Bible schools. Initially the colleges were expected to offer biblical instruction only for those who had already completed Bible school, but young men returning from wartime service and other high school graduates were admitted from the beginning. The more serious problem was how to accommodate those who had completed Bible school but not high school.

There was a further problem. Non-Mennonite Bible schools continued to attract many Mennonite young people. Those who had come to regard distinctive Mennonite teachings as anachronistic or relevant only to an earlier, separatist, agricultural life-style, but wanted some biblical instruction, found these institutions attractive. Such competition prompted the Ontario Mennonite Bible School to warn students: 'Don't expose yourself to a watered down, emaciated, powerless, popular, easy discipleship, cheap grace kind of Christianity. Get your Bible training in a Bible Institute where all the Bible doctrines receive their proper balanced emphasis.'[109]

That was not a particularly effective appeal if young people thought that the difference between watered-down and properly balanced training involved mainly social, cultural, and ethnic practices that they no longer regarded as a central or essential part of the Gospel. The result was a decline in student numbers and closing of most of the Bible schools.

The closure of the Ontario Mennonite Bible School and Institute, the oldest Canadian Mennonite Bible school, on 19 March 1969, marked the end of an era in the education and training of Mennonite young people in Ontario[110] and was part of the more general decline of such schools. The institute had been in operation since 1907 and had trained successive generations of Mennonite preachers, missionaries, Sunday school teachers, and lay church members. There had been nearly 6,000 student registrations, and J.C. Wenger, a well-known (Old) Mennonite historian, wrote later: 'Probably no other conference among Mennonites was so moulded by a Bible school as was Ontario.'[111]

Closure became necessary because of declining enrolments and increasing difficulty in finding faculty members willing and able to provide instruction for the remuneration offered and suited to the schedules of the Bible school. As well, the rented facilities at First Mennonite Church in Kitchener, where classes were given throughout the long history of the school, were needed by the church for its own, expanding Christian education program.

In their day, the Bible schools filled an important educational niche, particularly for Mennonite young people who did not go on to high school or post-secondary training. They greatly increased the knowledge and familiarity of the students with the scriptures, trained those with leadership and special skills in more effective use of their talents, and prepared some for more advanced study. And they did all this at a very reasonable cost during times when people suffered serious economic hardship.

In each of the larger conferences Bible school graduates had a common and shared experience. So many students, for example, met their spouses at the Ontario Mennonite Bible School that it was sometimes referred to as 'The Match Factory.' Since most students went home for the weekend, Friday was the time to finish leftovers, and Friday's supper became 'The Mennonite Weekly Review.'[112] And because much of the food was donated and some foods were in greater abundance than others, the cooks were sometimes hard-pressed to provide dietary variety. Most farms had large apple orchards, and apples were served in every possible form. As students came to the table and saw apples in yet another dish, one might well hear the comment, 'Apples for a change.'[113] Students at other Bible schools could tell many similar stories.

There were also many shared, deeply emotional, spiritual experiences – both of tragedy and happiness. The Bible schools created a laity that 'reflected the distinctive markings of a particular Bible study and fellowship experience as well as of exposure to the theology and personal influence of certain strong leaders.'[114] Yet all but six of Canada's Mennonite Bible schools were eventually closed, consolidated, or drastically restructured. The mission of the Bible schools, which had occupied a central place in Mennonite educational programs, had apparently been completed.

CONCLUSION

Education should prepare students for the work they will do and the occupations they will enter and, more generally, inform, enrich, and guide them in the lives they will lead as adults. It should teach and reinforce the beliefs, doctrines, practices, and values of the society in which they will live, work, worship, and die.

Throughout their history Mennonites have thought it important to control, or at least significantly influence, the education that their children receive. In Canada, only a small minority were able to retain, or regain, private elementary schools, and even these institutions had to meet the requirements of curricula set by public authorities. During and after the First World War provincial governments had gained effective control over elementary schooling, and Mennonite leaders began to devise means whereby their children would receive additional religious instruction.

Sunday schools, half- or full-hour additions to the elementary school curriculum, and, in some parts of the country, German Saturday schools taught what had previously been conveyed in Mennonite private schools. The Sunday schools, however, also accepted and brought into Mennonite churches many new, different, and innovative approaches. They were not just institutions of religious and cultural preservation. They were crucial instruments of accommodation and integration. The integration that they facilitated was, however, limited. They introduced the values, beliefs, and culture of North American evangelicalism, not those of North American urban society generally or of distinctive Anabaptist and Mennonite theology, and made them acceptable in Mennonite congregations and communities.

Bible schools familiarized young people and future Mennonite church leaders with the scriptures. Over the years, their programs changed greatly, but biblical instruction tended to be didactic and designed to strengthen evangelical and some sectarian rural and agricultural rather than distinctive Anabaptist and Mennonite doctrines. Within the confines of a fairly restricted theology, the missionary and evangelistic fervour evident in the Bible schools extended the vision and understanding of students. It was difficult for the schools to transcend the intellectual and academic confines of their supporting congregations and communities. That, however, was what most urban and educated young Mennonites apparently demanded.

At the last graduation exercises of the Ontario Mennonite Bible School and Institute the question was raised, 'Can the vision which brought O.M.B.S. & I. into being with such relevancy find new forms, patterns and programs?'[115] Some of those new forms, patterns, and programs were, in fact, already in place when the institution closed its doors. Leadership in Mennonite education had passed to new or expanded Mennonite high schools, Bible and liberal arts colleges, and a new liberal arts college directly affiliated with a large public university.

11

High Schools and Colleges

In 1947 Rosthern Junior College and the Rosthern Bible School shared a campus and some teachers. But the two institutions seemed to be moving in opposite directions. H.T. Klaassen, chairman of board at Rosthern Junior College and a teacher at the Bible school, explained the situation: 'Many of the young people attending the Bible schools become very intolerant. They will allow nothing except their own position to stand ... Personally I believe the Bible schools are in danger of going too far to the right and of losing their biblical *Nuechternheit* (common sense). The high schools, on the other hand, are in danger of going too far to the left and of losing their foundation.'[1]

In his efforts to maintain a balance between the two, and particularly to curb undesirable religious attitudes and secular influences in the high school, Klaassen became embroiled, in 1950, in the dismissal of a well-qualified, very popular, but allegedly liberal teacher. A bitter dispute led to loss of the entire high school faculty. It thwarted an exceptionally visionary and ambitious academic development program, resulted in protests by students and alumni, and brought demands for a separate administrative structure for the Bible school. For a time it threatened the very existence of the entire Mennonite educational endeavour at Rosthern.

It was clear, however, that closing a sometimes-troublesome school would not solve anything. Young people were eager to obtain a good academic education. If Mennonite leaders were to retain effective influence or control over the post-elementary education of their children they must have the kind of schools that their young people would attend. Many parents and leaders also realized, even if often with regret, that farming careers were no longer feasible for most of their young people.

A fear expressed repeatedly by Canadian Mennonite leaders was that those unable to become farmers might form an urban Mennonite proletariat. Farming, where the individual operators owned their own means of production, provided freedom and independence that seemed to be lacking in salaried employment. The power and control exercised by employers could make it difficult for employees to live and work in accordance with their own conscience and religious convictions. That had happened during the war to workers whose employers were committed to anti-German and pro-military policies and could happen again to those with employers who did not share their religious values.

Proletarianization was also feared for another reason. Few Mennonites had an informed understanding of how Canadian labour unions worked, but they knew that membership was often a condition of urban employment. The Russian revolution and subsequent Soviet experiences had instilled a horror of all proletarian class action. Mennonites did not want their young people to become members of militant workers' organizations, but if farming were no longer a viable option, many would be obliged to join the labour force unless they could get the education and training necessary to become professionals or go into business on their own. That required more education.

Once it became clear that young people, in large numbers, would go to high school and college, Mennonite leaders became concerned about the kind of schools these young people would go to. Mennonites had limited influence on public secondary and post-secondary education. The three Mennonite and Brethren in Christ private high schools at Gretna, Manitoba, Rosthern, Saskatchewan, and Fort Erie, Ontario, had for years provided secondary schooling, and after the war all three saw sharp increases in enrolment.[2] In addition, seven new Mennonite high schools and (in Winnipeg) two Mennonite Bible and liberal arts colleges were established in Canada between 1944 and 1947, while two Mennonite Bible schools added high school classes. One additional Mennonite high school was set up in 1958, and in 1963 a new Mennonite college, directly affiliated with the University of Waterloo, opened its doors.

Creation of these institutions showed that Canadian Mennonites recognized that their children needed more and different education than had previously been deemed sufficient. The new institutions also demonstrated Mennonites' continuing determination to preserve their heritage and identity.

HIGH SCHOOLS

The primary purpose of the Mennonite high schools established before the First World War and still operating in 1939 had been to train teachers for public or private schools in Mennonite districts. Young people planning to enter church work or one of the health professions also got secondary education there, but it was assumed that most Mennonite young people contemplating a life in farming would not go to high school.

The Brethren in Christ school began as a Bible school but offered a few approved high school classes in the late 1930s 'in response to the young people themselves, who in turn were responding to the changing times that made a high school education desirable.'[3] There were already in the 1930s occasional suggestions in Mennonite periodicals and conference minutes that it might be prudent to found additional Mennonite high schools. Several Bible schools experimented by offering a few high school courses, but the Depression, and lack of qualified teachers, presented seemingly insurmountable obstacles.

That situation changed dramatically in the mid-1940s. Mennonites became more prosperous. They realized that more young people would go to high school, and there were frustrations with the public system. These factors led to educational initiatives in all the provinces where Mennonites lived in larger numbers. Table 11.1 identifies Mennonite high schools that opened between 1889 and 1986.[4]

Table 11.1
Canadian Mennonite high schools

Date opened	Place	Name	Affiliation[5]	Date closed
1889	Gretna, Man.	Mennonite Collegiate Institute[6]	CMC	–
1905	Altona, Man.	Mennonite Educational Institute	CMC	1926
1905	Rosthern, Sask.	German/English Academy/Rosthern Junior College[7]	CMC	–
1934	Gormley/Ft Erie Ont.	Ontario Bible School/ Niagara Christian College[8]	BIC	–
1944	Clearbrook, BC	Mennonite Educational Institute[9]	MB	–
1945	Yarrow, BC	Sharon Mennonite Collegate Institute (1)[10]	MB	1950
1945	Winnipeg, Man.	Mennonite Brethren Collegiate Institute[11]	MB	–
1945	Niagara on the Lake, Ont.	Eden Christian College[12]	MB	–
1945	Leamington, Ont.	United Mennonite Educational Institute[13]	CMC	–
1945	Kitchener, Ont.	Rockway Mennonite Collegiate[14]	MC	–
1946	Steinbach, Man.	Steinbach Bible Institute[15]	Int	–
1946	Coaldale, Alta.	Alberta Mennonite High School[16]	MB	1964
1946	Sardis, BC	Menno High School[17]	–	1948
1951	Yarrow, BC	Sharon Collegiate Institute (2)[18]	MB	1970
1958	Winnipeg, Man.	Westgate Collegiate Institute[19]	CMC	–
1986	Osler, Sask.	Valley Christian Academy[20]	Berg.	–

The reasons for expansion and modification of existing high schools, and establishment of new ones, were similar across the country. Young people everywhere in Canada became more interested in high school education, and Mennonite parents in all but the most traditional communities realized that education held the key to a better life if farming were no longer a viable option for their children. The Mennonite Conference of Ontario, for example, undertook a survey in 1944 which showed that 81 out of 375 of their young people between the ages of 13 and 18 were attending high school. Fifteen of those were taking high school classes at the Ontario Bible School of the Brethren in Christ or in some other private high school, while 66 were at public institutions.[21] It was thought that 30 or 40 students would attend the first year if a private Mennonite high school were opened. Surveys elsewhere were not as precise, but church leaders and high school promoters everywhere realized that high school was in demand.

The increased prosperity of the late-war and immediate postwar years meant that Canadian Mennonites could afford to establish the new schools, even though they also had to pay taxes to support public schools. Few had a realistic idea of just how expensive the new high schools would be. The Bible schools, which had been run with minimal expenditure, led to some unrealistically low estimates of costs.

Determination to found high schools was based on several objectives. Students wanted the kind of academic instruction offered in public high schools. Parents and leaders were determined to perpetuate their religious and ethnic heritage and wanted to shield students from some of the things taught in the public system. It was assumed from the beginning that the new schools would require official accreditation. For that they had to follow the provincial curriculum, but it was expected that a private school could enrich or add courses in Bible, doctrine, ethics, and character training. Except for Rockway Mennonite Collegiate in Kitchener, the new high schools also taught German, which most Russian Mennonite[22] communities still regarded as an integral part of their spiritual heritage. Several schools also gave instruction in Mennonite history and in religious music. The private schools were to offer an 'education with a plus,' harmoniously integrated with the academic instruction.

Canadian Mennonites were also dissatisfied with some of the instruction given in the public schools. During the war years many public high schools organized cadet corps and engaged in other military activities. Mennonite students were sometimes subjected to considerable pressure from teachers and fellow students to participate.[23] In addition, readings chosen for literature classes, topics assigned for written assignments, and the general atmosphere did not always suit Mennonite tastes. The more fundamental concern was the fact that religion was not taught. Students were therefore not able at school to integrate academic learning with their religious values and beliefs.

An issue that greatly agitated some Canadian Mennonites in the 1940s and 1950s was the teaching of the theory of evolution in high school science classes. This theory, some thought, contradicted the biblical account of creation and questioned the very existence of God. It is clear that many who opposed modern scientific theories did not themselves understand those theories, but it was hoped that teachers in Mennonite private schools would provide an effective antidote to the theory of evolution.

The crisis at Rosthern Junior College, referred to above, was in part the result of a charge that Peter P. Rempel, the teacher dismissed, had explained the theory of evolution to his students. Rempel did not deny the charge but defended himself by saying that students would come into contact with the theory anyway and that it was best to have it explained from a Christian point of view. He insisted that evolution did not offer a scientific explanation for the creation or origin of the solar system and that the theory, even if true, 'in no way invalidates the moral and spiritual teachings of Christ.'[24] Such a defence did not save Rempel's job. Mennonite schools should be different from public ones. They should not teach evolution. Such attitudes created serious conflicts for some teachers whose public relations and diplomatic skills were sometimes severely tested as they 'kept their innermost convictions to themselves and tried to conform outwardly to the attitudes and demands of their employers.'[25]

There was another subject taught, or allegedly about to be added to the curriculum in public high schools, to which Mennonite leaders objected, sometimes vehemently. That was health and personal hygiene, which included basic sex education. Mennonite leaders feared that such instruction would prematurely rouse the curiosity of students and inform them of how they could avoid the consequences of sexual sin rather than admonishing them to avoid all extramarital sexual encounters.

Support for the new Mennonite high schools also came from people in outlying and isolated rural communities that did not have public high schools of their own. If their young people wanted to go to high school they had to obtain room and board in a larger centre that had a high school. That could be expensive and leave the adolescents without adequate supervision. The older Mennonite and Brethren in Christ schools, and almost all the Mennonite high schools established after 1944, had dormitories or made lodging arrangements for students from remote communities.

The drive to establish new Mennonite high schools began in 1943 in several places. The first such facility opened in the 1940s was the Mennonite Educational Institute in British Columbia. The initiative came from the South Abbotsford Mennonite Brethren church, but all the early proposals envisioned a school run by a BC Mennonite educational society with broad, inter-Mennonite support.[26]

The problems encountered in British Columbia were similar to those in other places where new high schools were proposed or established. First, there was the question of location. The largest BC Mennonite community was Yarrow, and leaders there had plans to build a high school.[27] In 1943, however, they felt that the time was not opportune. Wartime shortages of building materials and supplies had hampered efforts to expand their church and Bible school. In addition, hostility to Mennonites and their peace position was fairly strong. It seemed impolitic to begin work on a new private Mennonite high school before the war was won. But the Yarrow leaders insisted that when one was built, it must be in Yarrow.

The promoters from South Abbotsford were not easily dissuaded. They established an ad hoc committee, including representatives from Yarrow, which was sent to Victoria to obtain relevant information from the provincial government. Officials expressed regret that the Mennonites did not find the public high schools satisfactory but indicated that there would be no serious objection if they established their own high school, provided that they covered all costs and continued paying regular school taxes.

On the strength of these assurances the Abbotsford group decided to proceed in spite of opposition from Yarrow. It discovered, however, that it could not obtain the necessary construction supplies. Instead, recycled lumber and supplies from old farm buildings that were torn down, supplemented by whatever new materials could be purchased, provided the material to add a classroom to the Bible school of the South Abbotsford Mennonite Brethren Church. Those additions were completed only in October 1944, and instruction in both the high school and the Bible school began on 17 November. Four teachers shared all the teaching in both schools. F.C. Thiessen, an experienced and qualified teacher who enjoyed the confidence of leaders of both the Mennonite Brethren (MB) and the Conference of Mennonites in Canada (CMC) served as principal and gave the school needed academic credibility.[28]

The people at Yarrow supported the school that first year but regarded the arrangements in South Abbotsford as temporary. The next year, with the war coming to an end, they were ready to build. The Abbotsford people, however, were not willing to see their school moved to Yarrow. The result was that the Abbotsford school remained and a new one was established at Yarrow. Both institutions erected new buildings in 1946 and 1947.

Location was always a controversial issue. In Saskatchewan, where the buildings of the Rosthern Junior College urgently needed to be replaced, there were strong pressures to move the school to Saskatoon.[29] Suggestions were also made from time to time to transfer the Mennonite Collegiate Institute (MCI) from Gretna to Winnipeg or to another, larger Manitoba town. Then, in 1963, when fire destroyed the main school building, no less than six other locations were suggested for rebuilding.[30] The decision to rebuild in Gretna was not an easy one.

In Winnipeg, MBs had difficulty in reconciling the interests of their members living in widely separated parts of the city. The new Mennonite Brethren Bible College, discussed below, decided to offer high school classes for college students who had graduated from a Bible school but did not have a high school certificate. That resulted in establishment of the Mennonite Brethren Collegiate Institute (MBCI) in the Elmwood district. The first year, in fact, the high school classes were given in college classrooms. Then adjacent properties were acquired and new high school buildings erected.[31]

In Yarrow, building of what became the Sharon Mennonite Collegiate Institute was possible only with the support of other MB churches in the eastern Fraser Valley. In an effort to entice supporters from Chilliwack, Arnold, Sardis, and Greendale, busing was set up to bring students from those communities to Yarrow every day. Routes, schedules, length of time spent on the bus, and higher-than-expected costs made the system highly controversial; it was discontinued in 1948, when a major flood and collapse of the raspberry markets wrought havoc with all of Yarrow's economic initiatives. But the loss of the buses irritated the supporters in the other communities, leading, in some cases, to withdrawal of financial aid.[32]

Problems regarding location were compounded by differing levels of support in various communities. Schools were usually established on the initiative of supporters in the community where they were built, but support was expected from a much broader base. The Mennonite Educational Society in Abbotsford, for example, invited all the nearby Mennonite churches to become partners in its school. Churches that did so were expected to pay a $25 levy per member.[33] In the case of Rockway, the Mennonite Conference of Ontario was the initiator and operator of the school. It expected support from all congregations in the conference, even though not all sent students to the school. Many felt that the Kitchener-Waterloo churches should shoulder more of the burden than other, more remote congregations.[34] Location, in short, was a difficult and controversial issue when new high schools were built.

A second serious problem related to inadequate buildings and facilities. The Mennonite Educational Institute in Abbotsford occupied space in the enlarged Bible school of the South Abbotsford Mennonite Brethren Church until a new and larger facility could be built in nearby Clearbrook. The Rockway supporters in Kitchener acquired a small farm on the outskirts of the city, and during the first year the main floor of the farm home served as a kitchen and dining-room and also provided classroom space, while the rooms upstairs served as a residence for some out-of-town students. For the second year the barn was extensively renovated to provide additional space.[35] The first classes in what would become Leamington's United Mennonite Collegiate Institute were taught in the basement of the Oak Street United Mennonite Church, in conjunction with the small Bible school program.[36] The Alberta Mennonite High School at Coaldale used the former church building of a group living southeast of the town that had joined or been amalgamated with the Coaldale Mennonite Brethren Church.[37] The science laboratory consisted of bottles, flasks, and various mysterious substances discarded and donated to the school by the local doctor. The library was initially made up of books donated by teachers and supporters – most, of course, in German – and of discarded books from the Lethbridge public library.[38]

In short, facilities were, almost without exception, atrociously inadequate in the first years. That, however, was a problem faced not only by the new Mennonite high schools. A decade of depression, followed by six years of wartime military priorities and civilian rationing and shortages, had also left public high schools underfinanced and poorly equipped. Enthusiasm, goodwill, and determination to learn and to gain much-sought-after academic credits made it possible to overcome, or at least mitigate, these physical inadequacies. All the new Mennonite high schools quickly, and in spite of inadequate facilities, gained a reputation for excellent academic standards. Their students achieved good results on departmentally administered examinations.

Another problem was not so easily addressed. There were very few Mennonites qualified to teach high school. A significant number of the Russlaender had taken pedagogical courses and were qualified to teach in the Russian Mennonite Zentralschulen, which offered three or four years of instruction beyond the six-year elementary school curriculum. Some of these teachers had returned to school after their immigration to Canada, taking their Canadian high school training at the Mennonite high schools at Gretna or Rosthern and then an additional year or two at one of the provincial normal schools. Most, however, were qualified to teach only elementary school and junior high, not high school. Those few who had earned the required qualifications in Canada were assiduously courted. Gerhard Lohrenz, for example, was offered and in some cases quite literally begged to take up teaching positions in six of the new Mennonite high schools and in both Bible colleges.

Several Canadian Mennonite high schools attracted one or two teachers with training in an American Mennonite college. That created no problems at Rockway, but in western Canada the American teachers were viewed with suspicion, because they did not show great concern about preservation of the German language, and some had allegedly imbibed liberal ideas.[39]

The experience of the supporters of the Alberta Mennonite High School in looking for qualified teachers was particularly difficult, but it illustrates how serious the problem was.[40] Promoters and supporters hoped and expected that their school would open in September 1945. Numerous inquiries were made, and prospective teachers contacted, but plans to begin instruction in 1945 had to be abandoned because no qualified teachers could be found. There were also serious protests in Coaldale because local people feared that establishment of a private Mennonite high school would delay construction of a new public high school.

The search for qualified teachers seemed equally difficult in 1946, but early in 1946 B.B. Janz, chairman of the local school society, persuaded or exerted sufficient pressure on Henry Thiessen, a former elementary school teacher–turned–farmer in the Grassy Lake area, to accept the principalship of the proposed new school. Jacob Regehr, a former teacher in a Mennonite Zentralschule in Russia and at the time an elementary school teacher in the Mennonite reserve south of Swift Current, was persuaded to accept the second teaching position. Neither had the necessary Canadian qualifications for high school, but Janz obtained special permission from the Department of Education so that both could be appointed.

While negotiations with the prospective teachers were in progress, the society submitted its official application to the government, which quickly approved it. Grades 9 through 12 were to be offered – an impossible teaching load for the two teachers, particularly since neither had taught high school before. But the ministry gave them temporary permits, and the two taught the maximum number of courses permitted by the Alberta Teachers Association. Some required courses could not be taught, and students took those by correspondence. Visiting preachers, an occasional itinerant missionary, and teachers from the nearby Bible school taught religious subjects. Library and laboratory facilities were pathetically inadequate, and the dormitory and rooming arrangements for out-of-town students, who comprised almost half of the first year's forty-four students, were hopelessly inadequate. Only exceptional dedication and hard work by teachers and students alike made it possible for that new high school, and those in other provinces, to survive and to achieve results that departmental inspectors deemed satisfactory.

Teachers with training and experience in the Mennonite schools in Russia sometimes faced other problems. Their pedagogical methods placed considerable emphasis on rote learning, penmanship, grammar, and quite rigorously disciplined and controlled thinking and writing. Students were also expected to show deference toward teachers and those in positions of authority. Gerhard H. Peters, a former teacher at the Alexanderkrone Zentralschule who taught at Gretna's MCI from 1927 to 1948 and served as principal from 1935 to 1948, personified some of these rigidities. He was strongly committed to preservation of the German language and of distinctive Mennonite cultural practices. He was also a strict disciplinarian. One of his teaching methods was to call students to the front to work out assigned problems on the blackboard. Mistakes were, of course, pointed out, but it was sometimes done in a manner that embarrassed the student. That resulted in disciplinary problems, which eventually led to Peters's removal from the principalship and his resignation from the teaching staff. It seemed to him that students were becoming more disrespectful of authority and did not apply themselves to the serious tasks assigned them.[41] It was a common complaint, particularly among teachers who had served in the Mennonite schools in Russia. Gerhard Lohrenz, a teacher at Winnipeg's MBCI, complained that 'in the first years, we had many difficulties. The students who had grown up here in the city had become accustomed to many things we would not tolerate, and much that we sought to achieve was alien to them.'[42]

In an effort to deal with these problems the Mennonite high schools drew up intimidatingly long lists of rules. Persistent violation resulted in expulsion or other disciplinary acts, including physical punishment. At MBCI, however, many of those early problems were ameliorated when an evangelistic revival swept the school.[43] Former teachers in Russian Mennonite schools were not accustomed to such revivals in private schools, but this one seemed to solve the immediate problems. As a result evangelistic revival meetings became an important aspect of school life and of social control in many private Mennonite schools. Frequency and the tactics employed by the evangelists tended to be determined by the attitudes of the teachers, board members, and directors and by the seriousness of the problems in the schools. The objective was to create a pious and spiritual atmosphere. A teacher who was familiar with early developments at MBCI reported after his first year of instruction at another Mennonite high school: 'If the number of students attending our school who have gone astray in other schools is too large, or if the balance is not weighted on the side of those exerting a positive spiritual influence, we cannot expect to achieve good results.'[44] Recalcitrant students were sometimes pushed very hard, by evangelists, teachers, and fellow students alike, to achieve an acceptable religious conversion experience. Most of the rules and regulations remained throughout the 1950s, but enforcement methods gradually changed. There was clearly a perceived pattern of faith and behaviour into which students were to fit.

A new generation of teachers educated in Canada eventually brought a more open and free approach to discipline and social control. The old ideal had been to inculcate traditional values and ideals rooted in rural and separatist communities. The historian of the Rockway Mennonite Collegiate noted the changes; in addition to emphasizing traditional nonconformist ideas, the teachers also encouraged 'entering and penetrating society rather than withdrawing from it. Some of this reflected a missional stance of going out into the world with a Christian witness; some of it simply reflected a growing feeling of being at home in the world in which we live.'[45]

The new approaches came only slowly and resulted occasionally in conflict among younger teachers and board members, parents or supporters of the school. Peter P. Rempel at Rosthern, for example, had an informal teaching style that offended some: 'He shared the students' lives. He lived as one of them, shattering the traditional image of the Mennonite teacher as one who was a level or two above the students. The Rempel style was to perch on his desk with legs crossed or dangling in front of him. His usual, or, better said, unusual posture was such that on one occasion the inspector wrote: "A teacher should either stand, sit, or walk!"'[46]

Rosthern was not the only school that experienced difficulties in adjusting to new student attitudes and expectations and to a generally less ethnically oriented, more confident and open attitude by teachers who had themselves received most of their training in Canada. The historian of MCI in Gretna, for example, suggested that Ken Loewen, the first Canadian-born and -educated principal, was less concerned about preservation of distinctive cultural and linguistic Mennonite values and 'nudged the MCI closer to the educational mainstream.'[47]

These changes came somewhat later at MCI than in many of the other Mennonite high schools, but distinctive ethnocultural traits weakened everywhere. At the same time, the public high schools became more attractive. Most of the cadet and other para-military activities were phased out shortly after the war ended. Much more important, a growing number of Mennonite teachers and administrators took positions in the public system, particularly in communities where Mennonites comprised a significant percentage of the population. If there were Christian teachers sensitive to Mennonite needs and interests in the public high schools, the need for more private high schools became less urgent. The result was a significant convergence of public and private Mennonite high school education. That, and a fragmentation of community support, economic disasters, and the proximity of other, larger Mennonite high schools led to closing of three of the Mennonite high schools established in the 1940s.

The first to go were the high school classes offered through the Sardis/ Greendale Bible school. These classes had never been more than a temporary service for local students. Financial problems following the flood of 1948, the proximity of larger Mennonite high schools at Yarrow and Clearbrook, and improved transportation led to termination of the high school classes at Sardis.

The 1948 flood, the collapse of the raspberry markets, and serious rifts within the supporting community also forced closure of the Sharon Collegiate Institute at Yarrow. The elaborate bus system and an exceptionally ambitious building program proved too expensive, and facilities that had cost an estimated $200,000 had to be sold to the public system in 1952 for only $60,000.[48] Supporters of the collegiate then reorganized and began again on a vastly reduced scale in the facilities of the Yarrow Mennonite Brethren Bible School. A small and inexpensive new building was added later, and the school enjoyed some good years but succumbed in 1970. Parents interested in sending their children to a Mennonite high school could use the larger, better-equipped facilities of the Mennonite Educational Institute at Clearbrook. With more Mennonites teaching in the public system, and another Mennonite high school near by, there was no longer an urgent need to keep the Sharon Collegiate open.

The third school that closed was the Alberta Mennonite High School at Coaldale, Alberta. There acrimonious tensions between supporters of the local Bible school and adherents of the high school helped end both institutions, as did weakening of inter-Mennonite support. The school had been started by an educational society and initially received considerable assistance from members of both Mennonite Brethren (MB) and Conference of Mennonites in Canada (CMC) churches. The leadership, from the beginning, was Mennonite Brethren, and over the years the school became more and more an MB institution. CMC supporters received little encouragement and eventually ceased to back the school. Given improved roads, CMC parents in Alberta who wanted to send their children to a Mennonite high school opted for Rosthern. It was part of a trend in Coaldale that saw the Mennonite Brethren loosening their ties with other Mennonite groups while becoming more involved in inter-denominational evangelism. The take-over of the high school, first by the MB church at Coaldale and then by the Mennonite Brethren Conference of Alberta, marked the end of inter-Mennonite support for the school.

That was not the case everywhere. At Steinbach two ministers, one from the MB church and the other an Evangelical Mennonite Brethren, had started a Bible school in 1931. It was taken over by an inter-Mennonite Bible school association in 1938. In the fall of 1946 a high school curriculum was added, the language of instruction was switched from German to English, and the name was changed to the Steinbach Bible Academy. The high school classes were dropped after two years but reinstated in 1953, when the school became the Steinbach Bible Institute.[49] Mennonite Brethren interest declined after establishment of the Mennonite Brethren Bible College in Winnipeg, but that was offset by increased interest shown by leaders and members of the Kleinegemeinde (after 1952 the Evangelical Mennonite Conference or EMC). In 1961 the EMC offered to accept full responsibility, but that offer was turned down. Instead, a consortium of the EMC, the Evangelical Mennonite Brethren, and the Emmanuel Free Church of Steinbach operated the school.[50] That consortium was subsequently expanded to include also the Chortitzer Mennonite Conference and the Evangelical Mennonite Mission Conference.[51] This unique inter-Mennonite initiative had several consequences. The distinctive doctrines and practices of the supporting churches and conferences, and more generally distinctive Mennonite characteristics, received less emphasis, while common evangelical ideas and beliefs were given greater prominence. The Steinbach Bible Institute thus became an effective agency that moved its supporters closer to North American evangelicalism.

The high schools built in the 1940s left a mixed legacy. In Ontario the United Mennonites (CMC), the Mennonite Conference of Ontario, and the Mennonite Brethren each built a school, in Leamington, Kitchener, and Niagara-on-the-Lake, respectively. Each offered limited residential facilities and attracted students from their own denomination from across the province. But the three schools were in different areas of the province and so attracted Mennonite students living in their area but belonging to different conferences.

In Manitoba the Mennonite Brethren built their own high school in Winnipeg. The Mennonite Collegiate Institute (MCI) at Gretna, which had attracted many MB students before 1945, lost many of those to the new school. CMC congregations became the main supporters of the MCI, but there were persistent suggestions and demands that another CMC high school be built in Winnipeg. The local focus for such a development, however, was the Schoenwieser (later First) Mennonite church, and the prolonged conflict between that congregation and the Manitoba and Canadian conferences made founding of a new high school problematic. There was also fear that it would be too difficult for CMC congregations to support both the MCI and a new high school in Winnipeg.

It was not until 1958 that two CMC churches in Winnipeg – First Mennonite and North Kildonan Mennonite – set up a Mennonite high school. Interest in such a venture had been strong at First Mennonite for many years, and some of the initial funding came from conference dues withheld by First Mennonite during its dispute with the conferences. The two CMC congregations that started the school worked hard to attract support from other local Mennonite churches, and eventually the resulting consortium included at least 11 congregations, almost all of them members of the CMC.

During the first year classes of what was then the Mennonite Educational Institute were held at First Mennonite, in facilities that had earlier accommodated the Mennonitische Religionsschule. The school was moved to North Kildonan, where it remained until 1964, when the buildings of the Convent of the Sacred Heart on Westgate Avenue were acquired and the school became Westgate Mennonite Collegiate.

Westgate, in its early history, resembled First Mennonite. It was strongly committed to preservation of German, and at the beginning all the religious subjects were taught in German, and on Tuesdays and Thursdays students were to speak only German. Major German theatrical productions, Mennonite children's and male choirs that sang both folk and religious songs, and the works of German authors received a good deal of attention. Pietist and evangelical concerns received less emphasis, and Westgate was more open and tolerant in social issues than other Mennonite high schools. A controversial incident in 1970 illustrated this approach. A music and dance group from Westgate appeared on 26 April on the 'Sundayscope' television program sponsored by CJAY. The theme was encounter through the performing arts – drama, music, and dance. A choir sang hymns, which four or five dancers clad in body stockings accompanied with creative and interpretive dancing. The tight clothing of the dancers, accentuated by bright studio lights, was too revealing for some Mennonite viewers, and others were utterly scandalized by the very idea that hymns and gospel songs should be accompanied by dance.[52] A Westgate spokesperson tried to explain that this was 'an attempt to make the medium of television noticeable.'[53]

The production was a joint effort between Westgate and Faith and Life Communications of the Conference of Mennonites in Manitoba. It had been performed previously in several churches and on Westgate tours in the United States and Ontario, and several of those involved gained much confidence and creative freedom from it. It was well received by most viewers and by the station, garnering Westgate several additional invitations. But this strong support of the performing arts raised major protests in Mennonite churches.

Three of the supporting Winnipeg churches, which had planned a major spring promotion drive for the school, threatened to cancel those plans unless there were changes at Westgate. And changes there were; but it was the churches and supporters who changed. Westgate and the other Mennonite high schools facilitated greater openness. What was still controversial in 1970 would soon be acceptable.

It seems, in retrospect, that the Mennonite high schools rendered their greatest service by encouraging new and more critical methods of inquiry while reconciling these with the basic tenets of Mennonite faith and doctrine. Old didactic methods were replaced, first in academic subjects but soon also in religious instruction, by more open and thought-provoking teaching and learning styles.[54] It was in this respect that the high schools were often perceived as differing most from the older Bible schools. Doubts, questions, reading, research, critical thinking, and discussion leading to understanding, intelligent acceptance, and reasoned commitment to the principles and articles of the faith, rather than ritualistic affirmation of accepted formulae, became the basis of the new methods of inquiry in matters of faith, as they were in most other aspects of modern life. The new high schools and colleges demonstrated that open questioning of inherited dogma and social practices need not be fatal to faith. Rather, it could enrich faith and make it more meaningful.

THE BIBLE COLLEGES

High school training was not sufficient for those planning full-time, or even part-time church work as pastors, choir conductors, and music directors, or Sunday school and Christian education superintendents, particularly if they wanted to work in urban churches. Before 1939 Canadian Mennonites seeking training beyond Bible school and high school had usually gone to one of the Mennonite colleges in the United States. Members of the (Old) Mennonite and the Amish Mennonite churches were relatively satisfied with training offered at their church colleges in Goshen, Indiana, Harrisonburg, Virginia, or Hesston, Kansas. Mennonite leaders in western Canada were less confident that the U.S.-based colleges sponsored by their North American conferences could provide appropriate training. Preservation of the German language remained a serious concern of the Russian Mennonites until the mid-1950s but had ceased to be an issue for American Mennonites. Some Canadian Mennonites also thought that their U.S. co-religionists had accepted troublesome aspects of American culture, and the legacy of earlier fundamentalist-modernist theological disputes among U.S. Mennonites caused further uneasiness in Canada. The American Mennonite liberal arts colleges were not offering quite what the Canadian leaders or students wanted. As a result many of these students preparing for a career in the church attended non-Mennonite Bible institutions, which offered instruction beyond the level offered in the Bible schools. That, however, brought in other alien doctrines and practices in such alarming proportions that conferences felt that they had to provide more adequate training.[55]

Canadian Mennonites, especially the Conference of Mennonites in Canada (CMC), faced an additional problem. The backgrounds of groups and congregations varied greatly. In the CMC some people had come from Russia in the 1870s, others from Prussia or the United States before the First World War, and still others in the 1920s and late 1940s. Each group maintained unique practices and traditions, even after they joined together in support of specific projects and activities. Leaders of the large conferences hoped that launching of their own 'higher Bible School' would promote an understanding of those things that all congregations had in common, thus strengthening unity and coherence. The difficult theological dispute that divided CMC and Conference of Mennonites in Manitoba leaders from leaders of the Schoenwieser Mennonite Church further reinforced need for additional, more advanced religious and theological training, which stressed common beliefs and traditions.

When leaders of the CMC and of the Mennonite Brethren first talked about their own 'higher Bible Schools' they thought simply of adding a more advanced class to an existing Bible school. It was not long before at least some saw the proposed Bible colleges as new and separate institutions that would offer significantly more advanced and academically much more rigorous theological training. The links between the new institutions and existing Bible schools, and the location of the new colleges, were decided on in essentially the same way in both conferences, though the process proved much easier for the Mennonite Brethren than for the CMC. Both groups, much to the chagrin of some of their rural members, established new and separate Bible colleges in Winnipeg – the Mennonite Brethren in 1944 and the CMC three years later.

Several factors led to establishment of the Mennonite Brethren Bible College (MBBC) in Winnipeg. Initially the plan had been to add one and later two years of additional, more advanced training to the curriculum of the Winkler Bible School, and in 1943–4 such a class was offered there. A decision had, however, been made to locate the new college in Winnipeg. Then an old school building, complete with desks and strategically located on the Henderson Highway in Winnipeg, became available at an unexpectedly low price. Several prominent local businessmen decided to buy the property. Most of the funds needed to acquire and repair the building (total cost: $12,680) were borrowed from the Building Fund of the Mennonite Brethren Conference in Hillsboro, Kansas. Shortly thereafter an adjacent house and lot, which seemed admirably suited to be a future student residence, became available for $5,000, and the Winnipeg businessmen purchased it and then offered to turn it over to the proposed new college at cost.[56]

These aggressive initiatives aroused concern in Winkler and other rural communities. There was even greater disappointment when A.H. Unruh, the highly respected principal of the Winkler Bible School, became first president of the new Bible college in Winnipeg. Unruh was not a skilled administrator and after the first year turned the presidency over to John B. Toews, a much younger, administratively more talented, theologically and academically better qualified, and charismatic new leader. But Unruh continued as a popular and respected teacher who gave the college credibility in rural Manitoba.

Using Tabor College at Hillsboro, Kansas, as a model, John B.Toews established the new college's academic credibility, built an effective administrative team, and created much goodwill. But he was constantly urged by an influential minority in the conference to do more to safeguard and preserve German/Mennonite traditions. At board meetings, where he wanted to talk about theological, curriculum, and administrative policies, he would instead be asked repeatedly for precise statistics on the number of instruction hours conducted in German, and then warned that more should be done in German. He left after three years, mainly because of the language issue.[57]

Almost all the other teachers came from existing Bible schools. Some had taken more training at one of the U.S. Mennonite colleges or at some non-Mennonite Bible institute. Others were encouraged to use their summers, or were granted educational leaves, to improve their academic qualifications. In its second year the college appointed Ben Horch, a professionally trained choir conductor and musician of Lutheran background who had joined the MB church, to provide musical instruction 'for a few months of the year.' The conference was informed: 'Whoever has the youth, also has the future, and whoever has singing and music has the youth. Singing and music have an ennobling influence on people, particularly on maturing young people. We must provide something better and more solid than what the world can offer.'[58] Horch developed greater appreciation of choral and instrumental, classical, and religious music in Canadian Mennonite churches. Excellence in musical training, performance, and achievement became and remained a major attraction at both Mennonite colleges in Winnipeg.

The Mennonite Brethren's 'higher Bible School' was watched very closely by CMC leaders, who took their first major initiative in that area in 1942. The CMC agreed to provide the necessary funding if the Rosthern Bible School would add an additional year of theological training to its four-year curriculum. The proposed new class was extensively advertised, and a number of prospective teachers were contacted, but none was able, qualified, or willing to teach at that level, and the initiative had to be suspended.

Immediately after the war it was proposed that two teachers be hired for the proposed new class at Rosthern. One was to be a senior and respected minister, leader, or returned missionary; the other, a younger, academically well-trained teacher. Benno Toews, son of the highly esteemed David Toews, agreed to serve in the latter capacity, but the promoters were unable to recruit a senior educator who would serve as president and give the venture credibility in the congregations. While the search for a president was under way the conference set up ten student scholarships – two for each of Canada's five westernmost provinces – set minimum admission requirements, and invited applications from students who had completed either Grade 12 or a four-year Bible school program. Failure to find a qualified president and senior teacher forced postponement of the program in 1945.

Two CMC ministers in Winnipeg – Benjamin Ewert and Isaac I. Friesen – were consulted extensively throughout these developments. When it became clear in 1945 that the Rosthern plans would again be postponed Friesen suggested a cooperative arrangement with MBBC.[59] He and Ewert were encouraged to meet with the college's president but received a discouraging response. The Mennonite Brethren would welcome students from and the support of the larger CMC but insisted that Mennonite Brethren must retain control of the college.[60] CMC leaders felt that that left them no alternative but to continue with their own plans for the 1946–7 school term.

Dean P.S. Goertz of Bethel College in Newton, Kansas, was invited to work out a program that would allow students who took the proposed new class at Rosthern to transfer course credits to Bethel. J.J. Thiessen, chairman of the CMC, and Goertz also drew up a lengthy list of prospective teachers, and students were again invited to apply. Scholarships, arrangements for transfer of academic credits to Bethel College, and an encouraging number of applications were all on hand during the summer of 1946 – but again, no qualified senior instructor. In despair Thiessen wrote: 'At least twenty young people were ready to attend our new school. A number of them have no doubt made their decision and registered as students in schools of other denominations. A dozen or more are still patiently waiting for our final announcement. I spent last night in prayer and meditation and was close to the stage which Elijah experienced when he said "It is enough, oh Lord."[61]

Dean Goertz and President Kaufman of Bethel College both suggested that perhaps Thiessen himself should accept the presidency,[62] but he emphatically rejected that suggestion, explaining that though he had been a school teacher in Russia he lacked the academic qualifications to head the new 'higher Bible school.'[63] Early in September 1946 Thiessen had the sad task of advising the prospective students to enrol elsewhere. He recommended Bluffton College in Ohio or Bethel College in Kansas.

Benjamin Ewert and Isaac Friesen in Winnipeg followed these developments with interest. As early as June 1946 they suggested that it might be easier to establish the proposed new college in Winnipeg. Temporary space could be provided in the basement of Bethel Church – the city mission church for 'Kanadier' Mennonites working in Winnipeg. Other advantages mentioned were the central location of Winnipeg, supplementary employment and service opportunities, the success of the Mennonite Brethren Bible College and of the interdenominational Winnipeg Bible School, and access to richer library resources. Friesen also began to look for possible permanent accommodation in Winnipeg for the new college, suggesting that the old Normal School might be purchased at an exceptionally reasonable price. In response, the college board decided, on 25 September 1946, to locate in Winnipeg.[64]

The search for a president and at least one other qualified, full-time faculty member continued. In March 1947 President Kaufman of Bethel College suggested to J.J. Thiessen that he contact Arnold J. Regier, whose wife came from southern Manitoba and who had completed his seminary training and 'is expecting to take some position in the near future unless he continues in school for his Doctor's degree.'[65] Thiessen responded immediately, and a month later he informed Kaufman that 'Rev. Arnold J. Regier has definitely promised to work in our college.'[66] Thiessen thought of Regier as the younger, academically qualified teacher. But again the search for a president failed. Arnold Regier was then informed that 'this means that we expect you to take the lead, and [we] are making an announcement in our papers to this effect.'[67]

Regier would in fact be the only full-time faculty member during the first year of instruction at the new Canadian Mennonite Bible College (CMBC). Isaac I. Friesen, who held both an MA and an MEd degree, and H. Wall, who had an MA and taught part time at MBBC, were to teach part time at the new college. In addition, P.A. Rempel, who had committed himself to teaching at the Elim Bible School in Altona during the winter, agreed to teach German when Elim was not in session. This arrangement obviously did not give the German Mennonite heritage the prominence that many rural constituents thought appropriate. Regier had only a less-than-satisfactory knowledge of German, and, even worse, pronounced some words differently because he had learned the language in Germany, where he had been a graduate student.

The board suffered yet another disappointment. Negotiations for purchase of the old Winnipeg Normal School ended in failure, and it was necessary to lay a new floor and fix up two classrooms in the basement of the Bethel Mission church. Thus CMBC opened in September 1947 in temporary facilities in the basement of the Bethel Mission, with only one full-time faculty member, who was unfamiliar with many aspects of Canadian Mennonite life and did not speak fluently the language of its constituents, and two part-time instructors. Thiessen concluded: 'It was not the will of the Lord to grant us an easy beginning and He has shown us that we must start at the bottom. We have definitely committed our way unto Him and hope for healthy development of our Bible College.'[68]

Any such hope was soon placed under great strain. More students enrolled than had been expected, given the short notice. There was strong support from Ontario, but in rural southern Manitoba many people had serious misgivings, while some in Saskatchewan and Alberta were disappointed that the new institution was not in Rosthern. The president was obviously handicapped in the public relations work that he could do. Thiessen and other members of the board supported Regier as best they could, but he was not able to gain the whole-hearted confidence of southern Manitobans, and after several years it became clear to Thiessen and other board members that a new president was needed. Several prospective candidates were approached, apparently without Regier's knowledge and at a time when he still thought that he had the full support of the board. One of those was Paul Schaefer, then recently appointed principal of the Mennonite Collegiate Institute in Gretna and greatly esteemed by the Mennonites of southern Manitoba. Schaefer declined the invitation, even after repeated requests, but in his reply to Thiessen expressed his own disappointment and that of many other southern Manitoba Mennonites: 'The established course must be radically changed. The school must receive a thoroughly German face and spirit. It must, therefore, be freed from the influences under which it now operates. It must manifest the spirit of the Canadian conference.'[69]

There was serious student discontent over one of the other teachers appointed in the second year, and college supporters were concerned about the theological views of another new teacher who was very popular with the students. As a result, leadership and staffing problems remained serious throughout the 1940s, resulting in much turmoil and instability. If one considers the diversity within the CMC at that time, the surprising thing is not that opinions about the new college were divided but that it was established and survived in spite of those divisions and eventually became an exceptionally strong and effective focus of common identity.

The early proposals, and hence the first curricula of the new Bible colleges – MBBC and CMBC – were designed to build on or add to instruction given in the Bible schools. That situation, however, changed almost immediately. Administrators and faculty at both colleges knew that their students wanted transferable academic credit for classes they took, and they sought to tailor their programs in such a way that credit would be granted, at first by American Mennonite colleges, and with Canadian universities as soon as arrangements could be made. The curricular requirements of U.S. Mennonite colleges were modified to meet Canadian linguistic, cultural, and theological preferences, giving German greater prominence. Sports, particularly any mixed sports or those requiring shorts and T-shirts, were unacceptable. Pietistic and practical theology was given greater, and fundamentalist doctrines less, prominence than in the U.S. colleges.

Both institutions developed parallel programs, with some differences in emphasis. MBBC introduced four programs of study in 1945: theology, designed for future preachers and pastors; Christian education, for future Bible, Sunday, and Saturday school teachers; missions, for both home and overseas missionaries; and sacred music, for choir conductors and music teachers.[70] Later a 'General Bible' program was introduced for students who wanted good, basic Bible knowledge.

The program of instruction at CMBC paralleled that offered at MBBC, except that CMBC did not have a separate missions program.[71] The theology courses offered at both colleges generally concentrated on practical or applied theological issues. Even the systematic theology courses eventually introduced at both colleges were selective and practical. The practical application of basic Christian beliefs was thought to be far more important than abstract, theoretical, or academic approaches to the subject.[72] While there was some discussion regarding the possibility of offering more advanced theological or seminary training at both institutions, all three of the largest Canadian Mennonite conferences continued to look to U.S. denominational seminaries for training at that level.[73] Missions and proclamation of the Gospel to the 'lost' received greater emphasis at MBBC, while MCC and Christian service work enjoyed stronger support at CMBC. Both colleges, in the early years, had practical or extension work – practical help; singing; preaching or distributing tracts at inner-city missions, in hospitals, and in jails; or 'gratis' work in the kitchen or on the grounds of the college.

Faculty members at both Bible colleges were expected to help define, interpret, and preserve Mennonite doctrines, applying them to the changed circumstances of their time. That rather difficult mandate, and the fact that a number of the faculty had either attended Goshen College or been otherwise influenced by the Anabaptist research done there by Harold S. Bender and his associates, influenced what was taught. The context and the responses to Bender's 'Vision' differed somewhat between various Canadian Mennonite groups and between Canadians and Americans. In a recent article, historian Abe Dueck has suggested that, in addition to the acknowledged influence of Bender's work in (Old) Mennonite congregations, 'Canadian MBs appear to have been much more receptive to Bender's Anabaptist vision than their American counterparts and than the CMCs.'[74] He suggests that a renewed emphasis on Anabaptism allowed MBs 'to affirm the best of their Mennonite heritage without denying the validity of their 1860 experience.'[75] For CMBC faculty Bender's interpretation provided a different perspective from that offered by Paul Schaefer. An increased emphasis on the Anabaptist heritage also served as a corrective to the less attractive aspects of North American evangelicalism, which had gained considerable influence in some Canadain Mennonite congregations. The new colleges thus helped them rediscover forgotten aspects of their heritage.

Academic accreditation was a constant concern of both Bible colleges. There was little difficulty in arranging accreditation with American Mennonite liberal arts colleges or with the U.S.-based Association of Bible Colleges. Both places also arranged with Canadian universities that students could receive credit for courses taken at one of the Bible colleges that closely paralleled those offered at the universities. MBBC's students were able to receive credit for a few courses at Waterloo Lutheran University quite early, and in 1961 it became affiliated with that institution. In 1970 its Division of Arts became associated with the University of Winnipeg, while CMBC became a 'teaching centre' for a growing number of courses accredited by the University of Manitoba. These arrangements brought the two Winnipeg colleges into direct relations with universities but did not allow them to get public funding. That omission probably permitted them greater independence with respect to hiring of faculty.

In order to attract students interested in university credits, while providing Bible instruction for which credit was not given, the colleges did not permit students to take only arts classes. They had to take two or three Bible-related courses each year.[76] The number of courses for which university credit was given gradually increased, and by 1970 students could complete two years of a three-year BA program.[77] Registered university students could also take courses at the Bible colleges. The liberal arts classes, in short, were increasingly harmonized and integrated with those of the universities.

The two Bible colleges were largely creations of visionary and dynamic conference leaders who rallied their members to embark on a new and unknown course. No one could foresee the impact that the two colleges would have on the conferences and on Mennonite life in Canada generally. The smaller conferences lacked the financial resources, and perhaps also the vision, to found their own colleges. Most were relatively satisfied with their own or other Mennonite and interdenominational Bible schools. Several expanded offerings in their Bible schools, and a significant number of non-MB and non-CMC Mennonite students attended and were greatly influenced by the new Bible colleges in Winnipeg.

CONRAD GREBEL COLLEGE

Winnipeg's two Mennonite Bible colleges had closer relations with public universities than did U.S. Mennonite liberal arts colleges. They did not, however, receive public funding, as did the residential colleges of several other religious denominations located on the campuses of secular universities. The University of Toronto, for example, was originally King's College of the Anglican church. When it was secularized and became the University of Toronto the Anglicans created Trinity College, which was affiliated with the university. Two Methodist colleges (Victoria and Emmanuel), a Roman Catholic one (St Michael's), and a Presbyterian (Knox) also affiliated with the university, as did the Anglican Wycliffe college. These residential colleges offered theological instruction and also courses for which students received University of Toronto credits.[78]

A similar pattern developed elsewhere. At the University of Saskatchewan, Anglicans and Presbyterians (later United Church) established their own theological colleges. In the 1930s the Roman Catholics set up St Thomas More College, which had liberal arts courses for Roman Catholic students attending the university.

In the 1940s the German/English Academy at Rosthern made ambitious plans to offer first-year university classes. In anticipation of such a development, and due to wartime exigencies, the institution was renamed Rosthern Junior College.[79] When attractive property near the University of Saskatchewan campus became available in the early 1950s there were some who wanted the college to move to Saskatoon and perhaps to enter into an arrangement with the university similar to that negotiated by the Roman Catholics. The controversies associated with the firing of Peter P. Rempel, and a generally hostile reaction by the president of the university, scuttled these plans.

Unique opportunities for such an affiliation developed in Waterloo, Ontario, in the early 1960s. Waterloo was the home of a small Lutheran denominational college, Waterloo Lutheran College (renamed Waterloo Lutheran University in 1960), but there was considerable local pressure for a public university. Plans were prepared for a secular university, the University of Waterloo, with a number of affiliated denominational colleges, including Waterloo Lutheran College. Other denominations, including the Mennonites, were invited to establish their own affiliated colleges. An inter-Mennonite ministers' fellowship formed a three-member leadership committee in 1959 to prepare plans for a Mennonite college affiliated with the University of Waterloo. It quickly became evident that there was strong inter-Mennonite support for such a venture.

There were also problems. Waterloo Lutheran College became worried that it might lose its distinctive identity and refused to become an affiliated college of the new university. The Mennonite Brethren Bible College in Winnipeg had negotiated affiliation with Waterloo Lutheran. Frank C. Peters, former teacher at the MBBC and an influential Ontario Mennonite Brethren, decided that his denomination should support Waterloo Lutheran. He knew that Mennonite Brethren in Ontario were generally suspicious of an inter-Mennonite college operating on the campus of a secular university and discouraged their participation in the proposed new institution to be affiliated with the University of Waterloo.[80]

Other Mennonite groups in Ontario maintained an interest in a new inter-Mennonite residential and teaching college affiliated with the University of Waterloo. The result was Conrad Grebel College, supported by the Mennonite Conference of Ontario (Old Mennonites), the Western Ontario Mennonite Conference (Amish Mennonites), the United Mennonite Conference of Ontario (CMC), and Kitchener's Stirling Avenue Mennonite Church, which had separated from First Mennonite in a pre-war schism.[81]

Conrad Grebel became one of four church colleges on the campus of the University of Waterloo. Its objective was 'to be a home for students away from home and a living Christian community of university students having the common objective of a university education and the experience of living in a religious community. Here fellowship, worship and work can be carried on in a meaningful way on a day to day basis.'[82] The college offered its own courses, which received university credit if academic standards and university curricular requirements were met. Those courses were open to any interested students in the university. The university paid the college for all classes taken. Students in residence at the college took many of their classes at the university and, of course, paid the appropriate tuition fees.

Conrad Grebel College set a pattern emulated later in Winnipeg at Menno Simons College in the University of Winnipeg, which already had a chair of Mennonite studies. Thus Canadian Mennonite post-secondary institutions became at least partially integrated into the large secular universities while retaining a distinctive identity.

MENNONITES AT SECULAR UNIVERSITIES

The new Mennonite colleges in Winnipeg and Waterloo could serve only a small minority of students seeking post-secondary education. They offered little or no instruction in the sciences and professional training only in church-related work. The new Mennonite colleges did not have the space or the academic atmosphere sought by many Mennonite students. There were consequently always many more Mennonites studying at public universities than at church colleges.

Mennonite university students were not necessarily hostile to all aspects of their heritage, and some attempts had been made even before 1939 to establish or maintain contact with these students. During the war a few Mennonite and other conscientious objectors at the universities of Manitoba and Saskatchewan met occasionally to discuss military and alternative service problems, but they maintained a low profile. A small group of Mennonite students at the University of Toronto met occasionally.[83] There was, however, no formal Mennonite student organization during the war years.[84]

After the war a curious mixture of students of Mennonite background arrived in the universities. Those who had enlisted for active military service and had the required qualifications and the desire to attend university received some financial assistance from the government. Most had little to do with Mennonite churches, but some were attracted by supportive pastors such as Johann Enns in Winnipeg. A few studied at the Mennonite Brethren Bible College.

There were also young men returning from alternative service, but most of them faced daunting financial problems, since they had not been able to save money during the war and received no veteran's allowances. And then there was a rapidly growing number of younger students, many of them graduates from one of the new Mennonite high schools. Some were eager to escape parental, family, and community constraints. Others wished to maintain meaningful elements of their religious heritage in the university environment but found that Mennonite urban mission churches did not address their needs and interests. That prompted two young men studying at the University of Manitoba to call together ten interested students to found the Association of Mennonite University Students (AMUS). The stated objective of AMUS was 'to strive for the harmonious perfection of the intellectual, the spiritual and the physical characteristics of its members for the benefit of society.'[85] Only male students were admitted, and early activities involved mainly academic debates on Mennonite history, doctrines, faith, and culture. It was, and remained for more than three years, a small group that fitted comfortably around a living-room coffee-table or into a small university seminar room.

In the mid-1950s there was an attempt to revitalize and expand AMUS. Some visionaries wanted a North American Mennonite student federation with chapters on every university campus where there was sufficient interest. Chapters were started in Toronto, Edmonton, and Montreal. At Saskatchewan, which had probably the second-largest Mennonite enrolment, the Saskatchewan Mennonite Youth Organization, whose members might have given leadership, were preoccupied with the Youth Farm at Rosthern. In addition, First Mennonite and Central Mennonite Brethren churches in Saskatoon had strong youth programs serving university students, making an AMUS chapter redundant. At the University of British Columbia Mennonite students who participated in the Inter-Varsity Christian Fellowship regarded the new Mennonite student organization as a threat to their activities.[86]

An important change for the Manitoba chapter of AMUS came in 1956, when the constitution was amended. Women were admitted as members and a special debate was held to discuss their changing roles in modern society.[87] The president explained that AMUS was interested in discussing Mennonite ideas, history, and culture but not 'in evangelism of students in general nor in indoctrination of Mennonite students.' He argued that his generation was 'the first in establishing a tradition of (Mennonite) scholarship in Canada,' but that there were 'few pastors who are eminently capable of facing and discussing problems peculiar to Mennonite university students whose experience differs from that of Bible school and college students.'[88]

All four AMUS groups were genuinely inter-Mennonite. Speaking contests with annual prizes, debates, and visiting speakers provided the main activities. In 1956–7 the Toronto chapter also organized a student cooperative residence, Menno House, and obtained use of the University of Toronto's Hart House Farm for what became an annual weekend retreat, popularly referred to as the 'Caledon Weekend.' Mennonite high school students were invited to an open house and shown around the university, and there were also attempts to establish small Mennonite libraries on some campuses.

The success of AMUS was, however, short-lived. It lacked a permanent organization, and the turnover in leadership, as active members graduated, created instability. It met the needs of some students but was not able to establish a niche for itself. In Manitoba a new group of Mennonite academics, mainly Mennonite Brethren, began in 1960 to publish a new 'Journal of Cogitation' which they called *Aion*. It was published for approximately seven years.

In the early 1960s AMUS faded into oblivion, though a final effort was made to revitalize it at the University of Toronto in 1966–7. The surviving documents offer no clear explanation for the demise of AMUS,[89] but several contributing factors can be identified. AMUS was strongest in Winnipeg, where it initially received support from faculty and students of the new Bible colleges, but the interests of university and Bible college students were not always complementary, and the four major post-secondary institutions with significant numbers of Mennonite students were in widely separated parts of the city. AMUS apparently did not reconcile those divergent interests.

AMUS also had difficulty defining a role for itself that was different from but not in conflict with the work of the Inter-Varsity Christian Fellowship, particularly in western Canada.[90] Stronger and more attractive church youth programs also weakened the appeal of AMUS, particularly when university- and seminary-trained pastors replaced mission workers in the cities. In Ontario Conrad Grebel College provided a different focus for Mennonite university students, while MCC and some conference projects addressed peace and social concerns of interest to students in the turbulent 1960s.

Mennonite university students of the late 1940s and the 1950s felt that they were pioneers. AMUS was an attempt to make the inherited faith relevant to the new world into which they had moved, but it turned out to be only a transitional organization. Those students strongly committed to their Mennonite heritage were reintegrated into their congregations and conferences.

CONCLUSION

Canadian Mennonites embraced secondary and post-secondary education after 1945 with great enthusiasm. Through the new high schools and colleges, leaders and students were able to retain a measure of control, which allowed them to make the transition to a new and unfamiliar way of life without losing their faith and culture. The new institutions helped to define Canadian Mennonite accommodations to modernity. They set a course that complemented, but was also different from, that provided by the public institutions. Mennonite schools and colleges became agents of accommodation, but not of assimilation.

12
Artistic and Literary Voices

The post–Second World War era saw a remarkable flowering of musical, literary, and artistic talent in Mennonite communities in Canada. Better education undoubtedly contributed to this development, but successful artists must also have a story to tell or a truth to communicate. In the decades following the war, and particularly after 1960, a rapidly growing number of Mennonites became convinced that they did indeed have something to communicate. Music, literature, and to a lesser extent the other fine arts allowed them to reflect on their historic experiences and convictions, respond to the realities and changes in the world around them, and bring new messages to their own people and to Canadian and international audiences.

The messages were rooted in personal and collective experiences, and they were not always welcome in traditional Mennonite communities. Artists sometimes expressed truths and revealed much that was good and beautiful, but at times their artistic integrity and emotional honesty caused discomfort, particularly for some of the leaders. It was ever thus with artists, for whom honesty and integrity are a greater concern than the popularity of their message with those in power.

In his recently published lectures on Mennonite literary voices past and present, Al Reimer makes reference to the 'prophetic' role of artists in society. He defines a prophet as 'someone who is gifted with more than ordinary spiritual and moral insight, perhaps one who acts as an evangelist bringing a message of new significance to the community.'[1] Most prophets, whether of the artistic or biblical variety, define or point to ideals not fully realized and truths not fully understood or applied in life as they have experienced or observed it. They thus have 'one foot in, one foot out' of the society in which they live and which they portray. Old Testament prophets appeared and were sometimes honoured at the royal court, but most also spent time in the wilderness.

That was an experience shared by many Canadian Mennonites who sought to take messages to their people. They encouraged self-understanding and helped transform Mennonite life in Canada, but their contributions were not always understood or appreciated. Mennonite artists sometimes confused their audiences, but they also enriched the lives of fellow believers and bore witness to the outside world. If, as Mennonites believed, God communicates his truths through the lives of his people, the record of those lives should include not only the writings of the 'court historians' but also the sometimes-harsher, more critical insights and truths of the artistic, literary, and prophetic voices in their midst.

MUSIC

Mennonites have a long but somewhat narrow and uneven musical heritage. The sixteenth-century Anabaptist dismissal of existing patterns of church governance and worship included rejection of much sacred music, particularly the liturgical music of the Roman Catholic mass.[2] Some of the old Psalms and chorales were retained, but new hymns and songs expressing the suffering, perseverance, and spiritual victories of a severely persecuted people were also written by early Anabaptist leaders. At least 130 sixteenth-century Anabaptist hymn and chorale writers have been identified, and their works were carefully gathered and published in hymnals. The best known of these is the German *Ausbund*, first published in 1564 and still used by some Old Order Amish. The long and often cumbersome hymns in that collection, with their many verses, were normally sung in traditional forms of unaccompanied unison singing.[3] The musical instruments of the established churches, particularly the huge pipe organs, were not part of early Anabaptist worship or hymnody.

Over the centuries, Mennonites retained the most-loved hymns and chorales written by first-generation Anabaptists, but they also added hymns and music of other religious denominations.[4] A selection of the hymns from the *Ausbund* and other sources called the *Unparteiische Liedersammlung* was compiled and used by several Amish and Mennonite groups early in the nineteenth century. It was replaced in the nineteenth century, at least in Ontario, by Benjamin Eby's *Gemeinschaftliche Liedersammlung* (1836),[5] used by both the (Old) Mennonites and Amish Mennonites until late in the century. It is still used by the Old Order Mennonites in Ontario.

The Brethren in Christ produced their own *Hymns and Psalms: Original and Modern* (Toronto, 1862). It, like most Mennonite hymnals before 1850, had no notations. Tunes were identified by metric classification, which involved organization and identification of hymns and hymn tunes by the number of syllables for each line. A Brethren in Christ historian described both Brethren and Mennonite singing: 'The Brethren in their singing reflected values that governed other parts of their lives. They sang without instrumental accompaniment, and they sang slowly, the better to reflect on the words. Until the latter years of the century, they generally sang only the melody.'[6]

Seventeenth-century Polish/Prussian Mennonites changed the language of worship from Dutch to German. In an effort to guide the congregation in what was still, for some, an unfamiliar language, they appointed *Vorsaenger*, who led by singing the words of each line of the chosen hymn, after which the congregation sang that line in unison, unaccompanied by any musical instrument.

Such congregational singing, even when led by the *Vorsaenger*, did not stress basic principles of vocal quality, such as beauty and purity of sound. Musicologists complain that 'the most remarkable characteristics of unaccompanied unison singing were the nasal, penetrating tone and the slow tempo made necessary by the many auxiliary notes between the main notes of the chorale.'[7] This type and style of church music were common in Prussian and Russian Mennonite churches until the mid-nineteenth century and still persist in some Canadian congregations.

Significant changes in Mennonite church music, both in Russia and North America, occurred in the 19th century.[8] In 1837 Heinrich Franz, a Prussian Mennonite teacher in a southern Russian Mennonite school, began to compile sacred hymns to be sung in Mennonite schools and churches. He introduced a modified system of musical notation using numbers (*Ziffern*), rather than notes, to represent the degrees of the scale. That made it possible for singers to read and sing, at sight, the melody. Similar notations denoted simple, four-part harmonies, and by 1860 several Mennonite hymnals with four-part numerical notations were published.

Initially some church leaders strenuously opposed the new music, which was introduced by the teachers at the Orloffer Zentralschule and by the Gnadenfeld congregation, both in the Molotschna Mennonite colony in southern Russia. It was popularized, and much of the early opposition was removed, when religious revivals swept the Mennonite villages in the 1850s and 1860s. New, often more lively and emotional hymns, rooted in revival experiences, were also transcribed to numerical musical notations and added to the hymnody.[9]

There were parallel developments, but without the *Ziffern*, in North America. Gospel songs and hymns written by D.L. Moody, Ira Sankey, Fanny Crosby, and other nineteenth-century evangelicals were added to Mennonites' worship services and hastened their linguistic and religious integration into North American evangelicalism.

In the early decades of the twentieth century numerous local choirs and larger workshops for choir conductors and singers were organized by Mennonites in Russia. The immigrants of the 1920s brought this heritage with them, and Russian Mennonite choir leaders with established reputations provided a tremendous impetus to choral singing in Canada in the late 1920s and the 1930s. Others followed, and numerous congregational and community choirs were organized. The early choirs were set up in communities where immigrants of the 1920s lived, but their influence quickly spread to, and enriched, the music of Mennonites who had come to Canada earlier. Wesley Berg, who has written extensively on the subject, offers the following assessment of the influence of these Russian Mennonite musicians: 'These energetic, dedicated and talented men devoted their lives to the cause of music and singing, serving their fellow immigrants and the Mennonites already established here. This was especially true of the period from 1923 until 1942, after which the various conferences were able to use the foundations built by these pioneers to establish programs that could continue without extraordinary leadership.'[10]

Mennonite choral singing became so popular in part because choirs became social institutions in Mennonite communities. Members were usually young people for whom village life in Russia, or everyday life on isolated Canadian farms, provided limited stimulation. Choir practices and public performances, some of which involved travel, opened new artistic vistas and allowed young people to mingle and get to know one another while engaged in activities intended to glorify God. Parents readily granted short-term relief from the drudgery of farm work so that their teenagers could participate. As a result, activities associated with church and community choirs took on social as well as artistic dimensions.

During summer, between spring seeding and fall harvest, or later in the fall, large songfests (*Saengerfeste*) brought together hundreds of Mennonite young people to spend several days rehearsing and then performing great choral church music. Local choir conductors were asked to practise the music with their choirs beforehand so that singers would be prepared to participate.[11]

The Mennonite high schools at Gretna and Rosthern, and the Mennonite liberal arts colleges in the United States,[12] became musical centres for both the Swiss and Russian Mennonites, particularly after the arrival of the immigrants of the 1920s.[13] The high schools established immediately after the Second World War offered strong music programs from the beginning. Each school had at least one, and often several choirs that performed at the annual school opening and closing exercises. Many also put on an annual Christmas program and special spring choral concerts and went on fund-raising and public relations tours to other congregations.

The centres of Mennonite music making and training, however, were the two new Bible colleges in Winnipeg. Ben and Esther Horch at the Mennonite Brethren Bible College (MBBC) and John Konrad at the Canadian Mennonite Bible College (CMBC), along with other outstanding choir leaders, worked with musicians at those institutions. As music education became more formal and professional, both colleges found professionally trained and qualified choral music directors who continued and enriched what they had inherited. George and Esther Wiebe at the CMBC and William and Irmgard Baerg at the MBBC often worked in close cooperation. They established national and international reputations for excellence and integrity.

Several decades later, Conrad Grebel College developed a strong music program, which became the official music program of the University of Waterloo. All the Mennonite colleges and high schools also trained music teachers for Mennonite high schools and Bible schools, as well as singers and choir leaders for congregational and community choirs and orchestras.

The enthusiasm for music making in the 1950s is evident in a reported interview with K.H. Neufeld, one of the best-known choir conductors in western Canada, in 1953. Neufeld confidently predicted that 'within the next 20 or 25 years Mennonite composers, conductors, choirs, etc., would rank among the top musicians in Canada.' He reported: 'B.C. has 19 mixed choirs, Alberta 11, Manitoba 65, Ontario 17 and Saskatchewan a large number. Canada today has 24 Mennonite music teachers with a teacher's degree; three with a Bachelor of Music degree, and one with a doctorate in music.'[14]

Mennonite community choirs often crossed denominational boundaries. In Kitchener-Waterloo, in 1956, Abner Martin became the driving force behind a new, inter-Mennonite community choir called Menno Singers. Martin built on pioneering choral music work done by Harold Scheidel, who had organized a 'Nightingale Chorus,' which sang on one of the earliest Mennonite-sponsored religious radio broadcasts.[15] Many of the singers in Scheidel's chorus in the 1940s and Abner Martin's Menno Singers in the 1950s were recent graduates of Rockway Mennonite Collegiate, while in the 1960s more were associated with Conrad Grebel College. Both the chorus's radio broadcasts and the Menno Singers' performances became 'a well known part of the cultural fare in Kitchener-Waterloo.'[16] In addition to public performances of classical and sacred music, Menno Singers also arranged music workshops and sought to promote understanding and appreciation of good music in the community.[17] Mennonite children's choirs in Kitchener-Waterloo, Winnipeg, and Vancouver also brought together Mennonites from various conferences and became renowned for excellence.

Choral music was not the only interest of Mennonite conductors. Ben Horch also organized in Winnipeg the first Canadian Mennonite symphony orchestra.[18] Smaller orchestras and musical ensembles were set up in other Mennonite communities. Some, such as Horch's, attracted and helped in the development of musicians who later became professional solo performers or joined major symphonies. Mennonite community orchestras elsewhere also trained performers who later achieved national and international recognition. But there was always a place for interested amateurs and music lovers in the growing number of community choirs and orchestras.

Participation in choirs, musical presentations, and the arts generally also helped to break down gender biases. In most of Canada's Mennonite churches women were not given equal recognition or participation with the men, but in the choir it was usually the soprano section that carried the melody and thus had the leading part, and certainly female soloists earned equal or higher recognition than males. Leading female vocalists could thus proclaim in song messages that they could not deliver from the pulpit. Before 1970 there were very few female choir conductors, and those few led children's choirs, but numerous piano accompanists achieved greater involvement. Female soloists and accompanists, and perhaps also the few Mennonite female choir conductors, provided role models for girls who could dream of things not available to their mothers.

The wives of four of the five most prominent conductors identified by Wesley Berg are almost never mentioned in the available literature. But once the Winnipeg Bible colleges were established Esther Horch, and a little later Esther Wiebe and Irmgard Baerg, began distinguished musical careers of their own. Older, old-fashioned college administrators and board members were reluctant to recognize and pay for the important work these women did. Yet all three earned artistic equality with their male counterparts. They too became role models.

The music sung or performed by Mennonite musicians changed over the years. Late-nineteenth- and early-twentieth-century Russian Mennonite choirs sang mainly German chorales, hymns, and folk, nature, and gospel songs.[19] For a time familiarity and reliance on the numerical music notations (*Ziffern*) restricted the kind of music that Canadian Mennonite choirs could sing,[20] but the switch to notes, begun before establishment of the Bible colleges in Winnipeg, was quickly completed by the music teachers there. Mennonite symphony orchestras used notes from the beginning.

Music directors and students at Mennonite high schools and Bible col-

leges after the war began to look for English-language material to supplement but not, except with the Swiss Mennonites, to replace the old German
favourites. Choir conductors introduced some of the more popular choruses
from Handel's *Messiah*, Haydn's *Creation*, Mendelssohn's *Elijah* and *St Paul*,
Loew's *Suehnopfer*, and other classical religious pieces. Those wishing to
perform larger, integrated sacred works that their still largely amateur choirs,
with limited orchestral accompaniment, could perform often turned to John
Stainer's *Crucifixion* or John Farmer's *Christ and His Soldiers*.

The leading Mennonite conductors in the 1950s, however, wanted to perform the great works of religious music by Bach, Beethoven, Handel, and
Mendelssohn as the composers intended that they be performed. K.H.
Neufeld, for instance, prepared several performances of Stainer's *Crucifixion* hoping and expecting that it would serve as an introduction to the more
difficult, sophisticated, and moving Bach Passions.[21] Both Neufeld and Horch
adored Bach, a devout Christian, and thought that his music most closely
approximated Christian musical perfection.

There was always a second strand in music among Canadian Mennonites.
Many church and community choirs manifested great enthusiasm for evangelical gospel songs, hymns, and choruses. That music was regarded with
grave suspicion by some older members of congregations[22] and by almost all
musically trained Mennonite academics. It was readily admitted that choruses, gospel songs, and hymns with a lively melody could move audiences
to respond to the call of an evangelist, but the appeal seemed superficial,
transitory, and based on dubious theological premises. Evangelists sought to
convey the Gospel message using popular and worldly music and lyrics.
They were more interested in the immediate impact than in the artistic merit
of the music or the theological soundness of the lyrics.

'There is,' one Mennonite music historian wrote, 'a sense of outrage at the
way in which the music and poetry have been debased to reach large masses
of people.'[23] Choruses such as 'One, two, three, four, five, six, seven, I'm on
my way to heaven,' 'Climb, climb up sunshine mountain,' 'Have a little talk
with Jesus,' 'Heavenly Sunshine,' 'One door and only one,' 'I fell in love,
deep in love, With the Beautiful Nazarene,' set to popular secular tunes or
jingles, did not, in the opinion of Mennonite musicians and theologians,
'present musical and lyrical contents with enough beauty, persuasion, craft
and style to be worthy of the responsibility the doctrine taught has to carry.'[24]
These choruses seemed far removed from old, more familiar, and much more
substantial, German Sunday school children's gospel songs, such as 'Gott ist
die Liebe,' 'Muede bin ich geh zur Ruh,' and 'Weisst du wie viel Sternlein
stehen?' And when children and young adolescents were taught body move-

ments to accompany the English choruses, some critics complained that this came dangerously close to worldly dance forms.

There were similar concerns about many North American gospel songs and hymns composed by evangelicals such as D.L. Moody, Ira Sankey, and Fanny Crosby, which one particularly harsh critic described as 'cheap and tawdry tunes pandering to the genuinely illiterate and spiritually maimed.'[25] Many of the melodies were taken from secular pop hits and love songs and had a strong, 3/4-time waltz beat. Even the lyrics of popular love songs were only slightly modified in some of the 'Jesus is my boy friend' type of gospel songs. Even Mennonite leaders who strongly supported evangelistic crusades warned about popular evangelistic music: 'From the pulpit there will come denunciations of dancing and waltzing and the like, yet in the same church the congregation will be hearing waltz music and calling it a blessing besides.'[26] 'One must learn to distinguish between music that is worldly in character and that which is truly spiritual. Ignorance about such matters may lead one to commit many musical and spiritual improprieties.'[27]

Revivalist choruses and hymns seemed, at best, a poor substitute for the sober, solid, and time-tested German *Kernlieder* and generated much debate in Canada, particularly at the MBBC and within the MB committee preparing a new hymnal in the 1940s.

Debates about the appropriateness of particular forms of music for worship services were particularly intense whenever new worship hymnals were prepared. In the United States the (Old) Mennonites, the General Conference, and the Mennonite Brethren accepted both the English language and the lyrics and music of the new gospel songs and choruses in their new hymnals. The (Old) Mennonites in Ontario had little difficulty with the new hymnals of their conference. Few of the standard German chorales found their way into (Old) Mennonite Church hymnals, but that was no longer a serious concern.

Several Canadian (Old) Mennonite leaders also gathered and promoted what they regarded as the best of both traditional and North American popular evangelistic music. A favourite of S.F. Coffman's at the Ontario Mennonite Bible School was the great 'Hallelujah Chorus' from Handel's *Messiah*, but he was also very fond of other hymns such as 'In Thy Holy Place.' Coffman had a good sense of music and served on the Hymnal Committee of the Mennonite Church. His colleague at the Ontario Mennonite Bible School, C.F. Derstine, was also concerned about music in the Mennonite church and published what he called 'Sheet Music of Heaven,' in an effort to promote the kind of music he thought appropriate for worship and edification. Neither man was concerned about preservation of the German linguistic and musical heritage. Nor were they particularly worried about the musical quality, or theological soundness of the lyrics, of popular American gospel songs. As a result, the Swiss Mennonites in Ontario were able to accept new North American, English-language hymnody with relatively little controversy.

That was not the case for conferences that sought to retain German for worship and worried about the content of the English-language gospel songs and choruses. It became a particular problem for the Mennonite Brethren in Canada, most of whom came to Canada only in the 1920s. Mennonite Brethren in the United States made the language transition much earlier than their counterparts in Canada and also adopted a new hymnal 'composed largely of hymns of the Gospel song type of English or American origin.'[28]

The General Conference, with which the Conference of Mennonites in Canada (CMC) was associated, prepared its own English-language hymnal, which kept many more of the traditional German melodies but used English lyrics. Continued commitment to the German language prompted Canadian MBs and CMCs to create their own German hymnals.

The Mennonite Brethren acted first. Most Canadian MB congregations in the 1930s and 1940s had abandoned the old hymnbooks that they had brought with them from Russia, using instead the German *Evangeliums-Lieder*, compiled by Walter Rauschenbusch and Ira Sankey. It included some great German chorales and hymns and translated versions of less artistic or poetic nineteenth-century evangelical gospel songs, hymns and choruses.[29] In their new German hymnal, Canadian Mennonite Brethren hoped to preserve the best of their German hymnody, add to it the best of the translated American material, and eliminate the dubious and trite lyrics set to secular pop and dance music that had been included in the *Evangeliums-Lieder*. The result was the *Gesangbuch der Mennoniten Bruedergemeinde* (1953). Several years later an MBBC music professor wrote: 'Since our *Gesangbuch* has been published a definite improvement has resulted in the quality of our hymns. There is a new and necessary emphasis on the Christian Life, which, I feel, was sadly lacking in our *Evangeliums-Lieder* which we used previously.'[30]

The college professors may have been pleased. Many ordinary worshippers who had formed strong attachments to the emotional, subjective, and pious gospel hymns, with their catchy and upbeat melodies, were not, and it took years before the *Gesangbuch* replaced the old *Evangeliums-Lieder* in their affections. The quality of the *Gesangbuch*, however, was gradually recognized, and in 1955 the Evangelical Mennonite Church switched from the *Evangeliums-Lieder* to the *Gesangbuch*.

Mennonites of the CMC were more diverse than the Mennonite Brethren and compiling a hymnbook took longer. Their *Gesangbuch der Mennoniten*

(1965) contained 599 German hymns drawn from eight periods of church history, ranging from the pre-Reformation era to contemporary English and American hymns. There was a brief description of each period. Each of the nineteen sections pertained to a season of the church year or to a theme. One or more appropriate scripture verses accompanied each hymn.

The attempts by the Mennonite Brethren and the CMC to retain and enrich the best of their German-language, Anabaptist musical heritage with the great works of classical church music, and to discourage use of nineteenth-century gospel pop songs, met with only partial success. In 1971 Howard Dyck, later a music host for the Canadian Broadcasting Corporation, lamented, 'The excellent Anabaptist chorale tradition has all too often been replaced by the 19th century gospel song (which, incidentally, was regarded by the composers as "disposable" music) which often lacks theological, poetic, and musical integrity. We have been careless in allowing our hymnody to be cheapened by these elements.'[31]

Publication of their German hymnals largely coincided, to the sorrow and chagrin of several committee members, with early phases of the transition from German to English. It seemed logical to some that the shift would result in adoption of the hymnals of the U.S. conferences with which they were affiliated. That, however, seemed problematic, particularly for the Mennonite Brethren who were not satisfied with the numerous gospel songs, many of dubious lyric or musical quality, in the U.S. MB hymnary. Equally serious, many of the great German anthems, chorales, and hymns were not included. The music professors at MBBC were particularly concerned. One recommended use of the *Mennonite Hymnal* of the General Conference rather than the MB hymnal.[32]

When it became clear in the early 1950s that English would take over in MB churches, the Canadian conference, rather than accepting the U.S. hymnary, decided 'to recreate the Gesangbuch into an English language parallel.'[33] This necessitated translation of the lyrics of all the as-yet-untranslated German hymns and chorales in the Gesangbuch. Students and faculty at MBBC, housewives, schoolteachers, farmers, musicians, preachers, and anyone else who might wish to do so were invited to help. The results were sometimes inspired and sometimes literary butchery. Few of the amateur translators had genuine talent. Many, perhaps influenced by nineteenth-century American gospel music, seemed more concerned about the emotional and pious sentiments of the lyrics than their literary quality or theological soundness. The translations also created musical problems, as the hymnbook committee readily admitted: 'The actual matter of creating this new English language parallel, was not so much a problem of translating, but much more one of recreating familiar spiritual concepts from one language origin into that of another. Musical considerations heightened the difficulties a great deal in terms of fixed melodies, fixed harmonies and especially fixed rhythmic patterns.'[34]

The English version nevertheless documents the theological and linguistic evolution of the conference. It was, in the words of the Hymnbook Committee, designed to link 'this history of our European past with that of our present North American domicile.' The compilers wanted to provide 'the best opportunity for adapting into another language the spiritual heritage of congregational songs best epitomized by the old German *Kernlieder*,'[35] allowing members to worship in a unified way from the same hymnbook, but in two languages. Unfortunately, some of the most precious old German hymns sustained serious damage, and work on a new English-language hymnal soon began, inspired by a desire on the part of American Mennonite Brethren to deal with some of the inadequacies of their hymnal.

The CMC had much less difficulty with the *Mennonite Hymnary*, published by the General Conference Mennonite Church in 1940 and generally regarded as the most successful of all the Mennonite English-language hymnals that appeared between 1939 and 1970.[36] Edited by W.H. Hohmann and Lester Hostetler, it included 104 German hymn tunes, 58 of them chorales, thus preserving German traditions, even though the lyrics were in English. It also had 26 Psalms and Psalm tunes and a judicious selection 'of 68 of the better Gospel songs.'[37]

In the 1960s new cooperative hymnals were prepared. The first, published in 1969 after almost a decade of work by General Conference and (Old) Mennonite Church musicologists, was *The Mennonite Hymnal*, designed to serve both of those large conferences. Tune, text, and worship-aids committees sought to maintain the integrity of the original versions while making appropriate theological, linguistic, and stylistic modifications. Contemporary material was added, and some new tunes were commissioned for specific texts. At the same time MBs in Canada and the United States worked on a new hymnal to be used in both countries. The *Worship Hymnal* was published in 1971. It had something for all musical tastes, but its acceptance required tolerance and openness to change: 'As we come to appreciate hymns that are new to us but familiar to those who live above or below the border we will have reason to praise God that, in an age of increased polarization, we find it possible to have fellowship in worship, not only with God our Father and with His Son, Jesus Christ, but with one another.'[38]

Resistance to late-nineteenth- and twentieth-century gospel songs and hymns did not mean that Canadian Mennonites resisted all new musical forms. Many of the old German chorales and hymns had been written or sung by those who migrated from the Soviet Union to Canada and who had experienced the horrors of war, revolution, murder, and economic devastation.[39] Those hymns, or at least the way in which survivors of those experiences sang and understood them, had much in common with American Black spiritual music, which was rooted in the anguish and suffering of slavery and reconstruction. Mennonites tended to agree with musicologists who suggested that the Black spirituals had a depth of conviction and authenticity that stood 'in most marked contrast to the gospel songs, which too often represent a deliberate cheapening of literary and musical standards in an effort to cater to public taste.'[40] As a result, Black spirituals enriched Mennonite hymnody. Mennonite appreciation and acceptance of these spirituals, however, was never extended to another popular but more worldly form of Black American music – jazz. Ben Horch, for example, denounced jazz as 'caterwauling from darkest Africa' and warned against including any of it in Mennonite music programs and recitals.[41]

After 1945, Mennonite choir leaders and musicians, even while trying to preserve the best of their old German hymns and chorales, recognized that many of those old hymns had been written in times of persecution, suffering, social upheaval, and high infant mortality rates and focused the attention of the worshipper on heaven. In more orderly times such hymns seemed 'somewhat unrealistic in that they project our thinking away from this world to the heavenly kingdom, whereas I would think the New Testament thrust to be that of building the Kingdom of God here on earth.'[42] Many of the hymns also projected rural and agricultural images and values. As more Mennonites left the countryside it seemed reasonable to ask, 'To what extent does the imagery of the rural populace communicate to the city dweller? Can someone without a rural background comprehend "Sowing in the Morning," "We Plough the Fields and Scatter, the Good Seed on the Land," or "Bringing in the Sheaves" ? '[43] Such questions and problems prompted some to suggest that 'we need ... new hymns for a new day.'[44]

The response in the decades following the Second World War, however, was not to commission or inspire Mennonite writers and lyricists to write new hymns or to establish a distinct hymnody of their own. Instead, the major inspirations came through rediscovery and enthusiastic acceptance of classical religious music, which opened up vast new artistic vistas. Since much of that music was pious and worshipful, the discoveries did not directly threaten the faith. This, moreover, was music that had the kind of depth and substance that cautious older leaders and musically sophisticated academics found lacking in American revivalist pop gospel music. The result was a remarkable musical evolution in Canadian Mennonite communities and congregations. Not all moved at the same pace or always in the same direction.

The evolution was nevertheless a group experience rather than involving only scattered individuals.

Discovery of and enthusiasm for classical religious music still became controversial in some Mennonite communities. Two related issues elicited criticism. The first concerned the ultimate purpose of music making. Was it to worship and glorify God in the best and most artistically pleasing way possible or merely for the enjoyment of the listeners and to show off the talents and abilities of the performers? The revivalist hymns and many of the cherished numbers in the *Evangeliums-Lieder*, while artistically and literarily flawed, had an obvious and well-defined objective – to bring people to salvation or conversion and to praise and worship God. Some critics of classical religious music asked pointedly how many listeners had come forward to accept Christ as their personal saviour after a performance of the *Messiah*, of Mendelssohn's *Elijah*, or of one of Bach's masterpieces.

The applause after musical performances was, in the view of some critics, offensive and inappropriate. It clearly focused on and gave recognition to the performers, rather than directing the attention of the listeners to God. It was not uncommon to ask that there be no applause after a religious music program. A closing prayer by a church elder, sometimes with an invitation to unsaved listeners, seemed more appropriate to these critics.

Closely related to this debate were questions about who could properly participate. It seemed to some people highly inappropriate that individuals who had not had a conversion experience or made a personal religious commitment sang religious music. 'It is,' a music professor at the MBBC argued, 'impossible for a worldly singer to give a proper spiritual performance of a religious song, since it cannot be a genuine product.'[45] Even the best of professional musicianship seemed to such critics no adequate substitute for genuine faith and piety.

Some Mennonite churches followed this line of reasoning and allowed only those who had made an adult commitment to the church and its teachings to sing in their church choirs.[46] Others argued persuasively that the Gospel message, as expressed and conveyed through the music and lyrics of the great anthems, chorales, and hymns of the church, might be communicated far more effectively to a young person while he or she was learning to sing those hymns and musical masterpieces than through even the most stirring evangelistic service. Choirs, it was argued, could become effective instruments of evangelization, and young people should participate in them just as they did in Sunday school or Youth Endeavour activities, even if they had not yet made their adult religious decisions and commitments. Some churches, however, established two choirs – an official church choir, restricted to those making a profession of salvation, and another that could also serve in worship services but admitted anyone interested and willing to participate.[47] Some of those drawn in because of a love of singing and music, or merely for social reasons, developed a keen appreciation of both the glories of the fine arts and of the religious truths proclaimed through the music.

This issue was debated again when the Canadian Broadcasting Corporation (CBC) began a popular Sunday afternoon television program called 'Hymn-Sing' in the 1960s. A Mennonite critic, while complementing the CBC for producing a program of high quality, complained: 'It is disturbing to discover that most of the personnel concerned with the production of Hymn-Sing are not "church people" nor even thoroughly familiar with the tradition of singing hymns and making music for the honour and glory of God ... Can hymns remain true if they are presented as entertainment?'[48]

One of the most valued aspects of Mennonite choral music was that it brought people together in a common artistic endeavour. That makes the development of choral and orchestral music among Canadian Mennonites a particularly interesting and instructive case study of the processes of accommodation. Mennonites were musically transformed. They became an integral part of the classical music community of the nation. They retained the best of their own heritage while adding new appreciation and understanding of classical religious music. They did not develop their own distinctive hymnody but incorporated and reconciled the best of their own musical heritage with that of the great classical composers and writers of church music.[49] In a testimonial to Ben Horch a Mennonite scholar said: 'Your influence in our brotherhood has been most significant. It came at a very crucial time when our brotherhood was in the beginning stages of acculturation. These changes could have been more unsettling than they actually were. To have people like you ... present to guide with sympathetic understanding helped to bridge the gap between two cultures.'[50]

At the time of Horch's death another scholar observed: 'Ben was a bridge and built a bridge for many of our heritage ... [Ben] took us into the larger Canadian and world arena.'[51] It was a tribute applicable not only to Horch, or music leaders of his era, but to several generations of Canadian Mennonite choir directors and musicians.

LITERATURE AND POETRY

Creative writing and poetry by Canadian Mennonites also underwent remarkable changes after 1945. These shifts were as dramatic as those involving music making and appreciation but differed significantly from the developments in music because creative writers never gained the same recognition or acceptance from Mennonite congregational and conference leaders.

Mennonites living in relatively isolated communities had for generations shown little appreciation for creative literature. They read and appreciated early Anabaptist literary writing chronicling persecutions and martyrdom, but it was only in the twentieth century that they developed appreciation for creative literature. In Ontario the Swiss Mennonites in an earlier period had been familiar with eighteenth-century authors, such as Jung-Stilling and Schabaelje, who had explored the dual themes of *Heimweh* (a longing for home) and *Heilsgewissheit* (assurance of salvation) in introspective, auto-biographical, and didactic strains within fairly narrow intellectual, cultural, and religious boundaries. In the twentieth century John Bunyan's *Pilgrim's Progress* was more widely read. Ontario Mennonites were also familiar with, and appreciated, Mabel Dunham's *Trail of the Conestoga*, which interpreted Ontario Mennonites to themselves and to others in their communities. Luella Creighton's *High Bright Buggy Wheels* was also read, but Ontario Mennonites resented it.[52] They did not, however, respond to these depictions of their way of life by outsiders with a body of their own creative literature.

The Swiss Mennonites came to Ontario with Pennsylvania 'Deitsch' – a Palatine German dialect that they shared with German Lutheran, Catholic, and other migrants from Pennsylvania. It has therefore been argued that Mennonite dialect writers with a Pennsylvania heritage reflected Pennsylvania German rather than Mennonite culture.

Pennsylvania 'Deitsch,' like the Low German dialect of the Russian Mennonites, was almost entirely an oral language. That fact severely limited literary output and shaped the few things that were written. Peter C. Erb has identified four key Pennsylvania 'Deitsch' characteristics: *Schmiegsamkeit* (obsequiousness), *Fuegsamkeit* (compliance), *Schwaeche* (weakness), and *Nachgiebigkeit* (docility). These qualities persisted longer in Mennonite than in other Pennsylvania communities; they came to be understood and interpreted in ways that reinforced traditional Mennonite principles and practices:

Interpreting *Schwaeche* and *Nachgiebigkeit* ... might be a useful tool in explaining why *Deitsch* culture has remained longest among Mennonites and Amish. Non-resistant love, perhaps the central practical religious principle of these people, is after all the theological equivalent of the two characteristics ascribed. In the full blossom of culture all the supposedly negative characteristics can be read as positive. *Schmiegsamkeit* is not obsequiousness but openness, *Fuegsamkeit* not compliance but respect, *Schwaeche* not weakness but humility and *Nachgiebigkeit* not docility but piety.[53]

Ontario Mennonite authors with Pennsylvania or European Amish roots were also influenced by U.S. literary trends. The purpose and role of creative literature came to be defined differently by them than by Mennonites who came to Canada later. John Ruth, a Harvard-educated Pennsylvania Mennonite, enunciated clearly what he regarded as the central task of a Mennonite writer:[54] 'Ruth defines Mennonite writers as writing from within the covenant-community and bound to its discipline. They must tell the Mennonite story "from the unique centre of covenant-conviction where we stand." Such writers must find their distinctive voice and story not from models outside the community but from the centre of the community. "In fact," Ruth argues, "our particular story may not be tellable in terms of the stylistic cadences of the stories currently in vogue. Our imagination must be our own."'[55]

Ruth's model of story telling achieved some notable, if limited success in Canada. Ben Sauder (1898–1978), of St Jacob's, Ontario, is one of the few local Ontario Swiss Mennonites whose work has received some critical scholarly attention.

The situation was different with the Mennonites who had come to Canada from the Soviet Union in the 1920s. An essentially redemptive or didactic model of story telling was inadequate for conveying the pathos of the disintegration of the Russian Mennonites' world. And it also omitted the uncertainties and frustrations of those who grew up in Canada at a time of rapid change.

Creative writers who had lived through the Russian catastrophe were determined to preserve the memory of what had been lost and, if possible, to make some sense of their traumas. Many wrote diaries and memoirs about those events. A few also sought to recreate imaginatively and creatively, through novels and poems, features of their lost homeland. They now had their own story, which they believed must be told.[56] They produced numerous novels and books of poetry in German, some of literary merit.

Eighteenth-century German authors such as Jung-Stilling and Schabaelje provided a model for Mennonites writing about their people in Russia.[57] That framework cast creative writing into the somewhat narrow confines of 'Christian literature,' which had only limited appeal. Writing in German or Low German also limited the size of their readership. As a result, creative Russian Mennonite writers in Canada during the 1930s and 1940s 'wandered through a wilderness of artificial inwardness.'[58] Much of their work was introspectionist, romantic, or escapist.

A few early Canadian Mennonite creative writers transcended the accepted forms and content of so-called Christian literature.[59] Most prominent were Arnold Dyck, Fritz Senn (Gerhard Friesen), Jacob H. Janzen, Gerhard

Loewen, and Georg de Brecht (Gerhard Toews).[60] But even they appealed only to a small, educated elite, since they wrote mainly on Russian Mennonite topics, in either High or Low German.

Russian Mennonites in Canada lived in a linguistically trifurcated way. They used High German for worship and official discourse, Low German for everyday village and community life, and English for business. As well, there was no agreed-on way of writing Low German. Low German was 'a colloquial language, direct, simple, more adequate ... to express deep feelings.'[61] High German was the language of high culture and piety. Realistic material that might be tolerated in a low German work was not acceptable in High German. It was not easy to create literary masterpieces under such linguistic handicaps.

An exception to this general situation was Jacob H. Janzen, probably the most respected Russian Mennonite leader in Ontario in the 1940s. Janzen once told of an encounter that he had with a Swiss Mennonite bishop. When the good bishop heard that Janzen wrote novels he said disapprovingly that 'novelists were fiction writers and that fiction was a lie. I surely would not want to represent myself to him as a professional liar.'[62] An understanding of the value of creative writing had not yet emerged.

Early Mennonite writers often faced serious economic difficulties. Their earnings were meagre at best. Yet those men and women lived and worked in communities and congregations that valued economic success and hard practical and productive work. Jacob H. Janzen noted that his literary colleague Fritz Senn was deeply religious. But Senn never really felt at home in the religious institutions of the people whom he loved and wrote about. Janzen thought that Senn remained an outsider because he was poor and because materialistically minded Mennonites did not accept him fully as one of their own.[63] Arnold Dyck's economic troubles and his somewhat peripheral status in the Mennonite community of Steinbach are well known. These writers were people who often had 'one foot in, one foot out,' of their communities.[64] They wrote passionately, imaginatively, and often humorously about the Russian Mennonite homeland they had lost and about the adjustments of their people to the problems and opportunities of their new homeland. They provided a bridge for those who would later write in English about their people living in diaspora – some in Canada, but many in other parts of the world.

One of the first creative English-language Mennonite writers was Barbara Claassen Smucker, whose ancestors had emigrated from Russia to the United States. Her novel *Henry's Red Sea*, written for children between the ages of nine and fourteen, told of the rescue of the Mennonite refugees trapped in Berlin in 1947. It became popular and earned the acclaim of Mennonite and non-Mennonite critics. Smucker went on to a distinguished career, writing mainly stories for children and adolescents. She spent many years in Canada, where her husband taught at Conrad Grebel College.

The first major creative Mennonite literary work written in Canada in the English language came from the pen of Rudy H. Wiebe. His first novel, *Peace Shall Destroy Many* (Toronto: McClelland and Stewart, 1962), became immediately controversial. It triggered 'an explosion of the Mennonite world view,'[65] transcending the introspectionist, autobiographical, and didactic strains of earlier Mennonite writing.

Rudy Wiebe was born in a small and remote Mennonite community in northern Saskatchewan. The family moved to Coaldale, Alberta, when he was a boy. He attended the Alberta Mennonite High School and the University of Alberta in Edmonton, where he earned a BA and an MA. At that time the university had an option allowing students of English to write a novel as their MA thesis. *Peace Shall Destroy Many* fulfilled that requirement. Its central and controlling theme was described thus by one reviewer: 'What is a sincere and seeking Mennonite to do with the received faith of his fathers, particularly when this faith is hampered by a false traditionalism or a false idealism? How can he reinterpret this received faith more meaningfully and apply it more effectively, in a rapidly changing world without thereby losing anything that is truly essential to the faith?'[66]

Wiebe portrayed clearly some of the darker aspects of Mennonite life. Some in Coaldale thought that his fictional Deacon Block, a powerful and autocratic Mennonite leader, resembled the local Mennonite Brethren leaders, but readers in other Mennonite communities also recognized character traits of their leaders in Deacon Block. Critical Mennonite reviewers focused on Wiebe's realistic but unfavourable presentation of a Mennonite leader and on the fact that the novel dealt openly with sexual transgressions at a time when such matters were not mentioned in polite Mennonite society.

Wiebe has discussed the furore that followed publication of his novel. Remarkably, he explains that the story that he wanted to tell was that of Elizabeth Wiens. Her plight, other than her specific sexual transgression, rarely caught the attention of Mennonite reviewers. The disintegration of the fictional Deacon Block, at a time when Mennonite leaders were under severe pressure and traditional community controls were weakening, attracted most attention.

Wiebe had only recently been appointed editor of the *Mennonite Brethren Herald*. His editorials had elicited some criticism, but *Peace Shall Destroy Many*, which Wiebe described as 'the first realistic novel written in

English about the Mennonites,' brought an explosion and forced his resig-nation.[67] David Pankratz, pastor of Wiebe's home church in Coaldale, wrote to express his dismay: 'For some time I had been urged by members of our church to read the book. Younger and older members had read the book and classified it as "filth" ... I have read the book from cover to cover ... our Mennonite people, the M.B. church and authoritative men have been de-graded, and sorry to say, our young people plastered with shame.'[68] After resigning his editorship Wiebe accepted an appointment to teach at Goshen College in the United States and later a position in the English Department at the University of Alberta.

Some of those who wrote or telephoned him when *Peace Shall Destroy Many* appeared were supportive and said that the sorts of things that he had written about happened in many Mennonite communities. But after the *Winnipeg Free Press* announced that it would publish a condensed version of the novel a del-egation of Mennonite businessmen from Winnipeg and Steinbach indicated to the paper's editors that large Mennonite advertising accounts might be can-celled if they published a story that brought shame and embarrassment to their community.[69] The serialization did not run in 1963.[70]

Many delighted Mennonite readers, however, saw the work differently, as:

the right novel at the right time in that it raised crucial questions and long-suppressed issues of Mennonite life and faith and dared to address them honestly and with cre-ative independence. It slaughtered the sacred cows of institutionalised Mennonitism on all sides by dramatizing such issues as Mennonite isolationism and the patriarchal tyranny it bred, racial bigotry as the ugly product of Mennonite pride, passive non-resistance in a time of national crisis, sexual repression and the subjugation of the woman, religious formalism and the lust for land which in league with religious for-malism becomes such a soul-numbing form of idolatry.[71]

Wiebe had prescribed a dose of realism that many Canadian Mennonites found hard to swallow, but enthusiastic acceptance by outside readers and reviewers, and sober assessments by Mennonite critics, eventually fashioned a new understanding and appreciation: 'Imaginative literature worthy of the name, and this must include Mennonite literature, has to deal with the real world and with the real God. It must distinguish between the ritual use to which the available God is put and man's endless search for the real God, for ultimate meaning or whatever else this may be called.'[72]

Authors who documented or imaginatively recreated in a realistic way a Mennonite world and way of life that did not fit the stock forms of institu-tional Mennonite life sometimes paid a high price for their courage and honesty, but they provided an example for a host of younger writers:[73] 'Rudy Wiebe created a Mennonite literary world real enough and spacious enough to make it possible and indeed respectable for other writers to write Mennonite even if they were themselves no longer practising Mennonites. He gave them a literary context in which to express Mennonite experiences never before accessible to the creative imagination.'[74]

Wiebe remained for almost a decade a lone and sometimes lonely voice. When he was asked to write an article discussing 'Where we're at in our understanding and use of the arts' for the final issue of *Canadian Mennonite* in 1971, his assessment was sad and pessimistic. Why, he asked, were there so few Mennonite writers of stature, even though Mennonites had lived in Ontario for 170 years and in Manitoba for almost 100. Was it because Mennonites still thought that literature 'must have obvious sermonic and/or historic teaching to justify it, to give it relevance?' Were Mennonites still trying 'to fit writing into categories perpetuated by the sub-titles in some of our Sunday school papers.'[75]

Such an attitude still seemed justified in 1971, almost ten years after publication of *Peace Shall Destroy Many*. A scant three years later, however, the centennial of the Mennonite migration to Manitoba fostered publications by descendants of the 1870s pioneers. After that, a new generation created an impressive and critically acclaimed body of literary works. Wiebe himself has twice won the Govenor General's Literary Award (1973 and 1994), for novels not dealing directly with Mennonite life.[76]

Mennonite poets lagged behind novelists, and it was only after 1970 that powerful works by a new generation began to appear. No Canadian Mennonite poet has yet achieved the literary stature of Rudy Wiebe, but at least half a dozen have national or international reputations. Their work is read and appreciated by critics and by many who can identify with the sentiments expressed. But it is also regarded with suspicion by some congregational leaders because of the realism, honesty, and forthright, sometimes coarse language. The writing and reception of this poetry, and of Mennonite fiction, helped to create 'a sense of imaginative place, and situating in it literary myths that can help us to understand ourselves more clearly, inspiring us to take a closer look at ourselves and our Mennonite values, our aspirations and claims to being a community of faith and ethnic identity.'[77]

Mennonite writers recorded how their people changed after 1945. They have also provided historians with insights into the Mennonite experience that cannot be gained from official correspondence, reports, and documents.

DRAMA

Drama, theatrical performances, and motion pictures were frequently and emphatically denounced in Canadian Mennonite communities. They were, in the minds of many, the epitome of worldliness.[78] There were, however, some 'Christian Dramas,' some forms of serious non-religious drama, and humorous performances, often in Low German, which were regarded as wholesome, or at least as fairly harmless, alternatives to worldly forms of entertainment.

Mennonite theatrical expression in Canada borrowed heavily from developments in the Mennonite liberal arts colleges in the United States and secondary and post-secondary Mennonite schools in Russia. German/pietistic religious or folk dramas, morality plays, and enactments of favourite Bible stories or incidents from Mennonite history were popular in schools and colleges. The primary objective was educational, didactic, or commemorative, but it was recognized that successful dramas must also be entertaining.

The repertoire expanded in the early twentieth century when creative writers began to experiment with humorous, colourful, and entertaining plays and dialogues in Low German. Some of this material was similar to, or even plagiarized from, the writings of Fritz Reuter.[79] In Canada, Low German dramas such as Arnold Dyck's *Wellkaom op'e Forstei, De Opnaom, Dee Fria,* and *Onse Lied en ola Tiet* and Jacob Janzen's *De Bildung, De Enbildung,* and *Daut Schultebott,* together with pieces from Reuter, generated laughter in communities where Low German was understood and spoken.

Nevertheless, major dramatic productions in schools and congregations usually had serious cultural or religious purposes. One Mennonite commentator explained that 'the rescue mission serves one type of person; the fine arts communicate to another type.' He thought that 'music, painting, sculpture, and literature have all contributed perhaps not so much to inducing people to be "saved" as to leading them to a fuller understanding of the implications of salvation or redemption.'[80] Some hoped and believed that short dramatic productions could enrich and enliven regular church worship services. John Miller of Conrad Grebel College, for example, wrote 20-minute dramas of Bible stories that forced worshippers to become involved and 'to do their own interpreting rather than have the preacher interpret the story for them.'[81]

Others supporting the dramatic arts placed greater emphasis on cultural and, for a time, linguistic considerations. The Youth Group at the Schoenwieser [First] Mennonite Church produced annually for many years a major German drama. *Glaube und Heimat, Der Revisor, Der Pfarrer von Kirchfeld, Unsere Kleine Stadt,* and many others were performed until, in 1964, the language change ended the German performances.[82]

English plays put on in Mennonite schools and communities included *Casey, Christ in the Conrete City, Christ vs. the People, Death of a Salesman, Fiddler on the Roof, He Came Seeking, Let My People Go, Loving Enemies, A Man for All Seasons, Murder in the Cathedral, Peace Plays, Promised Land,* numerous versions of the *Passion Play,* and, of course, Sunday school performances of the Christmas pageant.[83] In Ontario Urie Bender wrote a pageant, *This Land of Ours,* which was staged several times in the Avon Theatre (one of the Stratford Festival theatres) in 1972 and 1973, making use of festival staging and costuming.[84] Various stagings of *The Trail of the Conestoga* were also popular in Ontario.

Virtually all the drama performed, and most of the limited amount written by Canadian Mennonites before 1970, was of a pious, romantic, historical, or culturally entertaining nature.[85] It is, with a few notable exceptions, deficient in the kind of dramatic and creative realism that novelists such as Rudy Wiebe brought to novels and poems. Mennonite theatre had not, by 1970, become a realistic reflection of Mennonite life.

Broadway musicals became popular in Canadian Mennonite high schools, colleges, and sometimes congregational drama groups in the 1950s. They tapped into a rich musical heritage, and most did not offend community standards of morality. Acceptance of the musicals reflected disillusionment with the didacticism of the old plays but also manifested apparent unwillingness to use drama in the hard, realistic way in which creative artists used novels and poetry. The musicals were, for the most part, light entertainment.

It is true that Wiebe wrote several plays,[86] or theatrical adaptations of portions of his novels, to make Canadian Mennonite drama more realistic, and in the 1980s a few dramatists began to deal with issues such as sexual, drug, and spousal abuse.[87] Remarkably, except for some of Wiebe's work, the ferment of the Vietnam War produced no realistic or prophetic Canadian Mennonite plays in the 1960s.

PAINTING, DRAWING, FRAKTUR, AND FOLK ART

There is a persistent tradition that says that Rembrandt was a Mennonite. While the evidence is inconclusive, he certainly depicted Mennonites. One of his best-known paintings is that of his friends Cornelis Claesz Anslo and wife. Anslo was the minister of the Waterlander Mennonite church in Amsterdam. There were close and continuing relations between prominent seventeenth-century Dutch painters and that church.[88]

This appreciation for art and paintings was not shared by all Mennonites. Some of the culturally conservative groups eventually interpreted the Second Commandment as a prohibition of all portrait painting and photography. There were, however, always a few Mennonites who not only appreciated but also created pictures, paintings, and many other beautiful things.[89]

An important source of inspiration for rural Mennonite art in the nineteenth century involved beautiful penmanship and illuminated drawings on paper, or Fraktur art. The drawings could be used as bookmarks, to decorate copy books, as Christmas and New Year's greetings, as special baptism, birth, or anniversary certificates, or as wall hangings with scripture verses. As an artistic form of penmanship Fraktur art was used in eighteenth-century Mennonite schools to teach young children the alphabet or to keep the older children occupied when the teacher was busy with younger classmates in the one-room village school. Verses, inscriptions, or letters of the alphabet could be decorated or enhanced by small drawings of birds, flowers, or other scenes from nature.[90]

Fraktur suffered a major decline as a result of nineteenth-century educational reforms. In Russia the great Mennonite leader Johann Cornies was greatly influenced by the progressive ideas of Friedrich Froebel and Johann Pestalozzi. He replaced memorization, rote learning, decorative art, and penmanship with learning of basic concepts and essential skills.[91] Introduction of the public school system in Pennsylvania, and somewhat later in Ontario, resulted in a similar decline of Fraktur.[92]

That change, however, affected girls far less than boys, because they received only minimal public education. There was a feeling that the old methods, including fine and time-consuming decorative arts, were still well suited for girls. In Russia that tendency was further reinforced by establishment of separate boys' and girls' schools for students venturing beyond the village school.

Drawing and painting were never exclusively a Mennonite female preserve, but application of some of the basic principles of Fraktur to other media did become a bastion of female artistry. Fine needlework, and in time the designing and stitching of decorative quilts for which Mennonite women have become well known in both Pennsylvania and Ontario, were an adaptation and often followed patterns similar to those used in Fraktur. In other Mennonite communities women also devoted much time to needlework. Those lacking the necessary creative talents could follow drawings or tracings made on a piece of cloth by others. Many, however, expressed their talents by drawing patterns and then embroidering or stitching them. Some also drew, decorated, and lettered scripture verses for pictures and wall hangings.

Mennonite men with creative talents were more likely to design and build fine, artistic, and often elaborately decorated furniture or to indulge in fine leather or metal work, all of which had obvious Fraktur antecedents. These art forms, expressed on paper or canvas with pens, coloured pencils, and brushes, on cloth with needles and coloured threads, or on wood, metal, or leather with sharp and precise tools, added beauty to things used in everyday life.

When Mennonites moved from rural communities to the cities, they lost or modified these folk arts. In some rural Mennonite communities traditional folk art has become a major tourist attraction. Scarcity of land forced some to look for alternative work, and folk art has become an important source of income, particularly in the Kitchener-Waterloo area.

In addition to the Mennonite folk artists there was a small band of artists whose pen sketches, water-colours, and oil paintings transcended the narrower, utilitarian confines of folk art. As with literary artists, the collapse of the Russian Mennonite commonwealth encouraged the immigrants of the 1920s to recreate visually the most beloved aspects of their lost homeland. Others devoted their talents to the production of religious drawings and paintings, and a few began to sketch aspects of their new life in Canada. Much of the pre-1970 sketching, drawing, and painting involved portraits and nature scenes that combined artistic insights and skills with a fairly rigid realism. Abstract and modern pictorial art remained largely misunderstood, unappreciated, and unexplored, as did almost all forms of sculpture other than realistic carvings of animals and village or farmyard items. Realism, which seemed unsettling in novels and poems, created no similar problems in the pictorial arts, and it was not until the 1970s and 1980s that Mennonite artists ventured boldly into new and different pictorial art forms.

THE CREATIVE ARTS AND THE MEDIA

The artistic renaissance in Canadian Mennonite communities after 1945 helped to shape and influence, and was in turn shaped and influenced by, the media. German-language church papers had carried some cultural and literary materials, but the arts received much greater attention in a new Mennonite teachers' magazine entitled *Mennonitische Lehrerzeitung*, which began publication shortly after the war, carrying mainly material of interest to the Russian Mennonite teachers who had come to Canada in the 1920s. The objective of the magazine, however, was to serve all Mennonite teachers, whether they taught in the public system, in a Mennonite high school, or at one of the Bible schools or colleges. The editors were particularly interested in strengthening and preserving the German language, culture, and literary heritage and enjoyed the support of leaders of both Mennonite Brethren (MBs) and the Conference of Mennonites in Canada (CMC).[93]

In 1950 the magazine was reorganized so that it would serve not only teachers, but also pastors, academics, artists, writers, and church workers. It was renamed *Mennonitische Welt* and became a monthly publication. It was seen as the Canadian German-language equivalent to the new English-language *Mennonite Life*, launched in 1946 under the auspices of Bethel College in Newton, Kansas, and carrying much Canadian literary, historical, and artistic material.

Mennonitische Welt was not able to sustain a sufficient readership and ceased in 1952. Its demise, however, coincided with the founding of a new in-house MBBC publication, the *Voice of the Mennonite Brethren Bible College*. The bi-monthly *Voice* promoted 'sound Christian teaching, and [set] forth the doctrinal position of the institution,'[94] but it also carried many articles on music making and appreciation. It provided very little coverage of creative literature or the other fine arts.

The first national English-language Mennonite newspaper,[95] *The Canadian Mennonite*, appeared first on 3 July 1953. It sought to define the place of Canadian Mennonites in their new circumstances in the 1950s and is discussed in detail below. It also provided extensive and sympathetic reporting on the fine arts – more sophisticated than those in the German-language church papers – following the pattern of *Mennonitische Lehrerzeitung* and *Mennonitische Welt*.

The Mennonite Brethren launched the English-language *Mennonite Observer* in September 1955. It was a weekly, eight-to-twelve-page companion to their German-language paper, the *Mennonitische Rundschau*. Its subordinate status was not satisfactory, and in 1962 the MBs started a new English-language denominational paper, the *Mennonite Brethren Herald*. Rudy Wiebe was appointed editor and gave the fine arts far greater prominence than they had received in the German papers. That coverage continued, albeit more cautiously, after Wiebe's resignation in 1963.

Informed, critical, but supportive reporting and new opportunities for creative artists began to appear in 1971, when a Winnipeg-based group began publication of the *Mennonite Mirror*. The paper attracted good writers and retained complete editorial freedom because it neither sought nor obtained any funds from official church organizations. The editors noted proudly that 'the *Mirror* has often been controversial, not because it has tried to be sensational but because its writers have been unusually free to say what they think.'[96] Editors wanted to break down separatist and isolationist practices and attitudes. They refused to turn their backs on the world, choosing instead 'to embrace it' with a message of love rooted in their religious heritage and in their Canadian experiences.[97]

Such an inclusive and all-embracing approach was particularly important for artists coming from a Mennonite background who, for one reason or another, had been alienated from Mennonite churches in Canada. *Mennonite Mirror* championed 'an honest art free of pious ideology, bigotry and parochial prejudice,' which looked at the Canadian Mennonite experience 'without blinkers, as it is actually lived, and not as we like to think in our best moments it ought to be lived.'[98]

Radio became another medium in the Mennonite artistic renaissance. Canadian Mennonites had first become actively involved with radio in 1940 when, almost simultaneously, Mennonite Brethren in Saskatoon and Swiss Mennonites in Kitchener-Waterloo began to broadcast or rebroadcast short religious programs. Artistry was not a notable feature of those early programs. They were sober and serious opportunities to preach the gospel to scattered members of their own denomination and to anyone else who might happen to tune in. Small amateur choirs or music groups provided what little pious artistic spice and excitement those programs offered.

New and different involvement in radio began when the more accomplished Mennonite musicians were featured on the Canadian Broadcasting Corporation (CBC). When Ben Horch resigned as senior music teacher at the MBBC in 1954, he received invitations from the CBC and radio station KWSO in Wasco, California, to assist in the programming of classical religious and particularly choral music. Horch saw this radio work as an extension of what he had done at MBBC. At the CBC he provided opportunities for Mennonite musicians to be heard across Canada, giving them generally a more positive image in the wider Canadian community.[99]

Horch and other classical and religious music enthusiasts gained a second important radio voice in 1957 with the opening of radio station CFAM in Altona, Manitoba.[100] Promoters were prominent southern Manitoba businessmen. One objective was to promote an appreciation of 'good music,' which, it was hoped, would divert young Mennonite listeners from the rock and roll played on most AM radio stations. Horch became music director, and while his work was never an effective antidote to rock and roll, it did provide Mennonite artists and aspiring broadcasters with new opportunities and increased understanding and appreciation of classical and religious music in rural Mennonite communities in southern Manitoba. CFAM, however, also aired numerous religious broadcasts, some of which seriously undermined its declared ambition to become 'the Good Music Station,' unless 'good' is taken as a measure of piety rather than of artistic excellence. CFAM also provided a mix of ethnic programs, some of which highlighted other creative, literary, pictorial, and folk artists.

CONCLUSION

In the three decades following the end of the Second World War there was a remarkable flowering of interest, participation, and appreciation of music, literature, and other fine arts by Canadian Mennonites. Suspicion and lack of understanding were first and perhaps most easily overcome in religious and classical music. In creative writing and poetry the uncomfortable realism of Rudy Wiebe in the 1960s, and of a surprisingly large and diverse number of younger Mennonite creative writers later, raised more concern. A fairly rigid realism in folk and pictorial arts remained the norm until the late 1970s, but attitudes, artistic creations, and their reception in Mennonite communities and beyond changed dramatically.

The Mennonites' discovery of the fine arts moved them much closer to the mainstream of Canadian literary and artistic life, but that did not necessarily weaken distinctive identities. Good Mennonite art, according to one writer in the *Mennonite Mirror*, 'can and will remind us of the radical roots of our Anabaptist-Mennonite faith, affirm our hard-won moral values and celebrate our plain-spoken, wholesome peasant tradition while at the same time exposing our hypocrisy, our shallowness and ethnic snobbery.'[101]

13

New Leadership

The nurture, training, and education of Mennonite young people in the 1940s and 1950s produced a new generation of Mennonite leaders. The biographer of the four men who dominated (Old) Mennonite church life in Ontario, in part through the Ontario Mennonite Bible School, described a phenomenon that also affected Mennonite communities elsewhere: 'Their strengths and dominant leadership capabilities were melded together and filtered through study and group experiences at OMBS. The result was simply the creation of layer upon layer of students returning to their home congregations. Ultimately, these layers helped to form a laity with self-recognition, purpose, and creative drive which first questioned, then displaced the kind of strong leadership – indeed the very men – which had brought about the phenomenon.'[1]

The men who provided strong and effective leadership in the 1940s worked within inherited organizational structures and institutions. They still adhered to the old ideal of a community of believers that was physically separate and did not conform to the values, standards, and practices of secular society. Those ideas had to be redefined as more and more Mennonites moved into the outside world and as the old boundaries that had kept out alien influences weakened or broke down entirely. Much that the leaders of the 1940s denounced as 'worldly' became not only acceptable but was sometimes endowed with new and positive spiritual values in the 1950s. Basic goals changed so fundamentally that the 1940s and 1950s became 'hinge years' in Canadian Mennonite history.[2]

The crumbling of old leadership and authority structures in all but the most traditional communities resulted, as was pointed out above, in partial integration of congregations into the evangelical substream of North American Protestantism. That phenomenon had so alarmed B.B. Janz, one of the powerful older leaders, that he wrote at one time: 'A Mennonite Brethren dissolution of the first order is in progress.'³ The new Mennonite Bible colleges and high schools significantly increased the number of prospective church leaders and workers who had at least some exposure to Mennonite theology and practice, but those newcomers had to work in different environments than the leaders of the difficult war and immediate postwar years.

Changes in leadership, particularly in the 1950s, were sometimes very difficult. They often involved far more than an orderly succession of one generation of leaders by another. The old forms, language, and nuances of leadership changed. Conferences and congregations were restructured, new issues and problems were addressed, and old dogmas were reformulated.

Delbert Wiens, an American Mennonite Brethren philosopher, expressed the essence of the challenge facing Mennonite leaders in the 1950s and 1960s in his widely read and influential paper 'New Wineskins for Old Wine: A Study of the Mennonite Brethren Church.'⁴ Some of Wiens's observations, notably those on specific kinds of conversion experiences and the immersionist form of baptism, applied mainly to distinctive Mennonite Brethren doctrines. Most had wider relevance.

The central point of Wiens's paper was that religious principles are expressed in specific social, cultural, and religious forms, containers, or 'wineskins.' A distinction should, however, be made between the containers and the essence of religious experiences. Changing times and circumstances make it necessary to replace the old wineskins if the wine is to be preserved: 'The old form of leadership, in its time and place, achieved impressive results. But we cannot simply translate the old forms into the present. The specifics are often irrelevant to a new time or place. We need methods and answers for a particular time and place, not carry over all the old specifics, but we need to discover the old spirit. Grounding ourselves in the past, we must learn to do in our own way for our time what our grandfathers achieved in their own time in their way.'⁵

This chapter presents examples of problems facing communities and congregations in the 1950s and 1960s. Some are typical; others are unique but highlight general problems that were resolved with varying degrees of controversy.

The underlying difficulties in the cases cited here were not new. Mennonites had suffered numerous schisms, including, in the 1930s, a painful division in the Sommerfelder Church in Manitoba, out of which the Rudnerweider Mennonite Church had emerged.⁶ The tensions in the decades following the outbreak of the Second World War more often led to dramatic leadership struggles and alienated many young people.

The Mennonite Brethren (MBs) at Herbert, Saskatchewan, had long been influenced by itinerant Mennonite and non-Mennonite evangelists. The arrival of immigrants from Russia (Russlaender) in the 1920s created considerable tension. The newcomers were not accustomed to the emotional appeals and dramatic style of the evangelists and thought that there was not sufficient emphasis on the subsequent life of Christian discipleship by the converts.[7] Some expressed concern about the itinerant evangelists who availed themselves of open doors and generous collections and then moved on, laughing at the gullibility of the Mennonites. Others were concerned about the dispensationalist and aggressively fundamentalist theology of some evangelists.[8] But a determined and vocal minority wanted to invite many more of these evangelists.

In the 1940s, disputes about the language of worship, mission strategy, and proposals to enlarge the local MB church but make it non-denominational, or to build a non-denominational tabernacle, added to the tensions. A small group at Swift Current, consisting mainly of former Mennonite Brethren who had left that congregation and begun their own 'Open Door Church of Swift Current,' provided a model for the dissidents at Herbert.[9]

When a proposal to expand facilities was delayed in 1946 because of severe shortages of construction material, the dissidents began to build a tabernacle 'in faith.' That created an impasse between dissidents and church leaders, some of whom actually sympathized with the dissidents but rejected the manner in which they proceeded. The matter was referred to the *Fuersorgekomitee* (Board of Spiritual and Social Concerns) of the Canadian MB conference. After hearing both sides, the *Fuersorgekomitee* supported the position of the Herbert church: 'It is not right to join with other groups thus exposing members to foreign influences. This kind of action has already caused serious disruption in the District, and is not consistent with the rules and regulations of the conference.'[10]

The dissidents rejected this finding and continued with construction. Further meetings accomplished nothing, and the *Fuersorgekomitee* eventually denounced the tabernacle as 'not in accordance with the spirit of God.' It sought to exert greater pressure on local church leaders to resolve the matter by not allowing the church to send delegates to Canadian conference sessions until the matter was settled.[11]

The Herbert church responded by reorganizing its leadership, excluding members of the tabernacle group and also the leader of the church, who sympathized with the goals and objectives of the tabernacle group but had opposed their unilateral action. The reorganization meeting, at which a new leader was elected, was held without notification to the elected church leader or the dissidents. The reorganized church, now more strongly committed to MB policies than to the non-denominational agenda of the dissidents, was then allowed by the *Fuersorgekomitee* to send delegates to the next Canadian conference.[12] Fifty-one dissidents withdrew from the church.[13]

The problems were further complicated by allegations that the church leader had been guilty of sexual misconduct, prompting the *Fuersorgekomitee* of the Canadian conference to ban him, for life, from any further work in any MB church.[14] That harsh response reflected the general concern of district and conference leaders regarding the life-style of some of those who responded to emotional and charismatic but allegedly undisciplined religious influences.

CHURCH LEADER OPPOSES *MESSIAH*

Massive historical changes often occur slowly, almost imperceptibly, over many years. But sometimes sudden crises, like a flash of lightning in the midst of a storm, reveal a landscape otherwise obscured. If someone on the scene meticulously records for posterity what he or she has seen, heard, and experienced at such a time, unique insights are possible.

That was the case in a series of turbulent events at the Coaldale Mennonite Brethren Church in 1956 and 1957. The church minutes provide basic information about those events,[15] but more revealing material is provided in correspondence and an 86-page manuscript written by Peter H. Regehr, a long-time member of the church and of its council.[16]

The congregation, established in 1926,[17] consisted almost entirely of Russlaender. Deep divisions in the church apparently had their roots in the different Russian Mennonite communities from which people came. They found practical expression in differing definitions of 'worldliness' and in rival support groups for the local Bible and high schools.

Tensions regarding increasingly long lists of forbidden 'worldly' activities, and conflicts over new influences from, and contacts with, the outside world, boiled over in 1956 in a dispute regarding the performance of Handel's oratorio *Messiah*. Peter Dick, a teacher of religion, German, and music at the Alberta Mennonite High School who had taken some music training at the Mennonite Brethren Bible College, was enthusiastic about classical religious music. He organized a large school and community choir and orchestra to stage a public performance of *Messiah*. The elected church leader, Jacob J. Siemens, had no appreciation for what he described as 'music that not even the heathen want to sing.' Such disagreements about classical music also occurred in other Mennonite communities. Urie Bender, for example, describes how the spirit of S.F. Coffman, teacher and music director of the Ontario Mennonite Bible School, was lifted to the very gates of Paradise when the great 'Hallelujah Chorus' was sung at year-end concerts of the Bible school. Standing beside him, however, was his colleague Oscar Burkholder, who had no appreciation of the piece and sometimes paraphrased it: 'Its like singing the cows are jumping over the fence, the brown cows, the red cows, the white cows, the black cows are jumping, jumping, are jumping over, jumping over the fence, over, over, over the fence.' Then he quoted Matthew 6:7: 'Use not vain repetitions.'[18]

The first public performance of *Messiah* at Coaldale took place in the local MB church in the spring of 1955. It led to no immediate crisis, though there were mutterings that Peter Dick was a modern-day Pied Piper leading the youth of Coaldale astray. For many participants it opened up new vistas of religious and artistic understanding and appreciation, but it was hardly in accord with separatist Mennonite life-styles.

The Coaldale performance in 1955 caught the attention of Martin Brothers, Funeral Home directors in Lethbridge, whose services the Mennonite families were just beginning to use.[19] When *Messiah* was again to be performed in 1956, Martin Brothers offered to sponsor a public performance in an appropriate location in Lethbridge. Southminster United Church, with its impressive pipe organ, was chosen for such a performance but had a policy requiring outside groups wishing to use its facilities to obtain the sponsorship of an approved community organization. Martin Brothers immediately obtained the sponsorship of the Lethbridge Rotary Club. The music director of the large Mormon church in Lethbridge also offered the support of his church. Peter Dick and those associated with him were convinced that a public performance of *Messiah* in Southminster United Church, sponsored by the Rotary Club and supported by the Mormon church, would be a powerful Christian witness. J.J. Siemens and others in the church council, however, were suspicious about the music and objected to sponsorship by alleged unbelievers. The church council nevertheless gave its approval, and the performance was scheduled for 29 April 1956.

A second, seemingly unrelated problem helped bring on a crisis. A community-based ministerial association was planning inter-denominational English-language evangelistic services in town. Henry Nikkel, a local businessman and an ordained preacher of the MB church, was elected to chair a three-member executive, the other members being the pastors of the local Pentecostal church and of the local Evangelical Free church. The stated policy of the MB church, however, was to support and participate only in evangelistic services under its own control, thus keeping out alien religious influences. When he heard about Nikkel's involvement, B.B. Janz, the influential former church leader, sent him a stern letter of protest, with copies going to J.J. Siemens and D.J. Pankratz, the leader and assistant leader of the church, respectively.[20]

In an effort to blunt the appeal of the community services the church council decided to schedule its own German evangelistic services from 10 to 25 April.[21] Peter Dick was asked to be in charge of the music and was told by Siemens that there must not be any practices for *Messiah* during the time of the evangelistic services, lest the attention of potential converts or counsellors be diverted from the serious appeals of the evangelist. Dick was understandably concerned about the limited time that arrangement would leave him for rehearsals of the oratorio, which was to be presented 29 April.

The evangelistic services proved disappointing. Few responded to the invitations, so, in an effort to salvage credibility and perhaps also to place further obstacles in Dick's path, Siemens decided unilaterally to add an extra night of evangelistic services. The evangelist was to discuss Christian principles in relations between male and female young people. That presumably would attract more young people, and it would address a topic about which Siemens had become deeply concerned and, in the opinion of many, paranoid. The additional service, however, was scheduled for the evening already set aside for the dress rehearsal of the oratorio. When Dick protested, Siemens brusquely told him that the choir should have practised earlier. The resulting council meetings and discussions between the individuals directly concerned were acrimonious and inconclusive.

When all of Dick's efforts to schedule a suitable time for the rehearsal were rejected by Siemens, a delegation of choir members visited Siemens. They stated their frustration in a manner that he found offensive and disrespectful. Eventually a compromise was negotiated whereby the special evangelistic meeting would be held earlier, thus providing time for a single, quick dress rehearsal. Since a number of the soloists came from out of town, that was the only opportunity that the choir, orchestra, and soloists had to rehearse together. A short and hurried rehearsal was held, and the oratorio was successfully presented.

Siemens's behaviour had deeply offended and threatened to alienate the young people. Senior members, including a number of the preachers who had become involved in the negotiations with Siemens, realized that he had lost the confidence of the membership. They felt that they had no alternative but to exert pressure on him to resign. Threats of resignation had been used repeatedly by leaders of the church before, only to be rejected by the council. In this case, however, Siemens's offer to resign was immediately accepted, apparently to his great surprise.

The resignation led to an immediate and even more serious crisis. None of the other suggested candidates for the leadership would accept that responsibility, even though neither the council nor the membership would support Siemens's re-election. It was suggested that perhaps the tensions within the church, and consequently the burdens of leadership in a congregation with almost 600 members, were simply too onerous for any lay minister who also had to earn his own livelihood. The council therefore concluded, sadly and in the case of some members bitterly,[22] that the old style of leadership by unpaid lay ministers had failed. Other MB churches, particularly in the United States, had already appointed paid pastors. That seemed to be the way of the future, and early in 1957 the twenty-two-member council, with one dissenting vote, reluctantly recommended appointment of a paid pastor. That recommendation elicited strong opposition, but there seemed to be no alternative. Particular reference was made to the fact that a pastor who depended for his livelihood on a salary paid by the congregation would presumably be more responsive to members' pressure and opinions. He would thus not lead it into the dead-end opposition to new innovations that had characterized Siemens's administration.

There was still much negotiating to be done, but eventually David J. Pankratz, the politically astute assistant leader who had managed to give everyone the impression that he agreed with them, accepted the appointment.[23]

There were, however, additional consequences of the events of 1956–7. The disappointing results of the MB evangelistic services increased enthusiasm for the more lively and emotional English-language, interdenominational evangelistic services. The special session on sexual matters, in which the speaker provided only exceedingly vague factual information, concentrating instead on prohibitions and the most extreme skid-row consequences of deviations from the rigorous sexual mores of the community, was particularly disappointing. Support for the Coaldale Crusade for Christ, in contrast, was so strong that, when the council considered the letter that B.B. Janz had sent to Henry Nikkel, it prudently decided to table it 'until the Lord gives light.'[24] Further action came in 1957 when yet another interdenominational evangelistic crusade was planned. The church agreed, after intense debate, to leave it to the conscience of each member whether he or she participated, even though such involvement reversed a clearly articulated policy of the church.

The change in leadership also hastened the language transition. That issue had become divisive, and it was clear to the council that some of the strongest support for a paid pastorate came from people who wanted more English sermons and worship services and more interdenominational evangelism. Only a pastor who could preach in both languages would be acceptable. That effectively eliminated all the older leaders, including Siemens, from consideration.

The frustration and dissatisfaction stirred up by these events brought yet another problem to the fore. One of the most effective and irritating ways in which angry members could express their feelings was to refuse to pay the assessed church dues or taxes. The church had a dual taxation system. Every member was expected to pay a relatively small membership fee. In addition, all members were required to fill in detailed statements of income and expenses and then to pay a fixed percentage of their net income to the church. There were always complaints that these forms, drawn up by farmer members, were not fair to workers or businessmen. Church support for new initiatives such as the local Bible school and high school or for controversial new conference projects such as the Bible college and community mutual-aid and health-care projects was usually calculated on a per-member basis, which became, in effect, an additional levy. Similar patterns of church finance were common in many Canadian Mennonite churches in the 1940s and 1950s, but in churches where there were sharp differences of opinion it was difficult to enforce church tax policies. Serious problems arose when members refused to pay taxes. The Coaldale church also had a policy of reading out the names of non-payers at membership meetings, denying them access to communion services, and not allowing them to do church work until suitable arrangements to pay the dues had been made.[25] This situation created further embarrassments and added to the acrimony, eventually discrediting the whole church tax system.

RESISTING 'WORLDLINESS' AT ROSEMARY, ALBERTA

New and alien influences and changes in the life-styles of church members worried many Mennonite leaders after the war. The tactics used to preserve the old ways and, with them, the authority of the leaders varied from congregation to congregation, but the files of conference leaders include numerous cases where excommunication and other harsh measures were taken. The results were often unfortunate. That was the case in the Westheimer Mennonite Church at Rosemary, Alberta.

Problems arose there when a minority became concerned about the allegedly lax social and moral standards of some members and the apparent acceptance of this state of affairs by the preacher and elected church leader, P.W. Dyck.[26] Dyck was an ordained preacher but not an ordained elder. The matter became public concern when it was alleged that three young female church members and one male member had been drunk at a wedding. The matter was reported to Dyck, but he did not take disciplinary action. Later it was proved that at least one of the three young women accused had not even been present at the wedding and the evidence against the others was dubious. Nevertheless, a vocal minority remained critical of Dyck's lenience over life-style and his alleged lack of true spirituality. Those tensions increased when he officiated at the marriage of his brother, a recent immigrant whose first wife had disappeared in the disruptions of war and whose fate was unknown.

Matters were further complicated when J.D. Nickel, an ordained elder, moved from Lymburn in northern Alberta to Rosemary. Nickel shared the concerns of those disgruntled with Dyck's lenient leadership. On 29 December 1951 a controversial and allegedly improperly called meeting, of which Dyck and his supporters were not informed, dismissed him and called on Nickel to replace him. That meeting was chaired by D.P. Neufeld, a young preacher in the church. The stated objective of the new leadership was greater spirituality in the church.[27]

Dyck continued as a preacher when called on and was asked to lead a devotional meditation and to provide a year-end review at the Sylvester service in the church on 31 December 1952. Dyck based his remarks on Luke 18:9–14, which tells the story of the self-righteous pharisee and the humble sinner going to the temple to pray. Dyck raised questions regarding true and false piety and complained about self-righteousness, lovelessness, and false accusations. He concluded with a reference to Galatians 5:22, 'But the fruit of the Spirit is love, joy, peace, long-suffering, gentleness, goodness, faith.' All these fruits seemed more apparent in the tolerant, accepting, and long-suffering policies of the former leader than in the constant legalistic denunciations of worldliness by Nickel, Neufeld, and their supporters.[28] Predictably, Dyck's meditation raised the ire of his opponents, one of whom even suggested that perhaps Dyck had been drunk when he delivered that meditation – a suggestion that was later unequivocally retracted.

The friction in the Westheimer church soon found expression in a practical manner. The Westheimer church, like the MB church in Coaldale, had specific membership dues. Some supporters of Dyck did not pay their dues on time in 1952. The council responded with a resolution early in 1953 giving all delinquents two months of grace to discharge their financial obligations. Twenty-two men failed to do so. They were then informed that they had lost their membership rights because of disobedience to the church and its rules. Those affected appealed to the Committee for Church Affairs of the Alberta conference. When that appeal failed, they approached J.J. Thiessen, chairman of the Conference of Mennonites in Canada (CMC). Thiessen personally sympathized with Nickel but was haunted by the Schoenwieser affair and wanted to avoid a confrontation, which might lead to a formal split.

The matter became more personal when David P. Neufeld, the young minister who had provided leadership in the overthrow of P.W. Dyck, applied for a Mennonite Central Committee (MCC) appointment in Europe. Dyck wrote to protest, arguing that Neufeld should first seek reconciliation in his home church before being commissioned for service overseas. The MCC administrators wanted no part of such local disputes. Neufeld had received strong support from the local church leader, Nickel, and from Thiessen, the conference chairman. That was sufficient for the MCC, and Neufeld was appointed for work in Frankfurt, Germany. An attempt by the dissident group to involve B.B. Janz, the influential MB leader, also failed.

Since the immediate reason for the disciplinary action had been the failure of the twenty-two men to pay their dues, Thiessen hoped that reconciliation might be possible if sufficient pressure were exerted on the delinquents so that they would pay, or promise to pay as soon as possible, their outstanding dues. Several immediately agreed to do so, but that was no longer enough for Nickel and his supporters. They insisted that, in addition to paying, the dissidents provide evidence that they had received new life from God.[29]

Nickel's intransigence created the crisis that Thiessen had feared. The expelled Westheimer applied for and were granted membership in the Scarboro Mennonite mission in Calgary. When Nickel tried to exert his influence as a member of the missions committee of the CMC to withhold a conference subsidy granted to the Calgary mission, the Calgary group declared its independence from the missions committee, reorganized itself, and applied for and was granted membership in the conference.

Intensive and emotional meetings, lasting two days and running into early morning on 3 and 4 November 1954, resulted in an official but fragile reconciliation.[30] There would henceforth be two Mennonite churches at Rosemary – one affiliated directly, and the other indirectly, through the Scarboro Mennonite mission, with the CMC. There was to be no further public controversy. In effect, the disputants agreed to disagree on a number of controversial matters.

It was ironic that Nickel presented the official report of the Home Missions Committee at the next sessions of the CMC. He did not mention the problems in his own church but made optimistic references to conference missionary ventures at La Crete and Buffalo Head Prairie, near Fort Vermilion. Nickel and others thought the Old Colony Mennonites in the north were too legalistic and emphasized the wrong forms of nonconformity when advocating separatist Mennonite ways. His opponents at Rosemary thought the same about him. It was obviously not easy to find a satisfactory balance.

NONCONFORMITY AND THE SWISS MENNONITES

Nonconformity, as applied to dress codes, wearing of wedding rings and other jewellery, purchase of life insurance, and participation with non-believers in business ventures, became particularly problematic for the (Old) Mennonites and the Amish Mennonites of Ontario after 1945.

In 1938 C.F. Derstine, the dynamic evangelist and pastor of the urban First Mennonite Church in Kitchener, wrote an article for the *Gospel Herald* in which he told of the conversion of one woman of non-Mennonite background and how she became willing to accept the bonnet that female (Old) Mennonite church members were expected to wear. She prayed to God that He give her a sign to let her know whether He wanted her to wear the bonnet. Then, in a vision, she saw Christ with his crown of thorns and responded, 'If you wore that crown of thorns for me, I'll cease following fashion.'[31] In telling the story Derstine expressed the traditional (Old) Mennonite position on the wearing of the bonnet. That position, however, was becoming increasingly difficult to maintain as members had more contact with the outside world and began to change their concept and understanding of the church and its role in modern society.

Derstine personified at least part of the problem. He was a successful evangelist and became increasingly concerned about the tensions faced by non-Mennonite converts who were expected to accept not only the Gospel message but also distinctive Mennonite dress codes and other cultural and social forms of nonconformity. That was becoming as serious an obstacle to evangelism for the Swiss Mennonites as retention of the German language was for the more recent Mennonite immigrants.

The Mennonite Conference of Ontario tried to deal with these issues in 1943, but there was no longer general consensus. The conservatives quite simply did not have a theology of change.[32] They wanted to make adherence to the dress and other nonconformity codes a 'test of membership,' and several denied communion to those in their own congregations who failed to abide by the codes. In 1943 they exerted enough pressure that conference leaders recommended that the dress codes for women be entrenched in the conference constitution.[33] When that recommendation was debated by conference delegates there were sharp disagreements, and only a relatively weak resolution, without effective means of enforcement, was passed. It stated, 'we as a Conference consider the wearing of a plain bonnet as the approved headdress of our sisters, and insist on a faithful compliance of the same as the continued practice of the church.'[34] Some congregations tried to enforce the codes, but others, including First Mennonite, no longer found the legalistic approach acceptable. Consequently, in the 1950s, pastors serving urban churches, or in missions, asked conference leaders to ease the rules and regulations to accommodate persons in their congregations who were seeking membership but were not comfortable with the Mennonite cultural trappings. Urban pastors became convinced that they could not build up their urban churches if they insisted on nonconformity codes set, interpreted, and enforced in the way advocated by the more conservative, rural bishops.

The debates concerning nonconformity were closely linked to other changes in the leadership of the Mennonite Conference of Ontario. The shift from bishop-centred leadership to one in which salaried pastors and elected lay church councils held control created particular problems that were accentuated by the fact that many of the salaried pastors were younger men serving in urban congregations.

Up to the mid-1950s both the (Old) Mennonites and the Amish Mennonites had been served by bishops, ministers, and deacons who were ordained for life and exercised a great deal of authority. Large congregations had a bishop and one or several ministers and deacons. Not all small congregations had a bishop; so bishops often had charge of more than one congregation. Only bishops had the right to marry, baptize, and serve communion.

This began to change in the 1950s as more salaried pastors were hired. Both pastors and congregations realized that there were both losses and advantages when the old, multiple ministry was replaced by salaried pastors and elected church councils of lay members. Pastors were given the right to marry, baptize, and serve communion, but they were also subject to greater congregational control. One of the first (Old) Mennonite churches to assert its congregational autonomy was First Mennonite in Kitchener. It passed a resolution in 1956 stating that 'the authority of First Mennonite Church, Kitchener, be invested in the congregation itself.'[35] The result has been described thus: 'The transition toward congregational autonomy, which had been initiated by C.F. Derstine's opposition to Conference dress regulations, was formally completed. The First Mennonite congregation now faced the prospect of exercising this newly invested authority. In the process, the office of bishop would become redundant and Derstine's traditional authority would be curtailed.'[36]

A rural and conservative reaction against these trends found its most effective champions in two rural bishops – Curtis Cressman and Moses Roth. These men were almost the exact opposite of Derstine in personality.[37] Roth, Cressman, and those associated with them feared that the urban pastors were abandoning the traditional Mennonite doctrines of nonconformity and other biblical practices. They complained about female members who no longer wore the bonnet or the prayer covering, about allegedly immodest and ornamental attire of Mennonite women in urban churches, wearing of jewellery, cutting of hair by women, and neglect of the biblical ordinances about footwashing, anointing with oil, the Brotherly Kiss, and the practice, as they saw it, of administering baptism only to those who gave appropriate evidence of new birth. Such evidence, in their view, must be made manifest in a nonconformist way of life. There were also complaints that some church members were becoming 'unequally yoked' with unbelievers in business, through purchase of life insurance or participation in local political activities.[38]

The tension was greatly intensified by a series of evangelistic meetings conducted by George R. Brunk II. Conference-sponsored tent meetings had been held in the area by Brunk several times, but in 1958 he was invited to conduct a campaign in the New Hamburg Community Centre that was not sponsored by the conference. Brunk, according to one commentator, had 'decided or was primed to believe the Ontario Conference was drifting, and in his usual outspoken way made this clear.'[39] He found a sympathetic hearing with the dissident rural bishops and their supporters and was invited to return in 1959. He reportedly 'thundered against spiritual drift'[40] and made emotional appeals that all those truly committed to the teachings of the scripture, including Mennonite Conference dress codes and other matters pertaining to nonconformity, take a firm stand.

All these issues, coupled with some sharp personality clashes between the conservative rural bishops and some of the urban pastors, resulted in preparation of a letter of secession, dated 31 July 1959, in which the dissidents spelled out their concerns. When the conference failed to respond in the manner requested, six ordained church leaders withdrew from the conference. They became leaders of a new body – the Conservative Mennonite Church of Ontario.[41]

The new church or conference held its first separate service on 22 November 1959. The dissidents were united in their insistence on dress codes for women and various other ordinances that had fallen into disuse in other Ontario Mennonite churches, but they soon discovered that on other matters they were not agreed, and in 1975 those opposed to use of radios and television left to found the Heidelberg Fellowship Church.[42]

Another parallel group intent on preserving traditional Mennonite and Amish ways broke with the Amish Mennonite church at Milverton, Ontario, in 1956 to set up the Bethel Conservative Mennonite Church.[43] Several smaller groups of dissidents in nearby Amish and (Old) Mennonite congregations also broke with their congregations. These small, scattered, culturally and socially conservative groups came to be loosely associated with one another through pulpit exchanges among themselves and with parallel Conservative Mennonite Fellowships and churches in Canada and the United States. Most of these groups depended on the strong leadership of their bishops and had few, if any, commitments to the larger conferences. Some members did, however, migrate west and northward in search of cheaper and more abundant farmland and thus formed small congregations in Alberta and British Columbia.[44]

Mennonite groups that had tried for centuries to separate themselves as much as possible from the outside world tended to be particularly suspicious of all technological, cultural, social, and political change. But even those most strongly committed to preservation of old ways could not avoid all change, and there were often sharp disagreements when some deemed it necessary, beneficial, or simply harmless to accept a particular innovation while others remained convinced that even small changes would lead to loss of essential aspects of their Christian life-style. Such disagreements resulted in much tension, and sometimes in fragmentation and schisms, particularly among the most traditional groups.

LANGUAGE AS AN INSTRUMENT OF CHANGE

Among some of the Russian Mennonites the German language became an instrument of nonconformity and a barrier against undesirable outside influences. The daughter of a prominent Mennonite leader of the 1940s and 1950s in western Canada described her father's attitude toward German: 'For my father, indeed, difference was a concept that was central to the very idea of religious identity. His insistence on the use of the German language had nothing to do with a celebration of German; on the contrary, it symbolized the separation of church and state. The wall of language created a space for religious freedom and he fought to keep that wall up, always insisting that he could not speak English. When outsiders came around, however, the wall vanished and my father suddenly, mysteriously turned into the gracious host speaking English.'[45] A 1959 newspaper report raised the same issue: 'Could we possibly be using the German language in our church services, not for any love of its aesthetic beauty or its utilitarian values, but rather because it is so effective as a barrier against outside influences and thus a definite help in preserving our religion and our culture in pristine purity?'[46]

Most of the Swiss Mennonites had already made the language transition and were not concerned about preservation of German, but that was not the case with those who had come to Canada from Russia. Russian Mennonites had diverse reasons for wanting to preserve German. Some saw it as an effective barrier against outside influences. Others, who had been raised and had their most treasured spiritual experiences in a German milieu, loved the language and were convinced that its loss would deprive them of cultural, literary, aesthetic, and religious treasures. Still others simply felt uncomfortable or threatened by any suggestion that their most sacred activities should be conducted in a language that they did not fully understand or appreciate. And then there were some who saw a language transition as inevitable but hoped that it would be sufficiently gradual that older and younger members would still be able to communicate with one another. During the war, for example, B.B. Janz explained why Coaldale Mennonites had a German Saturday school: 'The Mennonites in their efforts to maintain a Saturday school of their own for the children do not pursue any other aim but an exclusive religious purpose ... They are to enable the child to read the same Bible which its mother reads, that it may sing the same song which mother sings, and understand the worship in which the family participates.'[47]

There was also a small minority of Canadian Mennonites who believed that true Mennonite Christianity and the German language were inextricably linked and that loss of one must inevitably result in loss of the other. J.B. Toews, for example, remembers that when he returned to Coaldale after studying in the United States he was asked by a local church leader whether there were really Christians among the English. Toews replied that he thought that there were probably as many Christians among the English as among the Germans. That seemed incomprehensible to the venerable preacher. The Christianity that he knew, and which set the guidelines of his life, was encompassed in a German world. And he was not alone. Even Toews's mother was convinced that her son was lost when she learned that he would marry a young American woman who did not know German.[48]

Others acknowledged that Christianity was not tied to any language. What they resisted was the particular kind or style of Christianity that usually accompanied the language change in Canadian Mennonite churches. The Tabernacle Group at Herbert, and those converted in the Brunk revivals in southern Manitoba or in one of the Billy Graham or Janz Team crusades, were particularly eager to make the transition and, with it, a shift to the style and methods of those evangelists.

There was, of course, another very personal reason why many leaders opposed the change. Most did not have sufficient command of English to preach and conduct business in it. A change would remove them from office.

In 1940 only the Mennonite Church conferences in Ontario and western Canada, the Ontario Amish Mennonite conference, and Mennonite Brethren in Christ churches in Ontario and Alberta, with an aggregate of 8,200 members, worshipped in English. All the other conferences, with 26,422 members, belonged to German-speaking congregations.[49] Directly comparable statistics for later years are not available, partly because the change was often gradual. Sunday schools were usually the first to introduce some English material, sometimes because children from the community who could not understand German attended. There was also growing realization that Mennonite children who received most of their education in English could understand that language much better than German. Younger Sunday school teachers were also better able to communicate in English.

Churches that had boys' and girls' clubs tended to use English in gatherings long before it was accepted in Sunday morning worship, as did some of the women's societies organized by younger women.[50] The women's societies with mainly older members used German long after Sunday morning worship began to be conducted in English, as did some of the Sunday school classes for older church members.

In the 1950s many Canadian Mennonite churches held worship services in both languages, with English gradually replacing German in congregational activities. The transition was often difficult, as is demonstrated by the reaction to the first English sermon preached in the Coaldale Mennonite church: 'The morning service was started and ran off as usual. But when the minister who was to present the English message got up to speak, a considerable number of the audience rose and left the church. When the exodus had been completed the service continued without further disturbance.'[51]

Arrival of postwar immigrants, many of whom lacked working knowledge of English, delayed change in some congregations, but by the end of the 1950s the transition had been made in most Canadian Mennonite Brethren churches. Rural congregations that belonged to the CMC tended to make the shift somewhat later, while smaller and more traditional western congregations, such as the Old Colony, Reinlaender, Saskatchewan Bergthaler, and Sommerfelder, retained German in worship services well into the 1970s.

The language change received particularly strong support from those who regarded any German in the worship service as a serious obstacle to missionary outreach. They could not bring non-German neighbours and acquaintances to German services. One writer noted critically: 'We can preach repentance and forgiveness of sin but our confession of Christian love rings hollow when converts are advised to join some non-Mennonite church because we speak German in our churches.'[52]

That, of course, was precisely what those intent on preserving a separatist Mennonite life-style feared. It soon became obvious, however, that merely changing language of worship brought Mennonite churches very few non-German neighbours and friends during the years of the transition. Other factors kept outsiders from Mennonite services.[53]

Much emotional pain could have been avoided if advocates of linguistic nonconformity had admitted that retention of German in worship services was, at best, a dubious bulwark of separatism when their children were educated in English and most secular affairs were conducted in that language. And those who saw use of German as blocking missionary and outreach efforts could have acknowledged that it was only one of many obstacles. There is, however, some evidence that those congregations and conferences most strongly committed to missionary and outreach work made the transition more quickly, but also with more controversy, than others that placed greater emphasis on the quiet witness of everyday Christian living.[54] The more thoughtful and far-sighted leaders realized that the language would indeed be lost within a few generations and began to identify which aspects of their identity they must try to translate, fit into, and preserve in English linguistic forms.[55]

CHANGING LOCAL LEADERSHIP PATTERNS

At the local congregational level the most far-reaching leadership change involved introduction and acceptance of trained and salaried pastors. The traditional leaders, as indicated above, had been drawn from those who had shown leadership abilities in the congregation, and they usually served without remuneration. A few congregations, mainly (Old) Mennonite churches in Ontario, had accepted a form of paid pastor in the late 1920s and 1930s when they agreed to special, voluntary collections on one or several specific Sundays, with proceeds to go to their pastor or leading minister. The level of support thus provided was so low that these ministers had to earn additional income from marginal farming activities, outside employment, conducting evangelistic campaigns, and retaining the proceeds of special collections at those meetings, or teaching in a denominational Bible school and keeping some of the proceeds from student fees.[56] In other cases, local farmers or workmen sometimes helped their pastor/leader with seasonal farm work or with construction or repair of his house and farm buildings. Cars were sometimes made available for those engaged in congregational or conference work. In still other cases missionaries who also served as pastors of emerging ur-

ban mission churches received some compensation, as did some of the itinerant ministers appointed to visit Mennonites living in isolated rural areas.
The situation at the Schoenwieser church in Winnipeg, where two ministers
were employed full time in the 1930s, was unusual and reflected the unique
role of that city in the immigration movement.

Several factors contributed to acceptance of a pastoral system in most
Canadian Mennonite churches after 1945. The first, and perhaps most fundamental, was what one writer has called 'the dramatic decrease of physical
and spiritual isolation.'[57] As people had more contact with other churches
and groups they saw and became more willing to consider alternative schemes
of church leadership, particularly if there were serious problems with the
leadership in their church. Difficult Depression experiences, particularly by
the immigrants of the 1920s, fostered strong feelings of inferiority when these
people compared their life-styles and institutions with those of their English-speaking neighbours. This made it relatively appealing to borrow or
accept leadership forms from other denominations.

A second important factor had to do with increased reading and education. People were becoming more sophisticated, and preaching by poorly
educated older lay ministers provided inadequate spiritual nourishment for
some. It also weakened potential missionary and outreach effectiveness.
Preachers with better theological education and proper training in the art of
preparing and delivering sermons were needed if Mennonite churches were
to remain relevant in rapidly changing circumstances.[58]

The growing demand for better-qualified preachers and pastors was met
by a rapidly increasing number of Mennonite young people who took advanced training at the new Mennonite Bible colleges or at other Bible institutes and colleges. These young people, however, were looking for professional work and leadership positions in the churches, which could not easily
be accommodated in the old, multiple, lay-leadership forms of church governance. People were often confused and frightened by the rapid changes
around them and wanted biblical and theological guidance. In such situations the older methods of *Seelsorge* (literally, 'soul care') seemed inadequate.
Pastoral counselling by individuals with professional training was needed.

A final, and in many cases the decisive reason for the change was simply
the volume and complexity of the work to be done. That was especially true
in large congregations where sharp differences of opinion required much
time, skill, and energy in mediating and facilitating communications between
members who no longer understood one another as well as people had when
all shared a common rural way of life.

Appointment of trained and salaried pastors radically altered the relationship between the congregation and its spiritual leaders. Salaried pastors were employees of the congregation rather than men who had demonstrated practical capacity for leadership over long periods spent in the community and the congregation. Many came from elsewhere and had no personal roots in the congregation or community, and churches had to find new administrative structures to deal with these new relationships. Salaried pastors, in spite of their education and professional training, could be removed at the pleasure of a majority or, all too often, even on the whim of a vocal and determined minority. As paid employees they could not offer the kind of strong, albeit sometimes unpopular leadership provided in earlier decades by bishops and conference leaders.

Congregations had little practical experience in dealing with this new type of spiritual leadership, and the results were often unsatisfactory. The Mennonite Brethren Board of Reference and Counsel complained in 1951 about 'the revolutionizing changes of the political, social, and economic life during the past few decades.' Leadership, it lamented, 'is largely not any more the product of a gradual training process within the church, but is more the creation of educational institutions, the latter, in frequent instances, not of our own denomination.'[59]

The report criticized, in a surprisingly blunt manner, the quality and strength of the new pastoral leadership, calling it 'weak, unstable, divisive and unpermanent.'[60] Pastors with training from non-Mennonite Bible institutes and seminaries sometimes brought in alien theological influences, but there were also serious structural problems. The board acknowledged that when, despite much evidence to the contrary, it warned that 'a church must be kept mindful that a minister is a servant anointed of the Lord and cannot be dealt with like an hireling.'[61]

None of the conferences was willing to interfere directly with the autonomy of individual congregations, especially over leadership problems.[62] Some of the difficulties became less serious after establishment or expansion of Mennonite Bible colleges and institutes in Canada. As more prospective pastors attended these institutions greater theological consistency began to emerge. The conferences, however, experienced their own leadership crises in the 1950s and 1960s.

THE RESTRUCTURING OF THE CONFERENCES

Before 1950 almost all the Mennonite conferences were dominated by strong and sometimes autocratic leaders. In the Conference of Mennonites in Canada (CMC), for example, J.J. Thiessen, Jacob Gerbrandt, and John G. Rempel held a total of ten committee memberships, or 25 per cent of all committee memberships in that conference in 1942,[63] and they all also served on the boards of several North American, regional, or provincial committees of the General Conference (GC) or the CMC and on various inter-Mennonite organizations. It was much the same in the other conferences, but all were busily revising their constitutions in the late 1940s and early 1950s.

This concentration of power did not necessarily give the conferences the means to enforce their policies and decisions if individual congregations decided to go their own way or to disregard conference directives. The Schoenwieser proved that in Canada, as did several Mennonite Brethren (MB) congregations in the United States. Some of the leaders believed that the solution was to give conference leaders even more power to rein in maverick congregations and leaders,[64] but when the Mennonite Brethren Board of Reference and Counsel made a proposal to that effect delegates failed to endorse it, thereby plunging that conference into a serious constitutional crisis in 1954. Instead of creating a more powerful board of elders, the conference set up a number of 'consultative' committees that could advise but not dictate to the congregations.[65] That arrangement also proved unsatisfactory. It was difficult to draw up a conference constitution that respected local autonomy while preserving conference unity.

Conference reorganizations and constitutional revisions in both Canada and the United States became necessary for many reasons. The work of the conferences had become more complex as new projects and new educational institutions were established, and particularly as home and foreign missions proliferated. Greater technical expertise and stronger administrative skills were needed. And there were understandable demands that governance be opened up and democratized so that more interested people, especially younger, well-educated pastors, could participate.

The result was radical restructuring, which was facilitated by major constitutional revisions. Perhaps the most extreme development occurred in the CMC. In 1955, after years of discussion and debate, a new constitution was adopted.[66] It limited the length and number of terms an individual could serve on any board or on the executive committee. Board members were elected for three-year terms, but none could serve for more than three consecutive terms. Executive officers were elected for one-year terms and could not serve for more than three consecutive terms. Multiple executive and board memberships were not permitted. If a board member were elected to the executive committee he or she had to resign board membership. This departure from earlier practices meant that there would be many new board and executive members, and hence less continuity, which in turn led to greater reliance by the board on program administrators. In addition, provincial conferences soon established their own boards to parallel those of the Canadian conference. That led to both closer integration and increased competition between national and provincial programs.

A further change affecting all but the most traditional conferences was a deliberate policy of inviting and encouraging not only ministers and leaders but also lay members and non-delegates to attend the annual conference sessions in much larger numbers. Sessions consequently took on 'the character of family gatherings on a large scale, where acquaintances are made and renewed, fellowship intensified, and sympathetic personal face-to-face relationships made possible and maintained.'[67]

Mennonite conferences in the 1950s thus became more decentralized, more democratic, and more bureaucratic, and allowed for much more lay participation, as they tried to cope with the needs and opportunities of more prosperous but also more diverse circumstances. The small coterie of influential leaders that had guided the conferences through the difficult war and postwar years was replaced. New, younger, less experienced leaders, elected for shorter and more rigorously limited terms, took their place but had to rely much more than their predecessors on increasingly influential program administrators, executive secretaries, and bureaucrats.

CHANGING CONFERENCE NAMES

The changes in conference structures, leadership, and attitudes toward contacts with the outside world resulted in the renaming of several Canadian Mennonite churches and conferences. The old names, such as Altkolonier, Bergthaler, Bruderthaler, Chortitzer, Kleine Gemeinde, Krimmer Mennonite Brethren, Reinlaender, Rosenorter, Rudnerweider, Schoenwieser, and Sommerfelder, were all rooted in their own, unique rural histories. Those smaller groups that successfully resisted many of the changes, notably the Sommerfelder, Saskatchewan Bergthaler, Chortitzer, and Reinlaender, were content to retain their old names. Others adopted more contemporary, English names.

The first group to anglicize its name was the Bruderthaler Mennonite Church, which became the Evangelical Mennonite Brethren in 1937. Next the Mennonite Brethren in Christ became in 1947 the United Missionary Church and later simply the Missionary Church. With the name change these two groups also dropped many distinctive Mennonite and Anabaptist doctrines, and they eventually severed most formal links with other Mennonite churches and conferences.

In 1948 the Defenceless Mennonite Church of North America, which did not have any congregations in Canada, changed its name to Evangelical Mennonite Church. In Canada in 1952, the Kleine Gemeinde, a group distinct from the Evangelical Mennonite Church in the United States, took the name Evangelical Mennonite Conference. It retained the 'Mennonite' name and continuing contacts with other Mennonite groups but placed greater emphasis on missionary and evangelistic efforts. The Rudnerweider Mennonite Church followed a similar course in 1959 when it became the Evangelical Mennonite Mission Conference.

Localization of churches with multiple meeting places led to dropping of other distinctive names. The Schoenwieser Mennonite Church in Winnipeg, for example, became First Mennonite Church, while other groups formerly affiliated with the Schoenwieser formed their own, autonomous local churches. The Rosenorter Mennonite Church at Rosthern similarly broke into a number of autonomous local congregations, as did the Bergthaler Mennonite Church of Manitoba a little later. In the case of the Krimmer Mennonite Brethren an amalgamation with the Mennonite Brethren Church ended its separate name and identity.

Localization, particularly in conferences where the most conservative elements either withdrew or were 'hived' into only a few rural congregations, made possible new contacts with other Mennonite groups. In some cases departure of the conservatives also helped to heal old rifts, as happened in 1969 when the Stirling Avenue Mennonite Church became an associate member of the Mennonite Conference from which it had broken away earlier.[68]

In Ontario the Amish Mennonite Conference dropped the 'Amish' designation to become the Western Ontario Mennonite Conference in 1960. It had, even before that date, established close links with the (Old) Mennonite Conference of Ontario and with other Mennonite groups in Ontario through the Conference of Historic Peace Churches (CHPC) and the Mennonite Central Committee (MCC). The result was that the 'Amish' designation came to be identified with the Old Order Amish and their horse-and-buggy culture and life-style.

In the 1980s, the Mennonite Conference of Ontario was renamed the Mennonite Conference of Ontario and Quebec after several mission congregations were established in Quebec. This conference had never been officially called the (Old) Mennonite church, but members and outsiders alike frequently had used that designation to distinguish it from General Conference (GC), or (New), Mennonites after the division in 1847. The U.S. parent conference officially, and rather pretentiously, became 'The Mennonite Church' in 1971, formally dropping the unofficial '(Old)' designation. In Canada (Old) Mennonites belonged to the Mennonite Conference of Ontario and Quebec until 1988, when that body amalgamated with the Western Ontario Mennonite Conference (formerly the Ontario Amish Mennonite Conference) and the Conference of United Mennonite Churches in Ontario (affiliated with the CMC and the GC) to form the Mennonite Conference of Eastern Canada. Even those active in a Mennonite church or conference found these name changes confusing, but they reflected the post-1940 transformation of Canadian Mennonite life.

CHANGING FINANCIAL POLICIES

The financial and budgetary arrangements of Mennonite congregations, conferences, and institutions also changed significantly in the 1950s and 1960s. Rural congregations had very low initial or continuing costs. The most traditional groups held meetings in the homes of members or in the parochial school. The leaders and preachers served without compensation. Most rural congregations erected their own meeting-houses, but the usual procedure was to collect voluntary donations from interested members to pay for construction materials and then to do most of the construction work using volunteer labour by the members. Operating costs were similarly kept very low as long as the leaders and preachers served without compensation. A small membership fee usually paid ongoing operating expenses such as taxes and utilities. Special fund drives or, in the case of support for missionary ventures, major collections at special harvest mission festivals covered conference programs. Some rural congregations, particularly after a good harvest, could raise more money for mission and relief work in the collections taken during a harvest thanksgiving and missions festival than the annual operating costs of the congregation. The emotionally charged tours of Mennonite Central Committee (MCC) representatives reporting on the suffering and needs of postwar Mennonite refugees from the Soviet Union elicited similarly generous responses.

In urban congregations both capital and operating costs were much higher than in traditional congregations. Pastors, program administrators, teachers, and college professors were paid salaries, and new congregational and conference programs initiated or expanded after the war required far greater operating funds. Many of the new programs, moreover, did not enjoy unanimous support in the congregations, making the old system of paying operating costs through membership levies more difficult to enforce. The change to an entirely voluntary financial contribution system was, however, difficult because it significantly increased the uncertainties about the amount of money that might come in at a time when budgets and financial commitments for salaries and ongoing projects were becoming more rigid. Christian stewardship became an increasingly urgent concern once congregations and conferences had come to depend mainly on voluntary donations.

The MCC was in a better position to deal with these problems than most of the other Mennonite institutions. It was engaged mainly in short, limited-term, emergency relief activities. Successful special financial appeals could be made if a famine broke out somewhere, or some other disaster struck anywhere in the world. MCC spent very little of the money it raised on permanent staff and facilities.

The new Mennonite colleges and most of the high schools, by contrast, were not able to make effective, crisis-provoked appeals. They needed a steady income to pay salaries and operating costs. None had substantial endowment funds before 1970. Most operated on a very short financial leash, at least until they could establish a stronger base of support with their own alumni. Private solicitations among supporters, alumni, and churches remained an important source of income. The colleges and schools also derived significant public relations benefits from regular tours, in which a choir or singing group and speaker visited constituent churches. Special collections in support of the institution were part of these visits, which fact administrators often found frustrating.

It is a tribute to those handling Mennonite funds that, in spite of often-inadequate financial and accounting procedures, there were no major financial scandals. Treasurers, it seems, were often also enthusiastic supporters of the congregation, school, or other institution for which they solicited funds. They were far more likely to make additional contributions themselves in case of a financial crisis than take designated funds for their own purposes.

CONCLUSION

The struggles and problems that congregational and conference leaders had to deal with in times of rapid change involved much soul searching, prayer, reading, and searching of the scriptures. The leaders, in spite of their human limitations and failures, were intent on building the Kingdom of God in their congregations and communities. They devoted countless hours and much energy to meetings, correspondence, discussions, and frequent travel, which took them away from their homes, families, farms, and businesses. Before 1950 few received any significant financial remuneration, but they held and exercised a good deal of influence.

The congregations and communities in which these men had grown up, and in which they sought to provide leadership, were changing so rapidly that many of them were removed or replaced long before they reached their normal age of retirement. Even while they still occupied positions of leadership, effective control was shifting to younger, better-educated, English-speaking, and financially supported pastors and administrators. It is therefore not surprising that some felt a sense of betrayal and bitterness when forced out of positions of authority in the midst of some crisis. Others felt relief when the heavy burdens of office passed to their successors.

The older leaders, and their younger successors, were often keenly aware that this was much more than a natural transition from one generation to the next. Most of the decisive leadership changes came in the mid- to late 1950s and in the 1960s. By 1970 salaried pastors had replaced lay leaders in all but the most traditional, rural Mennonite churches. The language of worship in most churches had changed from German to English. Old linguistic and cultural forms of nonconformity were being modified or abandoned. Conferences had been restructured, in many cases renamed, and their administrative offices had been moved from rural towns to Winnipeg or Kitchener-Waterloo. Financial and budgeting processes had been radically altered, from a levy or church tax system to reliance on voluntary donations. And decisive influence had shifted from rural to urban centres and institutions. Younger leaders, with fresh ideas, innovative strategies, and new concerns, but also with a strong commitment to Anabaptist and Mennonite doctrines that they regarded as relevant to changed circumstances, could influence and direct how Canadian Mennonites would respond to the challenges of the modern world. That would force many in the 1960s to come to terms with, or to engage in controversy regarding, the dissonant aspects of their own Mennonite and Anabaptist heritage, North American evangelicalism, and mainstream Canadian religious life. The challenge that they faced was not only how to redefine who or what they were or should be. It was also how they would give voice and practical expression to that faith in a modern world. Their sense of mission, and how they could best communicate their faith, became matters of great concern.

PART FIVE
MISSION AND WITNESS

14

Mission at Home

In his recently published autobiographical reflections J. Lawrence Burkholder describes common pre–Second World War North American Mennonite attitudes and strategies: 'My impression was that Mennonite strength lay in its commitment to the particular in a rather severe either-or, all or nothing, adherence to Jesus only, especially Matthean discipleship. Accordingly, Mennonites insisted upon a strong but short tether – strong communitarian ties but short when it comes to responsible participation in the larger culture.'[1] Developments after 1945 strained these short but strong tethers. Some groups took extraordinary steps to preserve their nonconformist and sectarian communities and congregations. They defined the responsibilities and mission of believers and of their churches fairly clearly. Adherents must live in a faithful discipleship that differed significantly from the standards and practices of unbelievers. The primary function or mission of the church was to provide mutual support, assistance, and where necessary guidance, admonition, and discipline for its members. Proselytization was not emphasized. Little thought or support was given to methods of mass evangelism.

The massive changes that swept most Canadian Mennonite churches after 1939 greatly lengthened, but also weakened and made less rigid, the old short but strong nonconformist and communitarian tether of Mennonite discipleship. Many previously forbidden activities, aspirations, and practices became necessary in the new urban, professional, or entrepreneurial environment. Urban churches responded with what Burkholder complained was 'a sliding scale of discipleship.' They no longer demanded strict adherence to 'the gold standard of Jesus' sayings,' accepting instead 'something between the extraordinariness of Jesus' ethic and the everyday reasonableness of civil righteousness.'[2]

There was an apparently safe and approved way in which to redefine aspects of discipleship. Discarding of distinctive cultural, linguistic, or ethnic Mennonite concepts of Christian discipleship was more easily justified if it could be shown that they impeded effective evangelism and thus the building of the Kingdom of God. That justification, however, became relevant only if converts were brought into the churches that had missionized them. That had generally not been the case before 1939. Almost all the early missions, overseas and in North America, involved people living a considerable distance, geographically or otherwise, from Mennonite communities. Those missions were conducted, as a Mennonite Brethren missions historian has aptly put it, 'at arm's length.' After the Second World War, however, the former arm's-length relationship broke down. It happened first in the so-called home missions.

EARLY MISSION IDEAS

Throughout most of their history Mennonites had what a missions historian has called 'a non-missionary Mennonite mind.'[3] The first generation of early-sixteenth-century Anabaptists had been eager to spread its ideas and religious convictions. Members worked hard to gain converts, but by 1550 severe persecution and a scattering to remote agricultural frontiers had extinguished that spirit. One critical writer has noted: 'By about 1550 a great change took place among the Anabaptists. Before this time they had enthusiasm for a world mission, but after this they fled from the world and wasted their energies in the creation and application of strict rules of custom.'[4]

Such a comment does not do justice to Mennonite efforts to bring all aspects of their lives into a radical and holistic style of Christian discipleship within their own sectarian churches and communities. It is, however, accurate in identifying the Mennonite lack of interest in missions for 300 years: 'Due to continued isolation, at first caused by outside suppression and opposition but later maintained as an ideal, Mennonites were not much affected by and took little interest in, what was going on in the world about them.'[5]

Mennonites' interest in missions was rekindled in the mid-nineteenth century when religious awakenings and revivals swept their communities in the Netherlands, Russia, Prussia, and North America. These were movements of Protestant, not Anabaptist renewal, and they included ideas, beliefs, and practices that brought new life into Mennonite congregations but also undermined some of the holistic aspects of the Anabaptist-Mennonite heritage and theology. A Mennonite historian critical of the impact of evangelical influences on Mennonite missionary efforts has noted:

Jesus shaped His Gospel from the full-orbed vision of human well-being that runs through the Bible as shalom. The deeper I delved into this study and into missionary-movement assumptions, the more I became convinced that the modern missionary movement has not very effectively communicated Jesus' full vision. Mennonites had long spoken fondly of a 'gospel of peace,' and in retrospect their idea seems to have at least suggested shalom. So I became ever more convinced that mission-minded Mennonites might have communicated more of Jesus' message if instead of borrowing wholesale from Anglo-American Protestantism they had worked more consciously from some of their own long-held understandings, especially their peace position.[6]

The most traditional groups never shared the vision or enthusiasm for missions. They rejected what other, more open groups, particularly the major new conferences that emerged from the nineteenth-century schisms, borrowed and accepted from German Pietists and Anglo-American evangelicals. The General Conference Mennonites in the United States and the Mennonite Brethren in Russia and after 1874 in North America were among the first to become involved in modern missionary work. That interest grew, and by 1939 all the large North American Mennonite conferences and many of the smaller ones had active missionary programs.

Canadian Mennonites thought about and implemented policies for missions in two quite different contexts. Such endeavours carried out among neighbours, friends, and fellow countrymen were usually referred to as 'home' missions. Those involving sending of missionaries overseas, usually to the colonies of European imperial powers, were labelled 'overseas,' or 'foreign.' Cross-cultural missions to Native people or to the urban poor in North America, which could be treated as home or as foreign missions, are discussed in this chapter.

Home missions included a wide range of programs and activities. Many began as rural or colonization missions and sometimes involved little more than migration of a group of Mennonite farm families into a new district. The way they lived and conducted their affairs, rather than their preaching and other soul-winning efforts, comprised their Christian witness in the new community. Other home missions began as attempts to maintain contact with Mennonites living alone or in remote areas where they did not have regular contact with others of their faith. Some home missions were established to meet specific needs of people. City victims of poverty, alcoholism, and disease, and Native people on remote reserves became the beneficiaries of Mennonite compassion, charity, and evangelism. And then there were some more aggressive and intrusive efforts to win converts and establish or plant new churches in a great variety of settings. Missions to the Jewish and to the Russian people, service and teaching in remote communities, and major missionary initiatives to French-speaking residents of Quebec all attracted some Canadian Mennonites.

Success in home mission programs created some problems for Mennonite conferences and home congregations. It was difficult to integrate or incorporate converts or entire mission churches into the regular programs of sponsoring congregations and conferences. Distinctive Mennonite doctrines and practices were sometimes poorly understood or rejected by the converts, who wanted to maintain aspects of their own culture, which had evolved in their own unique environment. That forced Canadian Mennonites to reassess which aspects of their heritage should be retained and which could be modified in order to make the Gospel more relevant to the people whom the missionaries were trying to reach.

In their attempts to resolve this problem Canadian Mennonites active in mission work tended to be drawn into the evangelical substream of North American Protestantism. They abandoned not only distinctive ethnic and cultural traits but also important aspects of their holistic theology. Specifically, conversion rather than life-long discipleship received increased emphasis. The result, suggested an (Old) Mennonite missions historian, was that 'we seem to be more conformed to the North American way of life than the New Testament would allow, and less non-conformist than our history and heritage would suggest.'[7]

RURAL EVANGELISM AND CHARITIES

Mennonite groups that were most strongly committed to a traditional rural way of life had a relatively simple concept of mission. They did not get involved in foreign missions or in campaigns designed to persuade their non-Mennonite neighbours to accept either their way of life or their religious beliefs. It was sufficient to live a life of faithful discipleship. Such a life, rather than sermons and evangelistic campaigns, provided the best and most effective Christian witness. These Mennonites lived peaceably in their communities, helped one another as needed, and assisted needy, suffering, or unfortunate people around them. Outsiders who found such a life fulfilling and were willing to subject themselves to the necessary discipline were always welcome, but there was little proselytization. The primary responsibility of the faithful was to communicate the Gospel by living it.

Rural missions and colonization schemes were often a product of both economic and religious motives. When Old Order Amish and other traditional Mennonite groups needed more land for their growing families, or when they became convinced that unwanted outside influences could no longer be kept out of their communities and congregations, they sought out new settlement frontiers. Similarly, immigrants from Russia or the Soviet Union had acquired land and built communities and churches within whose boundaries they tried to build the Kingdom of God.

Rural Mennonites regarded charity to anyone in need an important Christian duty. The Mennonite Board of Missions and Charities, for example, acquired several large farmsteads in the United States and turned them into rural homes for orphans and needy old people. Special fund-raising, food-gathering, and clothing drives for destitute people in the cities were also undertaken by the board, and, as indicated above, a number of urban missions had been established. Many of the cooperative and mutual-aid organizations were also designed to benefit the entire community, not only members of a Mennonite church. The essential core of Mennonite rural missions, however, was to provide living examples of Christianity. The impact that that had on those living in and near Mennonite communities was a matter left in the hands of God and subject to the decisions made voluntarily by their non-Mennonite neighbours.

Rural missions or colonization evangelism were never easy. The (Old) Ontario Mennonite Conference had set up a Board of Rural Missions in 1914. It was instrumental in founding several rural congregations but was merged in 1929 with the City Mission Board of the conference. Supporters evaluated its work: 'Rural mission work in Ontario is not an easy task. Through experience, mistakes and recovery, with a more zealous search for the leading and blessing of God we have come thus far along the pathway of duty. We are particularly adapted for rural work. To-day as never before doors are open to our particular testimony. It has become a question of which fields we shall possess with the present resources of the church.'[8]

The (Old) Mennonite Church reorganized its rural missions in 1920 when it reviewed the status of all its congregations and unorganized groups. Twenty congregations supported by the missions committee were declared self-sustaining and invited to become members in the conference. The others would be assisted by the mission committee until they either disbanded or grew to the point where the conference could recognize them as self-sustaining.

Mennonite farmers looking for more land rarely moved as a large, organized group. Usually individuals bought farms or took up homesteads, and if enough came to a particular district a church would be organized. Consequently many Mennonites lived in relative isolation, far removed from their home congregations, and rural mission work often consisted of itinerant preachers who would periodically visit those living on the fringes of established Mennonite communities. If there was enough interest to hold occasional worship services with the people in some remote settlement, preachers would be sent and sometimes financial assistance was provided to help pay for rental of a place to meet and for other incidental expenses. Itinerant evangelists could also be sent out to hold special evangelistic services in these fringe communities. This form of endeavour was sometimes referred to as 'Randmission' (fringe mission).

For the immigrants of the 1920s it often had not only a charitable but also an unpleasant economic objective. Many still owed money for their transportation to Canada, advanced by the Canadian Pacific Railway and guaranteed by leaders of the Canadian Mennonite Board of Colonization. Collections from indebted individuals became one of the most difficult and unpleasant tasks of board officials, particularly from those living in remote areas who were often late, indifferent, or so impoverished that they were unwilling or unable to make regular payments. Visits by a preacher from the *Randmission* therefore could involve not only spiritual ministry but also tough financial discussions. In British Columbia people from the prairies who had not yet paid their transportation debts were trying to start anew. Board and church leaders from the prairies wrote frequently to BC ministers giving names of debtors. Everyone breathed a great sigh of relief when, thanks to special fund drives, the burdensome debt was repaid in November 1946.

During the war appointment of and funding for preachers and church leaders who visited conscientious objectors' work camps became a concern of home mission and colonization boards. Home missionaries also sought to serve young women working as domestics in the cities and other needy people in the cities. Those initiatives have, however, been discussed above.

NATIVE MINISTRIES

During the war Manitoba's Mennonites became involved in new and unfamiliar mission projects in the north of the province. The Manitoba Conference of the United Church of Canada, many of whose missionaries and teachers had become military chaplains or enlisted for regular military service, faced a desperate shortage of teachers and missionaries for their northern missions. Some of their own men had become conscientious objectors (COs), and relations between key Mennonite and United Church leaders in Manitoba were sufficiently cordial that the United Church leaders made a difficult request. They sought government authorization to allow conscientious objectors, including those belonging to their own or to Mennonite churches, to discharge their alternative service obligations by working as teachers or missionaries in the northern missions for the Native people.[9]

While the senior United Church leaders in Manitoba welcomed Mennonite teachers and missionaries, several of their own workers were bitterly opposed, particularly if the Mennonite worker served as both teacher and missionary. Harry Meadows, the United Church missionary at Cross Lake, for example, wrote to a senior official of his church in 1943:

The Mennonite teacher they have sent to me is not up to much. I've had to keep him away from the school job as he spoils almost every bit of material he touches ... They are not of use and although they are willing to accept our salaries they will not conduct themselves as United Church men ... God's Lake is in bad shape. The Mennonites will not baptize children under nine years and you know what infant baptism means to Indians. As a result our Indians are getting the priest to baptise their children and going over to the Catholic ... I was sorry to learn from your letter that Neufeld will have something to say about the running of our missions, but I must admit that he couldn't make a worse mess than we are ... By the way the Mennonite Brethren Church of which Neufeld is a member is the most narrow sect of all the Mennonites. It burns me up that these fellows should be up here holding down safe jobs and drawing more money than they ever had before while your son who could do the job properly is in the army to help make the country safe for such as they.[10]

The reaction of senior United Church leaders to this complaint, however, was emphatic: 'When we get a young man like Harry Meadows, who has no standing in the Church, writing to a man like Dr. Stevens, urging him to stir up trouble, I think it is time that somebody intervened. The worst thing in his letter is when he says that it burns him up that these fellows should be up there holding down safe jobs, while Fred Stevens is in the army to help make the country safe for such as they. I think that is a monstrous piece of impertinence from a young man of military age, who is himself safe and sound at Cross Lake.'[11]

Some difficulties arose because the United Church made a distinction between teachers and missionaries. Teachers were appointed simply to teach in the mission school, but missionaries also administered the sacred rites of the United Church, including infant baptism. Several Mennonite Brethren (MB) and Conference of Mennonites in Canada (CMC) men became both teachers and missionaries and performed infant baptisms. There is no record, other than Harry Meadows's complaint, that Mennonite missionaries insisted that children be nine years old before they were baptized. At some of the mission stations where there was only a Mennonite teacher, and hence no one authorized to administer baptism, parents took their infants to the Catholic mission for baptism.[12]

The complaint about Mennonite teachers accepting United Church salaries was not justified. These alternative service workers, like any others employed with the approval of Selective Service officials, were allowed to keep only a small monthly allowance. The rest of their salary had to be donated to the Red Cross.

The efforts of the Mennonite alternative service workers were appreciated, and a year after they began their work the superintendent of missions of the Manitoba conference of the United Church acknowledged: 'But for the help of our Mennonite brethren, our report must have revealed a serious loss, instead of encouraging progress.'[13]

These experiences with the Native people in the north gave valuable experience to Mennonite teachers and opened a new field of missionary work after the war. One of those teachers from the Bergthaler Mennonite Church of Manitoba later wrote: 'My wartime experiences on the Cross Lake Indian Reserve helped me begin to sort out many misconceptions about Indians. I became keenly interested in their social and spiritual welfare. I learned that they were not necessarily lazy but defeated. Their hunting and fishing lifestyle did not call for the schedule of a farm routine. Their concept of time was more circular whereas ours was straight.'[14]

The experience of the Bergthaler and later of the Conference of Mennonites in Canada in this kind of work differed considerably from that of the Mennonite Brethren. The Bergthaler had established their own mission to the Natives in Mexico, with disappointing results. The wartime work in northern Manitoba captured the imagination and enthusiasm of several young Bergthaler, and in 1948 they set up the Mennonite Pioneer Mission (MPM). The idea was to send qualified teachers and health-care workers, who would also serve as missionaries, into the Native communities. The first station that they opened was at Matheson Island. Others at Bloodvein, Cross Lake, Loon Straits, Manigotogan, and Pauingassi followed. These teachers and missionaries worked in close cooperation with appropriate federal and provincial agencies and departments.

The first mission endeavour usually involved organization of a Sunday school or daily vacation Bible school, depending on the season. If there was sufficient interest Bible studies were arranged for the parents as well, but the missionary teachers and nurses also spent a great deal of time learning the language, getting to know the people, and helping them with many of their economic and practical problems. They frequently served as mediators when the local people had to deal with unfamiliar government agencies, becoming a voice for the Native people.

The early missionaries found the work difficult and the results disappointing. A historian has noted that during their first twenty years with the Native people of northern Manitoba the missionaries and board members learned that 'one could not simply announce the gospel at Sunday services and expect a church to emerge automatically. Missionaries were learning that they had to bridge a cultural and ethnic gap between themselves (primarily of Low German–Russian background) and the Saulteaux, Cree, and Metis.'[15] A long-term board member explained later: 'After some discouraging initial experiences with those who had been "wonderfully saved" our workers came to see that making disciples among our northern people was not so easy ... [The northern people] wanted to see the Christian faith and this required time.'[16]

The missionaries initiated several community development programs. Thus at Manigotogan, where the local fishing industry was threatened with destruction, the missionary helped to organize the Wanipigow Producers Co-op Ltd in 1963, thereby securing employment for local residents and better prices for fish. In other communities missionaries helped in negotiations with the government for funding and then in construction of a hockey rink and other community buildings. Handicraft projects were started, and markets in the south developed for the products.

At several places people already had considerable experience with other Christian missionaries. Most of the United Church missions had suffered serious decline either as a result of the departure of missionaries and teachers during the war or because they became discouraged with the progress being made. The MPM made great efforts to avoid any appearance of competition or territoriality. At Little Grand Rapids the Mennonite mission was closed when the United Church, which had been working in the area, appointed a new missionary and became more active.[17] The Native people had difficulty understanding or appreciating denominational competition, and MPM missionaries generally tried to avoid it.

Some of the Roman Catholic missionaries in Manitoba were and remained hostile. At Bloodvein, prior to arrival of the Mennonites, the priest warned the people that 'the devils are coming.'[18] The Mennonites and Roman Catholics established competing schools at Bloodvein, but the two were eventually merged and placed under government control. There were fortunately also happier, more cooperative experiences. Henry Neufeld established cordial relations with Robert Bernardino, a Roman Catholic priest. After Bernardino left for France the two exchanged letters in which Neufeld reported on progress and successes at the Roman Catholic mission. Bernardino responded, 'I sincerely admire you and your wife for your Christian testimony among the poor ... We live in a time of ecumenism, if we find it possible to progress in that direction in the days ahead, so much the better ... The division among Christians surely is hard for both of us to bear. Is it not? But at least if we don't talk *against* one another and strive to be positive, it is already a powerful testimony of what Christian charity can accomplish.'[19]

Relations with some other missionaries were more strained. Mennonites had particular problems with Pentecostals who moved into a community to hold highly emotional evangelistic meetings, baptize converts, and then leave them to find their own way. The only thing that seemed to matter to these itinerant evangelists was to 'save' as many people as they could in the shortest possible time. Such tactics left the Indian people confused and made the ongoing work of the missionaries more difficult.[20]

MPM missionaries also had a difficult experience at Loon Straits in Manitoba. There a mission had been started by the Plymouth Brethren, but an accident made it impossible for the missionary to continue. MPM responded positively to an invitation that it send a missionary to Loon Straits. His approach and methods, however, differed from those of the Brethren. Serious tensions developed between the newcomer and a group of the local Native Christians, who complained that the Mennonite did not understand them, that he was more interested in building, establishing, and forcing them to join the church than in serving the people, that he spent too much time building and improving his own house, and that he did not spend enough time visiting and helping the people. Some even doubted whether he was really saved and asked the MPM board to recall him.

The board responded cautiously. It sent people to investigate and, if possible, to achieve reconciliation, but the local Christians lost patience. Citing Matthew 18:15–20, they said that they had gone through the three stages of reconciliation set out in those verses but that the missionary had not repented. They therefore excommunicated him and pronounced a ban against him. Since the board had not responded as they thought appropriate, a ban was also pronounced against its members. Thereafter the Brethren and Mennonite groups met separately, until both missions were closed.[21]

Thirty years later, Henry J. Gerbrandt, a member of the executive committee of MPM when the Loon straits trouble occurred, wrote in his memoirs:

Our ministry in Loon Straits did not give enough attention to the Christians who were there. It is true that we were invited to Loon Straits, but we did not fully understand that invitation. We gave it our own slant. They had meant we should help them; we took over completely. The clash that followed is one of the darker chapters ... They were believers with a Plymouth Brethren understanding of church polity. We did not respect their faith and sincerity and forced on them a view of the church which they did not share. Consequently, they asked us to withdraw. We ignored that and built a mammoth mission house and developed our own group. First, their ministry folded, then ours did.[22]

Gerbrandt and other members of the board concluded that they must become more sensitive and open to local situations and to the social and cultural setting in which the Native people lived. They tried to learn more about Native religion and culture and to look more for the good in it. That was not necessarily a way to gain support for the missions in Mennonite communities and congregations. A 1959 pamphlet designed to garner such support still reflected older ideas and attitudes. It denounced witchcraft and Indian superstitions and concluded: 'Considering all the above mentioned facts about the Indians and their location, their beliefs, their backwardness, etc., one realizes that work here is not too different from that on a foreign field.'[23]

Such attitudes were fortunately becoming unfashionable. The Bergthaler Mennonite Church of Manitoba began to work together with the CMC in the MPM in the mid-1950s, and in 1964 Menno Wiebe, a trained anthropologist with great sensitivity and a good understanding of Native culture and religion, became executive secretary. He advised the missionaries to look for ways in which the Native people could become Christian within their cultural and social context. Jacob A. Loewen, a Mennonite Brethren anthropologist, was also called on for advice and to give special conference and workshop presentations. The missionaries were told to find ways to fit the Gospel into Indian culture and not to expect or demand that the Indians accept the white people's way of life. Wiebe also believed that 'Mennonites, because of their own history of minority oppression, might have an edge in sensitivity to the harboured resentment of the Indian people.'[24] Wiebe insisted that Mennonites could be effective missionaries to the Native people only if they listened and learned to understand them.

This new emphasis gave those associated with the MPM, renamed Native Ministries in 1975, greater credibility in Native communities. It was a course of action that was also appealing to workers at other Mennonite, United Church, Anglican, Roman Catholic, Presbyterian, Lutheran, and Christian Reformed missions. It was not, however, an approach approved by Pentecostals and the other, more fundamentalist mission groups. Nor was it one with which Mennonite Brethren felt comfortable at that time.

Although MPM's community-building and Native-support policies en-joyed considerable success in northern Native communities and growing support in the Mennonite constituency,[25] it was difficult to implement simi-lar ideas and methods to help and serve Natives who moved to the cities, particularly to Winnipeg, where there were numerous Mennonite churches. It quickly became clear that there were serious problems with Mennonite images of the urban Indian, especially if Natives attended and tried to be-come involved in Mennonite churches. A 1967 MPM report identified and criticized such attitudes: 'Apparently we are much more ready to do mis-sion work among the Indians in the north who are removed from our churches than we are among the Indians who are coming to live as our neighbours. It is painful to discover that the very churches who show considerable interest in the MPM program "out there" show almost no interest to the very same Indian people when they come to live in our communities. We accepted In-dians as converts. Perhaps it is now time that we accept these converts as brothers and open our churches to them.'[26]

Mennonite Brethren missionaries and mission board administrators were not able to make the necessary accommodations in their efforts to take the Gospel to Canada's Native people, either on northern reserves or in poorer urban dis-tricts. They, like the Bergthaler and later the CMC, followed up wartime as-signments by establishing new missions in Native communities in northern Manitoba. Several missionaries trained at the Mennonite Brethren Bible Col-lege (MBBC) in Winnipeg were sent out, but they encountered serious difficul-ties. They emphasized a specific kind of conversion experience, apparently not recognizing that such an experience incorporated elements of Western civiliza-tion that did not meet Native needs. There was less understanding for the need to fit the Gospel into Native society and greater insistence that at conversion the Native leave behind and abandon all the old ways.[27]

The Mennonite Brethren also placed greater emphasis on 'church plant-ing.' They wanted to set up in Native communities denominational churches similar to those in Mennonite communities. As a result, some MB mission-aries showed considerable hostility toward the work done by other denomi-nations. William Neufeld, who provided strong leadership in the wartime alternative service program, seemed almost obsessed by fears that an aggres-sive Roman Catholic priest was enjoying considerable success.[28] The Na-tives, in contrast, had seen far too much interdenominational squabbling and ecclesiastical empire building. Their most serious complaints against the MPM missionary at Loon Straits and against the Mennonite Brethren were that these people were interested more in building a church than in serving the people. These problems eventually resulted in withdrawal of the Mennonite Brethren from Native ministries in northern Manitoba. An MB historian has offered a partial explanation of that decision: 'One may fairly say, having looked at Lindal, Ashern and Winnipegosis that many, if not most, college-trained people found those areas too isolated, too daunting, and too circumscribed in their cultural and social amenities, not to mention the difficulties of working with a scattered and declining population. It is not entirely unfair to ask whether professionals trained at MBBC could in fact serve as successfully as Bible school graduates in places like the above.'[29]

A Mennonite Brethren who had a close relative in an MB mission in northern Manitoba in the 1950s offered a different assessment. He thought that the Mennonite Brethren had simply not learned to work effectively in cross-cultural situations.[30]

The U.S. (Old) Mennonite Church began a small Native mission in northern Minnesota in 1938. In 1951 the mission churches were reorganized, and Irwin Schantz, an American Mennonite, began a new Native mission in northern Ontario. He established a home base at Red Lake, the northernmost point of the highway. A building was erected at Pikangikum, and Bible studies, itinerant preaching, and witnessing forays into Ojibway Indian encampments were made. These resulted in several small mission groups and churches, which were organized as the Northern Light Gospel Mission Conference.[31] Teachers and health-care workers from among southern Ontario Mennonites were encouraged to take employment in the Native communities, and annual fund-raising campaigns led to shipment of substantial quantities of food, blankets, clothing, machinery, and household equipment. In 1965, for example, supplies with a wholesale value of $5,000 were sent north.[32] In 1989 Mennonite Church Native missions organizations were disbanded, and a new Native Mennonite Conference was organized. The change seemed to acknowledge that membership in existing Mennonite conferences did not entirely meet Native needs and desires.

CHILDREN'S MISSIONS

Mennonite home missions programs for children attracted a good deal of attention and participation in the 1940s and 1950s. In part, and in many instances primarily, these were programs designed for children whose parents and families were members of the sponsoring churches. Such programs have been discussed above. There were, however, initiatives designed to extend to children who had no other church contacts the benefits first of Sunday school and daily vacation Bible school and later of Christian camping programs.

The daily vacation Bible schools, also known as summer Bible schools, usually lasted two to four weeks and gave the children a rudimentary knowledge of Bible stories and the fundamentals of the Christian faith.[33] In Canada such classes were begun in the 1930s, copying models established by Mennonite and other denominations in the United States. They varied considerably in the relative emphasis placed on religious education and proselytization. Some were organized independently by Bible school students and teachers, some by individual congregations, and still others by regional or provincial conferences. A Mennonite writer observed: 'The church has recognized the summer Bible school as a great potential missionary agency for reaching children, establishing new Sunday schools, and founding new churches. This is a major reason for the rapid growth of this movement. Summer Bible schools have become a major feature of the Christian education program in most congregations in almost all branches of the Mennonite brotherhood.'[34]

In some cases daily vacation Bible school was coordinated with careful colonization evangelism. As people moved into a new district workers invited the children of recently arrived members, and others from the community, to come to Sunday school and to summer Bible school. Often that provided an opportunity for contact with the parents, and in a number of instances, particularly as a result of initiatives by Mennonite Church and Amish Mennonite students from the Ontario Mennonite Bible School, strong local congregations emerged. The fact that these Swiss Mennonites had already made the language transition and conducted their church services in English made it easier for outsiders to become interested and involved.

There were, however, also some unfortunate experiences. Various Mennonite groups in western Canada became involved in daily vacation Bible school at a time when their language of worship was still German and when many still hoped to preserve other aspects of their Russian Mennonite heritage. Children from non-Mennonite homes, or interested English-speaking adults, could not participate effectively in German services. The result was sometimes unfortunate. Some promoters and workers taught the children for two to four weeks, pushed them as hard as they could toward a conversion experience, and then left. The Mennonite Brethren in British Columbia, for example, kept a careful tally of all the conversions achieved through these programs.[35] But they had no clear idea what to do with these young converts. George W. Peters, a teacher at the Hepburn Bible School in the 1940s, exemplified this approach when he wrote: 'The purpose of the *Kindermission* (Children's Mission) is to win youth for the Lord and through youth to serve our land. The Children's Mission shall remain missionary; the mission should not have church-building as its main principle, but to bring the gospel to those who don't have it. When conversions take place, the task of the mission is done; there the church must step in.'[36]

This seemed grossly irresponsible to church leaders who agonized over their proper response to those reached through the children's mission. When G.W. Peters and his Western Children's Mission sent several teams of Bible school students from Hepburn to conduct classes in British Columbia they recorded many conversions. This, however, worried some of the older and more traditional leaders, such as John A. Harder, of the Yarrow Mennonite Brethren Church. The emotional pressure tactics used by Peters and his group to obtain the right decisions, and the children's minimal knowledge or understanding of Christian discipleship, seemed problematic and allegedly led to the organization of a second MB children's mission – the West Coast Children's Mission of British Columbia.[37] The early workers in that mission were told to recommend that their converts join some English-language evangelical church and to provide some liaison between the children and appropriate local pastors.[38]

The tension was gradually reduced when Mennonite churches began to conduct their Sunday schools and worship services in English. There were nevertheless residual cultural and ethnic obstacles that were not easily overcome, and most non-Mennonite converts continued to join other churches. Some Mennonites who were particularly enthusiastic about child evangelism also found it expedient to join other evangelical churches, such as the Christian and Missionary Alliance, Evangelical Free, Baptist, Pentecostal, Four Square, and Full Gospel movements.

There was controversy in British Columbia in 1958 when it was proposed that the West Coast Children's Mission be renamed the Mennonite Brethren Mission of British Columbia. It was intended as a signal that the conference was now ready to accept non-Mennonite converts. Some opposed it for that reason, while others wanted no references to the name 'Mennonite,' with its cultural and ethnic connotations, in the name of either the mission or their churches.[39] The basic question – whether distinctive Mennonite doctrines, and if so which ones, should have a place in a mission-oriented church – was never clearly answered. By 1970, however, the language fight had clearly been lost, and even defenders of distinctive Mennonite practices acknowledged that these were not essential ingredients of their faith. There were, however, other historic doctrines that many were not willing to give up.

CHURCH PLANTING

Mennonite home missions of the late 1940s and the 1950s were not a great success in terms of numbers of converts. No doubt many people were helped in one way or another, and missionaries who placed great emphasis on such things could point to numerous conversions. Some churches, particularly in the cities, had certainly grown rapidly, but much of that growth was due to the movement of rural church members into the cities. It seemed to many home mission workers, administrators, and supporters that new and different strategies were needed if they were to witness effectively to outsiders. As a result, new strategies became popular.

Churches had been started in many rural and urban places as Mennonites moved into new communities. There was, however, considerable evidence that such congregations usually retained many of the social and cultural characteristics of the congregations of origin and had difficulty incorporating people of different origins. It seemed to critics that 'if the community into which this group migrates is distinctly different culturally from the migrating group, the possibilities for the new church to become indigenous to the new community are clearly limited.'[40]

The solution, it was suggested, was a new strategy of church planting – only a few, carefully selected and trained planters would be sent into a target community. They would do mission work, the object being to set up a church made up of the people from that community. Sending only a few representatives might mean that 'formation of a new church will be dependent on the success in calling people of that community to faith and forming them into a body of believers.'[41] The culture of the new church would then respond to the needs of the community.

Mennonite Brethren were particularly enthusiastic. In 1965, after reviewing the discouraging statistical results of their earlier home missions programs, they established an ambitious target of church planting and growth. They intended within a decade to double their church membership in both Canada and the United States through aggressive planting. 'We are,' they said, 'seeking more effective avenues of church-centred witness through further Mennonite Brethren Conference–supported Christian Service placements.'[42]

James and Elfrieda Nikkel were particularly eager to put the new strategy into practice. They went north to The Pas in Manitoba in 1969, beginning with Christian day camps for families. Tract distribution, visiting, special services on the streets, Bible studies, and evangelistic services brought converts, who were then formed into neighbourhood life groups – they had

received new life and now wished to share it with others in small, neighbourhood settings.

Once a small core group had formed, a new church was organized. It might
receive limited financial but not further personnel assistance from the conference. Its main thrust was to gain as many new members as possible from
the local community. Once a new church was organized and in operation,
the Nikkels moved to another community or neighbourhood. A later cita-
tion honouring the Nikkels said: 'Starting churches in the north was getting
to be the normal thing for James and Elfrieda.'[43]

This strategy achieved some impressive early results. But the emphasis on
gaining converts quickly revealed some less endearing consequences. The
new churches sometimes experienced great instability. Many converts responded to a variety of religious appeals, following whatever happened to
be the religious fad of the month or year in their community. The planters
tried to open wide the front doors of their new churches to bring in as many
converts as possible, but often those newcomers went out the back door
almost as quickly as they came in through the front.

The focus on church planting and church membership prompted Mennonite Brethren to withdraw from some inter-Mennonite relief and service programs. Church planting used MB Christian service programs, not inter-Mennonite projects. MBs therefore abstained, or cooperated only very reluctantly,
when Mennonites of various backgrounds in a new city or community began to meet together for fellowship and worship. Both the Mennonite Church
and the CMC allowed congregations with mixed membership to affiliate with
more than one conference, but the Mennonite Brethren refused such arrangements. When the Ottawa Mennonite Fellowship was organized and applied
for dual membership in the United Mennonite (CMC) Conference of Ontario
and the Mennonite Brethren Conference of Ontario it was rebuffed, and the
MB missions committee sent a delegation to try to persuade those of MB
background to organize a separate church.[44] When those involved chose to
remain with the Ottawa Mennonite Fellowship, the missions committee sent
in a planter to start the National Capital Community church.

Parallel situations developed in other places. MB church-planting strategies did not promote inter-Mennonite cooperation, and some MB planters
regarded distinctive Mennonite and Anabaptist doctrines as an impediment
to evangelization. A former MB church planter later wrote: 'We rationalized
or sloughed off those identifiable characteristics of our brotherhood and
our Anabaptist heritage that set us apart from mainstream evangelicals-fun-
damentalists ... We did not want to be held up on our main emphasis, evangelism, by awkward elements in our theology, even though that rationaliza-

tion would be impossible to justify in a scholarly way.'[45]

A survey of MB home missions workers in the 1970s indicated that nearly twice as many thought of themselves as 'broadly evangelical' than as having 'an Anabaptist-Mennonite orientation.'[46] Other Mennonite conferences that also adopted some of the church-planting strategies took a different view of their heritage. The General Conference and its Canadian affiliate, the CMC, regarded the distinctive teachings, particularly their peace teachings during the upheavals of the Vietnam War in the 1960s, as an added attraction: 'Perhaps the time has come to call for a radical discipleship in the sense of our Anabaptist tradition. Perhaps if we were to do this we would discover that our distinctives are really our greatest point of appeal rather than an unnecessary offense.'[47]

'Distinctives' pertained generally to the Anabaptist-Mennonite emphasis on Christian discipleship, and specifically to the peace witness. These were indeed becoming attractive for some non-Mennonites and are discussed in more detail below. It was more difficult to make the same argument in support of retention of distinctive Mennonite dress, preservation of the German language, or rejection of modern technology.[48]

Church planting by the larger Mennonite conferences and some of the smaller ones did not result in significantly greater statistical success than the earlier home mission programs. The Mennonite Brethren, who had set very ambitious goals for their new strategy, were particularly disappointed. Statistics showed that in 1965 membership in Canadian MB churches stood at 15,807. Ten years later it was 18,663 – an increase of only 18 per cent.[49] Comparable figures for the CMC, which followed less aggressive evangelism tactics and tried to build on rather than minimize references to distinctive Mennonite and Anabaptist teachings, were 20,579 members in 1965 and 23,979 a decade later, for a 17 per cent increase.[50] In both conferences the increase would have been significantly higher if they had never attracted a single outside convert but brought all their own children into membership.

Results for the Evangelical Mennonite Conference (EMC) and the Evangelical Mennonite Mission Conference (EMMC) were similar. EMC leaders established the Western Gospel Mission in 1946 and in 1950 invited the EMMC to become a partner in that endeavour. The two conferences worked together until 1960, founding 11 mission stations in Ontario, Manitoba, and Saskatchewan. By 1958 some of the workers wanted to organize these bodies into churches, but that raised the awkward question of affiliation. The Western Gospel Mission was accordingly dissolved, and six of the stations were assigned to the EMC and five to the EMMC. But some years later an

EMC missions historian noted: 'If a person were to pick up the E.M. Conference yearbook in 1978, all except two of these six stations/churches would be missing.'[51]

The Western Gospel Mission marked an early phase in missionary work in both sponsoring conferences. It began with Sunday school and vacation Bible school and evolved to the point where the workers wanted to plant or establish new churches, whose members were mostly of non-Mennonite ethnic background. The impact of these ventures was undoubtedly considerable. An EMMC historian notes: 'For many Rudnerweider [EMMC] young people, this summer ministry was a perfect chance to try their gifts and stretch their spiritual muscles. At the same time, it also provided a sense of adventure. Dozens of people involved in this ministry will always look back to these experiences as high points of their growing up years.'[52]

But mission work also created tensions. A successful mission had to serve people with traditions, environments, and problems that differed from those of traditional rural or new urban Mennonite churches. Nonconformist dress became problematic for some urban missions, but many other changes also became necessary. One of a relatively small number of missions that made that transition was the Warden Park Mennonite Church in Toronto.[53]

It is difficult to assess the impact of home missions and church planting on outsiders brought into the fellowship of the sponsoring churches. What has become clear is the harsh fact that the new and more aggressive church-planting strategies of the 1960s did not bring in the numbers anticipated and that dispensing with distinctive aspects of the Anabaptist-Mennonite heritage did not result in greater success than that achieved by church planters who tried to preserve and use some of those 'distinctives' as an attraction.

HOME MISSIONS IN QUEBEC

Canadian Mennonites became involved in unexpected home missions projects in Quebec. The first body to become actively involved was the (Old) Mennonite Conference of Ontario. In June 1954 two students of the Ontario Mennonite Bible School made a brief tour of the province. They spoke mainly with the teachers at two French Protestant Bible colleges and with French-speaking missionaries representing independent Baptists, Brethren Assemblies, and Pentecostals. They were informed of the political as well as religious influence and authority of the Roman Catholic church. That first visit was followed with a second in September 1955 under the direction of the secretary of the Ontario Conference Mennonite Mission Board. His report included the following assessment: 'The Province of Quebec with its some-thing less than four million Roman Catholics and less than 2,000 French Evangelicals, and only fifty-six evangelical missionaries and pastors, repre-sents a major foreign mission field, – and this is one of the neediest in the world, and only one day's drive from our well established churches in Ontario.'[54]

The report recommended that the Mennonite Board of Missions and Chari-ties take over responsibility for a mission in Quebec, which would begin with door-to-door selling of Bibles, tract distribution, and personal evange-lism work. A chapel or meeting house was envisioned 'after there are enough believers to require a special meeting place.' The mission board in Elkhart was also warned that any mission worker must have 'a knowledge of or commitment to learn the language, culture, life, mentality of the French Canadian, and readiness to adapt to it in his work.' There must be 'readiness to build indigenous, French Canadian churches, that may be different than the pattern of church life known by the worker, yet follow the pattern of New Testament Church in life and doctrine.'[55] The Elkhart-based board agreed to take responsibility for a new mission in Quebec but treated the venture as an 'Overseas Mission.' The Mennonite Conference of Ontario, however, retained a strong interest, and the earliest Mennonite mission work-ers came from Ontario. The first two couples sent as mission workers to Quebec were Harold and Pauline Reesor and Tilman and Janet Martin. The Reesors attended some preparatory French classes in Bible institutes in Con-necticut and France, but both couples also took additional instruction in a French-language Bible institute in Longueuil, near Montreal. When the Martins found that the Bible institute used mostly English, they enrolled for summer courses at l'Université de Montréal.

It became necessary to obtain a charter because only officially recognized churches in Quebec were able to keep, and where necessary provide, vital statistics about births, marriages, and deaths of members. An organized church program, with a building, was begun in October 1961. Almost all the converts, however, were described later by Janet Martin as troubled people with very little education.[56] That was also the impression gained by the sec-retary of the Elkhart board when he visited Quebec. He thought that the mission workers had 'found an entré to people who are on the lower levels as we usually do in our city programs, so they have alcoholics and neurotics and the type of people that have quite severe problems.'[57]

The mission suffered a serious schism late in 1961 when many of the young people became involved in an 'End Times Movement.'[58] That incident, and more general concern about whether the missionaries really understood the

French culture and mind and were focusing their efforts on the appropriate social and economic level, prompted the mission board in Elkhart to ask one of its most distinguished scholars, John Howard Yoder, to visit Quebec and prepare a more detailed report on the work done there. Yoder observed:

The Montreal work suffered a serious setback around last Christmas, when a number of members, including some whom Tilman was hoping he could count on for leadership responsibility, fell away from the group in a series of crisis experiences which were extremely painful for the Martins ... The Martins have done a very good job of becoming acquainted and understanding their people. The initial contacts were not with upper class people, but neither were they exclusively with 'alcoholics and neurotics.' Both the excellent youth group and the bookstore work seem very likely to build bridges to a somewhat higher social group; so would the possibility of a kindergarten after the Bethel pattern, which Tilman is thinking about.[59]

In a separate memorandum Yoder also suggested that he, the workers, and members of the Ontario mission board saw a need 'for someone with a higher degree of both sociological and theological training. Tilman Martin is a Bible Institute graduate; Harold Reesor has less preparation than that.'[60]

The strength of the mission was that the first missionaries worked with the people over a period of many years. They established small, French-speaking mission churches in the Montreal suburbs of Montreal North and Joliette in 1957 and 1958, respectivaly. Later French missions were set up at Rawdon and in the northern mining community of Rouyn-Noranda, on the Ontario-Quebec border. English- and Spanish-speaking congregations were also created in Montreal. Membership had reached approximately 140 when the Mennonite Conference of Ontario changed its name to the Mennonite Conference of Ontario and Quebec, in recognition of these churches.[61]

In 1959, five years after the (Old) Mennonites made their first investigation regarding missionary opportunities in Quebec, the Mennonite Brethren launched a similar initiative. The resulting report, written by Henry Warkentin for the Canada Inland Mission of the Canadian Mennonite Brethren Conference, was pessimistic. 'The French Canadians,' Warkentin reported, 'are not very aggressive and are soon content with the status quo.'[62]

Two factors contributed to a much more positive assessment of MB missionary prospects in Quebec. The first was expulsion or flight of all the MB missionaries from the Belgian Congo, renamed Zaire after independence. These people had worked in a country where French was the official language. Many had studied French at a small evangelical Bible institute in Lennoxville, Quebec, and had some familiarity with conditions in the province. Temporary closing of the missions in Zaire encouraged several returnees to seek new fields of service in other French-speaking countries. Some went to France; others became interested in Quebec.

The second decisive factor was the upheaval often referred to as Quebec's Quiet Revolution. After Premier Maurice Duplessis died and the authoritarian and repressive regime of his Union Nationale was overthrown in 1960 by Jean Lesage and the Liberal party many other changes quickly followed. The influence and authority of the Roman Catholic church, which had been closely associated with the discredited former government, were broken. There was a much greater openness to all kinds of change, including in religious practices. Pope John XXIII and the Second Vatican Council contributed greatly to that openness.

The first MB missionaries in Quebec were Ernest and Lydia Dyck, who had served for almost a decade in the Congo and were sent to Quebec in August 1961.[63] After some preliminary investigation it was decided to begin the first MB mission in St Jerôme, about 30 miles north of Montreal.

Two factors accounted for this choice. First, St Jerôme was one of only a few communities in Quebec that permitted evangelical broadcasts on the local radio station. Second, it was only about 30 miles from the small (Old) Mennonite mission station, and there was initially considerable cooperation between the two groups. Almost immediately they worked together to obtain provincial charters. They compiled background information on the Mennonites, including evidence showing that they were not associated with the hated Jehovah's Witnesses, who had for many years been banned in Quebec. They also split related legal costs.[64]

The attitudes of the missionaries and of some early converts sometimes showed an abysmal ignorance of Quebec history. The lead article in an issue of the *Mennonite Brethren Herald* in 1984, which carried a series of articles on the Quebec MB churches when they were being organized into a separate, provincial MB conference, began: 'To most people it may seem as though Quebec had never heard the Gospel until the end of the 1950s.' It dismissed the large Protestant minority in the province as 'conventional Protestants whom nobody bothered about.'[65] Twentieth-century Mennonites may not have agreed with some aspects of the Gospel brought to New France at tremendous sacrifice and widely publicized martyrdoms by Roman Catholic orders, and they may have found the impressive accomplishments of Quebec's Protestants irrelevant to their narrowly defined evangelical missionary concerns, but anyone familiar with the history of Quebec cannot help but wince at some of the

things that early Mennonite missionaries said and wrote. That ignorance, however, complemented the disillusionment and sense of rootlessness felt by many
in Quebec whose way of life had been uprooted by the Quiet Revolution.

Ernest and Lydia Dyck were joined by Clyde and Elizabeth Shannon,
also returned Congo missionaries, in 1962 when a new mission was opened
in the town of Ste Thérèse. During the first years much of the work was
related to an evangelical radio broadcast that originated in Switzerland but
was rebroadcast over the St Jerôme radio station, with funding coming from
the Canadian MB youth organization. Bible studies and worship services in
the homes of the missionaries were announced on the broadcasts, and the
missionaries responded to letters and phone calls from listeners who wanted
more information. Sunday school and small Bible study classes were organized, literature was distributed, occasionally permits were obtained to hold
street meetings in the town, and a major evangelization initiative called 'Operation Mobilization' was launched after those involved had taken a course
on 'Soul Winning.'

Several MB schoolteachers from other parts of Canada were encouraged
to take positions in Quebec schools near the new MB missions. That made it
possible to organize the first MB church in Quebec on 25 October 1964. It
included both the St Jerôme and Ste Thérèse groups and had a membership
of eighteen, eight of whom were Québécois. Several other former missionaries from the Congo went to Quebec in the 1960s, but a few returned to
Zaire when that again became possible.

The groups at both St Jerôme and Ste Thérèse quickly grew to a size where
the homes rented to house the missionaries and for worship and Bible study
proved too small. As a result, a new facility was built at St Jerôme in 1963–4,
and another at Ste Thérèse a few years later. Another small MB church was
planted at St Laurent in 1969. Others were added in the 1970s until, in 1983,
there were 11, with a total membership of 567.[66]

In the later 1960s, and particularly in the 1970s, the Mennonite Brethren
tried to emulate the 'saturation advertising' methods then popular with
American advertising firms. 'Saturation evangelism,' involved radio broadcasts, Sunday schools, Bible studies, summer camps, literature distribution,
a special evangelical column in the local newspaper, street meetings, evangelistic crusades and campaigns, and door-to-door, person-to-person, hospital, and jail visitations. The objective was to saturate carefully selected communities with the Gospel message as it was understood by MB missionaries.

These efforts were initiated by the Mennonite Brethren Board of Evangelism, but success depended on participation by members and leaders in Quebec. Saturation evangelism brought in significant numbers of people, but it

also created considerable instability in the new churches. An MB Bible school teacher offered the following explanation:

In many cases there is greater zeal for evangelism in Quebec, greater zeal for asking the question, 'What does the Lord want me to do?' But on the other hand, I find a more rooted, mature and stable Christian mindset, that can give long-term life to the church, in the west ... Many young Christians have a very subjective view of how God works and will say with great conviction, 'the Lord revealed this to me' or 'the Lord said that.' In a couple of weeks the Lord may have revealed something exactly opposite, however, so they are having difficulties distinguishing between the voice of the Lord and the voice of their impulses.[67]

That instability was particularly evident in patterns of leadership. In the early years the missionaries, and most notably Ernest and Lydia Dyck, were clearly dominant, but efforts were made to involve French-Canadian converts as soon as possible. Many of the converts with unhappy memories of the influence of Catholic clergy reacted negatively to autocratic church leadership. But most needed considerable guidance before they could provide effective leadership themselves. Some were strongly encouraged to attend the Mennonite Brethren Bible College in Winnipeg or similar institutions. In 1976 the Mennonite Brethren established the Institut Biblique Laval to train prospective leaders.

The most impressive growth in Quebec came in the 1970s and 1980s. In 1970 there were three MB churches in the province. The one at St Jérôme, organized in 1964, had 36 members; the one at Ste Thérèse, launched in 1968 as a separate church, had 27; and a small group that had organized a church at St Laurent in 1969 had eight.[68]

The commitment of these converts to distinctive Mennonite-Anabaptist doctrines was mixed, as one teacher candidly admitted: 'There are two trends. Some aren't interested in labels. They simply want to be known as evangelical Christians. They have had enough of labels. Others identify very strongly with the Mennonite Brethren conference. As time has passed some have come to the consciousness, it is the Mennonite Brethren church that brought me the gospel, that started the Bible school, that supplied funds for evangelism, church planting, and encourages us in our faith and receives us with open arms when we go to conferences.'[69]

A curious aspect of the Quebec story is the lack of continued cooperation between the (Old) Mennonite and MB missions and churches. After close collaboration in their search for official recognition and charters, the two groups went their own, often parallel ways. Apparently Canadian Mennonites could work together when dealing with governments, or when organizing and providing relief, but not in missionary work and church planting. 'In Quebec,' one of those involved noted, 'the evangelical church in general is reproducing the historical divisions that have existed elsewhere. That's sad.'[70]

SERVICE AND MISSION IN NEWFOUNDLAND AND THE MARITIMES

Mennonite home mission programs were similar to the voluntary service programs sponsored by the Mennonite Central Committee (MCC). Both encouraged people with professional skills to move into new communities. In voluntary service projects, however, no church planters or evangelists were involved. The objective was not to begin new churches but simply to help local people with some of their problems. Home mission ventures emphasized direct evangelism and visualized establishment of new churches. Nowhere were these divergent strategies more obvious than in the Atlantic provinces.

The MCC's voluntary programs in Newfoundland have been discussed above. The Mennonite Brethren, however, had reservations about that approach, and in 1960 they launched their own parallel Christian Service program. The MB program also encouraged young people, particularly those trained as teachers or health-care workers, to spend two or three years in voluntary service. These volunteers, however, were to work closely with church planters. The objective was to set up new churches, and the Halifax-Dartmouth area of Nova Scotia became the first Atlantic missions and service field. By 1969 12 MB couples and eight single people had obtained short-term employment there. After some early instability a small church was established.

In the 1960s other Mennonites also moved to the Maritimes, simply to follow farming or professional opportunities. Peter and Justina Penner moved to Sackville, New Brunswick, where Peter accepted an academic appointment at Mount Allison University. The Penners, former MB home missionaries, quickly became active in the local United Church but also contacted other Mennonites living in the Maritimes. They wanted to provide opportunities for people of Mennonite background to meet for a time of fellowship and edification. This group, unlike some MB church planters, had a strong Anabaptist-Mennonite orientation, and it went on record stating that future planting in the Maritimes should be done in consultation with other Mennonite denominations. Peter Penner stated categorically: 'if the Anabaptist-Mennonite movement is to mean anything in this traditional and oldest area of the country, Mennonite Brethren will have to come to terms with the healthy mix of Mennonites now current in the Maritimes.'[71] That advice was not heeded, and an influx in the 1980s threatened to replicate denominational divisions prevalent in other parts of the country. Arrivals included some Church of God in Christ, Mennonite farmers who bought marginal land in order to build a traditional Mennonite community, those active in the Mennonites of the Atlantic Provinces who hoped to bring a distinctive Anabaptist witness to the area without establishing new churches, and MB church planters interested in evangelism and either indifferent or hostile to historic beliefs and practices.

RADIO MINISTRIES

Radio was regarded as an instrument of worldly entertainment by many Canadian Mennonites in 1939. But rules against purchase of a radio were difficult to enforce. Farmers said that they needed it to obtain information on agricultural commodity prices. Others, including leaders involved in wartime negotiations with the government, felt a need to keep up to date with the latest war news, and those with close relatives in the Soviet Union followed news there with great interest. Radio came to be tolerated in all but the most traditional homes.

There was another reason for the acceptance of radio. Evangelists and radio preachers such as Theodore Epp, Charles Fuller, and William Aberhart had demonstrated the effectiveness of radio as a means to proclaim the Gospel. In the United States a cautious Mennonite radio broadcast was begun in 1936 by William Detweiller, a minister in Smithville, Ohio. In Canada the first Mennonite radio broadcasts were aired in 1940; in Kitchener Harold Scheidel, a lay person, offered a musical program by a 'Nightingale Chorus.' Scheidel's initiative has been described thus: 'In addition to his regular daytime job as a coal deliverer, Harold [Scheidel] also became well known as formulator and conductor of the Nightingale Chorus ... His group was composed of vocalists from various area churches and singing schools. This choir was noted for its weekly broadcast on a Kitchener radio station during six months of the years 1940–1950.'[72]

The radio program was intended primarily for shut-ins. The response was sufficiently encouraging that C.F. Derstine, pastor of First Mennonite Church, provided leadership in additional radio broadcasts, which in 1945 came under official sponsorship of the Mennonite Conference of Ontario. The 'Mennonite Hour' was produced locally and used live music provided by local groups.[73]

In Saskatchewan the first Mennonite broadcast went on the air on 21 October 1940. It was a project of the MB city mission in Saskatoon, where there were unusually favourable circumstances for religious broadcasts. In the early days of Canadian broadcasting churches and religious organizations were granted licences to operate small radio stations, but in the 1930s Saskatoon's first commercial radio station, CFQC, was able to eliminate all rivals. In order to keep prospective rivals at bay, and also because of a strong personal commitment to religious broadcasting by the owners, CFQC carried a great deal of religious material at very reasonable cost.[74] Missionary H.S. Rempel thought that a short Mennonite radio broadcast that would cost $10 for 15 minutes was an enormous undertaking, but the young people were so enthusiastic that he was always able to meet those obligations.[75]

Both Conference of Mennonites in Manitoba and the Mennonite Brethren in Winnipeg also went on the air in the 1940s, and by 1952 Mennonites were airing nine programs in western Canada – five in Saskatchewan, two in Manitoba, and one each in Alberta and British Columbia. General Conference groups and the Mennonite Brethren each had four programs. The ninth was sponsored by the Evangelical Mennonite Brethren.[76]

Mennonites produced many of their own broadcasts but also supported some produced by others. They regarded the broadcasts as another means to preach the Gospel to those they were trying to reach through home missions. But from the beginning it was clear that almost all listeners were Mennonite church members. Shut-ins had specifically been targeted by the first Ontario broadcasts and quickly became an important constituency. Parallel German and English broadcasts tacitly acknowledged that much of the support came from Mennonite listeners, though there was always a suggestion that other German speakers could also be reached through the German-language broadcasts. The large western Canadian conferences also prepared and broadcast Gospel programs in Low German to reach members of traditional Mennonite groups.

CONCLUSION

Ambiguities about the audience, and hence the real impact of radio broadcasts, raise fundamental questions about the level of support and the impact of Mennonite home missions. The rhetoric suggests a strong commitment to evangelism, but there was only limited direct participation in the projects. It was clearly in bad taste to question or criticize those promoting aggressive evangelization programs. But if one reads congregational histories and personal reminiscences it is hard to avoid the conclusion that only a small minority of Canada's Mennonites participated in door-to-door or person-to-person evangelism. Few ordinary church members took time to distribute tracts or other religious literature, to participate in street meetings, or to do the other things involved in saturation evangelism.

Mennonites in Canada were more likely to look to their churches as places of worship and fellowship. They sought friendship, serenity, inspiration, and also counsel and guidance when facing difficult personal and family problems, or health crisis and bereavement. The church was the place where they could celebrate decisive events – marriages, funerals, communion, and child dedication – and, more generally, where they could get support as they tried to apply in their daily lives the teachings of scripture. Some who financially supported home missions would have felt uneasy, and others would have been acutely embarrassed, if they had ever been called on to accompany workers and to participate in their everyday activities. Many Mennonites apparently thought such methods appropriate when missionaries dealt with impoverished, backward, poorly educated people who were far away. But it was not how they normally dealt with people they encountered in their own work.

These differing approaches were in part due to a sharp divergence of missionary strategies and to patterns of acculturation. Canadian Mennonites were generally upwardly mobile, but missions were usually designed for the poor, the shiftless, the underprivileged, and the disadvantaged. Concern about, and help for, impoverished and oppressed people who might disrupt the established order has always been fashionable among Canadian elites. It has not, however, been fashionable to bring such people into direct fellowship or into relationships of equality unless they also accept the religious and cultural values and practices of the elite.

Home mission programs were, for many years, conducted 'at arm's length.' Once that was no longer possible, two distinct responses emerged. There were some – most notably, the CMC missionaries to the Natives – who sought to become servants, to 'walk in the shoes,' and to accept and carry the burdens of those whom they sought to serve. Others accepted the upwardly mobile ideology of North American evangelicals. Converts were not only expected to accept the gospel of salvation from sin but were also encouraged to embrace materialistic ideologies and practices that would lead to economic and social success. Such people found the methods and style of upwardly mobile pietist/evangelical/fundamentalist movements particularly attractive. Home missions thus facilitated integration of some Canadian Mennonites into that stream of American life, while it alienated others from it. The strong but short communitarian tether was lengthened by home mission experiences, but various groups tended to pull in different directions.

15
Mission to the World

Canada's Mennonites experienced much change in the second half of the twentieth century. They tried to resist unfamiliar outside influences and to protect old customs and practices. That, however, did not prevent the majority from supporting aggressive and intrusive missionary activities overseas, the stated intent of which was to change radically the lives of other people. Missionaries were messengers and proponents of Christianity, Western civilization, progress, modern science, and technology, as North Americans and Europeans knew and understood them.

Conditions and opportunities for missionary work, however, changed radically during and after the Second World War. People who went out before the war expected to be engaged in grim confrontations with 'dark heathenism, idolatry, fear of ghosts and spirits, superstition, sorcery, uncertainty, great poverty, and stubborn resistance.'[1] But they were confident that, with God's help, they would prevail. Impressive mission compounds, dominated by white missionaries and assisted by Native converts, became islands of Western, Christian civilization in vast oceans of heathendom.

Some churches in Canada regarded missionary successes overseas 'as a measurement of their vigour and wealth, and the growing number of missionaries and especially converts was regarded as evidence of the truth and efficacy of Christianity.'[2] Large collections taken at their annual harvest thanksgiving and missions festivals, and the number of missionaries sent or supported by Mennonite congregations and conferences, were celebrated as manifestations of faithful Christian life and witness.

The war and postwar developments made the old style of missionary work more difficult and, in the opinion of many, inappropriate. Authority in the mission churches was transferred to local leaders, and those churches were expected to become financially self-supporting. The role of the missionary changed drastically. One of the most influential and controversial Mennonite mission administrators described those changes: 'Today he [the missionary] is a guest in the country where he serves. In the church, he no longer can be the superior. He must find his place within the church as an equal and a brother. This means he must be willing to work under the direction of African church leaders. He must be willing to step aside when his foreignness is a hindrance. And he must respect the national and cultural aspirations of the people. His task is not to import a foreign culture. He must plant the gospel in the local soil and let it take root there.'[3]

The most significant changes occurred overseas, but they did not leave supporters at home unaffected. There were frequent declarations that missions were the most important responsibility of the churches, and those churches could not remain unaffected when the whole overseas missionary enterprise underwent changes so drastic that one Mennonite writer called it 'the transfiguration of mission' and others referred to it as 'the crisis of missions' or even the end of the missionary era.[4]

The effects of this crisis, and the response to it by Canadian Mennonites, were diverse. They led some to rediscovery and reaffirmation of their Anabaptist heritage, while others were drawn closer to the methods and ideology of other evangelical churches. The crisis thus added more complexity to the changes sweeping congregations after 1939.

A MISSIONARY OF THE OLD SCHOOL

Susie Brucks personified, and in her autobiography described and explained, many aspects of the old missionary life. She was, first of all, a woman in an enterprise that attracted a disproportionate number of women:[5] 'Women have comprised the vast majority of the missionaries, both on the old-line Protestant denominational boards and in the twentieth-century evangelical missionary enterprise. Throughout the history of modern missions, women have been more strongly attracted than men to the challenge of sharing the gospel worldwide, especially with other women.'[6] Brucks's education was also quite typical. In the 1930s she attended the Coaldale Bible School and Prairie Bible Institute, both in Alberta, and then took a short medical course, almost certainly at the Missionary Medical Institute in Toronto,[7] before being sent overseas.

Brucks, like many other missionaries, also felt that she had received an explicit call from God. One day in 1934, after a long, hot, and exhausting day of hoeing and thinning sugar beets at Coaldale, she felt an urge to kneel down in the middle of the field to pray. While in prayer she believed that she heard clearly God's call that she become a missionary, but to confirm that the call was really from God she asked for a specific sign. She would become a missionary if, at the next Sunday morning church service, the preacher would base his sermon on the text from Mark 16:15: 'Go ye into all the world, and preach the gospel to every creature.' The preacher did, and after that Susie told her home congregation of the call and waited patiently for further developments. Five years later the Africa Mission Society invited her to serve in its programs. She left for the Belgian Congo early in 1944.

Her attitudes toward the Natives were also quite common among missionaries of that time. She believed that the people she had gone to serve, instruct, and enlighten lived in dark heathenism, idolatry, superstition, sorcery, and constant fear of evil spirits and the ghosts of ancestors and slain enemies. Resistance or failure to respond to her invitation to be saved was attributed to the devil, not to cultural differences or misunderstandings. And all success, such as recovery from illness or a serious injury, was immediately and directly attributed to God. She believed that 'heathen faiths' stood in direct conflict with Christianity and that it was wrong to make any modification of Christianity in response to Native religious beliefs and practices.[8]

As a person with some education and rudimentary medical training Brucks also became a messenger and proponent of Western civilization, progress, science, and technology, which in her mind were virtually inseparable from Christianity. Her methods were simple and direct. In her memoirs she tells of a childbirth in which she assisted shortly after her arrival. The mother had been in labour for three days, was exhausted, and was seriously dehydrated but surrounded by other women and Native healers. First, all the other people were ordered to leave the hut. Then Brucks knelt down to pray – a necessary preliminary in her practice for any treatment. Native culture, which dictated that the mother not drink any water during childbirth lest the child drown, was dismissed as unfounded superstition. The woman was persuaded to drink water, and after that mother and missionary coordinated their efforts and a healthy child was born. The God of the missionary was given all the credit for this happy outcome, and many more people in need of medical help came to the missionary.[9] They naturally not only received the help they sought but were also told about Jesus and God's plan of salvation as Susie Brucks understood it.

Brucks, and many other missionaries, would have been perplexed at any criticism that they were insensitive to Native cultures, spiritual values, and social practices. She made no clear distinction between Western practices and her understanding of Christianity. She thought it important, for example, that when the Natives prayed they kneel, bow the head, close their eyes, fold their hands, and then repeat the appropriate words as taught by the mission-ary.[10] After they were 'saved,' the new believers were expected to accept Christian adult baptism, join a church organized in a manner familiar to the missionary, sing translated North American gospel songs and choruses, and often also to dress and eat in Western fashion. The result, of course, was serious disruption of traditional social and cultural structures.

When the missionaries fled the Congo in July 1960 Susie Brucks returned to Canada, and the Mennonite Brethren Board of Foreign Missions terminated her service. That was a great disappointment, but she made contact with World Wide Missions and went back to the Congo to work in an orphanage in 1962. She had to raise the money for her passage and living costs, but an appearance on an American radio program where she told her story brought in enough donations to cover the costs. She was a foot-soldier in the 'army of Christian adventurers going into all lands, and proclaiming under King Jesus a war against sin and idolatry.'[11]

ORIGINS AND WARTIME DISRUPTIONS

North American Mennonites came to the foreign missionary enterprise later than many other Christian denominations and only after being involved for some time in 'home' missions and charities. Their first overseas missionaries were sent out only in the late 1890s, but enthusiasm and support for missions increased greatly in the first half of the twentieth century. In September 1939 there were approximately 150 missionaries serving overseas under the auspices of 11 North American Mennonite mission boards, while perhaps another 50 served with non-Mennonite mission boards or in 'faith missions' where they were responsible for soliciting funds to support the project.[12]

The main overseas Mennonite mission fields in 1939 were in India, the Congo, China, and Argentina. Several conferences also had small mission programs in other African countries adjacent to the Congo; others had workers in Mennonite communities in Mexico and Paraguay. In China and the Congo, Mennonite missionaries worked for inter-Mennonite missionary organizations.[13] In most countries each conference had a geographically separate field, but the missionaries, of whom there were at least 141 in 1939, met in annual conferences.[14] Table 15.1 shows the mission fields that were active in 1939.

While these statistics are impressive, they are also misleading with regard to Canadian participation. There was growing interest from the three largest conferences, and from several of the smaller ones, but only few Canadian Mennonites were serving overseas before 1939. The offices of the mission boards of the three largest North American conferences were all in the United

Table 15.1
Mennonite foreign missions, 1939

Name of agency	Date board established	Field	Date mission started	No. of mission-aries
General Conference of Mennonites[15] (Commission on Overseas Missions)	1872	India Congo China	1900 1912 1914	26 13 21
Mennonite Brethren[16] (Board of Foreign Missions)	1878	India China Paraguay	1899 1919 1935	25 7 3
Mennonite Church[17] (Mennonite Board of Missions and Charities)	1882	India Argentina	1899 1917	32 23
Brethren in Christ[18]	1895	Rhodesia India	1898 1904	
China Mennonite Missionary Society (Inter-Menn)	1905	China[19]	1905	17
Mennonite Mission Board of Pacific Conference	1906			
Congo Inland Mission (Africa Inter-Mennonite Mission)	1911	Congo[20]	1912	
Eastern Mennonite (Board of Missions)[21]	1914	Tanganyika	1934	
Virginia Mennonite Board of Missions (U.S.)	1919			
Church of God in Christ, Mennonite[22]	1933	Mexico	1933	4
Evangelical Mennonite Brethren	1936			
Evangelical Mennonite Church (U.S.)[23]	1937	Congo	1937	2
Rudnerweider Mennonite Church[24]	1938			

States. They sought support for their mission programs in both countries, but only the Mennonite Brethren in Christ and the Mennonite Board of Missions and Charities (MBMC) of the Mennonite Church readily appointed Canadians as overseas missionaries before 1939.

The first Canadian-born Mennonite missionaries to serve overseas of whom a record is still available were members of the Mennonite Brethren in Christ church. William Shantz, a native of Mannheim, Ontario, went to China in 1895.[25] In 1905 the Mennonite Brethren in Christ organized a new missionary society for work in Africa, in which A.W. Banfield, a native of Quebec, served as field superintendent.[26] The Mennonite Brethren in Christ, however, were rapidly losing their Mennonite identity and in 1947 changed their name to United Missionary Church. With the change went many distinctive Mennonite and Anabaptist doctrines and practices, making the identity of this group problematic.

The first (Old) Mennonite missionary from Canada to serve overseas was Vera Hallman, a native of Roseville, Ontario. She studied at the Toronto Bible School and at the Hesston Academy in Kansas and then served with a Mennonite Mission in Youngstown, Ohio, before being sent overseas in 1923 to serve in the Argentine Mennonite Mission, which had been started in 1917.[27] Hallman returned to Canada on furlough in 1929. Illness, family responsibilities, and marriage to Abram Hunsberger prevented return to Argentina, but after the death of her husband she served several years in Puerto Rico.

Vera Hallman was joined in Argentina by two (Old) Mennonite Canadian missionary couples, Amos and Edna Swartzentruber and Nelson and Ada Litwiller. All four had been at the Bethany Biblical Seminary operated by the Church of the Brethren in Chicago. The Swartzentrubers had also studied at the Ontario Mennonite Bible School. The Swartzentrubers began their missionary service in 1923 in Youngstown, Ohio. Early in 1924 they left for Argentina. They served in that country, and briefly as replacements for other church workers in Uruguay, for 39 years. The Litwillers followed a year later, serving in Argentina from 1924 until 1956, when Nelson became founding president of the Seminario Evangelico Menonita de Teologia in Montevideo, Uruguay.[28]

Other (Old) Mennonite missionaries from Canada who were sent overseas under the auspices of the Mennonite Board of Missions and Charities included Elvin and Mary Snyder, who went to Argentina in 1928; Lewis and Edna Weber, who also went to Argentina but in 1931; Simeon and Edna Hurst, who were sent to Tanganyika in 1940; and Una Cressmen, who went to Argentina in 1940. Two early (Old) Mennonite missionaries from Canada, Nancy Ramseyer and Alice Bachert, went in 1923 and 1930 to India and Costa Rica respectively, but they served under non-Mennonite boards. Nancy Ramseyer died of acute appendicitis within a year of her departure from Canada. Alice Bachert, a nurse-midwife, later moved from Costa Rica to Colombia, where she worked for a time with the Mennonite Mission.[29]

The Argentine Mennonite Mission remained, throughout the pre-1939 period, the primary focus of missionary interest among Canadian (Old) Mennonites,[30] even though the MBMC made few distinctions between missionaries from Canada and those from the United States. Most of these missionaries had Bible school training, followed by more advanced education at a U.S. church college. By 1940 Goshen College and Eastern Mennonite College were the preferred training centres for prospective Swiss Mennonite missionaries. The offices of the MBMC were in Elkhart, Indiana.

Prospective Mennonite Brethren (MB) missionaries from Canada and their supporters encountered greater difficulties than did their Swiss Mennonite counterparts when dealing with a U.S. denominational mission board. In the 1930s these problems boiled over in a major controversy, which pitted Canadian Mennonite Brethren who had emigrated from the Soviet Union in the 1920s (Russlaender) against the MB Board of Foreign Missions in Hillsboro, Kansas. Much of the difficulty was related to Henry and Anna Bartsch, who applied to the board in Hillsboro in 1931. They, and at least one other Canadian missionary couple, were accepted after lengthy delays but then waited for years without receiving any assignment.

The Bartsches eventually decided to go to the Congo on their own, thus becoming the first Canadian MB missionaries to serve overseas. They and their supporters were convinced that the MB Board of Foreign Missions in Hillsboro discriminated against Canadian applicants, particularly Russlaender.[31] The Mission Board, however, was concerned about the allegedly inadequate education of many prospective missionary candidates. Board members believed high school and some college training to be essential, but the Canadian applicants had attended only elementary and Bible schools. The Canadians did not think it necessary to complete high school, and certainly not to go to college for three or four years, if they were going out to proclaim the Gospel to illiterate and backward peoples. They could not, in any case, afford such training even if they had considered it necessary.

When the Bartsches arrived in the Congo they joined the Aron E. Janzen family, MB missionaries from Minnesota, who had established a mission at Kafumba. The Janzens were then working under the auspices of the Congo Inland Mission, not the MB Board of Foreign Missions. Personality conflicts, uneasiness about Janzen's charismatic style, and a vision to go into a remote region where the Gospel had never been preached prompted the Bartsches to leave Kafumba after a few years and to travel some 300 miles into the interior to begin a new mission program at Bololo. Most of the other missionaries at Kafumba decided to accompany the Bartsches, leaving the station understaffed and creating much tension and ill will.[32]

The Bartsches obtained only limited support from some students at the Winkler Bible School and from a special support committee, the Afrika Missions Verein, organized by H.H. Janzen of Waterloo. Both the Winkler Bible School and the Verein were founded by immigrants of the 1920s and reflected their ambitions and dynamism. The Verein was also viewed in Hillsboro as an independent Canadian MB Missions Board operating in competition with Hillsboro. It reflected dissatisfaction in MB churches in Canada at the failure of the board in Hillsboro to send and support Canadian overseas missionaries.[33] These tensions gave a unique sense of identity to Canadian Mennonite Brethren,[34] which strongly influenced their determination to set up their own missionary training college in Canada, the Mennonite Brethren Bible College.

The pre-war situation in the General Conference (GC) was less turbulent, but only because there was not as much pressure from the recently arrived Canadians. No Canadian was sent to any overseas mission by the GC Board of Overseas Missions until Anne Penner of Rosenfeld, Manitoba, went to India in 1946.[35]

In the Evangelical Mennonite Conference (EMC, formerly the Kleine Gemeinde) the awakening of interest in overseas missions is usually traced to the Steinbach Bible Academy after its reorganization in 1938. The EMC organized its own mission board in 1952. Before that EMC missionaries were encouraged to serve overseas under other mission boards, but none did so before 1939.[36]

The Evangelical Mennonite Mission Conference (EMMC, formerly the Rudnerweider Gemeinde) had a strong interest in overseas missions from the time of its formation in 1937 but commissioned its first overseas missionary only in 1940. It too encouraged members to work under the auspices of other mission boards or to secure support in their home congregations and communities.[37]

The Brethren in Christ had several Canadian missionaries in their African missions, but their main mission office was also in the United States.[38] Their strong missionary interest, as well as their continuous participation in the Conference of Historic Peace Churches (CHPC), the Non Resistant Relief Organization (NRRO), and the Mennonite Central Committee (MCC), demonstrated their commitment to historic Anabaptist principles, which they shared with the Mennonite churches of Ontario in the 1940s. Indeed, the exigencies of war and the challenges of postwar relief and rehabilitation greatly strengthened their links with the Mennonites. That, however, was not the case for another Mennonite group with members in Ontario and the United States – the Mennonite Brethren in Christ. These Brethren developed an exceptionally strong missionary program but feared that identification with the Mennonite Church, its separatism, and its historic peace teachings would inhibit their missionary endeavours. So in 1947 they dropped the name and some of the distinctive doctrines of the Mennonites and became the Missionary Church.[39]

During the war years most of the Mennonite missions, other than those in China, continued their work with some disruptions. Contacts between missionaries and the congregations in North America became less frequent, and necessary supplies were difficult to obtain because of currency exchange restrictions and transportation disruptions. Missionaries returning to North America on furlough during the war experienced considerable difficulty when trying to return to their missions, and newly appointed missionaries faced serious delays and sometimes outright refusals when they applied for visas.[40]

In India concerns about visas and transportation were compounded by fears in the Mennonite Church and GC missions that there might be a Japanese invasion, as there had been in neighbouring countries. This led to a request by the Indian government that missionaries in the threatened regions return home. The MBMC was particularly hard hit by this decision, which resulted in the return in 1942 and 1943 of seven of the 20 missionaries on the field early in 1942.[41]

Invasion was not a threat in the Congo or in adjacent African countries, but transportation and visa difficulties also wrought havoc there. One of the most bizarre incidents in Mennonite mission history occurred in the Congo during the war. On 19 May 1940 members of the Karl Kramer family, working at the Bololo station, were interned by the government because they were German nationals. After the war, government officials invited the MB Board of Missions to apply for their release. But the board refused, and the Kramers remained in Congolese internment camps until 1949, when the Red Cross negotiated their freedom and repatriation to Germany. Bernhard Doerksen, who interviewed members of the Kramer family to gain a better understanding of the callous neglect they suffered at the hands of the MB Board of Foreign Missions, states that 'according to Annemarie Kramer, their neglect was directly related to the seldom-mentioned tensions that existed between the Kafumba and Bololo stations.'[42] The Kramers later moved to Canada, where they lived for years in poverty.[43]

Canadian Mennonites were of course kept informed about the missionary programs of their North American conferences, even though few Canadians served overseas in the 1940s.[44] Canadians and Americans alike found the events in China during and after the war particularly unsettling. The Japanese occupation made it necessary for GC missionaries in Hopei Province and Mennonite Brethren in Fukien province to withdraw, while the Mennonite Church had to postpone and eventually abandon its plans to establish a mission in China. The Krimmer Mennonite Brethren also had a mission in China, and some of their missionaries stayed and worked, albeit under severe restrictions, during the years of the Japanese occupation, until they were driven out by the communists.[45]

When they left during the war, the Mennonite missionaries in China believed that they would be able to return to their mission stations after the war. They hoped that constructive relief undertaken by American Mennonite Civilian Public Service (CPS) units or by the MCC would facilitate their return, but the communist revolution made that impossible, and in 1951 the last Mennonite missionaries from North America were forced to leave. Loss of the China missions was a great disappointment, but new opportunities elsewhere, notably in Japan and Taiwan, caught the attention of mission-minded North American Mennonites.

The most disconcerting developments of the war and immediate postwar years were not, except in China, disruptions caused by military action. The two most difficult issues that missionaries and mission administrators had to deal with had to do with the increased popularity of relief work and growing nationalism in formerly colonized lands.

MISSIONS, SERVICE, AND CHARITIES

Mennonite overseas missionary programs expanded dramatically after 1945. Canadians, who had been absent or seriously under-represented in pre-war missionary ventures, became equal partners with their U.S. fellow-believers during those years. A list of new Mennonite mission fields established between 1944 and 1975 provides an exceptional record of expansion (see Table 15.2).[46]

Expansion of existing mission fields, and opening up of many new ones, were exciting but fraught with difficulties. The war had unleashed sentiments, aspirations, and ideologies that made it necessary for missionaries, administrators, and supporters to change some of their earlier policies and practices.

One issue that greatly concerned mission administrators immediately after the war was the growing popularity of relief voluntary service programs. They strongly supported and endorsed the programs of the MCC but began to fear that relief activities would supplant missionary work. At its annual meeting in 1946 the MBMC noted with concern:

the large number of young people eager to undertake a relief task of a few years, compared to the few who are coming forward to give their lives to the missions cause, be it rural, city, home or foreign ... Our people have felt, and rightly so, that we cannot make our Christian claims and refuse to share our abundance. As a result our relief programs have steadily enlarged; giving for relief has mounted and young people are offering their lives for the relief of their suffering fellow men. This is commendable and right but we need to keep our vision clear. Giving physical relief is not the program of the church. The Great Commission makes clear the primary program of the church. We must be careful to observe here 'evangelical priority.'

Table 15.2
Mennonite mission fields established 1944–75

Date established	Country	Agency or conference
1944	Nigeria	Mennonite Brethren
1944	Brazil	Mennonite Brethren
1945	Colombia	Mennonite Brethren
1945	Puerto Rico	Mennonite Church
1945	Colombia	General Conference
1945	Dominican Republic	Missionary Church (MBinC)
1945	Sierra Leone	Missionary Church (MBinC)
1946	Dominican Republic	Evangelical Mennonite Church (U.S.)
1946	Peru	Mennonite Brethren
1948	Ethiopia	Eastern Mennonite
1949	Japan	Mennonite Church
1949	Jamaica	Missionary Church (MBinC)
1949	Italy	Virginia Mennonite
1950	Mexico	Mennonite Mission Board Pacific Coast
1950	Mexico	Mennonite Brethren
1950	Mexico	General Conference
1950	Paraguay	General Conference
1950	Honduras	Eastern Mennonite
1950	Japan	Mennonite Brethren
1950	Belgium	Mennonite Church
1951	Japan	General Conference
1951	Ethiopia	Mennonite Brethren
1951	Luxembourg	Eastern Mennonite
1952	Germany	Conservative Mennonite
1952	United Kingdom	Mennonite Church
1953	Japan	Brethren in Christ
1953	France	Eastern Mennonite
1953	Somalia	Eastern Mennonite
1953	Israel	Eastern Mennonite
1953	Ecuador	Mennonite Brethren
1953	Austria	Mennonite Brethren
1953	Germany	Mennonite Brethren
1953	Ghana	Mennonite Church
1953	Israel	Mennonite Church
1954	France	Mennonite Church
1954	Uruguay	Mennonite Church
1954	Mexico	Evangelical Mennonite Conference
1954	Taiwan	General Conference
1954	Brazil	Mennonite Church
1955	Jamaica	Virginia Mennonite
1955	France	Eastern Mennonite
1956	Uruguay	General Conference
1956	Puerto Rico	Mennonite Broadcasts Inc.

(Continued on next page)

Table 15.2 (*continued*)

Date established	Country	Agency or conference
1957	Italy	Mennonite Broadcasts Inc.
1957	Algeria	Mennonite Church
1957	Nepal	Mennonite Church
1957	Vietnam	Eastern Mennonite
1958	Mexico	Franconia Mennonite Conference
1958	Panama	Mennonite Brethren
1959	Paraguay	Evang. Menn. Conference
1959	Nigeria	Mennonite Church
1960	Haiti	Church of God in Christ, Mennonite
1960	British Honduras/Belize	Eastern Mennonite
1962	Costa Rica	Conservative Mennonite
1962	Switzerland	Mennonite Broadcasts Inc.
1963	Nigeria	Church of God in Christ, Mennonite
1963	Belgium	Mennonite Broadcasts Inc.
1964	Kenya	Eastern Mennonite
1965	Hong Kong	Eastern Mennonite
1965	Nicaragua	Brethren in Christ
1966	Haiti	Church of God in Christ, Mennonite
1966	Uruguay	Mennonite Brethren
1966	Peru	Mennonite Church
1966	Nicaragua	Evangelical Mennonite Conference
1967	Guatemala	Eastern Mennonite
1968	Nicaragua	Conservative Mennonite
1968	South Korea	Evangelical Mennonite Church (U.S.)
1968	Guatemala	Eastern Mennonite
1968	Haiti	Eastern Mennonite
1968	Afghanistan	Mennonite Brethren
1969	Nepal	Mennonite Brethren
1970	Taiwan	Evangelical Mennonite Church (U.S.)
1970	Paraguay	Mennonite Church
1971	Ghana	Mennonite Brethren
1971	Trinidad and Tobago	Virginia Mennonite
1971	Philippines	Eastern Mennonite
1971	Swaziland	Eastern Mennonite
1971	Yugoslavia	Eastern Mennonite
1972	Bolivia	General Conference
1972	Lesotho	Africa Inter Mennonite
1972	Lesotho	Evangelical Mennonite Church (U.S.)
1973	Lesotho	General Conference
1974	Bolivia	General Conference
1974	Botswana	General Conference
1974	Bangladesh	Mennonite Brethren
1974	Cameroon	Mennonite Brethren
1974	Japan	Evangelical Mennonite Church (U.S.)

Table 15.2 (*concluded*)

Date established	Country	Agency or conference
1974	Zambia	Eastern Mennonite
1974	Philippines	Church of God in Christ, Mennonite
1975	Upper Volta	Church of God in Christ, Mennonite
1975	Germany	Evangelical Mennonite Conference
1975	Afghanistan	Mennonite Church
1975	Zaire	Mennonite Church
1975	Botswana	Africa Inter Mennonite
1975	Brazil	General Conference
1975	Indonesia	Mennonite Brethren
1975	Liberia	Mennonite Brethren
1976	Dominican Republic	Church of God in Christ, Mennonite
1976	Guatemala	Church of God in Christ, Mennonite

One may still say it ... perhaps it should be said more loudly now than ever before ... that it is more important to save a man's soul than his body. The relief program of the church must be subordinated under the evangelistic program and must be integrated as completely as possible into it. As soon as a relief program begins to be an end in itself, the evangelical position of the church is threatened, for the proclamation of the Good News of salvation is still and always the program of the church.[47]

The early Mennonite mission programs had almost all begun as relief efforts. In the case of India, news of drought and widespread famine in 1897 and again in 1898 had prompted Mennonites in Russia and the United States to work together in the gathering and sending of several shiploads of corn and other foodstuffs and relief supplies to India. Then, as they became more familiar with conditions there, Mennonites became more and more interested in 'the spiritual need of these benighted people,'[48] and each group decided to send missionaries to them. Thus a joint or cooperative Mennonite relief effort resulted in establishment of three separate mission programs at the turn of the century, even though the denominational distinctions were irrelevant to the Indian people.

There were confident expectations that the cooperative relief work done through the MCC in the 1940s would also prepare the way for denominational missions. MCC, as an inter-Mennonite agency, was never expected to proselytize on behalf of any supporting church. In postwar Europe MCC workers conducted religious services, but baptisms and other matters pertaining to church membership were turned over to ministers from supporting conferences who were given access to MCC-administered refugee camps.

That sometimes resulted in unfortunate competition, but the camps were transitory. More difficult problems arose as mission boards took over inter-Mennonite relief programs.

The best example of a successful transition occurred in Puerto Rico. During the war an American Mennonite Civilian Public Service (CPS) unit was established at La Plata to operate a local hospital and medical clinics throughout the district. In addition, a health and recreation program in the schools, staffed by Mennonite nurses, was greatly appreciated by the local people. In 1945 the MBMC decided to build on the local goodwill generated by the CPS workers:

This is a great opportunity which should not be allowed to go by. For years we have passed by this island on our way to the mission fields of South America. We little thought that here under the folds of the American flag, is need as great as that of any land we know of. Unwittingly we were led to the place. Our name became well and favourably known among the people who depend on our CPS unit for their welfare. They have confidence in the Mennonites and have learned to trust them, and it would be unfortunate not to follow up the opportunity that is so widely open to us at this time.[49]

Several Canadians served at the Puerto Rico mission, which became the brightest and most encouraging new Mennonite Church mission field, serving as a model for initiatives in Argentina, Belguim, Ethiopia, India, London, and Poland.[50] But that model did not work in Poland, where the difficulties of moving from an inter-Mennonite, MCC-sponsored relief program to denominationally based mission programs became painfully obvious. The MBMC hoped to transform the Polish MCC relief program into a missionary venture. But the conservative Amish-Mennonites,[51] who had supported the MCC relief work, became interested in opening their first-ever foreign mission program in Poland. They suggested that their missionaries work under the auspices of the MBMC despite major theological and other differences. The mission that they had in mind would certainly be different from the church programs of the Prussian Mennonites who had lived in the territory that became part of post-1945 Poland. On matters such as the specific form of adult baptism the Polish/Prussian Mennonites, the Conservative Amish, and the Mennonite Church followed different forms, each reinforced by a distinctive theology. That, of course, could make for a confusing Mennonite missionary witness in a predominantly Roman Catholic country governed by a communist and atheistic government. The result was a decision not to establish any Mennonite missionary program in Poland 'unless these two branches [the MCs and the Conservative Amish] could agree to have a united Mennonite church there.'[52]

Such incidents led relief and missionary programs to be seen as parallel and even competing endeavours. In addition, the mission boards had their own relief programs, while inter Mennonite relief was provided through the offices of the MCC. The ensuing debate was disconcerting to those who strongly supported a holistic approach to physical and spiritual need and suffering.

Several recommendations approved at the triennial MB conference in 1954 summarized how the conferences tried to deal with the problem. They gave official priority to evangelism and to the service activities of their own missions programs, but they also offered strong and effective support to the relief work done by MCC. The Mennonite Brethren resolved: 'That our participation in the important ministry of relief be as closely as possible coordinated with the missionary objectives of our Conference of bringing the Gospel to the people to whom we minister relief. That where opportunities present themselves of extending urgently needed relief to our own missionary constituency, that this need receive preference to the needs in the general MCC program.'[53]

Canadian Mennonites in the 1940s accepted this compromise, but in practice many gave more to MCC than to their own denominational mission programs. And within denominational programs medical, educational, economic, and technological activities got more financial support than itinerant preaching and evangelism. Mennonite immigrants from the Soviet Union, who had themselves benefited from MCC programs, tended to give particularly generously to that agency. MCC met desperate needs they knew and had experienced themselves. But strong support for its programs did not mean that these people, or other MCC supporters, lacked zeal for missionary work.

Balancing evangelistic and relief activities was further complicated by preferences expressed, or demands made, by recipients of these programs. The benefits of famine relief, medical care, educational facilities, and economic and technological assistance were tangible and immediate. There was often less enthusiasm for religious teaching, which not only challenged ancestral beliefs but disrupted social relations in families and communities. These natural preferences of ordinary people in foreign lands were strongly endorsed by newly independent governments that came to power in many of the former colonies after 1945. In country after country governments made it difficult for missionaries to obtain entry visas unless they came with resources, skills, and services that officials considered useful.

INDIGENIZATION

Mennonite missionaries before 1939 rarely questioned or even gave serious consideration to the cultural, social, or intellectual contexts of the societies into which they took the Gospel. They hoped to transplant Christianity as they understood and had experienced it with as little change as possible. A Mennonite Brethren commentator has said: 'We were transplanting, not planting churches. We have brought the gospel in an MB box and insisted that the converts adhere to all MB rules and cultural practices, when we should really get rid of the MB box.'[54]

A General Conference historian has stated candidly that the missionaries sent out by that conference 'never questioned the appropriateness of imposing their culture in its entirety upon the Native American people. They were too confident of the wholesomeness and goodness of their own culture to see the pagan flaws in their own social and political structures.'[55]

And the first Mennonite Church Mission Board official ever to visit the Argentine mission stations wrote in 1941: 'I was impressed with the appearance of the members. They seem to have the best of our Mennonite spirit. Their worship is simple like ours in the States ... I feel we must give the missionaries credit not only for having led them to Christ and helped them to become Christians, but also for having led them to become Mennonites ... It is true that many of the members are desperately poor, but when they become saved their way of living improves and they become clean in comparison with what they had been before.'[56]

Such transplanting was a feature of most Protestant missions, but for Mennonites the tendency was reinforced by their inclination to establish missions in places where they had first operated relief programs. The first Mennonite missions in India provide a particularly good example of what could happen. First, famine victims were helped simply on the basis of need. In the context of the Indian caste system that meant that relief was given first to the untouchables. The starving were fed. Those needing clothes, shelter, or medical care were given what they needed. But if those who had been given material aid also accepted Christianity they became 'socially and economically disinherited upon receiving baptism and identifying themselves with the Christian Church ... As dependents and wards of the mission they looked to the missionaries for financial help to make a new start in life.'[57]

The mission compound became the new home of converts. In the Mennonite Church mission in India, some of the converts became a source of cheap labour, and others were given specialized training in carpentry, blacksmithing, brick and stone masonry, tailoring, field work, improved methods of plant and animal husbandry, and house building, in the hope that they would then be able to earn a livelihood. But it quickly became clear that even with their new skills the converts still experienced great difficulty in gaining acceptance and finding employment in the Indian community. So the mission purchased an entire village and provided Christians with land and development loans so that they could establish an alternative, Christian community. The support of the missionaries made it possible for the converts to exchange their former low economic and social status for a life in the new community in which the missionaries did their best to impart both religious and cultural values. One former General Conference missionary to India has suggested that the new Christian community really became a new caste in Indian society.[58] This strategy seriously limited the success of any missionary evangelistic efforts beyond the bounds of the compound. In 1940 (Old) Mennonite Church missionaries acknowledged a theme that pervades much early Mennonite missionary work: 'We had hoped for more conversions, more spiritual growth, more victories for the Lord, but He has granted what pleased Him and what He was able to accomplish through us ... Truly, Christ's Kingdom cannot be established in this sinful world without a death and life struggle. If spiritual results come easily, beware!'[59]

In 50 years of missionary work in India, and after enormous personal and financial sacrifices, MC missionaries could point to only 3,000 converts, many of them offspring of earlier converts. The situation was even less encouraging in Argentina. That mission, begun in 1917, had only 650 members in 1953. The staff that year included 27 missionaries and 20 Native workers, all drawing remuneration from the board.[60]

The attempt to preach not only the Gospel but also to transplant a culture and a Western, Christian way of life created numerous awkward and sometimes embarrassing misunderstandings. Jacob A. Loewen, a well-known Mennonite Brethren missionary, anthropologist, linguist, and storyteller, tells a humorous but highly revealing autobiographical story. He was sent to a remote jungle community in Colombia where patterns and styles of clothing differed from those in North America. Loewen and his wife made the necessary adjustments, but serious trouble erupted when the mission station was visited by officials of the MB Board of Foreign Missions. The visitors were particularly offended by the fact that the women wore only skirts but nothing on top. The missionaries explained to the offended visitors 'that ordinary women in this tribe never covered their breasts. Only bad women, who had something to hide and wanted to let strange men know that they were welcome, hung something over their breasts. There would be serious consequences if we insisted that all the women attending the Spanish services cover themselves, especially if men from other villages should see that ... It took at least twenty-five years before the lifestyle of these Indians had changed enough that women's clothing covered the entire body.'[61]

Jacob Loewen frequently warned missionaries that they must be concerned about and have an appreciation of ways of life that were different from their own. He told numerous stories to illustrate his concern that 'the missionary and his program can easily – although unwittingly – interfere with a society's processes, thereby seriously disrupting the latter's capacity for socialization and social control.'[62] He warned: 'A common substitute for the genuine willingness to learn and to know is a kind of smug paternalism, in which the missionaries speak familiarly in terms of "our people," "our Christians," and "our Indians." We need to remind ourselves that such statements are a reflection that the speaker is really building his own ego, and that he views himself or his mission as the centre and the national people as a "nice flock of dependent satellites." '[63]

Missionaries and administrators were not ignorant of the close linking of Western culture and their understanding and proclamation of Christianity, but some never seriously questioned their familiar culture. Others were more realistic: 'Religion has always been an integral part of culture; and when the two elements have been together for hundreds of years it is virtually impossible to separate them. It would be as easy to extract salt from the sea as to remove Christianity from western culture. This fact should also be borne in mind when one is tempted to castigate the missionaries for their failure to do a better job.'[64]

Canadian Mennonites, as pointed out above, accommodated themselves to major cultural changes in their own lives in Canada after the war. New wineskins had to be found to preserve the old wine. That also became necessary, but proved more difficult, on the mission field. There missionaries not only had to discard the old wineskins. They had to pour their precious Gospel wine into new wineskins that were not of their own making and which many thought unreliable.

The war released long-repressed frustrations and hostilities in all the countries that had been colonized or otherwise dominated by Western imperial powers. The belligerents naturally tried to foment resistance and rebellion in colonies controlled by their enemies, thereby fostering the growth of nationalist movements. The missionary movement had been closely linked with the policies of the imperialist powers, and the paternalism of the missionaries became an inevitable target not only for nationalist governments but also for local Christians. The historian of the Mennonite Church in India noted: 'The (local) church in independent India behaved much as the entire society did following independence. The church like the state felt a need to gain self-respect after years of paternal domination. Similarly it needed to gain economic self-sufficiency and to create an indigenous church life and structure after years of missionary tutelage.'[65]

Mennonite missionaries felt the disruptive effects of this new form of nationalism. As early as 1940, the Mennonite Board of Missions and Charities (MBMC) of the Mennonite Church noted with concern: 'One of the molesting and disturbing elements of mission work today is the spirit of nationalism ... It seems that in these days, foreigners are not welcome in any country. For financial reasons, they are often tolerated. There has been for some years a tremendous growth of the nationalistic spirit ... This spirit is developing in missionary activities of all denominations and calls for much wisdom and care on the part of the foreigner to not become antagonistic and domineering.'[66]

During the war years the missions of both the General Conference (GC) and the Mennonite Church in India were threatened by invading Japanese troops. That forced the missionaries to contemplate what should be done if they were forced to flee. A GC missions historian has observed: 'Locked away in the safe on each GC Mennonite mission compound in India during World War II were contingency plans in case of missionary evacuation. Who among the Indian Christians would be given responsibility for mission schools, churches, and hospitals? To whom would be given the keys to the missionary bungalows and supply rooms? Who would be given authority to draw funds from the missionary account?'[67]

The MB missions in India did not face such a threat, but events in China after the war forced evacuation of virtually all Western missionaries. Property, programs, offices, authority, and leadership had to be turned over to local leaders, irrespective of the missionaries' views regarding their competence and readiness.

These developments in India and China and rising nationalism in all the other former colonies made it necessary for missionaries and administrators to turn over increasing control of programs and property to the local church in a timely, prudent, and orderly manner. Collectively such programs came to be called indigenization. The MBMC, in reporting on the situation in India in 1940, acknowledged: 'The path of wisdom appears to be for the Mission to help the [local] Church take up her responsibilities so as to rapidly make the Church as nearly self-governing and self-supporting as possible.'[68] More specifically, it recommended transfer of the title to the land and buildings owned by the mission to the local church or conference. A promise to transfer the property was made amid flowery words which suggested that this would be 'an encouragement and a stimulus' for the local church, since it demonstrated 'a spirit of trust and good will' by the board. But the board also admitted that it had no choice: 'From a realistic point of view the board might as well turn these buildings over, for we cannot conceive of a circumstance under which we could ever sell them even if we should desire to do so … Certain American Missions in the North of India during the past year attempted to sell land near some of the churches (but not the churches themselves) and it created a very ugly situation, the echoes of which have reached every part of India.'[69]

The transfer was delayed several years, until the Indian conference was legally incorporated, but in the meantime governance of the 'Mission' was changed. It was renamed the India Mennonite Mission, and the old council made up of all the missionaries was enlarged to include fourteen Indians – seven chosen by the local Indian church and seven by the missionaries. The objective was to admit Indians to the council but to leave the missionaries in effective control. There were always more than fifteen missionaries, and they directly named seven of the fourteen India members.[70] But even these changes were postponed when it was discovered that the first Indian minister ordained by the missionaries had 'fallen' and therefore had to be relieved of his ministry and of his church membership. Turning real control over to local believers was a long and difficult process.

The government of Argentina eventually solved the problem in that country for the MBMC. A constitution similar to the one proposed for the mission in India was also drawn up for the mission in Argentina. But the government, facing intense pressure from the Roman Catholic church, found the limited concessions unsatisfactory and threatened to nationalize all Protestant mission schools. Faced with this threat, and clear indications of the kind of constitutional changes needed to satisfy the government, MBMC administrators agreed 'to sanction certain revisions during the year since the Government required a greater sharing of responsibility for the administration of the work by Argentine nationals, and the mission charter was endangered by further delay.'[71]

Indigenization in the 1940s was not yet a matter that was understood or given much thought by Canadian Mennonite mission supporters. But in its 1950 annual report the MBMC gave clear notice of a plan with which it had wrestled for some time and that would dominate missionary debates in the 1950s: 'The missionary movement in past years rode quite high on the wave of the supposed superiority of western culture and imposing materialism. The spell of the latter has been broken, partly at least, and from now on the Christian faith is going to have to stand upon its own inherent worth. With rising nationalism the disparity between the foreigner and the national is brought into serious question. It is clear that on the foreign fields every effort will need to be made to involve the nationals in the total church enterprise.'[72]

Indigenization proved particularly difficult in MB missions. Unlike the mission boards of other Mennonite conferences, the Mennonite Brethren did not, until 1949, send administrators to inspect and report on the work of their missionaries. The missionaries were screened and given instruction and guidance before they went overseas, and they were expected to remain in close written contact with their sponsors, but it was only in the early spring of 1949 that A.E. Janzen, executive secretary and treasurer of the Board of Foreign Missions of the Conference of the Mennonite Brethren Church of North America, travelled to the Conference's five major mission fields and prepared a detailed report on each field.

His successor, J.B. Toews, has described Janzen's report as an inventory without any coherent missionary philosophy. Janzen, according to Toews, was 'a very relational person who abhorred conflict.'[73] As a result, his 1949 report perpetuated old attitudes and envisioned continuation of the old methods. He described Africa thus: 'Africa is a country of deep shadows, physical and spiritual. No country, perhaps, contains so much native life in the raw, untouched by civilization, as does the dark continent ... The African people in their heathendom, when motivated by witchcraft and demon worship, may become dangerous when irritated. And certainly, as long as they are under the influence and spell of the evil spirits, their countenances reflect it.'[74] In his discussion of India Janzen began by quoting Psalm 2:8: 'Ask of me and I shall give thee the heathen for thine inheritance, and the uttermost parts of the earth for thy possession,' and he described India as 'a land of idolatry.'[75] He complained that Christians there had no sense of stewardship and 'that there is not one indigenous treasurer who can be trusted with money.'[76]

Janzen recognized that local churches should be given greater responsibility, particularly for evangelization in the villages, but saw the missionaries and compounds as the real focus of the enterprise. Thus, while other mission boards were agonizing over new constitutions that would turn over effective control to local churches, Janzen recommended further expansion of facilities and personnel: 'The work in Africa holds great possibilities also for the future ... The missionary effort can be strengthened by extending our educational and Bible training facilities, by providing a doctor and central hospital, by operating a school for missionary children, by erecting buildings on stations of permanent materials, by extending the publication of Christian literature, and above all, by God's grace, by planting many self-supporting and indigenous churches in the hundreds of villages.'[77]

In 1953 Toews succeeded Janzen as executive secretary of the Board of Foreign Missions. Toews was convinced that radical changes were necessary and set himself the task of restructuring the MB overseas missionary program. He made frequent tours of mission fields, but his style antagonized many of the missionaries. Instead of accompanying them on carefully planned tours of the compound and villages to meet suitably docile and deferential converts, Toews sought direct meetings with local Christians to which the missionaries were not always invited.[78] At those meetings local leaders complained about the proprietary interest that each of the senior missionaries took in his or her mission and stated emphatically: 'We chafe under this colonial system.'[79] Toews became convinced that the strategies followed by the missionaries were manifestations of 'colonialism.'[80] He was particularly upset by an extreme example of missionary dominance at Shamshabad, where the senior missionary paid the local preachers. When Toews arrived several of these preachers were sitting outside on the verandah. The missionary explained that they were sitting there as punishment because they had not preached as he had instructed them. They had to sit and wait until they were sufficiently remorseful. Only then would they be paid.[81]

Toews made contact with several other prominent and concerned mission supporters and administrators, the most important being George W. Peters, who had begun his missionary work in Canadian home missions and children's evangelism, and Henry H. Janzen, who had organized the Afrika Missions Verein to support the Bartsches in the Congo when they were not given the assignment they sought by the Hillsboro-based mission board. These three men became the principal authors of a radical new missions policy statement that was presented and approved at the triennial General Conference of the Mennonite Brethren Church of North America, held at Yarrow, British Columbia, in October 1957. The 'Statement of the General Conference of the M.B. Church on the Effects of the Changes of Our Age on the World-Wide Missionary Assignment' reviewed 'the status of our missionary program up to this day' and explained:

The world-wide revolutionary changes of the post-war era effecting every phase of the international, national, social and religious life of our generation exerts a severe testing upon the missionary accomplishment of the past and its program for the future. The impact of the changes establish beyond question that the time of a fixed routine pattern of mission programs has out-lived itself. The assignment of a missionary for a stationary ministry of evangelism with a lifetime to continue in the same place as the central figure of a perpetual program results in a reactionary protest of the nationalistic-conscious native of all lands. With the growing international rejection of all colonial imperialism there has also arisen a principle rejection of the 'missionary-centered' gospel ministry.[82]

The statement recommended far-reaching changes requiring 'considerable adjustments for the future in the area of our missionary approach and administrative direction.' It placed major emphasis on 'the establishment of an indigenous church which can assume the responsibility for the evangelization of its own constituency even though the missions may be required to withdraw ... [This would necessitate] new standards of qualifications of missionaries and will also demand new methods in some areas of work.' Few details were provided, but the board asked for 'sympathetic understanding on the part of our churches if some changes in personnel would have to be effected to assure a most fruitful ministry on the various fields.'[83] Most of the delegates who approved the so-called Yarrow Statement did not understand the ramifications of accelerated indigenization.

The missionaries in the field were the first to experience the new policies. Those policies significantly reduced their autonomy and authority in two significant ways. First, the board demanded more frequent and detailed reports and insisted on setting policies and making decisions on matters formerly left to the discretion of the missionaries in the field. Frequent visits, particularly by the determined executive secretary, ensured that the new policies were implemented. In addition, the authority of the missionary was subordinated to that of the local church and its indigenous leaders. Instead of being a colonial master, the missionary was to become a servant of the local church. Taken to its logical conclusion, the policy would make the old-fashioned missionaries obsolete and redundant.

Abram and Annie Unruh, long-term missionaries in India and the son and daughter-in-law of the popular and influential former principal of the Peniel Bible School at Winkler and later first president of the Mennonite Brethren Bible College, voiced the concerns of many missionaries and their supporters when they protested the new policies. They were particularly upset by the recommendation that evangelism become the responsibility of the local churches. The Unruhs and others readily admitted that local churches should become more actively involved but insisted that such involvement did not absolve missionaries and supporters of their responsibility to continue their evangelistic work.

In a letter to the board written in May 1958 the Unruhs raised some of their concerns and asked pointedly whether the new policy reflected the views of the North American churches or only those of a few members of the board. There was no response from the board, and the Unruhs then appealed directly to the constituency:

... No one may give the task of evangelization a national character and then make evangelization a national responsibility. Today's cry that the evangelization of India is the responsibility of India's churches, does not absolve us of the responsibility for the millions of lost souls in India, Africa, and yes, of the whole world. A half-truth can become a lie, and can lead to a frightful awakening when the Lord of the Church of God will require an answer regarding the fulfilling of his missionary command ... We are messengers who still offer the sinner the Gospel at the very gates of eternity. It is the task of missions to proclaim the message of the Gospel until the doors close. We do not seek substitutes to carry out our task. We are on the lookout for those, who, together with us, can go after the lost sinner and bring him the message of salvation.[84]

Other missionaries, particularly from India where missionaries' confidence in the ability of the local leaders was lowest, joined Unruh in questioning the wisdom of rapid indigenization. That created considerable uneasiness and concern in the supporting constituency and resulted in the involuntary retirement of several senior missionaries who were unable or unwilling to accommodate themselves to the new policies. The dissident missionaries were, however, overtaken by events elsewhere.

The independence movement in the Congo did not make a clear distinction among political, economic, religious, and cultural forms of Western imperialism. The close links between the colonial administration and the Roman Catholic church made it easy for local leaders to persuade the people that all Western influences served the same purpose – to claim land and people for the benefit of the colonial power.[85] Thus when nationalist leaders declared their independence from Belgium and renamed their country Zaire, imperialists of every kind felt so threatened that in July 1960 they fled en masse to the safety of neighbouring countries. Leadership of churches passed to local pastors, without further advice and guidance from the missionaries.

The forced departure of the missionaries, first from China and then from Zaire, was not entirely unexpected. But it was a terrible shock for North American and European supporters of missions. In Zaire tribal warfare and political instability after independence resulted in much suffering and the disintegration of Mennonite churches, which suffered schisms along tribal lines, lost influential leaders, and became embroiled in personality conflicts.

UNUSUAL SACRIFICE

In a few rare instances local jealousies and tribal or religious conflicts resulted in the deaths of missionaries. The experiences of two Canadian mis-

sionary couples in Somalia, were particularly difficult but ultimately also grati-
fying. When they decided to send missionaries to Somalia, members of the
Eastern Mennonite Mission Board were aware of government restrictions
there on evangelistic and missionary activity. But in 1956 they decided to send
mission money and personnel to establish medical and educational institutions in that country. Victor and Viola Dorsch and their family left Baden,
Ontario, for Somalia in 1956. Four years later, Merlin and Dorothy Grove
and their family left the Markham area for Somalia. On 16 July 1962, while
registering students for adult evening classes in Mogadishu, Merlin Grove was
stabbed to death and Dorothy sustained severe stab wounds to the abdomen.

The attack was the outcome of a lengthy controversy. Muslim opposition
to Christian schools culminated, on 23 March 1962, in a government order
that the Mennonite mission stop all activities. That order, however, had resulted in sufficient pressure from parents and other local supporters that the
government allowed the schools to reopen with some restrictions on non-
Muslim teaching. It was while registering students for the reopened mission
school that Merlin Grove was murdered.[86] While the prime minister expressed
his personal regrets and his hope that the mission would continue, tensions
between Christians and Muslims in Somalia continued, and in 1976, while
the Dorches were on furlough, the mission was closed.

The Eastern Mennonite Mission Board represented a very conservative wing
of the Mennonite Church, at least in dress and style. Nevertheless it was willing to enter Somalia and simply be a presence, knowing that 'fruit' for its
labours would be minimal. Yet when Somali refugees began to arrive in
Toronto in the 1990s several remembered Victor Dorsch, who was then living in retirement in the Waterloo area. There was a remarkable reunion of
twenty-seven Somalis with the Dorsch family in May 1992, as they explored
ways and means to deal with the violence, anarchy, and famine that had overtaken their country.[87]

In the three decades after 1939, Merlin Grove was the only Canadian Mennonite missionary murdered in the field by those he sought to serve. There
were, however a number of missionaries or their children who died en route
or overseas. The personal costs were sometimes very high, and the results not
always what the missionaries and their supporters expected or hoped for.
Unusual sacrifices, however, are an integral part of the mission story.

CONCLUSION

During the first half of the twentieth century Canadian Mennonites, except
the most traditional groups, became enthusiastic and generous supporters of

and participants in overseas missionary programs. There was phenomenal expansion after 1945, but also fundamental and disconcerting change. Nationalist and communist ideologies drove the missionaries out of China in the late 1940s. Independence fostered strong nationalist and anti-imperialist movements in India, which forced indigenization of the Mennonite churches there, and fundamentally altered the role and position of the missionaries. Similar developments in Argentina and former colonies around the world, and then the tragic upheavals in Zaire, left many North American mission supporters with the disconcerting impression that the age of Protestant missions was rapidly coming to a close.

That was too pessimistic. Christian missionary work did not end with indigenization or with flight and expulsion from China, Zaire, and other countries. The loss of China, in fact, was in part eased by exciting new missionary opportunities in Japan and Taiwan. But missionaries and those who supported them had to adjust to new and very different conditions.

Indigenization required greater respect of, sensitivity to, and acceptance of local culture and life-styles and greater understanding and acceptance of non-Christian religions. In the context of the global Cold War religious relativism, rather than insistence on the exclusive claims of Christianity in the garb of Western culture and civilization, made sense.

In their own communities Canadian Mennonites had experienced much change. They had accepted new religious methods and practices, borrowed mainly from the evangelical wing of North American Protestantism. Such religious relativism within or between the evangelical faiths at home also facilitated, at least for some, greater openness elsewhere. Mennonites with their non-violent and non-resistant theology, for example, became particularly intrigued with the ideas and career of Mahatma Gandhi, the great leader of Indian resistance against British imperialism.

Jacob Loewen, the articulate and thoughtful Mennonite Brethren missionary, anthropologist, and Bible translator, argued in his inimitable style that too many missionaries scratched where the people did not itch.[88] They addressed issues and provided solutions for problems that those to whom they ministered did not know they had. It was essential, Loewen argued, that the missionaries immerse themselves in the local culture to understand the hurts, problems, and needs of the local people and then address those as best they could.

Loewen has suggested that missionary efforts in the postwar era followed one of three distinct models. The first he described as church transplanting, in which the missionaries tried to establish new churches modelled as closely as possible on those of the sponsoring communities. This 'imperialist' model was rendered obsolete by indigenization.

The second model focused on conversion and soul winning. The objective was to go out and 'save' as many people as possible as quickly as possible, without much concern about the subsequent life of the convert. Speaking specifically of his denomination, Loewen expressed concern that the historic Anabaptist emphasis on discipleship was weakened in this approach. The scriptures, as well as Anabaptist-Mennonite writings, say far more about the narrow way than about the narrow gate by which the Christian enters that narrow way. Missionaries intent on achieving as many conversions as possible reversed that emphasis.

The third model, and obviously the one that Loewen endorsed, sees the missionary as a catalyst. The missionary does not bring God or an understanding of good and evil to the heathen. God is already there. The responsibility of the missionary is to look where God is already working and then to 'plug in' there. The catalyst should not come with his or her own agenda. He or she should look for a felt need and find reasonable answers to local dilemmas.

Pre-war Mennonite missionaries and those who supported them 'were sure of the rightness of their message, their strategy, and their ultimate triumph. They did not doubt the essential goodness of their own national and Germanic culture.'[89] That confidence was seriously undermined during and after the Second World War. The wickedness and suffering of two world wars undermined confidence in the essential goodness of Western civilization. Debates regarding the relative importance of meeting physical rather than spiritual needs fragmented the ideal of a holistic ministry. Anti-colonialism and national independence movements raised serious questions regarding the linking of religious values and cultural practices. A new era dawned in overseas missionary work during and after the war. In that new era 'the needed qualities were those of patience and servanthood, rather than those of initiative and mastery.'[90]

For Canadian Mennonite missionaries and their supporters the rapid expansion and subsequent restructuring of overseas enterprises became an important window on the world. Missionaries were expected to teach and preach to people around the world who had not yet heard or accepted the Gospel. But they also, willingly or otherwise, learned much about the outside world. The comfortable linking of Western culture and civilization with Christianity, the relevance and principles of other faiths, and the aspirations and problems of racial equality, self-determination, and national independence all had to be rethought. In short, the missionary enterprise forced Canadian Mennonites who were already rethinking and redefining their place in Canadian society to reassess also their place and role in the world.

16
Peace, Justice, and Social Concerns

The 1960s saw political, social, and religious tumult in North America. In the United States the assassinations of John F. Kennedy, of Robert Kennedy, and of Martin Luther King, Jr, the civil rights movement, the Vietnam War, and the disastrous Democratic party convention of 1968 in Chicago were only the most widely publicized disasters that suggested serious flaws in the society that North Americans had created in the prosperous years after 1945. There were, as a result, intense debates regarding peace, justice, and social concerns.

Canadians, including Mennonites, became deeply involved in those debates. They had sharp differences of opinion, rooted in differing understandings of their religious heritage and its relevance to the issues of the day, but the disagreements coincided to a remarkable degree with those among Canadians generally. Mennonites had responded very differently from almost all other Canadians to the exigencies of the Second World War. During the Vietnam War neither Mennonites nor their fellow Canadians had a united response, but the divisions in both groups focused on many of the same issues.

Divergent Canadian and U.S. responses to domestic and international problems gave Canadians a stronger sense of their own national identity. In the United States the military-industrial complex about which President Dwight Eisenhower had warned seemed to embroil Americans in policies of social warfare as they sought to stop communism in its many manifestations by military means. Canada, by contrast, was devising innovative social welfare policies in which medicare was a key ingredient.

In their recent book on Mennonite peacemaking Leo Driedger and Donald Kraybill argue that before, during, and immediately after the Second World War, the Mennonite peace position focused on non-resistance and the refusal to bear arms in war but that it was transformed after 1945. There was, they argue, 'a shift from passivity to activism, from isolation to engagement.

The earlier Mennonite view that nonresistance was primarily objection to warfare has been replaced by an activist mode of constructive conciliation with a wide scope of involvement.'[1]

Within the Canadian Mennonite community that shift was often controversial, in part because those who made it moved people closer to their Anabaptist heritage and to the mainstream of Canadian religious and political thought but away from the evangelical substream that adopted a belligerent anti-communist and pro-militarist position.

WHAT A DIFFERENCE TEN YEARS MAKES

On 16 February 1960 a seven-member delegation of Canadian Mennonites and Brethren in Christ met with Prime Minister John Diefenbaker in Ottawa.[2] The delegates had prepared a brief, which they read to the prime minister. In it they explained who the members of Canada's historic peace churches were and their 'deep-rooted conviction against active participation in war.'[3] The brief further outlined their privilege of exemption from military service 'which we have enjoyed since our church fathers came to this country in 1790' and made reference to their record of alternative and voluntary service to relieve human pain and suffering. They came, the delegates said, 'with but one request.' In the event of another war they asked that the government consult with them 'to find ways in which we might utilize our contributions in manpower and resources to their greatest potential value to our country within the framework of law and with our peace testimony.' The brief concluded with the wish that God 'grant to you, our Prime Minister, wisdom and courage to discharge your many duties as chief executive of our country.' And it promised that Mennonites would pray for him.

Meetings of this kind were not new. It had been a practice of Canadian peace church leaders to meet as soon as it could be conveniently arranged with newly elected prime ministers to explain their position. The first such meeting had been with William Lyon Mackenzie King after he took office in 1921.[4] Most of the members of the 1960 delegation had been at previous such events,[5] and during the war there had been numerous meetings with the prime minister and with senior cabinet ministers, members of Parliament, and government bureaucrats. Those carrying the Mennonite and Brethren in Christ brief in 1960 were thus no strangers to Parliament Hill.

The main message had always been the same,[6] as had the response. Diefenbaker, like his predecessors, spoke appreciatively of the relief and other services provided by members of the peace churches and assured them that the provisions for peace church freedoms, and respect for their conscience, were 'changeless.'[7] In his report one member of the delegation noted happily: 'Several times during the reading of the brief, the Prime Minister nodded his head and at the assurance of the prayers of our people on his behalf he said "Thank you, thank you very much."'[8] The quiet, even cosy, affair was not widely reported in the popular press.

Almost exactly ten years later, on 20 March 1970, another Mennonite delegation went to Ottawa to present a brief to Pierre Trudeau.[9] The contrast between that meeting and the one with John Diefenbaker revealed how much the Canadian Mennonite world had changed.

The first major, and to the Mennonites highly disconcerting, change after Trudeau's election was that their first request to meet with him was refused.[10] The official reason given was Trudeau's very busy schedule, but when the meeting was finally arranged Trudeau, who had received a copy of the Mennonite brief beforehand, explained that he was not interested in meeting with yet another social action group. But he very much appreciated the 'spiritual input that you [the Mennonites] are bringing into this society, as a group of people who have a certain faith and who are a leaven in the dough, as it were ... I am very much impressed by the Mennonite community for their support of the cause of peace as opposed to militarism.'[11]

The brief in 1970 nevertheless focused almost entirely on controversial social and political issues. It had six main items.[12] First, it advocated an immigration policy that kept 'Canada's doors open to émigrés who have been made homeless by war or persecution, including US draft-age immigrants.' Second, it urged greater efforts at reunification of families where one partner was in the Soviet Union and the other in Canada. Third, it requested exemption for the Old Order Amish from participation in the Canada Pension Plan. Fourth, the brief urged that Canada officially recognize the People's Republic of China while also maintaining full relations with the nationalist Chinese government of Taiwan. Fifth, it requested export concessions for grain shipments to food-for-work projects abroad and increased Canadian foreign aid spending. And sixth, the document urged establishment of 'peace chairs' on Canadian university campuses.

The composition of the Mennonite delegation in 1970 was also different. In 1960 the Conference of Historic Peace Churches had taken the initiative in preparing the brief and calling together the old and experienced Mennonite and Brethren in Christ leaders who had been to Ottawa many times. The seven men who took the 1960 brief to Ottawa each represented a particular Mennonite conference.[13] In 1970 a new Canadian inter-Mennonite organization, the Mennonite Central Committee (Canada), was the initiator, and the delegation consisted almost entirely of younger men, all of whom were elected or appointed officials of MCC (Canada).[14]

The circumstances were also very different. The 1960 meeting had been a quiet affair in Mr Diefenbaker's office, arranged through the offices of the member of Parliament for Waterloo North. It was suited to the temperament of people who still prided themselves on being 'the quiet in the land.' The 1970 meeting, by contrast, was a significant public relations and media event. The prime minister, flanked by three cabinet ministers, sat on one side of a large conference table, the five Mennonite representatives on the other. Sitting in a circle behind the political leaders and the Mennonite representatives was 'an awe-inspiring ring of newsmen.' Both major Canadian television networks recorded the entire 45-minute encounter, while numerous tape recorders provided fodder for the assembled journalists. It was, according to a later MCC (Canada) press release, 'in every respect one of the most thoroughly covered events in which Canadian Mennonites have ever been involved.'[15]

The session itself also went far beyond a polite reading of the brief, followed by appropriate obsequies and expressions of goodwill. Trudeau engaged the delegates in discussion and debate, explaining government policies with regard to the universal Canada Pension Plan, overseas relief, and policy on China.

In previous submissions the Mennonites had concentrated on what they believed was right, and hence what they were willing to do in situations of military conflict, and what they believed was wrong and would not do. The choices were not that simple in any of the matters raised in 1970. Governments, Trudeau explained, rarely have the luxury of choosing simply to do what is right and refusing to do what is wrong. They must choose between competing solutions, each of which has both good and bad elements. 'The task of government every day in every area is to choose between various solutions,' Trudeau said, and he then warned the delegates, 'If you are telling us that in the dilemma we should not act, then we don't agree.'[16]

In his assessment of the meeting, J.M. Klassen, executive secretary of MCC (Canada), noted: 'Mr. Trudeau has a philosophical bent and an openness to pursue further some of the thoughts and concepts which underlie our brief ... He is very perceptive and appears uninhibited to speak on any issue.'[17] But Klassen was clearly unhappy with the government's decision not to exempt the Old Order Amish from participation in the Canada Pension Plan and thought that this constituted 'a threat to the religious freedom which could easily extend to other areas of life.'[18] The 1970 encounter demonstrated that Mennonites had entered the political process, only to discover that politics is the art of the possible, not of the ideal.

THE *CANADIAN MENNONITE*

Mennonite newspapers became important agents and facilitators as their readers made the difficult transition from quietism to activism. The language of discourse and communication became important in that transition.

Most of the Swiss Mennonites in Ontario had made the transition from German to English as the language of worship and communication in their churches before 1939. An inevitable corollary had been the gradual change-over of their church papers from German to English. The *Herald of Truth*, a church paper founded in 1864, and its successor, the *Gospel Herald*, were both published in the United States but had a wide circulation in Ontario Swiss Mennonite congregations. Two other Swiss Mennonite church papers, the *Ontario Mennonite Evangel* and the *Mission News*, were published in Ontario and read by Swiss Mennonites there. These papers carried religious devotional material, local community and congregational news, and short snippets of world news thought to be of interest to readers. They had, in essence, made the linguistic change without changing the basic format or content.

The language transition in the religious life of the Russian Mennonites gained momentum only after 1945. But by the early 1950s many realized that the change was inevitable and began to think of setting up an English-language Mennonite church paper. That new paper, however, marked not only a language transition but also significant changes in the way news was gathered, reported, and interpreted.

The Altona publishing firm of D.W. Friesen and Sons started the paper. The first issue, 3 July 1953, was something of a trial balloon. The publishers invited Mennonites from all conferences and communities to subscribe, promising that if enough subscriptions were received the paper would begin regular weekly publication in October. In the letter soliciting subscriptions, and in the first editorial, the objectives of the new paper were defined:

This new English-language weekly, The *Canadian Mennonite*, will be published in the interests of all Mennonite church groups in Canada. In its contents it will present articles of information, such as news items from the various Mennonite districts and correspondence from readers, and also articles of instruction and inspiration, such as book reviews, stories, sermons and devotional material, discussion, etc. In doing this, it will seek to present the pure teachings of the Bible as interpreted and proclaimed by the Mennonite Church, reaching out to many Canadian Mennonite young people and others who do not, or cannot, read our German-language periodicals, and also presenting a united witness to our Canadian neighbours.[19]

The person responsible for making the *Canadian Mennonite* different from most church papers of the time was its first editor, Frank H. Epp. Epp was an exceptionally talented but also pugnacious and at times abrasive editorial writer and public speaker. The polite and deferential tone in which the work and activities of Mennonite bishops, elders, and leaders was discussed in official church papers was sometimes lacking in Epp's editorials and news reports. He clearly saw his role to be that of a journalist and was determined to make the paper more than a denominational mouthpiece. In his style he sometimes assumed a prophetic rather than a docile, pious, or conciliatory stance. His criticisms of American military policies in Vietnam in the 1960s, of Israeli occupation policies in the Gaza strip and the West Bank, and of American civil rights problems roused much animosity, as did his caustic comments about the employment and business practices of some Mennonite entrepreneurs. In his reports about Mennonite conferences and congregations he reported 'internal' and 'back-stage' matters not previously thought appropriate for publication. And he refused to submit his reports to conference officials for approval before publication.

Epp set the tone of the paper, editing it from 1953 until 1967. During those years, and in fact over the entire seventeen and a half years of the paper, it exhibited several characteristics. It was, first of all, an English paper. That alone was controversial, creating among other things a serious rift between Epp and his father, a Mennonite minister and staunch defender of the German language.[20]

Second, the paper sought to be inter-Mennonite in the sense that it was not the official organ of any conference or group but sought to serve all Mennonites in Canada. Inter-Mennonite papers were not new. *Der Immigrantenbote*, later renamed *Der Bote*, sought to serve the immigrants of the 1920s on an inter-Mennonite basis in the German language. The *Canadian Mennonite* was to bring in not only the immigrants of the 1920s but all Canadian Mennonites. It nevertheless enjoyed a much larger readership among the children of those immigrants than it did in other Mennonite circles. In fact, it never gained many subscribers among the Swiss Mennonites of Ontario or the more traditional Mennonite groups in the west.

Third, and ultimately much more controversial, the *Canadian Mennonite* deliberately covered many issues that other church papers had either avoided or treated only in a superficial or celebratory manner. It appeared in tabloid newspaper format, or, as the editor pointed out repeatedly, in everyday or workaday clothes. A glossy, church magazine format was rejected. The paper carried some devotional religious material, but its primary objective was to cover news stories of interest and relevance to Canadian Mennonites in their ordinary, everyday environment. From the beginning it carried material related to secular political, economic, diplomatic, and social events and developments. It was to be, in Epp's words, 'a real newspaper.'[21] It reported many good things, but it also carried unflattering and critical reports about embarrassing or sinful events, actions, and attitudes in the Mennonite household of faith: 'We felt it was our obligation to try to get at the heart of what was happening within our brotherhood with deep, complete and early reporting.'[22] In his often hard-hitting editorials, Epp insisted that Mennonites ought to observe and apply the teachings of Jesus in all of life. They had moved from their secluded communities into the world. Could they take their holistic gospel with them and apply it in the new environment? He asked difficult questions, such as: 'Is it not true that the way we preach the gospel on Sundays has hardly any bearing on the way we hire workers, buy land, and sell cars?'[23]

Some of the news stories in the paper provided discomfiting answers, particularly for those whose less-than-exemplary affairs were publicized. But Epp and the members of his board emphatically rejected the notion that a Christian code of conduct applied only in church or within the family or community of believers and that a different standard was appropriate when dealing with unbelievers and outsiders. 'We begin,' he complained, 'with separation of church and state and end with the separation of Sunday and Monday, of the church and the world, of the church and business.'[24] Referring more specifically to those who insisted in the 1960s that the Gospel could not and should not be applied to American foreign policy in Vietnam, Epp wrote: 'Our distorted gospel can't call leaders of state to refrain from killing because the ethic doesn't apply; and we can't expect this of Christians because the ethic doesn't apply to them when the leaders of state give the orders.'[25]

The *Canadian Mennonite* followed another disconcerting policy. It spoke to issues and advocated action in matters that Mennonites had long regarded as none of their business. Epp explicitly rejected the argument often advanced by evangelical Christians that it was the duty of the church to save souls, not to save or transform the secular world order: 'By asking the church to stick to the saving of souls and not to apply the will of God to the affairs of men, we find a rather comfortable way out of the very difficult and demanding social implications of the gospel ... The result ... is that very few real disciples are born and very little renewal really comes. And that is why the church does not turn the world upside down as it apparently did in the first and sixteenth centuries.'[26]

There were also ongoing, sometimes bitter and confrontational, encounters with those who equated evangelical theology with capitalism, the Western and American way of life, American nationalism, U.S. military policies, aggressive anti-communism, and missionary work that ignored social and economic problems: 'Nothing will be so great a tragedy as a world evangelism that simply reinforced the wicked western way of life ... world evangelism must not counter but spearhead a world revolution in the sense that it calls the rich society to lose itself and accept the way of the cross voluntarily.'[27]

The *Canadian Mennonite*, in short, sought to make radical Christian discipleship relevant to the everyday problems and activities of its readers. Canadian Mennonites had become actively involved in the affairs of the world. The challenge was to place all of life under the Lordship of Christ in that context. That could become very irritating when the ideal was contrasted with embarrassingly honest reporting of what was really happening.

The result was that the *Canadian Mennonite* had a precarious existence throughout its seventeen and a half years. It received only limited financial support from the Conference of Mennonites in Canada, and revenues from subscriptions never covered all its cost. From 1953 until 1962 D.W. Friesen and Sons, as publishers, carried the operating deficit. Then, in 1962, an inter-Mennonite organization – the Canadian Mennonite Publishing Association – was formed. It sought to promote the paper and raise funds through special solicitations and donations.

Critics frequently challenged the editorial freedom and independence of the editor, but on several occasions strong supporters and major financial benefactors also sought to influence or dictate policy. The first major such incident occurred when Rudy Wiebe's *Peace Shall Destroy Many* was reviewed in the paper. One strong financial supporter was very unhappy with Wiebe's book and insisted that the paper give it a negative review.[28] When the editor refused, there were serious financial repercussions. In a second troublesome incident, in 1966, a businessman's right-wing ideological advertisement produced a hostile response in a letter to the editor. When the editor published the letter, the advertiser threatened court action. Litigation was not regarded by members of the board as appropriate for a Mennonite paper. So they agreed to an out-of-court settlement in which the paper paid $1,500 plus court costs.[29] The editor accepted, even though he had rather looked forward to airing in court the right-wing attitudes and some business practices of Mennonite businessmen.

The most serious problems encountered by the editor, however, involved his unrelenting criticism of American military and foreign policies in Vietnam in the 1960s. 'Our editorial stance,' Epp recalled later, 'produced much hostility, opposition, and name-calling.'[30] He insisted, however, that his editorial policy 'championed the genius of the Mennonite movement, a nonresistant faith for which our people had allegedly fled to Prussia, migrated to Russia and Canada, and heroically stood up to society and state in the two world wars.'[31]

The specific irritants of the Vietnam War and U.S. civil rights problems gradually waned. Many of the other issues championed, and application of Anabaptist and Mennonite theology to the hurts and needs of modern society, as advocated by the *Canadian Mennonite*, eventually became an accepted part of Mennonite life in this country. But the accumulated animosities, along with crushing financial burdens, forced the paper to cease publication in February 1971. In his emotional reflections on the history and place of the paper, Epp wrote: 'When institutions die, as die they must with the rest of humanity, the proper response is not to weep over yet another dead body but rather to ask questions concerning the soul. What manner of spirit did the ashes represent? ... If the spirit of the dead institution was linked to the eternal and universal spirit he will reappear perhaps more vigorously than before. Death may have been necessary to give certain ideals new life.'[32]

Less than one year after the demise of the *Canadian Mennonite* an English-language, inter-Mennonite paper was started in Waterloo. Several of the people who had been prominent supporters of earlier publication were involved in the new venture, which was first called the *Canadian Mennonite Reporter* but soon adopted the name *Mennonite Reporter*. Serving as editor, on an interim basis, was none other than Frank Epp, then a faculty member at Conrad Grebel College.

The *Mennonite Reporter* had one very important advantage over its predecessor. The Mennonite Conference of Ontario and Quebec (Old Mennonites), and the Western Ontario Mennonite Conference (formerly the Amish Mennonites), ceased publishing their own church papers and made the *Mennonite Reporter* their Canadian church paper. Both conferences agreed to pay for the cost of sending the paper to all member households. The Conference of Mennonites in Canada (CMC) also offered a subsidy to reduce subscription costs for its members. That provided much greater financial stability, while editorial independence was safeguarded through a separate association – the Mennonite Publishing Service.

The *Mennonite Reporter* continued many of the news-reporting and editorial practices of the *Canadian Mennonite*, but that style of journalism became less controversial and the editors had a less prominent profile in the Mennonite community than Epp had had. Other Canadian Mennonite church papers also began to emulate the journalistic methods of the *Canadian Mennonite*, though their editorial freedom was more restricted.

In 1962 the Mennonite Brethren began their own English-language paper, the *Mennonite Brethren Herald,* financed and controlled by the Canadian MB Conference. It and other simalar papers continued to carry more devotional material, and more local and congregational news, than the *Mennonite Reporter.* Nevertheless, the spirit of the defunct *Canadian Mennonite,* suitably modified and constantly changing, lived on. The call to apply the inherited Anabaptist and Mennonite faith in an integrative, modern, urban, and professional environment was not silenced.

THE MENNONITE CENTRAL COMMITTEE (CANADA)

One of the most effective agencies seeking to translate into practice the ideals of radical discipleship was the Mennonite Central Committee (Canada). When it was created in December 1963, MCC (Canada) was expected to solve two quite specific problems. It was to bring together into a single body the numerous Canadian Mennonite relief, service, colonization, immigration, peace, disaster service, health-care, and voluntary-service organizations that had been formed over the years. In addition, it was to become an effective and unified voice for Canadian Mennonites when they spoke to governments or to the public about their peace position.

A brief review of the Mennonite relief and service organizations may be helpful. In Ontario, Mennonites and Brethren in Christ had created two complementary organizations, one to deal with relief matters and the other to make appropriate representations to governments and to conduct negotiations regarding alternatives to military service. The Non Resistant Relief Organization had been created in 1917, and the Conference of Historic Peace Churches (CHPC) in 1940. In western Canada those Mennonites covered by the 1873 order in council had the Canadian Mennonite Relief Committee and their own Committee of Bishops, the *Aeltestenkomitee,* which sought to conduct negotiations with the government. Those Mennonites not covered by the 1873 order in council had the Mennonite Central Relief Committee. A Western Service Committee, established under the umbrella of the Canadian Mennonite Board of Colonization, conducted negotiations on their behalf with the government.

Both western Canadian relief committees and the Non Resistant Relief Committee channelled and distributed overseas shipments through the Canadian or American offices of the MCC.

Complicating the matter further, the Mennonite Central Relief Committee of Western Canada had set up provincial chapters. In addition, several provinces had their own Mennonite Disaster Service organizations, and new

Mennonite Mental Health Services were being created. Then there were relief, service, peace, and social concern committees set up by individual conferences.

There were obviously far too many committees, boards, and agencies. Until the mid-1950s key Canadian Mennonite leaders knew each other and the programs reasonably well. That made for relatively effective practical, though often informal coordination, consultation, and cooperation. The retirement or replacement of the older leaders, and a desire for greater efficiency and effectiveness, resulted in proposals to merge, amalgamate, or reorganize the various bodies. A means had to be found to cut through the bureaucratic proliferation and confusion. A single, centralized inter-Mennonite agency was the obvious solution.

Reorganization was made more urgent by growing confusion about the peace witness. During the Second World War, joint delegations of the CHPC and the Western Service Committee of the Canadian Mennonite Board of Colonization had made representations and spoken to the politicians and federal bureaucrats, while the *Aeltestenkomitee* had been effectively frozen out of meaningful participation in those negotiations. The disagreements among Mennonite groups in their response to conscription had been confusing both to government officials and to their own young people. The embarrassing situations created by B.B. Janz's tactics in Ottawa, and the large number of Mennonite young men who enlisted for active military service, all indicated the need for a new, broadly based, inter-Mennonite agency to formulate, promote, explain, and do further research on historic Mennonite peace teachings and practices.

The first step in a radical restructuring occurred in 1959. Mennonites in western Canada not covered by the 1873 order in council merged their Canadian Mennonite Board of Colonization with their Mennonite Central Relief Committee of Western Canada to form the Canadian Mennonite Relief and Immigration Council.

The second step was taken when the CHPC invited western representatives to join them in preparation of the 1960 brief to John Diefenbaker. The document was prepared in Ontario, but representatives from the other groups met privately in Ottawa before it was presented to ensure that there was unanimous support for the positions taken. Those involved in these essentially ad hoc arrangements agreed that a permanent organization was needed. So they created the Peace Church Council of Canada – essentially an enlargement of the old, Ontario-based CHPC to include the Mennonites of western Canada. This shuffle left many leaders, particularly some of the younger ones, more frustrated than ever, and there were calls for a much more radical restructuring and consolidation of all relief, service, and peace witness activities.

The radical change occurred in December 1963, when representatives from nine inter-Mennonite relief, service, peace, social concern, and mutual-aid boards, committees, and councils and from nine Mennonite conferences met in Winnipeg to create a new, national, inter-Mennonite organization that would unite all Canadian Mennonite groups in all the activities they wished to do together.[33] The new organization was to have a national mandate, but there would be provincial chapters from Ontario to British Columbia.

The delegates accepted a proposed new constitution and appointed a seven-person executive to work out all the necessary details involved in transfer of responsibilities of 'all inter-Mennonite programs ... including relief, service, peace, disaster service, immigration and mental health.'[34] Members of the transitional executive were almost equally divided between those who had served for many years and younger people who came to prominence only after the war.

The name proposed was 'Canadian Mennonite Council.' When concern was expressed about that name, 'Mennonite Central Committee (Canada)' was suggested as an alternative. Since shipment and distribution of overseas relief supplies would be handled by MCC it seemed appropriate to signify that link in the new name. 'MCC (Canada)' would also be popular in the numerous communities where the Pennsylvania-based Mennonite Central Committee enjoyed an excellent reputation. That was particularly true where there were large numbers of immigrants from the 1920s and 1940s who had received crucial assistance from the MCC.

When the name change was proposed at the meeting in Winnipeg, a night letter was sent to the MCC executive committee, which was meeting in Chicago. The Canadians asked whether there would be any objection if they named their new national organization 'MCC (Canada).' They received no reply and interpreted that as an indication that there were no objections. Later they discovered that the night letter had never reached the executive committee and that there was in fact considerable consternation in the United States when the new name was announced.[35]

U.S. Mennonites had considerable difficulty in understanding the need for a new Canadian relief organization. They thought of the MCC as an international Mennonite organization not tied or inhibited by national boundaries. The Canadians had no desire to break ties with their American co-religionists. They saw the Akron office as the appropriate agency to ship and administer overseas relief and service programs but suggested that there were unique national conditions which made it appropriate that national programs in both Canada and the United States be administered by national MCC (Canada) and MCC (United States) organizations. Overseas programs could be administered by a redefined MCC (International). These Canadian proprosals eventually forced that kind of restructuring on the MCC, even though MCC (United States) has never made much sense to the Americans.

The mandate of MCC (Canada) was to work in peace education, relief and development, voluntary service, immigration, government contacts, and other areas of mutual concern.[36] It quickly became the most influential Canadian Mennonite institution, providing a common focus and administrative structure for relief activities. It also made possible broadening and strengthening of the peace witness. The relief and service efforts have been discussed above. That work was well understood and received strong support in the Mennonite community, though it occasionally resulted in controversy when MCC offered aid and help to the victims of war without reference to the political loyalties of those victims. In Vietnam, for example, MCC remained scrupulously neutral, offering medicine, food, and non-military material both in the north and in the south.

The peace-education and peace-witness programs of MCC (Canada) became much more controversial. MCC (Akron, Pennsylvania) had established its own Peace Section in 1946. It promoted peace education in the churches through literature and study conferences, and it provided advice, information, and assistance for conscientious objectors.[37] Over the years it gradually expanded its work in a third area, that of peacemaking in conflict and promoting peace concerns among other Christians and government officials. The work and impact of the MCC (Akron) Peace Section have been described thus: 'It played very important roles in developing peace awareness and as a prophetic witness and interpreter to Mennonite groups. The peace witness of the various Mennonite groups would be substantially weaker without the nudging and encouragement of Peace Section.'[38]

Within months of its creation, MCC (Canada) established its own Peace and Social Concerns Committee, giving it a wide mandate to promote the cause of peace within and beyond the Mennonite and Brethren in Christ constituency. In addition to traditional Mennonite concerns regarding alternatives to military service, it was to address problems in labour relations and social concerns and to establish ongoing contacts with governments.

MCC (Canada)'s Peace and Social Concerns Committee became an influential but often controversial advocate of activist peacemaking. Young professional and university-educated Mennonites used it and the U.S.-based MCC Peace Section to promote their vision of Mennonite peacemaking.

Those providing leadership in MCC (Canada)'s Peace and Social Concerns Committee in the 1960s had almost all received at least some of their post-secondary education in the United States. And they maintained close contact with the MCC (Akron) Peace Section. As a result they understood American peace problems and issues much better than the often unique position and dynamics of Canadian domestic and international affairs.

Frank Epp was one of the most vocal and widely published Canadian peace activists in the 1960s. He seldom made a clear distinction between Canadian and U.S. policies and problems, as is evident in the introduction to his book *A Strategy for Peace*:

The American publisher of this Canadian manuscript has properly asked why the author sometimes speaks as a Canadian, sometimes as an American, sometimes as a North American. The answer is simple. This is how most of us Canadians live. We are citizens of an independent country, which is also a province of the empire, not always an unhappy province. This is true especially of people like me. I have spent some of the best years of my educational life in American schools; some of my most receptive audiences have been on American college campuses ... No effort has been made, therefore, to clear up the confusion concerning the national base from which I speak.[39]

Such confusion, or more often ignorance about distinctly Canadian policies and problems, was glaringly evident in the references to the North Atlantic Treaty Organization (NATO) in early drafts of the brief presented to Prime Minister Trudeau in 1970. In the second draft the authors argued that 'preoccupation with military security brings a false security only.' They added: 'We are concerned that Canada is giving so little thought to non-violent forms of resistance and social change.'[40]

Obviously neither those who drafted the brief, nor their critics at the Akron office who successfully suggested deletion of these references because they thought that Mennonites had no business discussing NATO, knew the history of NATO. They apparently did not know about Canada's determined and ongoing fight with the Americans over Article II – the so-called Canadian clause – of the NATO charter. When NATO was created Lester Pearson, who had just been appointed as Canadian Secretary of State for External Affairs and made his maiden speech in Parliament defending Article II, insisted that NATO must not become 'an instrument of unimaginative militarism.' He believed that the root causes of international conflict must be addressed through 'peaceful co-operation in the economic, social and cultural fields' and demanded that NATO have 'deeper meaning and deeper roots' than a mere balance of military terror.[41] In the end, and in spite of American attempts to weaken it, Canada got its Article II and subsequently fought hard to defend the spirit of that article in the face of American attempts to weaken and subvert its impact. Canadian Mennonites concerned about alternatives to 'unimaginative militarism' missed an obvious opportunity to engage their political leaders in informed debate because they were unaware of distinctively Canadian policies.

There was also a curious omission from that brief. The document made no reference to the leadership that Canada had provided in creation of the first United Nations peacekeeping missions. It entirely ignored Lester Pearson's role in the Suez crisis, which had won for him the Nobel Prize for Peace, and the whole notion of military peacekeeping missions. The Canadian record in peacekeeping and peacemaking was in fact much closer to that advocated by would-be Mennonite peacemakers than they realized. Canada supported economic, social, cultural, and educational cooperation as the most effective way to reduce international tensions, and peacekeeping missions under the direction of the United Nations in situations where conflict had resulted in destructive military action. But Canadian Mennonite peace activists addressing international issues talked mainly about the stupidity and wickedness of American foreign policy in Vietnam. American draft dodgers, not the problems faced by a 'middle power' such as Canada trying to promote a less militarist and confrontational policy, occupied their minds.

A similar preoccupation with American problems dominated most of the discussion about racial problems. MCC (Canada)'s spokespersons said far more in the 1960s about the evils of racial segregation and about the civil rights movement in the United States, and about apartheid in South Africa, than they did about the suffering and problems of Canada's Native people. That was sad for several reasons. An opportunity was lost to engage in informed discussion with Canadian politicians and government officials, who, like the Mennonites, hoped to be peacemakers and peacekeepers in the world. The preoccupation with American issues also caused considerable irritation in Canada. Critics did not think it proper for Canadians to meddle in the affairs of another country.

Ignorance of Canadian policies, and preoccupation with American issues, were gradually reduced as Canadian Mennonites became more involved in public affairs. The experiences and lessons learned by those working with Native people in Canada, particularly as explained and interpreted by Menno Wiebe and others serving in the Mennonite Pioneer Mission, provided a Canadian perspective on racial problems.

The opening in Ottawa in the late 1960s of an MCC (Canada) office, which was to serve as a 'listening post,' helped to familiarize Canada's Mennonites with domestic and foreign policies. The published reports by William Janzen, who served in the Ottawa office for many years, helped sensitize and inform Canadian Mennonites about domestic problems of justice, oppression, exploitation, and discrimination. Stories telling the experiences of the Native people, of people caught in exploitative situations, and of unmet needs helped Mennonites in the search for practical and workable solutions when dealing with flawed social, economic, and political institutions.

The Ottawa reports were rarely as critical as had been the denunciations of American policies in the 1960s. Canadian Mennonites did not disagree fundamentally with most Canadian foreign policy objectives. There were some controversial and divisive national policies, but Mennonite reactions to most issues were not fundamentally different than those of their fellow citizens. There were certainly very few Canadian military or diplomatic policies that elicited the kind of criticism that Mennonite peace activists in the 1960s levelled against American military and civil rights policies.

ATTITUDES TOWARD CANADIAN GOVERNMENTS

Canadian Mennonite peace activists regarded themselves, and were regarded by others, as people who were willing to accept and accommodate themselves to change and who also had a fairly open and tolerant attitude about people who held different views. They were often contrasted with those in the Canadian Mennonite community who rejected modern technology and clung tenaciously to the old ways. But in their attitude toward the role and function of government in a modern society these two seemingly divergent Mennonite groups were in basic agreement. And their position was one that also enjoyed wide acceptance in the larger Canadian community.

The traditional and widely accepted Anabaptist-Mennonite view of government or the state was defined by Harold Bender:

The beginning of all Anabaptist consideration of the state is the affirmation of its divine origin, an affirmation made specifically, emphatically and repeatedly. This is true of all governments, whether good or bad ... The necessity for the state is human sin ... Its task ... is to punish the evil, to protect the good, to administer a righteous justice, to care for the widows, the orphans, and the poor, and to provide a police force that is not against God and His Word ... Its essential function is to maintain order and thus make possible a decent human society.[42]

In their briefs and petitions to Ottawa, Mennonites invariably promised to pray for their government. In the early briefs they then asked the government to grant them exemptions from military service, remove obstacles to Mennonite immigration, and deal with other matters of concern to their people. Later briefs urged Ottawa to do what these spokespersons believed would be good for all Canadians and for suffering people in other countries. Canadian Mennonites, whether strongly committed to traditional ways or open to a great deal of change, had an essentially positive view of government.

There was also general agreement that government had a particular responsibility in protecting minorities and those holding unpopular religious, political, or other views. Mennonites in Canada had little doubt that in secular societies comprised of sinful men and women there would inevitably be selfish behaviour, disagreement, and conflict. The role of the government was to control, regulate, and manage such conflict through proper legal and institutional means. Righteousness and goodness could not be legislated; nor could sin, selfishness, and wickedness be banished by decree; but the former could be encouraged and the latter controlled. Government, as Bender said, was necessary because of human sin.

These views were similar to those of other Canadians and their leaders. The earliest English-Canadian governments had been established by the United Empire Loyalists who had fled northward after the American revolution. The Loyalists, according to one highly acclaimed recent study, assumed that society was comprised of unequal, diverse, and imperfect human beings. Conflict was therefore inevitable, but government was expected to provide

countervailing forces that unified and stabilized society and fostered public morality ... Government could not obliterate conflicts ... but it could regulate and channel them within legal and institutional bounds.

A strong and independent government could also preserve freedom by ensuring that basic British rights like trial by jury were guaranteed to all citizens. Even those citizens who supported unpopular political ideas would be guaranteed the rights to life, liberty and property. And it could prevent organized and powerful groups within the community from denying dissenters such rights as the freedom of speech or of the press. That was the liberty which Loyalists sought but did not find in Revolutionary America.[43]

Monarchical institutions were regarded by the Loyalists, and also by Canadian Mennonites, as important protectors of minorities.[44] Democratic majorities sometimes rode roughshod over the rights and interests of the minority. The Loyalists spoke frequently and bitterly of 'the tyranny of the mob' in revolutionary America. One of Canada's most distinguished historians, the late W.L. Morton, expressed a typical Canadian view when he wrote that the chief political good, and hence the primary responsibility of government, 'is stability, the existence of order in state and society. The order intended, however, is not order imposed by authority from without, but order arising from equilibrium reached among the elements of society by usage, tradition and law. It is what the philosophers call an organic order, not an order mechanically contrived, but one resulting from growth from within. Now such an order in an actually living organism, or metaphorically, in a living society results in two characteristics. One is unity, the other wholeness.'[45]

Morton's analysis is secular, but it has obvious similarities with views and expressions that can be found in Anabaptist and Mennonite writings. The language of order, stability, unity, and wholeness, particularly with regard to minorities, spoke of reciprocal privileges and responsibilities, not of individual rights that could be exercised even if they undermined social equilibrium and stability without due concern for the welfare of others. In an orderly and well-governed society privileges are granted but must be used in responsible ways that do not disrupt or destroy the social unity and wholeness of the entire society.

Over the centuries Mennonites in various countries negotiated so-called *Privilegien*. The word is significant, in part because the privileges have sometimes been misinterpreted as rights to be enjoyed without concern for their social implications. These privileges, sometimes granted in perpetuity, carried with them reciprocal responsibilities.

The Old Order Amish in Ontario understood this very well when they ran into serious problems regarding compulsory participation in the Canada Pension Plan in the 1960s, introduction of Social Insurance Numbers, and school consolidations that threatened their elementary schools. Canada at that time had no Charter of Rights. Instead, negotiators sought compromises that would allow the Old Order Amish and their neighbours to live in peace and harmony in the same communities.[46]

The compromise in the case of the Social Insurance Numbers was perhaps the easiest and illustrates the nature of the process. The federal government wanted a nine-digit identification number for each citizen with whom it had financial dealings. Specifically the numbers were to be used to identify taxpayers and recipients of social welfare benefits. The Old Order Amish were willing taxpayers and had no basic objection if the government wanted to identify them by a number rather than by names. But they objected on religious grounds to acceptance of social welfare benefits paid by the government. The solution was simple. The government agreed that those requesting it would get a number beginning with the digit '0.' Anyone with such a number was not eligible for benefits under any government social welfare programs. The Old Order Amish were not exempt from payment of taxes that supported such programs.

The compromise reached in the school question, as explained above, allowed the Old Order Amish and the Old Order Mennonites to establish their own private schools, provided that they followed the approved provincial curriculum and the tax base for the consolidated schools was not disrupted. Somewhat similar compromises were negotiated in the other disputes.[47]

While the Old Order people were conducting their negotiations, Canadian Mennonite peace activists became involved in issues related to American draft dodgers. They achieved their greatest successes when they publicized the plight of these young men and provided evidence that many were sincere, honest, and responsible prospective Canadian citizens. Critics tended to portray the draft dodgers as lazy, dirty, shiftless, and irresponsible. The issue for many Canadians was whether these young men who requested the privileges of Canadian residence or citizenship would accept the appropriate responsibilities. But at times American-style arguments about individual rights, which did not resonate well in Canada, also got into Canadian peace literature about the draft dodgers. In the booklet *I would like to dodge the draft-dodgers but* ... Frank Epp introduced language about 'rights' that was more familiar to audiences in the United States than to those in Canada: 'At a time when almost all the religious and political world was against them, our forefathers stood fast in defense of the most fundamental human right, namely the right not to kill ... For Mennonites the right has been won and the belief has been recognized, but thousands of young men from other traditions are today fighting the battle we were privileged to fight 50 years ago.'[48]

Epp had converted into a 'right' what had been carefully and correctly referred to as a 'privilege' in the brief that Canadian Mennonites had presented to Prime Minister Diefenbaker. There were probably few Canadians who took note of this change of words, but the new language sounded foreign in Canada.

In his recent book comparing Canadian and U.S. political ideology, sociologist Seymour Lipset argues: 'The very organizing principles that framed these nations, the central core around which institutions and events were to accommodate, were different. One was Whig and classically liberal or libertarian – doctrines which emphasize distrust of the state, egalitarianism, and populism – reinforced by voluntaristic and congregational religious tradition. The other was Tory and conservative in the British and European sense – accepting the need for a strong state, for respect for authority, for deference.'[49]

Lipset may have exaggerated the differences, but few suggest that there are no significant differences between Canadian and American political ideologies. It was therefore unfortunate that Canadian Mennonite peace activists in the 1960s addressed American military, foreign affairs, civil rights, and other domestic issues with talk of rights and freedoms rooted in American political ideology.

Attempts to apply names or labels to ideological differences have sometimes created more confusion than clarity. Thus, in the contemporary popular press stalwart defenders of the free-enterprise system, old-style Soviet communists, and Arabs who insist on restrictive clothing for women are all referred to as 'conservatives,' while those willing to accept change and who tolerate diversity of opinion and belief and also support universal, government-sponsored social programs are referred to as 'liberals.' If the meaning that those labels had in the nineteenth century were applied, then Margaret Thatcher, Ronald Reagan, and Brian Mulroney were certainly 'liberals,' while modern socialist parties come much closer to the seventeenth-century 'conservative' ideology than any so-called conservative. Canadian political ideas, as discussed above, are closer to the 'conservative' ideology expressed so eloquently in Edmund Burke's *Reflections on the Revolution in France*[50] than to the 'liberal' ideology that fed both the French and the American revolutions.

The language of political discourse among Canadian Mennonites urging a more activist peace witness in the 1960s responded primarily to American ideology. Canadian Mennonites did not formulate their own ideology in the 1960s, but there was an uncomfortable feeling that the new initiatives in peacemaking somehow did not quite fit the Canadian scene. The brief to Prime Minister Trudeau in 1970, for example, failed to address Canada's most important peace initiatives.

TRADITIONALIST MENNONITE RESPONSES

Many Mennonites in Canada dissented from the views expressed by the peacemaking activists. Some supported the old, separatist position, which held that the state had its God-given responsibilities to maintain law and order, if necessary by force or by the sword, but that Christians should have nothing to do with it. State responsibilities were fundamentally different from the ethic of those who had voluntarily committed themselves to following Jesus' teachings. The state had to deal with sinful and unregenerate people. To discharge its responsibilities it had to resort to means that were inappropriate for Christians. Gerhard Lohrenz, one of the most outspoken and widely published Mennonite critics of the peace activists in the 1960s, expressed the views of many when he wrote: 'To me it seems that MCC should refrain from political actions designed to bring about a new political set up; it simply should stick to Galatians 6:10. ['As we therefore have opportunity, let us do good unto all men, especially unto them who are of the household of faith.'] This provides a platform which the various groups of our people are and will be willing to support; as soon as we begin to act politically it must lead to division in our ranks.'[51]

Others argued that simply doing good, or providing relief, solved few problems if the underlying injustices and oppression were not removed. Those involved in voluntary service were often the first to realize that emergency aid alone was not enough. Thus Hedy Sawadsky, a Canadian who served two years as an MCC relief worker in Jordan and Israel in the 1960s, reported on a confrontation that she had with a well-educated Palestinian women, who said, 'Hedy, what you're doing here is fine, but it's Band-Aid work. You came after the war, after the damage was done. Why don't you go home and work for peace and get at the root causes of evil and war?'[52] That was the challenge that Mennonite peace activists tried to meet.

Many of those who opposed a more active Mennonite peace position shared with other Canadians, and particularly with many evangelical Christians, a deep-seated fear and hatred of communism. Many Canadian Mennonites had, in fact, experienced Soviet communism at first hand and were convinced that there was a world-wide communist conspiracy that could be met and stopped only by superior military force. Any peace initiatives that weakened or undermined American resolve in its Cold War with the Soviets should be denounced. One of Gerhard Lohrenz's correspondents expressed those ideas:

With myself I have had the conviction for quite some time that this whole peace movement really is mostly deception. They always find fault with our government and that of the U.S., but very few seem to see that the communist countries are far more violent and so completely atheistic as to try to eradicate faith in God from the face of the earth ... I have read in certain well documented news commentaries papers how communists iniate [sic] so called 'peace' movements to further their cause ... But what can we do to save MCC from should I say such subversion. Sometimes I feel this should be more widely explained to our brotherhood or constituencies and then by a vote at the MCC meeting relieve the Peace Section of the umbrella of the MCC.[53]

The horrors, mistakes, and atrocities of the Vietnam War greatly intensified the debate between those who believed that secular governments, including that of the United States, should conduct their affairs in a civil and Christian way and those who insisted that the primary duty of the American government was to stop the Godless and atheistic communist threat by any necessary means.

German linguistic, cultural, and ethnic concerns sometimes aggravated the disagreements. In 1955 Dietrich H. Epp, founder, editor, and publisher of the German-language inter-Mennonite paper *Der Bote*, died. The paper had received substantial support from the Conference of Mennonites in Canada (CMC), and J.J. Thiessen, who chaired both the CMC and the editorial board of *Der Bote*, was determined to find a new editor who would promote not only Mennonite religious ideas but also serve as a champion of their German culture and heritage. The man chosen was Walter Quiring,[54] who had served with the military forces of the Third Reich during the Second World War. He had published extensively on Mennonite agricultural pioneering successes in various parts of the world and was a former editor of the German-language Mennonite glossy magazine *Mennonitische Welt*.

Quiring and *Der Bote* became bitter antagonists of Frank Epp and the *Canadian Mennonite*. That antagonism was rooted in Quiring's strong anti-communist and pro-German stance. Quiring made few apologies for his wartime activities, while Epp was sharply critical of the support that the two largest German-language Canadian Mennonite papers – *Der Bote* and *Mennonitische Rundschau* – had given the Nazis before and during the war.

When Quiring's appointment to *Der Bote* was proposed no one challenged his editorial and literary skills or his support for the German language and culture. There were, however, questions regarding his Nazi past and his alleged lack of 'spirituality.'[55] As editor of *Der Bote* Quiring became a determined and talented critic of the peacemaking agenda of the *Canadian Mennonite* and of MCC Peace and Social Concerns Committees.

When Epp published a controversial, commissioned history of the Canadian Mennonite Board of Colonization, Quiring led the charge in denouncing the book as biased, inaccurate, and unreliable. He did not find it sufficiently critical of the communists and also objected to incorporation of material that he and other critics thought should not have been included. He scrutinized the book with great care and then published a long review in which he enumerated many errors. These ranged from simple typographical or grammatical mistakes to major interpretive problems. That review clearly indicated the hatred of communism and the pro-German sentiments felt by many Canadian Mennonites.[56]

One issue in particular inflamed the passions of Gerhard Lohrenz, Walter Quiring, Paul Schaefer, and other critics of the new, more activist peacemaking strategy. That was civil disobedience. Vietnam War draft dodgers and civil rights marchers and demonstrators achieved some of their most impressive successes in the United States when they refused to obey laws that they believed to be bad, unjust, or discriminatory. Two things made civil disobedience a particularly volatile issue in Canada. First, it could disrupt the order, stability, and unity of the country. Those who disobeyed laws they thought unjust were not peacemakers; they were peace disturbers. Second, those advocating civil disobedience in Canada were protesting American rather than Canadian policies and problems.

Gerhard Lohrenz and Walter Quiring were very angry when an American peace activist from a Quaker background was invited to speak at the University of Manitoba on civil disobedience and the *Canadian Mennonite* gave his address favourable coverage. The speaker, Dr Sibley, had been doubly offensive. He had argued that Christians have a duty to disobey and protest against laws that do not accord with Christian teachings. He had also made statements in support of intellectual freedom, which the critics interpreted as pro-communist. Lohrenz, in a letter urging the Conference of Mennonites to cut off all financial support for the *Canadian Mennonite*, argued that the editor had supported Sibley, who had said: 'I would like to see on the campus one or two Communist professors, a student's communist club, a chapter of the American Association of the advancement of atheism, a society for the promotion of free love, a league for the overthrow of the government by Jeffersonian violence.'[57]

Sibley did not personally support many of these things but believed that they should be discussed openly. Critics vehemently disagreed, insisting that the peacemaking endeavours of the activists were contrary to separatist Mennonite doctrines. They were able to gain a great deal of support, not only from those who shared their fears and prejudices but also from those who had difficulty going along with peacemaking that seemed rooted in American political ideology.

CLASHES WITH OTHER EVANGELICALS

Peacemaking also offended those who believed that the primary responsibility of the church was to preach the gospel and to save souls. Many North American evangelicals believed that the world was lost and going to its doom. It could not be saved. The end times were at hand. Christians should therefore devote all their efforts to the saving of individual human beings.

Frank Epp was an enthusiastic supporter of North American evangelicals. He believed that men such as George R. Brunk II, the Janz Team, and Billy Graham were a positive and liberating force in Canadian Mennonite life. They had pointed out the error of clinging to obsolete and dead traditions and brought new life to Mennonite churches. They were allies in the battles with pro-German traditionalist leaders, and those working at the *Canadian Mennonite* were described as 'friends of evangelist Graham.'[58] But there was a fly in the ointment. It was the militant anti-communist stance of many evangelicals, including Billy Graham and other North American evangelists, who, according to the *Canadian Mennonite*, did not preach the whole Gospel. Specifically, they did not apply the Gospel to issues of war and peace. Instead, they preached a pro-Western, anti-communist, and militarist gospel that reinforced traditionalist, pro-German, and anti-communist sentiments in Mennonite communities: 'The way Mennonites all over the country are running after the professional anti-Communist crusaders, after the political ideologies purporting to be exclusively Christian, and after a strange brand of nationalist Christianity makes one think that either Christ of the cross has been forsaken or he has been made over into the image of a nationalistic Messiah.'[59]

A *Canadian Mennonite* editorial complained that nationalist evangelists were making God into an American tribal deity: 'American Christians were mistaking Americans as the people of God, America as God's own country and God as the God of the Americans ... That this reduction of God to a tribal deity must happen again even after the bitter, bitter lessons of revolutions and war is both disheartening and alarming. That it is happening first of all and most of all in the sector of Christianity which we have described as evangelical is sorrowing.'[60]

Such editorials brought the paper into direct conflict with the American tribal deity's chief high priest – Billy Graham. Graham had been a struggling preacher until 1949, when he was suddenly catapulted to national prominence through a campaign in Los Angeles. Several prominent Hollywood personalities had responded, giving the campaign unusual publicity. In addition, and more important, Graham had distinguished himself as a particularly determined and outspoken opponent of communism, who linked Christianity with American nationalism and militarism. The earth, he announced, was divided into two camps: 'On the one side we see communism. On the other we see Western culture, with its foundation in the Bible, the Word of God ... Communism has declared war against God, against Christ, against the Bible.'[61] Such language, equating the United States and Western civilization with the cause of God, was clearly at variance with historic Anabaptist theology, but it attracted the favourable attention of newspaper magnate William Randolph Hearst, who ordered that his papers 'puff Graham.'[62] Henry Luce followed, with a three-page colour spread and story in *Time*, and Graham became a star and the darling of the political and military establishment. He became a confidant of several U.S. presidents, and a former aide to Lyndon Johnson later said that, at the worst times during the Vietnam War, 'Nobody could make Johnson feel he was right quite like Billy Graham could.'[63]

What were Canadian Mennonites to make of all this? Many participated enthusiastically in the campaigns and crusades. They also shared Graham's hatred of communism, but his support for American foreign policies and military tactics, particularly his willingness to bring to the podium young, clean-cut U.S. marines in uniform who talked of how God had helped them in the war, implying that they were killing communists for Jesus, violated Mennonite sensitivities. Many evangelicals, particularly those subscribing to dispensationalist theology, had no difficulty with the war. The God of the Old Testament who had helped the ancient Israelites in battle and demanded that they slaughter their enemies, down to the last woman and child, was now demanding something similar of Americans in their war with Godless communism. Jesus' teachings in the Sermon on the Mount were for a future dispensation. Communists were the modern-day Philistines.

The main problem that many Mennonites had with militant anti-communism was that they agreed with much of it but simply could not imagine Jesus approving, much less doing, the sorts of things that the Americans were doing in Vietnam. Mennonites, even more than many American evangelicals, regarded communism as a thoroughly evil system bent on world domination. They had little confidence that communists could or would be deterred by peaceful or diplomatic means. Only military might and the resolve of the West were likely to stop communist aggression. And, according to Anabaptist theology, it was the God-given responsibility of the state to maintain law and order and to punish evil-doers. Yet few could imagine Jesus dropping napalm on defenceless women and children, burning the homes and villages of harmless peasants, or doing the many other atrocious things that Americans allegedly had to do to stop the communists.

Graham eventually realized that his open support of American military policies was controversial and tried to restrict himself to the task of evangelism. Canadian Mennonite peace activists demanded more. As early as 1956 an editorial in the *Canadian Mennonite* praised Graham's 'whole-hearted dedication to God' but complained that 'Billy Graham is still not sufficiently applying the Gospel to the problems of everyday life.'[64]

In August 1961, sixteen Mennonite leaders met with Graham and members of his staff in Philadelphia. The *Canadian Mennonite* wrote: 'He [Billy

Graham] commented briefly on the problems involved in taking the nonresistant position, but noted the uncertainty and confusion among Christians regarding the proper attitude toward participation in war. He stated his personal openness and interest in meeting with a few Mennonite leaders for more extended discussion on the doctrine of nonresistance.'[65]

The increasing ambivalence toward Graham became obvious in two news reports that appeared in the 7 December, 1965 issue of the *Canadian Mennonite*. One described a Washington peace march. It was entitled 'To Mobilize the Conscience of America'[66] and explained in strongly supportive language why two Mennonites had participated. The other article covered Graham's criticism of the peace march, using the military heading 'The Cry for War. Graham Attacked Peace Marchers.'[67]

In 1966, after publishing several stories critical of Graham's support for the war, Mennonite leaders arranged another meeting, this time with Leighton Ford, Graham's associate. In describing that meeting, the *Canadian Mennonite* quoted Ford as saying: 'I am personally attracted to Niebuhr's beliefs on pacifism and did some rethinking of my own position, but I am not prepared to take a completely pacifist position.'[68]

Graham's 1966 Christmas tour of Vietnam, his high praise for the dedication, discipline, and motivation of American soldiers in Vietnam, and his denunciations of peace marches, which, he claimed, gave comfort to the enemy, led the editor of the *Canadian Mennonite* to ask some very difficult questions: 'To what extent do we ally ourselves with an organization [Billy Graham] so facilely identifying itself with an existing power structure alien to the very nature of the church? ... On what level, and to what extent, is cooperation possible with an organization and a speaker whose easy identification with a political power negate [*sic*] both our understanding of the very nature of the church and the Baptist concept of church-state separation.'[69]

Even the *Mennonite Brethren Herald*, which had given enthusiastic, deferential, and almost unquestioning support to Graham's evangelistic campaigns, eventually had enough. John Redekop, the paper's 'Personal Opinion' column writer, levelled a blast at the statements made by Graham during his 1966 Christmas tour of Vietnam:

I get the impression that he [Graham] has caused millions of people throughout the world to conclude that at least as he sees it, the cause of Christ and the cause of the U.S. in Vietnam are one and the same thing ... I suggest that Graham distorts the biblical depiction of the Christian battle against evil when again by subtle implication, he links it with the American intervention in Vietnam.

The preaching of the full gospel does not make the prophet popular. It never has. Jesus Christ himself was run out of town and crucified. Anybody who calls people to a life of true discipleship can expect to be rejected by the powers of this world. Chaplains are salve for the conscience; prophets call men to repentance.[70]

The ongoing debates between Christian peace activists and American religious leaders who gave strong support to American anti-communist military campaigns was never resolved to either side's satisfaction. Billy Graham's own confidence was badly shaken, however, by the revelations resulting in the disgrace of his close friend Richard Nixon and later by a visit to the Soviet Union, which destroyed his earlier image and understanding of that country.[71] Mennonite peace activists, however, could not formulate a satisfactory solution to the problem of communist aggression. Both sides eventually agreed that grievous mistakes were made in the Vietnam War. In practice, however, both opted for escapist courses. The evangelicals concentrated on their task of soul winning and world-wide evangelism, leaving the dirty work of keeping law and order and thwarting communist aggression to the government and the military. Canadian Mennonite peace activists preached peace but refused to endorse any military action, even if it were designed to maintain or re-establish peace, order, and good government.

CONCLUSION

In the 1960s Canadian Mennonites had to reassess and apply in new ways their 'peace witness.' Non-resistance remained the ideology of some, but others moved toward more activist peacemaking strategies. Many of those whose lives had been transformed by the forces of modernity also found it necessary to transform their peace witness. The attempt to do so produced much controversy. Redefinition of Mennonite peace concerns brought activists closer to the thinking and aspirations of their fellow citizens but increased the strains between Mennonites who cherished inherited Anabaptist doctrines and those more strongly influenced by other evangelical approaches.

The convergence between the peace positions of Mennonites and those of their government and fellow citizens was somewhat obscured in the 1960s because Mennonite peace activists borrowed from and depended on American ideas and methods. It was only when Canadian Mennonites had the opportunity to look back, and to reflect on their post–Second World War experiences, that the Canadian character of the Mennonite transformation became obvious.

Conclusion:
Looking Back

Canadian Mennonites experienced much change in the decades following the beginning of the Second World War. It was natural for them to review and assess those changes from time to time. Several events provided unique opportunities for such assessments and shed light on different aspects of the changes that Mennonites had experienced.

THE MENNONITE WORLD CONFERENCE IN KITCHENER, 1962

In August 1962 the Seventh Mennonite World Conference was held in Kitchener. It was the first time the Mennonite World Conference met in Canada, and Canadian Mennonites naturally gave much thought to the image that they would present to their world-wide fellow believers. The Kitchener-Waterloo area, where Old Order Amish lived side by side with successful Mennonite businessmen, professionals, and academics, provided a unique opportunity to show the diversity of Canadian Mennonite life. It also revealed, particularly to delegates from Third World countries, the economic success and prosperity that Mennonites had achieved in Canada. Certainly people with very diverse employment, occupational, and business backgrounds mingled in the Kitchener Memorial Auditorium during that first week of August 1962.

The conference was memorable for many because it was the last time the seriously ill conference president, Harold S. Bender, gave a public address. But in retrospect it was the conference theme, 'The Lordship of Christ,' that seems particularly noteworthy. That theme had been chosen at the suggestion of Harold Bender and of the West German members of the presidium of the Mennonite World Conference. They wanted a theme that focused on issues that 'concern us as Christians and Churches in the light of contemporary conditions.'[1] It had particular relevance to the Canadian situation, where Mennonites had lived for decades in communities in which they sought to separate themselves from the world. Mennonites' theology had always placed their own families, congregations, and communities under the Lordship of Christ, but there had not been an equally clear understanding that all of life beyond their own communities must also be placed under the Lordship of Christ. Having ventured into the outside world, Mennonites at Kitchener in 1962 boldly proclaimed: 'We acknowledge Jesus our Saviour to be the Lord of our lives in everything. We accept His call to full discipleship. We pledge our obedience to Him and His Word, and dedicate ourselves unreservedly to His cause and Kingdom. We commit ourselves to the Way of life which the gospel and His teaching require.'[2]

The idea that all of life must be brought into harmony and wholeness under the Lordship of Christ, allowing for no distinction between sacred and secular or spiritual and carnal affairs, was strongly affirmed at the conference. Adolf Schnebele, an elder in a West German church, put it this way: 'The Lordship of Jesus over the life of the believer has a total effect. This means that the claim to Lordship includes all of life. Even the daily work is included in it. Nothing is too secular to be placed under the Lordship of Christ.'[3]

When Canadian Mennonites first left the security of their rural communities many feared that that would result in loss of their radical and holistic discipleship. The Mennonite World Conference of 1962 was a triumphant assertion that, in spite of the massive changes that they had undergone, their holistic theology remained relevant and redemptive. There was certainly diversity. Vincent Harding, a Black civil rights leader who had seen the inside of numerous southern U.S. jails, was one of the invited speakers, much to the chagrin of some traditionalists. But so were evangelists Myron Augsburger and George R. Brunk. Doctrines of radical discipleship were being applied in different ways, but the conference affirmed the relevance of historic Anabaptist and Mennonite theology in the new environment in which the majority of Canadian Mennonites found themselves.[4]

THE CANADIAN CENTENNIAL, 1967

Five years later, Canadian Mennonites celebrated a very different event. The centennial of Confederation elicited numerous statements and reports documenting the comfortable relationship that Mennonites had formed with their fellow citizens and with their governments. They joined with twenty-nine other religious bodies to endorse the Canadian Interfaith Conference's 'Commentary on Canada,' which concluded: 'In gratitude for the blessings of the past, and in hope for the future, we do proclaim this historic year, 1967, as one of thanksgiving, prayer and celebration to commemorate the Centennial of Confederation.'[5]

In its celebration, the *Canadian Mennonite* published an exceptionally large, seventy-six-page, special edition. The editorial there said, among other things, 'Yes, Canada, you've become a home to us; so much so that we're losing the nonconformity that brought us here.'[6] Another writer asked: 'What will the impact of the Mennonites be on the larger society? It remains to be seen whether the Anabaptist-Mennonite emphasis on practical discipleship will make any impact at all on the harsh hedonistic emphases of the world. Will we be scattered as chaff before the wind, because we have lost our values? or are we being scattered as seeds of the Kingdom to die unto ourselves and to bear much fruit?'[7]

Mennonites, who had been strangers and sojourners in alien lands so often in their history, had become citizens of Canada in an emotional and religious as well as in a legal sense. John A. Toews, in his reflective article entitled 'Fly your flag, but not too high,' observed:

For the committed Christian the priorities of life have been established once and for all by the teachings of Christ ... As citizens of Canada we rejoice with our fellow-Canadians in the prosperity and progress of our country during this Centennial Year. As Christians, and more particularly as Mennonite Christians, we are grateful for the magnanimity of our Canadian Government in extending liberties and opportunities to people who have accepted the responsibilities of citizenship with some reservations. We believe that we can serve our church, our country, and our world most effectively by giving our primary loyalty and supreme allegiance to Jesus Christ as Lord of both: church and state.[8]

Mennonites clearly felt comfortable in the larger Canadian society. Two writers who reviewed the coverage that Mennonites were receiving in the public press in 1967 were pleased to report: 'The Mennonite image is good; we can move more boldly ... Mennonite culture is respectable; relief and service across the world is applauded; Mennonites are becoming more educated and co-operation with other groups is on the increase.'[9]

THE PROFILE OF MENNONITE AND BRETHREN IN CHRIST DENOMINATIONS, 1972

The Canadian census of 1971, referred to repeatedly above, and the membership profile based on material gathered by J. Howard Kauffman and

Leland Harder in 1972 and published in 1975, provide further and different evidence of the changes in Mennonite life. The most basic fact that emerges clearly from comparison of the 1941 and the 1971 returns is that Mennonites, who had been overwhelmingly a rural and agricultural people in 1941, had left their farms and rural communities in large numbers. Kauffman and Harder's study unfortunately does not segregate Canadian from American findings in many categories. Their general findings nevertheless are relevant to the Canadian situation. The first of these, as outlined in the conclusion, is perhaps not surprising: 'The present day descendants of the sixteenth-century Anabaptists emerge from the study as a religiously conservative group. Their scores on two doctrinal orthodoxy scales placed them near the most orthodox end of the liberal-orthodox continuum, with about 90% of the respondents choosing the most orthodox response. This portrays Mennonites and Brethren in Christ as more orthodox than all other major denominations that have been studied, both Protestant and Catholic, with one notable exception, the Southern Baptists.'[10]

This finding corrects a mistaken impression that has arisen because Mennonite historians and sociologists sometimes divide Canadian Mennonites into opposing camps of liberals and conservatives. It is true that some are more open than others to new technology and more tolerant of new ideas, practices, a non-rural life-style, and different forms of church governance and discipline. But when compared with other religious groups Mennonites endorsed conservative or orthodox beliefs and practices.

They did so, however, without abandoning a commitment to the ideal of a radical and holistic Christian discipleship that was rooted in historic Anabaptism: 'Can present-day Mennonites and Brethren in Christ validly claim the name of Anabaptists? The findings lean in the affirmative direction although not in all the details. To be sure, a minority do not assent to the distinguishing principles which set the early Anabaptists apart from the other reformers. But a substantial majority do ... From sixty to eighty percent of the present church members express agreement with these basic principles of Anabaptism. An additional ten to twenty percent indicate uncertainty on these issues.'[11]

The issues on which there was serious slippage were not directly related to fundamental principles – a holistic Gospel, a radical discipleship that taught love and non-resistance, and the church as a voluntary association of adult believers. They concerned participation in politics and government, use of courts for legal redress, some of the rigorous elements of church discipline related to excommunication and shunning of those excommunicated, and swearing of oaths.

The researchers in 1972 found that 'adherence to Anabaptism was only slightly stronger among rural members than among urban members.'[12] The follow-up survey by Kauffman and Driedger almost twenty years later found, to the surprise of many, that distinctive Anabaptist values and teachings actually enjoyed greater support in urban than in rural congregations in 1989. That clearly suggests that urbanization and modernization did not result in abandonment of distinctive Anabaptist-Mennonite doctrines.

Kauffman and Harder also asked the very difficult question whether 'a commitment to Anabaptism makes any significant difference in the life and witness of contemporary church members.' Their findings suggest an affirmative answer:

Those rating high [on the Anabaptist Scale used by the interviewers] are also higher on all faith scales, especially associationalism, communalism, conversion, devotionalism, and doctrinal orthodoxy. Those strongly Anabaptist also rate higher on moral attitudes and behaviour, pacifism, and the idea of separation of church and state. In several areas of social ethics, notably attitudes toward racial minorities and toward welfare programs, those committed strongly to Anabaptism are not much different from others. Those committed to Anabaptism are slightly more prejudiced against Catholics and Jews, and are more opposed to labor unions.[13]

Kauffman and Harder's profile also reported several 'unresolved tensions.' The first related to sectarian or separatist values and those calling for more cooperation with other denominations and support for ecumenism. A second related to increased participation by North American Mennonites in politics. On this point there may well have been a significant difference between Canadian and American responses, and perhaps also between those of Swiss and Russian Mennonites. The survey does not make a distinction, but other studies indicate that at least the Russian Mennonites in Canada felt more comfortable with their governments than did Mennonites in the United States.

The final conclusion is particularly instructive:

If Anabaptism is to speak with freshness and relevance to the here and the now, it cannot be freighted with too much cultural baggage from the past. The younger generation is looking for a message that will speak to the latter part of the twentieth century. The message from the 'left wing of the Reformation' does speak to the contemporary world, but it must be freed from the encrusted cultural forms within which it so easily becomes encased by the passage of time and the generations ... There is much to be done, and the hurts of the world cry out for the message of love and Christian service set forth by the Anabaptist reformers four centuries ago.[14]

'WHERE WE'RE AT' IN THE *CANADIAN MENNONITE*, 1971

Another very different source confirms many of these findings. In February 1971 the influential but often controversial English-language Mennonite newspaper, the *Canadian Mennonite*, was forced to close. In the next-to-last issue Frank H. Epp, the former and long-term editor, offered his own reflections, which infuriated the traditionalists because he suggested that the spirit of the *Canadian Mennonite* might live on.[15] In 1971 there were still many who wanted to turn the clock back. They wanted an English-language Mennonite paper that would be as devotional, deferential, and docile as the German-language papers and cause as few controversies as the *Mennonite Brethren Herald*. Gerhard Lohrenz in Winnipeg, for example, was convinced that the *Canadian Mennonite* had failed because of its 'unwise policy of supporting the "radicals" on all issues ... Often this position of the paper bordered on the ludicrous.'[16] Other critics were less circumspect and simply denounced it as a communist paper.

These sentiments made the final issue an unusual artefact. Twelve younger Mennonites wrote articles that explained 'Where We're At ...' Both the topics and the writers selected were significant. The dozen topics were 'Where we're at ... '

> In our attitude toward non-Mennonites
> In our attitude toward women
> On violence and revolution
> In Mennonite family life
> In inter-Mennonite relations
> In theology
> In our understanding and use of the arts
> In music-making
> In our understanding of the Anabaptist vision
> In Mennonite educational procedure and philosophy
> In our attitude toward youth
> In our understanding of the pastoral ministry

Almost all the authors subsequently occupied leadership positions in the larger Mennonite community. Neither the traditionalists nor fundamentalist/pro-military, anti-communist spokespersons were invited to contribute to the final edition of the *Canadian Mennonite*. Those assessing where Canada's Mennonites were in 1971 were more closely attuned to future developments than were their critics.

None of these twelve articles advocated a return to German as the appropriate language of worship or to former rural-agricultural, separatist theology. Nor did they advocate reversion to old structures of leadership and church governance, and they certainly did not endorse a hard-line, anti-communist theology. The tenor of the several articles was clear. They called for a radical discipleship, applied to the conditions and challenges of modern society. Those challenges were clearly spelled out by Helmut Harder in his article on Mennonite theology: 'We are now hearing voices outside our circles which are saying – sometimes clearly and sometimes implicitly – that the Anabaptist vision is by no means obsolete.'[17]

In his review article William Klassen was one of the first critics to make a clear distinction between Canadian and U.S. goals for Mennonites: 'If indeed the emerging generation can divert its energies from reaction against an ethnic identity and instead come to terms with those elements in its past which transcend ethnic categories, then a truly revolutionary witness could again spring forth from one segment of the free church. To do so it will need a far greater degree of independence from a US agenda and an institutional structure which thrives in the United States.'[18]

The articles manifest both a strong sense of mission or purpose and a feeling of comfort in, or accommodation to, the Canadian context in which that mission or purpose was to be realized. Mennonites in Canada were no longer aliens or strangers. They were people who believed that they had in the past, and would in future, make a positive contribution to the country and the society in which they lived. Their lives were integrated into Canadian society, but they had not lost their unique or distinctive witness.

THE MANITOBA MENNONITE CENTENNIAL, 1974

The *Canadian Mennonite* and those who wrote the 'Where We're At ...' articles in 1971 did not speak for all Canadian Mennonites, or perhaps even for a majority. Opposition seemed to be particularly strong in some of the rural communities in southern Manitoba, among descendants of the immigrants of the 1870s. Celebrations marking the centennial of the arrival of these Mennonites in Manitoba were held in 1974. In anticipation of those events stories of the pioneers were gathered in 1972 and 1973, edited, and then published in 1975.[19] Work was also begun on a Mennonite Pioneer Museum in Steinbach. Public and government support for that museum, and the Manitoba Mennonite centennial celebrations, demonstrates how the immigrants of the 1870s and their descendants had adjusted to their new homeland. In the special centennial issue of the *Mennonite Mirror*, Robert Kreider spoke for many when he wrote: 'I am of the conviction that our

Mennonite heritage speaks to the sickness of our society. Here are people who take seriously the biblical record and their dramatic Anabaptist-Mennonite heritage ... If the Mennonite heritage is to speak to the needs of people today, it cannot be a slavish imitation of Mennonite traditions. It calls for fresh translations of our heritage into the language of our day. Our need is not for a copying of surface characteristics, but rather for a living out in fresh ways of ideas and themes within the tradition.'[20]

SOME HARD LESSONS

The transformation of Canadian Mennonites was not easy. Several particularly hard lessons had to be learned. Perhaps the most difficult was the fact that in the new world there seemed to be fewer absolutes and few situations where there was a clear choice between what was right and what was wrong. How could a Gospel of radical discipleship be reconciled with active participation in a capitalist economic system? How could it accommodate participation in political and practical affairs, where the art of the possible, not of the ideal, was operative? In the old secluded and sectarian Mennonite world military warfare had always been wrong, and it was relatively easy to bring that perspective to the evils of the Vietnam War in the 1960s. It was much harder to assess the morality of a Canadian international peacekeeping mission. Perhaps for that reason Canadian Mennonites said almost nothing about peacekeeping in the 1960s. The old absolute values were difficult to apply in those and many other modern situations. Once that fact was admitted, there was an obvious danger that on many questions Canadian Mennonites would adopt 'a sliding scale of discipleship' rather than accepting and applying literally Jesus' Sermon on the Mount, which was their 'gold standard of Christian discipleship.'[21]

At a Mennonite Brethren Bible College faculty retreat in 1978 John A. Toews provided insight into this aspect of the Mennonite transformation. He commented that during most of his life he had been uncomfortable with uncertainly or ambiguity. As an evangelist and teacher he had tried to embody a way of teaching and preaching that expressed complete certainty. He had, however, come to the point where he had to acknowledge that there was much he did not know and that there were ambiguities in our deepest convictions. A Christian had to come to terms with those uncertainties and find peace by leaving them to God's providence.[22] Those old certainties could become burdensome for leaders and for those whom they tried to lead. In his last sermon series in the Kitchener Mennonite Brethren Church before moving from the city Frank C. Peters, an influential and beloved teacher and pastor, asked his listeners: 'Have you ever thought of the anquish of a preacher who remembers burdens he has placed on people over the years based on convictions he had at that time – and recognizes that since then he has changed his mind?'[23] In the transformation experienced in Canada by Mennonites as they moved from their rural enclaves into modern urban environments old certainties were shaken, not only for parishioners but for their leaders as well.

A second hard lesson related to the discovery that Mennonites' understanding of the Gospel was inevitably clothed in their own cultural, social, and ethnic garb but that the Gospel itself was not limited to specific cultural or ethnic forms. It sometimes seemed difficult to separate the essence of the Gospel from the cultural context in which people had heard, accepted, and tried to apply it. Missionized peoples overseas, Native Canadians, urban derelicts, and ordinary Canadians with whom Mennonites shared workplaces, communities, and amenities taught them that the Gospel was not limited to their sectarian sacred forms. It was greater and transcended any culture and yet always had to be lived and proclaimed within specific cultural and ethnic contexts.[24]

A third hard lesson pertained to the embarrassments of failure and sin in the lives of individual believers and within the community of believers. Before 1939 there was a strong feeling that the true church of Christ ought to be a shining example. It, and its members, must be without spot or wrinkle, and in many of Canada's Mennonite churches there were long lists of prohibited activities to ensure that the church's witness to the public was exemplary. When that had not been the case, there had been a strong feeling that failures must not be disclosed to those to whom the message of salvation was to be preached and demonstrated through the exemplary lives of believers. In the more open, modern urban environment such sectarian practices could not be enforced. While the Gospel message was to make people whole, that ideal was never fully realized either in everyday life or in the sacred affairs of the church. People had to admit and find redemptive ways of dealing not only with the evils of the outside world but also with the imperfections of their sacred communities.

CONCLUSION

Mennonites in Canada in the early 1970s were a different people than their parents had been when war broke out in 1939. The war pried many out of their rural communities. Technological and economic changes in agriculture meant that fewer people were needed on the farms while new opportunities in the towns and cities drew thousands of Mennonites into new environments. The work there required more and different education and training and new styles of leadership and organization. All these changes meant that the witness or mission of Mennonites altered, even though the core concepts and beliefs remained.

Not all Mennonites in Canada accommodated themselves to the changing environment in the same way or at the same pace. Most experienced the changes as a process of accommodation rather than of assimilation. Some were assimilated into contemporary secular society, and others, into the evangelical stream of Christianity in which they lost their understanding of and commitment to distinctive Anabaptist-Mennonite beliefs and practices. But the majority experienced the transformation as members of a diverse but identifiable group. They were a people transformed. They had lost some of their distinctive traits but retained many others and also rediscovered some that had been neglected in the rural enclaves but which were relevant to life in a modern Canadian setting.

Appendix A
Mennonite Groups in Canada

Any systematic classification and description of Mennonite groups inevitably causes much confusion, particularly for non-Mennonite readers. The date at which various groups arrived in Canada, and their antecedent history, offer an explanation of some of the differences among groups and conferences of Mennonites. Five major migrations or migration waves can be identified. There was, however, intermittent migration between the major waves, and there was also considerable movement of people back and forth between Canada and the United States. The five major migrations, with some of the denominational terms attached, are as follows:

(OLD) MENNONITES, 1786–1825

Approximately 2,000 (Old) Mennonites migrated to Upper Canada (later Ontario) from Pennsylvania between 1786 and 1825. These people traced their ancestry to southern Germany and Switzerland and have often been referred to by Mennonite historians as 'Swiss' Mennonites.

AMISH MENNONITES, 1824–1850

Approximately 1,000 Amish Mennonites moved to Upper Canada from Alsace, adjacent German territories, and Bavaria between 1824 and 1850. They also traced their ancestry to southern Germany and Switzerland and have also been referred to as 'Swiss' Mennonites.

KANADIER, 1874–1880

Between 1874 and 1880, 7,343 Mennonites migrated from Russia to Manitoba under the provisions of a special Canadian order in council, PC 959, dated 13 August 1873.

Their ancestors came from the Netherlands but had migrated to Prussia, Poland, and northern Germany before their migration to Russia in the late eighteenth and early nineteenth centuries. They have sometimes been referred to as 'Dutch' Mennonites. A more common popular designation, however, was 'Kanadier,' which distinguished them from the next group of Mennonite immigrants from Russia, who also traced their ancestry to the Netherlands.

RUSSLAENDER, 1923–1930

Some 20,200 Mennonites fled from the Soviet Union and were assisted by the Canadian Mennonite Board of Colonization to emigrate to Canada between 1923 and 1930. They shared a common 'Dutch' ancestry with the immigrants of the 1870s, but chose to remain in Russia. They were uprooted and dispossessed as a result of the Russian Revolution. In Canada they were sometimes referred to as 'Russlaender.'

POSTWAR IMMIGRANTS

About 7,700 Mennonites from the Soviet Union and other eastern European countries fled or were evacuated westward during the last year of the Second World War and subsequently migrated to Canada in the late 1940s as Displaced Persons, with the assistance of the Canadian Mennonite Board of Colonization. No special designation has been given to these people, but many had relatives among the 'Russlaender' and shared many of the ideas and practices of that group.

Appendix B
Conferences / Branches in Canada

An alternative and perhaps more helpful way of classifying Mennonite groups is to consider the kind of conference to which they belonged. In 1940 there were three large conferences, with members or affiliate conferences in several or all the five westernmost Canadian provinces. Then there were eight smaller, multi-province conferences or groups, six of which were established by the immigrants of the 1870s. Finally there were a number of smaller, culturally and socially conservative or traditional regional groups. The smaller of these regional groups in Ontario traced their origin to the first migration from Pennsylvania and Europe or to some subsequent schism, while those on the prairies traced their origin to the migration from Russia in the 1870s.

Many of the conferences changed their names after 1940, and many that changed their names as well as a number of the new conferences chose to include in their new names the word 'Evangelical.' Acronyms became a popular way to identify conferences.

LARGE, MULTI-PROVINCE CONFERENCES

Conference of Mennonites in Canada (CMC) This is the largest and most broadly based Canadian Mennonite conference. It was created as the Conference of Mennonites in Central Canada in 1903 by the Rosenorter Mennonite Church of Saskatchewan, most of whose members had moved to Canada from Prussia before the First World War, and the Bergthaler Mennonite Church of Manitoba, whose members had come to Canada from Russia in the 1870s. A majority of the immigrants arriving in Canada in the 1920s and 1940s joined this conference. It was renamed the General Conference of Mennonites in Canada in 1932 and became the Conference of Mennonites in Canada (CMC) in 1959. Most congregations are also members of the General Conference of Mennonites in North America (GC).

Affiliated with the CMC are provincial conferences in each of the five westernmost provinces of Canada:

- Conference of Mennonites in British Columbia, organized 1936
- Conference of United Mennonite Churches in Ontario, organized 1944
- Conference of Mennonites in Manitoba, organized 1947
- Conference of Mennonites in Alberta, organized 1950
- Conference of Mennonites of Saskatchewan, organized 1959

Until 1972 the Bergthaler Mennonite Church of Manitoba, a founding member of the CMC, disagreed with some doctrines and church policies of the North American General Conference Mennonite Church. As a result, the Bergthaler were for many years members of the CMC, but not of the North American General Conference.

Northern District Conference of the Mennonite Brethren Church of North America, which became the *Canadian Conference of the Mennonite Brethren Church in North America (MB)* This conference had its origins in a split in the Mennonite Church in Russia in 1860 and has also drawn its members from a diverse background, with immigrants of the 1920s being particularly numerous and influential. It is affiliated with the General Conference of Mennonite Brethren Churches in North America, whose offices in the 1940s were located in Hillsboro, Kansas.

Affiliated with the Canadian Conference of Mennonite Brethren Churches are provincial conferences in each of the five westernmost provinces. These conferences grew out of regional meetings of deacons and ministers, which were organized along provincial lines, except in Saskatchewan, where two districts, Herbert and Hepburn, operated separately until 1945. The districts supported specific projects, mainly Bible schools. Founding dates are as follows:

- Saskatchewan Mennonite Brethren Conference, 1928
- Alberta Mennonite Brethren Conference, 1928
- Manitoba Mennonite Brethren Conference, 1929
- British Columbia Mennonite Brethren Conference, 1929
- Ontario Mennonite Brethren Conference, 1932

The Northern District Conference of the Mennonite Brethren Church of North America also manifested an anomaly in 1940. Ontario Mennonite Brethren were not members of the Northern District Conference, because they admitted baptized individuals who had not been baptized by immersion and allowed them to participate in communion. Other Canadian Mennonite conferences made baptism by immersion a condition of membership. The Ontario Mennonite Brethren joined the Northern District (Canadian) Mennonite Brethren conference only in 1946.

Mennonite Brethren (MBs) were not a part of the first three major migrations of

Mennonites to Canada. A number did, however, migrate to the United States, beginning in 1874, and some subsequently moved to Canada. In the 1890s the Mennonite Brethren also sent missionaries, particularly to Manitoba, where they enjoyed considerable success proselytizing members of other Mennonite conferences and groups.

Two conferences or groups closely associated with the Mennonite Brethren were absorbed after 1940. The first consisted of remnants of the Allianz Gemeinde, called the Evangelical Mennonite Brethren Church in Canada. This church had been established in Russia in an attempt to bridge the differences between the larger Russian Mennonite Church and the breakaway Mennonite Brethren. The Allianz Gemeinde accepted any form of adult baptism and enjoyed particular strength in Ontario. The Namaka EMB (Allianz) church joined the Alberta conference in 1938, and other churches, including the one at Arnaud, Manitoba, joined the Manitoba Mennonite Brethren Conference. The Ontario Mennonite Brethren joined the reorganized Northern District (Canadian) in 1946. When these various Allianz churches joined the Mennonite Brethren conference, those not baptized by immersion had to be rebaptized.

The second conference absorbed by the Mennonite Brethren was the Krimmer Mennonite Brethren Church. It had its roots in the Kleine Gemeinde movement in Russia, but when its leaders accepted rebaptism by immersion the links with the Kleine Gemeinde were broken and the new group organized itself as the Krimmer Mennoniten Bruedergemeinde. This group merged with the larger General Conference of the Mennonite Brethren Church in North America in 1960.

Mennonite Conference of Ontario, which became the *Mennonite Conference of Ontario and Quebec* (MC) This is the largest conference of those Mennonites whose ancestors came to Canada from the United States after the American Revolution. Its members were often referred to as (Old) Mennonites to distinguish them, particularly in the United States, from the new General Conference Mennonites.

The Mennonite Conference of Ontario was renamed the Mennonite Conference of Ontario and Quebec in 1971. It and its western Canadian affiliate, the North West Conference of the Mennonite Church, are affiliated with the Mennonite Church (North America).

This conference established close links with the Amish Mennonite Conference, particularly after the Amish Mennonite Conference dropped the name 'Amish' and became the Western Ontario Mennonite Conference in 1964. Many of the statistics merge memberships in the two conferences.

In 1988 the Mennonite Conference of Ontario and Quebec, the Western Ontario Mennonite Conference, and the Conference of United Mennonite Churches in Ontario merged to form the Mennonite Conference of Eastern Canada.

'SWISS' MENNONITES IN ONTARIO

Ontario Amish Mennonite Conference, which became the *Western Ontario Mennonite Conference* The Amish Mennonites who migrated from Europe to Ontario after 1823 organized this conference. Members were sometimes referred to as New Order Amish, but they dropped the name 'Amish' in 1964 and became closely associated in a number of endeavours with the Mennonite Conference of Ontario and Quebec. Some members moved to the western provinces but did not establish their own conference there.

Reformed Mennonite Church This church was the product of a division in 1812 in the (Old) Mennonite Church in the United States, led by John Herr. Members came to Canada in the first wave of migration. This group has placed great emphasis on church discipline and on retention of practices such as foot-washing, the kiss of peace, and the shunning of erring members. Membership in Canada has dwindled over the years.

Mennonite Brethren in Christ Church, which became the *Missionary Church* This church traces its origin to divisions in the (Old) Mennonite Church in the United States in 1883. Its earliest members also came to Canada in the first wave of migration. The name was changed in 1947 to the United Missionary Church, and later simply to the Missionary Church. It dropped many distinctive Mennonite and Anabaptist doctrines. With the name change in 1947 it severed almost all formal links with other Mennonite churches and conferences.

Old Order Amish In the 1880s a minority of members in the Ontario Amish Mennonite Conference rejected a number of changes in worship and acceptance of new technologies. The specific issue leading to a break involved the building of meeting-houses for worship.

Those who rejected use of meeting-houses continued to worship in their homes and have come to be known as Old Order Amish. They continue to reject most modern technology, such as electricity, telephones in their homes, and ownership of cars. Changes in farm machinery are made very selectively.

In 1953 a number of Amish began migrating from the United States to Ontario, thus significantly increasing numbers.

Beachy Amish Mennonite Church At the turn of the century two Amish Mennonite congregations in Ontario suffered further divisions. The two seceding congregations built meeting-houses, have slowly made technological change, but have retained Amish clothing styles and wearing of the beard. In more recent years they have been relating to the Beachy Amish Mennonites in the United States, who originated in Pennsylvania as a division from the Old Order Amish in 1927.

Old Order Mennonites Many of the issues that divided the Amish Mennonite Conference of Ontario also led to disagreements in the (Old) Mennonite Conference of Ontario. Sunday school and evangelistic meetings were big issues in the Mennonite division, and technology has been resisted through the years. Old Order Mennonites continue to wear plain clothing.

Individual Old Order Mennonite bishops sometimes take differing stands on controversial issues, and there are Old Order Mennonite sub-groups, usually identified by the names of their bishops.

Markham-Waterloo Mennonite Conference This is an Old Order Mennonite offshoot. Members accept automobiles and telephones and some other modern technology but oppose personal ostentation. Members who buy cars, for example, are required to paint the chrome and decorations black.

Conservative Mennonite Churches In 1956 a bishop and several members withdrew from an Amish Mennonite Conference congregation in order to maintain stricter clothing regulations. In 1959 another group withdrew from the Ontario Mennonite Conference, also over clothing and nonconformity. This second group established the Conservative Mennonite Church of Ontario. By 1970 there were twelve Conservative congregations or mission locations, relating to a variety of conferences and fellowships.

'KANADIER' MENNONITES

The Mennonites who migrated to Manitoba from Russia in the 1870s constituted three distinct groups, each of which established its own church organization.

The largest group, with 3,403 migrants, came from the Russian Mennonite colony of Bergthal, a daughter colony of the original Russian Mennonite colony of Chortitza. They settled in both the East and West reserves of Manitoba. The Manitoba Bergthal church, as noted above, was a founding member of what would become the Conference of Mennonites in Canada.

The second-largest group consisted of 3,240 migrants either from the Chortitza mother colony or from another daughter colony of Fuerstenland. Almost all members settled in the western part of the West Reserve in the Municipal District of Reinland and were generally referred to either as 'Reinlaender' or as 'Old Colony Mennonites.'

The third group, with 700 migrants, belonged to the Kleine Gemeinde and settled mainly in the East Reserve or at Scratching River.

Each group suffered major schisms and divisions in the 1880s and 1890s, often because of missionary endeavours by evangelists from other Mennonite groups in the United States.

Old Colony Mennonite Church The original members of this church had emigrated either from the original Russian Mennonite colony of Chortitza or from its daughter colony of Fuerstenland. They were sometimes called 'Fuerstenlaender,' and later 'Reinlaender,' but they are a different group from the Reinland church described below, which was formed in 1958. In the 1890s some moved from southern Manitoba to Saskatchewan, but in the 1920s a substantial number left Manitoba and Saskatchewan for Mexico because they were unwilling to accept new Canadian school legislation.

Sommerfelder Mennonite Church of Manitoba The Bergthaler Mennonite Church suffered a major schism in the 1890s in which a majority of its members left to form the Sommerfelder Church. The most contentious issues involved acceptance by the Bergthaler bishop of 'progressive' education and participation in municipal politics. The Bergthaler had members and churches in both the East and West reserves. The dissenters living in the West Reserve, led by Abraham Doerksen, who lived in the village of Sommerfeld, became known as Sommerfelder. In the 1890s a number of Sommerfelder moved to Saskatchewan, and in the 1920s many emigrated to Mexico and Paraguay to protest against provincial school legislation.

Chortitzer Mennonite Church of Manitoba The Chortitzer Mennonite Church is the East Reserve equivalent of the Sommerfelder Mennonite Church. Its leader, Gerhard Wiebe, had been a bishop of the Bergthal Mennonite Church but disagreed with the 'progressive' ideas of his West Reserve counterpart, Johann Funk. The group became known as the Chortitzer Mennonite Church because Bishop Wiebe lived in the village of Chortitza, Manitoba. Members also moved to Saskatchewan after 1890, and many left for Mexico and Paraguay in the 1920s.

Bergthaler Mennonite Church in Saskatchewan Some members of the Bergthal Mennonite Church moved from Manitoba to Saskatchewan in the 1890s. They too rejected the changes in education and religious practices accepted by Bishop Funk of the Bergthaler Mennonite Church in Manitoba but kept the Bergthaler name. They did not join the Manitoba Bergthaler in formation of what became the Conference of Mennonites in Canada. Their history is similar to that of the Old Colony, Sommerfelder, and Chortitzer groups.

Kleine Gemeinde, which became the *Evangelical Mennonite Conference (EMC)* This group had its origins in a split in the Mennonite Church in Russia in 1812. The church had established its own colony of Borosenko in Russia but objected to Tsarist reforms and migrated en masse to Canada and to Nebraska in the 1870s. It also fell victim to schisms and divisions in the 1880s and 1890s, and some of its members migrated to Mexico in the 1940s.

Church of God in Christ, Mennonite (Holdeman) This church, popularly known as the Holdeman Church, had its origins in a split in the (Old) Mennonite Church in the United States in 1859. The leader, John Holdeman, achieved a sympathetic hearing among some Amish Mennonites in Ontario. Instead of organizing a congregation, however, those who wished to join his church moved to Michigan and joined the congregation being established there. Holdeman ministers continued to return to Ontario to minister to a few adherents who did not migrate.

In the religious upheavals of the 1880s and 1890s Holdeman missionary-evangelists, who combined North American evangelistic techniques with an emphasis on traditional Mennonite doctrines of nonconformity to the world, enjoyed considerable success, particularly among restless members of the Kleine Gemeinde in Manitoba and a group of impoverished Volynian Mennonites who had emigrated to the United States. Many of these subsequently moved to Alberta.

Rudnerweider Mennonite Church which became the *Evangelical Mennonite Mission Conference (EMMC)* This group had its origins as a result of an evangelistic revival that split the Sommerfelder Mennonite Church in Manitoba in 1937. It placed a strong emphasis on personal conversion, evangelism, Sunday schools, youth programs, and missionary work. Members were called 'Rudnerweider' because that was the village in which the four early ministers and leaders of the church often met.

Reinland Mennonite Church The Sommerfelder seemed to suffer serious losses and schisms from both conservative and progressive elements in their midst. In 1937 the Rudnerweider left because the Sommerfelder were not accepting new religious ideas and practices quickly enough. In 1958 another group left because the Sommerfelder were making too many changes. The new group resurrected the old name of Reinland Mennonite Church. The Reinland Church, however, suffered its own conservative losses in 1984 when a dissident minister objected to a new church building, which had a basement and electricity, and formed his own group – the Friedensfelder Menno–niten Gemeinde.

Bruderthaler Church, which became the *Evangelical Mennonite Brethren Conference* This group originated in a schism in 1889 in the Mennonite church at Mountain Lake, Minnesota, established by immigrants from Russia after 1870. Its official name was the Defenceless Mennonite Brethren of Christ in North America. A number of its members migrated to western Canada in the early 1900s, establishing several new Mennonite communities. Members also engaged in successful evangelization, particularly at Steinbach, Manitoba. It became the Fellowship of Evangelical Bible Churches in 1987, having lost most of its Mennonite and Anabaptist distinctives.

Many of the Evangelical Mennonite Brethren (Allianz) churches, notably Namaka, Alberta, were also affiliated with the Bruderthaler.

Evangelical Mennonite Brethren Church This church, popularly known as the 'Allianz' Gemeinde, traces its origins to Russia, where it was organized in 1905 in an attempt to bridge differences that had arisen as a result of the schism that led to formation of the Mennonite Brethren Church. The 'Allianz' Gemeinde accepted into membership individuals who were baptized as adults, by immersion, sprinkling, or pouring. Most 'Allianz' members who migrated to Canada in the 1920s joined local Mennonite Brethren churches. In Ontario 'Allianz' members baptized by pouring or sprinkling were initially accepted into full membership without rebaptism, but in western Canada those who had not been baptized by immersion had to be rebaptized to become members of a Mennonite Brethren church. Later rebaptism was also demanded of Ontario members who had not been baptized by immersion.

A number of 'Allianz' churches affiliated with both the Mennonite Brethren and the Bruderthaler Mennonite conferences. They had, in effect, a triple identity – they had the option of remaining a separate denomination, becoming Mennonite Brethren, or joining the Bruderthaler. Most joined the Mennonite Brethren, and in 1939 there were only a few Evangelical Mennonite Brethren (Allianz) Churches in Canada. The last of these gave up their separate identity in 1945 and joined the Mennonite Brethren. Virtually all members came to Canada from Russia in the 1920s. Numerous members settled in Latin America, especially Paraguay.

Krimmer Mennonite Brethren Church (KMB) This church had its origins in the Kleine Gemeinde but became a separate Mennonite Brethren church when its leaders accepted baptism by immersion. It retained a separate identity until 1960, when it merged with the General Conference of the Mennonite Brethren Church of North America.

SOURCES

Most of the information in this appendix is taken from Margaret Loewen Reimer, *One Quilt, Many Pieces: A Reference Guide to Mennonite Groups in Canada*, 3rd ed. (Waterloo, Ont.: Mennonite Publishing Service, 1990). Additional data were obtained from individual histories of many of the Mennonite groups, from the *Mennonite Encyclopedia*, and from Frank H. Epp's two volumes of *Mennonites in Canada* (Toronto: Macmillan, 1974 and 1982).

Appendix C
Membership of Conferences/Branches

Conference or group	1940	1950	1960	1970
Conference of Mennonites in Canada	11,891	15,500	16,118	20,018
Mennonite Brethren	7,346	9,579	13,659	16,660
Mennonite Church	3,359	6,261	7,149	9,016
Mennonite Brethren in Christ	2,741	2,818	–	–
Sommerfelder	5,207	3,785	3,000	4,000
Amish	2,100	–	–	–
Amish Old Order	350	350	382	650
Beachy Amish	–	–	336	343
Old Colony	1,590	1,859	2,377	3,331
Evangelical Mennonite Mission Conference	1,211	1,709	1,890	1,712
Evangelical Mennonite Church	1,145	1,925	2,751	3,580
Evang. Mennonite Brethren	835	900	929	1,643
Church of God in Christ, Mennonite	800	1,300	1,644	2,017
Krimmer Mennonite Brethren	250	310	163	–
Old Order Mennonites	1,047	1,795	2,044	2,100
Chortitza Mennonites	–	1,525	1,432	1,800
Reformed Mennonite Church	–	200	214	193
Reinlaender Mennonites	–	–	750	800

Sources: The 1940 statistics are taken from *Yearbook of the General Conference of the Mennonite Church of North America, 1940* (Newton, Kan.: Mennonite Publishing Office, 1940), 38, and *Mennonite Yearbook and Directory, 1941* (Scottdale, Penn.: Mennonite Publishing House, 1941), 39. The 1940 figures for the Amish include both the Old Order Amish and the Ontario Amish Mennonite Conference. In later tables the Ontario Amish Mennonite Conference, renamed the Western Ontario Mennonite Conference in 1956, is included in Mennonite Church statistics. The figures also lump together several groups of 'Old Mennonites in Ontario' and 'Old Mennonites in West-Canada.'

The 1940 figures are, at best, only a rough and inaccurate guide. The figures published by different conference statisticians did not always agree. All the 1940 statistics except those for the Mennonite Church were prepared by the General Conference statistician. Those for the Mennonite Church were published in the official *Yearbook* of that church, which did not, however, have accurate statistics on membership in other groups.

In an effort to achieve as much consistency as possible, I have taken all statistics for 1950,

1960, and 1970 from the *Mennonite Yearbook and Directory* for the years 1951, 1961, 1971, pp. 57, 52, and 44, respectively. No other conference publication provides reasonably consistent statistical information on all Mennonite groups and denominations. The statistics in the *Mennonite Yearbook and Directory* give memberships as of 31 December of the previous year.

Appendix D
Census Figures

Province	1931	1941	1951	1961	1971
Newfoundland	–	–	3	39	45
Prince Edward Island	2	–	6	1	15
Nova Scotia	1	23	23	31	90
New Brunswick	–	5	30	5	90
Quebec	8	80	220	197	655
Ontario	17,683	22,256	25,796	30,948	40,115
Manitoba	30,375	39,395	44,667	56,823	59,555
Saskatchewan	31,372	32,553	26,270	28,174	26,315
Alberta	8,301	12,119	13,528	16,269	14,645
British Columbia	1,095	5,119	15,387	19,932	26,520
Yukon and NWT	–	4	8	33	100
Totals	88,837	111,554	125,938	152,452	168,150

Source: T.D. Regehr, 'Canada,' *Mennonite Encyclopedia*, vol. V (Scottdale, Penn.: Herald Press, 1990), 121. Hutterites are included in all the numbers except those for 1971, when Canada's 13,650 Hutterites were enumerated separately.

Appendix E
Mennonite Journals and Newspapers

- *Mennonite Quarterly Review*, 1927–present (North Am.)
- *Mennonite Life*, 1946–present (North Am.)
- *Journal of Mennonite Studies*, 1983–present (Can.)
- *Conrad Grebel Review*, 1983–present (Can.)
- *The Voice of the Mennonite Brethren Bible College*, 1952–71 (Can.)
- *Direction*, 1972–present (North Am.)
- *Festival Quarterly*, 1974–present (North Am.)
- *Mennonite Historian*, 1975–present (Can.)

INTER-MENNONITE NEWSPAPERS

- *The Canadian Mennonite*, 1953–71 (Can.)
- *Mennonite Mirror*, 1971–90 (Can.)
- *Mennonitische Post*, 1976–present (Int'l)
- *The Mennonite Reporter*, 1971–present (Can.)

DENOMINATIONAL PUBLICATIONS

(Old) Mennonites:
- *The Gospel Herald*, 1908–present (North Am.)

General Conference/Conference of Mennonites in Canada:
- *The Mennonite*, 1885–present (North Am.)

- *Der Bote,* 1924–present (Can.
- *Intotemak* (Native Ministries), 1972–present (Can.)
- *Chinese Mennonite Newsletter,* 1986–93, 1995–present (Can.)

Mennonite Brethren:
- *Mennonitische Rundschau*, 1887–present (North Am.)
- *Zionsbote*, 1884–1964 (North Am.)
- *Konferenz Jugendblatt*, 1954–7 (North Am.)
- *Christian Leader*, 1937–present (North Am.)
- *Mennonite Observer*, 1955–61 (Can.)
- *Mennonite Brethren Herald*, 1962–present (Can.)
- *Le Lien,* 1980–present (Que.)

Brethren in Christ:
- *Evangelical Visitor*, 1887–present (North Am.)

Evangelical Mennonite Conference:
- *Christlicher Familienfreund*, 1935–84 (North Am.)
- *The Messenger*, 1962–present (North Am.)

Evangelical Mennonite Mission Conference:
- *Der Leitstern*, 1943–67 (Can.)
- *EMMC Recorder*, 1964–present (Can.)

Chortitzer Mennonite Conference:
- *The CMC Chronicle,* 1981–5 (Can.)

Church of God in Christ:
- *The Messenger of Truth* (North Am.)

Conservative Mennonite Church of Ontario:
- *Ontario Informer,* 1973–present (Ont.)

Beachy Amish Mennonite Church:
- *Calvary Messenger,* 1970–present (Ont.)

Markham Waterloo Mennonite Conference:
- *The Church Correspondent,* 1955–present (Ont.)

Midwest Mennonite Fellowship:
• *Midwest Mennonite Focus*, 1980–present (Can.)

Old Order Amish:
• *Family Life*, 1968–present (Ont.)

LOCAL PAPERS SERVING MENNONITE COMMUNITIES

• *Abbotsford, Sumas and Matsqui News* (BC)
• *Chilliwack Progress* (BC)
• *Coaldale Flyer* (Alta)
• *Three Hills Capital* (Alta)
• *Saskatchewan Valley News* (Sask.)
• *Steinbach Post* (Man.)
• *The Carillon* (Man.)

Appendix F
Mennonite Rural-Urban Statistics

	1941	1951	1961	1971
Canada				
Total	111,380	125,938	152,452	181,800
Rural	96,787 (87%)	101,271 (80%)	99,809 (65%)	101,685 (56%)
Farm	n.a	80,539 (64%)	70,397 (46%)	62,540 (34%)
Non-farm	n.a	20,732 (16%)	29,412 (19%)	39,155 (22%)
Urban	14,593 (13%)	24,667 (20%)	52,643 (35%)	80,105 (44%)
Over 100,000	n.a.	5,902 (5%)	24,805 (16%)	45,015 (25%)
30,000–99,999	n.a.	4,325 (3%)	7,728 (5%)	2,745 (2%)
10,000–29,999	n.a.	2,187 (2%)	2,499 (2%)	11,050 (6%)
Below 10,000	n.a.	12,253 (10%)	17,611 (12%)	21,305 (12%)
Ontario				
Total	22,219	25,796	30,948	40,380
Rural	16,902 (76%)	19,586 (76%)	20,910 (68%)	21,210 (53%)
Urban	5,317 (24%)	6,210 (24%)	10,038 (32%)	19,170 (47%)
Manitoba				
Total	39,336	44,667	56,823	64,350
Rural	35,622 (91%)	33,419 (75%)	34,414 (61%)	35,675 (55%)
Urban	3,714 (9%)	11,248 (25%)	22,409 (39%)	28,675 (45%)
Saskatchewan				
Total	32,511	26,270	28,174	28,530
Rural	28,242 (87%)	22,873 (87%)	20,216 (72%)	18,100 (63%)
Urban	4,269 (13%)	3,397 (13%)	7,958 (28%)	10,430 (37%)
Alberta				
Total	12,097	13,528	16,269	20,745
Rural	11,549 (95%)	12,639 (93%)	12,744 (78%)	13,390 (65%)
Urban	548 (5%)	889 (7%)	3,525 (22%)	7,355 (35%)
British Columbia				
Total	5,105	15,387	19,932	26,595
Rural	4,432 (87%)	12,626 (82%)	11,425 (57%)	13,045 (49%)
Urban	673 (13%)	2,761 (18%)	8,507 (43%)	13,555 (51%)

(Continued on next page)

Note: There are minor discrepancies between the figures given in these tables and those given in other tables prepared by Statistics Canada. The figures given here include both Mennonites and Hutterites, for all years. There were 13,650 Hutterites living in Canada in 1971.

Sources: *Census of Canada, 1941*, table 37; *Census of Canada, 1951*, vol. 1, table 39; *Census of Canada, 1961*, series 1.2, table 43; and *Census of Canada, 1971*, table 11.

Notes

Abbreviations

AHL	Aylmer Historical Library, Aylmer, Ont.
AMC	Archives of the Mennonite Church, Goshen, Ind.
CBC	Columbia Bible College, Clearbrook, BC
CGC	Conrad Grebel College, Waterloo, Ont.
CM	*Canadian Mennonite*
CMBS (W)	Centre for Mennonite Brethren Studies, Winnipeg, Man.
EMC	Evangelical Mennonite Conference
JMS	*Journal of Mennonite Studies*
MBMC	Mennonite Board of Missions and Charities
MBH	*Mennonite Brethren Herald*
MCC	Mennonite Central Committee
ME	*Mennonite Encyclopedia*, 5 vols. (Scottdale, Penn.: Herald Press, 1959)
MG	manuscript group
MH	*Mennonite Historian*
MHC	Mennonite Heritage Centre, Winnipeg, Man.
ML	*Mennonite Life*
MM	*Mennonite Mirror*
MQR	*Mennonite Quarterly Review*
MR	*Mennonite Reporter*
NAC	National Archives of Canada, Ottawa
OMGUS	Organization for the Military Government of Germany (U.S.)
PABC	Provincial Archives of British Columbia
RG	record group
SAB	Saskatchewan Archives Board
USNA	United States National Archives, Washington, DC

Introduction: A People Transformed

1 Canada, *Census of Canada*, 1941, Table 37.
2 J. Winfield Fretz, 'Community,' *ME* I, 657. Fretz's 1943 report on Canadian Mennonite communities is available in the AMC, MCC Records, file IX-5-1, Executive Committee Minutes. The report was accepted and is filed with the minutes of the Executive Committee meeting of 18 September 1943.
3 E.K. Francis, *In Search of Utopia: The Mennonites in Manitoba* (Altona, Man.: D.W. Friesen and Sons, 1955), 6.
4 Ibid, 2.
5 Canada, Census of Canada, 1971, Cat. 92-735, vol. 1, part IV, Table 18. The total number of Mennonites (not including 13,650 Hutterites) enumerated in 1971 was 168,150. Of that number, 50,190 were classified as rural farm, 38,520 as rural non-farm, and 79,440 as urban. More detailed statistical information about Mennonites in North America, including the rate of urbanization of the various denominational conferences, is given in J. Howard Kauffman and Leland Harder, *Anabaptists Four Centuries Later: A Profile of Five Mennonite and Brethren in Christ Denominations* (Scottdale, Penn.; Herald Press, 1975), and J. Howard Kauffman and Leo Driedger, *The Mennonite Mosaic: Identity and Modernization* (Kitchener, Ont., and Scottdale, Penn.: Herald Press, 1991).
6 See, for example, David Rempel, 'Der Zug in die Stadt. Die groesste Wanderung in unserer Geschichte,' *Der Bote*, 38 (23 and 30 May 1961).
7 Robert Craig Brown and Ramsay Cook, *Canada 1896–1921: A Nation Transformed* (Toronto: McClelland and Stewart, 1974).
8 Francis, *Utopia*, 276.
9 Ibid., 7.
10 Ibid., 278.
11 Seymour Martin Lipset, *Continental Divide: The Values and Institutions of the United States and Canada* (New York: Routledge, 1990), discusses the work of these scholars in considerable detail.
12 For a more detailed discussion of fundamental Canadian values and institutions see ibid. and A.B. McKillop, ed., *Contexts of Canada's Past: Selected Essays of W.L. Morton* (Toronto: Macmillan, 1980).

1: Canadian Mennonites in 1939

1 John Herd Thompson, *The Harvests of War: The Prairie West, 1914–1918* (Toronto: McClelland and Stewart, 1978), 9.
2 Robert Bothwell, Ian Drummond, and John English, *Canada since 1945: Power, Politics and Provincialism* (Toronto: University of Toronto Press, 1981), xi.

3   Frank H. Epp, *Mennonites in Canada, 1920–1940: A People's Struggle for Survival* (Toronto: Macmillan, 1982), 600.

4   John A. Toews, *People of the Way: Selected Essays and Addresses by John A. Toews* (Winnipeg: Historical Committee, Board of Higher Education, Canadian Conference of Mennonite Brethren Churches, 1981).

5   As quoted in *Mennonites in Ontario: A Mennonite Bicentennial Portrait, 1786–1986* (Toronto: Mennonite Bicentennial Commission, 1986), 126.

6   J. Winfield Fretz, *The Waterloo Mennonites: A Community in Paradox* (Waterloo, Ont.: Wilfrid Laurier University Press, 1989), 181.

7   Two works that provide a simple overview of Mennonite theology and beliefs are J.C. Wenger, *What Mennonites Believe*, rev. ed. (Scottdale, Penn.: Herald Press, 1991), and James H. Waltner, *This We Believe* (Newton, Kan.: Faith and Life Press, 1968). More detailed information on Anabaptist and Mennonite confessions of faith is available in Howard John Loewen, *One Lord, One Church, One Hope, and One God: Mennonite Confessions of Faith* (Elkhart, Ind.: Institute of Mennonite Studies, 1985).

8   Toews, *People of the Way*, 230.

9   John C. Wenger, 'The Biblicism of the Anabaptists,' in Guy F. Hershberger, ed., *The Recovery of the Anabaptist Vision* (Scottdale, Penn.: Herald Press, 1957), 167–79.

10 John Christian Wenger, *Glimpses of Mennonite History and Doctrine* (Scottdale, Penn.: Herald Press, 1940), 147.

11 J. Lawrence Burkholder, 'The Anabaptist Vision of Discipleship,' in Hershberger, ed., *Recovery*, 135–151; C. Norman Kraus, 'Toward a Theology for the Disciple Community,' in J.R. Burkholder and Calvin Redekop, eds., *Kingdom, Cross, and Community: Essays on Mennonite Themes in Honor of Guy F. Hershberger* (Scottdale, Penn.: Herald Press, 1976), 103–17.

12 Wenger, *What Mennonites Believe*, 85.

13 Guy F. Hershberger, *War, Peace and Nonresistance* (Scottdale, Penn.: Herald Press, 1953; and J.A. Toews, *True Nonresistance through Christ: A Study of Biblical Principles* (Winnipeg: Board of General Welfare and Public Relations of the Mennonite Brethren Church of North America, 1955).

14 Leo Driedger and Donald B. Kraybill, *Mennonite Peacemaking: From Quietism to Activism* (Scottdale, Penn.: Herald Press, 1994), 35.

15 David Luthy at the Heritage Historical Library in Aylmer, Ontario, has a remarkable collection of Mennonite publications that have told or used the story, and even more often the illustration, of Dirk Willems saving his captor's life. The story of Willem's martyrdom, and a reproduction of the woodcut engraving, are given in Thieleman J. van Braght, *The Bloody Theatre of*

Martyrs Mirror of the Defenceless Christians Who Baptized Only upon Confession of Faith, and Who Suffered and Died for the Testimony of Jesus, Their Saviour, From the Time of Christ to the Year a.d. 1660, 5th ed. (Scottdale, Penn.: Herald Press, 1950), 741.

16 Harold S. Bender, 'State, Anabaptist-Mennonite Attitude Toward,' *ME* IV, 611–18.

17 Ibid.

18 Burkholder and Redekop, *Kingdom, Cross and Community*, and C. Norman Kraus, *The Community of the Spirit: How the Church Is in the World* (Scottdale, Penn.: Herald Press, 1993).

19 Wenger, *Glimpses*, 170.

20 Ephesians 5:27.

21 Abe Dueck, 'Baptists and Mennonite Brethren in Canada,' in Paul Toews, ed., *Mennonites and Baptists: A Continuing Conversation* (Winnipeg, and Hillsboro, Kan.: Kindred Press, 1993), 177–92.

22 Rodney J. Sawatzky, 'The One and the Many: The Recovery of Mennonite Pluralism,' in Walter Klaassen, ed., *Anabaptism Revisited: Essays on Anabaptist/Mennonite Studies in Honor of C. J. Dyck* (Scottdale, Penn.: Herald Press, 1992), 141–54.

23 *The Consolidated-Webster Comprehensive Encyclopedic Dictionary* (Chicago: Webster's Dictionary, 1953), 260; Dennis P. Hollinger, 'Evangelicalism,' *ME* V, 281; John G. Stackhouse, Jr, *Canadian Evangelicalism in the Twentieth Century: An Introduction to Its Character* (Toronto: University of Toronto Press, 1993), 7.

24 Cornelius Krahn, 'Pietism,' *ME* IV, 176.

25 Harold S. Bender, 'Fundamentalism,' *ME* I, 418–19; Paul Toews, 'Fundamentalism,' *ME* V, 318–19.

26 C. Norman Kraus, *Dispensationalism in America: Its Rise and Development* (Richmond, Va.: John Knox Press, 1958).

27 For a discussion of these events from a Canadian perspective see Epp, *Mennonites in Canada, 1920–1940*, chap. 2.

28 Scholarly assessments of the significance of Bender's work are found in Guy F. Hershberger, ed., *Recovery of the Anabaptist Vision*. A memorial issue of the *Mennonite Quarterly Review* (38, no. 2, April 1964), published shortly after Bender's death, assessed his work. More recently, on the fiftieth anniversary of the publication of his *Anabaptist Vision*, several scholarly conferences revisited and assessed the scholarship of Bender and his associates. See also the special issue of the *Conrad Grebel Review*, 13, no. 1 (Winter 1995) entitled 'The Anabaptist Vision: Theological Perspectives.'

29 The address has been republished many times, including Harold S. Bender, *The*

Anabaptist Vision (Scottdale, Penn.: Herald Press, 1944).

30 Early critics of Bender's vision include James M. Stayer, *Anabaptists and the Sword* (Lawrence, Kan.: Coronodo Press, 1972); James M. Stayer and Werner O. Packull, trans. and eds., *The Anabaptists and Thomas Muentzer* (Toronto: Kendall/Hunt Publishing Co., 1980). A detailed recent overview of relevant sixteenth-century Anabaptist historiography is provided in Arnold Snyder, 'The Anabaptist Vision beyond Polygenesis: Recovering the Unity and Diversity of Anabaptism,' read at a colloquium at Conrad Grebel College, 29 October 1993.

31 John Howard Yoder, 'Outside Influences on Mennonite Thought,' *Proceedings of the Ninth Conference on Mennonite Educational and Cultural Problems* (Hesston, Kan.: Hesston College, 1953), 33–41; John Howard Yoder, 'Anabaptist Vision and Mennonite Reality,' in A.J. Klassen, ed., *Consultation on Anabaptist-Mennonite Theology* (Fresno, Calif.: Council of Mennonite Seminaries, 1970), 1–46; Rodney J. Sawatzky, 'The Quest for a Mennonite Hermeneutic,' *Conrad Grebel Review*, 11, no. 1 (winter 1993), 1–20.

32 Abe Dueck, 'Canadian Mennonites and the Anabaptist Vision,' *Journal of Mennonite Studies*, 13 (1995), 71–88; Elfrieda Toews Nafziger, *A Man of His Word: A Biography of John A. Toews* (Winnipeg: Kindred Press, 1992).

33 E. Morris Sider, *The Brethren in Christ in Canada: Two Hundred Years of Tradition and Change* (Nappanee, Ind.: Evangel Press, 1988).

34 All statistics in Table 1.2 represent only approximate numbers of members and adherents. There are considerable variations in the figures given in official sources. The numbers given here are drawn mainly from the *Year Book of the General Conference of the Mennonite Church of North America, 1940* (Newton, Kan.: Mennonite Publishing Office, 1940), 38. Additional, and sometimes slightly different information is given in *Mennonite Yearbook and Directory, 1940* (Scottdale, Penn.: Mennonite Publishing House, 1940), in the two volumes of Frank Epp's *Mennonites in Canada*, in relevant entries in the five volumes of the *Mennonite Encyclopedia (ME)*, and in the histories of individual conferences. All the figures in Appendix C, which differ somewhat from the figures in this table, are taken from successive issues of the *Mennonite Yearbook and Directory*, which remained more consistent over the years but was less accurate than other sources in its 1939 statistics.

The decennial Canadian census consistently reported more Mennonites than any cumulative total of 'souls' reported by Mennonite statisticians. The 1941 census, for example, reported 111,380 Mennonites. Yet the *Year Book of the General Conference of the Mennonite Church of North America, 1940*, reported 82,351, of whom 40,275 were members of a Mennonite church. *The Mennonite Yearbook and Directory*, 1940, reported 73,471, of whom 34,622 were members of a Mennonite church. Clearly, these statistics are not precise, but they indicate the relative strengths of the various Mennonite groups and conferences in Canada in 1939.

35 Wenger, *Glimpses*, 188.
36 Mark A. Noll, David W. Bebbington, and George A. Rawlyk, eds., *Evangelicalism: Comparative Studies of Popular Protestantism in North America, the British Isles, and Beyond* (New York: Oxford University Press, 1994); George A. Rawlyk, ed., *The Canadian Protestant Experience, 1760–1990* (Burlington, Ont.: Welch Publishing Co., 1990); and C. Norman Kraus, ed., *Evangelicalism and Anabaptism* (Scottdale, Penn.: Herald Press, 1979).
37 Harold S. Bender, 'John Herr,' *ME* II, 712–13; 'Reformed Mennonite Church,' ibid., IV, 267–70.
38 Cornelius Krahn, 'Reimer, Klaas,' ibid., IV, 278; Delbert Plett, *The Golden Years: The Mennonite Kleine Gemeinde in Russia* (1812–1849) (Steinbach, Man.: D.F.P. Publications, 1985).
39 'Oberholtzer Division Issue,' *MQR*, 46, no. 4 (Oct. 1972), 326–430; Edmund G. Kaufman, comp., *General Conference Mennonite Pioneers* (North Newton, Kan.: Bethel College, 1973).
40 Clarence Hiebert, *The Holdeman People: The Church of God in Christ, Mennonite, 1859–1969* (Pasadena, Calif.: William Carey Library, 1973).
41 A.H. Unruh, *Die Geschichte der Mennoniten-Bruedergemeinde, 1860–1954* (Hillsboro, Kan.: General Conference of the Mennonite Brethren Church of North America, 1955); J. A. Toews, *A History of the Mennonite Brethren Church: Pilgrims and Pioneers* (Fresno, Calif.: Board of Christian Literature, General Conference of Mennonite Brethren Churches, 1975).
42 E. Reginald Good, 'A Review of Aaron Eby's "Geschichte der Mennoniten in Canada" published in 1972,' *MQR,* 64, no. 4 (Oct. 1990), 362–71.
43 Isaac R. Horst, *Separate and Peculiar* (Mount Forest, Ont.: Isaac R. Horst, 1979); Mary Ann Horst, *My Old Order Mennonite Heritage* (Kitchener, Ont.: Pennsylvania Dutch Craft Shop, n.d.).
44 Gingerich, *The Amish of Canada*; Lorraine Roth, 'The Amish Mennonite Division in Ontario, 1886–1891,' *Ontario Mennonite History*, 11, no. 1 (March 1993), 1–8.
45 Royden K. Loewen, *Family, Church, and Market. A Mennonite Community in the Old and the New Worlds, 1850–1930* (Toronto: University of Toronto Press, 1993); H.J. Gerbrandt, *Adventure in Faith: The Background in Europe and the Development in Canada of the Bergthaler Mennonite Church in Manitoba* (Altona, Man.: Bergthaler Mennonite Church of Manitoba, 1970).
46 Wenger, *Glimpses*, 188.
47 Steven Nolt, 'The Mennonite Eclipse,' *Festival Quarterly*, 19, no. 2 (summer

1992), 8–12.

48 Harold S. Bender, 'Sunday School,' *ME* IV, 659.

49 The *Mennonite Encyclopedia* published in 1956 defined Fundamentalism as 'a movement in conservative American Protestantism in the first half of the 20th century of reaction against the growth of theological liberalism and modernism.' The updated volume of that *Encyclopedia* states 'Fundamentalism among Mennonites was as much an effort to define the relationship between culture and Christianity as a crusade to root out theological modernism.'

50 Theological liberalism has been defined as 'the rationalistic movement of the eighteenth century that led to a revolt against authoritarianism in both religion and secular culture.' See Donovan E. Smucker, *The Origins of Walter Rauschenbusch's Social Ethics* (Montreal and Kingston: McGill-Queen's University Press, 1994). In its modernist manifestation, theological liberalism sought to apply rationalistic and progressive religious principles to modern problems – mainly those associated with urbanization and industrialization.

51 Adolf Ens, *Subjects or Citizens: Mennonite Relations with Government, 1870– 1925* (Ottawa: University of Ottawa Press, 1994).

52 The pietism that most strongly influenced the Russian Mennonites has been defined as 'the Protestant reaction against orthodox intellectualism and formalism in favour of a personal, devotional, subjective, individualist, conversionist evangelism that stresses vital religious experience.' Smucker, *Walter Rauschenbusch*, 9.

53 This fragmentation is explained in greater detail in Frank H. Epp's two volumes of *Mennonites in Canada*.

54 The clearest example of such categorizations can be found in Fretz, *Waterloo Mennonites*, but it also occurs in many other scholarly works. See, for example, Loewen, *Family, Church, and Market*.

55 For a discussion of Canadian evangelicalism and the attitudes of evangelicals to so-called 'liberal' influences see John G. Stackhouse, Jr, *Canadian Evangelicalism in the Twentieth Century: An Introduction to Its Character* (Toronto: University of Toronto Press, 1993); Rawlyk, ed., *The Canadian Protestant Experience*; David B. Marshall, *Secularizing the Faith: Canadian Protestant Clergy and the Crisis of Belief, 1850–1940* (Toronto: University of Toronto Press, 1992). The attitude of evangelical missionaries toward other religious ideas is discussed in Joel A. Carpenter and Wilbert R. Shenk, eds., *Earthen Vessels: American Evangelicals and Foreign Missions, 1880–1980* (Grand Rapids, Mich.: Eerdmans, 1990), and Wilbert R. Shenk, ed., *The Transfiguration of Mission: Biblical, Theological and Historical Foundations* (Scottdale, Penn.: Herald Press, 1993).

56 Paul Toews, 'Fundamentalism,' *ME* V, 319.

57 *Yearbook of the General Conference of the Mennonite Brethren Church of North America*, held at Winkler, Manitoba, 21-26 July 1951 (Hillsboro, Kan.: Mennonite Brethren Publishing House, 1951), 125.

58 This method of choosing leaders is still used in Canadian Old Order congregations. See Isaac R. Horst, 'How the Old Order Chooses Ministers,' *MR* 24, no. 19, 3 Oct. 1994.

59 The term 'bishop' was first introduced and used by Mennonites in the United States, but his functions were not the same as those of bishops in other, more hierarchical, denominations. For a time U.S. Mennonites used the term 'elder' in the way that other Mennonites used the term 'deacon.' Bishops in the Swiss Mennonite churches and elders in Russian Mennonite churches had many similar responsibilities, but there were also some important differences in the ways in which these leaders met their responsibilities. There had by 1939 been a greater proliferation of 'elders' than of 'bishops' and the power and influence of 'elders' in some Russian Mennonite churches had been undermined when leaders who had been ordained as ministers but not as elders were recommended for licences to preside at marriages or funerals and to serve communion.

60 H. S. Bender, 'Bishop,' *ME* I, 347.

61 Cornelius Krahn, 'Elder,' *ME* II, 178–81. Krahn deals benignly with the abuses of power by some of the elders. Such abuses in the Molotschna Colony of Russia are documented in greater detail in P.M. Friesen, *Die Alt-Evangelische Mennonitische Bruederschaft in Russland (1789-1910) im Rahmen der mennonitischen Gesamtgeschichte* (Halbstadt, Taurien: Raduga Verlag, 1911); and Franz Isaak, *Die Molotschnaer Mennoniten. Ein Beitrag zur Geschichte derselben aus Akten aelterer und neuerer Zeit, wie auch auf Grund eigener Erlebnisse und Erfahrungen dargestellt* (Halbstadt, Taurien: H.J. Braun, 1908); H. Goerz, *Die Molotschnaer Ansiedlung. Entstehung, Entwicklung und Untergang* (Steinbach, Man.: Echo Verlag, 1950/51).

62 For detailed and meticulous accounts of such devolution in some of the larger churches see Walter Klaassen, *'The Days of Our Years': A History of the Eigenheim Mennonite Church Community, 1892-1992* (Rosthern, Sask.: Eigenheim Mennonite Church, 1992); H.J. Gerbrandt, *Adventure in Faith: The Background in Europe and the Development in Canada of the Bergthaler Mennonite Church in Manitoba* (Altona, Man.: Bergthaler Mennonite Church of Manitoba, 1970); J.H. Enns, comp. *Dem Herrn die Ehre. Schoenwieser Mennoniten Gemeinde von Manitoba* (Winnipeg: Schoenwieser Mennoniten Gemeinde, 1969); and E. Reginald Good, *Frontier Community to Urban Congregation: First Mennonite Church, Kitchener 1813–1988* (Kitchener, Ont.: First Mennonite Church, 1988).

63 Evangelical Mennonite Conference (EMC) Archives, vol. 2, file 2, and vol. 68, file 2, Correspondence. See also EMC Archives, vol. 190, file 9, essay by Archie Penner, 'From Aeltester, Lehrer and Gemeinde to Boards, Pastors and Conference.'

64 Individual congregations could choose which North American and/or regional or provincial conferences they wanted to join. The large Bergthaler Mennonite Church in Manitoba, for example, was a founding member of what became the Conference of Mennonites in Canada (CMC), but it did not join the North American General Conference until 1971. John Friesen, 'A Delayed Merger: The Bergthaler Mennonite Church of Manitoba and the General Conference,' *ML*, 48, no. 1 (March 1993), 22–6.

65 Jacob Gerbrandt, 'Canadian Mennonite Board of Colonization,' *ME* I, 507–8.

66 Ibid.

67 The best-known, but now somewhat dated history of the MCC is John D. Unruh, *In the Name of Christ: A History of the Mennonite Central Committee and Its Service, 1920–1951* (Scottdale, Penn.: Herald Press, 1952). More recently a multi-volume series of documents and personal recollections pertaining to the history of the MCC, edited by C.J. Dyck, has been published by Herald Press.

68 Urie A. Bender, *Four Earthen Vessels: Biographical Profiles of Oscar Burkholder, Samuel F. Coffman, Clayton F. Derstine, and Jesse B. Martin* (Scottdale, Penn.: Herald Press, 1983).

69 Sider, *Brethren in Christ in Canada.*

70 Toews, *History of the Mennonite Brethren Church.*

71 Jack Heppner, *Search for Renewal: The Story of the Rudnerweider/Evangelical Mennonite Mission Conference* (Winnipeg: Evangelical Mennonite Mission Conference, 1987), 41–5.

72 AMC *MCC Records*, file IX-5-1, J.W. Fretz, 'Report of My Trip to Canada to Study Mennonite Colonization,' presented to the Executive Committee of the MCC at its meeting on 18 September 1943, 21.

73 Leo Driedger, 'Kinship: Changing Mennonite Family Roles and Networks,' in *Mennonite Identity in Conflict* (Lewiston and Queenston: Edwin Mellen Press, 1988), 131–46.

74 Loewen, *Family, Church, and Market.*

75 In urban areas with populations of 1,000 to 5,000 these numbers jumped to 94.1 per cent, 81.6 per cent, 34 per cent, 56.3 per cent and 66.5 per cent respectively. Alison Prentice et al., *Canadian Women: A History* (Toronto: Harcourt Brace Jovanovich, 1988), 245.

76 Veronica Strong-Boag, *A New Day Recalled: Lives of Girls and Women in English Canada, 1919–1939* (Toronto: Copp Clark Pitman, 1988), 92.

77 Prentice, *Canadian Women*, 249.

78 With respect to persons over 65 years of age, Mennonites were on the low end of the scale, with only 3.7 per cent of adherents in that category, compared with Anglicans – 8 per cent; Baptists – 8.5 per cent; United Church – 8.1 per cent; Roman Catholic – 5.2 per cent; and Presbyterian – 10 per cent.

79 In urban areas, Mennonites under 15 years represented only 27.9 per cent of the total, compared to rural areas, where the number was 40.3 per cent. Furthermore, the larger the city or town the smaller the family; in urban areas with more than 30,000 people, 23.8 per cent of Mennonites were less than 15 years of age, in areas with more than 1,000, 28.9 per cent, and in urban areas with fewer than 1,000, 31.4 per cent which was very close to the rural average. *Census of Canada, 1941*, Table 14.

80 One of Kaufman's industrial nurses who was temporarily director of his birth control clinic (Parents Information Bureau) was Anna Weber (also known as Sophie), a sister to Urias Weber, minister at Stirling Avenue Mennonite Church. Their brother, Irvin K. Weber, was general manager of the factory.

81 CGC II-2.5.2 Mennonite Conference of Ontario – Special Committees, Merle Shantz, et al., 'Report of the Committee on Birth Control.'

82 J.R. Mumaw, 'The Christian Home,' *Christian Monitor*, 30, no. 1 (Jan. 1940), 12.

83 Alta Metzler, 'Present-Day Issues Which Challenge the Mothers of Our Land and How to Meet Them,' *Gospel Herald*, 13 July 1939, 315.

84 'A Man's Ideas of a Wife,' *Christian Monitor*, 31, no. 6, June 1939, 171.

85 'Woman's Place in Christian Service,' *Gospel Herald*, 6 May 1943, 114.

86 Lorraine Roth, *Willing Service: Stories of Ontario Mennonite Women* (Waterloo, Ont.: Mennonite Historical Society of Ontario, 1992), ix.

2: Wartime Alternative and Military Service

1 *Census of Canada, 1941*, Table 14

2 T.D. Regehr, 'Lost Sons: The Canadian Mennonite Soldiers of World War II,' *MQR*, 66, no. 4 (Oct. 1992), 461–80.

3 Frank H. Epp, *Mennonite Exodus: The Rescue and Resettlement of the Russian Mennonites since the Communist Revolution* (Altona, Man.: Canadian Mennonite Relief and Immigration Council, 1962), 31.

4 Noah Bearinger, 'No Spears of Iron: Memoirs of the Alternative Service Camp at Montreal River during the Second World War,' *Family Life* (June and July 1986). A copy is available at the Aylmer Historical Library (Old Order Amish) (AHL) in Aylmer, Ontario.

5 Ibid.

6 As quoted in Harry Loewen, 'Shot Down over Germany,' published in *No*

Permanent City: Stories from Mennonite History and Life (Waterloo, Ont., and Scottdale, Penn.: Herald Press, 1993), 184.

7 Marcus Shantz, 'From Air Force Enthusiast to Peace Activist,' *MR*, 24, no. 2 (24 Jan. 1994), 12.

8 Ibid.

9 An interview in which David Schroeder and Gerhard Ens told their stories is published in Lawrence Klippenstein, ed., *That There Be Peace: Mennonites in Canada and World War II* (Winnipeg: Manitoba CO Reunion Committee, 1979), 47–53.

10 Ibid., 53.

11 As reported in *The Beacon: Canada's National CO Magazine*, 4, no. 1 (March 1945), 11.

12 As told to the author by Anne (Peters) Bargen.

13 NAC Personnel Records Centre, Statement of Service in the Canadian Armed Forces, for Rudolf Goetz, Regimental No. K1553. This file does not include details pertaining to the circumstances of Goetz's death.

14 David Bercuson to Ted Regehr, 13 July 1994.

15 The complete document, entitled 'Peace, War, and Military Service. A Statement Adopted by the Mennonite General Conference at Turner, Oregon, August 1937,' is published in D.P. Reimer, *Erfahrungen der Mennoniten in Canada waehrend des zweiten Weltkrieges, 1939–1945* (n.p., n.d.), 36–42. The quotations below are taken from that document. The statement adopted at Oregon was published in English, even in Reimer's book, which was originally published in German. Other parts of Reimer's book were later translated into English, and the entire work was republished as *Experiences of the Mennonites of Canada during the Second World War* (n.p., n.d.). See also Melvin Gingerich, *Service for Peace: A History of Mennonite Civilian Public Service* (Akron, Penn.: Mennonite Central Committee, 1949).

16 The official minutes of the meeting were published in Reimer, *Erfahrungen*, 42–62. Later news reports in the Mennonite periodicals indicated that up to 500 persons attended, but only 230 registered.

17 A more detailed discussion of this migration is given in Frank H. Epp, *Mennonites in Canada, Vol. 1, 1786–1920: The Story of a Separate People* (Toronto: Macmillan, 1974), and E. Morris Sider, *The Brethren in Christ in Canada: Two Hundred Years of Tradition and Change* (Nappanee, Ind.: Evangel Press, 1988).

18 Canada PC 957, 13 Aug. 1973.

19 William Janzen, *Limits on Liberty: The Experience of Mennonite, Hutterite, and Doukhobor Communities in Canada* (Toronto: University of Toronto Press, 1990), 163–97; Adolf Ens, *Subjects or Citizens? Mennonite Relations*

with Government, 1870–1925 (Ottawa: University of Ottawa Press, 1994).

20 As quoted in Janzen, *Limits on Liberty*, 199. See also J.A. Toews, *Alternative Service in Canada during World War II* (Winnipeg: Publication Committee of the Canadian Conference of the Mennonite Brethren Church, 1959).

21 Lawrence Klippenstein, 'Mennonite Pacifism and State Service in Russia: A Study in Church-State Relations, 1789–1936,' PhD thesis, University of Minnesota, 1984.

22 As quoted in Janzen, 'Limits of Liberty in Canada: The Experience of the Mennonites, Hutterites and Doukhobors,' PhD thesis, Carleton University, 1981, 457.

23 Canada, 31 Vic., cap. 40, sec. 17.

24 Canadian manpower and conscription policies are discussed in detail in E.L.M. Burns, *Manpower in the Canadian Army, 1939–1945* (Toronto: Clarke, Irwin and Co., 1956); C.P. Stacey, *Arms, Men and Governments* (Ottawa: Queen's Printer, 1970); J.L. Granatstein, *Canada's War: The Politics of the Mackenzie King Government, 1939–1945* (Toronto: Oxford University Press, 1977); J.L. Granatstein and J.M. Hitsman, *Broken Promises: A History of Conscription in Canada* (Toronto: Oxford University Press, 1977); R. MacGregor Dawson, *The Conscription Crisis of 1944* (Toronto: University of Toronto Press, 1961); and Brian Nolan, *King's War: Mackenzie King and the Politics of War, 1939–1945* (Toronto: Fawcett Crest, 1988).

25 As quoted in Janzen, *Limits on Liberty*, 200.

26 Jonathan F. Wagner, *Brothers beyond the Sea: National Socialism in Canada* (Waterloo, Ont.: Wilfrid Laurier University Press, 1981).

27 Frank Henry Epp, 'An Analysis of Germanism and National Socialism in the Immigrant Newspapers of a Canadian Minority Group, the Mennonites, in the 1930s,' PhD thesis, University of Minnesota, 1965.

28 Robert C. James, ' "The City Where God Has Caused Us To Come." The Story of the Leamington Mennonite Community May 09 to June 03, 1940: An Examination of Wider Circumstances,' a history seminar paper, a copy of which is available at CGC.

29 CMBS(W) B.B. Janz Papers, B.B. Janz to Rev. David Toews, 4 July 1940.

30 John J. Bergen, 'The World Wars and Education among Mennonites in Canada,' *JMS*, 8 (1990), 156–72.

31 Details of this vigilante action, in the course of which members of the legion entered the Bible School at Drake and forcibly removed the teacher, who was put on the train back to Rosthern, whence he had come, are given in the Archives of the Evangelical Mennonite Conference in Steinbach, vol. 253, file 45. Subsequent police actions are described in SAB Department of the Attorney General, file C 12 G.

32 Wagner, *Brothers*, and Lita-Rose Betcherman, *The Swastika and the Maple Leaf: Fascist Movements in Canada in the 1930s* (Toronto: Fitzhenry and Whiteside, 1975).

33 When, for example, the allegedly pro-German sentiments of Jacob Gerbrandt at Drake, Saskatchewan, roused the ire of local legion members, the police quietly contacted David Toews, asking him to speak to Gerbrandt, one of the key Mennonite leaders who met with government officials throughout the war. Toews warned Gerbrandt that he would be interned if he persisted in keeping the controversial German Saturday school open. The school was promptly closed. Copies of the relevant police reports are in SAB Department of the Attorney General, file C 12 G.

34 The events of 10 June 1940 have been reconstructed on the basis of King's diary and histories of Canadian politics during the war.

35 NAC MG 26, J, King Diary, 10 June 1940.

36 CMBS (W) B.B. Janz Papers, David Toews to B.B. Janz, 1 July 1940.

37 Ibid.

38 These procedures, particularly as they affected conscientious objectors, are outlined in NAC RG 35/7, vol. 21, 'Historical Account of the Wartime Activities of the Alternative Service Branch, Department of Labour, 11 April 1946.'

39 The response of the peace groups to National Registration is discussed in Janzen, *Limits on Liberty*, 199–203.

40 CGC file XV-11.1.1, E.J. Swalm, 'The Organization of the Conference of Historic Peace Churches,' unpublished paper. The CHPC registration cards are in files XV-11.1.10, XV-11.1.11, and XV-11.1.12.

41 MHC Board of Colonization, 1321/929, David Toews to Mr. Justice T. C. Davis, 19 Aug. 1940, and T. C. Davis to David Toews, 22 August 1940.

42 *Canada Gazette*, 74, no. 23, 27 Aug. 1940, 'National War Service Regulations, 1940 (Recruits).'

43 Ibid., Sec. 17.

44 Ibid., Sec. 18.

45 J.G. Rempel, *Die Rosenorter Gemeinde in Saskatchewan in Wort und Bild* (Rosthern, Sask.: n.p., 1950), and Walter Klaassen, '*The Days of Our Years*': *The Eigenheim Mennonite Community, 1892–1992* (Rosthern, Sask.: Eigenheim Mennonite Church, 1992).

46 CMBS(W) B.B. Janz Papers 3/37, B.B. Janz to J.T. Thorson, 28 June 1941.

47 Kenneth Wayne Reddig, 'Manitoba Mennonites and the Winnipeg Mobilization Board in World War II,' MA thesis, University of Manitoba, 1989.

48 NAC RG 27, vol. 983, Minutes of Meetings of Registrars, 18 Feb. 1941.

49 Reddig, 'Manitoba Mennonites.'

50 Janzen, *Limits on Liberty*, 211–12.

51 'Frank Statement by Mennonite Replies to "Language" Charge,' *Abbotsford, Sumas, Matsqui News*, 23 June 1943, 1. The headline in this case is misleading, since most of the report deals with 'the deepening controversy over the Mennonite position of not bearing arms in war.'

52 William Janzen and Frances Greaser, eds., *Sam Martin Went to Prison: The Story of Conscientious Objection and Canadian Military Service* (Winnipeg: Kindred Press, 1990). See also Janzen, *Limits on Liberty*, and David Warren Fransen, 'Canadian Mennonites and Conscientious Objection in World War II,' MA thesis, University of Waterloo, 1977.

53 CGC File XV 11.1.10. CHPC, Minutes of meeting, 8 Oct. 1940.

54 Minutes of meetings of Mennonite leaders in western Canada are given in Reimer, *Erfahrungen*.

55 As quoted in Fransen, 'Canadian Mennonites,' 58.

56 MHC Board of Colonization, 1321/928, David Toews, Rosthern, Saskatchewan, B.B. Janz, Coaldale, Alberta, C.F. Klassen, Winnipeg, Manitoba, and J.J. Gerbrandt, Drake, Saskatchewan, to T.C. Davis, 12 November 1940; and David Toews, Rosthern, Saskatchewan, B.B. Janz, Coaldale, Alberta, J. Gerbrandt, Drake, Saskatchewan, C.F. Klassen, Winnipeg, Manitoba, E.J. Swalm, Duntroon, Ontario, J.B. Martin, Waterloo, Ontario, Fred Haslam, Toronto, Ontario, and J.H. Janzen, Waterloo, Ontario, to T.C. Davis and L.R. Lafleche, 13 Nov. 1940.

57 Federal documentation, including correspondence and minutes of notes of meetings, is available in NAC RG 27, vol. 986, file 1.

58 CMBS(W) B.B. Janz Papers, 3/37, B.B. Janz to D. Toews and J. Gerbrandt, 15 Nov. 1940. In the file there is also a nine-point memorandum, dated 14 Nov. but not further identified. At the bottom is a note in Janz's handwriting: 'No. 3 presented by B.B. Janz.' A slightly altered version, dated 19 Nov. 1940 is also in the file.

59 Ibid., B.B. Janz to Major-General L.R. LaFleche, 19 Nov. 1940. See also B.B. Janz to Hon. Mr. Justice Davis, Associate Deputy Minister, 1 Dec. 1940.

60 Ibid., E.J. Swalm, J.B. Martin, Fred Haslam, J.H. Janzen, B.B. Janz, C.F. Klassen, and J.H. Sherk to Hon. J.G. Gardiner, 22 Nov. 1940; CGC XV-11-4-1, Military Problems Committee, 'Report of Delegation of Conference of Historic Peace Churches Which Interviewed the Deputy Ministers of National War Services, Nov. 22, 1940.'

61 As quoted in Fransen, 'Canadian Mennonites,' 102; and Janzen, *Limits on Liberty*, 207.

62 As quoted in Fransen, 'Canadian Mennonites,' 103.

63 CMBS(W) B.B. Janz Papers 3/37, B.B. Janz to Hon. Mr. Justice Davis, Associate Deputy Minister, National War Services, written on 'C.P.R. train

going West,' 1 Dec. 1940.

64 Canada, PC 7215, 24 Dec. 1940, published in *the Canada Gazette*, 74, no. 64, 7 Jan. 1941.

65 DND Directorate of History, file 326.009 D102, Memorandum to the district officer commanding, Military District 12, from B.W. Browne, 26 Nov. 1941. See also Janzen, *Limits on Liberty*, 213.

66 NAC RG 35/7, vol. 21, 'Historical Account.'

67 NAC RG 27, vol. 986, Dept. of National War Services, Division 'M' to Dept. of National War Services, Dept. of National Defence, and Dept. of Mines and Resources, 13 Jan. 1942.

68 As quoted in Fransen, 'Canadian Mennonites,' 120–1.

69 NAC RG 27, vol. 986, Report on Work Done by Conscientious Objectors (Mennonites, Doukhobors and Other Sects) under the Direction of Department of Mines and Resources from June to November 15th, 1941, 13.

70 NAC RG 27, vol. 986, file 2-101, Minutes of meeting held in the office of Major-General L.R. LaFleche, National War Services, Ottawa, 1 Nov. 1941, 2. The order in council, PC 2452, requiring conscientious objectors to serve for the duration of the war, was passed only on 30 March 1942. See also NAC RG 39, vol. 41, file 49810.

71 NAC RG 35/7, vol. 21, 'Historical Account,' 9-10; and Toews, *Alternative Service*, 83–9.

72 As quoted in Toews, *Alternative Service*, 106.

73 Canada, PC 2821, 7 April 1943.

74 CGC file XV-11.1.11, Report of delegation to Ottawa, 27–29 April 1943, and Memorandum from E.J. Swalm, J.B. Martin, C.F. Klassen, and J. Harold Sherk to Hon. Humphrey Mitchell, Minister of Labour.

75 F.J. McEvoy, 'Operation Habbakuk: "Professor" Pyke's Secret Weapon,' *The Beaver* (April–May 1994), 32–9. A description of the work that he did has been provided by Abe J. Dick, one of the conscientious objectors who worked briefly on the project, in correspondence with Professor W.A. Waiser, Department of History, University of Saskatchewan.

76 NAC RG 35/7, vol. 21, 'Historical Account,' 23.

77 The attitudes and consequent wartime problems of the Jehovah's Witnesses are described in detail in William Kaplan, *State and Salvation: The Jehovah's Witnesses and Their Fight for Civil Rights* (Toronto: University of Toronto Press, 1989).

78 Toews, *Alternative Service*, 95.

79 Janzen, 'Limits of Liberty,' 527.

80 CGC Transcript of an interview by Frank H. Epp, 22 Jan. 1984, with Peter Bargen and others in Edmonton.

81 NAC RG 35/7, vol. 21, 'Historical Account,' 19. This contrasted unfavourably with the 541 men who were granted CO status but later enlisted in the armed forces.
82 Peter Bargen interview, 11.
83 Ibid.
84 'Pete Isaak, Peter Bargen Receive Wounds,' *Chilliwack Progress*, 10 Jan. 1945, 8.
85 This is the number given in Epp, *Mennonite Exodus*, 331. Epp apparently obtained the figure from the files of the Canadian Mennonite Board of Colonization, but I have not been able to corroborate it. The files of the board contain a letter from the Department of Labour indicating that the government did not keep detailed records regarding the denominational affiliation of each conscientious objector. There were a total of 10,851 COs working in the Alternative Service program on 31 December 1945, and estimates by government officials of the number of Mennonites ranged from 63 per cent to 80 per cent, with 70 per cent being the most frequently quoted figure; 7,500 has been accepted by both William Janzen and David Warren Fransen, who have studied the matter in detail.
86 As quoted in Toews, Alternative Service, 103. For comparable experiences by the Brethren in Christ see E. Morris Sider, 'Life and Labor in the Alternative Service Work Camps in Canada during World War II,' MQR, 66, no. 4 (Oct. 1992), 580–97.
87 Noah Bearinger, 'No Spears of Iron: Memories of the Alternative Service Camp at Montreal River during the Second World War,' Family Life (June and July 1986).
88 John A. Toews, a young Mennonite Brethren minister who had studied at Mennonite Bible schools and at the Calgary Prophetic Bible Institute, exemplified the new evangelistic methods. Elfrieda Toews Nafziger, A Man of His Word: A Biography of John A. Toews (Winnipeg: Kindred Press, 1992).
89 Sider, Brethren in Christ, cites the case of David Jantzi, an Old Order Amishman from Milverton, who was 'saved' in the camps but then excommunicated by his home congregation. He later became a minister in the Amish Mennonite Church.
90 E. Morris Sider, 'Life and Labour in the Alternative Service Work Camps in Canada during World War II,' MQR, 66, no. 4 (Oct. 1992), 595.
91 Ibid.
92 NAC RG 35/7, 'Historical Account,' 26a.
93 Ibid.
94 Klippenstein, ed., *That There Be Peace*, 100.
95 Peter J. Klassen, *Verlorene Soehne: Ein Beitrag in der Frage der Wehrlosigkeit* (Winnipeg: Sonderausgabe, n.d.).

96 The basis for calculation of this figure is given in Regehr, 'Lost Sons,' 461–80.
97 G. Enns (pseudonym of I.G. Neufeld), 'Ein Besuch bei Mennonitischen Soldaten,' *Mennonitische Rundschau*, 24 July 1944, 1, 5.
98 Al Reimer, 'The War Brings Its Own Conflict to Steinbach,' *MM*, 3, no. 8 (June 1974), 15.
99 As quoted by G. Enns, 'Heimkehr der Mennonitischen Soldaten,' *Mennonitische Rundschau*, 8 Aug. 1945, 7.
100 Esther Epp-Tiessen, *Altona: The Story of a Prairie Town* (Altona, Man.: D.W. Friesen and Sons, 1982), 199.
101 Ruth Roach Pierson, *'They're Still Women After All': The Second World War and Canadian Womanhood* (Toronto: McClelland and Stewart, 1986).

3: Voluntary Service

1 John Herd Thompson, *Canada, 1922–1939: Decades of Discontent* (Toronto: McClelland and Stewart, 1985).
2 Frank H. Epp, *Mennonites in Canada, 1920–1940: A People's Struggle for Survival* (Toronto: Macmillan, 1982).
3 For a detailed discussion of this concept see Bruce L. Guenther, ' "In the World but not of it": Old Colony Mennonites, Evangelicalism and Contemporary Canadian Culture – A Case Study of Osler Mission Chapel (1974–94),' paper presented to the Canadian Society of Church History, University of Calgary, 7 June 1994.
4 Two official statements by the Mennonite Central Committee, one dated 1942 and the other approved in 1964, document this change. See 'A Statement of position for the guidance of workers and prospective workers under MCC, adopted by MCC at its Annual Meeting, 29 Dec. 1942,' published in C.J. Dyck, ed., *Responding to Worldwide Needs: The Mennonite Central Committee Story*, Vol. 2 (Scottdale, Penn.: Herald Press, 1980), 11; and 'Consultation of Relief, Service, and Missions Relationships Overseas, Chicago, May 7–8, 1965, Findings Committee Report,' ibid., 20.
5 Ruth Roach Pierson, *'They're Still Women After All': The Second World War and Canadian Womanhood* (Toronto: McClelland and Stewart, 1986), 39.
6 Veronica Strong-Boag, *A New Day Recalled: Lives of Girls and Women in English Canada, 1919–1939* (Toronto: Copp Clark Pitman, 1988), 92.
7 Pierson, *'They're Still Women,'* 39.
8 A total of 541 men who had been granted CO status subsequently enlisted voluntarily for active military service, and by 1942 MCC and other Mennonite leaders realized that financial hardship was a factor in some of

these decisions. NAC RG 35/7, vol. 21, 'Historical Account of the Wartime Activities of the Alternative Service Branch, Department of Labour, 11 April 1946,' 19; 'Unser Zivildienst,' *Mennonitische Rundschau*, 23 Sept. 1942, 2–3.

9 NAC RG 27, file 601.3 (12); quoted in L.E. Westman, Chief Alternative Service Officer, to Allan M. Mitchell, Director, Employment Service and Unemployment Insurance Branch, 23 Aug. 1943.

10 Marlene Epp, ' "United We Stand, Divided We Fall": Canadian Mennonite Women as COs in World War II,' *ML*, 48, no. 3 (Sept. 1993), 8.

11 CGC J.B. Martin Papers, Hist. MSS. 1.34.1.1.1, Blake to J.B. Martin, 1 March 1943.

12 Marlene Epp, 'United We Stand,' 9. Details on the exact allowances at various times are given in John A. Toews, *Alternative Service in Canada during World War II* (Winnipeg: Canadian Conference of the Mennonite Brethren Church, 1959).

13 Katherine Martens, *All in a Row: The Klassens of Homewood* (Winnipeg: Mennonite Literary Society, 1988), 89.

14 It was only after intense debate that the (Old) Mennonite Church of Ontario allowed its members freedom to accept or reject the cheques as they saw fit. CGC Calendar of Appointments of the Mennonite Church of Ontario (1945–6), 'Family Allowance Study Committee Report,' 41.

15 Ruth Roach Pierson, *Canadian Women and the Second World War*, Canadian Historical Association Booklet no. 37, (Ottawa, 1983).

16 Gloria Redekop, 'Mennonite Women's Societies in Canada: A Historical Study,' PhD. thesis, University of Ottawa, 1993; Marlene Epp, 'Women in Canadian Mennonite History: Uncovering the "Underside," ' *JMS*, 5 (1987), 90–107, and ' "United We Stand," ' 7–10; Lorraine Roth, 'Conscientious Objection: The Experiences of Some Canadian Mennonite Women during World War II,' *MQR*, 66, no. 4 (Oct. 1992), 539–45; Lorraine Roth, *Willing Service: Stories of Ontario Mennonite Women* (Waterloo, Ont.: Mennonite Historical Society of Ontario, 1992).

17 Pierson, *'They're Still Women'*.

18 E. Morris Sider, 'Life and Labour in the Alternative Service Work Camps in Canada during World War II,' *MQR*, 66, no. 4 (Oct. 1992), 580–97.

19 Roth, *Willing Service*, 19–21.

20 Roth, 'Conscientious Objection,' 539–40.

21 CBC Minutes of the Mennonite Brethren Churches of British Columbia, 21 Nov. 1943.

22 *History of the B.C. Mennonite Women in Mission, 1939–1976* (Chilliwack, BC: BC Mennonite Women in Mission, 1976). Similar histories of other Mennonite women's organizations are available at the MHC and CGC.

23 Mennonite leaders in Ontario had rejected alternative service work by their young men that might involve medical orderly or ambulance services under Red Cross direction. But the women in some Ontario churches participated in a wide range of Red Cross projects. Other groups did only knitting, while one group sent mouthwash to the soldiers on one occasion. See Roth, 'Conscientious Objection,' 539–45.

24 C.J. Dyck, *Responding to Worldwide Needs*, 28–55.

25 Redekop, 'Mennonite Women's Mission Societies'; Melvin Gingerich, 'Women's Missionary and Service Auxiliary,' *ME* IV, 974–5.

26 Reading no. 61 in C.J. Dyck, ed., *From the Files of MCC: The Mennonite Central Committee Story*, vol. 1 (Scottdale, Penn.: Herald Press, 1980), 118.

27 John D. Unruh, *In the Name of Christ: A History of the Mennonite Central Committee and Its Service, 1920–1951* (Scottdale, Penn.: Herald Press, 1952), chap. 2; Frank H. Epp, *Mennonite Exodus: The Rescue and Resettlement of the Russian Mennonites since the Communist Revolution* (Altona, Man.: Canadian Mennonite Relief and Immigration Council, 1962).

28 Short histories of these relief committees are available in the *ME* I–V (Scottdale, Penn.: Herald Press, 1956, 1957, 1959, and 1990). The several histories of the MCC provide more information, as does Frank Epp in *Mennonite Exodus* and in his two volumes of *Mennonites in Canada*.

29 See Frank Epp, *Mennonite Exodus*, for a much more detailed account of the work of these committees and boards.

30 Unruh, *In the Name of Christ*, 43.

31 Reading no. 12, in C.J. Dyck, ed., *Responding to Worldwide Needs*, 39.

32 Roth, *Willing Service*, 188–90.

33 Ibid., 86–8.

34 Marion Keeney Preheim, 'Elfrieda Dyck,' in C.J. Dyck, ed., *Something Meaningful for God: The Stories of Some Who Served with MCC* (Scottdale, Penn.: Herald Press, 1981), 215–57; Peter and Elfrieda Dyck, *Up from the Rubble: The Epic Rescue of Thousands of War-Ravaged Mennonite Refugees* (Scottdale, Penn.: Herald Press, 1991), 227–9.

35 Dyck, ed., *Something Meaningful for God*, 33–5, 39–41; Unruh, *In the Name of Christ*, 48–53; Peter and Elfrieda Dyck, *Up from the Rubble*; Marcus Shantz, 'Edna Hunsperger Bauman,' *Looking for Peace: Three Mennonites Remember W.W II* (Kitchener, Ont.: Mennonite Central Committee, Ontario, and Rockway Mennonite Collegiate, 1992), unpaginated.

36 The list of MCC workers in England, but not their nationality, is given in Unruh, *In the Name of Christ*, 55.

37 Dyck, ed., *Responding to Worldwide Needs*, 41.

38 I have less than happy memories of a school project in which all the students

were expected to knit small woollen squares that were then to be sewn
together to make blankets for injured soldiers. The war would have been lost if
everyone else had made as big a mess of their tasks as I did with that knitting.
Fortunately one of the Mennonite girls in the class was so skilled that she not
only completed her work but also had time to take mine apart and knit it up
properly, and the war was won in spite of my incompetence.

39 NAC RG 35/7, vol. 21, 'Historical Account,' 23.
40 Malcolm J. Proudfoot, *European Refugees, 1939–1952: A Study in Forced
    Population Movements* (London: Faber and Faber, 1957), and Jacques Vernant,
    The Refugee in the Post-War World (London: George Allen and Unwin, 1953).
41 *Forty Years of International Assistance to Refugees* (Geneva: United Nations
    High Commissioner for Refugees, n.d.).
42 For harsh criticism of the consequences of the treatment of Germans and
    collaborators by the allies, see Alfred M. de Zayas, *Nemesis at Potsdam: The
    Expulsion of the Germans from the East* (Lincoln, Neb.: University of Nebraska
    Press, 1977), 132. The Mennonites from Danzig, East and West Prussia, and the
    Polish corridor were regarded and treated by UNRRA as German nationals.
    There was, as explained in the chapter on immigration, much controversy about
    the status and eligibility of the Mennonite refugees from the Soviet Union and
    central Poland evacuated westward by the retreating German forces.
43 Robert Kreider, 'CRALOG,' *ME* I, 730. Kreider sent numerous exceptionally
    detailed, informative, and incisive reports to MCC officials in Akron,
    Pennsylvania. Copies of these reports are available in AMC *Bender Papers*,
    53/44.
44 Unruh, *In the Name of Christ*, 102–74; Dyck, ed., *Responding to Worldwide
    Needs*, 43–6.
45 'A Statement of position for the guidance of workers and prospective workers
    under MCC. Adopted by MCC at its Annual Meeting, December 29, 1942,' in
    Dyck, ed., *Responding to Worldwide Needs*, 10–11.
46 For one particularly moving account, see Frank Epp, *Mennonite Exodus*, 367.
47 AMC Bender Papers, 52/17, Robert Kreider to Howard Yoder and Sam
    Goering, 20 March 1946.
48 Robert S. Kreider and Rachel Waltner Goossen, *Hungry, Thirsty, a Stranger:
    The MCC Experience* (Scottdale, Penn.: Herald Press, 1988), 9–10.
49 AMC Mennonite Board of Missions and Charities Records, Minutes of the
    Annual Meeting, 15 July 1947, to which is attached a document written by
    Robert Kreider and entitled 'Meeting Mennonite Need in Germany.'
50 Robert Kreider to Ted Regehr, 8 Aug. 1992.
51 C.F. Klassen, the MCC commissioner of immigration, was one of the first to
    visit the refugees in their camps in the fall of 1945. He returned to Canada in

December and reported in all the larger Canadian Mennonite churches during early 1946. In addition, he wrote regular news reports which were published in Mennonite newspapers. His work is discussed in greater detail in Herbert Klassen and Maureen Klassen, *Ambassador to His People: C.F. Klassen and the Russian Mennonite Refugees* (Winnipeg: Kindred Press, 1990). Klassen's overriding concern was the welfare and resettlement of the Soviet Mennonite refugees.

52 AMC Bender Papers, 53/44, Robert Kreider to Sam Goering, Howard Yoder and J.N. Byler, 13 April 1940.

53 J.N. Weaver, 'CARE,' *ME* I, 516.

54 Unruh, *In the Name of Christ*, 227–9.

55 Melvin Gingerich, *Service for Peace: A History of Mennonite Civilian Public Service* (Akron, Penn.: Mennonite Central Committee, 1949), 189.

56 AMC Bender Papers 53/66, Wilson Hunsberger to Orie Miller, 13 Jan. 1946; Wilson Hunsberger to Ministry of Agriculture, Republic of Poland, 11 Jan. 1947; and Wilson Hunsberger to Orie Miller, 2 Feb. 1947; Unruh, *In the Name of Christ*, 136–9.

57 Prince Albert *Daily Herald*, 25 Jan. 1943.

58 Harold A. Penner, 'Voluntary Service,' *ME* V, 917.

59 Unruh, *In the Name of Christ*, 294.

60 AMC MCC IX-6-3.99, file entitled 'Mennonite Central Committee Canadian Headquarters, 1959,' memo from VS Section to VS and I-W Office, 3 Dec. 1959, re Taves and Wiebe VS meeting, Waterloo, 30 Nov. This memo outlines administrative details of the program.

61 Ibid., IX-6-6, file entitled 'Mennonite Central Committee Canadian Headquarters, 1960,' Report of my visit to Newfoundland January 26 to February 20 by Harvey Taves, 1 March 1960.

62 As quoted in Peter Penner, *No Longer at Arm's Length: Mennonite Brethren Church Planting in Canada* (Winnipeg: Kindred Press, 1987), 117–8.

63 AMC IX-6-3, file entitled 'Mennonite Central Committee Canada, 1971,' Canadian Voluntary Service Report to the MCC (Canada) Executive Committee Meeting, 27–28 Nov. 1970, by John Wieler, Associate Executive Secretary.

64 Ibid., file entitled 'Mennonite Central Committee Canadian Headquarters, 1960,' R.G. Sivertz, Director, Northern Administration Branch, Department of Northern Affairs and National Resources to Harvey Taves, 22 Jan. 1960; Taves to Sivertz, 1 Feb. 1960; and Taves to Dick Burkholder, Summer Service, Mennonite Central Committee, 12 April 1960.

65 Harold A. Penner, 'Voluntary Service,' *ME* V, 917–18.

66 Katie Funk Wiebe, *Day of Disaster* (Scottdale, Penn.: Herald Press, 1976).

67 William T. Snyder, 'Mennonite Disaster Service,' *ME* III, 620.

68 Wiebe, *Day of Disaster*, 15–32.
69 Griselda Shelly, 'Relief sales,' *ME* V, 759–60.
70 Ibid.
71 Kreider and Goossen, *Hungry, Thirsty, a Stranger*, 362.
72 Harold S. Bender, *ME* III, 890.
73 Roy Vogt and Ruth Vogt, *Embracing the World: Two Decades of Canadian Mennonite Writing. A Selection of Writings from the Mennonite Mirror*, vol. 19, no. 10 (June–July 1990), 4.

4: Refugee Immigrants

1 Some of these people were also called displaced persons, or DPs. In this chapter I use the broader term 'refugee,' as defined by a 1951 United Nations Convention Relating to the Status of Refugees: 'A refugee is any person who, owing to a well-founded fear of being persecuted for reasons of race, religion, nationality, membership of a particular social group, or political opinion, is outside the country of his nationality and is unable or, owing to such fear, is unwilling to avail himself of the protection of that country of his former habitual residence, or is unable or, owing to such fear, is unwilling to return to it.' Elizabeth G. Ferris, *Refugees and World Politics* (New York: Praeger, 1985).
2 MHC Canadian Mennonite Board of Colonization, 1348/1109.
3 A. Schmidt, unpublished, handwritten manuscript entitled 'Exodus.' I purchased one of the best known of Agatha Schmidt's paintings, together with her handwritten recollections, at the 1962 Mennonite World Conference in Kitchener, Ontario.
4 Ingeborg Fleischhauer and Benjamin Pinkus, *The Soviet Germans Past and Present* (London: Hurst, 1986); Ingeborg Fleischhauer, *Das Dritte Reich und die Deutschen in der Sowjetunion* (Stuttgart, 1983).
5 Details of actions and policies followed by the German occupation forces are given in the extensive records of the Reichsministerium fuer die besetzten Ostgebiete and of the Volksdeutsche Mittelstelle, available in the Deutsches Bundesarchiv, Koblenz.
6 These figures are at best rough estimates. In June 1948, MCC workers in Europe had registered 11,766 Mennonite refugees from the Soviet Union who had remained in western Europe after the postwar repatriations. There is no detailed or authoritative record of the alleged repatriation back to the Soviet Union of more than 23,000 Mennonite refugees. Statistics on the number of Germans from the Soviet Union involved in the evacuation, and their fate, are given in Fleischhauer and Pinkus, *Soviet Germans*. Mennonite statistics are available at the Weierhof Mennonitische Forschungsstelle, archival box labelled

'Hilfswerk II HVDM Anfaenge 1946–1950.' See particularly A. Braun, treasurer of the Hilfswerk der Vereinigung der Deutschen Mennoniten-gemeinden, and 'Liebe Brueder,' 13 Dez. 1946. Other sources give somewhat different estimates.

7 There is extensive documentation on the evacuation at the Bundesarchiv, Koblenz, in the records of the Reichsministerium fuer die besetzten Ostgebiete (see particalarlly R6/136 and 137) and of the Volksdeutsche Mittelstelle (especially R59/93, 94, 135, and 136).

8 Schmidt, 'Exodus.'

9 A detailed account by one of the refugees who was overtaken by the Red Army and sent back to the Soviet Union is Katharina Krueger, *Schicksal einer Russlanddeutschen: Erlebnisbericht* (Goettingen: Graphikum, 1991).

10 Schmidt, 'Exodus.'

11 Ibid. A detailed diary of the trek was kept by Jacob A. Neufeld and is now available in MHC J.J. Thiessen Papers, vol. 885. Neufeld also published an account of the trek, based on his diary, as *Tiefenwege: Erfahrungen und Erlebnisse von Russland-Mennoniten in zwei Jahrzehnten bis 1949* (Virgil, Ont.: Niagara Press, n.d.).

12 Extensive German documentation on arrangements for the 'Umsiedlungen' are available in the records of the Volksdeutsche Mittelstelle.

13 As quoted in Alfred M. de Zayas, *Nemesis at Potsdam: The Expulsion of the Germans from the East,* 3rd ed., rev. (Lincoln, Neb.: University of Nebraska Press, 1988), 65.

14 Evidence and personal accounts of the swearing in and the granting of German citizenship to refugees resettled in Poland differ greatly. Many of those who remained in the west insisted that the procedures were perfunctory and informal. Katharina Krueger, who also accepted German citizenship but was repatriated back to the Soviet Union, indicates that, in the camp where she stayed, the Einbuergerungskomission made careful and detailed genealogical inquiries. This was followed by further instruction and indoctrination, and finally by the granting of German citizenship, which she mistakenly believed would protect her from any return to the Soviet Union. Krueger, *Schicksal*, 35–6.

15 USNA RG 260, OMGUS, AGO, decimal file 383.7, 1945–46, top-secret document dated 28 Feb. 1945 and entitled 'Treatment of USSR Displaced Persons Liberated by Forces Operating under U.S. Command,' and ibid., Confidential document dated 8 April 1945 and titled 'Liberated Citizens of the Soviet Union.'

16 Ibid., decimal file 383.7 – 1947, L.S. Ostrander, Adjutant General, by Command of General McNarney to the Commanding Generals, Third US Army, Seventh US Army Area, Berlin District, re Repatriation of Soviet

Citizens Subject to Repatriation under the Yalta Agreement, 4 Jan. 1946.

17 A much more detailed account of the Berlin rescue, based on archival documents in the Bundesarchiv in Koblenz and in the U.S. National Archives, is T.D. Regehr, 'Anatomy of a Mennonite Miracle: The Berlin Rescue of 30–31 January 1947,' *JMS*, 9 (1991), 11–33. See also Peter Dyck and Elfrieda Dyck, *Up from the Rubble: The Epic Rescue of Thousands of War-Ravaged Mennonite Refugees* (Scottdale, Penn.: Herald Press, 1991), and Barbara Smucker, *Henry's Red Sea* (Scottdale, Penn.: Herald Press, 1955).

18 Weierhof Mennonitische Forschungsstelle, Archival box labelled 'Hilfswerk II HVDM Anfaenge 1946–1950,' Ernst Crous to Siegfried Janzen, 16 Feb. 1948; and Heinrich Wiehler (Aeltester), 'Die Frueheren ostdeutschen Mennoniten-gemeinden unter Einschluss der Gemeinden in Polen. Uebersicht ueber die frueheren ostdeutschen Mennonitengemeinden (Ostpreussen, Danzig-Westpreussen, Polen),' *Unser Blatt*, 15 Sept. 1949.

19 The experience of the few Mennonites living in central Poland was more similar to that of those in the Soviet Union than it was to the experience of the Danzig and Prussian Mennonites.

20 William I. Schreiber, *The Fate of the Prussian Mennonites* (Goettingen: Goettingen Research Committee, 1955), 38.

21 Details of the atrocities committed by soldiers of the Red Army against German civilians are documented in de Zayas, *Nemesis at Potsdam*. Some of the suffering of Prussian Mennonites is documented in MHC vol. 1732, files 22, 23, 24, 31, 42, and 43. See also Karl Fast and Greta Fast, 'In Una-Massen gehoert,' *Der Bote*, 16 Feb. 1990.

22 Horst Penner, *Die ost- und westpreussischen Mennoniten in ihrem religioesen und sozialen Leben in ihren kulturellen und wirtschaftlichen Leistungen* (Selbstverlag, 1987), 128–32.

23 de Zayas, *Nemesis at Potsdam*, 74.

24 Estimates of the number rescued vary considerably. The higher figure comes from de Zayas, *Nemesis*. Other, mainly older sources, suggest that 1.5 million, or perhaps 2 million, were rescued by sea.

25 Bruno Ewert, 'From Danzig to Denmark,' *ML*, 1, no. 1 (Jan. 1946), 37; and Walter Gering, 'With Prussian Mennonites in Denmark,' *ML*, 2, no. 4 (Oct. 1947), 12–14.

26 Malcolm Proudfoot, *European Refugees, 1939–52: A Study in Forced Population Movements* (London: Faber and Faber, 1957), and Jacques Vernant, *The Refugee in the Post-War World* (London: George Allen and Unwin, 1953). See also USNA RG 260, OMGUS, AGO, Memorandum, Supreme Headquarters Allied Expeditionary Force, 16 April 1945, re Displaced Persons and Refugees in Germany.

27 The Inter-Governmental Commission for Refugees, UNRRA, and the Preparatory Commission for the International Refugee Organization (PCIRO) dealt with emigration matters until the requisite number of nations had signed up to permit creation of the International Refugee Organization (IRO), which began its work in July 1947.

28 John B. Toews, *Lost Fatherland: The Story of the Mennonite Emigration from Soviet Russia, 1921–1927* (Scottdale, Penn.: Herald Press, 1967); Herbert Klassen and Maureen Klassen, *Ambassador to His People: C.F. Klassen and the Russian Mennonite Refugees* (Winnipeg: Kindred Press, 1990); and Frank H. Epp, *Mennonite Exodus: The Rescue and Resettlement of the Russian Mennonites since the Communist Revolution* (Altona, Man.: Canadian Mennonite Relief and Immigration Council, 1962).

29 The story of this original group of Mennonite refugees from the Soviet Union who were granted admission to Holland is told in vivid and colourful detail in Dyck, *Up from the Rubble*, chap. 4, 'The First Thirty-three.'

30 Siegfried Janzen, 'Das Fluechtlingslager Gronau,' *Der Mennonit*, 1 Jahrgang, Juli/Aug. 1948, 52–3, 64.

31 Peter J. Dyck, 'Lager Backnang bei Stuttgart,' ibid., 2 Jahrgang, Maerz/April 1949, 23.

32 C.F. Klassen, 'Die mennonitschen Fluechtlinge und wir,' ibid., 1 Jahrgang, Okt./Nov. 1948, 84–6.

33 Ibid., 85. This report by Klassen is remarkable because he describes his relations with IRO officials as entirely friendly. He mentions some disputes 'on the periphery' with minor IRO officials but ascribes those difficulties to jealousy.

34 The relevant IRO files are at the Archive Nationale, Paris, IRO Records, box 49, file entitled 'Eligibility of Mennonites, 1946–47'; ibid., box 571, 'Refugees – Mennonites, fevrier 1947–juillet 1949'; ibid., box 572, 'Refugees – Volksdeutsche,' juillet 1949–aout 1951. An additional file of interest is ibid., box 1170, 'Paraguay correspondence.' Copies of the official IRO orders pertaining to Mennonite refugees from the Soviet Union, together with some ensuing correspondence involving MCC, IRO, and Canadian immigration officials, are in NAC RG 76, vol. 855, file 554-22.

35 NAC RG 76, vol. 885, file 554-22, William Snyder to A.L. Jolliffe, Director of Immigration, Dominion of Canada, 16 Sept. 1949.

36 Ibid.

37 In conversations with Peter J. Dyck and William T. Snyder in 1992 I was told unequivocally that MCC had not withheld any relevant information available in its files. When Dyck and others set up the MCC Kartei at the Gronau camp they did not inquire about possible wartime collaboration by the refugees,

choosing instead to believe that the refugees had collaborated only under
duress – an imprecise and flexible term.

38 MHC Board of Colonization 1325/957, C.F. Klassen to William Snyder, 28
Jan. 1953.
39 This dispute is documented and analysed in T.D. Regehr, 'Of Dutch or
German Ancestry? Mennonite Refugees, the Mennonite Central Committee,
and the International Refugee Organization,' *JMS,* 13 (1995), 7–25.
40 MHC Board of Colonization, 1325/991 and 1325/957, has fairly extensive and
revealing documents regarding problems of Mennonite IRO eligibility.
41 Gerald E. Dirks, *Canada's Refugee Policy: Indifference or Opportunism?*
(Montreal and Kingston: McGill-Queen's University Press, 1977); Freda
Hawkins, *Canada and Immigration: Public Policy and Public Concern*
(Montreal and Kingston: McGill-Queen's University Press, 1972); H.L
Keenleyside, 'Canada's Immigration Policy,' *International Journal,* 3, no. 2
(1948), 222–238.
42 Canada, *Proceedings of the Senate Committee on Immigration and Labour,* 1946.
43 NAC RG 27, vol. 3041, file 125, 'Preliminary Report of the Interdepartmental
Committee on Immigration Policy to the Cabinet Committee on
Immigration,' 4 April 1946.
44 MHC Board of Colonization, 1325/958, H.C.P. Cresswell to J.J. Thiessen, 24
April 1946, and Cresswell to David Toews, 26 July 1945.
45 Archive Nationale, Paris, Records of the International Refugee Organization,
box 59, Activities report for December 1946 of the Intergovernmental
Committee on Refugees, British Zone, Germany.
46 For a detailed description of these lobbying activities see MHC Board of
Colonization 1325/958, C.F. Klassen 'An die Mitglieder des Mennonitischen
Zentralen Hilfskomitees, 1 Mai 1946.'
47 Ibid., 1325/959, James G. Gardiner to Gerhard Ens, 16 April 1946.
48 Ibid., J.A. Glen, Minister of Mines and Resources, to J.J. Thiessen, Chairman,
Canadian Mennonite Board of Colonization, 24 June 1946. The underlying
rationale for this order in council is given in NAC RG 27, vol. 3041, file 125,
'Preliminary Report of the Interdepartmental Committee on Immigration
Policy to the Cabinet Committee on Immigration,' 4 April 1946. 'Absorptive
capacity,' not UNRRA or IRO eligibility, was stressed in this document.
49 MHC Board of Colonization, 1324/950, David Toews to H.C.P. Cresswell, 7
Feb. 1945.
50 Ibid., 1324/947; and NAC RG 76, vol. 855, file 544-22.
51 MHC Board of Colonization, 1329/988, 1329/989, and 1330/990.
52 NAC RG 76, vol. 855, file 554-22, J.J. Thiessen to Walter E. Harris, Minister of
Citizenship and Immigration, 16 April 1951.

53 MHC Board of Colonization, 1394/1556, 'Bericht der Canadian Mennonite Board of Colonization fuer die Jahressitzung am 9 Maerz 1955,' 5.

54 Epp, *Mennonite Exodus*, 444.

55 The story of one immigrant family that began work in Calgary under humble circumstances but built a large construction business employing many immigrants is told in Joanna Buhr, 'Kurt Janz: The Struggling Phoenix,' unpublished paper which the author generously made available to me.

56 Ruth Roach Pierson, 'Women's Emancipation and the Recruitment of Women into the Canadian Labour Force,' Canadian Historical Association *Historical Papers*, 1976, 141–74, and Ruth Roach Pierson, *Canadian Women and the Second World War* (Ottawa: Canadian Historical Association, 1983).

57 Marlene Epp, 'Women in Canadian Mennonite History: Uncovering the "Underside," ' *JMS*, 5 (1987), 90–107.

58 Neufeld, *Tiefenwege*, 163, as translated by T.D. Regehr.

59 Ingrid Rimland, *The Wanderers: The Saga of Three Women Who Survived* (St Louis, Mo.: Concordia Publishing House, 1977), 196.

60 As quoted in Marlene Epp, 'The Memory of Violence: Mennonite Refugees and Rape in World War II,' early draft of a paper presented at the annual meeting of the Canadian Historical Association in Calgary, May 1994, 25.

61 Harry Loewen, 'A Courageous Mother,' in *No Permanent City: Stories from Mennonite History and Life* (Waterloo, Ont., and Scottdale, Penn.: Herald Press, 1993), 205.

62 'Ernste Fragen der Gegenwart,' *Der Mennonit* 4 Jahrgang (September 1951), 141.

63 NAC RG 76, vol. 855, file 554-22, part 1, J.J. Thiessen to A.L. Joliffe, 19 and 28 Sept. 1949.

64 Marlene Epp, 'Memory of Violence,' and 'Women in Canadian Mennonite History.'

65 George K. Epp, 'Mennonite Immigration to Canada after World War II,' *JMS*, 5 (1987), 108–119.

66 The traditional and conservative religious tone of the wartime and refugee experiences of the immigrants, and the way in which those values were strengthened in Canada by the immigrants, is clearly described in Henry H. Winter, *Ein Hirte der Bedraengten. Heinrich Winter, der letzte Aelteste von Chortitza* (Wheatley, Ont.: Henry H. Winter, 1988).

67 David B. Marshall, *Secularizing the Faith: Canadian Protestant Clergy and the Crisis of Belief, 1850–1940* (Toronto: University of Toronto Press, 1992), 3.

5: Wartime Changes in Agriculture

1 AMC, MCC Records, file IX-5-1, J.W. Fretz, 'Report of My Trip to Canada to Study Mennonite Colonization,' presented to the Executive Committee at its meeting on 18 Sept. 1943, 27.

2 'Protokoll der 9. Vertreterversammlung der mennonitischen Siedler Albertas, abgehalten im Bethause der Mennonitengemeinde zu Tofield vom 14-15 Juli 1939,' *Der Bote*, 31 Jan. 1940, 7–8, 7 Feb. 1940, 5–6, 21 Feb. 1940, 7–8, 6 March 1940, 5–6, 13 March 1940, 5–6, 20 March 1940, 5–6, and 27 Mar. 1940, 5–6.

3 A.A. Toews, 'Sind wir als Siedler wirtschaftlich vorwaerts gekommen?' *Der Bote*, 14 Feb. 1940, 8.

4 *The Albertan*, 15 Oct. 1959. A copy of the article is in NAC MG 32, B40, A-175, vol. 69, Alvin Hamilton Papers. I am grateful to Chad Mitcham for drawing it to my attention.

5 Ian MacPherson and John Herd Thompson, 'An Orderly Reconstruction: Prairie Agriculture in World War Two,' in D.H. Akenson, ed., *Canadian Papers in Rural History*, vol. 4 (Gananoque, Ont.: Langdale Press, 1984), 11–32.

6 Ibid., 11.

7 Canada, *House of Commons Debates*, 1 Aug. 1940, 2308.

8 James G. Gardiner, *Canadian Agriculture and the War* (Ottawa: King's Printer, 1941), 6, 9.

9 G.E. Britnell and V.C. Fowke, *Canadian Agriculture in War and Peace, 1935–1950* (Stanford, Calif.: Stanford University Press, 1962), 366–7. See also L.B. Pett et al., 'The Development of Dietary Standards,' *Canadian Journal of Public Health*, (June 1945), 232–9, and Bernd Martin and Alan S. Milward, eds., *Agriculture and Food Supply in the Second World War* (Ostfildern: Scripta Meraturae, 1985).

10 Keith A.H. Murray, *Agriculture: History of the Second World War: U.K. Civil Series* (London: HMSO, 1955).

11 A.A. Toews, 'Sind wir als Siedler wirtschaftlich vorwaerts gekommen?' *Der Bote*, 14 Feb. 1940, 8. A somewhat more optimistic assessment of conditions at Namaka, where Toews lived, is Henry C. Klassen, 'The Mennonites of the Namaka Farm,' *ML*, 30, no. 4 (Dec. 1975), 8–14. Extensive and detailed reports on the Alberta, Saskatchewan, and BC communities in which Mennonite immigrants of the 1920s settled with the help of the CPR's Canada Colonization Association are available in the records of that organization, now at the Glenbow-Alberta Institute in Calgary. *The Western Weekly Law Report* contains information on bankruptcy and contractual problems encountered in the 1930s by many of these immigrants.

12 Norman Ward and David Smith, *Jimmy Gardiner: Relentless Liberal* (Toronto:

University of Toronto Press, 1990), 256.

13 V.C. Fowke, 'Economic Effect of the War on the Prairie Economy,' *Canadian Journal of Economics and Political Science*, 9 (Aug. 1945), 373–87.

14 Frank H. Epp, *Mennonite Exodus: The Rescue and Resettlement of the Russian Mennonites since the Communist Revolution* (Altona, Man.: Canadian Mennonite Relief and Immigration Council, 1962).

15 M.C. Urquhart and K.A.H. Buckley, *Historical Statistics of Canada* (Toronto: Macmillan, 1965), series L206, L207, L217, and L218.

16 British dietary preferences helped determine the food products that would be imported. Eggs, bacon, and cheese were given highest priority, but chicken and beef were regarded as less essential, or even as luxury foods. This contrasted sharply with American preferences for beef, chicken, and turkey.

17 The location and production of Alberta's cheese factories are given in the *Annual Report of the Department of Agriculture for the Province of Alberta*, various years. Mennonite farmers organized cheese factories at Coaldale, Crooked Creek, Didsbury, Glenwood, Mountain View, Rosemary, Sunnyslope, and Swalwell. These factories produced almost all the cheese manufactured in southern Alberta. In northern Alberta the Alberta Dairy Pool dominated the market, producing cheese at five locations.

18 P.H. Regehr, *Er fuehret ... Geschichte der Coaldale Mennonitischen Kaeserei, 1928–1958* (Yarrow, BC: Columbia Press, n.d.). Information about the wartime contracts is given in Fretz, 'Report of my Trip to Canada.'

19 *Annual Report of the Department of Agriculture of the Province of Alberta for the year 1942.*

20 Britnell and Fowke, *Canadian Agriculture*, 348; Esther Epp-Tiessen, *Altona: The Story of a Prairie Town* (Altona, Man.: D.W. Friesen and Sons, 1982), 207–10.

21 These are all described in Fretz, 'Report of My Trip to Canada.'

22 K.S. Coates and W.R. Morrison, *The Alaska Highway in World War II: The U.S. Army of Occupation in Canada's Northwest* (Toronto: University of Toronto Press, 1992).

23 *Annual Report of the Department of Agriculture of the Province of Alberta for the Year 1944*, 'Report of the Poultry Commissioner.'

24 E.K. Francis, *In Search of Utopia: The Mennonites in Manitoba* (Altona, Man.: D.W. Friesen and Sons, 1955) 243.

25 J. Winfield Fretz became the most passionate advocate of this approach. See particularly his pamphlets *Mennonite Colonization: Lessons from the Past for the Future* (Akron, Penn.: Mennonite Central Committee, 1944), and *Christian Mutual Aid: A Handbook of Brotherhood Economics* (Akron, Penn.: Mennonite Central Committee, 1947).

26 Regehr, *Er fuehret*, 42. Peter H. Regehr was the father of a large family. Most

members ended up in cities or larger towns despite his strong commitment to a separatist, rural, and agricultural life-style. A son served in the armed forces during the war, and a granddaughter became Miss Dominion of Canada in the 1970s.

27 Macpherson and Thompson, 'Orderly Reconstruction,' 11–12; W.H. Drummond, 'The Impact of the War on Canadian Agriculture,' in J.F. Parkinson, ed., *Canadian War Economics* (Toronto: University of Toronto Press, 1941) 128.

28 Urquhart and Buckley, *Statistics*, series L82.

29 Britnell and Fowke, *Canadian Agriculture,* 398.

30 The secondary sources pertaining to the Japanese evacuation, on which much of this discussion is based, are Ken Adachi, *The Enemy That Never Was: A History of the Japanese Canadians* (Toronto: McClelland and Stewart, 1976) and Ann Gover Sunahara, *The Politics of Racism: The Uprooting of Japanese Canadians during the Second World War* (Toronto: Lorimer, 1981). The major archival sources documenting the evacuation of the Japanese and the subsequent 'sale' of 817 Japanese berry farms are NAC RG 25, vol. 3004, *Report of the British Columbia Security Commission*; NAC RG 14, vol. 653, *Appendix to the Journals of the House of Commons to Accompany the Fourth Report of the Standing Committee on Public Accounts*, presented to the House of Commons on Tuesday, 17 June 1947; NAC RG 38, vol. 40, file V-8-10, Records of the Soldiers' Settlement Board, later the Veterans' Land Administration; NAC RG 64, Records of the Wartime Prices and Trade Board; and NAC RG 117, vol. 1, file 2, Records of the Custodian of Enemy Property.

31 Interview with Peter D. Loewen, 17 Dec. 1988, at Clearbrook, BC, and interview with Agatha E. Klassen, 18 Dec. 1988, at Yarrow, BC. See also Agatha E. Klassen, ed., *Yarrow: A Portrait in Mosaic,* rev. ed. (Yarrow, BC: Klassen, 1980); and Evelyn Macquire, AASc, RN, 'The Mennonites in British Columbia,' *Bulletin of the British Columbia Board of Health*, 8 (Aug. 1938), 171–3.

32 Fretz, 'Report of My Trip to Canada.' For a retrospective view of the earlier troubles, see also *Chilliwack Progress*, 27 May 1953.

33 Results of ongoing raspberry variety tests by the provincial department of agriculture are given in a number of its annual reports in the 1930s and in I.C. Crane, District Horticulturalist, Abbotsford, BC, 'Observations on Raspberry Varieties Grown in the Fraser Valley' (revised 1965). A copy of this pamphlet is available in the Agriculture and Forest Products Library at the University of British Columbia.

34 G.G. Baerg, *A Brief History of Mennonites in British Columbia*, prepared as one of the 'Histories of Ethnic Groups in British Columbia' series in 1967;

B.B. Wiens, 'Pioneering in British Columbia,' *ML,* 1, no. 2 (July 1946), 9, 13.

35 British Columbia, *Department of Agriculture Annual Report, 1938* (Victoria: King's Printer, 1938), L23.

36 Ibid.

37 Extensive details on the problems of the BC berry industry are available in the records and reports of the Wartime Prices and Trade Board. See particularly NAC RG 64, vol. 50; vol. 210; vol. 567, file 16–611; vol. 568, files 16-6-13 and 16-6-14; vol. 960, file 4-1; vol. 1002, file 4-17-1; vol. 1152, file 16-1-4; vol. 1174, file 16-3-2-2; vol. 1355; vol. 1541; and vol. 1555. A comprehensive postwar report on the wartime Fresh Fruits and Vegetables Administration is available in NAC RG 64, vol. 20.

38 Adachi, *The Enemy That Never Was,* 149.

39 Sunahara, *The Politics of Racism,* 101.

40 A complete list of all the British Columbia Berry Association producers, and the tonnage handled by each in 1941, is available in NAC RG 64, vol. 986, file 1-13-1. In that year the largest of these growers' associations was the Pacific Co-operative Union.

41 Interview with William Schellenberg, 18 Dec. 1989, at Yarrow, BC. Schellenberg was president of the Yarrow Growers' Co-op.

42 PABC Add. MSS. Rigenda Sumida, 'The Japanese in BC.'; see particularly chap. 8.

43 NAC RG 64, vol. 210, J.B. Shimek, General Manager of the Pacific Co-operative Union, to Donald Gordon, Chairman of the Wartime Prices and Trade Board, 29 Nov. 1941.

44 Administrator's Orders of the Wartime Prices and Trade Board are in NAC RG 64, vol. 50.

45 The impact of the Japanese evacuation on British Columbia's Mennonite farmers is discussed in more detail in T.D. Regehr, 'Canadian Mennonites and the Japanese Berry Farmers in British Columbia after the Evacuation of 1942,' *JMS,* 10 (1992), 87–101.

46 NAC RG 38, vol. 403, file V-8-10 (10), I.T. Barnet to G. Murchison, 19 May 1942.

47 Ibid., List attached to a memo from I.T. Barnet to G. Murchison, 9 Sept. 1942. This list pertains only to former Japanese farms later acquired by the Veterans' Land Administration from the Custodian of Enemy Property. The term 'Mennonite' is used here in an ethnic sense. Not all those listed were members of any Mennonite church, but in 1942 individuals with the surnames Banman, Conrad, Elias, Ewert, Friesen, Froese, Harder, Hamm, Harms, Heinrichs, Hildebrandt, Janzen, Klassen, Martens, Mierau, Niessen, Nikkel, Pankratz, Redekopp, Rempel, Retzlaff, Siemens, Teichrob, Thiessen, Toews, and Wiebe

were still generally identified as Mennonites.

48 *Abbotsford, Sumas and Matsqui News*, 7 Jan. and 22 April 1942. PABC GR 1222, box 161, file 6, William Wright, Secretary-Treasurer, Associated Boards of Trade of the Fraser Valley and the lower mainland, to John Hart, Premier, 16 June 1943. *Vancouver Sun*, 20 March 1943; *Vancouver News Herald*, 22 May 1943; and *Chilliwack Progress*, 23 June 1943.

49 Technically, the decisions were made by the administrators of the old Soldier Settlement Act, set up to serve veterans of the First World War. A new Veterans' Land Act had been drafted and was making its way through Parliament when the decision to acquire the Japanese berry farms was made. The Veterans' Land Act became law on 20 July 1942.

50 See particularly NAC 14, vol. 653, *Appendix to the Journals of the House of Commons to Accompany the Fourth Report of the Standing Committee on Public Accounts*, presented to the House of Commons on Tuesday, 17 June 1947; and NAC RG 117, vol. 1, file 2.

51 NAC RG 38, vol. 403, file V-8-10, D.W. Strachan to George Murchison, 28 July 1943.

52 NAC RG 64, vol. 1172, file 16-3-2, G.F. Perkin to 'All Members Interested in Strawberries,' 29 July 1942.

53 NAC RG 38, vol. 403, file V-8-10 (1), I.T. Barnet to G. Murchison, 27 Aug. 1942. See also I.T. Barnet to G. Murchison, 2 June 1942.

54 Details on the 1943 leases of former Japanese farms, with a complete list of all lessees, are given in NAC RG 38, vol. 403, file V-8-10 (1).

55 'Conchie Land Buying,' *Chilliwack Progress*, 23 June 1943.

56 NAC RG 64, vol. 567, file 16-11, E.J. Chambers, Administrator, Fresh Fruits and Vegetables, to L.R. Wilson, Federated and Coast Growers and Shipping Organizations, 25 May 1944. The basic guidelines followed are outlined in ibid., vol. 1555, Handbook entitled *Stabilization Controls and What They Do*, prepared by an interdepartmental committee composed of representatives of the departments of Finance, Labour, and Agriculture, the Wartime Prices and Trade Board, and the War Information Board, Dec. 1943. The relevant administrator's orders are in ibid., vol. 50. Cabinet approval is recorded in NAC RG 2, PC 3/5410, 7 July 1943.

57 NAC RG 64 , vol. 986, file 4-13-1, memorandum entitled 'Berries – 1941,' and NAC RG 38, vol. 403, file V-8-10, I.T. Barnet to G. Murchison.

58 Agatha E. Klassen, *Yarrow*, and reports in the *Chilliwack Progress*, 14 July and 20 Aug. 1943 and 7 March and 26 Sept. 1945.

59 *Chilliwack Progress*, 19 May 1943.

60 *Mennonitische Rundschau*, 15 Dec. 1943.

61 *Abbotsford, Sumas and Matsqui News*, 22 Dec. 1943.

62 *Mennonitische Rundschau*, 23 June 1943.

63 Ibid.

64 B.B. Wiens, 'Pioneering in British Columbia,' *ML*, 1, no. 2 (July 1946), 9, 13.

65 Klassen, *Yarrow*, 76.

66 Canada, *House of Commons Debates*, 22 Feb. 1949, 772.

67 Abe A. Shelly, formerly Schellenberg, served during the war as Retail Food
    Director and then Wholesale and Retail Food Director for Canada of the
    Wartime Prices and Trade Board. He was obviously in a good position to
    know about the cheap berries available in Yarrow. For details on the careers of
    members of the Schellenberg (or Shelly) family see Eric Knowles, 'The Shellys
    of Saskatchewan: A Business That Progressed Backwards,' *Western Business
    and Industry*, 20, no. 9 (Sept. 1946), 48–9, 104–5.

68 Canada, *House of Commons Debates*, 1 April 1949, 2262–4.

69 Klassen, *Yarrow*, 70.

70 Canada, *House of Commons Debates*, 25 March 1949, 2028.

71 Fretz, 'Report of my Trip to Canada.'

72 The chairman of the Yarrow Growers' Co-op in 1948 was William
    Schellenberg. In an interview on 31 July 1989, shortly before his death,
    Schellenberg spoke of his involvement. He said that the co-op regularly
    borrowed large sums from the banks and then advanced money to berry
    farmers for supplies, fertilizer, equipment and operating expenses. He said that
    the bankers phoned to warn him, long before the crash, that the co-op and the
    farmers were carrying excessive debt burdens. He reassured the bankers that
    the people were honest and would repay their debts. The disasters of 1948
    made it difficult, and in some cases impossible, for them to do so. Schellenberg
    also claimed that when the trouble developed those unable to repay their debts
    began a whispering campaign regarding alleged financial irregularities by the
    management, which he adamantly denied. When the trouble developed, the
    British Columbia Central Co-op offered up to $60,000 to help the Yarrow co-
    op through the crisis, but members, led by individuals who owed large sums to
    the co-op, voted to liquidate it. Schellenberg served as liquidator and said that
    all debts owed by the co-op were paid in full but that it was not possible to
    collect some of the debts that individual producers and customers owed.

73 Ontario, Ministry of Agriculture and Food, *Agricultural Statistics for Ontario,
    1941–1978* (Toronto: Queen's Printer, 1979). For an analysis of the figures
    given in Table 5.2, see K.J. Rea, *The Prosperous Years: The Economic History of
    Ontario, 1939–75* (Toronto: University of Toronto Press, 1985), 134–61.

74 Britnell and Fowke, *Canadian Agriculture*, 398.

75 Bill Moyer, *Kitchener Yesterday Revisited: An Illustrated History* (Burlington,
    Ont.: Windsor Publications, 1979), 71.

76 Rea, *Prosperous Years*, 145.

77 Ibid.

78 Bert Friesen, *Where We Stand: An Index to Statements by Mennonites and Brethren in Christ in Canada, 1787–1982* (Winnipeg: Mennonite Central Committee, Canada, 1986), 188.

79 J. Winfield Fretz, *The Waterloo Mennonites: A Community in Paradox* (Waterloo, Ont.: Wilfrid Laurier University Press, 1989), 182.

80 *Waterloo County Holstein-Frisian History, 1882–1962* (Galt, Ont.: Holstein Breeders Association Inc., 1962).

81 Roy G. Snyder, *Fifty Years of Artificial Insemination in Canada, 1934–1984* (n.p.: Canadian Association of Animal Breeders, 1984).

82 Fretz, 'Report of My Trip to Canada'; C. Alfred Friesen, *Memoirs of the Virgil-Niagara Mennonites: History of the Mennonite Settlement in Niagara-on-the-Lake, 1934–84* (n.p., 1984); Robert Shipley, ed., *St Catharines: Garden on the Canal* (Burlington, Ont.: Windsor Publications, 1987); Henry Paetkau, 'Separation or Integration? The Russian Mennonite Immigrant Community in Ontario, 1924–45,' PhD thesis, University of Western Ontario, 1986.

83 *The Canadian Who's Who* (1948), 964.

84 W.M. Drummond, 'The Impact of the Post-war Industrial Expansion on Ontario's Agriculture,' *Canadian Journal of Economics and Political Science*, 24 (Feb. 1968), 84–92.

85 Urquhart and Buckley, *Statistics*, series L28.

86 Fretz, *Waterloo Mennonites*, 182.

87 Harley J. Stucky, 'The Agricultural Revolution of Our Day,' *ML*, 14, no. 3 (July 1959), 118.

88 A moving description of working conditions in the sugar-beet fields of southern Alberta has been provided by one of the Japanese evacuees from British Columbia who worked on Mennonite farms. Joy Kogawa, *Obasan* (New York: Penguin, 1983), 196.

89 Wally Kroeker, 'Lord of the Onions,' in Calvin Redekop and Urie A. Bender, eds., *Who Am I? What Am I? Searching for Meaning in Your Work* (Grand Rapids, Mich.: Academie Books, 1988), 122–3.

6: The Continuing Agricultural Base

1 As quoted in Robert S. Kreider and Rachel Waltner Goossen, *Hungry, Thirsty, a Stranger:* The MCC Experience (Scottdale, Penn.: Herald Press, 1988), 83.

2 Harold S. Bender, 'State, Anabaptist-Mennonite Attitude Toward,' *ME* IV, 611–18.

3 F.H. Lacey, ed., *Historical Statistics of Canada*, 2nd ed. (Ottawa: Statistics Canada and the Social Science Federation of Canada, 1939), series M119.

4 Ibid., series M45.
5 Ibid., series M67.
6 Ibid., series M1.
7 Since education is under provincial jurisdiction, laws and provisions pertaining to organization of local school boards and compulsory attendance of children at approved schools varied somewhat from province to province. Thus local school boards in compact Mennonite settlements in Ontario usually enjoyed greater latitude in the operation of local public schools than was the case in the prairie provinces.
8 Leonard Doell, *The Bergthaler Mennonite Church of Saskatchewan, 1892–1975* (Winnipeg: CMBC Publications, 1987), 65–8.
9 NAC RG 76, vol. 855, file 554-22, C.P. Hebert, Canadian Ambassador, Mexico, to The Secretary of State for External Affairs, Canada, re 'Mennonite trek from Canada to Mexico and Honduras,' 28 June 1951.
10 Ibid. See also J.E. Valenzuela, Secretariat of External Affairs of the Republic of Honduras, to Leland de Villafranca, Consulate General of Honduras, Mexico City, 19 Sept. 1950.
11 Ibid. This rebuff did not end attempts to establish a Mennonite colony in British Honduras (later renamed Belize), which eventually succeeded, mainly because of Mennonites who had migrated from Canada to Mexico in the 1920s and moved on to Belize.
12 Doell, *Bergthaler*, 64–9.
13 A detailed description of these Mennonite groups is given in Appendix B.
14 H.L. Sawatzky, 'Post World War II Mennonite Emigration from Canada to Latin America,' paper read at a Mennonite History Symposium held at Conrad Grebel College in 1988.
15 Dawn S. Bowen, 'The Transformation of a Northern Alberta Frontier Community,' MA thesis, University of Maine at Orono, 1990.
16 CMBS(W) Protokoll der Mennoniten Bruedergemeinde zu Coaldale, Alberta, 26 Mai 1947, which includes a report by B.W. Sawatzky on the Mennonite communities near Fort Vermilion, Alberta.
17 As quoted in Bowen, 'Transformation.'
18 John Friesen, 'Theological Developments in Canada during the 1950s and early 1960s,' paper presented at a Symposium on Mennonites in Canada, Waterloo, Ont., 12 May 1988.
19 Bowen, 'Transformation.'
20 Donald B. Kraybill, *The Riddle of Amish Culture* (Baltimore, Md.: Johns Hopkins University Press, 1989), 63.
21 Ibid., 68.
22 Ibid., 23.

23 The detailed documentation pertaining to this migration is available in NAC RG 76, vol. 855, file 554-22.

24 *Mennonite Yearbook and Directory 1941* (Scottdale, Penn.: Mennonite Publishing House, 1941), 58.

25 AHL Manuscript by Joseph Stoll entitled 'Recent Amish Immigration to Ontario,' written in 1966.

26 Ibid. See also John A. Hostetler, 'Old Order Amish,' *ME* IV, 43–7; and John A. Hostetler, *Amish Society* (Baltimore, Md.: Johns Hopkins University Press, 1963).

27 *CM*, 4, no. 17, and 6, no. 2, reported that a group of Old Order Amish from Indiana obtained an option to purchase land in Prince Edward Island. They were denied entry into the country because they refused to have their photographs taken for the identification cards required by Canadian immigration officials. They returned home after allegedly waiting at the border for six months.

28 AHL, Stoll, 'Recent Amish Immigration,' p. 1.

29 Ibid.

30 Ibid.

31 T.D. Regehr, 'Relations between the Old Order Amish and the State in Canada after 1940,' *MQR*, 69, no. 2 (April 1995), 151–77.

32 Dennis L. Thomson, 'Canadian Government Relations,' in Donald B. Kraybill, ed., *The Amish and the State* (Baltimore, Md.: Johns Hopkins University Press, 1993), 235–50; AHL Harry van Bommel, 'Systems Analysis of the Cabinet Compromise re Amish Use of Milk Cans,' paper presented to Professor Ruprecht, Political Science Department, York University, 1978.

33 Frank H. Epp, *Mennonites in Canada, 1920–1940: A People's Struggle for Survival* (Toronto: Macmillan, 1982); and Harry Leonard Sawatzky, *They Sought a Country: Mennonite Colonization in Mexico* (Berkeley, Calif.: University of California Press, 1971).

34 J. Winfield Fretz, *Mennonite Colonization in Mexico* (Akron, Penn.: Mennonite Central Committee, 1945), 7.

35 H.L. Sawatzky, 'Mexico,' *ME* V, 580.

36 CGC Hildegard M. Martens, 'Mennonites from Mexico: Their Immigration and Settlement in Canada,' Research report submitted to Research Grants Program, Canada Manpower and Immigration, and to Mennonite Central Committee (Canada), 30 June 1975.

37 NAC RG 76, vol. 855, file 554-22, Canadian Ambassador, Mexico, to the Secretary of State for External Affairs, Canada, Despatch No. 432, 17 Oct. 1951.

38 MHC Board of Colonization, 1327/974, A.A. Wiens to J.J. Thiessen, B.B. Janz, and Wm. Snyder, 30 April 1954.

39 Sawatzky, *They Sought a Country*, 318–23.

40 NAC RG 76, vol. 855, file 554-22, Canadian Ambassador, Mexico, to the Secretary of State for External Affairs, Canada, Despatch No. 432, 17 Oct. 1951.

41 Ibid., John W. Taylor, British Embassy, Mexico, to Rt. Hon. Anthony Eden, Foreign Office, London, 25 April 1952.

42 Ibid., Johann Fehr to 'Beloved Gentlemen in Ottawa,' 18 Oct. 1954.

43 MHC Board of Colonization, 1327/974, William T. Snyder to J.J. Thiessen, 7 May 1954.

44 Ibid. has numerous letters dealing with these issues. The letters written by A.A. Wiens, who ended up with the unhappy task of looking after many of the Mexican Mennonites in British Columbia, are particularly critical of the Mexican Mennonites.

45 Ibid., Report entitled 'A Visit to Mexico,' by John R. Swartz, Anan U. Christner, and John Martin. Attached is a highly critical note written by A.A. Wiens of British Columbia.

46 AMC, MCC Records, file IX-6-3.99, file entitled 'Mennonite Central Committee Canadian Headquarters,' Harvey Taves to William T. Snyder, 12 June 1961, and Harvey Taves to William T. Snyder and Orie O. Miller, 19 May 1961. Passport and citizenship problems encountered by the Mexican Mennonites in Ontario are discussed in ibid., Harvey Taves to J.J. Thiessen, Chairman, Canadian Mennonite Board of Colonization, 9 May 1960.

47 Martens, 'Mennonites from Mexico.'

48 AHL David Bender, 'Aylmer Amish Acres,' published in the *Aylmer Amish Directory*, 1990.

49 A discussion of the impact of war on Mennonite economic policy in Ontario is provided in E. Reginald Good, 'War as a Factor in Mennonite Economic Policy: A Case Study,' MA thesis, University of Waterloo, 1984. Later Ontario developments are discussed in J. Winfield Fretz, *The Waterloo Mennonites: A Community in Paradox* (Waterloo, Ont.: Wilfrid Laurier University Press, 1989).
    Among descendants of the 1870s Mennonite immigrants the Waisenamt was the most common community-based mutual-aid institution. For a history of these institutions see Jake Peters, *The Waisenamt: A History of Mennonite Inheritance Custom* (Steinbach, Man.: Mennonite Village Museum, 1985); E.K. Francis, *In Search of Utopia: The Mennonites in Manitoba* (Altona, Man.: D.W. Friesen and Sons, 1955); and Robert R. Meyers, *The Spirit of the Post Road: A Story of Self-help Communities* (Altona, Man.: Federation of Southern Manitoba Co-operatives, 1955).

50 J. Winfield Fretz, *Christian Mutual Aid: A Handbook of Brotherhood Economics* (Akron, Penn.: Mennonite Central Committee, 1947), 85–6.

51 Kropotkin's best-known work translated and published in English is *Mutual Aid a Factor in Evolution* (New York: McClure, Phillips and Co., 1902).

52 As quoted in Fretz, *Christian Mutual Aid*, 11.

53 J. Winfield Fretz, *Meditations on Christian Mutual Aid* (Bluffton, Ohio: Association of Mennonite Aid Societies, 1958), 6.

54 Ibid., 40.

55 Fretz, *Waterloo Mennonites*, 270–80.

56 Meyers, *Spirit of the Post Road*, 11.

57 Fretz, *Mutual Aid*, 87.

58 Peters, *Waisenamt*, 2.

59 Esther Epp-Tiessen, *Altona: The Story of a Prairie Town* (Altona, Man.: D.W. Friesen and Sons, 1982), 166.

60 Meyers, *Spirit of the Post Road*, 66.

61 Peters, *Waisenamt*.

62 'The Free Enterprise Spirit and Co-operation: Steinbach Credit Union, Manitoba's Largest,' *MM*, 2, no. 5 (Jan. 1973), 15; 'The Beginnings of a Credit Union in Altona,' ibid., 13; 'Twenty Nine Years at Crosstown Credit Union,' ibid., 17.

63 'The Free Enterprise Spirit and Co-operation: Steinbach Credit Union, Manitoba's Largest,' *MM*, 2, no. 5 (Jan. 1973), 15.

64 Epp-Tiessen, *Altona*, 262.

65 Kelly Harms, *'Grace upon Grace': A History of the Mennonite Nursing Home of Rosthern* (Rosthern, Sask.: Mennonite Nursing Homes Inc., 1994).

66 *CM*, 6, no. 50 (19 Dec. 1955), 1 and 8.

67 This argument is strongly advanced in Meyers, *Spirit of the Post Road*.

68 Ian MacPherson and John Herd Thompson, 'The Business of Agriculture: Prairie Farmers and the Adoption of Business Methods, 1880–1950,' in Peter Baskerville, ed., *Canadian Papers in Business History*, vol. 1 (Victoria: University of Victoria Press, 1989), 245–69.

69 Saskatchewan, *Report of the Royal Commission on Agriculture and Rural Life* (Regina: Queen's Printer, 1955–7). See particularly vol. 3, Report 14, *A Program of Improvement*, Appendix 1, 'Complete List of Commission Recommendations,' 85–148.

70 John L. Stover, *First Majority – Last Minority: The Transforming of Rural Life in America* (DeKalb, Ill.: Northern Illinois University Press, 1976), xii.

71 MacPherson and Thompson, 'Business of Agriculture,' 245–69.

72 Royden Loewen, 'Rurality, Ethnicity, and Gender Patterns of Cultural Continuity during the "Great Disjuncture" in R.M. Hanover, 1945–1961,' *Journal of the Canadian Historical Association*, 4 (1993), 162.

73 Ibid., 161–82.

74 Hugh Getty Laurence, 'Change in Religion, Economics, and Boundary Conditions among Amish Mennonites in Southwestern Ontario,' PhD thesis, McGill University, 1980.

75 Donald Wetherell, with Elise Corbet, *Breaking New Ground: A Century of Farm Equipment Manufacturing on the Canadian Prairies* (Saskatoon: Fifth House, 1993).

76 Ibid.

77 Loewen, 'Rurality,' 164.

78 Ibid., 170.

79 D. Owram, 'Home and Family at Mid-Century,' paper read at the annual meeting of the Canadian Historical Association in Charlottetown, 1992; Veronica Strong-Boag, 'Home Dreams: Women and the Suburban Experiment in Canada, 1945–1960,' *Canadian Historical Review*, 72 (1991), 471–504.

80 Royden Loewen, *Family, Church and Market: A Mennonite Community in the Old and the New Worlds, 1850–1930* (Toronto: University of Toronto Press, 1993), chap. 11.

81 Laurence, 'Changes in Religion,' chap. 6, 11.

82 Ibid., 13.

7: New Economic Opportunities

1 The story of Reuben Musselman is based on personal recollections, as told to Doug Miller and confirmed by Musselman, and on a report prepared by Marlene Epp, dated 11 Sept. 1989.

2 A more detailed discussion of these aspects of Mennonite entrepreneurship is given in T.D. Regehr, 'Mennonites and Entrepreneurship in Canada,' in Calvin Redekop, Victor A. Krahn, and Samuel J. Steiner, eds., *Anabaptist/Mennonite Faith and Economics* (New York: University Press of America, 1994), 127–52.

3 John Herd Thompson with Allen Seager, *Canada, 1922–1939: Decades of Discontent* (Toronto: McClelland and Stewart, 1985).

4 Ken Norrie and Douglas Owram, *History of the Canadian Economy* (Toronto: Harcourt Brace Jovanovich, 1991), 560–3.

5 M.M. Atkinson and W.D. Coleman, *The State, Business and Industrial Change in Canada* (Toronto: University of Toronto Press, 1988).

6 Dennis Guest, *The Emergence of Social Security in Canada* (Vancouver: University of British Columbia Press, 1980).

7 Leonard C. Marsh, *Report on Social Security for Canada, 1942*, reprint (Toronto: University of Toronto Press, 1975). Many of the same issues are also addressed in Leonard C. Marsh, *Canadians In and Out of Work* (Toronto: Oxford University Press, 1940).

8 J. Murray Beck, *Pendulum of Power: Canada's Federal Elections* (Toronto: Prentice Hall, 1968), 241–58.

9 Victor Krahn, 'The Effects of Small Businesses upon the Old Order Communities of Waterloo County,' research paper prepared for Calvin Redekop, Conrad Grebel College, Oct. 1989. A copy is available at the AHL. I am indebted to Cal Redekop for taking me on a tour of many of these Old Order rural service businesses. See also Paul Harold Brubacher, 'Dimensions of Social Interaction between Old Order Mennonites and Non-Mennonites in the Mount Forest Area,' MSc thesis in agricultural economics, University of Guelph, 1984; and John F. Peters, 'Socialization among the Old Order Mennonites,' *International Journal of Comparative Sociology*, 28 (1987), 211–24.

10 'Mennonite Beginnings at Rosthern,' *ML*, 31, no. 4 (Dec. 1976), 4–15; *Old and New Furrows: The Story of Rosthern* (Rosthern, Sask.: Rosthern Historical Society, n.d.).

11 Several particularly good local histories discussing business activities in rural Mennonite communities are Esther Epp-Tiessen, *Altona: The Story of a Prairie Town* (Altona, Man.: D.W. Friesen and Sons, 1982); Peter D. Zacharias, *Reinland: An Experience in Community* (Reinland: Reinland Centennial Committee, 1976); and Royden Loewen, *Blumenort: A Mennonite Community in Transition, 1874–1982* (Steinbach, Man.: Blumenort Mennonite Historical Society, 1983).

12 AMC, MCC Records, file IX-5-1, J.W. Fretz, 'Report of My Trip to Canada to Study Mennonite Colonization,' presented to the Executive Committee at its meeting on 18 Sept. 1943, 12.

13 Gerald Wright, *Steinbach: Is There Any Place Like It?* (Steinbach, Man.: Derksen Printers, 1991); Epp-Tiessen, *Altona; Coaldale: Gem of the West, 1900–1983* (Coaldale, Alta: Coaldale Historical Society, 1983); and Agatha E. Klassen, *Yarrow: A Portrait in Mosaic* (Yarrow, BC: A.E. Klassen, 1980).

14 *Coaldale*, 143.

15 Clarence Barber, *Report of the Royal Commission on Farm Machinery* (Ottawa: Queen's Printer, 1971), 41.

16 One of the best succinct discussions of the growing importance of franchised agricultural machinery dealers in Canada is given in ibid.

17 Consolidations and corporate genealogies of the major farm machinery companies, and the four main types of manufacturers in Canada, are described in ibid.

18 Zacharias, *Reinland*, 137–9.

19 'Die Monarch-Maschinenfabrik in Winnipeg,' *Mennonitische Welt*, 5 Jahrgang (Sept. 1952), 3–4.

20 '50 Years of a Family Business,' *MM*, 5, no. 2 (Nov. 1975), 13.

21 Eric Knowles, 'The Shellys of Saskatchewan: A Business That Progressed Backwards,' *Western Business and Industry*, 20, no. 9 (Sept. 1946), 48–9, 104–5.
22 Ibid.
23 Zehr's grocery store chain was started by Emory Zehr, a member of the Stirling Avenue Mennonite Church in Kitchener. His first outlet was a small corner grocery offering free delivery, and Zehr allegedly made it successful 'just through running his legs off.' The quality of the produce sold, competitive prices, and good service, in addition to ethnic and denominational loyalties, attracted customers and fostered loyalty. For more information see Henry Koch, 'Talking Business: He Feeds Half of K-W and a Third of Guelph,' *Kitchener-Waterloo Record*, 9 May 1970.
24 *Coaldale*, 147.
25 '50 Years of a Family Business,' 13.
26 'John Klassen: Whose Unique Personality and Vision Transcended His Achievements,' *MM*, 12, no. 1 (Sept. 1982), 4.
27 'A Long Way from Lumberyard to Millworks,' *MM*, 7, no. 10 (summer 1978), 10.
28 John Keats, *The Insolent Chariots* (Philadelphia and New York: Lippincott, 1958), 12.
29 Armin Wiebe, *The Salvation of Yasch Siemens* (Winnipeg: Turnstone Press, 1984), 65–6.
30 Arthur R.M. Lower, *Canadians in the Making: A Social History of Canada* (Don Mills, Ont.: Longmans Canada, 1958), 424–6.
31 A detailed analysis of the way in which franchised automobile dealerships operated is H.O. Helmers, *A Marketing Rationale for the Distribution of Automobiles*, and Charles N. Davisson and Herbert F. Taggart, *Financing and Operating Characteristics of Automobile Dealers and the Franchise System*, Two Studies in Automotive Franchising, Division of Research, Graduate School of Business Administration, University of Michigan, 1974.
32 Epp-Tiessen, *Altona*, 246–7.
33 Royden K. Loewen, *Family, Church, and Market: A Mennonite Community in the Old and the New Worlds, 1850–1930* (Toronto: University of Toronto Press, 1993), 250.
34 'There's a Reason for Low Car Prices,' *Carillon News*, 14 Oct. 1960.
35 Abe Warkentin, *Reflections on Our Heritage: A History of Steinbach and the R.M. of Hanover from 1874* (Steinbach, Man.: n.p., 1971), 109–10.
36 Ibid., 111.
37 'Its a Long Way from Rosenfeld: A.J. Thiessen and Buses,' *MM*, 8, no. 9, 15–16; F.C. Pickwell, 'The West's Young Motor Coach Industry,' *Western Business and Industry* (April 1946), 24, 26, and 28.

38 'A Faith Today Interview with Don Reimer,' *Faith Today* (Nov.-Dec. 1987), 21–2.
39 'This Express Company Shows There's More to Business than Trucks and Goods,' *MM,* 5, no. 9 (summer 1976), 16.
40 'A Faith Today Interview with Don Reimer,' 23. See also Conrad Peters, 'Reimer Express Lines,' essay prepared for Mennonite Studies 251 at the Canadian Mennonite Bible College, 1988.
41 The problems and opportunities associated with the government disposal and civilian modification of military vehicles are explained in Canada, *House of Commons Committee on War Expenditures and Economies, 1946.* Both the proceedings and the reports of this committee were published.
42 Lawrence B. Smith, *Housing in Canada: Market Structure and Policy Performance,* Research Monograph no. 2; Urban Canada: Problems and Prospects (Ottawa: Central Mortgage and Housing Corporation, 1971), 9.
43 Ibid., 70.
44 Canada, 8 Geo. VI, cap. 46.
45 Albert Rose, *Canadian Housing Policies (1935–1980)* (Toronto: Butterworths, 1980), 28; *Canada Year Book,* 1945 (Ottawa: King's Printer, 1945), 445.
46 The Roman Catholic church and French-Canadian intellectuals believed that the true genius and virtue of their people were rural and agrarian. They feared or were suspicious of the cities where English and Protestant influences prevailed but recognized that many of their people had to find at least temporary urban employment. There was, however, reluctance to encourage people to put down firm roots in the city – and ownership of a private house was the most obvious way in which people became established. Private or individual ownership of houses in mixed suburbs and communities also threatened traditional styles of French-Canadian and Roman Catholic community or parish living. The concerns and fears of French Canadians were, in fact, very similar to those expressed by influential Mennonite leaders, but they responded differently to the opportunity of building and owning their own houses in ethnically and religiously mixed and linguistically alien urban suburbs.
47 Rose, *Canadian Housing Policies,* 35.
48 P.G. Wilmut, 'The Canadian Construction Scene: Review and Forecast,' *Western Business and Industry* (June 1953), 76–82.
49 Rose, *Canadian Housing Policies,* 35.
50 Alberta, *First Annual Report of the Department of Economic Affairs for the Year 1945* (Edmonton, 1945), 7.
51 One of the best-known Mennonite window and door manufacturers was C.T. Loewen of Steinbach, whose operations expanded dramatically after 1945. See Hilda Matsuo, 'A Long Way from Lumberyard to Millworks,' *MM,* 7, no. 10 (summer 1978), 10.

52 Donald B. Kraybill and Phyllis Pellman Good, eds., *Perils of Professionalism: Essays on Christian Faith and Professionalism* (Scottdale, Penn.: Herald Press, 1991).
53 Leo Driedger, 'From Martyrs to Muppies: The Mennonite Urban Professional Revolution,' *MQR*, 67, no. 3 (July 1993), 304–22.
54 Rev. J.J. Thiessen of Saskatoon was fond of telling of such a reaction when he was born and to emphasize that his was not an isolated case.
55 Mavis Reimer, *Cornelius W. Wiebe: A Beloved Physician* (Winnipeg: Hyperion, 1983).
56 Harold J. Dick, *Lawyers of Mennonite Background in Western Canada before the Second World War* (Winnipeg: Legal Research Institute of the University of Manitoba, 1993).
57 Katherine George, 'The Mennonites and the Protestant Ethic,' *Transactions of the Historical and Scientific Society of Manitoba*, series III, no. 21 (1964–5), 83–99.
58 On the relationship of the Mennonite faith to modern economic and entrepreneurial activities see Redekop et al., *Anabaptist/Mennonite Faith and Economics*.

8: Lure of the Cities

1 J. Winfield Fretz, 'Community,' *ME* I, 657.
2 Leo Driedger, J. Winfield Fretz, and Donovan E. Smucker, 'A Tale of Two Strategies: Mennonites in Chicago and Winnipeg,' *MQR*, 52, no. 4 (Oct. 1978), 294–311.
3 Calvin W. Redekop, 'Community,' *ME* V, 173–6.
4 CBC Minutes of the Mennonite Brethren Churches of British Columbia, 1931–61, 15 Nov. 1942.
5 Herold Scheidel to John Hess, 2 June 1954. I am grateful to Reg Good, historian of First Mennonite Church, Kitchener, for making a copy of this letter available to me.
6 Esther Paetkau, *First Mennonite Church in Saskatoon, 1923–1982* (Saskatoon: First Mennonite Church, 1982), 54. The incident is described in greater detail in Paetkau's MTh thesis, prepared for the Lutheran Seminary at the University of Saskatchewan.
7 Rudy Wiebe, *The Blue Mountains of China* (Toronto: McClelland and Stewart, 1970), 149.
8 My understanding of Mennonite urbanization is based mainly on the extensive and excellent work done by Leo Driedger and his associates. Driedger and Donald B. Kraybill provide one of the best succinct definitions and discussions of the impact of modernization and urbanization on North American

Mennonites in *Mennonite Peacemaking: From Quietism to Activism* (Scottdale, Penn.: Herald Press, 1994), chap. 2. Other works by Driedger include *Mennonite Identity in Conflict* (Lewiston, NY, and Queenston, Ont.: Edwin Mellen Press, 1988); Driedger, 'A Perspective on Canadian Mennonite Urbanization,' *ML*, 23, no. 4 (Oct. 1968), 147–51; Driedger, J. Winfield Fretz, and Donovan E. Smucker, 'A Tale of Two Strategies: Mennonites in Chicago and Winnipeg,' *MQR*, 52, no. 4 (Oct. 1978), 294–311; Driedger and J. Howard Kauffman, 'Urbanization of Mennonites: Canadian and American Comparisons,' *MQR*, 56, no. 3 (July 1982), 269–90; Driedger, 'Post-War Canadian Mennonites: From Rural to Urban Dominance,' *JMS*, 6 (1988), 70–88; and Driedger, 'From Martyrs to Muppies: The Mennonite Urban Professional Revolution,' *MQR*, 67, no. 3 (July 1993), 304–22.

The statistical data on which much of Driedger's Mennonite research is based are in J. Howard Kauffman and Leland Harder, *Anabaptists Four Centuries Later: A Profile of Five Mennonite and Brethren in Christ Denominations* (Scottdale, Penn.: Herald Press, 1975); and J. Howard Kauffman and Leo Driedger, *The Mennonite Mosaic: Identity and Modernization* (Scottdale, Penn.: Herald Press, 1991).

Driedger is also author of a sociology textbook on urbanization, *The Urban Factor: Sociology of Canadian Cities* (Toronto: Oxford University Press, 1991), and of a shorter work prepared for the Mennonite World Conference held in Winnipeg in 1990, *Mennonites in Winnipeg* (Winnipeg and Hillsboro, Kan.: Kindred Press, 1990).

9 Donald B. Kraybill, 'Modernity and Modernization,' in Leo Driedger and Leland Harder, eds., *Anabaptist-Mennonite Identities in Ferment* (Elkhart, Ind.: Institute of Mennonite Studies, 1990), 91–116.
10 Driedger and Kraybill, *Mennonite Peacemaking*, 39–40.
11 Ibid., 40–1.
12 Ibid., 41.
13 Ibid., 42.
14 Ibid.
15 Ibid., 51–3.
16 While Kauffman and Harder's study did not provide comparative Mennonite profiles for 1940 and 1970, it did present much interesting and useful statistical information about North American Mennonites in 1972, the year in which the field work was done.
17 Driedger, 'Post-War Canadian Mennonites,' 70–88.
18 A frame building constructed in 1834 was the first used exclusively for worship services.
19 Driedger, 'Post-War Canadian Mennonites,' 79; Frank H. Epp, *Mennonites in*

Canada, 1920–1940: A People's Struggle for Survival (Toronto: Macmillan, 1982), 269–91.

20 John H. Hess, 'Toronto,' *ME* IV, 739.

21 AMC Mennonite Board of Missions and Charities, Annual Report, 1–4 June 1946.

22 Fern Burkhardt, *A Mighty Flood: The House of Friendship* (Kitchener, Ont.: House of Friendship, 1989); 'Open Doors for the Homeless: House of Friendship Expands,' *CM*, 16, no. 42 (5 Nov. 1968), 11.

23 CBC Minutes of the Mennonite Brethren Churches of British Columbia, 1931–61, meeting of 15 June 1946.

24 Driedger, 'From Martyrs to Muppies,' 304–22.

25 Marlene Epp, 'The Mennonite Girls' Homes of Winnipeg: A Home Away from Home,' *JMS*, 6 (1988), 100–14; Frieda Esau Klippenstein, '"Doing What We Could": Mennonite Domestic Servants in Winnipeg, 1920s to 1950s,' *JMS*, 7 (1989), 145–66; Anna Thiessen, *Die Stadtmission in Winnipeg* (Winnipeg: Selbstverlag, 1955); Hilda Matsuo, 'Helen Epp and the "Maedchenheim,"' *MM*, 3, no. 6 (April 1974), 7–9; Arnold Dyck, *Warte-Jahrbuch fuer die Mennonitische Gemeinschaft in Canada*, 1 Jahrgang (1943), 60–3; and C.L. Dick, *The Mennonite Conference of Alberta: A History of Its Churches and Institutions* (Edmonton: Mennonite Conference of Alberta, 1980), 75–7.

26 'Ein temporaeres "Juenglingsheim,"' *Warte-Jahrbuch fuer die Mennonitische Gemeinschaft in Canada*, 1 Jahrgang (1943), 66.

27 Ruth Roach Pierson, 'Women's Emancipation and the Recruitment of Women into the Canadian Labour Force in World War II,' Canadian Historical Association *Historical Papers* (Ottawa: Canadian Historical Association, 1976), 165.

28 CBC Minutes of the Mennonite Brethren Churches of British Columbia, 1931–61, 25 June 1939 and 15 Nov. 1942; Paetkau, *First Mennonite Church*, 16; Mary Lou Driedger, 'From Country to City: Five Women Recall the Fear and Rewards of Leaving Home for the First Time,' *Embracing the World: Two Decades of Canadian Mennonite Writing: A Selection of Writings from the Mennonite Mirror* (Winnipeg: Mennonite Mirror, 1990), 5–7.

29 Jean Murray was for many years a professor of history, and my colleague, at the University of Saskatchewan. She remembered the Mennonite domestic servants who worked in her childhood home with great affection and spoke with me about them several times.

30 Driedger, 'From Country to City,' 6.

31 Ibid., 7.

32 The development of the early Mennonite churches in Winnipeg followed this pattern. See, for example, Driedger, *Mennonites in Winnipeg*; and *25 Jahre der Mennonitischen Ansiedlung zu Nord Kildonan, 1928–1953* (North Kildonan,

Man.: Mennoniten Brueder Gemeinde und Mennoniten Gemeinde zu Nord Kildonan, 1953).

33 CBC Minutes of the Mennonite Brethren Churches of British Columbia, 1931–61, meeting of 14 June 1936.

34 Ibid., meeting of 30 Dec. 1936.

35 Ibid., meeting of 11 Nov. 1939.

36 Ibid., meeting of 25 Feb. 1940.

37 J.H. Enns lists rural groups affiliated with the Schoenwieser Mennonite Church in Winnipeg at various times as Culross, Elie, Elkhorn, Fleming, Foxwarren, Gardenton, Glenlea, Graysville, High Bluff, Lorette, Manson, Meadows, Morris, Newton Siding, Niverville, Oak Bluff, Oak Lake, Peterfield, Pigeon Lake, Rivers, Sperling, Springstein, and Steinbach, all in Manitoba. (Other sources suggest that this list may not be entirely accurate.) J.H. Enns's unpublished autobiography, 'Dem Lichte Zu! Erinnerungen aus meinem Leben,' was written in 1966. I am indebted to members of the Enns family who made this document available to me; a copy is now available in MHC, vol. 4103.

38 For a general but incomplete and uncritical history of the Schoenwieser Mennonite Church see *Dem Herrn die Ehre. Schoenwieser Mennoniten Gemeinde von Manitoba, 1924–1968* (Altona, Man.: First Mennonite Church, Winnipeg, 1969).

39 MHC J.J. Thiessen Papers, 888/211, G. Derksen to 'Werter Freund,' undated, but almost certainly July 1945.

40 When J.H. Enns's youngest son married a non-Mennonite who had difficulties at First Mennonite in spite of a valiant effort to join the choir and sing the German hymns then still popular there, he advised the couple to join her church. 'Mennonites aren't the only ones who will get to heaven,' he told them. Mary M. Enns, 'One Man's Sons: The Enns Brothers Look Back at the Father Who Shaped Their Lives,' *MM*, 10, no. 3 (Nov. 1980), 6–8.

41 R.H. Vogt, 'Rev. J.H. Enns, 1889–1974: An Appreciation,' *MM*, 4, no. 1 (Oct. 1974), 10.

42 Ludwig Keller, *Ein Apostel der Wiedertaeufer* (Leipzig: S. Hirzel, 1882).

43 The main documentation on the difficult and acrimonious conflict of local ministers and executive members of the Conference of Mennonites in Canada is to be found in MHC J.J. Thiessen Papers 888/211, 888/212, and 888/213. There is also much information in Enns, 'Dem Lichte Zu!'

44 David B. Marshall, *Secularizing the Faith: Canadian Protestant Clergy and the Crisis of Belief, 1850–1940* (Toronto: University of Toronto Press, 1992), chap. 3.

45 The several relevant files in the J.J. Thiessen Papers (MHC) provide documentation regarding this charge.

46 MHC J.J. Thiessen Papers, 888/213, 'Protokoll der Sitzung der

Konferenzleitung und des Programmkomitees mit den Aeltesten aus unsrer Konferenz in Eigenheim am 4 Juli 1945,' and ibid., 888/211, J.H. Enns an 'Werte Brueder,' 17 July 1945.

47 Ibid., 888/213, 'Resolution der Versammlung der Prediger der Schoenwieser, Schoenfelder, Springsteiner, Bethel, Lichtenauer, Arnauder, Niverviller, Glenleaer, und Elim Gemeinden am 21 July 1945 in der Kirche der Schoenwieser Gemeinde zu Winnipeg, Man,' and a document entitled 'Die Stellung der Prediger der Schoenwieser Gemeinde zu ihrem Aeltesten J.H. Enns nachdem er bei der Konferenzleitung der Canadischen Konferenz als Irrlehrer angeklagt und in einer geschlossenen Sitzung der auf der Konferenz anwesenden Aeltesten als Irrlehrer gebrandmarkt und verurteilt wurde.'

48 Joh. G. Rempel, 'Sollte Gott gesagt haben?' *Der Bote*, 12 Sept. 1945.

49 MHC J.J. Thiessen Papers, 888/213, J.G. Rempel to Peter Froese, 9 Oktober 1947. The tone in several of the letters received by members of the conference executive was certainly harsh, but Rempel's complaints were seriously exaggerated. One letter, for example, suggested that perhaps Beelzebub had darkened Rempel's common sense and discernment, but it did not call him Beelzebub.

50 Ibid., Jacob Pankratz to Johann G. Rempel, 10 Oct. 1945, and G. Derksen to 'Werter Freund,' undated. Rempel called the Schoenwieser leaders 'Eine Bande' and complained: 'Ihre Frechheit geht doch weit.'

51 Ibid., Joh. G. Rempel, An die Aeltesten und Prediger der Konferenz der Mennoniten in Canada, 8 Dezember 1945.

52 Ibid., 'The Winnipeg Controversy,' a lengthy document written for the information of members of the Church Unity Committee of the General Conference of the Mennonite Church of North America, provides a detailed outline of the sequence of events.

53 Enns, 'Dem Lichte Zu!' 164.

54 Ibid. Both Isaac I. Friesen and Benjamin Ewert wrote numerous letters expressing their opposition to the doctrine of universalism but also their concerns about the impact that a permanent break with the Schoenwieser would have on all aspects of CMC work in the city.

55 *Dem Herrn die Ehre*, 80–4.

56 MHC J.J. Thiessen Papers, 888/213, 'Bericht der Versammlung die bezueglich der Winnipeg Angelegenheit in der Bethel Mennoniten Missionskirche zu Winnipeg am 26st August, 1948 gehalten wurde.'

57 Ibid. On the critical issue of universalism Enns wrote: 'Was nun die Lehre der Schrift von den ewigen Dingen anbetrifft, so bezeuge ich zunaechst, und darin werdet Ihr mir alle zustimmen, dass die Fragen der Ewigkeit grosse Geheimnisse bergen. Es tut mir leid, dass ich einmal die Lehre von der

Allversoehnung angeregt habe. Ich will mehr als bisher mit Euch an die ernsten Worte Jesu denken, die er von dem juengsten Gericht und von dem ewigen Schicksal sowohl derer die zu seiner Rechten also auch derer die zu seiner Linken stehen, sagt, und will meine Zuhoerer allen Ernstes an die ernste Ewigkeit und unsere Verantwortung ihr gegenueber erinnern und keinem ein Ruhekissen unter das Gewissen legen, so wahr mir Gott helfe.'

58 Ibid.

59 Ibid., Jacob H. Janzen to J.G. Rempel, 17 April 1947.

60 Ibid., J.J. Thiessen to W.F. Unruh, 24 Nov. 1946.

61 The migration of mission churches in Winnipeg from the poorer areas to the suburbs is well described in Driedger, *Mennonites in Winnipeg*, chap. 7.

62 Rodney J. Sawatzky and Scott Holland, eds., *The Limits of Perfection: A Conversation with J. Lawrence Burkholder* (Waterloo, Ont.: Institute of Anabaptist-Mennonite Studies, Conrad Grebel College, 1993), 29.

63 A sensitive discussion of conditions in the Coaldale Mennonite Brethren Church is given in Urie A. Bender, *Stumbling Heavenward: The Extraordinary Life of an Ordinary Man, Peter Rempel* (Winnipeg: Hyperion, 1984).

64 Peter F. Bargen, 'Some Perspectives of the Spiritual Beginnings,' *Truth Shall Set You Free: Lendrum Mennonite Brethren Church, 1962–1987* (Edmonton: Lendrum Mennonite Brethren Church, 1987), 4.

65 Ibid.

66 Dick, *Mennonite Conference of Alberta*, 106.

67 This subject has not been examined in depth by scholars. A limited and rather disappointing work on the subject is Menno H. Epp, *The Pastor's Exit* (Winnipeg: CMBC Publications, 1984). Somewhat more helpful is Leland Harder, *The Pastor-People Partnership: The Call and Recall of Pastors from a Believer's Church Perspective* (Elkhart, Ind., and Bluffton, Ohio: Institute of Mennonite Studies and Central District Ministerial Committee, 1983).

68 Abe J. Dueck, *Concordia Hospital, 1928–1978* (Winnipeg: Concordia Hospital, 1978).

69 Rick Martens, 'Unresolved Issues at Concordia,' *MM*, 3, no. 1 (Oct. 1973), 17; 'Concordia Hospital Then and Now,' *MM*, 5, no. 8 (June 1976), 15.

70 Driedger, *Mennonites in Winnipeg*, 57.

71 Peter Letkemann, 'Mennonites in Vancouver: A Survey,' *ML*, 23, no. 4 (Oct. 1968), 160–4; Driedger, *Mennonites in Winnipeg*, chap. 7.

72 Veronica Strong-Boag, 'Home Dreams: Women and the Suburban Experiment in Canada, 1945–60,' *Canadian Historical Review*, 72, no. 4 (Dec. 1991), 490.

73 As quoted in ibid., 498.

74 LaVerna Klippenstein, 'The Modern Housewife,' *MM*, 1, no. 8 (May 1972), 5.

75 Ruth Roach Pierson, '"They're Still Women After All": Wartime Jitters over

Femininity,' in Ian McKay, ed., *The Challenge of Modernity: A Reader on Post-Confederation Canada* (Toronto: McGraw-Hill-Ryerson, 1992), 419.
76 Strong-Boag, 'Home Dreams,' 471.
77 Ibid., 498.
78 Such a map is published in *CM*, 18, no. 49 (18 Dec. 1970), 9.
79 Driedger, *Mennonites in Winnipeg*, 88–9.
80 Driedger, 'From Martyrs to Muppies,' 305.
81 Driedger and Kauffmann, 'Urbanization of Mennonites,' 287.
82 Driedger, 'From Martyrs to Muppies,' 316.
83 Ibid., 321.

9: Nurture and Training of Youth

1 Anabaptist doctrines pertaining to baptism are discussed in Rollin Stely Armour, *Anabaptist Baptism* (Scottdale, Penn.: Herald Press, 1966), and Harold S. Bender, 'Baptism,' *ME* I, 224–8.
2 The problems and challenges of Anabaptist midwives are discussed in William Klassen, 'The Role of the Child in Anabaptism,' in Harry Loewen, ed., *Mennonite Images: Historical, Cultural, and Literary Essays Dealing with Mennonite Issues* (Winnipeg, Man.: Hyperion Press, 1980), 17–32.
3 David Janzen, 'Dedication of Infants,' *ME* V, 221.
4 Gideon G. Yoder, *The Nurture and Evangelism of Children* (Scottdale, Penn.: Herald Press, 1959).
5 John Howard Kauffman, 'Childrearing,' *ME* V, 137.
6 Klassen, 'Role of the Child,' 17–32.
7 J.C. Wenger, ed., *The Complete Writings of Menno Simons* (Scottdale, Penn.: Herald Press, 1956), 951.
8 At the time of writing the son was still alive. It therefore seems prudent to withhold the name in a published work.
9 Jake Goertzen, 'My Crucified Childhood: The horrors of a Christian Upbringing,' *MR*, 19, no. 17 (4 Sept. 1989), 10–11.
10 Ibid.
11 Ibid.
12 Harvey Neufeld, 'Creating the Brotherhood: Status and Control in the Yarrow Mennonite Community, 1928–1960,' in Donald H. Akenson, ed., *Canadian Papers in Rural History*, vol. 9 (Gananoque, Ont.: Langdale Press, 1994), 220.
13 Ibid.
14 Alta Mae Erb, *Christian Nurture of Children* (Scottdale, Penn.: Herald Press, 1959), and Gideon Yoder, *The Nurture and Evangelism of Children* (Scottdale, Penn.: Herald Press, 1959).

15 It is almost impossible to document how many Canadian Mennonite parents
    in the 1950s and 1960s read Dr Benjamin Spock. There may well have been
    significant differences between those Mennonite groups, mainly Swiss
    Mennonite, whose conferences published their own child-rearing and nurture
    books, and Mennonite parents who received no such guidance. In addition,
    some parents relied more on Dr Spock's advice regarding specific childhood
    medical problems than on his general and allegedly permissive advice
    regarding the training of children. In matters pertaining to general child
    rearing, Canadian Mennonites, with only minor exception, followed
    prevailing cultural trends.
16 Benjamin McLane Spock, *The Common Sense Book of Baby and Child Care*,
    new and completely revised ed. (New York: Duell, Sloan and Pearce, 1957).
17 Ibid., 43.
18 Ibid., 323–35.
19 William Klassen, 'Role of the Child,' 30–1.
20 Spock, *Common Sense*, 225. See also Benjamin McLane Spock, *Problems of
    Parents* (Boston: Houghton Mifflin, 1962), and *Dr. Spock Talks with Mothers:
    Growth and Guidance* (Boston: Houghton Mifflin, 1961).
21 Spock, *Common Sense*, 225.
22 Kauffman, 'Childrearing,' *ME* V, 137–8.
23 Ibid.
24 Calvin Redekop, *Mennonite Society* (Baltimore, Md.: Johns Hopkins
    University Press, 1989), 159.
25 J. Winfield Fretz, *Waterloo Mennonites: A Community in Paradox* (Waterloo,
    Ont.: Wilfrid Laurier University Press, 1989), 118–9.
26 N. van der Zijpp, 'Catechetical Instruction,' *ME* 1, 527–8.
27 A fuller explanation of this phenomenon, which was evident in Old Order
    Amish and also in other traditional Mennonite communities, is given in
    Donald B. Kraybill, *The Riddle of Amish Culture* (Baltimore, Md.: Johns
    Hopkins University Press, 1989), 138–40.
28 Ada Zimmerman Brunk and Ethel Yake Metzler, *The Christian Nurture of
    Youth* (Scottdale, Penn.: Herald Press, 1960), 6.
29 'Camps and Retreat Centers,' ME V, 118.
30 'The Purpose of Church Camps,' *CM*, 3, no. 21 (27 May 1955), 2.
31 Ibid.
32 Ibid.
33 Peter Penner, *No Longer at Arm's Length: Mennonite Brethren Church
    Planting in Canada* (Winnipeg: Kindred Press, 1987), 53.
34 John A. Toews, *A History of the Mennonite Brethren Church: Pilgrims and
    Pioneers* (Fresno, Calif.: General Conference of Mennonite Brethren

Churches, 1975), 237.

35 All these quotations are from Jack Dueck, 'Problems and Opportunities Discussed at Bi-annual Camping Convention,' *CM*, 15, no. 18 (2 May 1967), 3–4.

36 'Amish Board Expands Camping Program,' *CM*, 10, no. 24 (15 June 1962), 1.

37 Morris Sider, *The Brethren in Christ in Canada: Two Hundred Years of Tradition and Change* (Nappanee, Ind.: Evangel Press, 1988), 250.

38 As quoted in 'Camps and Camp Retreats,' ME V, 120.

39 MHC J.J. Thiessen Papers, 865/52, Wilma and Cornelius Dyck to J.J. Thiessen, 30 July 1955.

40 CBC Minutes of the Mennonite Brethren Churches of British Columbia, 18 Oct. 1950.

41 MHC J.J. Thiessen Papers, 867/69. This entire file deals with arrangements for a series of evangelistic meetings by a German evangelist.

42 One of the most successful Mennonite Brethren evangelists who studied at William Aberhart's Calgary Prophetic Bible Institute was John A. Toews. In a conversation I had with him shortly before his death Toews expressed regrets about the things that he had said and done as a young evangelist. See also Elfrieda Toews Nafziger, *A Man of His Word: A Biography of John A. Toews* (Winnipeg and Hillsboro, Kan.: Kindred Press, 1992), 26–7.

43 CMBS(W) box 2, folder D, no. 7d. Unpublished paper by J.J. Toews, entitled 'Hazards and Opportunities in the Evangelism of Our Children.'

44 Neufeldt, 'Creating the Brotherhood,' 223.

45 MHC J.J. Thiessen Papers, 867/69, Johann Wichert to J.J. Thiessen, 31 July 1959; translated from the German by T.D. Regehr. The Swiss Mennonites of Ontario had very different impressions of the Brunk campaigns from those of many of the older Russian Mennonites. The former heard Brunk's admonitions to be separated from the world; the latter reacted to his methods, which they thought were rooted in American popular culture. Wichert, in another letter to J.J. Thiessen, referred to Brunk as 'very American.' Yet Swiss Mennonites from Ontario have told me that Wichert's criticism is 'so out of character in describing Brunk that it is almost unbelievable.' Lorraine Roth to Ted Regehr, 26 Jan. 1995.

46 For a critical assessment of the Brunk campaigns see Dale F. Dickey, 'The Tent Evangelism Movement of the Mennonite Church: A Dramatistic Analysis,' PhD thesis, Bowling Green State University, 1980.

47 MHC, *Revival Fires in Manitoba: A Report on the Work of Brunk Revivals Inc. in Four Manitoba Communities, Summer of 1957* (n.p., n.d.), not paginated.

48 Ibid.

49 Ibid.

50 Jake Goertzen, 'My Crucified Childhood,' 10–11.
51 Al Reimer, 'Coming in out of the Cold,' in Harry Loewen, ed., *Why I Am a Mennonite: Essays on Mennonite Identity* (Scottdale, Penn.: Herald Press, 1988), 256.
52 Katie Florence Shank, *Revival Fires* (Broadway, Va.: K.F. Shank, n.d.); *Revival Fires in Manitoba.*
53 Whitney R. Cross, *The Burned-Over District: The Social and Intellectual History of Enthusiastic Religion in Western New York, 1800–1850* (New York: Harper Torchbook, 1965).
54 A controversial, often comical account of adolescent sexual behaviour in a fictional Mennonite village and of the role of the automobile in those escapades is Armin Wiebe, *The Salvation of Yasch Siemens* (Winnipeg: Turnstone Press, 1984). A darker, fictional view is Douglas Reimer, *Older Than Ravens* (Winnipeg: Turnstone Press, 1989). The hostile reaction among MBs when Rudy Wiebe published his first novel, *Peace Shall Destroy Many* (Toronto: McClelland and Stewart, 1962), and later *My Lovely Enemy* (Toronto: McClelland and Stewart, 1983), was due mainly to controversial sexual material.
55 J.B. Toews, Fresno, California, who had experienced the Makhno terror in southern Russia, strongly emphasized this point in an interview on 1 February 1993. Mennonite attitudes towards Nestor Makhno and his anarchist followers are clearly stated in Victor Peters, *Nestor Makhno: The Life of an Anarchist* (Winnipeg: Echo Books, 1970). The emotional impact, particularly of some of the sexual atrocities, is portrayed in a deeply moving way in Al Reimer, *My Harp Is Turned to Mourning* (Winnipeg: Hyperion Press, 1985).
56 Karen Armstrong, *The Gospel According to Woman: Christianity's Creation of the Sex War in the West* (New York: Anchor/Doubleday, 1987).
57 Willard S. Krabill, 'Sexuality,' *ME* V, 815–17.
58 Armstrong, *The Gospel According to Woman.*
59 Krabill, 'Sexuality,' 817.
60 Michael Bliss, '"Pure Books on Avoided Subjects": Pre-Freudian Sexual Ideas in Canada,' *Canadian Historical Association Historical Papers*, 1970 (Ottawa, Ont.: Canadian Historical Association, 1970), 89–108.
61 CMBS(W) Acc. No. 1206, Jacob H. Janzen, 'Das Sexuelle Problem,' 1941.
62 Ibid., 4.
63 Ibid., 2.
64 Bliss, 'Pure Books,' 101.
65 John Harvey Kellogg, founder of a complex of mental health care facilities at Battle Creek, Michigan, was one of the most extensively published writers linking diet to a host of mental and physical disorders. See for example his *The*

New Dietetics: A Guide to Scientific Feeding in Health and Disease (Battle Creek, Mich.: Modern Medicine Publishing Co., 1923). Relations among members of the Kellogg family became strained as the success of both the asylum and its special food production facilities expanded. Kellogg was the medical authority, but his business abilities and interests were overshadowed by his younger brother, W.K. Kellogg.

66 John Harvey Kellogg, *Ladies Guide in Health and Disease, Girlhood, Maidenhood, Wifehood, Mother* (Battle Creek, Mich.: Modern Medicine Publishing Co., 1901).

67 The review was published in 'Rezension und ... ! Das sexuelle Problem,' *Der Bote*, 14 Jan. 1952, 3–4. See also 'Das sexuelle Problem,' ibid., 11 Feb. 1942, 3–4, and 'Das sexuelle Problem,' ibid., 25 Feb. 1942, 3.

68 C.F. Derstine, *Manual of Sex Education for Parents, Teachers, and Students* (Kitchener, Ont.: n.p., 1942, and Grand Rapids, Mich.: Zondervan, 1943); *The Path to Beautiful Womanhood* (Kitchener, Ont.: n.p., 1942), and Grand Rapids, Mich.: Zondervan, 1944); and *The Path to Noble Manhood* (Kitchener, Ont.: n.p., 1942, and Grand Rapids, Mich.: Zondervan, 1944).

69 Oscar Lowry, *The Way of a Man with a Maid: Sexology for Men and Boys* (Grand Rapids, Mich.: Zondervan), 43.

70 Oscar Lowry, *A Virtuous Woman: Sex Life in Relation to the Christian Life* (Grand Rapids, Mich.: Zondervan, 1938), 27.

71 Ibid., 82.

72 CMBS(W) Acc. No. 164, A. Nachtigal, 'Gesegnete Spatziergaenge eines Vaters mit seinem 14-jaehrigen Sohn. Fuer Juenglinge und reifere Knaben' (Yarrow, BC: Selbstverlag, 1947).

73 John R. Rice, *Bobbed Hair, Bossy Wives and Women Preachers* (Grand Rapids, Mich.: Zondervan).

74 CMBS(W) B.B. Janz Papers, 7/106, B.B. Janz to Ivan Casey, Minister of Education, Edmonton, 13 Nov. 1949.

75 Krabill, 'Sexuality,' 815.

76 Sue Goertzen, 'Sex Education,' *ME* V, 814–15.

77 Ibid.

78 James Fairfield, 'Sex Is Great,' *CM*, 18, no. 14 (10 April 1970), 4, 8.

79 Mrs M. Dyck, Winnipeg, 'Sex Story Offensive,' *CM*, 18, no. 16, 5.

80 Susie Harms, 'Ashamed of Dirt Spots,' *CM*, 18, no. 18 (8 May 1970), 5.

81 Bernie Wiebe, 'Now a Word from ...,' ibid.

82 S.F. Pannabecker, 'Conversion,' *ME* I, 704.

83 The specific theological significance attached to baptism, but not necessarily to its form, seemed to change if or when individual conferences or congregations accepted conversionist ideas and practices.

84 Harold S. Bender, 'Baptism,' *ME* I, 225–8. See also Armour, *Anabaptist Baptism*.

85 Walter Unger, 'Mennonite Brethren and General Conference Theology – A Common Center, A Single Foundation,' paper presented at a Symposium on Inter-Mennonite Relations: MBs and GCs in Canada, 4–5 Nov. 1983, 24.

86 Ernst Correll and Harold S. Bender, 'Marriage,' *ME* III, 509.

87 It is almost impossible to footnote these incidents, giving specific dates, places, and names of congregations whose minutes record these incidents, without also inflicting renewed pain and embarrassment on the victims, or on innocent family members of offenders. When these things were recorded in official church minutes there was an expectation that they would be held in strict confidence. Now those minutes are open to historical researchers. In this study specific details are less important than a general indication that such things happened and how they were dealt with.

10: Church and Community Schools

1 Daniel Hertzler, *Mennonite Education: Why and How?* (Scottdale, Penn.: Herald Press, 1971); and P.G. Klassen, 'A History of Mennonite Education in Canada, 1786–1960,' DEd dissertation, University of Toronto, 1970.

2 On the Mennonite experience in this regard see Frank H. Epp, *Mennonites in Canada*, Vol. 2, *1920–1940: A People's Struggle for Survival* (Toronto: Macmillan, 1982), chaps. 3 and 10.

3 Frank H. Epp, *Mennonites in Canada, 1786–1920: The History of a Separate People* (Toronto: Macmillan, 1974); Epp, *Mennonites in Canada, 1920–1940*; J. Winfield Fretz, *The Waterloo Mennonites: A Community in Paradox* (Waterloo, Ont.: Wilfrid Laurier University Press, 1989), chap. 11.

4 J.T.M. Anderson, *The Education of the New Canadian* (Toronto: J.M. Dent & Sons, 1918).

5 David C. Jones et al., *Shaping the Schools of the Canadian West* (Calgary: Detselig, 1979); William Janzen, *Limits on Liberty: The Experience of Mennonite, Hutterite, and Doukhobor Communities in Canada* (Toronto: University of Toronto Press, 1990); and John W. Friesen, 'Studies in Mennonite Education: The State of the Art,' *JMS*, 1 (1983), 133–48.

6 As quoted in *CM*, 14, no. 32 (16 Aug. 1966), 1.

7 Lorraine Roth to T.D. Regehr, 26 Jan. 1995.

8 Isaac Horst to 'Dear Friend,' 18 Feb. 1985. This four-page letter explaining the establishment of the Old Order Mennonite and the Old Order Amish parochial schools in Ontario was written to Nancy Martin, a student at the Canadian Mennonite Bible College who was writing an essay on the subject. A

copy of that essay, together with the letter from Horst and other supporting documents, is available at MHC.

9 Ibid.

10 Harold S. Bender, 'Sunday School,' *ME* IV, 657–60, and Harold S. Bender, *Mennonite Sunday School Centennial, 1840–1940* (Scottdale, Penn.: Herald Press, 1940).

11 Paul M. Lederach, 'The History of Religious Education in the Mennonite Church,' PhD thesis, Southwestern Baptist Theological Seminary, 1949.

12 Leonard Froese, 'Das paedagogische Kultursystem der mennonitischen Siedlungsgruppe in Russland,' Dissertation zur Erlangung des Doktorgrades der Philosophischen Fakultaet der Georg-August-Universitaet zu Goettingen, 1949; Oskar Anweiler, *Geschichte der Schule und Paedagogik in Russland vom Ende des Zarenreiches zum Beginn der Stalin-Aera* (Berlin: Quelle und Meyer Heidelberg, 1964); T.D. Regehr, *For Everything a Season: A History of the Alexanderkrone Zentralschule* (Winnipeg: CMBC Publications, 1988).

13 A general overview of Sunday school materials prepared by different North American Mennonite conferences is given in Paul M. Lederach, 'Literature for Christian Nurture,' in Cornelius J. Dyck, ed., *The Lordship of Christ: Proceedings of the Seventh Mennonite World Conference*, Kitchener, Ont., 1–7 Aug. 1962 (Elkhart, Ind.: Mennonite World Conference, 1962), 553–68.

14 Ruth Wiens, 'A Study of the Present Task of the Sunday School in the Light of Its Historical Background and Today's Changing World,' Master of Religious Education thesis, Mennonite Brethren Biblical Seminary, 1965.

15 These problems were discussed in detail at the triennial sessions of the General Conference of the Mennonite Brethren Church of North America and at the annual sessions of the Northern District Conference of the Mennonite Brethren Church of North America in the late 1940s and early 1950s. The determination of the Canadians to prepare the necessary student and teacher Sunday school materials in German was not shared by their American counterparts and led to redoubled efforts by the Sunday School Committee of the Northern District Conference.

16 The Sunday School Committee of the General Conference of the Mennonite Brethren Churches of North America, for example, recommended in 1951 that 'Sunday School teachers and expositors of our Sunday School lessons … continue the emphasis on the non-resistance principle in the interpretation of the lessons when the war idea occurs in the Old Testament lessons, and have at least two lessons per year with special emphasis on non-resistance. Further that we continue with the National Sunday School lessons for another three years, but that the Sunday School Committee use its influence, with the National Committee, that more lessons be selected from the Epistles, in order to

emphasize the teaching of the Bible relative to the church of Jesus Christ.' As quoted in *Yearbook of the 45th General Conference of the Mennonite Brethren Church of North America*, held at Winkler, Manitoba, 21–26 July 1951 (Hillsboro, Kan.: Mennonite Brethren Publishing House, 1951), 76.

17 H. Regehr, 'Gesundes Wachstum in den S.-Schulen der Kanadischen M.B.-Konferenz,' *Voice of the Mennonite Brethren Bible College*, vol. 2, no. 3 (May–June 1953), 12–14.

18 Bender, 'Sunday School,' 659.

19 CMBS (W) box 2, folder D, Unpublished manuscript No. 7d, J.J. Toews, 'Hazards and Opportunities in the Evangelism of Our Children'; J.A. Toews, 'Child Conversions,' *The Voice*, 1, no. 4 (July–Aug. 1952), 12–15; and J.H. Quiring, 'Forbid them not,' *The Voice*, 4, no. 2 (March–April 1955), 11–13.

20 D. Ewert, 'Schools and Missions,' *The Voice*, 5, nos. 3 and 4 (May–June and July–Aug. 1956), 12–15 and 4–9, respectively.

21 A general overview of German-language instruction in Mennonite schools is given in 'Aus dem Protokoll der Lehrerversammlung am 17. und 18. August [1949] im Mennonitischen Missionspark zu Springstein, Manitoba,' *Mennonitische Lehrerzeitung* (Sept. 1949), 4–5. See also *Mennonitische Lehrerzeitung* (Dec. 1949), 19–20, and subsequent issues, in which various correspondents responded, sometimes with considerable heat, to problems pertaining to preservation of German.

22 SAB Records of the Department of the Attorney General, file C12G, contains detailed reports on one such case from the files of the Royal Canadian Mounted Police, division F, file 41s 518-1.

23 CMBS (W) B.B. Janz Papers, 7/106, Janz to C. F. McNally, Deputy Minister of Education, Alberta, 19 Sept. 1940, and McNally to Janz, 4 Oct. 1940.

24 The size and significance of the German Saturday schools in larger communities such as the one at Coaldale may be deduced from the pictures and extensive written material on those schools in *Gedenk- und Dankfeier des 25-jaehrigen Bestehens der Coaldale Mennoniten Brueder Gemeinde am 27 Mai 1951* (Coaldale, Alta.: Coaldale Mennonite Brethren Church, 1951).

25 Bruce L. Guenther, 'The Origin of the Bible School Movement in Western Canada: Towards an Ethnic Interpretation,' *Historical Papers 1993, Canadian Society of Church History* (n.p.: Canadian Society of Church History, 1993), 135.

26 Ibid.

27 J.B. Martin and Newton Gingrich, *Mission Completed: History of the Ontario Mennonite Bible School and Ontario Mennonite Bible Institute* (St Jacob's, Ont.: St Jacob's Printery), 3.

28 John A. Toews, *A History of the Mennonite Brethren Church* (Fresno, Calif.: Board of Christian Literature, General Conference of Mennonite Brethren

Churches, 1975), 160.

29   'Die Bibelschulen der Mennoniten in Kanada,' *Mennonitsche Welt*, 5 Jahrgang (Jan. 1952), 5–6.

30   The general information in this table is drawn from Walter Unger, 'Bible Colleges and Institutes,' *ME* V, 73–7; and Epp, *Mennonites in Canada, 1920–1940*, 468. Conference affiliation does not necessarily mean that specific conferences sponsored the various schools. In many cases interested individuals organized local support societies. Often these individuals had specific local or broader conference affiliations, and most sought to persuade the local church, a provincial conference, or a national conference to provide support. The affiliation indicated is, therefore, relatively flexible.

31   This school was originally called simply the Bible Study Class but later came to be called the Ontario Mennonite Bible School. In 1950 the instructional program was expanded to include more advanced courses, which were offered, together with the former Bible school classes, by the new Ontario Mennonite Bible Institute. Martin and Gingrich, *Mission Completed*.

32   Peter G. Klassen, 'A History of Mennonite Education in Canada, 1786–1960,' DEd thesis, University of Toronto, 1970.

33   The history of this and other Mennonite Brethren Bible schools is recorded in A.J. Klassen, ed., *The Bible School Story: Fifty Years of Mennonite Brethren Bible Schools in Canada, 1913–1963* (Clearbrook, BC: Canadian Board of Education, 1963); Toews, *History*; 'M.B. Bible Schools in Canada,' *Konferenz-Jugendblatt*, 2, no. 62 (Nov.–Dec. 1955), 9–18; and Margaret Epp, *Proclaim Jubilee* (n.p.: n.p., c.1977).

34   References to this winter Bible school appear in the general lists, but none of the relevant yearbooks indicate that it was still operating in 1939. For more information on the Bible schools in the Mennonite Church see Clarence Fretz, 'A History of Mennonite Bible Schools in the Mennonite Church,' *MQR*, 26, no. 2 (April 1942).

35   For more information on the founding and objectives of this school see Epp, *Mennonites in Canada, 1786–1920*, 336–7; and Guenther, 'Origin,' 152. In 1992 this school merged with the Hillcrest Christian College to form Rocky Mountain College in Calgary. The Mennonite Brethren in Christ changed their name to the United Missionary Church in 1947.

36   George David Pries, *A Place Called Peniel: Winkler Bible Institute, 1925–1975* (Winkler, Man.: Winkler Bible Institute, 1975).

37   Margaret Epp, *Proclaim Jubilee*.

38   Officially this school was interdenominational, but most of its teachers and students were Mennonite Brethren. Toews, *History*, 261; Margaret Epp, *Proclaim Jubilee*.

39 Esther Epp-Tiessen, *Altona: The Story of a Prairie Town* (Altona, Man.: D.W.
    Friesen and Sons, 1982), 220–2; H.J. Gerbrandt, *Adventure in Faith* (Altona,
    Man.: Bergthaler Mennonite Church of Manitoba, 1970). This school was
    moved from Gretna to Altona in 1940. Information on General Conference
    Mennonite Bible schools is available in 'Die Bibelschulen der Mennoniten in
    Kanada,' *Mennonitische Welt*, 5 Jahrgang (Jan. 1952), 5–6, and Rudy A. Regehr,
    'A Century of Private Schools,' in Henry Poettcker and Rudy A. Regehr, eds.,
    Call to Faithfulness: Essays in Canadian Mennonite Studies (Winnipeg: CMBC
    Publications, 1972), 103–16.
40 *The Torchbearer: The Coaldale Bible School Jubilee Yearbook, 1929–1954* (n.p.,
    1954). The school achieved its maximum enrolment of 100 students in 1948–9.
41 This Bible school offered mainly evening classes, in German, for people who
    worked during the day. It operated in a relatively informal manner and was
    largely a project of its main instructor, Abram Peters. Toews, *History*, 260;
    Abe Dueck, 'MBBC Antecedents: The Winnipeg German Bible School,' *MH*,
    18, no. 2 (June 1992), 1, 5, 7.
42 Toews, *History*, 263. I have obtained additional information in a letter from
    Henry C. Born to T.D. Regehr, 8 Nov. 1993. See also Agatha E. Klassen, ed.,
    Yarrow: A Portrait in Mosaic, rev. ed. (Yarrow, BC: A.E. Klassen, 1980), 89–92.
    This work states erroneously the date on which the school closed. See also
    H.C. Born, 'Reflections on the Mennonite Brethren Bible School Movement in
    British Columbia,' *MH*, 19, no. 3 (Sept. 1993), 7–8.
43 The Steinbach Bible School began as a venture of a Mennonite Brethren and an
    Evangelical Mennonite Brethren minister. It was taken over by a Bible School
    Association in 1938. In 1946 it added high school classes, and the name was
    changed to the Steinbach Bible Academy. The high school classes were
    dropped after two years but reinstated in 1953 when the school became the
    Steinbach Bible Institute. Archie Penner, 'Steinbach Bible Institute,' *ME* IV,
    625. See also P.J.B. Reimer, ed., *The Sesquicentennial Jubilee: Evangelical
    Mennonite Conference, 1812–1962* (Steinbach, Man.: Evangelical Mennonite
    Conference, 1962), 146–53.
44 E. Morris Sider, *Here Faith and Learning Meet: The Story of Niagara
    Christian College* (Nappanee, Ind.: Evangel Press, 1982); E. Morris Sider, *The
    Brethren in Christ in Canada: Two Hundred Years of Tradition and Change*
    (Nappanee, Ind.: Evangel Press, 1988). This school, operating under several
    informal names, began as the Ontario Bible School at Springvale, Ontario, in
    1932. It was moved to Gormley, Ontario, in 1934, and to Fort Erie in 1938. It
    became the Niagara Christian College in 1951.
45 This Bible school lasted only a few years. It drew support from several
    Mennonite groups but was generally regarded as an MB school. Toews,

History, 261; John G. Doerksen, 'History of Education in the Mennonite Brethren Church of Canada,' MEd thesis, University of Manitoba, 1963, 84.

46 The Rosthern Bible School was closely related to the German/English Academy, later renamed the Rosthern Junior College. Frank H. Epp, *Education with a Plus: The Story of Rosthern Junior College* (Waterloo, Ont.: Conrad Press, 1975).

47 The Amish of Canada conducted a number of more or less itinerant winter Bible schools. The school at Tavistock has been included in other lists and is therefore mentioned here. It is not the only school of this kind. For a more general discussion of these relatively informal and unstructured winter Bible schools among the Amish Mennonites see Orland Gingerich, *The Amish of Canada* (Waterloo, Ont.: Conrad Press, 1972), 103.

48 C.L. Dick, *The Mennonite Conference of Alberta: A History of Its Churches and Institutions* (Edmonton: Mennonite Conference of Alberta, 1980), 35–6.

49 J.H. Enns, 'Dem Lichte Zu! Erinnerungen aus meinem Leben,' Unpublished autobiography, 1966, 134–5. Evening classes were first offered in the basement of the Schoenwieser Mennonite Church. Daytime instruction began the second year. Enns, who ran the school, indicates that the opening of the Canadian Mennonite Bible College made this school redundant.

50 Toews, *History*, 262.

51 Ibid. This school is also mentioned in Margaret Epp, *Proclaim Jubilee*, and Klassen, *Bible School Story*.

52 Gingerich, *Amish*.

53 J.G. Rempel, *Die Rosenorter Gemeinde in Saskatchewan* (Rosthern, Sask.: D.H. Epp, 1950), 116.

54 *Jahrbuch 1936 der Allgemeinen Konferenz der Mennoniten in Canada* (Rosthern, Sask.: D.H. Epp, 1936), 76.

55 Ezra Stauffer, *History of the Alberta-Saskatchewan Mennonite Conference* (Ryley, Alta.: Alberta-Saskatchewan Mennonite Conference, 1960). The Bible school/classes/conferences of the Alberta-Saskatchewan Conference were less structured and more diverse than those of the other Mennonite conferences in western Canada or their counterparts in Ontario. Some of these sessions lasted only for several weeks, and a long list could be drawn up of locations where such instruction was provided.

56 This school, like many of the others in small Mennonite communities, closed when slightly improved economic conditions and transportation made it possible for students to travel to the larger Bible schools. The larger CMC Bible School in Alberta was located at Didsbury, while the Bible school at Coaldale attracted many Mennonite Brethren from more remote communities.

57 Toews, *History*, 262–3.

58 *Maple View Mennonite Church 1859–1984* (Wellesley, Ont.: Maple View Mennonite Church, 1984).

59 This CMC school is not listed in Regehr, *Call to Faithfulness,* but appears in several lists in the Mennonite Encyclopedia. I could find no evidence that it operated after 1940.

60 In 1955 this school became the focus of a consolidation of various small MB Bible Schools and was renamed the Mennonite Brethren Bible Institute of British Columbia. In 1970 it was merged with the Bethel Bible Institute operated by United Mennonites of British Columbia (General Conference) to form the Columbia Bible Institute, which was later renamed Columbia Bible College.

61 Regehr, *Call to Faithfulness.*

62 Ibid.; Dick, *Mennonite Conference of Alberta,* 127–34. In 1967 this school was merged with the Swift Current Bible Institute.

63 Unger, 'Bible Colleges and Institutes,' 74.

64 Toews, *History,* 262–3.

65 Peter Penner, *No Longer at Arm's Length: Mennonite Brethren Church Planting in Canada* (Winnipeg: Kindred Press, 1987), 25.

66 Unger, 'Bible Colleges and Institutes.'

67 *Ebenezer: Virgil Mennonite Brethren Church, 1937–87* (Fonthill, Ont.: Niagara Yearbook Services, 1984). It started in 1938 as an evening school, while a sister institution in Vineland, launched in 1939, operated as a day school. The two schools were after 1938 operated by the same society and used some of the same teachers. In 1943, after closing of the school in Vineland, the Virgil Bible School became a day school. It became the Mennonite Brethren Bible Institute of Ontario in 1955 when it was moved to Kitchener.

68 Toews, *History,* 263.

69 Walter Klaassen, *'The Days of Our Years': A History of the Eigenheim Mennonite Church Community, 1892–1992* (Rosthern, Sask.: Eigenheim Mennonite Church, 1992), 111–13; H.T. Klaassen, *Birth and Growth of the Eigenheim Mennonite Church, 1892–1974* (Rosthern, Sask.: Valley Printers, 1974), 51. This reference suggests that the Eigenheim Bible school was started in 1934, but the documents cited by Walter Klaassen clearly indicate that a proposal to establish such a school was made in 1934 but that there was opposition and the proposal was only followed later.

70 Klaassen, *'Days of Our Years,'* 150.

71 See reference to the Virgil Bible school, note 67, above.

72 *Die Vereinigten Mennoniten Gemeinden in British Columbien, 1959* (Abbotsford, BC.: Conference of Mennonites in Canada, 1959), 24. This school opened in Coghlan, but a new facility was built in Clearbrook. In 1970 the school was merged with the Mennonite Brethren Bible Institute of British

Columbia to form Columbia Bible Institute, later Columbia Bible College.

73 Unger, 'Bible Colleges and Institutes,' 74.

74 The school apparently operated for only a very short period. It was forcibly closed by vigilantes from the Royal Canadian Legion in 1940, and the teacher was taken under escort to the train station and sent back to Rosthern. This information is taken from a press clipping in the Evangelical Mennonite Conference Archives, Steinbach, vol. 253, file 45.

75 *Mennonitische Lehrerzeitung* (June 1949), 5.

76 Unger, 'Bible Colleges and Institutes,' 74. I could find no other reference to this school.

77 This school was begun by the Mennonite Brethren in Christ, who subsequently changed their name to the United Missionary Church. Harold S. Bender, 'Mennonite Brethren in Christ Church,' *ME* III, 603.

78 Toews, *History*, 263.

79 The Russian Bible School was not really Mennonite sponsored. H.H. Janzen, an MB leader in Ontario, was invited to be principal by Peter Deyneka of the Russian Gospel Association in Philadephia and with the active support of Oswald J. Smith's People's Church in Toronto. See Rudy H. Janzen, trans. and ed., *By God's Grace Rev H.H. Janzen, D.D., Was Who He Was* (Scarborough, Ont.: Rudy Janzen, 1988).

80 There are brief references to this Bible school in Penner, *No Longer at Arm's Length*; John D. Friesen, *Holding Forth the Word of Life*; and Jack Heppner, *Search for Renewal: The Story of the Rudnerweider/Evangelical Mennonite Mission Conference, 1937–1987* (Winnipeg: Evangelical Mennonite Mission Conference, 1987), 105.

81 Erich Ratzlaff, *Ein Leben fuer den Herrn: Biographie und Predigten von David Borisovich Wiens* (Winnipeg: Mennonite Brethern Conference, 1982), 28–9; Penner, *No Longer at Arm's Length*, 42. This was a mission venture by David Wiens, designed to serve Russians living in the Arlee area. It apparently operated for only a short period.

82 Penner, *No Longer at Arm's Length*.

83 Melvin Gingrich, 'United Mennonite Bible School,' *ME* IV, 774.

84 The amalgamations that led to establishment of the Columbia Bible Institute are explained briefly in John M. Klassen, 'British Columbia,' *ME* V, 98–9.

85 Heppner, *Search for Renewal*, 273–9.

86 Robert Martin-Koop, 'Quebec,' *ME* V, 740.

87 Pries, *A Place Called Peniel*, 26.

88 *The Torchbearer*, 4.

89 Klaassen, '*The Days of Our Years*,' 100.

90 Urie Bender, *Four Earthen Vessels: Biographical Profiles of Oscar Burkholder,*

Samuel F Coffman, Clayton F. Derstine, and Jesse B. Martin (Scottdale, Penn.: Herald Press, 1982), 85.

91 Martin and Gingrich, *Mission Completed*, 7–8.
92 Guenther, 'Origin of the Bible School Movement,' 155.
93 Lauretta Jutzi, 'Ontario Bible School Reunion Draws Enthusiastic Crowd,' *MR*, 24, no. 15 (1 Aug. 1994), 9.
94 Ibid.
95 Martin and Gingrich, *Mission Completed*, 49–50.
96 *Mennonitische Rundschau*, 30 Sept. 1942, 3, provides a report on the Steinbach Bible School with a list of all the courses.
97 Unger, 'Bible Colleges and Institutes,' 75; Bender, 'Bible School,' 332–3.
98 These impressions are drawn from Bible school yearbooks, catalogues, and numerous reports in the *Canadian Mennonite*.
99 *Yearbook of the Northern District Conference of the Mennonite Brethren Church of North America: Reports for the Year 1944–1945 with Resolutions for the Year 1945–1946* (Winnipeg: Christian Press, 1945), 68; Martin and Gingrich, *Mission Completed*, 48–50.
100 I have the detailed notes that my mother took in her Church History class at the Morningstar Bible School in Coaldale in the 1930s. The teachers there were strongly committed to Mennonite history and theology, but there were very few references to Mennonite history in that class.
101 John A. Toews taught systematic theology at the Mennonite Brethren Bible College. Many MB Bible school teachers took those course, in which Augustus A. Strong's texts were used by Toews in a curiously selective manner. Toews's approach is discussed in Howard John Loewen, 'Augustus A. Strong: Baptist Theologian for Mennonite Brethren,' in Paul Toews, ed., *Mennonites and Baptists: A Continuing Conversation* (Winnipeg and Hillsboro, Kan.: Kindred Press, 1993), 193–210.
102 *The Canadian Mennonite* carried numerous reports on mission conferences held at the Bible schools and on visits to those schools by missionaries. Distinctive Anabaptist-Mennonite perspectives and doctrines are not mentioned.
103 Paul Schaefer, *Woher? Wohin? Mennoniten! Lektionen fuer den Unterricht in der Mennonitengeschichte*, 4 vols. (Altona, Man.: Ackerbau Verein, 1942; Altona, Man.: Mennonite Agricultural Advisory Committee, 1942 and 1946; Altona, Man.: Mennonitischer Historischer Verein, 1953).
104 Harold S. Bender, 'Bible Institutes,' *ME* I, 331–2.
105 Included in Pries, *A Place Called Peniel*, and Martin and Gingrich, *Mission Completed*, are a number of testimonies by former students. None indicates that his or her years at the Bible school provided greater appreciation or understanding of distinctive Anabaptist and Mennonite doctrines.

106 Pries, *A Place Called Peniel*, 82.
107 Margaret Epp, *Proclaim Jubilee*; Klassen, *Bible School Story*.
108 Unger, 'Bible Colleges and Institutes,' 73–6.
109 Martin and Gingrich, *Mission Completed*, 147.
110 Reasons for closure of the school are discussed with considerable candour in ibid., 55–8.
111 As quoted in Bender, *Four Earthen Vessels*, 302.
112 Jutzi, 'Ontario Bible School Reunion,' 9.
113 Lorraine Roth to T.D. Regehr, 26 Jan. 1995.
114 Bender, *Four Earthen Vessels*, 302.
115 Martin and Gingrich, *Mission Completed*, 58.

11: High Schools and Colleges

1 As quoted in Frank H. Epp, *Education with a Plus: The Story of Rosthern Junior College* (Waterloo, Ont.: Conrad Press, 1975), 181.
2 The three schools were the Mennonite Educational Institute located in Gretna, Manitoba; the Rosthern Junior College (until 1946 the German/English Academy) in Rosthern, Saskatchewan, and the Niagara Christian College in Fort Erie, Ontario.
3 E. Morris Sider, *The Brethren in Christ in Canada: Two Hundred Years of Tradition and Change* (Nappanee, Ind.: Evangel Press, 1988), 204.
4 The basic information in this table is taken from William Hooley, comp., 'Secondary Schools,' *ME* V, 804.
5 Almost all these high schools are, or were at one time, run by an educational society. They have come to be identified with particular conferences either because the majority of the members of the educational society were members of that conference or because a particular conference provides partial or complete support for the financial and administrative affairs of the school.
6 Gerhard Ens, *'Die Schule Muss Sein': A History of the Mennonite Collegiate Institute* (Gretna, Man.: Mennonite Collegiate Institute, 1990).
7 This school was originally called the German/English Academy, but its name was changed in response to wartime conditions and a hope, never realized, that it might also offer some introductory university-level classes. Epp, *Education with a Plus*.
8 E. Morris Sider, *Here Faith and Learning Meet: The Story of Niagara Christian College* (Nappanee, Ind.: Evangel Press, 1982); Sider, *Brethren in Christ*. This school began as the Ontario Bible School but was moved to a new campus at Fort Erie, in 1939 and renamed the Niagara Christian College in 1951.
9 The information on this school comes mainly from the *Protokolle des*

mennonitischen Erziehungs-Institutes, in the office of the principal of the Mennonite Educational Institute. See also anniversary yearbooks of the school and the history of the South Abbotsford Mennonite Brethren Church.

10 This school was originally called the Mennonite Educational Institute but became the Sharon Collegiate Institute early in its history. Agatha E. Klassen, *Yarrow: A Portrait in Mosaic* (Yarrow, BC: A.E. Klassen, 1980); CMBS(W) Protokollbuch der Mennoniten Brueder Gemeinde zu Yarrow; CGC Protokollbuch des Hochschul Komitees (Yarrow).

11 John A. Toews, *A History of the Mennonite Brethren Church* (Fresno, Calif.: Board of Christian Literature, General Conference of Mennonite Brethren Churches, 1975), 267–8.

12 C. Alfred Friesen, ed., *History of the Mennonite Settlement in Niagara-on-the-Lake, Ontario, 1934–84;* 'Milestones in the History of Eden,' *CM,* 10, no. 23 (8 June 1962), 5; *Memoirs of the Virgil-Niagara Mennonites* (Virgil, Ont.: Fiftieth Anniversary Jubilee Celebration, 1984).

13 Jacob P. Driedger, *United Mennonite Educational Institute, Leamington, Ontario: Its Origin and Growth, 1945–1975* (Leamington, Ont.: United Mennonite Educational Institute, 1975); Margaret Mantler, 'Student Reviews UMEI History,' *CM,* 15, no. 22 (30 May 1967), 4.

14 The school was originally called the Rockway Mennonite School and became the Rockway Mennonite Collegiate only later, but here I use the latter name throughout. I am indebted to Sam Steiner who allowed me to read several chapters of his history of the institution, *Lead Us On: A History of Rockway Mennonite Collegiate, 1945–1995* (Kitchener, Ont.: Rockway Mennonite Collegiate, 1995).

15 Archie Penner, 'Steinbach Bible Institute,' *ME* IV, 624.

16 CMBS(W) B.B. Janz Papers, 7/106; *Quo Vadis,* Tenth Anniversary Yearbook of the Alberta Mennonite High School.

17 *Mennonitische Lehrerzeitung* (June 1949), 5. The Menno High School offered grades 7 through 10 in 1946–7 and grades 7 through 11 in 1947–8 but was closed in the summer of 1948, following the flood.

18 Klassen, *Yarrow.*

19 This school was originally called the Mennonite Educational Institute but was renamed later. Adolf Ens, 'Education,' *ME* V, 259.

20 Ibid. This is a school of the Bergthaler Mennonite Church of Saskatchewan.

21 Steiner, *Lead Us On.*

22 'Russian Mennonites' is here used about those whose ancestors came to Canada in the 1870s and those who came in the 1920s. For further information see Appendix A.

23 Steiner, *Lead Us On,* chap. 2. Similar concerns can also be found in the minutes

of other educational societies and committees, particularly in British Columbia.

24 Epp, *Education with a Plus*, 178.

25 Ibid., 180.

26 Protokolle des mennonitischen Erziehungs-Institutes.

27 CMBS(W) Protokollbuch der Mennoniten Brueder Gemeinde zu Yarrow; CGC Protokollbuch des Hochschul Komitees (Yarrow).

28 All these details are taken from the three protocol books listed in 26 and 27, above.

29 Epp, *Education with a Plus*, 244–6.

30 Ens, '*Die Schule Muss Sein*,' chap. 10.

31 Information on the early history of the Mennonite Brethren Collegiate Institute is drawn mainly from the *Yearbook of the Northern District (Canadian) Conference of the Mennonite Brethren Church*, various years, and from correspondence in the B.B. Janz Papers in CMBS(W).

32 Protokollbuch der Mennoniten Brueder Gemeinde zu Yarrow and Protokollbuch des Hochschul Komitees.

33 Protokolle des mennonitischen Erziehungs-Institutes.

34 Steiner, *Lead Us On*, chap. 2.

35 Ibid., chap. 3.

36 Driedger, *United Mennonite Educational Institute*.

37 *Quo Vadis*, 1956 Yearbook of the Alberta Mennonite High School, 6.

38 CMBS(W) B.B. Janz Papers, 7/106.

39 The serious shortage of teachers is particularly well documented in CMBS(W) B.B. Janz Papers, 7/106; and MHC J.J. Thiessen Papers, 915/351 and 915/352.

40 As documented in CMBS(W) B.B. Janz Papers, 7/106.

41 Ens, '*Die Schule Muss Sein*,' chap. 8; T.D. Regehr, *For Everything a Season: The Alexanderkrone Zentralschule* (Winnipeg: CMBC Publications, 1988).

42 G. Lohrenz, 'Die M.B. Hochschule in Winnipeg,' *Mennonitische Welt*, 5 Jahrgang (Sept. 1952), 9–10.

43 Ibid.

44 CMBS(W) B.B. Janz Papers, 7/106, Peter J. Dick in his first report to the annual meeting of the Alberta Mennonite Educational Society, 24 March 1950.

45 Ferne Burkhardt, 'Rockway Mennonite School: Conception and Birth,' *Mennogespraech*, 1, no. 2 (Oct. 1983), 9–13.

46 Epp, *Education with a Plus*, 182.

47 Ens, '*Die Schule Muss Sein*,' 223.

48 CMBS(W) Protokollbuch der Mennoniten Brueder Gemeinde zu Yarrow; CGC Protokollbuch des Hochschul Komitees (Yarrow).

49 Penner, 'Steinbach Bible Institute,' 625; P.J.B. Reimer, *The Sesquicentennial Jubilee: Evangelical Mennonite Conference, 1812–1962* (Steinbach, Man.:

Evangelical Mennonite Conference, 1962), 146–53; Gerald Wright, *Steinbach: Is There Any Place Like It?* (Steinbach, Man.: Derksen Printers, 1991).

50 Reimer, *Sesquicentennial Jubilee*, 151–2. The Emmanuel Free Church dropped out after only a short time.

51 Unger, 'Bible Colleges and Institutes,' *ME* V, 75.

52 Telephone interview by T.D. Regehr, 10 Aug. 1994, with William Kruger, principal of Westgate Collegiate Institute at the time.

53 'Tough Minds and Tender Hearts,' *CM*, 18, no. 23 (12 June 1970), 5.

54 A good description and criticism of the old instructional methods, in this case at MCI in Gretna, are given in Kathy Martens, 'Looking Back Doesn't Always Bring Fond Memories of School,' in *Embracing the World: Two Decades of Canadian Mennonite Writing. A Selection of Writings from the Mennonite Mirror*, 19, no. 10 (June–July 1990), 27–9. Peter P. Rempel at Rosthern Junior College represented the newer, and in its day controversial, teaching style.

55 MHC J.J. Thiessen Papers, 915/352, J.H. Langenwalter to members of the Board of Education of the General Conference, 11 July 1945.

56 John Doerksen, 'Mennonite Brethren Bible College and College of Arts: Its History, Philosophy and Development,' PhD dissertation, University of North Dakota, Grand Forks, 1968. A somewhat different interpretation of these events is given in C.F. Funk, *1944 Auf Dem Wege zum College der Mennoniten Brueder Gemeinden von Kanada – Beobachtungen – Wuensche – Hoffnungen – Einsicht – Realismus* (Winkler, Man.: C.J. Funk, 1944); *Yearbook of the Northern District Conference of the Mennonite Brethren Church of North America* (Winnipeg: Christian Press, 1946), 59–61.

57 Interview with J.B. Toews in Fresno, California, 1 Feb. 1993.

58 *Yearbook of the Northern District Conference* (1946), 62.

59 MHC J.J. Thiessen Papers, 915/352, Isaac I. Friesen to J.J. Thiessen, 3 Oct. 1945.

60 As told to the author by J.B. Toews in an interview on 2 Feb. 1993.

61 MHC J.J. Thiessen Papers, J.J. Thiessen to P.S. Goertz, 10 Aug. 1946.

62 Ibid., E.G. Kaufman to J.J. Thiessen, 17 Aug. 1946, and P.S. Goertz to J.J. Thiessen, 21 Aug. 1946.

63 Ibid., J.J. Thiessen to P. S. Goertz, 17 Aug. 1946.

64 Ibid., J.J. Thiessen to J.J. Janzen, 21 March 1947.

65 Ibid., Ed. G. Kaufman to J.J. Thiessen, 18 March 1947.

66 Ibid., J.J. Thiessen to Ed. G. Kaufman, 11 April 1947.

67 Ibid., J.J. Thiessen to Arnold J. Regier, 12 June 1947.

68 Ibid., J.J. Thiessen to Ed. G. Kaufman, 5 Aug. 1947.

69 Ibid., 869/97, Paul Schaefer to J.J. Thiessen, 18 Feb. 1949. H. Wall, who handled much of the public relations work of the college in southern Manitoba in the early years, informed J.J. Thiessen after a group from the college had presented a

program that Paul Schaefer had complained afterward because it had not been entirely in German. He insisted that the college would have greater success if programs were exclusively in German.Wall simply noted that it was impossible to fight against such an attitude. Ibid., 915/351, H. Wall to J.J. Thiessen and J. Gerbrandt, 23 May 1949. Bruno Dyck, 'Half a Century of Canadian Mennonite Bible College: A Brief Organizational History,' *JMS*, 11 (1993), 194–223.

70 *1946 Yearbook of the 36th Canadian Conference of the Mennonite Brethren Church of North America* (Winnipeg: Christian Press, 1946), 98–9.

71 'Canadian Mennonite Bible College,' *CM*, 9 no. 48 (8 Dec. 1961), 5.

72 Howard J. Loewen, 'Augustus H. Strong: Baptist Theologian for Mennonite Brethren,' in Paul Toews, ed., *Mennonites and Baptists: A Continuing Conversation* (Winnipeg, Man. and Hillsboro, Kan.: Kindred Press, 1993), 193–210; Rodney Sawatzky, 'Words Becoming Flesh: The Life and Thought of David Schroeder,' in Harry Huebner, ed., *The Church as Theological Community: Essays in Honour of David Schroeder* (Winnipeg: CMBC Publications, 1990), 3–22.

73 (Old) Mennonite Church seminary instruction was offered as a graduate program at Goshen College until 1958, when the General Conference seminary which had been located in Chicago was moved to Elkhart, Indiana. The two seminaries then formed the Associated Mennonite Biblical Seminaries but operated on the Goshen and Elkhart campuses until 1969, when they built a common campus at Elkhart. The Mennonite Brethren Biblical Seminary was established at Fresno, California, in 1955. These seminaries provided the post-graduate theological training for prospective Canadian pastors and church leaders.

74 Abe J. Dueck, 'Canadian Mennonites and the Anabaptist Vision,' *JMS*, 13 (1995), 84.

75 Ibid.

76 'Important Academic Changes Announced,' *CM*, 12, no. 23 (9 June 1964), 5.

77 'Credit Extension Alters CMBC Study Program,' *CM*, 18, no. 22 (5 June 1970), 4.

78 'University of Toronto,' *The Canadian Encyclopedia*, vol. 4 (Edmonton: Hurtig, 1988), 2223.

79 Epp, *Education with a Plus*, 154–8.

80 Ross T. Bender, 'Private Mennonite Education in Ontario after World War II,' *JMS*, 6 (1988), 120.

81 'What Is Conrad Grebel College?' *Conrad Grebel College Bulletin*, 1, no. 1 (April 1964), 1.

82 Ibid.

83 The majority in the small Toronto Mennonite student group during the war

had come from Saskatoon to study music. A former Saskatchewan resident, I.G. Neufeld, had some sort of a vaguely defined city mission assignment. He met both with Mennonite students and with some of the Mennonite enlisted men at nearby military training bases. He wrote a number of news reports for a Toronto daily newspaper and for *Der Bote*, but when writing for *Der Bote* he used the byline G. Enns – his mother's name.

84 A long and detailed letter by I.G. Neufeld outlining developments in Toronto is MHC J.J. Thiessen Papers, 882/184, I.G. Neufeld to J J. Thiessen, 24 June 1944. There is also a small collection of I.G. Neufeld's papers at MHC.

85 As cited in 'Mennonite Student Group Strives for Perfection in Members,' *CM*, 2, no. 5 (29 Jan. 1954), 7.

86 'Mennonite Student Cliques Prevent Outreach,' *CM*, 6, no. 41 (24 Oct. 1958), 1. This article elicited a spirited response from Ernie Redekop, a former president of the IVCF chapter at United College in Winnipeg, who became president of AMUS at the University of Manitoba in 1958, and numerous letters that debated the purpose and merits of AMUS and IVCF.

87 *CM*, 4, no. 45 (16 Nov. 1956), 9; and *CM*, 4, no. 47 (30 Nov. 1956), 11.

88 *CM*, 6, no. 43 (31 Oct. 1958), 1.

89 'Toronto AMUS Strives for Relevancy in Its Witness,' *CM*, 14, no. 34 (30 Aug. 1966), 1, 8. See also David Schroeder, 'A Ministry to the University People,' *CM*, 10, no. 32 (17 Aug. 1962), 4.

90 The development and unique regional appeal of IVCF in western Canada, particularly Alberta, is discussed in John G. Stackhouse, Jr, *Canadian Evangelicalism in the Twentieth Century: An Introduction to Its Character* (Toronto: University of Toronto Press, 1993).

12: Artistic and Literary Voices

1 Al Reimer, *Mennonite Literary Voices Past and Present* (North Newton, Kan.: Bethel College, 1993), 56.

2 Cornelius Krahn, 'Mennonites and the Fine Arts,' *ML*, 3, no. 2 (April 1948), 3.

3 Robert Friedman, 'Ausbund,' *ME* I, 191–2.

4 Information on early Anabaptist and Mennonite hymnology is drawn mainly from Harold S. Bender, 'Hymnology of the Anabaptists,' *ME* II, 869. See also A.J. Ramaker, 'Hymns and Hymn Writers among the Anabaptists of the Sixteenth Century,' *MQR*, 3 (1929), 93–131.

5 Orland Gingerich, *The Amish of Canada* (Waterloo, Ont.: Conrad Press, 1972), 79.

6 Morris Sider, *The Brethren in Christ: Two Hundred Years of Tradition and Change* (Nappanee, Ind.: Evangel Press, 1988), 93–4.

7   Wesley Berg, *From Russia with Music: A Study of the Mennonite Choral Singing Tradition in Canada* (Winnipeg: Hyperion, 1985), 16. A more detailed description of Amish and Old Colony church music, including tone production, is available in Charles Burkhart, 'Church Music of the Old Order Amish and Old Colony Mennonites,' *MQR*, 27, no. 1 (Jan. 1953), 34–54.

8   See particularly Berg, *From Russia with Music*; Wesley Berg, 'Gesangbuch, Ziffern, and Deutschtum: A Study of the Life and Work of J.P. Claszen, Mennonite Hymnologist,' *JMS*, 4 (1986), 8–30; Wesley Berg, 'From Piety to Sophistication: Developments in Canadian Mennonite Music after World War II,' *JMS*, 6 (1988), 89–99.

9   Mary Toews, 'German Hymnody,' *Voice of the Mennonite Brethren Bible College*, 2, no. 1 (Jan.–Feb. 1953), 14–16.

10 Berg, *From Russia with Music*, 65.

11 The Mennonite periodicals, particularly *Canadian Mennonite*, carried frequent, detailed, and enthusiastic reports about *Saengerfeste* held in various parts of Canada in the 1950s and 1960s.

12 David H. Suderman, 'Our Musical Heritage in the Colleges,' *ML*, 3, no. 2 (April 1948), 31–2.

13 'A Quarter Century of Music at Rosthern Junior College,' *CM*, 11 Dec. 1953, 1.

14 K.H. Neufeld, 'Music among Mennonites in Canada,' *CM*, 3 July 1953, 5.

15 Jane Marie Schultz, 'The Evolution of Singing Schools among the Swiss Mennonites of Southern Ontario,' BA thesis, University of Waterloo, 1987.

16 Marlene Epp, *Mennonites in Ontario* (Waterloo, Ont.: Mennonite Historical Society of Ontario, 1994), 22.

17 'Professional Workshop Unique Musical Event Coming to Waterloo,' *CM*, 13, no. 17 (1965), 12.

18 Bertha Elizabeth Klassen, *Da Capo: 'Start Once from the Front.' A History of the Mennonite Community Orchestra* (Winnipeg: Centre for Mennonite Brethren Studies, 1993); Lloyd Siemens, 'Ben Horch: Dean of Mennonite Conductors,' *MM*, 4, no. 1 (Oct. 1974), 12–13, and 'On Being Professional without Being Elite, Horch: Part II,' *MM*, 4, no. 2 (Nov. 1974), 9–10.

19 Berg, *From Russia with Music*, 111.

20 Wesley Berg, 'Gesangbuch, Ziffern, and Deutschtum', 8–30.

21 Berg, *From Russia with Music*, 94.

22 George Wiebe, 'The Hymnody of the Conference of Mennonites in Canada,' M.A. thesis, University of Southern California, 1962.

23 Berg, *From Russia with Music*, 116.

24 Esther Horch, 'Hymns as a Vehicle of Worship for Children,' *Voice*, 5, nos. 1 and 2 (Jan.–Feb. and March–April, 1956), 18–20 and 15–18, respectively.

25 Eric Routley, *Gospel Hymns Nos. 1 to 6 Complete* (New York: Da Capo Press,

1972), as quoted in Berg, *From Russia with Music*, 116.

26 Peter Klassen, 'Concerning Music and Ethics,' *Voice*, 10, no. 5 (Sept.–Oct. 1961), 18–21.

27 Peter Klassen, 'Music in Our Churches,' *Voice*, 6, no. 6 (Nov.–Dec. 1957), 20–1.

28 Ibid.

29 Berg, *From Russia with Music*, 26. See also Paul W. Wohlgemuth, 'Singing the New Song,' in John A. Toews, *A History of the Mennonite Brethren Church* (Fresno, Calif.: Board of Christian Literature, General Conference of Mennonite Brethren Churches, 1975), 242.

30 Peter Klassen, 'Concerning Mennonites and Music – A Brief Appraisal,' *Voice*, 4, no. 1 (Jan.–Feb. 1955), 10.

31 Howard Dyck, 'Where We're At in Music-Making,' *CM*, 19, no. 8 (19 Feb. 1971), 15.

32 Klassen, 'Concerning Mennonites and Music,' 11–14.

33 The Hymnbook Committee, 'The New English Hymnal of the M.B. Church,' *Voice*, 8, no. 6 (Nov.–Dec. 1959), 27.

34 Ibid.

35 Ibid.

36 Margie Wiebe, 'Hymns Used by the General Conference,' *ML*, 2, no. 2 (April 1948), 36. Detailed information on these and the many other Mennonite hymnals published over the years is available in Harold S. Bender, 'Hymnology of the American Mennonites,' *ME* II, 879–86. See also Paul W. Wohlgemuth, 'Mennonite Hymnals Published in the English Language,' PhD dissertation, University of Southern California, 1956.

37 Harold S. Bender, 'Hymnology of the American Mennonites,' *ME* II, 883.

38 As quoted in Wohlgemuth, 'Singing the New Song,' 247.

39 William Baerg, 'In Search of New Hymns,' *Voice*, 17, no. 5 (Sept.–Oct. 1968), 14–15.

40 As quoted in Berg, *From Russia with Music*, 116.

41 Ben Horch, 'Music Recitals,' *Voice*, 2, no. 3 (May–June 1953), 21.

42 William Baerg, 'In Search of New Hymns,' *Voice*, 17, no. 5 (Sept.–Oct. 1968), 15.

43 Ibid.

44 Ibid.

45 Peter Klassen, 'Music in Our Churches,' *Voice*, 6, no. 6 (Nov.–Dec. 1957), 21.

46 This issue was debated in detail on 4 November 1929 by the members of the Mennonite Brethren Church at Coaldale, Alberta. A copy of the minutes is available at CMBS(W), Reel R47.

47 Ibid.

48 Peter Klassen, 'Hymn-Sing: Some Reflections,' *Voice*, 16, no. 1 (Jan.–Feb. 1967), 12–15.

49 Dyck, 'Where We're At,' 15.
50 As quoted in Peter Letkemann, 'Benjamin Horch (1907–1992),' *JMS*, 11 (1993), 242.
51 Ibid., 243.
52 I am indebted to Reg Good of Kitchener for information about Ontario Mennonite reactions to these non-Mennonite literary writers.
53 Peter C. Erb, 'Weakness and Docility: Characterizing Pennsylvania "Dutch" Literature among Mennonites,' in Hildi Froese Tiessen, ed., *The New Quarterly: New Directions in Canadian Writing*, Special Issue: Mennonite/s Writing in Canada, vol. 10, nos. 1 and 2 (spring/summer 1990), 53–69.
54 John L. Ruth, *Mennonite Identity and Literary Art* (Scottdale, Penn.: Herald Press, 1978).
55 Elmer Suderman, 'Mennonites, the Mennonite Community, and Mennonite Writers,' *ML*, 47, no. 3 (Sept. 1992), 22.
56 Harry Loewen, 'Mennonite Literature in Canada: Beginnings, Reception and Study,' *JMS*, 1 (1983), 120.
57 Victor G. Doerksen, 'From Jung-Stilling to Rudy Wiebe: "Christian Fiction" and the Mennonite Imagination,' in Harry Loewen, ed., *Mennonite Images: Historical, Cultural and Literary Essays Dealing with Mennonite Issues* (Winnipeg: Hyperion, 1989), 197–208.
58 Victor G. Doerksen, 'In Search of a Mennonite Imagination,' *JMS*, 2 (1984), 111.
59 For a further and more detailed explanation and definition of 'the stock forms of the part' in Mennonite literary writing, see ibid., 110–11.
60 A more detailed discussion of the literary work of these four authors is given in Harry Loewen, 'Mennonite Literature in Canada: Beginnings, Reception and Study,' *JMS*, 1 (1983), 119–32.
61 Elmer Suderman, 'Mennonites, the Mennonite Community, and Mennonite Writers,' *ML*, 47, no. 3 (Sept. 1992), 24.
62 Jacob H. Janzen, 'The Literature of the Russo-Canadian Mennonites,' *ML*, 1, no. 1 (Jan. 1946), 22.
63 As cited in Harry Loewen, 'The Mennonite Writer as Witness and Critic,' *JMS*, 2 (1984), 116.
64 Al Reimer, 'One Foot In, One Foot Out: Themes and Issues in Contemporary Mennonite Writing,' *JMS*, 10 (1992), 151–64.
65 Doerksen, 'From Jung-Stilling to Rudy Wiebe,' 208.
66 Herb Giesbrecht, 'O Life, How Naked and How Hard When Known! A Comprehensive Review of a Controversial Novel that Destroyed the Peace of Many,' *CM*, 11, no. 12 (22 March 1963), 5, 8–9.
67 Rudy H. Wiebe, 'The Skull in the Swamp,' *JMS*, 5 (1987), 15.

68 As quoted in ibid., 16.
69 In his own writing Rudy Wiebe has not revealed the identity of the people who visited the editorial offices of the *Winnipeg Free Press*. They were prominent Mennonite businessmen who purchased advertising space in the paper.
70 Ibid., 19.
71 Reimer, 'One Foot In, One Foot Out,' 155.
72 Doerksen, 'From Jung-Stilling to Rudy Wiebe,' 208.
73 Harry Loewen, 'Mennonite Literature in Canada: Beginnings, Reception and Study,' *JMS*, 1 (1983), 124.
74 Reimer, 'One Foot In, One Foot Out,' 155.
75 Rudy Wiebe, 'Where We're At ... In Our Understanding and Use of the Arts,' *CM*, 19, no. 8 (19 Feb. 1971), 14.
76 The best and most complete review of recent developments in Canadian Mennonite creative literature is Reimer, *Mennonite Literary Voices*.
77 Ibid., 152.
78 For listings of such denunciations see Bert Friesen, *Where We Stand: An Index to Statements by Mennonites and Brethren in Christ in Canada, 1787–1982* (Winnipeg: Mennonite Central Committee, Canada, 1986).
79 Hans B. Grube, ed., *Reuter's Werke in zwoelf Teilen* (Berlin and Leipzig: Deutsches Verlagshaus Bong & Co., n.d.).
80 Jake Letkeman, 'Drama in the Christian High School,' *CM*, 14, no. 31 (9 Aug. 1971), 10.
81 '20-minute Bible Dramas – They'll Turn Church into a Stage,' *CM*, 19, no. 3 (15 Jan. 1971), 8.
82 U. Woelcke, 'Winnipeg Mennonite Theatre,' *MM*, 2, no. 1 (Sept. 1972), 29.
83 *The Canadian Mennonite* published numerous reviews of plays and dramatic productions in Mennonite communities. The names of the plays, as listed here, are taken from those reviews.
84 '150 Years: Thousands Attend Ten-day Amish Celebration,' *MR* (16 Oct. 1972), 1. See also the editorial in the same issue.
85 A long and detailed list of Mennonite playwrights in Canada and the United States is given in Lauren Friesen, 'Dramatic Arts,' *ME* I, 245–6.
86 The two plays that are particularly noteworthy are *Sailing to Danzig* and *As Far As the Eye Can See*. Wiebe's most successful adaptation of a portion of one of his novels is *The Vietnam Call of Samuel U. Reimer*, taken from *The Blue Mountains of China*.
87 Lauren Friesen, 'Dramatic Arts,' *ME* V, 245–6.
88 A detailed discussion of Mennonite links and influences on the art of Rembrandt and other seventeenth-century Dutch painters may be found in Cornelius Krahn, 'Rembrandt, the Bible and the Mennonites,' and H.M.

Rottermund, 'Rembrandt and the Mennonites,' both published in *ML*, 7, no. 1 (Jan. 1952), 3–10.

89 Information about and reproductions of paintings by Alexander Harder, a Mennonite artist in Russia who came to Canada in 1927, are provided in 'From Plough to Brush – Alexander Harder,' *ML*, 8, no. 4 (Oct. 1953), 147– 50. Other issues of *Mennonite Life* have information about and pictures of Mennonite pottery, needlework, sculptures, and engravings.

90 Ethel Ewert Abrahams, 'Fraktur. Dutch-Prussian-Russian,' Mary Jane Lederach Hershey, 'Fraktur. Swiss-Pennsylvania German,' and Carolyn C. Wenger, 'Fraktur,' all in *ME* V, 308–10.

91 T.D. Regehr, *For Everything a Season: A History of the Alexanderkrone Zentralschule* (Winnipeg: CMBC Publications, 1988), 8.

92 Nancy-Lou Patterson, 'Anna Weber Hat Das Gemacht. Anna Weber (1814– 1888) – *Fraktur* Painter of Waterloo County, Ontario,' *ML*, 30, no. 4 (Dec. 1975), 15–19. See also Nancy-Lou Patterson, *Mennonite Traditional Arts of the Waterloo Region and Southern Ontario* (Kitchener, Ont.: The Kitchener-Waterloo Art Gallery, 1974).

93 The first issue carried letters of support from the chairmen of both conferences. See also Paul J. Schaefer, 'Erster Bericht der Erziehungsbehoerde der Konferenz der Mennoniten in Kanada,' *Mennonitische Lehrerzeitung*, Zweites Heft (Oktober 1948), 13.

94 *Voice*, 1, no. 1 (Jan.–Feb. 1952), 2.

95 There were several earlier bi-national English Mennonite papers which enjoyed wide readership among the Swiss Mennonites in Ontario. The *Herald of Truth*, founded in 1864, was in English, as was its successor, the *Gospel Herald*. *Mission News* and the *Ontario Mennonite Evangel*, both published by Swiss Mennonites in Ontario, were also in English. The *Canadian Mennonite* was the first English-Canadian Mennonite newspaper that sought to appeal to a national Mennonite readership which transcended denominational boundaries.

96 Roy and Ruth Vogt, 'Introduction: Looking back on Two Decades,' *Embracing the World: Two Decades of Canadian Mennonite Writing. A Selection of Writings from the Mennonite Mirror*, vol. 19, no. 10 (June–July 1990), 4.

97 Ibid.

98 Al Reimer, 'Who's Afraid of Mennonite Art?' *Embracing the World*, 73.

99 Lloyd Siemens, 'On Being Professional without Being Elite,' *MM*, 4, no. 1 (Oct. 1974), 10. Peter Letkemann's lengthy obituary for Ben Horch, in *JMS*, 11 (1993), 236–43, provides information on his radio work.

100 *The Canadian Mennonite* carried numerous reports on CFAM, particularly in 1956, when authorization to open the station was obtained and a corporate

structure was created. An excellent brief summary of the station and its activities can be found in Esther Epp-Tiessen, *Altona: The Story of a Prairie Town* (Altona: D.W. Friesen and Sons, 1982), 248–51.

101 Reimer, 'Who's Afraid of Mennonite Art?' 73.

13: New Leadership

1 Urie A. Bender, *Four Earthen Vessels: Biographical Profiles of Oscar Burkholder, Samuel F. Coffman, Clayton F. Derstine, and Jesse B. Martin* (Kitchener, Ont., and Scottdale, Penn.: Herald Press, 1982), 303.

2 Ibid., 309–15.

3 As quoted in John B. Toews, *With Courage to Spare: The Life of B.B. Janz (1877–1964)* (Winnipeg, Man., and Hillsboro, Kan.: General Conference of Mennonite Brethren Churches of North America, 1978), 104.

4 Delbert Wiens, *New Wineskins for Old Wine: A Study of the Mennonite Brethren Church* (Hillsboro, Kan.: Mennonite Brethren Publishing House, 1965).

5 Ibid., 27 and 24.

6 Frank H. Epp, *Mennonites in Canada, 1920–1940: A People's Struggle for Survival* (Toronto: Macmillan, 1982), 428–30; Jack Heppner, *Search for Renewal: The Story of the Rudnerweider/Evangelical Mennonite Mission Conference, 1937–1987* (Winnipeg: Evangelical Mennonite Mission Conference, 1987).

7 Some of these tensions are documented in the dairy of Isaac P. Regehr, my grandfather, who was a teacher at the Herbert Bible School from 1928 until his death in 1930 and an ordained preacher in the MB church. He became so disillusioned with the tensions in the church and with some aspects of the life-style there that he ceased to attend business meetings of the church but continued to preach when invited to do so.

8 Wilhelm Bestvater, long-time principal of the Herbert Bible School, had supported both the dispensationalist/fundamentalist theology and the charismatic methods of the evangelists while he worked in Herbert. In 1946–7 Bestvater no longer lived in Herbert, but his influence remained.

9 This account of events and developments in the Herbert Mennonite Brethren Church is based on CMBS(W) Records of the Canadian Conference of Mennonite Brethren Churches, vol. 1, file B220, Fuersorgekomitee Protokolle (Board of Spiritual and Social Concerns Minutes and Correspondence).

10 Ibid., Sitzung des Fuersorgekomitees der kanadischen Konferenz zusammen mit dem Fuersorgekomitee des S. Sask. Kreises, abgehalten zu Herbert, 13 Juli 1946. The minutes were kept in German. The translation is mine.

11 Ibid., Protokoll einer Fuersorgekomitee Sitzung, Saskatoon, 9 Mai 1947.

12 Ibid., Aufzeichnungen einer Durchsprache ueber die Herbert-Angelegenheit im Hause der Geschwister J.M. Lepp, Dalmeny, am 1 Juli 1947. Zugegen waren das Fuersorgekomitee der Canad. Konferenz der MBG, das Praesidium des Kreiskomitees von Herbert, Br. J.E. Priebe, delegaten von der reorganizierten Herbert-Gemeinde, Vertreter der Tabernacle-Gruppe in Herbert.

13 Ibid., J.M. Neufeld to C.C. Peters, 15 December 1947.

14 Ibid., Undated document marked 'Vertraulich – Besondere Angelegenheit des Bruders … , Herbert,' and 'Protokoll einer Sitzung des Fuersorgekomitees der canad. Konferenz in der Angelegenheit von Br. … ,' both filed with the minutes of the Fuersorgekomitee dated 28 June and 2 July 1947.

15 CMBS(W) Microfilm Reel R47, Protokoll der Mennoniten Bruedergemeinde zu Coaldale, Alberta, beginning 23 May 1926.

16 Peter H. Regehr, 'Wogen und Wellen in der Sturm- und Drangsalsperiode in der Mennonitschen Bruedergemeinde zu Coaldale um die Jahreswende 1956–1957.' The provenance of this manuscript is unusual. Regehr's wife did not approve of the many things that he wrote, and shortly before his death Regehr noticed that a number of his manuscripts had disappeared. When failing health made it difficult for him to leave the house, my father often visited and read the Mennonite periodicals to him. On one of these visits Regehr confided that he feared that his wife was destroying his diaries and manuscripts and entrusted 'Wogen und Wellen' to my father for safekeeping. Shortly before his death my father entrusted the manuscript to me. I still have the original in my possession, but a xerox copy was prepared for the Conrad Grebel College archives.

17 Joanna Buhr, 'Pursuit of a Vision: Persistence and Accommodation among Coaldale Mennonites from the Mid-Nineteen Twenties to World War II,' M.A. thesis, University of Calgary, 1986.

18 Bender, *Four Earthen Vessels*, 107 and 151.

19 Previously a local carpenter had made the coffins, and family members prepared the body for burial.

20 CMBS(W) B.B. Janz Papers, 4/57, B.B. Janz to Heinrich Nikkel, 3 Feb. 1956.

21 CMBS(W) Minutes of the Vorberat (Church Council) of the Mennonite Brethren Church at Coaldale, 13 Feb. 1956.

22 Peter H. Regehr expresses much of that bitterness in his manuscript and cites at length the arguments made at membership meetings in support of the centuries-old style of lay leadership in Anabaptist and Mennonite congregations. B.B. Janz was also very unhappy with the change but recognized that any alternative would create even greater local problems.

23 Available documentation provides puzzling impressions and descriptions of

David Pankratz. His supporters, including the overwhelming majority of the church members and of the church council, regarded him as a sincere, humble, and devoted servant of God and of the church. Others, who thought that they had his support but found that at critical occasions it had not been given, or that somehow Pankratz was absent when they thought that his influence might have carried a controversial point, portray him as a politically skilled and not altogether reliable operator.

24 CMBS(W) Minutes of the Vorberat (Church Council) of the Mennonite Brethren Church at Coaldale, April 1956.

25 CMBS(W) Coaldale Mennonite Brethren Church minutes, 4 Aug. 1958.

26 A photograph and short biography of Peter W. Dyck are available in *Jubilaeums-Album der Konferenz der Mennoniten in Kanada, 1902–1952* (Winnipeg: Conference of Mennonites in Canada, 1952), 24, and in Gerhard I. Peters, *Remember Our Leaders: Conference of Mennonites in Canada* (Clearbrook, BC: Mennonite Historical Society of British Columbia, 1982), 172.

27 Detailed information regarding events in the Westheimer Mennonite Church at Rosemary are taken from MHC J.J. Thiessen Papers, 869/90, and MHC J.D. Nickel Papers.

28 A copy of Dyck's comments is available in MHC J.J. Thiessen Papers, 869/90. There was, however, a dispute about what Dyck had said. His opponents charged that he had made intemperate remarks that were not part of the written sermon.

29 Ibid., J.D. Nickel to J.J. Thiessen, 11 Sept. 1953, and J.J. Thiessen to J.D. Nickel, 18 Nov. 1953.

30 The very detailed minutes of these special sessions provide an unusually candid look at the conflict-resolution strategies and tactics of the conference leaders, most notably of J.J. Thiessen. The minutes are in ibid., 'Sonderkonferenz zu Rosemary, Alberta, Nov. 3, 1954.' The fragility of the reconciliation was demonstrated by the fact that G.G. Epp, the conference secretary, had barely returned home when he received a request from J.D. Nickel for a copy of a statement that the dissidents had read at the meeting. He wanted to prepare a formal rebuttal, which, he insisted, should be filed with the minutes of the meeting.

31 As quoted in E. Reginald Good, *Frontier Community to Urban Congregation: First Mennonite Church, Kitchener, 1813–1988* (Kitchener, Ont.: First Mennonite Church, 1988), 124–5.

32 Ken Cressman, 'The Development of the Conservative Mennonite Church of Ontario,' Paper prepared for Sociology 275, University of Waterloo, in 1976 and available in CGC.

33 CGC Ontario Conference Historian's Records, Minutes of a 'Special Ministers' and Christian Workers' Meeting,' 26 April 1943.

34 As quoted in Good, *Frontier Community*, 128.

35 Ibid., 132.

36 Ibid.

37 CGC Kenneth Cressman, 'A Descriptive Analysis of the Conservative Mennonite Schisms in Ontario, 1956–1979,' Paper written for Sociology 733, University of Waterloo, in 1979 and available in CGC, 10.

38 Lengthy lists of all the concerns mentioned by the conservative bishops are given in Cressman, 'Development,' 12.

39 Cressman, 'Descriptive Analysis,' 37.

40 Ibid.

41 Margaret Loewen Reimer, *One Quilt, Many Pieces: A Reference Guide to Mennonite Groups in Canada*, 3rd ed. (Waterloo, Ont.: Mennonite Publishing Service, 1990), 37.

42 Isaac R. Horst, 'Conservative Mennonite Church of Ontario,' *ME* V, 191–2.

43 Reimer, *One Quilt, Many Pieces*, 38.

44 Specific groups of this kind identified in ibid., 38–9, are the Western Conservative Mennonite Fellowship and the Midwest Mennonite Fellowship, which have members in Alberta, and the Eastern Pennsylvania Mennonite Church, which has members in British Columbia.

45 Magdalene Redekop, 'Through the Mennonite Looking Glass,' in Harry Loewen, ed., *Why I Am a Mennonite: Essays on Mennonite Identity* (Kitchener, Ont.: Herald Press, 1988), 235.

46 'Merits and Demerits of Isolation,' *CM*, 7, no. 26 (3 July 1959), 5.

47 A letter from B.B. Janz published in the *Lethbridge Herald*, 5 July 1940.

48 Interview with J.B. Toews, 1 Feb. 1993.

49 These statistics are taken from the *Year Book of the General Conference of the Mennonite Church of North America* (Newton, Kan.: Mennonite Publishing Office, 1940), 38.

50 Gloria L. Neufeld Redekop, 'Mennonite Women's Societies in Canada: A Historical Case Study,' PhD thesis, University of Ottawa, 1993, 128, 161, and 239.

51 C.L. Dick, *The Mennonite Conference of Alberta: A History of Its Churches and Institutions* (Edmonton: Mennonite Conference of Alberta, 1980), 43.

52 'Merits and Demerits,' 5.

53 In her novel *Itsuka*, Joy Kogawa, the young Canadian Japanese girl whose family was evacuated from British Columbia and who spent time in and around the Mennonite communities in southern Alberta, tells of going to evangelistic services with her MB friends and putting up her hand and going through the other procedures to accept salvation as preached by local evangelists. But the flash of a slight spark of romance between Kogawa's fictional MB girlfriend named, alas, Tina Regehr and her brother was quickly snuffed out. In that area

the evangelistic effort had apparently succeeded, but it is clear that many more serious obstacles than language would have made Kogawa feel uncomfortable if she had applied for membership in the Coaldale Mennonite Brethren Church in the early 1950s.

54 The database on Mennonite congregations at Conrad Grebel College includes information on the date when congregations reported that they made the language change.

55 Some of the most thoughtful, concerned, and intelligent articles, letters, and editorials pertaining to the language question and to problems of transition were published in *Mennonitische Lehrerzeitung* and its successor, *Mennonitische Welt*. Both magazines were specifically created to help preserve the German language and German Mennonite and Christian traditions and practices through education.

56 The financial plight of the four prominent Mennonite pastors/evangelists/Bible school teachers in Ontario is outlined in considerable detail in Bender, *Four Earthen Vessels*.

57 EMC Archives, Steinbach, vol. 190, file 9, Archie Penner, 'From Aeltester, Lehrer und Gemeinde to Boards, Pastors and Conference.'

58 Paul M. Miller, *Servant of God's Servants* (Scottdale, Penn.: Herald Press, 1964); J. Lawrence Burkholder, 'Theological Education for the Believers' Church,' *Concern*, 17 (Feb. 1969), 12; I.I. Friesen, 'Values and Problems of the Lay and the Supported Ministry,' *The Believers' Church*, Study Conference, Chicago, 23–25 August 1955; and Leland Harder, *The Pastor-People Partnership: The Call and Recall of Pastors from a Believers' Church Perspective* (Elkhart, Ind.: Institute of Mennonite Studies, 1983).

59 *Yearbook of the 45th General Conference of the Mennonite Brethren Church of North America*, held at Winkler, Manitoba, 21–26 July 1951 (Hillsboro, Kan.: Mennonite Brethren Publishing House, 1951), 126.

60 Ibid.

61 Ibid., 142 and 143.

62 Menno H. Epp, *The Pastor's Exit: The Dynamics of Involuntary Termination* (Winnipeg: CMBC Publications, 1984); and Harder, *The Pastor-People Partnership*.

63 Jacob Peters, 'Organizational Change within a Religious Denomination: A Case Study of the Conference of Mennonites in Canada, 1903–1978,' PhD thesis, University of Waterloo, 1986, 156.

64 *Year Book of the 45th General Conference*, 124–44.

65 J.A. Toews, *A History of the Mennonite Brethren Church* (Fresno, Calif.: Board of Christian Literature, General Conference of Mennonite Brethren Churches, 1975), 210–15.

66 Peters, 'Organizational Change.'
67 Christian Neff and Harold S. Bender, 'Conference,' *ME* I, 670. Some conferences, notably the Ontario Amish Mennonite Annual Conference, had always been heavily attended. They featured inspirational meetings, with business conducted between sessions.
68 Cressman, 'Development,' 39.

14: Mission at Home

1 Rodney J. Sawatzky and Scott Holland, eds., *The Limits of Perfection: A Conversation with J. Lawrence Burkholder* (Waterloo, Ont.: Institute of Anabaptist-Mennonite Studies, Conrad Grebel College, 1993), 29.
2 Ibid., 40–1.
3 Edmund George Kaufman, *The Development of the Missionary and Philanthropic Interest among the Mennonites of North America* (Berne, Ind.: Mennonite Book Concern, 1931), chap. 2.
4 As quoted in ibid., 39.
5 Ibid., 56.
6 Theron Schlabach, *Gospel versus Gospel: Mission and the Mennonite Church, 1863–1944* (Scottdale, Penn., and Kitchener, Ont.: Herald Press, 1980).
7 Ibid., 156.
8 CGC II 3-2.3, box 1, folder II, 'The Record of Rural Missions in Ontario.'
9 United Church Archives (UCA), Victoria College, Toronto, Board of Home Missions, series II, section I, box 15, file 389, George Dorrey to R.A. Hoey, Indian Affairs Branch, Department of Mines and Resources, 30 March 1943. The first four Mennonites recommended for such an appointment were W.A. Dueck, N. Dueck, A.W. Schellenberg, and Alfred Kroeker. The United Church encountered considerable difficulty in getting authorization from government. That prompted its superintendent of missions to complain: 'Government red tape passes my poor comprehension.' Permission was, however, eventually granted. Ibid., John A. Cormie to R.B. Cochrane, 5 July 1943.
10 Ibid., Harry Meadows to Dr. Stevens, 9 Oct. 1943.
11 Ibid., George Dorey to J.A. Cormie, 20 Nov. 1943.
12 The personal recollections of one of the Mennonite teachers and missionaries in a United Church mission station in northern Manitoba are published in Abram J. Friesen, *God's Hand upon My Life: Autobiography by Abram J. Friesen* (Chilliwack, BC: Abram J. Friesen, 1986).
13 UCA, Board of Home Missions, series II, section I, box 15, file 389, The United Church of Canada Manitoba Conference, 1944 Digest of Minutes and

Proceedings of the Twentieth Conference, 5–9 June 1944, 52. MB historians have erred in transcribing this report to read 'Mennonite Brethren,' rather than 'Mennonite brethren.' The United Church superintendent of missions was referring to both MB and CMC teachers and missionaries.

14 Henry J. Gerbrandt, *En Route: The Memoirs of Henry J. Gerbrandt* (Winnipeg: CMBC Publications, 1994), 203.

15 Lois Barrett, *The Vision and the Reality: The Story of Home Missions in the General Conference Mennonite Church* (Newton, Kan.: Faith and Life Press, 1983), 225.

16 Gerbrandt, *En Route*, 209.

17 MHC Mennonite Pioneer Mission records, vol. 344, Henry J. Gerbrandt to Henry and Elsa Neufeld, 8 Aug. 1955.

18 As quoted in Barrett, *Vision and Reality*, 223.

19 A copy of this letter was made available to me by Henry Neufeld.

20 Barrett, *Vision and Reality*, 222–5.

21 MHC vol. 345, Report to the Executive Committee of the Mennonite Pioneer Mission section of the Mission Board of the Conference of Mennonites in Canada, on a trip to Loon Straits, 20 April 1960.

22 Gerbrandt, *En Route*, 210.

23 MHC vol. 345, Pamphlet entitled *Mennonite Pioneer Mission in Manitoba, 1945–1959* (Altona, Man.: Mennonite Pioneer Mission, 1959).

24 As quoted in Barrett, *Vision and Reality*, 228.

25 The Mennonite Pioneer Mission was an agency of the Bergthaler Mennonite Church of Manitoba from 1948 until 1957, when responsibility was transferred to CMC, with which the Manitoba Bergthaler Church was affiliated.

26 As quoted in Barrett, *Vision and Reality*, 230.

27 In many cases the differences between MPM and MB missionaries had more to do with the relative emphasis each placed on different aspects of the Christian faith than with absolute principles. MPM and MB missionaries had many of the same assumptions, but the MBs had more difficulty making the necessary adjustments. To compare parallel and yet ultimately divergent Native missionary careers and strategies by an MPM and an MB missionary see Henry and Elna Neufeld, *By God's Grace: Ministry with Native People in Pauingassi* (Winnipeg: CMBC Publications, 1993), and Friesen, *God's Hand*. Gerbrandt, *En Route*, offers a thoughtful retrospective look at factors that facilitated and those that impeded Mennonite missions.

28 William Neufeld's efforts to thwart Roman Catholic efforts are documented in UCA, Board of Home Missions, series II, section I, box 15, file 389, Harry Meadows to Dr. Stevens, 9 Oct. 1943, and George Dorey to J.A. Cormie, 20 Nov. 1943.

29 Peter Penner, *No Longer at Arm's Length: Mennonite Brethren Church Planting in Canada* (Winnipeg: Kindred Press, 1987), 58.

30 As told to the author in conversation with Abraham Friesen, professor of history at the University of California at Santa Barbara and a relative who assisted Abram J. Friesen in the writing of his autobiography.

31 Cornelius Krahn, 'Northern Light Gospel Mission,' *ME* IV, 1112; Margaret Loewen Reimer, *One Quilt, Many Pieces: A Reference Guide to Mennonite Groups in Canada* (Waterloo, Ont.: Mennonite Publishing Service, 1990), 41.

32 *CM*, 13, no. 34, 3.

33 An account of the involvement of Evangelical Mennonite Conference workers in this kind of work is in the EMC Archives, vol. 73, file 1b. It includes an article by Frank H. Epp entitled 'A Mission to Neglected Areas.' Peter Penner provides an account of MB initiatives in *Reaching the Otherwise Unreached: An Historical Account of the West Coast Children's Mission of B.C.* (Clearbrook, BC: West Coast Children's Mission, 1959).

34 S.C. Yoder, 'Summer Bible School,' *ME* IV, 654–5.

35 Penner, *Reaching the Otherwise Unreached*, 23.

36 As quoted in Penner, *No Longer at Arm's Length*, 24.

37 Interview with Jacob A. Loewen, 21 Dec. 1988.

38 This whole matter is discussed in greater detail in Penner, *No Longer at Arm's Length*.

39 Penner, *Reaching the Otherwise Unreached*, 122.

40 Lawrence M. Yoder, 'Church Planting,' *ME* V, 158.

41 Ibid., 159.

42 Penner, *No Longer at Arm's Length*, 96.

43 As quoted in ibid., 102.

44 My wife and I were present at that meeting. Members of the MB mission committee knew my family background but apparently did not know that I had never been a member of an MB church.

45 Penner, *No Longer at Arm's Length*, 155.

46 Ibid.

47 As quoted in Barrett, *Vision and Reality*, 240.

48 CGC II-3-2.3, box 1, folder 4, contains extensive correspondence on the problems at Sudbury, where the (Old) Mennonites tried to enforce some of those distinctives. See also Karen Salo, 'A History of the Waters Mennonite Congregation,' essay written at the Canadian Mennonite Bible College in Religious Studies 251.

49 Penner, *No Longer at Arm's Length*, 99.

50 *1965 Illustrated Year Book, Conference of Mennonites in Canada* (Winnipeg: Conference of Mennonites in Canada, 1965), and *The Conference of*

Mennonites in Canada Yearbook, 1975 (Winnipeg: Conference of Mennonites in Canada, 1975).

51 Sue Barkman, *Ever-Widening Circles: EMC Missions Silver Jubilee, 1953–1978* (Steinbach, Man.: Evangelical Mennonite Conference, 1978), 167.

52 Jack Heppner, *Search for Renewal: The Story of the Rudnerweider/Evangelical Mennonite Mission Conference, 1937–1987* (Winnipeg: Evangelical Mennonite Mission Conference, 1987), 127.

53 Mary I. Groh, *'Like a Mustard Seed': A History of the Warden Park Mennonite Church* (Scarborough, Ont.: Warden Park Mennonite Church, 1977).

54 CGC II-3-2.3, box 1, file 4.

55 Ibid., 'Quebec Survey Report,' n.d. This report was sent to the Mennonite Board of Missions and Charities. The correspondence files indicate that the report was forwarded in October 1955. AMC Mennonite Board of Missions and Charities, IV-8-13, 'Overseas Missions,' drawer 8, Quebec 1956–7, J.D. Graber, Secretary, Mennonite Board of Missions and Charities, to Paul Martin, Secretary, Ontario Conference Mennonite Mission Board, 5 Nov. 1955.

56 CGC Taped recollections of a workshop on 'Home Missions,' held at Conrad Grebel College on 5 Oct. 1989.

57 AMC Mennonite Board of Missions and Charities, IV-8-13, 'Overseas Missions,' drawer 8, Quebec 1956–63, Nelson E. Kauffman, Secretary for Home Missions, Mennonite Board of Missions and Charities, to John Howard Yoder, 4 Sept. 1962.

58 CGC Taped recording of Janet Martin's talk at the 'Home Missions' workshop held at Conrad Grebel College, 5 Oct. 1989.

59 AMC Mennonite Board of Missions and Charities, file IV-8-13, 'Overseas Mission,' drawer 8, Quebec 1956–63, John Howard Yoder to Nelson E. Kauffman, 14 Sept. 1962.

60 Ibid., John H. Yoder to Nelson Kauffman and Osiah Horst, 30 Jan. 1963.

61 Robert Martin-Koop, 'Quebec,' *ME* V, 740.

62 As quoted in Penner, *No Longer at Arm's Length*, 104.

63 Claudette LeBlanc, 'Two Profiles,' *MBH* 22 June 1984, 4.

64 *1962 Yearbook of the Fifty-second Canadian Conference of the Mennonite Brethren Church of North America,* 30 June–4 July 1962 (Winnipeg: Canadian Conference of the Mennonite Brethren Church of North America, 1962), 73–4.

65 LeBlanc, 'Taking Root on Quebec Soil,' *MBH,* 22 June 1984, 2.

66 CMBS(W) Essay by Sonia Blanchette entitled 'The History of Mennonite Brethren Churches in Quebec.'

67 'An Interview with Gerald Janzen,' *MBH,* 22 June 1984, 7–8.

68 *Yearbook, Canadian Conference Mennonite Brethren Churches,* 1971, 153.

69 'An Interview with Gerald Janzen,' *MBH*, 22 June 1984, 8.
70 Ibid.
71 Penner, *No Longer at Arm's Length*, 116.
72 Jane Marie Schultz, 'The Evolution of Singing Schools among the Swiss Mennonites of Ontario,' BA thesis, University of Waterloo, 1987, 62.
73 Harold S. Bender, 'Radio Broadcasting, Mennonite,' *ME*, IV, 244–5.
74 E. Austin Weir, *The Struggle for National Broadcasting in Canada* (Toronto: McClelland and Stewart, 1965); and Don Kerr and Stan Hanson, *Saskatoon: The First Half-Century* (Edmonton: NeWest Press, 1982), 265–7.
75 *Verhandlungen der 31. Noerdlichen Distrikt-Konferenz der Mennoniten-Bruedergemeinden von Nord-Amerika*, abgehalten zu Herbert, Saskatchewan, vom 5 bis zum 9 July 1941 (Hillsboro, Kan.: Mennonite Publishing House, 1941), 80. See also John A. Toews, *A History of the Mennonite Brethren Church* (Fresno, Calif.: Board of Christian Literature, General Conference of Mennonite Brethren Churches, 1975), 320–2.
76 Bender, 'Radio Broadcasting.'

15: Mission to the World

1 Susie Brucks Dyck, *Goettliches Wirken in der Afrika Mission* (Clearbrook, BC: Susie Brucks Dyck, 1983), 5.
2 David B. Marshall, *Secularizing the Faith: Canadian Protestant Clergy and the Crisis of Belief, 1850–1940* (Toronto: University of Toronto Press, 1992), 99.
3 J.B. Toews, *The Mennonite Brethren Church in Zaire* (Fresno, Calif.: General Conference of Mennonite Brethren Churches, 1978), 193.
4 Wilbert R. Shenk, ed., *The Transfiguration of Mission: Biblical, Theological and Historical Foundations* (Scottdale, Penn. and Waterloo, Ont.: Herald Press, 1993). Other recent books discussing these drastic changes in Mennonite missionary perceptions are Victor Adrian and Donald Loewen, eds., *Committed to World Mission: A Focus on International Strategy* (Winnipeg, Man., and Hillsboro, Kan.: Kindred Press, 1990); David W. Shenk, *God's Call to Mission* (Scottdale, Penn.: Herald Press, 1994); and Wilbert R. Shenk, ed., *Anabaptism and Mission* (Scottdale, Penn.: Herald Press, 1984).
For more general recent books on the missionary enterprise see Joel A. Carpenter and Wilbert R. Shenk, eds., *Earthen Vessels: American Evangelicals and Foreign Missions, 1880–1980* (Grand Rapids, Mich.: Eerdmans, 1990); William R. Hutchison, *Errand to the World: American Protestant Thought and Foreign Missions* (Chicago: University of Chicago Press, 1987); Ruth Compton Brouwer, *New Women for God: Canadian Presbyterian Women and India Missions, 1876–1914* (Toronto: University of Toronto Press, 1986);

Alvyn Austin, *Saving China: Canadian Missionaries in the Middle Kingdom, 1888–1959* (Toronto: University of Toronto Press, 1986); and A. Hamish Ion, *The Cross and the Rising Sun: The Canadian Protestant Movement in the Japanese Empire, 1872–1931* (Waterloo, Ont.: Wilfrid Laurier University Press, 1990).

5 Brouwer, *New Women for God.*

6 Ruth A. Tucker, 'Women in Mission: Reaching Sisters in "Heathen Darkness,"' in Carpenter and Shenk, eds., *Earthen Vessels*, 279.

7 In her autobiography Brucks does not mention the specific program in Toronto, but both the Coaldale Bible School and the Prairie Bible Institute participated in the program of the Missionary Medical Institute, which provided practical instruction in treatment of disease in one of the rooms of the People's Church in Toronto. It was a one-year program with visiting lectures by local doctors and missionary doctors on furlough. Brucks was sent overseas before completing the one-year course in Toronto. A brief history of the institute is given in *Life Bearers: Year Book of Missionary Medical Institute*,14 Park Road, Toronto, Canada (Toronto: Missionary Medical Institute, 1943).

8 These ideas are all clearly expressed in Susie Brooks Dyck, *Goettliches Wirken.*

9 Brucks Dyck, *Goettliches Wirken*, 16.

10 The story of such a conversion and prayer is told in ibid., 45.

11 Marshall, *Secularizing the Faith*, 99.

12 Statistics regarding Mennonite missionaries serving overseas are inconsistent and confusing. Some mission boards listed all their missionaries, including those on furlough, retired, or serving for short terms. In some cases husband and wife teams were counted as only one missionary, but in others both partners were counted. A number of Canadian MB missionaries received support from individual churches but were not recognized by the conferences to which those churches belonged. For the Krimmer Mennonite Brethren, their missionaries were also included in the official statistics of the MB conference. Some of the smaller Canadian Mennonite conferences, such as the Rudnerweider/Evangelical Mennonite Mission Conference, promoted foreign missions but encouraged members to serve with other boards or in faith missions.

There was also considerable confusion between home and foreign mission personnel. Missionaries working with North American Native peoples, for example, were often listed as foreign missionaries. Mission boards established long before they opened any missions overseas were originally formed to promote home missions and charities.

13 A. Neuenschwander, 'Congo Inland Mission,' *ME*, I, 690; and S.F. Pannabecker, 'China Mennonite Mission Society,' ibid., 560.

14 There is no recent, comprehensive history of Mennonite overseas missions, but there are numerous publications of uneven quality telling the history of the missionary endeavours of individual conferences or of work undertaken in specific countries. An early discussion of Mennonite missionary activity is Edmund George Kaufman, *The Development of the Missionary and Philanthropic Interest among the Mennonites of North America* (Berne, Ind.: Mennonite Book Concern, 1931). An interesting and well-documented history of the missionary work of the Mennonite Church is Theron F. Schlabach, *Gospel versus Gospel: Mission and the Mennonite Church, 1863–1944* (Scottdale, Penn.: Herald Press, 1980), while John Allen Lapp, *The Mennonite Church in India, 1897–1962* (Scottdale, Penn.: Herald Press, 1972) is a more conventional but well-documented history of Mennonite Church missionary work in India. The best work dealing with the overseas missionary work of the General Conference is James C. Juhnke, *A People of Mission: A History of General Conference Mennonite Overseas Missions* (Newton, Kan.: Faith and Life Press, 1979). The Mennonite Brethren have published far more books about their overseas missionary endeavours than any of the other conferences, but most are essentially celebratory. One of the most scholarly and critically thoughtful studies of MB missions is Bernhard Doerksen, 'Mennonite Brethren Missions: Historical Development, Philosophy, and Policies,' DMiss thesis, Fuller Theological Seminary, 1986.

All these works are written from North American, and more specifically from mission board, perspectives. The most serious attempt to assess the impact of missionary work on indigenous people has been done by a former MB missionary. A collection of his essays has been published in Jacob A. Loewen, *Culture and Human Values: Christian Intervention in Anthropological Perspective. Selections from the Writings of Jacob A. Loewen* (Pasadena, Calif.: William Carey Library, 1975).

15 Statistics on General Conference missionaries are taken from S.F. Pannabecker, ed., *The Christian Mission of the General Conference Mennonite Church* (Newton, Kan.: Faith and Life Press, 1960); and Juhnke, *People of Mission.*

16 Statistics on MB missionaries are based on G.W. Peters, *The Growth of Foreign Missions in the Mennonite Brethren Church* (Hillsboro, Kan.: Board of Foreign Missions, 1947); and *Missionary Album, July 1951, of Missionaries Serving under the Board of Foreign Missions Mennonite Brethren Conference, Inc.* (Hillsboro, Kan.: Board of Foreign Missions, 1951). There is considerable inconsistency between these two sources. The detailed biographical sketches in the *Missionary Album* seem more reliable than Peters's data. The date for establishment of a mission is the date on which the Board of Foreign Missions accepted responsibility. Mennonite Brethren had actually begun to work in China as

early as 1911. The Congo mission is not listed here because the MB Board of Foreign Missions did not take over the Bololo and Kafumba stations until 1946.

17 The statistics for missionaries serving under the Board of Missions and Charities of the Mennonite Church (MBMC) are taken from annual reports of that board, which accepted some candidates from other conferences.

18 Statistics for Brethren in Christ missionaries are given in the annual *Directories of the Brethren in Christ Church*.

19 The China Mennonite Mission Society had workers from the Krimmer Mennonite Brethren, the Evangelical Mennonite Brethren, the Mennonite Brethren, and the Missionary Church Association. It was dissolved in 1946, when the Mennonite Brethren and Krimmer Mennonite Brethren took responsibility for the western field in Szechwan-Kansu, while the Evangelical Mennonite Brethren took over Shantung-Honan.

20 This was an inter-Mennonite venture involving the Evangelical Mennonite Conference, the Evangelical Mennonite Brethren Conference, and the General Conference Mennonite Church, but missionaries from other conferences also served under its general sponsorship.

21 The work of the Eastern Mennonite Board of Missions and Charities was always closely coordinated with that of the MBMC. More information on the work of the Eastern Mennonite Board is given in I.D. Landis, *The Missionary Movement among Lancaster Conference Mennonites* (Scottdale, Penn.: Herald Press, 1937).

22 The best general history of the Church of God in Christ, Mennonite, is Clarence Hiebert, *The Holdeman People: The Church of God in Christ, Mennonite, 1859–1969* (South Pasadena, Calif.: William Carey Library, 1973). The history of the Holdeman mission in Mexico is given in Leola Willard, *God Opened the Door* (Hesston, Kan.: Publication Board, 1962).

23 This Mennonite group should not be confused with the Evangelical Mennonite Conference (the former Kleine Gemeinde) in Canada. The Canadian EMC established its own mission board only in 1952. None of its members was serving in overseas missions in 1939. For an overview of the missionary activities of the EMC in Canada see *Go Ye: Report to the 1967 Regional Missionary Conferences* (Morris, Man.: EMC Board of Missions, 1967).

24 A mission committee was established in 1938 to facilitate support for foreign missions, but the missionaries from this conference served with other boards in 'faith missions.'

25 J.A. Huffman, *History of the Mennonite Brethren in Christ Church* (New Carlisle, Ohio: n.p., 1920), 265.

26 Ibid., 189.

27 Lorraine Roth, *Willing Service: Stories of Ontario Mennonite Women*

(Waterloo, Ont.: Mennonite Historical Society of Ontario, 1992), 55–9.

28 John M. Bender, 'Litwiller, Nelson,' *ME* V, 527; J.W. Shank, *The Gospel under the Southern Cross: A History of the Argentine Mennonite Mission of South America Celebrating Its 25th Anniversary, 1917–1942* (Scottdale, Penn.: Mennonite Publishing House, 1943); 'Nelson Litwiller: Incorrigible Optimist,' *CM*, 16, no. 32, 6.

29 Roth, *Willing Service*, has short biographies of the Swiss Mennonite women from Ontario who served in these missions. Lorraine Roth has also provided me with other helpful information and advice.

30 Shank, *Gospel under the Southern Cross*. Additional information about the Argentine Mennonite Mission is given in 'Martin Duerksen Addresses Fraser Valley Gatherings,' *CM*, 3 no. 4, 3.

31 A critical and comprehensive treatment of the stresses and strains within the Mennonite Brethren Conference in its missionary endeavours is given in Doerksen, 'Mennonite Brethren Missions.' The history of the Bololo mission is also dealt with in detail by one of the main participants in Anna Bartsch, *The Hidden Hand in the Story of My Life* (Winnipeg: Kindred Press, 1987), and by one of the most influential members of the MB Board of Foreign Missions in Toews, *Mennonite Brethren Church in Zaire*.

32 *Verhandlungen der 30 Noerdlichen Distrikt-Konferenz der Mennoniten-Bruedergemeinden von Nord-Amerika*, abgehalten zu Coaldale, Alberta, Canada, vom 8 bis zum 12 Juli 1939, 9–16. The MB mission board agreed to take over both the Kafumba and Bololo mission fields in 1943 but soon sold the Bololo station to the Fundamental World Wide Mission. Susie Brucks was one of the missionaries at Bololo. Unfortunately her published reminiscences are highly sanitized and say virtually nothing about the serious tensions between the Kafumba and Bololo projects.

33 Doerksen, 'Mennonite Brethren Missions,' 98–9.

34 A.E. Janzen, *Survey of Five of the Mission Fields of the Conference of the Mennonite Brethren Church of North America Located in India, Africa, Brazil, Paraguay and Columbia* (Hillsboro, Kan.: Board of Foreign Missions, 1950), 56.

35 Juhnke, *People of Mission*, 99.

36 *Go Ye*.

37 Jack Heppner, *Search for Renewal: The Story of the Rudnerweider/Evangelical Mennonite Mission Conference, 1937–1987* (Winnipeg: Evangelical Mennonite Mission Conference, 1987).

38 Sider, *Brethren in Christ in Canada*, 164.

39 Harold S. Bender, 'Mennonite Brethren in Christ Church,' *ME* I, 603.

40 AMC MBMC, Annual Meeting, 14–16 June 1942.

41 As reported in ibid., Annual Meeting, 16–18 May 1943.

42 Doerksen, 'Mennonite Brethren Missions,' 109.
43 Henry Bartsch issued an exceptional appeal on behalf of the Kramers, addressed to the Canadian District Mennonite Brethren Board of Spiritual and Social Concerns, in August 1947. See CMBS(W) B220, Board of Spiritual and Social Concerns, H.G. Bartsch to 'Dear Sir,' 27 Aug. 1947.
44 AMC MBMC, Report of Annual Meeting, 14–16 June 1942, 9–10.
45 For an uncritical but probably accurate account of the experiences of Pauline Foote, a Krimmer Mennonite Brethren missionary in China who observed at close range but with little appreciation of the broader implications the Chinese revolution of Mao Tse Tung, see Katie Funk Wiebe, *Have Cart, Will Travel: The Life Story of Paulina Foote, Adapted from Her Book, God's Hand over My Nineteen Years in China* (Hillsboro, Kan.: Mennonite Brethren Publishing House, 1974).
46 The basic source for most of this information, verified where possible by comparisons with denominational information, is Edward R. Dayton, ed., *Mission Handbook: North American Protestant Ministries Overseas*, 11th ed. (Monrovia, Calif.: Missions Advanced Research and Communications Center, 1976). When individual mission boards published a list of the fields in which they were active, those lists were regarded as more accurate than the ones in the *Mission Handbook*, and the list has been altered accordingly.
47 AMC MBMC, Annual Report, 1–4 June 1946.
48 Ibid., Executive Office Correspondence, J.D. Graber. This phrase is used in a manuscript by George J. Lapp, prepared for the fiftieth anniversary celebrations of the Mennonite Church mission in India and is entitled 'How Foreign Missions Began in the Mennonite Church.'
49 AMC MBMC, Annual Report, 2–5 June 1945.
50 Ibid., Annual Report, 11–14 June 1949.
51 The group is not further identified in the documents of the MBMC. Members are simply referred to as Conservative Amish-Mennonites.
52 Ibid., General Correspondence, Harold S. Bender to John L. Horst, O.O. Miller, and J.D. Graber, 25 June 1948.
53 *Year Book of the 46th General Conference of the Mennonite Brethren Church of North America*, held at Hillsboro, Kan., 23–8 Oct. 1954 (Hillsboro, Kansas: Mennonite Brethren Publishing House, 1954), 21.
54 Interview with Jacob Loewen, 21 Dec. 1988.
55 Juhnke, *People of Mission*, 11.
56 AMC MBMC, Annual Meeting, 18–20 May 1941.
57 Ibid., Executive Office Correspondence – J.D. Graber, Manuscript by George J. Lapp, prepared for the fiftieth anniversary celebrations of the Mennonite Church Mission in India, entitled 'How Foreign Missions Began in the Mennonite Church.'

58 Paul Irvin Dyck, 'Emergence of New Castes in India,' MA thesis, University of Manitoba, 1970.
59 AMC MBMC, Annual Meeting, 5–7 May 1940.
60 J.W. Shank, 'Argentina,' *ME*, I, 154.
61 Unpublished manuscript by Jash Leewe entitled 'Onnse Ieaschte Missjoonsreis ooda Waut je emma fonn'ne Missjoon weete wulle oba kjeena junt fetalle deed,' Kapitel 10 entitled 'Pauss opp fe'de kjlieena Fass!' 5–6.
62 Jacob A. Loewen, 'Socialization and Social Control: A Résumé of Processes,' in Loewen, *Culture and Human Values*, 212.
63 Jacob A. Loewen, 'Reciprocity in Identification,' in ibid., 31.
64 J. Herbert Kane, as quoted in Toews, *Mennonite Brethren Church in Zaire*, 130.
65 Lapp, *Mennonite Church in India*, 207.
66 AMC MBMC, Annual Meeting, 5–7 May 1940.
67 Juhnke, *People of Mission*, 164.
68 Ibid.
69 AMC MBMC, Annual Meeting, 5–7 May 1940.
70 Ibid., Annual Report, 2–5 June 1945.
71 Ibid., Annual Report, 11–14 June 1949.
72 Ibid., Annual Report, 10–13 June 1950.
73 Interview with J.B. Toews, 1 Feb. 1993.
74 Janzen, *Survey of Five of the Mission Fields*, 70–1.
75 Ibid., 1.
76 Doerksen, 'Mennonite Brethren Missions,' 197.
77 Janzen, *Survey of Five Mission Fields*, 71.
78 Peggy and Walter Regehr, daughter and son-in-law of A.A. and Annie Unruh, told the author, with tears in their eyes, how much it had hurt their father when Toews declined an invitation to visit the various preaching and teaching stations and had instead ensconced himself in his air-conditioned room and invited local church leaders to visit him to discuss and criticize the work of the missionaries. They felt that their father had never been given an opportunity to give his version of events, nor to express his vision for the mission.
79 As quoted in Peter Penner's as-yet-unpublished history of MB missions in India. I am indebted to Penner for making a draft of the relevant chapters of a work in progress available to me.
80 Toews used and emphasized that term in his interview with the author on 1 February 1993.
81 As told in Peter Penner's manuscript history of the MB missionary work in India.
82 *Year Book of the 47th General Conference of the Mennonite Brethren Church in North America* (Hillsboro, Kan.: Mennonite Publishing House, 1957), 42.

83 Ibid.
84 'An Open Letter to the Constituency from A.A. and Annie Unruh,' published in the *Mennonitische Rundschau*, 5 Nov. 1959. I am indebted to Peggy and Walter Regehr for making a copy of this letter available to me.
85 J.B. Toews, *Mennonite Brethren Church in Zaire*, 124.
86 A. Grace Wenger, *A People in Mission; 1894–1994: The Story of Missions by Mennonites of Lancaster Conference and Its Partners* (Saluga, Penn.: Eastern Mennonite Missions, 1994), 62–3.
87 Hugo Neufeld, 'Mission School Reunion Leads to Somali-Mennonite Association,' *MR*, 22, no. 19 (5 Oct. 1992), 1.
88 Jacob A. Loewen, 'Religion, Drives, and the Place Where It Itches,' in Loewen, *Culture and Human Values*, 3–26.
89 Juhnke, *People of Mission*, 213.
90 Ibid.

16: Peace, Justice, and Social Concerns

1 Leo Driedger and Donald B. Kraybill, *Mennonite Peacemaking: From Quietism to Activism* (Scottdale, Penn.: Herald Press, 1994), 263.
2 C.J. Rempel, 'Delegation Visits Prime Minister,' *CM*, 7, no. 9 (27 Feb. 1959), 1 and 4. Eight men had signed the brief, but only seven Mennonite representatives were present at the meeting.
3 The Mennonite brief was published, in its entirety, in ibid., 2. All quotations from the brief are from that source.
4 Reference to the long record of Mennonite delegations meeting with every new prime minister since 1921 are given in AMC MCC, file entitled 'Mennonite Central Committee 1970,' Press release entitled 'Mr. Trudeau's Discussion with the Mennonites,' and dated 25 March 1970.
5 The veteran of these meetings was E.J. Swalm, who represented the Brethren in Christ. J.B. Martin of Waterloo, representing the (Old) Mennonite Church, was the second Mennonite or Brethren in Christ who had been at numerous meetings with prime ministers and cabinet ministers and bureaucrats.
6 In addition to the main message pertaining to the 'peace' position of Canadian Mennonites and Brethren in Christ, a second theme relating to immigration had been mentioned repeatedly at earlier meetings between federal politicians and Mennonite and Brethren in Christ delegations.
7 Rempel, 'Delegation Visits Prime Minister,' 4.
8 Ibid., 1.
9 AMC MCC, Press release, 25 March 1970.
10 'Trudeau Will Meet MCC Officials After All. No Disregard for Mennonites,'

CM, 18, no. 10, 1.

11 'Prime Minister Impressed with "Spiritual Input" of Mennonites,' *CM*, 18, no. 12, 1–2.

12 'Five Will Meet Prime Minister,' *CM*, 18, no. 11, 1–2.

13 The eight, as listed in the brief, were C.W. Loewen, Winnipeg, Manitoba, Evangelical Mennonite Brethren; Bishop J.B. Martin, Waterloo, Ontario, Mennonite Conference; D.P. Neufeld, Rosemary, Alberta, General Conference; J.M. Penner, Ste Anne, Manitoba, Church of God in Christ, Mennonite (Holdeman); David P. Reimer, Giroux, Manitoba, Evangelical Mennonites; C.J. Rempel, Kitchener, Ontario, Mennonite Brethren; Elven Shantz, Kitchener, Ontario, Stirling Avenue Mennonite; and E.J. Swalm, Duntroon, Ontario, Brethren in Christ. All but Loewen attended the meeting.

14 The five men who met with Trudeau were J.M. Klassen, Winnipeg, Manitoba, Executive Secretary of MCC (Canada); Newton L. Gingerich, Tavistock, Ontario, MCC (Canada)'s vice-chairman; C.J. Rempel, Kitchener, Ontario; T.E. Friesen, Altona, Manitoba; and Walter Paetkau, Abbotsford, British Columbia.

15 'Prime Minister Impressed,' 1–2.

16 Ibid.

17 AMC MCC Records, file 'Mennonite Central Committee Canada 1970,' J.M. Klassen to 'The Members MCC (Canada),' 25 March 1970.

18 Ibid.

19 'High Aims and High Hopes,' *CM*, 1, no. 1 (16 Oct. 1953), 2.

20 There are hints of this tension in the correspondence of Gerhard Lohrenz. Helen Epp, Frank's widow, confirmed that there was considerable tension between Frank and his father over the language issue.

21 Frank Epp used and emphasized this point in the personal reflections that he wrote for the last issue of *The Canadian Mennonite*. Frank H. Epp, 'We Died Many Times, But in Those Deaths We Lived: Reflections of a Former Editor,' *CM*, 19, no. 7, 7.

22 Ibid.

23 Frank H. Epp, *The Glory and the Shame* (Winnipeg: Canadian Mennonite Publishing Association, 1969), 58. This book contains a collection of editorials that Epp wrote for the *Canadian Mennonite* shortly before he left the editorship of the paper in August 1967.

24 Ibid., 25.

25 Ibid.

26 Ibid.

27 Ibid., 28–9.

28 The information and the interpretation given here are taken from Epp, 'We Died Many Times,' 7.

29 Ibid.

30 Ibid.

31 Ibid.

32 Ibid., 12.

33 'Canadian Brotherhood Gives Birth to National Inter-Mennonite Committee,' *CM*, 11, no. 50, 1, 6.

34 Ibid.

35 Esther Epp-Tiessen, 'The Origins of Mennonite Central Committee (Canada),' MA thesis, University of Manitoba, 1980; Frank H. Epp, *Partners in Service: The Story of the Mennonite Central Committee Canada* (Winnipeg: MCC [Canada], 1983).

36 Esther Epp-Tiessen, 'Mennonite Central Committee Canada (MCCC),' *ME* V, 559.

37 Urbane Peachey, 'Mennonite Central Committee Peace Section,' *ME* V, 562–3; and John A. Lapp, 'The Peace Mission of the Mennonite Central Committee,' *MQR*, 44, no. 3 (July 1970), 281–97.

38 As quoted in Driedger and Kraybill, *Mennonite Peacemaking*, 143.

39 Frank H. Epp, *A Strategy for Peace: Reflections of a Christian Pacifist* (Grand Rapids, Mich.: William B. Eerdmans Publishing Company, 1973), 8–9.

40 AMC MCC Papers, file entitled 'Mennonite Central Committee 1969,' Second draft, not for publication, of the brief to be presented to the Rt. Hon. Pierre Elliott Trudeau.

41 The quotations are taken from John English, *The Worldly Years: The Life of Lester Pearson, 1949–1972* (Toronto: Random House, 1992), 22–3. For further information regarding Canadian foreign and military policies see James Eayrs, *Northern Approaches: Canada and the Search for Peace* (Toronto: Macmillan, 1961); J.L. Granatstein, *Canadian Foreign Policy since 1945: Middle Power or Satellite?* (Toronto: Copp Clark, 1969); John W. Holmes, *The Better Part of Valour: Essays on Canadian Diplomacy* (Toronto: McClelland and Stewart, 1970); R.A. MacKay, *Canadian Foreign Policy: Selected Speeches and Documents* (Toronto: McClelland and Stewart, 1971); and Robert Bothwell, Ian Drummond, and John English, *Canada since 1945: Power, Politics, and Provincialism* (Toronto: University of Toronto Press, 1981).

42 Harold S. Bender, 'State, Anabaptist-Mennonite Attitude toward,' *ME* IV, 611–13.

43 Janice Potter, *The Liberties We Seek: Loyalist Ideology in Colonial New York and Massachusetts* (Cambridge, Mass.: Harvard University Press, 1983), 59–60, 180.

44 W.L. Morton, 'The Meaning of Monarchy in Confederation,' *Transactions of the Royal Society of Canada*, vol. 1, series IV (June 1963), sec. II, 271–82. After

negotiating the terms and conditions of their immigration with Canadian government officials in 1873, the Mennonite delegates took the trouble to go to London to obtain acceptance and support of those terms and conditions from Queen Victoria. Presumably, if a hostile popular government was elected in Canada, the queen would prevent it from violating the negotiated arrangements.

45 W.L. Morton, 'The Conservative Principle in Confederation,' *Queen's Quarterly*, 71, (1964), 529. See also Morton, 'The Possibility of a Philosophy of Conservatism,' *Journal of Canadian Studies* (summer 1970), 3–14; and Morton, 'Canadian Conservatism Now,' *Conservative Concepts*, 1 (spring 1959), 7–8.

46 For more detail see T.D. Regehr, 'Relations between the Old Order Amish and the State in Canada,' *MQR*, 69, no. 2 (April 1995), 151–77.

47 William Janzen, *Limits on Liberty: The Experience of Mennonite, Hutterite, and Doukhobor Communities in Canada* (Toronto: University of Toronto Press, 1990), chap. 10.

48 Frank H. Epp, ed., *I Would Like to Dodge the Draft-dodgers But ...* (Waterloo, Ont.: Conrad Press, 1970), 17.

49 Seymour Martin Lipset, *Continental Divide: The Values and Institutions of the United States and Canada* (New York: Routledge, 1990), 2.

50 Edmund Burke, *Reflections on the Revolution in France*, reprint (Chicago: Gateway, 1955).

51 MHC Gerhard Lohrenz Papers, 3313/244, Gerhard Lohrenz to Abe R. Reimer, 18 Nov. 1970.

52 As quoted in Driedger and Kraybill, *Mennonite Peacemaking*, 137.

53 MHC Gerhard Lohrenz Papers, 3313/244, Abe R. Reimer to Gerhard Lohrenz, 8 Jan. 1971. The letter is quoted as it was written.

54 MHC J.J. Thiessen Papers, 869/86 and 869/87, files entitled 'Walter Quiring.'

55 Ibid., Cornelius Krahn to Willard Wiebe, Abe Wiebe, Willard Claassen, J.J. Thiessen, and J.G. Rempel, 7 Aug. 1953; and Joh. G. Rempel to J.J. Thiessen, 18 Sept. 1953.

56 For a review of Epp's book, and of the other published reviews of the book, that sets these concerns in perspective see John B. Toews, 'Book Review: The Migrations of the Russian Mennonites,' *CM*, 11, no. 44 (5 Nov. 1963), 8–9.

57 MHC Gerhard Lohrenz Papers, vol. 3313, Gerhard Lohrenz to D.P. Neufeld, Executive Secretary, Conference of Mennonites in Canada, 18 June 1965.

58 'Graham, His Friends, and Critics,' *CM*, 5, no. 38 (13 Sept. 1957), 2.

59 'A Nearly Non-existent Non-resistance,' *CM*, 11, no. 10 (8 March 1963), 6.

60 'The Idolatry of Nationalism,' *CM*, 12, no. 40 (6 Oct. 1964), 5.

61 As quoted in Frye Gaillard, 'The Conversion of Billy Graham: How the President's Preacher Learned to Start Worrying about the Bomb,' *The Progressive* (Aug. 1982), 29.

62 Ibid.

63 Ibid.

64 'Billy Graham – a Human Apostle,' *CM*, 1, no. 11 (16 March 1956), 2.

65 'Mennonite Leaders Met with Evangelist Billy Graham,' *CM*, 9, no. 38 (29 Sept. 1961), 1.

66 'To Mobilize the Conscience of America! Two Commentaries on Washington March,' *CM*, 13, no. 48 (7 Dec. 1965), 1.

67 'The Cry for War: Graham Attacked Peace Marchers,' ibid.

68 'On Graham's War Stand: Leaders Talk with Evangelist Ford at Kitchener-Waterloo Crusade,' *CM*, 14, no. 19 (10 May 1966), 1.

69 'A Problem of Stance,' *CM*, 15, no. 9 (28 Feb. 1967), 4.

70 John Redekop, 'Graham in Vietnam,' *MBH*, 6, no. 2 (13 Jan. 1967), 2.

71 According to Gaillard, 'Conversion,' Graham changed his attitude as a result of that visit but lacked the courage to say so publicly for fear of undermining the effectiveness of his evangelistic work. There were further meetings with Mennonite leaders who then sent books related to issues of war and peace which Graham allegedly read with interest. Documentation in this regard is available in the Frank H. Epp Papers at CGC.

Conclusion: Looking Back

1 AMC MCC Records, file X-9-7, Minutes of the First Meeting of the Presidium of the Mennonite World Conference, Bienenberg/Liestal, Switzerland, 1 Aug. 1958.

2 'The Message of the Seventh World Conference to the Mennonite Congregations of the World,' *CM*, 10, no. 32 (17 Aug. 1962), 2.

3 Adolf Schnebele, 'Jesus Christ: Lord Over the Life of the Believer,' in Cornelius J. Dyck, ed., *The Lordship of Christ: Proceedings of the Seventh Mennonite World Conference, Kitchener, Ontario, Canada, August 1–7, 1962* (Elkhart, Ind.: Mennonite World Conference, 1962), 39.

4 An edited version of the proceedings (Dyck, ed., *The Lordship of Christ*) was published. Records documenting planning for the event are at AMC. Detailed coverage was provided in *CM*, 10, nos. 31 and 32 (10 and 17 Aug. 1962), and in *MBH*, 1, no. 29 (10 Aug. 1962). There was also good coverage from the secular press, including the *Globe and Mail*.

5 'Commentary on Canada,' *CM*, 15, no. 24 (13 June 1967), 1.

6 'Thank You, Canada,' ibid., 5.

7 Gerhard Ens, 'Change and Responsibility,' ibid., 12.

8 J.A. Toews, 'Fly Your Flag, But Not Too High,' ibid., 1, 26.

9 Peter Wiebe and Leo Driedger, 'In the Public Press: The Mennonite Image Is

Good; We Can Move More Boldly,' ibid., 67.

10 J. Howard Kauffman and Leland Harder, *Anabaptists Four Centuries Later: A Profile of Five Mennonite and Brethren in Christ Denominations* (Scottdale, Penn.: Herald Press, 1975), 334–5.

11 Ibid., 336–7.

12 Ibid., 342.

13 Ibid., 338–9.

14 Ibid., 343.

15 MHC Gerhard Lohrenz Papers, vol. 3313, Menno Schrag to Gerhard Lohrenz, 5 March 1971.

16 Ibid., vol. 3321, Gerhard Lohrenz to H.J. Gerbrandt, 11 Dec. 1971.

17 Helmut Harder, 'Where We're at in Theology,' *CM*, 19, no. 8 (19 Feb. 1971), 13.

18 William Klassen, 'Where We're at on Violence and Revolution,' ibid., 30.

19 Lawrence Klippenstein and Julius Toews, eds., *Mennonite Memories: Settling in the West* (Winnipeg: Centennial Publications, 1975; 2nd ed. published in 1977).

20 Robert Kreider, 'Influenced But Not Imprisoned, by Our Heritage,' *MM* Special Centennial edition (Jan.–Feb. 1974), 31–2.

21 These problems are discussed clearly in Rodney J. Sawatzky and Scott H. Holland, eds., *The Limits of Perfection: A Conversation with J. Lawrence Burkholder* (Waterloo, Ont.: Conrad Grebel College, 1993), 1–54.

22 As told in a letter from James N. Pankratz to Ted Regehr, 7 May 1993.

23 Ibid.

24 Jacob A. Loewen, *Culture and Human Values: Christian Intervention in Anthropological Perspective* (Pasadena, Calif.: William Carey Library, 1975).

Bibliographical
Essay

The bibliography compiled in the research and writing of this manuscript comprises more than 100 pages of typescript. Since much of the information in it is available in the Notes above, it seemed prudent, in the interest of keeping the book to a reasonable length, not to include a detailed bibliography here. The complete bibliography, however, is available on the internet, and copies have also been deposited in the four major Canadian Mennonite archives:

- Columbia Bible College
  2940 Clearbrook Road
  Clearbrook, BC
  V2T 2Z8

- Conrad Grebel College
  University of Waterloo
  Waterloo, Ontario
  N2L 3G6

- Centre for Mennonite Brethren Studies
  1-169 Riverton Ave.
  Winnipeg, Manitoba
  R2L 2E5

- Mennonite Heritage Centre
  600 Shaftesbury Blvd.
  Winnipeg, Manitoba
  R3P 0M4

MENNONITE STUDIES SINCE 1982

When Frank Epp's *Mennonites in Canada, 1920–1940: A People's Struggle for Survival* (Vol. 2; Toronto: Macmillan, 1982) was published, a special scholarly conference was organized at St Michael's College, University of Toronto, with the help of the Multicultural History Society of Ontario and the Ethnic and Immigration Studies Program at the University of Toronto. Scholars from various disciplines were invited to report on 'Mennonite Studies – the State of the Art' in their disciplines. The papers presented were subsequently published in Volume 1 of the *Journal of Mennonite Studies* (1983). The objective was to inform readers what had been done and to stimulate further scholarly work in Mennonite studies.

More than a decade has passed since that broad overview of Mennonite studies. Much new material has been published, but there also remain some major gaps. In the writing of this volume I have tried to read all the relevant new published scholarly works but also have had to rely on primary sources to complement what had been done or to do basic research on neglected themes and issues. Often that primary research, and the appropriate documentation and interpretation of neglected issues, required more space than could be made available in a single volume. I therefore published a number of separate and more detailed articles. These are all referred to in the appropriate notes.

PRIMARY SOURCES

This volume is based on extensive research in primary sources, only the most important of which can be identified here. I thoroughly examined major archival collections at the Archives of the Mennonite Church (AMC) in Goshen; the Centre(s) for Mennonite Brethren Studies (CMBS) in Winnipeg (W) and in Fresno (F), California; Columbia Bible College (CBC) in Clearbrook; Conrad Grebel College (CGC) in Waterloo; and the Mennonite Heritage Centre (MHC) in Winnipeg. These include official records of conferences and conference agencies at all these archives, of the Canadian Mennonite Board of Colonization at the MHC, and of the Mennonite Central Committee (MCC) at the AMC.

The official records of Mennonite conferences and agencies were complemented by several large and numerous smaller collections of private papers. The most relevant large collections of private papers used include those of Benjamin B. Janz at CMBS (W), of J.J. Thiessen at MHC, and of Harold S. Bender at AMC.

At the National Archives of Canada (NAC) in Ottawa records of numerous government departments provided relevant information. On matters related to wartime military or alternative service I examined records of the departments of Finance, Forestry, Labour, Mines and Resources, National Defence, and Northern Affairs and of the Privy Council. Immigration matters were dealt with by the departments of Citizenship, Immigration, and Labour, while information about wartime economic policies was obtained from the records of the Wartime Prices and Trade Board and the departments of Agriculture, Health and Welfare, Labour, and Munitions and Supply. References to Mennonite reactions to economic conditions created as a result of evacuation of Japanese from British Columbia are scattered in the records of the British Columbia Security Commission, the Custodian of Enemy Property, the Privy Council, the Veteran's Land Administration, the Wartime Prices and Trade Board, and in the Records of Parliament. I also did much archival research in non-Canadian government records related to the migration of post–Second World War immigrants. Collections that supplemented material in the immigration records of the Canadian government include the records of the Reichsministerium fuer die besetzten Ostgebiete, of the Volksdeutsche Mittelstelle, and of the Organization for the Military Government of Germany, United States, all at the Bundesarchiv in Koblenz, Germany.

I also consulted records of the Organization for the Military Government of Germany, United States, and of the Department of the Secretary of State, both at the National Archives in Washington, DC, as well as records of the International Refugee Organization at the Archive Nationale in Paris and the records of various League of Nations and United Nations agencies in Geneva, Switzerland, responsible for care of refugees.

Individual participants with personal knowledge of some of the controversial events discussed in the manuscript were interviewed, but none of that material was subjected to any statistical analysis. The interviews clarified or offered personal perspectives on information obtained from archival sources or from published material.

SCHOLARLY JOURNALS, PERIODICALS, AND NEWSPAPERS

Two new Canadian Mennonite scholarly journals have published much material in the last decade, complementing the *Mennonite Quarterly Renew* (MQR). The *Journal of Mennonite Studies* (*JMS*), to which reference has been made above, is a Canadian interdisciplinary journal dealing with Mennonite issues. It began publication in 1983, in Winnipeg, and has carried numerous excellent scholarly articles on Mennonite history, literature, the arts, and culture. The *Conrad Grebel Review: A Journal of Christian Inquiry* also started publication in 1983. It has dealt more with theological and philosophical issues pertaining to the Anabaptist and Mennonite experience. The editorial in the journal's first issue noted: 'It is time to articulate a Mennonite theology by means of which we can assess the basic assumptions of our culture.'

Both journals complemented the *MQR*, the oldest English-language scholarly Mennonite journal, published at Goshen College. The *MQR* has carried, and continues to carry, many articles related to the Canadian Mennonite experience. I employed all three journals extensively in this study.

Several other Mennonite journals with a more popular orientation were also examined. These include *Mennonite Mirror* (*MM*), published in Winnipeg; *Mennonite Life* (*ML*), from Bethel College in North Newton, Kansas; and briefly *Mennonitische Lehrerzeitung* and *Mennonitische Welt*, both published in Winnipeg.

During the period under study Mennonites printed a number of newspapers in Canada. Some were in-house publications dealing mainly with devotional or local, everyday concerns. Others sought to report local as well as national and international news of interest to the Mennonite constituency. The most extensively used newspaper in this study was the *Canadian Mennonite* (*CM*), published in Manitoba from 1953 until 1971. Refered to somewhat less frequently were the *Mennonite Brethren Herald* (*MBH*), *Mennonitische Rundschau*, and *Der Bote*. Other denominational and community newspapers were consulted with reference to specific issues or events.

SCHOLARLY BOOKS

Books remain a crucial source of information and insight for historians, and I spent much time reading what others had written on a great range of topics. Only some of the most important topics and books can be identified here.

The Mennonite identity, and distinctive Anabaptist-Mennonite beliefs and practices, have been of great interest to Mennonite scholars during the last two decades. Several scholarly conferences, the proceedings of which had been published, dealt with issues related to Mennonite identity. See particularly Leo Driedger and Leland Harder, eds., *Anabaptist-Mennonite Identities in Ferment* (Elkhart, Ind.: Institute of Mennonite Studies, 1990); Abe J. Dueck, ed., *Canadian Mennonites and the Challenge of Nationalism* (Winnipeg: Manitoba Mennonite Historical Society, 1994); Calvin Redekop, Victor A. Krahn, and Samuel J. Steiner, eds., *Anabaptist/Mennonite Faith and Economics* (New York: University of America Press, 1994); and Calvin Wall Redekop and Samuel J. Steiner, eds., *Mennonite Identity: Historical and Contemporary Perspectives* (New York: University of America Press, 1988). Books by individual authors that examine and seek to define Mennonite identity include Leo Driedger, *Mennonite Identity in Conflict* (Lewiston, NY: Edwin Mellen Press, 1988); Harry Loewen, ed., *No Permanent City: Stories from Mennonite History and Life* (Scottdale, Penn.: Herald Press, 1993); Harry Loewen, ed., *Why I Am a Mennonite: Essays on Mennonite Identity* (Scottdale, Penn.: Herald Press, 1988); and Calvin Redekop, *Mennonite Society* (Baltimore, Md.: Johns Hopkins University Press, 1989) and *Who Am I? What Am I?* (Grand Rapids, Mich.: Academie Books, 1988).

Two major statistical surveys conducted in 1972 and 1989 examined the contemporary identity of Mennonites in North America. The results were published in J.

Howard Kauffman and Leland Harder, *Anabaptists Four Centuries Later: A Profile of Five Mennonite and Brethren in Christ Denominations* (Scottdale, Penn.: Herald Press, 1975); and J. Howard Kauffman and Leo Driedger, ed., *The Mennonite Mosaic: Identity and Modernization* (Scottdale, Penn.: Herald Press, 1991). A similar statistical survey dealing only with Mennonite Brethren is provided in Peter M. Hamm, *Continuity and Change among Canadian Mennonite Brethren* (Waterloo, Ont.: Wilfrid Laurier University Press, 1987), while application of some of the statistical survey results to the changing Mennonite peace position is available in Leo Driedger and Donald R. Kraybill, *Mennonite Peacemaking: From Quietism to Activism* (Scottdale, Penn.: Herald Press, 1994).

There have also been numerous conferences and publications on the impact of the so-called Anabaptist Vision on the identity and theology of Mennonites in North America. One of the earliest was Guy F. Hershberger, ed., *The Recovery of the Anabaptist Vision: A Sixtieth Anniversary Tribute to Harold S. Bender* (Scottdale, Penn.: Herald Press, 1957). A more recent collection of articles appeared in John Richard Burkholder and Calvin Redekop, eds., *Kingdom, Cross and Community: Essays on Mennonite Themes in Honor of Guy F. Hershberger* (Scottdale, Penn.: Herald Press, 1976), and in several special issues of *MQR*. The fiftieth anniversary of the publication of Harold Bender's famous essay was celebrated in several scholarly conferences and in numerous articles in Mennonite scholarly journals. Much of this material relates to sixteenth-century European Anabaptism, but it also sheds light on the Anabaptist-Mennonite identity in North America in more recent times.

Mennonite identities are sometimes revealed, albeit in fragmentary fashion, in numerous local church and community histories or in biographies of individual leaders. Canadian Mennonite congregations, institutions, and communities have marked major anniversaries with histories. Some of these transcend local celebratory interests. Noteworthy examples include J. Winfield Fretz, *The Waterloo Mennonites: A Community in Paradox* (Waterloo, Ont.: Wilfrid Laurier University, 1989). Esther Epp-Tiessen, *Altona: The Story of a Prairie Town* (Altona, Man.: D.W. Friesen and Sons, 1982); Walter Klaassen, *'The Days of Our Years': A History of the Eigenheim Mennonite Church Community: 1892 – 1992* (Rosthern, Sask.: Eigenheim Mennonite Church, 1992); Royden Loewen, *Family, Church and Market: A Mennonite Community in the Old and the New Worlds, 1850–1930* (Toronto: University of Toronto Press, 1993); and Peter D. Zacharias, *Reinland: An Experience in Community* (Altona, Man.: Reinland Centennial Committee, 1976). Leo Driedger, *Mennonites in Winnipeg* (Winnipeg: Kindred Press, 1990), provides a brief introduction to the Mennonite communities in a large urban centre. Driedger has also written numerous articles on urbanization and its impact on Mennonite life, and I have relied heavily on his work when discussing urbanization.

Several new histories of Mennonite high schools should also be noted: Frank H.

Epp, *Education with a Plus: The Story of Rosthern Junior College* (Waterloo, Ont.: Conrad Press, 1975), and Gerhard J. Ens, *'Die Schule Muss Sein': A History of the Mennonite Collegiate Institute* (Gretna, Man.: Mennonite Collegiate Institute, 1990). The fiftieth anniversaries of the high schools and Bible colleges established immediately after the Second World War have already resulted in the writing of a major history of the Rockway Mennonite Collegiate by Sam Steiner and preparation of other celebratory and historical accounts of some of the other institutions. Several doctoral dissertations have been written about the history of Canadian Mennonite education, but there is not yet a comprehensive published scholarly study of that topic.

Only a few scholarly biographies of Canadian Mennonites have been published in the last two decades. These include Urie Bender, *Four Earthen Vessels: Biographical Profiles of Oscar Burkholder, Samuel F. Coffman, Clayton F. Derstine, Jesse B. Martin* (Scottdale, Penn.: Herald Press, 1982), and *Stumbling Heavenward: The Extraordinary Life of an Ordinary Man, Peter Rempel* (Winnipeg: Hyperion, 1984); and John B. Toews, *With Courage to Spare: The Life of B.B. Janz (1877–1964)* (Hillsboro, Kan.: Mennonite Brethren Publishing House, 1978). Though most autobiographies that have appeared offer little insight into difficult or controversial issues, noteworthy exceptions include: Siegfried Bartel, *Living with Conviction: German Army Captain Turns to Cultivating Peace* (Winnipeg: CMBC Publications, 1994); Peter Dyck and Elfrieda Dyck, *Up from the Rubble: The Epic Rescue of Thousands of War-Ravaged Mennonite Refugees* (Scottdale, Penn.: Herald Press, 1991); David Ewert, *Journey of Faith: An Autobiography* (Winnipeg: Kindred Press, 1993); Henry Gerbrandt, *En Route/Hinjawaeajis: The Memoirs of Henry J. Gerbrandt* (Winnipeg: CMBC Publications, 1994); and Peter Hamm, *Reflections on My Journey* (Winnipeg: Kindred Press, 1993).

The most important books dealing with military service during the war are E.L.M. Burns, *Manpower in the Canadian Army, 1939–1945* (Toronto: Clarke, Irwin, 1956); William Janzen, *Limits on Liberty: The Experience of Mennonite, Hutterite, and Doukhobor Communities in Canada* (Toronto: University of Toronto Press, 1990), and C.P. Stacey, *Arms, Men and Governments* (Ottawa: Queen's Printer, 1970). Those relating to the Canadian economy during and immediately after the war include Robert Bothwell, Ian Drummond, and John English, *Canada 1900–1945* (Toronto: University of Toronto Press, 1987); G.E. Britnell and V.C. Fowke, *Canadian Agriculture in War and Peace, 1935–1950* (Stanford, Calif.: Stanford University Press, 1962); and Kenneth Norrie and Douglas Owram, *A History of the Canadian Economy* (Toronto: Harcourt Brace Jovanovich, 1991). The best general book on Canadian immigration and refugee policy is Gerald E. Dirks, *Canada's Refugee Policy: Indifference or Opportunism?* (Montreal: McGill-Queen's University Press, 1977), while Frank H. Epp, *Mennonite Exodus: The Rescue and Resettlement of the Russian Mennonites since the Communist Revolution* (Altona, Man.: Canadian Mennonite Relief and Immigration Council, 1962), remains the best account of twentieth-century Mennonite immigration.

Numerous recent books deal with evangelicals in Canada and with evangelical missionary activities. Most cover the Mennonite story somewhat erratically, since Canadian Mennonites have sometimes regarded themselves, and been seen by others, as an integral part of North American evangelicalism, while at other times, and particularly on the issue of a peace witness, they have felt some discomfort in the camp of the evangelicals. Mennonite writing on evangelism and mission work includes much celebratory and sometimes hagiographic material. Some of the more scholarly books are Lois Barrett, *The Vision and the Reality: The Story of Home Missions in the General Conference Mennonite Church* (North Newton, Kan.: Faith and Life Press, 1983); James C. Juhnke, *A People of Mission: A History of General Conference Mennonite Overseas Missions* (North Newton, Kan.: Faith and Life Press, 1979); C. Norman Kraus, ed., *Missions, Evangelism and Church Growth* (Scottdale, Penn.: Herald Press, 1980); John A. Lapp, *The Mennonite Church in India* (Scottdale, Penn.: Herald Press, 1972); Peter Penner, *No Longer at Arm's Length: Mennonite Brethren Church Planting in Canada* (Winnipeg: Kindred Press, 1987); Theron Schlabach, *Gospel Versus Gospel: Mission and the Mennonite Church, 1863–1944* (Scottdale, Penn.: Herald Press, 1980); Wilbert R. Shenk, *The Transfiguration of Mission: Biblical, Theological and Historical Foundations* (Scottdale, Penn.: Herald Press, 1993); and J.B. Toews, *Pilgrimage of Faith: The Mennonite Brethren Church 1860–1990* (Fresno, Calif.: Kindred Press, 1993).

There is extensive new scholarly writing pertaining to Canadian Mennonite music, literature, and art. With the exception of Al Reimer, *Mennonite Literary Voices: Past and Present* (North Newton, Kan.: Bethel College, 1993), most has appeared in chapters of books or in articles. The most important are Harry Loewen, ed., *Mennonite Images: Historical, Cultural, and Literary Essays Dealing with Mennonite Issues* (Winnipeg: Hyperion, 1980); Harry Loewen and Al Reimer, eds., *Visions and Realities: Essays, Poems, and Fiction Dealing with Mennonite Issues* (Winnipeg: Hyperion, 1985); Hildi Froese Tiessen, ed., Special issue of *Prairie Fire*, 11, no. 2 (Summer 1990), on 'New Mennonite Writing'; Hildi Froese Tiessen, ed., *Liars and Rascals: Mennonite Short Stories* (Waterloo, Ont.: University of Waterloo Press, 1989); Hildi Froese Tiessen, ed., Special issue of the *New Quarterly*, 10, nos. 1 and 2 (spring/summer 1990), 'Mennonite/s Writing in Canada'; Hildi Froese Tiessen and Peter Hinchcliffe, eds., *Acts of Concealment: Mennonite/s Writing in Canada* (Waterloo, Ont.: University of Waterloo Press, 1992), and numerous articles in *JMS*.

MENNONITES AND THE 'NEW' HISTORY

Of late, Canadian historians have paid increasing attention to what Carl Berger in his revised edition of *The Writing of English Canadian History* (Toronto: University of Toronto Press, 1986) called 'new' history. Such history focuses on social issues and seeks to view human affairs from the perspective of ordinary people, rather than concentrating only on the actions of the great and the powerful. It has sometimes been called history viewed from the bottom up, and much of it has examined issues related to gender, race, class, and ethnicity.

Mennonite society before 1970 was highly patriarchal, and the neglect of women and their experiences is a major weakness in Mennonite historiography. There is, however, encouraging progress in the writing of Mennonite gender history. Much of it is still at the thesis or scholarly-article stage, but a well-attended scholarly conference held in Pennsylvania in the early summer of 1995 was devoted entirely to Mennonite women's studies and demonstrated lively interest and much relevant new research. Several articles by Marlene Epp and Gloria Redekop as well as Gloria Redekop's doctoral thesis were used extensively in this study. Scholarly articles seeking to establish a theological understanding of issues related to gender have appeared in special issues of the *Conrad Grebel Review*, in the *MQR*, and in a book edited by John E. Toews entitled *Your Daughters Shall Prophesy: Women in Ministry in the Church*. Katie Funk Wiebe, a Canadian-born Mennonite Brethren writer based in the United States, has written extensively about the experiences of MB women.

Racial issues have become relevant to Canadian Mennonites mainly as a result of their misssionary work, particularly with Native Canadians, and of involvement by some Canadian Mennonites in the U.S. civil rights movement. Their own communities and congregations, for the most part, remained throughtout the period under review preserves of white Protestants. Those who came to Canada from Russia or the Soviet Union often had a very poor opinion of other Slavic people, and many responded enthusiastically to anti-Slavic and anti-communist Nazi and Cold War propaganda. Mennonites had more mixed relations with Jewish neighbours, living sometimes in harmony with these people, sometimes offering significant assistance, but at other times exhibiting prejudice and suspicion. A scholarly conference in Winnipeg in August 1995 examining Mennonite-Jewish-Ukrainian relations marked an important attempt to address some of these issues.

Ethnicity in Mennonite history was closely linked to sectarian theology and became a matter of serious concern when people began to leave their separatist rural enclaves. Sociologists, most notably Leo Driedger, J. Winfield Fretz, Donald Kraybill, and Calvin Redekop, have brought the methods and resources of their discpline to the study of this important aspect of Mennonite life. Much of the relevant literature indicates that during the period under study Mennonites in Canada found it difficult to distinguish between the essential elements of their faith and the cultural context within which they experienced and lived it.

Canadian Mennonites have been reluctant to apply any Marxist or other class analyses to their economic role in Canadian society. Class distinctions violate their concept of community and congregation, but it is clear that farmers, small independent businessmen, and professionals constituted the dominant groups in most Canadian Mennonite communities in the period under review. They were, and often behaved as, members of the *petite bourgeoisie*, and my work has been influenced by the class analysis offered by Seymour Lipset in *Agrarian Socialism*, and by C.B. MacPherson and Gad Horowitz in their various books and articles, which seem relevant to Canadian Mennonite attitudes, aspirations, and experiences. It is not hard to find references that document fear of proletarianization and hostility to organized labour. The usual explanation given is that employees might lose their religious freedom and independence if their convictions come into conflict with those of their employers. There is, however, also evidence that Mennonites feared that proletarianization would weaken their ability to define and control their relations to the means of production and distribution. Professional and trade organizations enjoyed greater acceptance.

Before 1970 only a handful of Canada's Mennonites achieved sufficient wealth to think of themselves as capitalists. They and their prosperous but less affluent co-religionists were more likely to see themselves as frugal, astute, hard-working, and hence successful small, independent operators.

Both the methods and findings of practitioners of the 'new' history have had only a limited impact to date, but different questions are being asked and new social science methods are being used by historians. Thus far, Mennonites in Canada have approached their history rather cautiously. There has not been a twentieth-century historiographical revolution in Canadian Mennonite studies, which have always been interdisciplinary, but in recent years scholars from several disciplines have used some of the new methods.

This study still relies heavily on traditional archival and library sources and methods of scholarship. I have tried to employ some of the methods and to understand and apply some of the concepts and interpretations of the most recent scholarship, but I have no doubt that some of my younger colleagues, and certainly some graduate students, will find my methods, sources, and interpretations too conventional. That still reflects the current state of Mennonite studies in Canada, but younger scholars are exploring new issues that will enrich and no doubt modify our understanding of the Mennonite experience in Canada. While this study completes the Mennonites-in-Canada history project begun almost thirty years ago, it will, at best, provide a conceptual framework that others, using both old and new methods and sources, will test, modify, challenge, and, I hope, in part at least, confirm.

Illustration Credits

Canadian Mennonite: Hoffnungsfeld Mennonite church, vol. 13, no. 48, p. 8; first Mennonite Church, Kitchener, vol. 5, no. 24, p. 8; Mennonite Disaster Service, vol. 16, no. 30, p. 1; Mennonite Brethren baptism; Brunk tent campaign, vol. 5, no. 23, p. 5; Goodwill Rescue Mission, vol. 10, no. 3, p. 5; Mennonite Pioneer Mission, vol. 7, no. 16, p. 5; World Conference in Kitchener; Centennial quilt, vol. 15, no. 11; Queen Elizabeth visiting, vol. 5, no. 24, p. 8; with Trudeau, vol. 19, no. 8, p. 7

Frank H. Epp, photograph by Belair, Kitchener

Exodus, by Agatha Schmidt, courtesy of the author

Conrad Grebel College: Sewing circle, 1994-1.88; barn raising, 1989-5.12.; R. Musselman Ltd.; quilting bee

Columbia Bible College: First Mennonite Church, Greendale

Saskatoon Star Phoenix: Preparing to leave for British Honduras

Centre for Mennonite Brethren Studies in Canada: Coaldale Mennonite choir and orchestra

Kennedy Heights Mennonite Brethren Church: Cultural centre at Strawberry Hill

Mennonite Heritage Centre: Car dealership; with Diefenbaker; Elven Shantz; Johann H. Enns

Index